UNIHI-SEAGRANT-CR-88-01

The UN Convention
on the Law of the Sea:
Impact and
Implementation

The UN Convention on the Law of the Sea: Impact and Implementation

Proceedings

Law of the Sea Institute
Nineteenth Annual Conference

Co-sponsored by the
Centre for Marine Law and Policy
University of Wales Institute
of Science and Technology

Edited by
E. D. Brown
R. R. Churchill

Published by
The Law of the Sea Institute
William S. Richardson School of Law
University of Hawaii • Honolulu

The Law of the Sea Institute is housed and sponsored by the William S. Richardson School of Law, University of Hawaii, and is a project sponsored in part by the University of Hawaii Sea Grant College Program under Institutional Grant No. NA85AA-D-SG082 from NOAA, Office of Sea Grant, United States Department of Commerce.

Sea Grant Cooperative Report
UNIHI-SEAGRANT-CR-88-01

International Standard Book Number: 0-911189-16-5

Library of Congress Cataloging-in-Publication Data

Law of the Sea Institute. Conference (19th : 1985 :
    Cardiff, South Glamorgan)
    The UN Convention of the Law of the Sea.

    (Sea grant cooperative report; UNIHI-SEAGRANT-CR-88-01)
    "Co-sponsored by the Centre for Marine Law and Policy,
University of Wales Institute of Science and Technology."
    Includes index.
    1. Maritime law--Congresses. 2. United Nations
Convention on the Law of the Sea (1982)--Congresses.
I. Brown, E. D. II. Churchill, R. R. (Robin Rolf)
III. University of Wales. Centre for Marine Law and
Policy. IV. Title. V. Series.
JX4408.L373 1985   341.4'5   87-32490
ISBN 0-911189-16-5

Cite as 19 L. Sea Inst. Proc. [page numbers] (1987)

This book may be ordered from:
The Law of the Sea Institute
William S. Richardson School of Law
University of Hawaii
2515 Dole Street
Honolulu, Hawaii 96822

Phone (808) 948-6750 or 941-8500
Telex 7431895 (ITT) SEALAW

PREFACE

The UN Convention on the Law of the Sea 1982 remained open for signature until December 9, 1984. By that time it had been signed by 159 states and had been ratified by fourteen states. It will enter into force only if a further forty-six states ratify or accede to it. The prospects for its early entry into force have not been improved by the decision of the governments of three important western states, the Federal Republic of Germany, the United Kingdom and the United States, not to sign the Convention, because of dissatisfaction with its regime for seabed mining. It seems not unlikely that the rate of ratification of the Convention will be influenced by these decisions, as well as by the outcome of the ongoing labors in the Preparatory Commission to develop the detailed rules for the exploitation of the Area beyond the limits of national jurisdiction.

The issue of seabed mining has featured prominently in recent annual Conferences of the Law of the Sea Institute. Partly for this reason, partly because further progress must await the outcome of the Preparatory Commission's work, this topic has been considered only incidentally at the Nineteenth Annual Conference. It is clear that whether the Convention enters into force or not, and irrespective of the timing of that event and of the number of adherent states, the substance of the Convention will have a major impact upon the further development of international customary law and many of its rules will be informally "implemented" by their incorporation in municipal law. This Conference is concerned to examine the likely impact and implementation of the Convention in the various fields covered by the seven panels and the Special Symposium.

E.D. Brown

Robin R. Churchill

Centre for Marine Law and Policy
University of Wales
Institute of Science and Technology
Cardiff, Wales

ACKNOWLEDGEMENTS

Funding for this conference and proceedings has been generously provided by:

BRITOIL

CARDIFF CITY COUNCIL

EXXON CORPORATION

FORD FOUNDATION

JANE HODGE FOUNDATION

ANDREW W. MELLON FOUNDATION

PETRO-CANADA RESOURCES

WILLIAM S. RICHARDSON SCHOOL OF LAW
University of Hawaii

SECRETARY OF STATE FOR WALES

SOUTH GLAMORGAN COUNTY COUNCIL

UNIVERSITY OF HAWAII

UNIVERSITY OF HAWAII SEA GRANT COLLEGE PROGRAM
in association with
NATIONAL OCEANIC AND ATMOSPHERIC ADMINISTRATION
Department of Commerce

We also gratefully acknowledge the efforts of:

Ralph Colling
Alyson Nakamura
Elizabeth Ng
Philomene Verlaan
Ida Yoshinaga

in preparing this proceedings for publication.

TABLE OF CONTENTS

CONTRIBUTED PAPERS

BANQUET SPEECH

THE LAW OF THE SEA INSTITUTE

1985 STAFF

John P. Craven, Director
Scott Allen, Associate Director
Maivan Lam, Assistant Director
Carol Stimson, Administrator/Editor

OPENING CEREMONIES

WELCOMING ADDRESS

E. D. Brown
Director
Centre for Marine Law and Policy
University of Wales Institute of Science and Technology

It is my privilege to welcome you to this Nineteenth Annual Conference of the Law of the Sea Institute. It is indeed a pleasure for me personally to see so many old friends in the audience, many of whom I met years ago at this Institute's earlier annual conferences. I am sure you will agree that we are most fortunate to have attracted so many distinguished speakers to our panels, and I look forward to four days of very stimulating debate with you.

I should like to introduce to our proceedings the distinguished visitor who will formally open the conference: Councillor Captain Norman Lloyd-Edwards, the Lord Mayor of the City of Cardiff. We would, of course, have been honored to have our Conference opened by the Lord Mayor in any event, but on this occasion, the City -- with what I can only describe as Celtic foresight -- was recently wise enough to elect, as their Lord Mayor, a councillor who is both a lawyer and a distinguished naval officer. We are very privileged, sir, to have you with us, and it is my pleasure to invite you to address the conference.

WELCOMING ADDRESS

Captain Norman Lloyd-Edwards
Lord Mayor of Cardiff

Ladies and gentlemen, welcome to Cardiff. We are enormously proud of St. David's Hall, which we now consider to be the foremost concert hall in Europe. It enables us to attract many of the world's leading orchestras and conductors, but we also wish to attract conferences, and I am particularly happy to welcome your conference today.

The port of Cardiff has been known for many decades as "the port of coal." Many charter parties began with the instruction to the master to proceed first to the port of Cardiff, and there, to bunker the best Welsh coal before proceeding to their destination. At one stage, ships were queuing up to enter our port. In Cardiff's heyday -- the early 1920s -- we exported over a million tons of coal a year, not only for bunkering but for actually fueling the furnaces of the world. That, unhappily, is no longer the case. The change to bunkering oil and the decline in the coal export trade hit Cardiff badly. Now we depend very much on the importing of timber and fruit, and the Associated British Ports are actively trying to attract new cargoes to Cardiff.

When I first set up as a solicitor in the early 1960s, one of my specialties was admiralty law, in the interpretation of charter parties and in dealing with claims arising from collisions and groundings. In those days there were some eight shipowners here in Cardiff. Sadly, that number is now reduced to just one. With the decline in the number of shipowners and the overall decline of this country's merchant fleet -- which is something to be deplored -- that aspect of my work has diminished.

It is extraordinary that, as the shipping and trading in and out of Cardiff have declined, so the reputation of the city as a major center for maritime studies has increased. When I was Deputy Chairman of the Education Committee, I was involved in running the Reardon Smith Nautical College, a pre-sea training school. During that time, we were able to bring together other colleges and schools dealing with communications and engineering. We are now able to boast a Centre of Maritime Studies which would be difficult to equal anywhere else in the United Kingdom.

It is therefore totally appropriate that UWIST was involved in the organization of your Institute's annual conference, and I am delighted that you decided to accept their invitation to hold it here in Cardiff. I have seen the list of speakers; it is a most impressive galaxy.

I also notice that you intend to work very hard. This is not a feature of all conferences. Usually, participants work terribly hard in the morning, and then there is a bus ride in the afternoon. You seem to be working all through Saturday as well! This is to be commended, but I am slightly apprehensive that you have not given yourselves sufficient time to see the rest of our city. I hope you will find time after the conference to go to our parks and lakes, our beaches and mountains, our castles, our museums, our cathedrals, and to our shopping centers and that when you return to your respective homes, wherever they may be all over the world, you will take with you the thought that not only have you had a worthwhile conference, but that you have had a very happy time in the capital city of Wales and will want to come back to see us at the earliest possible moment thereafter.

With this good wish and an expectation that you are going to have a truly memorable period in our city, I have the greatest pleasure in bidding you welcome. I hope that you will indeed have a most successful Conference.

E. D. Brown: Professor Thomas Clingan is known to all of us in the field, both in his capacity as leader of the United States delegation to the Law of the Sea Conference and as a writer and teacher of international law at the University of Miami. He will greet us this morning in his capacity as the Presiding Officer of the Law of the Sea Institute.

WELCOMING ADDRESS

Thomas A. Clingan
School of Law
University of Miami

It is my great pleasure this morning, as Presiding Officer of the Executive Board of the Law of the Sea Institute, to welcome you on behalf of that board to the Nineteenth Annual Conference of the Law of the Sea Institute, this year jointly sponsored by the Institute and the Centre for Marine Law and Policy at the University of Wales Institute of Science and Technology.

In the past, both of our institutions have played prominent roles in the consideration of ocean policy issues. The Law of the Sea Institute, established in 1965, provides a neutral forum open to all disciplines concerned with the ocean and its resources. The Institute takes no views of its own, advocates no position, but provides a convenient opportunity for people of all disciplines to exchange views on matters of current interest with regard to ocean policy. The proceedings of these meetings are widely disseminated for use by scholars, businessmen and decision-makers. Our co-host this year, the Centre for Marine Law and Policy, has the distinction of being the first institution in the United Kingdom to provide for interdisciplinary research and teaching in marine affairs. While their approaches are quite different, the two co-sponsors blend nicely to assure that this year's program will be of interest and value to you all.

The Law of the Sea Institute has a tradition of holding its annual meetings in countries bordering the Atlantic and Pacific Oceans -- countries necessarily affected by the oceans and oceans policy. It is appropriate that we hold this year's meeting in Cardiff, a land of great scenic beauty and rich tradition. Much of this tradition relates to the sea upon which the city borders; Cardiff is known for its history as a sea port. Swansea and Milford Haven are now among the finest ports for the transport of oil.

Wales served as the starting point for another famous sea voyage. It began on the rocky headland on the Pembrokeshire coast; here in a little hollow near the coast lies the Cathedral Church of St. David's. It was on this coast that many landfalls were made on the ancient sea-routes from northern Spain, Brittany and Cornwall to Ireland and the Isle of Man. Here it was that the Briton, St. Patrick, took ship for the Emerald Isle on his journey that led to the conversion of Ireland. Had he only been able to foresee the future, perhaps he might have first laid his course to Rockall.

I believe that the program -- prepared for you with great care by the Conference General Chairman and Director of our host Centre, Professor Brown, and by its panel chairmen -- will stimulate your interest and participation. I wish to express the Board's appreciation to Professor Brown and his staff for arranging an exceedingly pleasant setting for this meeting, and for the many hospitalities that they are extending to us. It is my hope, for those who are not thoroughly conversant with this Institute's prior work, that you will be inspired to become members of the Law of the Sea Institute and actively support its ongoing efforts. I can promise you a rewarding experience, so please join us.

E. D. Brown: There has been a tradition at these annual gatherings of introducing a poetic note into our proceedings. Some of you may well remember Francis Christy's leanings in this direction when he made much play of the fact that the name *Grotius* rhymes with *atrocious*. This brings me to our final speaker in this opening session, one who has been described as the polymath extraordinaire -- lawyer, scientist, politician, and, this morning, Director of the Law of the Sea Institute -- Professor John Craven. Rumor has it that he will, once again, be injecting a verse or two -- although he has assured me that he will not be speaking in Welsh.

WELCOMING ADDRESS

John P. Craven
Director
Law of the Sea Institute

The Law of the Sea Institute has had, for almost a decade now, the advantage of being peripatetic, holding its conferences in many seaports bordering many seas. Initially, as a note of levity, we looked to the major poets of each of these nations and discovered that each had indeed captured, through poetry, his nation's perceptions of the sea. In Kiel, we learned of Goethe's perception, which was drawn from the Baltic, a sea so often deceptively still and therefore deceptively terrifying, and we quoted a few lines in German from the poem *Meeres Stille*. In Oslo, we discovered, through Ibsen's *Peer Gynt*, the majesty of the *fjord* and the mountain as Peer Gynt returns from his ocean travels, and when we assayed to recite the poetry in native Norwegian, it was understandable -- by the non-Norwegians. In San Francisco, we empathized with Bret Harte's description of the fog-enshrouded Golden Gate and his perception that the ocean is perpetually enshrouded in fog with hidden rock. In each recitation, we tried to provide the full flavor by reciting in a native tongue: German, Norwegian and Californian.

So, with high expectations, we set forth to recover from the famous bards of Wales some significant piece of sea poetry in the original tongue. I did make a selection from a fourteenth-century bard and I set out to learn how to pronounce the language with the aid of my wife, who is a speech pathologist. But I soon discovered that, just as the Orient is unable to master the single "l" in "Honoruru," I am unable to master the double "l" in "Llewellyn." Fortunately, one of your latter-day bards, Dylan Thomas, wrote and spoke the mellifluous language of Britain and America, and his perception of the sea is, as it is for most Welshmen, personal and profound. His perception is quite fittingly encapsulated in the prologue to his poems which he dedicated to "Wales in my Arms":

> This day, winding down now
> At God's speeded summer's end
> In the torrent salmon sun
> In my seashaken house
> On a breakneck of rocks,
> Tangled with chirrup and fruit,
> Froth, flute, fin and quill
> At a wood's dancing hoof,
> By scummed, starfish sands
> With their fishwife cross
> Gulls, pipers, cockles, and sails,
> Out there, crow black, men
> Tackled with clouds, who kneel
> To the sunset nets,
> Geese nearly in heaven, boys
> Stabbing, and herons, and shells
> That speak seven seas...

PART I:

THE IMPACT OF UNCLOS III
ON CONTEMPORARY NAVAL OPERATIONS

INTRODUCTION

Captain A.G.Y. Thorpe
Chief Naval Judge Advocate
Royal Navy, United Kingdom

"The Impact of UNCLOS on Contemporary Naval Operations" is a fascinating subject. To me, a serving officer in the Royal Navy, it is of vital importance. Unfortunately, UNCLOS dealt mainly with peaceful uses of the sea. I say *unfortunately* because, if you take the view that I do, the traditional divide between the law of war and the law of peace is no longer relevant; we spend our lives perpetually on a ladder of tension, either high or low. We need all the help we can get because, I hope, we can actually turn the tension down as well as up. Therefore, concepts such as self-defense and naval weaponry are of particular importance.

Our first speaker, Mr. Geoffrey Kinley, is a very distinguished lecturer in Defence Studies at Kings College, London, and is currently writing a new edition of O'Connell's book on *The Influence of Law on Sea Power*. Mr. Kinley will give you an overview of self-defense.

Professor David Larson of the University of New Hampshire Department of Political Science will then summarize his very detailed paper dealing with naval weaponry in particular.

Next, in addition to these presentations, I will make available a paper I gave at the British Institute of International and Comparative Law on the legality of mine warfare, because this is a specific weapons problem with the technology for the future.

Finally, we will have two commentaries. Rear Admiral Bruce Harlow, formerly of the United States Navy, will address Mr. Kinley's views on the law of self-defense and contemporary naval operations. Then, Mr. Glen Plant, a law of the sea officer with the United Nations Office of the Special Representative of the Secretary-General for the Law of the Sea, will discuss the papers presented by both Mr. Kinley and Professor Larson.

THE LAW OF SELF-DEFENSE, CONTEMPORARY NAVAL OPERATIONS, AND THE UNITED NATIONS CONVENTION ON THE LAW OF THE SEA

Geoffrey Kinley
Faculty of Laws
Kings College
London, United Kingdom

Introduction

> The States Parties to this Convention ... Affirming that matters not regulated by this Convention continue to be governed by the rules and principles of general international law,
>
> Have agreed as follows: ...
>
> -- Preamble to the United Nations Convention on the Law of the Sea, 1982[1]

The United Nations Convention on the Law of the Sea (hereafter, *the UN Convention*) does not directly concern itself with the use of force at sea.

Among matters not regulated by the UN Convention are the legal problems arising from the use of force at sea by states insofar as such force is permitted under the United Nations Charter (hereafter, *the Charter*) in circumstances of self-defense. Also left unregulated by the UN Convention is the legal regime governing the operations of naval forces on the high seas in peacetime, a regime which will have as its primary objective the elimination of the risk of force being used at all at sea by states through their maritime forces. This is a very significant element in that legal order for the seas and oceans which will promote their peaceful use.

This paper will examine the extent to which the UN Convention deals with these matters at all, and consider the rules and principles to be found outside the UN Convention which impose legal constraints on the actions of naval units, particularly when operating on the high seas in conditions of high political tension as between the flag-state of a warship and another state regarded as a potential enemy. Unless the states in question are content in a particular case to slide into a condition of general hostilities, or belligerency, it is assumed that they would prefer to have an effective legal regime governing the conduct of naval units on the high seas.

Two preliminary points must be made. First, it is assumed for the purposes of this paper that the UN Convention was only intended to operate in situations for which specific provision was made in its articles, and that other matters, such as the use of force, were left to be regulated within the general framework of the Charter. Article 301 of the UN Convention subjects states parties "exercising their rights and performing their duties" under the Convention to the constraints on the threat or use of force established under Article 2(4) of the Charter. Insofar as the use of force is left for regulation elsewhere, this must be assumed to be force the use of which is permitted under the Charter. Force, or the threat of force, can be a feature of United Nations enforcement action under Chapter VII of the Charter.

But more typically force can be employed by a member-state of the United Nations under the Charter for purposes of self-defense, even if Article 51 of the Charter (which provides for this) does oblige the member-state which resorts to this right immediately to report the exercise thereof to the Security Council. In theory, the situation is then subjected to the measures deemed necessary by the Security Council.

It is not, alas, inconceivable that member-states of the UN may resort to force, or persist in its use, in circumstances which fall outside the Charter regime completely. If member-states, or indeed non-members, were to drift into the state of general armed conflict with one another which went far beyond the bounds of the doctrine of self-defense as ordinarily understood and were to ignore partially or wholly the constraints of the UN Charter and the resolutions of the political organs of the organization, it seems reasonable to assume that *pro tanto* the pre-Charter traditional law of naval warfare would be applied to the maritime operations arising in the course of that conflict. This is necessary, even if only to protect the interests of those other states which have been affected by the conflict -- the "neutrals."[2] If, for example, a naval armed conflict is carried on between states which have ignored their obligations under the Charter, and if there is no effective UN enforcement action under Chapter VII of the Charter to counteract the effects of that conflict, it would seem that the very Charter mechanism, the maintenance of which is so essential to what the Preamble to the UN Convention terms *a legal order for the seas and oceans*, will have completely broken down and rendered the Convention inoperable. Clearly, however, the law cannot leave the conflict completely unregulated.

The second preliminary point is this. When speaking of *naval operations* it is necessary to bear in mind that the bulk of the navies of the world are merely coastal defense forces, restricted in capability to the basic protection of the national territory and of the economic interests of the state in question in its maritime belt. Relatively few navies have global reach and the capacity to deploy maritime forces for lengthy periods far from home. Those who can do this are sometimes termed *deep water* or *ocean going* navies. The United States, the USSR and the United Kingdom are, of course, among the small group of states possessing this sort of naval capability. Such a global capability enables a state to project its political influence through its navy -- "gunboat diplomacy." This projection of influence may be purely a feature of national policy or it may be supportive of the policy of a regional or inter-continental collective security arrangement. The global reach of a navy also enables the flag-state of a warship to protect its national merchant shipping and its maritime trade and trade routes -- a central feature of the maritime policies of the European member-states of NATO.

The realities are that the bulk of the navies of the world are, by necessity, born of limited capability, interested only in the legal problems of conducting maritime operations in, or within striking distance of, the territorial sea of the particular state. The high seas, however, are by and large the preserve of the deep water navies. The high seas are, by definition, an area within which no state has a claim to sovereignty which can give it some automatic legal edge or prior claim of right, as is the case with naval operations conducted in the territorial sea of a coastal state. The high seas being the preserve of all states, they form an area within which the risk of confrontation between the warships of potentially hostile states is greatest, especially when the states in question are determined to put a marker down to indicate that they are the most significant maritime power (and, by inference, political force) in the areas of sea in question.

It follows that activities undertaken by way of maintaining a state's security or displaying its political influence through naval operations on the high seas are particularly apt for precise legal regulation where the absence of legal clarity may lead to a risk of major naval (or indeed more general) armed conflict. In the case of the superpowers, any confrontation which is not properly governed by legal rules might conceivably trigger a Third World War. The aim of this paper is to assess just how far the necessary legal precision and clarity exists, either within the UN Convention or outside it.

The United Nations Convention and the Use of Force by States

General Features of the Convention Regime

Insofar as the UN Convention expresses the rights and obligations of states parties to the Convention (and, by extension, their warships, military aircraft, national shipping and civil aircraft) in terms of geographical zones -- essentially the zones which comprise the maritime belt of a state -- it is necessary to examine the relevant zonal regimes set up under various parts of the Convention to ascertain whether or not they give any guidance as to the circumstances in which a state may use armed force within the general context of the law of the sea in peacetime and hence within the scope or area of interest of the Convention.

The Convention is absolutely silent as to circumstances in which the use of force by a state is permitted. It never speaks of the lawful use of force, save insofar as it in effect enjoins states parties to the Convention to exercise their rights and perform their obligations under the Convention constrained by the requirements of Article 2(4) of the UN Charter, a constraint which exceptionally allows for the use of force in self-defense. The use or threat of force is purely cited in the context of the illegality thereof -- illegality triggering, by inference, a right to use counter-balancing force, essentially in the context of self-defense.

These references to the use or threat of force are to be found specifically in relation to the security of the coastal state in its territorial sea and to that of the littoral state where a right of transit passage exists through an international strait, *i.e.*, through waters ordinarily part of the territorial sea of the littoral state. The Convention provisions with regard to the exclusive economic zone (*EEZ*) are silent as to the use of force, or as to the security considerations of the coastal state.

The Territorial Sea

Insofar as the UN Convention concerns itself with questions of defense security at all, that concern is evinced with regard to the security of the coastal state in its territorial sea. The term *security* is expressly used in Article 19 of the Convention in conjunction with the terms *peace* and *good order*. If a foreign vessel prejudices in the territorial sea any of these interests of the coastal state, its passage will not be innocent. Unlike these other terms, however, *security* is not singled out in Article 27 of the Convention as an interest the infringement of which will entitle the coastal state to exercise criminal jurisdiction over a foreign vessel passing through the territorial sea. It is, nonetheless, clear that the term *security*, picked up as it was from Article 14(4) of the Geneva Convention on the Territorial Sea and Contiguous Zone of 1958, is intended to identify in particular the need of the coastal state to defend itself and to ensure that it is not exposed to any military threat. This is supported by a reference to *weapons exercises* as a facet of coastal state security in Article 25(3). The expression *security* may be referable, of course, in general parlance to the protection of any vital interest of the coastal state, such as the living resources of either the territorial sea or the EEZ. The enforcement of the national legislation of the coastal state with regard to the protection of such interests may involve the enforcement agencies of the state in using a degree of force in order, for example, to arrest a foreign vessel violating the coastal state's fishing conservation legislation.

It is, however, clear that the enforcement task need not necessarily be carried out by the naval forces of the state. In the United Kingdom, for example, naval officers and warships enforcing sea fishery conservation regulations do so under the authority of specific sea fishery legislation and do not act in their military capacity.

Even in matters concerning defense security in the narrow sense of the term, the Convention is silent as to possible constraints on the use of force. There are, however, significant pointers in Article 19 of the Convention, which sets out the detailed criteria for innocent passage by foreign vessels through the territorial sea. Among the activities which would make the passage of a foreign vessel non-innocent on the grounds that it is prejudicial *inter alia* to the security of the coastal state, we find the following listed:

(a) any threat or use of force against the sovereignty, territorial integrity or political independence of the coastal State, or in any other manner in violation of the principles of international law embodied in the Charter of the United Nations;
(b) any exercise or practice with weapons of any kind;
(c) any act aimed at collecting information to the prejudice of the defense or security of the coastal state;
(d) any act of propaganda aimed at affecting the defense or security of the coastal state;
(e) the launching ... of any aircraft;
(f) the launching ... of any military device; ...
(k) any act aimed at interfering with any systems of communication or any other facilities or installations of the coastal state; ...

In any of these cases, the Convention rather grimly asserts in Article 25(1), "The coastal state may take the necessary steps in its territorial sea to prevent passage which is not innocent."

As a corollary the Convention adds in Article 30 that a foreign warship which

does not comply with the laws and regulations of the coastal state concerning passage through the territorial sea and disregards any request for compliance therewith which is made to it

may be required by the coastal state to leave the territorial sea.

Article 30 is an echo of Article 23 of the Territorial Sea Convention of 1958 which was relied upon by the United States in asserting that North Korea was not entitled forcibly to seize the intelligence-gathering vessel *Pueblo* in 1968, even supposing she was at the time of that seizure within the North Korean territorial sea, but only to require her to leave the territorial sea.[3] It is submitted, however, that Article 30 as worded seems now to pick up directly the wording of Article 21 where the coastal state is permitted to adopt "laws and regulations ... relating to innocent passage through the territorial sea," that legislation essentially covering questions of safe navigation, protection of the marine environment, and enforcement of local fishery legislation, as well as its customs, fiscal, immigration and sanitary legislation. Article 21 picks up some of the more mundane activities stated in Article 19 to be prejudicial to the coastal state from the point of view of innocence of passage. In the circumstances, it is submitted that there is no ground for suggesting that Article 30 acts as a general constraint on the authority given to the coastal state to take "necessary steps" to deal with non-innocent passage through its territorial sea.

The real question is whether or not Articles 19 and 25 of the Convention give the coastal state rights to use force to deal with vessels engaged in non-innocent passage which it would not have by reference to "rules and principles of general international law." It seems that the coastal state would be entitled to use force against vessels engaging in certain of the proscribed activities, whether or not those vessels were at the time of transgression in the territorial sea. For example, Article 19(2)(a) picks up the wording of Article 2(4) of the Charter itself, which prohibits the "threat or use of force" against the territorial integrity or political independence of a state. The prohibition in Article 2(4) of the Charter is generally agreed to be subject to the reservation of the right of self-defense in Article 51 of the Charter.[4] So it seems that in this particular case the "necessary steps" open to the coastal state would be co-extensive with those available under the law of self-defense in the event of an armed attack. Hence the coastal state's response to the "threat of force" under Article 19(2)(a) would presumably depend on whether or not the government of that state believed that the right of self-defense included the right of anticipatory self-defense or pre-emption, *i.e.*, the right to respond or react with force to the imminent use of armed force by another state.[5]

Other activities by a foreign vessel listed in Article 19 of the Convention could similarly be construed as giving the right to the coastal state to use necessary force by way of self-defense. All would turn on the facts. An act "aimed at collecting information to the prejudice of the defense of the coastal state" might conceivably be directly linked with the launching of an armed attack as, indeed, might an act of propaganda under Article 19(2)(d). Interference with communications facilities of the coastal state -- say, by electronic "jamming" -- might equally be part of an attack. More obviously the launching from a warship of a missile (a typical "military device") towards the coastal state would, and the launching from an aircraft carrier of a strike aircraft might, constitute the commencement of an armed attack.

If then, on the facts, a situation has arisen in which the coastal state would have the right to resort to force to repel what was an "armed attack," the Convention adds nothing to the general law. The merit of Article 19 is that it clarifies the acts falling short of an "armed attack" which may entitle the coastal state to exclude foreign vessels from the territorial sea and, in the case of warships, to exclude or expel them therefrom pursuant to Article 30 of the Convention. It seems reasonable to assume that the expulsion or exclusion mechanism under Article 30 is the only remedy available to the coastal state where the foreign warship engages in activities forbidden under sub-paragraphs (g), (h), (i) and (j) of Article 19(2). These are matters on which the coastal state may legislate with regard to innocent passage through the territorial sea under Article 21(1), which links up with Article 30.

International Straits
Part III of the UN Convention provides, in the case of international straits, the right of transit passage for foreign ships and aircraft and, as a *quid pro quo*, allows the littoral states some powers of control, while insisting in Article 34(1) that the sovereignty and jurisdiction of the littoral states is exercised subject to Part III "and to other rules of international law." The Convention stresses in Article 38(1) that the right of transit passage "shall not be impeded" and finally asserts in Article 44 that:

> States bordering straits shall not hamper transit passage and shall give appropriate publicity to any danger to navigation or overflight within or over the strait of which they have knowledge. There shall be no suspension of transit passage.

It is instructive to analyze and compare the controls given under Part III to the littoral states with those vested in the coastal state with regard to innocent passage through the territorial sea. We find, for example, a power vested in littoral states to adopt, under Articles 40-42, laws and regulations relating to safety of navigation; research and survey activities; pollution control; fishing; and the enforcement of customs, fiscal, immigration or sanitary legislation. These powers are very similar in form to those given the coastal state under Articles 21 and 22 of the Convention, and for the most part repeat the lesser "non-innocent" activities listed in Article 19(2)(g)-(j). In the case of transit passage, too, they pick up the specific obligations with regard to safety at sea and ship-originating pollution laid on vessels under Article 39(2).

Quite what the littoral states can do in the event of transgressions by foreign vessels of the lesser requirements of transit passage is nowhere spelled out. While Article 42 permits the littoral state to adopt legislation relating to transit passage, nothing is said about the enforcement of such legislation. There are no provisions in Part III of the Convention comparable with the coastal state enforcement provisions to be found in Part II with regard to innocent passage through the territorial sea (Articles 25, 27 and 30). Nor are there specific provisions reminiscent of the coastal state's enforcement powers in the EEZ under Article 73 with regard to its legislation for resource management and conservation. However, on the basis first, that infringement of the provisions of Articles 40-42 make the passage of a ship no longer transit passage and second, that the waters comprising straits are for all purposes except transit passage regarded as waters within the sovereignty and jurisdiction of the littoral states, there seems no reason to suppose that the right vested in littoral states to prescribe legislation is not accompanied by a corresponding right to enforce it. Article 38(3) supports this interpretation insofar as it leaves any activity falling outside transit passage "subject to the other applicable provisions of this Convention," which provisions presumably include enforcement powers vested in the coastal state within the territorial sea under Part II.

As far as the use of force is concerned, Part III of the Convention is no more specific than was Part II. The requirements for transit passage by ships and aircraft -- including, of course, warships and military aircraft -- are provided in Articles 38(2) and 39(1). Article 39 provides as follows:

> (1) Ships and aircraft, while exercising the right of transit passage shall:
> (a) proceed without delay through or over the strait;
> (b) refrain from any threat or use of force against the sovereignty, territorial integrity or political independence of states bordering the strait, or in any other manner in violation of the principles of international law embodied in the Charter of the United Nations;
> (c) refrain from any activities other than those incident to their normal modes of continuous and expeditious transit unless rendered necessary by *force majeure* or by distress;
> (d) comply with other relevant provisions of this Part.

Presumably Article 39(1)(a) is intended as an alternative formulation of the requirement that transit passage must be "continuous and expeditious" under Article 38(2). Article 39(1)(b) is, of course, a simple recital of the familiar incantation in Article 2(4) of the UN Charter, prohibiting the threat or use of force (in this case by transiting ships or aircraft) with the addition of the word *sovereignty*. While Article 39(1)(c) forbids "any activities other than those incident to their normal mode of continuous and expeditious transit," no attempt is made to list exhaustively matters which might affect prejudicially the security of the littoral states, as was done in Article 19 with regard to innocent passage through the territorial sea. It seems reasonable to assume, however, that such activities, insofar as they constituted, on the facts, elements in an "armed attack" on the littoral states, could be dealt with as such by the littoral states.

In fact, Part III of the UN Convention adds nothing at all to the general law with regard to the use of force within an international strait. All turns on whether or not the littoral states could in any event have exercised the right to use force against a transiting vessel, particularly a warship. It must be borne in mind that, on the reasoning of the International Court of Justice in the *Corfu Channel Case (Merits)*,[6] the mere fact that a foreign warship is apparently asserting a right of transit passage which has been the object of some prior challenge does not make that assertion necessarily or inevitably an overt threat against the sovereignty of the littoral states.

The Exclusive Economic Zone

Part V of the Convention, which provides the regime for the EEZ, is silent as to the protection of the defense security of the coastal state within the EEZ, and as to any related use of force to ensure such protection. The legality of force is implied rather than stated in Article 73 in relation to the enforcement of the coastal state's legislation with regard to the EEZ, legislation made under the authority of this Part of the Convention. This enforcement task falls outside of defense security in the usual sense of the term. There are echoes in this Part of the Convention of national defense considerations, it must be conceded. Article 60(1), for example, vests in the coastal state the exclusive right in the EEZ, *inter alia:*

> to authorize and regulated the construction, operation and use of:
> (a) artificial islands: ...
> (c) installations and structures which may interfere with the exercise of the rights of the coastal state in the zone.

Inasmuch as under Part V of the Convention, such islands, installations and structures are not in terms limited to those which are created for the purpose of exploiting the natural resources of the EEZ, this provision seems, on its face, to enable the coastal state to prevent the erection of any such construction which it considers inimical to its defense security interests.

That aside, Article 58, the provision which imposes duties on other states in the EEZ, effectively puts the EEZ on the same plane as the high seas so far as defense security matters (including ultimately the use of force) are concerned. Article 58(2) provides:

> Articles 88 to 115 and other pertinent rules of international law apply to the exclusive economic zone in so far as they are not incompatible with this Part.

It is to these Articles and to the high seas regime generally under the Convention that we must next turn.

The High Seas

The bulk of the references in the UN Convention to warships, the basic instruments of maritime power, are found in Parts II and VII. In Part II of the Convention, the warship is treated separately from merchant ships from the point of view of immunities from the civil and criminal processes of the coastal state but is otherwise subjected to the same regime of innocent passage in the territorial sea. No mention is made, however, of the particular role of the warship *qua* instrument for advancing the national policy of the flag-state.

Part VII of the UN Convention, dealing with the high seas, similarly refers to warships particularly from the point of view of preserving their immunity from the jurisdiction of states other than the flag-state (Article 95). Specific law enforcement powers are conferred on warships by this Part of the Convention: the power to seize pirates (Article 107); the right to conduct hot pursuit (Article 111); and the general (although exceptional) right of visit and flag verification of apparently foreign vessels provided under Article 110.

None of these powers of immunities in any way touches on the operation of the warship in its most typical role on the high seas -- as an emblem of the political power of the flag-state and as a key element in that state's defense security system. The Convention does nothing to define or constrain the scope of naval operations. Naval maneuvers or exercises; weapons testing; submarine operations; surveillance or harassment of foreign warships: none of these is singled out for attention in the Convention, as far as the high seas are concerned. Part VII of the Convention is, in fact, largely a re-statement of the provisions of the Geneva Convention on the High Seas of 1958, the Preamble to which declares itself to be a codification of customary

17

international law. If Part VII, following the 1958 High Seas Convention, does not forbid particular naval operations, then they remain legal, in the view of one distinguished commentator.[7]

In an ideal world, Part VII of the Convention should be sufficient to prevent any risk of force being used in naval operations, provided only that contracting states act in accordance with certain cardinal principles. First, that warships of different states keep clear of one another on the high seas and that states heed the exhortation in Article 87(2) of the Convention that they should exercise the relevant freedoms with due regard for the interests of other states in their exercise of the freedom of the high seas. Second, that they should ensure, under Article 88, that the high seas are reserved for peaceful purposes. Third, that they should not attempt to exercise sovereignty over any part of the high seas: Article 89.

In the context of naval operations, the particularly relevant freedoms of the high seas among those expressly mentioned in Article 87(1) of the Convention are the freedoms of navigation and overflight. The freedom of overflight has to be considered (at least in the case of civil aircraft) in the light of the Chicago Convention of 1944.[8] As such, it raises questions beyond the scope of the present paper.

The UN Convention gives no assistance as to whether, and, if so, how, the freedom of navigation for warships on the high seas is in any way constrained. *Navigation* is not defined. In general usage, it may be particularly linked with the characteristics of vessels engaged in maritime trade and thus evoke the notion of the continuous movement of a vessel from one port or place to another by the most convenient or the shortest practicable route. *Navigation* must embrace for all vessels the freedom to anchor or stop on the high seas when so required by bad weather, *force majeure* or physical constraints, such as tidal conditions. Yet the notion of continuous movement as a feature of the freedom of *navigation* is brought out by implication in the Convention's formulation of the freedom in Article 87(1), in that certain freedoms which may require a vessel to stop, or maneuver on occasion in a random fashion -- such as the freedoms of fishing and scientific research -- are separately identified.

Yet even if it is assumed that *navigation* usually implies in the context of the high seas the continuous movement of a vessel by the shortest practicable route from place to place, there seems to be no reason to suppose that the routine operational requirements of a warship in peacetime -- such as the requirement to lie stopped on the high seas for a lengthy period while engaged in surveillance, or to maneuver in a distinctive way while engaged on, say, an anti-submarine exercise -- take it outside the confines of "navigation" under the Convention. What is particularly required is that the warship so engaged plainly indicates its intentions in accordance with internationally accepted (and publicized) signals and procedures.

The problem is that where warships of two states which are potential enemies of one another are engaged in low-level confrontation on the high seas, their maneuvers may well be constrained, even dictated, by national security or policy requirements rather than by overriding considerations of safety at sea, and in particular, by the maintenance of separations between vessels. Two such states may, for example, each wish, for national policy reasons, to maintain a naval presence in the same, limited area of high seas at the same time. The area in question may, for example, be in the approaches to a strait of immense strategic significance.

A state may even purport unilaterally to appropriate a specified area of high seas for purposes of, say, weapons testing or naval exercises and to exclude vessels of other states from that area. This might be effected by the issue of a Notice to Mariners. The state may at the same time disclaim any intention of infringing Article 89 of the Convention. It may cite safety as the reason for such exclusion. There are many examples of nuclear weapon tests being conducted on the high seas -- particularly in the Pacific by the United States and the USSR -- where the testing state has "advised" or "requested" foreign vessels for safety reasons not to enter the test area for a given period.[9] But this falls short of *directing* foreign vessels not to enter the test area. Furthermore, the testing state has usually laid great stress on the brevity of the period of exclusion and the remoteness of the test area from regular shipping and air routes.[10] These factors have probably influenced other states in acquiescing where, say, nuclear tests are projected and therefore directing their vessels to avoid the area. The natural inclination of mankind to avoid radiation injury is obviously also a significant factor in compliance where high seas nuclear tests are concerned.

But what if a state seeks, for stated military purposes, to exclude in mandatory terms vessels of other states, both warships and member ships, from a large area of high seas in or on a busy shipping route, for a period of several months? What if the area in question is, as suggested earlier, an area of general strategic significance?

In practical terms, it might be that, whatever the level of tension, any other state which saw its vital interests threatened by such an attempted exclusion, and which had the maritime strength to match that of the state claiming the alleged right, would ignore the exclusion or challenge the appropriate state directly. As a matter of legal theory, however, this is a situation in which the freedoms of the high seas enunciated under the Convention may come into conflict, particularly so long as *navigation* has to be regarded as an all-purpose phrase.

Conflict between freedoms is certainly possible on a literal interpretation of the Geneva Convention on the High Seas of 1958, which provides by Article 2 that, in addition to the listed freedoms of the high seas, there are "others which are recognized by the general principles of international law." *If* there is indeed a broadly accepted freedom for states to appropriate areas of high seas for naval purposes poses and to exclude others therefrom, this freedom is obviously incompatible with "freedom of navigation" in the sense of vessels being able to sail where they like on the high seas. Whether or not this conflict can arise under the UN Convention is more uncertain. In the 1982 Convention, the extended list of freedoms of the high seas in Article 87(1) is stated collectively to "comprise" the freedoms; the term *comprise* seems to be used here in an exhaustive sense. The old, open-ended definition has gone. Yet the fact that the provisions of the High Seas Convention of 1958 were said to be "generally declaratory of established principles of international law" must inevitably have left its mark on state practice.

The only guidance provided under the UN Convention as to the resolution of such conflicts is provided by Article 87(2), which rather weakly exhorts states in exercising freedoms to have due regard for the interests of other states. How far any state would be prepared to subordinate its national interests to those of a potential enemy in the context of naval operations on the high seas at a time of rising tension is, to put it mildly, debatable. In the absence of any system of priorities of freedoms under the Convention, the conflicts remain. Rightly or wrongly -- and, this writer would suggest, wrongly -- the opportunity was not taken in drafting the UN Convention to spell out with particularity whether or not, and, if so, to what extent, a specific freedom of naval operations on the high seas exists, enabling the maritime forces of a state to interfere with, or impede, "navigation" in the sense of the ordinary flow of maritime trade and traffic. At the very least (and arguably producing a similar beneficial result) the freedom of navigation should be better defined, and, if related by that definition to the securing of freedom of passage and movement for shipping generally, given priority.

The Right to Use Force by Way of Self-Defense in Contemporary Naval Operations

Contemporary naval operations is a term particularly used in the context of this paper to embrace all forms of maritime operations on the high seas falling short of general armed conflict. The assumption is made that, both under the UN Convention and under customary international law, the dedication of the high seas to peaceful uses is intended intended to exclude aggression, but that military activity as such on the high seas in peacetime, and the deployment of warships in such areas, is *prima facie* peaceful. In examining the possible application of the law of self-defense to naval operations, this paper is primarily concerned with the activities of sophisticated naval units belonging to significant maritime powers with the capacity to deploy worldwide.

The right of all sovereign states to defend their national territory and their warships and military aircraft, wherever they may be located, is deeply rooted in customary international law.[11] Essentially self-defense is the legal use of force by a state to respond to an illegal use of force against it, designed to counteract the effect of that illegality. The degree of force used in self-defense is thus required to be proportionate to the original threat, and to be the minimum necessary to restore the *status quo ante*. In the Falkland Islands dispute of 1982, for example, the force employed by the United Kingdom's government was directed solely to counteracting the effects of the Argentine invasion of the islands by securing the removal of their forces therefrom and restoring British administration.[12]

Academic opinion has long been divided as to the content of self-defense and the degree of legal constraint on the use of force under this guise.[13] Most jurists agree that the right of self-defense extends to the protection of national merchant shipping and civil aircraft outside national territory. All writers agree that the direct organs of a state such as its armed forces, its warships and military aircraft, can exercise the right of self-defense; *i.e.*, the right to defend themselves from attack by the armed forces or agencies of another state, wherever they may be.

Yet even in the particular context of the self-defense of the warships or military aircraft of a state in conditions of non-armed conflict, there are, however, further academic controversies with regard to the content of self-defense. These stem from the wording of the UN Charter, insofar as the doctrine of self-defense was preserved in Article 51 in the following terms:

> Nothing in the present Charter shall impair the inherent right of individual or collective self-defense if an armed attack occurs

against a Member of the United Nations, until the Security Council has taken the measures necessary to maintain international peace and security ...

Article 51 was clearly intended as an exception to the general prohibition on

the threat or use of force against the territorial integrity or political independence of any state, or in any other manner inconsistent with the Purposes of the United Nations

enshrined in Article 2(4) of the Charter. Article 51, it should be noted, is part of Chapter VII of the Charter, which is entitled "Action with Respect to Threats to the Peace, Breaches of the Peace, and Acts of Aggression." Insofar as Article 51 is expressed as a reservation of a state's rights pending UN action in such circumstances, it would ordinarily be presumed that such threats to the peace, breaches of the peace or acts of aggression would trigger the right of self-defense.

The controversies stem from the form of words used, apparently, to qualify the right of self-defense in Article 51 of the Charter -- "if an armed attack occurs." This gives rise to two related questions. First, is there a right of anticipatory self-defense under the Charter? Second, if there is no such right, what is an *armed attack* and when does it *occur*? In short, when exactly can force in self-defense be employed?

First, there is the question of pre-emptive action. Does the expression *if an armed attack occurs* mean that a state has to wait until an armed attack *has occurred* against its territory or national forces before it can validly exercise its right of self-defense? In the context, for example, of naval operations involving warships on the high seas, and confrontations in such an environment between the warships of potentially hostile states at times of high tension between such states less than open armed conflict, this might mean that, on the true construction of Article 51, a state and its armed forces might be required to await the first use of lethal weapons by such a potential enemy, or even to sustain an initial casualty. Or can a state and its armed forces, faced with an imminent threat of attack or the use of force by the armed forces of another state, pre-empt that attack and use self-defensive force in anticipation of such an attack?

Academic opinion has been historically divided on this point. On this ancient point of interpretation, this writer supports the assessment of Bowett and Waldock that, even under the Charter, there is a right of anticipatory self-defense, for several reasons. First, Article 51 preserves the "inherent" right of self-defense. This can only mean, in my view, that right which was vested in states prior to, and independent of, the Charter complete with all the attributes conferred on that right by customary law. This writer argues that if there is a case for considering the law, like Brownlie,[14] in a temporal context, the state of the law in 1945 must itself be subject to re-evaluation as, for example, weapon technology develops. Second, Article 2(4) (to which Article 51 is, by general agreement, an exception) embraces not only the actual use of force but the threat thereof. Third, so restricted a view of the right of self-defense as argued for by Brownlie and Akehurst would mean that the tactical advantage would always be in the hands of the "assailant," to use O'Connell's term.[15] Indeed, in an extreme case, the ability of a warship effectively to defend itself at all might be destroyed if the warship of a potential enemy was always allowed to have the first use of a lethal weapon. Fourth, because state practice since the Charter does not, in my view, support the argument that the state employing the right of self-defense must eschew the first use of a live weapon. Insofar as the North Atlantic Treaty, for example, provides that member-states may regard "an attack against one as an attack against all,"[16] it seems to contemplate measures including armed force being used by states before they are themselves attacked.

Looked at from the very practical standpoint of the commanding officer of a warship in a confrontation situation who is faced with the possibility of his ship being severly incapacitated or totally destroyed if a potential enemy is allowed to have first use of a lethal weapon, questions as to whether or not there is a right of anticipatory self-defense may seem academic. No doubt anyone in his position would resolve the matter by assuming that he had a right of pre-emptive action, leaving the legal niceties for later consideration by his government. Nonetheless, Article 51's peculiar formulation requires analysis.

Rejection as a legal option of the possibility of pre-emptive action by a state by way of self-defense means that the right to use force under this cover under the Charter will only be triggered by the *occurrence* of an *armed attack*. If, as Brownlie and Akehurst infer,[17] this "occurrence" is to be equated with the receipt of a physical blow by the victim state -- say, when one of its warships is struck by an anti-ship missile -- doubts arise as to whether the right of self-defense has any validity at all in this age of nuclear weapons, given the lethal character of, for example, modern naval theater nuclear clear missiles with sophisticated guidance systems to which there may be no adequate counter-measures. While such missiles, armed with conventional warheads, may not provide assured destruction, and may well have their share of malfunctions, their technical reliability will improve with time. This writer would suggest that if a potential enemy is known to possess such lethal weapons capable of the total destruction of one's own major units, a legal right which cannot be resorted to until such destruction has possibily occurred is of little consequence.

If, however, despite these arguments based on practicability, pre-emptive action is rejected as no longer possible because of Article 51 of the Charter, we must analyze the concept of the "armed attack" to ascertain whether its occurrence is only consistent with receipt of a physical blow by a victim state. Is this, in short, the moment of its occurrence?

The *travaux preparatoires* of the UN Charter, it should be said, do not assist in the task of definition. The drafting history of Article 51 is obscure.[18] Logically, as an exception to Article 2(4), Article 51 should preserve the right of self-defense in cases where Article 2(4) applies, *i.e.*, where there is an actual use of force against a state, or even the threat of force. This would mean the attack could occur at the threat stage. Then, again, Article 51 is part of Chapter VII of the Charter, which authorizes UN action where the Security Council has determined under Article 39 that there exist *threats to the peace, breaches of the peace or acts of aggression*. Article 39 does not employ the expression *armed attack* at all. If, however, Article 51 is to be construed as part of Chapter VII, then it is permissible, on its face, to identify the armed attack which authorizes a state to use force in self-defense, pending Security Council measures, with the types of military activity on the part of a state which authorize the Security Council to take action under Chapter VII in the first place.

Academic opinion in the United Kingdom has not sought to identify the moment of occurrence of an armed attack. Perhaps this is because it has been thought that the identification of the moment at which the attack occurs will always turn on the facts, taking into account the particular characteristics of the weapon systems known to be at the disposal of a state regarded as a potential enemy. Those who say that pre-emptive action is permissible under the Charter do not need to consider the point in any event. Those writers such as Brownlie and Akehurst who favor the narrow, more conservative view of the right of self-defense naturally tend to identify the moment of attack with the delivery of a physical blow on another state, or its warships or military aircraft. This is the stage which, Akehurst holds, is capable of objective verification.[19]

Such an identification of the moment of an armed attack admittedly has the merit of simplicity and clarity. Politically, too, a state may find it acceptable or, indeed, advantageous to sustain an initial casualty, if only to attract the natural sympathy felt towards a victim of unprovoked aggression. This may also be tactically acceptable, where a potential enemy is known not to possess weapons of total devastation, such as nuclear weapons. The result, however, is to hinder the search for the essential ingredients of the armed attack which the lawyer must identify in order to assess when the legal constraints on the victim states are removed.

This writer submits that if it is necessary to establish the time of occurrence and the essential character of an armed attack for the purpose of the UN Charter, it is equally essential to have in mind two basic yet potentially competing requirements of the right of self-defense. First, such a right is only exercisable when the government of the victim state (or the relevant organ of that state, such as the commanding officer of one of its warships) has identified beyond doubt that another state is perpetrating an illegal act of force against it. Second, it has to be an effective right capable of preventing the attacking state from acquiring either some unfair military advantage, or, in an extreme case, some overwhelming balance of military superiority which cannot be redressed. The essence of the right of self-defense by a state is an entitlement to use force to restore the military and political *status quo ante*. Any constraint on the use of force, therefore, which results in that force being insufficient in scale to achieve the aim or causes it to be exercised too late, cannot be described as an effective right.

Assuming, then, that the government of a state is denied the right of anticipatory self-defense, it faces the problem of interpreting the wording of Article 51 literally while maintaining a worthwhile shield. Essentially a balance has to be struck between the need on the one hand for that state sufficiently to identify an attacker, and to detect the unmistakable features of an armed attack, and the requirement on the other hand that the self-defensive force shall be effective. Obviously if there is sufficient military tolerance to allow a state to wait for the actual launch of a missile by a hostile warship, or the firing of some other projectile by a potential enemy without thereby impairing its own capability to defend itself effectively, this is preferable in military or political terms. Legally, however, it is submitted that the requirement of effectiveness will justify the victim state in acting at an earlier stage.

23

It is submitted that what is required of a victim state contemplating the exercise of the right of self-defense is always sufficient evidence of the potential enemy's commitment to the delivery of a physical blow -- "the crossing of the Rubicon." As Waldock puts it,

> an armed attack may be said to have begun to occur, though it has not passed the frontier.[20]

The evidence of commitment to the delivery of a physical blow as indicating the occurrence of an armed attack will obviously depend on the victim state's appreciation of the existence of a military threat posed by another state. If political relations are poor between two states so that there is a condition of *high tension* or *rising tension*, the victim state's awareness should be the more acute. Knowledge of the types of weaponry at the disposal of the potential enemy and their range and destructive power will also be factors in the equation. Generally speaking, the more sophisticated the weaponry known to be at the disposal of a potential enemy, the more attention the state envisaging the use of force in self-defense must pay to such background matters. For example, a potential enemy may be known to have armed its warships with nuclear weapons capable in a single strike of destroying the victim state's capacity to defend itself. Alternatively, the enemy may have missiles or other weapons against which, once launched, the victim state has no defensive system.

It is recognized that the search for evidence of a potential enemy's commitment to the use of a weapon will involve considerations of what is sometimes termed *hostile intent*. The writer is conscious that, in what O'Connell calls *naval parlance*, a distinction has been drawn in the framing of Rules of Engagement between *hostile acts* and *hostile intent*, and that even the hostile act has been regarded as a broader concept than an armed attack.[21] Nonetheless it is, in my view, impossible to separate *act* from *intent* in this context. This is particularly the case when one considers the events which precede the actual firing of a weapon. On one view these events may be regarded as part of the act of firing the weapon; on another they may be considered as mere evidence of the intention to fire.

It is submitted that if, at a time of high or rising tension between two states, a warship of one of those states shows some overt hostile intent, or operates its weapons systems or associated electronic guidance systems, and this operation is detected by a warship of the other state within range of the weapon in question, the detecting state may reasonably take the view that an armed attack has begun to occur within Waldock's meaning. It is submitted that the onus lies on states to ensure that their armed forces always conduct themselves in a peaceful manner, and particularly their naval forces on the high seas. It is always possible in the event of a warship testing or exercising its weapons, or weapons guidance systems, to carry out testing in such circumstances and under such conditions that a potential enemy cannot misunderstand one's intentions. Alternatively, if weapons exercise or the testing of delivery or guidance systems have to be conducted in the vicinity of warships of a potentially hostile state, it is always possible to inform the other state either through diplomatic channels, or directly, of one's intentions. In this connection, it is significant to note (as will be discussed in a subsequent part of this paper)[22] that the principal maritime powers have entered into bilateral treaty arrangements designed to ensure that misunderstandings about intentions in the context of naval operations in the high seas cannot arise.

The writer suggests that the clarification of intentions is at the heart of the problem. If a state makes clear its policy on responding to particular actions by a potential enemy, and emphasizes that it will regard certain identified activities as forming part of an armed attack, many problems will be resolved. That clarity in the law is essential can be readily appreciated if one considers, for example, problems which may be caused where a state as a matter of policy the permits its warships, irrespective of proximity to a potential enemy, to exercise with weapons to a stage little short of the actual firing of the weapon. If, for example, warships of a potentially hostile state have habitually switched on their missile fire control radars at a specific time each day for test purposes, there is always the risk that another state will assume that this testing process is being repeated on a subsequent occasion when that hostile warship has in fact already embarked on the course of launching a full scale attack. Frequency of repetition of potentially offensive military activity may lead, in short, to complacency or lack of vigilance on the part of the other side. Clearly if, as a matter of law, overt activity forming part of a weapon firing sequence, or overt activation of a weapon system, is to be regarded as evidence of the occurrence of an armed attack, the frequency with which such activities are detected will not affect the legal right of a potential victim to respond.

The discussion thus far has been concerned with the use, or threatened use, of weapons as evidencing the occurrence of an armed attack. It should, however, be borne in mind that the very maneuvering of warships may be conducted in such a way on the high seas as to cause apprehension that an armed attack is being carried out. Aggressive maneuvering may be intended merely to harass or provoke; a typical example will be where the maneuvers of warships are designed to interfere with or impede the surveillance activities of a potential enemy warship. At times of high tension, however, such maneuvers -- involving, very often, a risk of collision -- might reasonably be regarded as the institution of an attack.

The position with regard to the employment of sophisticated naval weapons such as anti-ship missiles is perhaps easier to regulate from the point of view of identifying the occurrence of an armed attack. The use of such weapons will usually involve the firing ship in commencing a sequence of operations which can be observed, sometimes visually, sometimes by electronic counter-measures or defensive systems. The opening of missile housings represents a classic example of the former; the detection of emissions from a fire control radar serving a missile system, denoting that the guidance system has "locked on" to a target, of the latter. If, at a time of high tension, these "indices" as O'Connell describes them,[23] are detected on a warship of a potentially hostile state, it may well be reasonable to regard them as part of the complex series of operations -- say, the firing sequence of a missile -- which will result in the launch of a projectile. If the warship detecting these indications knows that the potential enemy possesses weapons of devasting power, the belief may be the more reasonable.

It is, therefore, submitted that the balance between identification of an armed attack and effectiveness of self-defense in the context of naval operations on the high seas is best served if all governments ensure that their warships and military aircraft scrupulously adhere to established international procedures in matters of navigation and

further ensure that any departures by their warships from such procedures for operational reasons are well publicized or properly communicated to any potentially hostile state. This is the price which must
be paid for growing sophistication in weapon technology. Where lethal
weapons are deployed, the balance requires that the frontier of an
armed attack be pushed back further in time to events prior to, yet
connected with, the operation of a weapons system.

O'Connell pertinently points out that sufficient, or sufficiently
precise indicators may well not be available in a particular case.[24] A
warship of a potential enemy may, for example, not be in visual contact
Again, electronic information -- such as radar emissions characteristic
of an enemy fire control radar -- may be misleading because of, say,
atmospheric interference. He particularly reminds us of the unrelia-
bility of sonar information.[25] Electronic information may, too, be
misunderstood or misinterpreted also as a matter of human error.

O'Connell cites these facts as leading "naval thinking" to conclude
that the firing of weapons in self-defense may only be permissible in
response to a discharge of a projectile by the other side. *His* conclusion, writing in 1975, is that such is the failure rate in surface-to-
surface missiles, and such is the adequacy of counter-measures to them,
that the chances of instant destruction are not sufficiently high to
require the use of pre-emptive force.[26] Yet clearly improvements in
weapons guidance systems may from time to time outstrip counter-measures. It seems unsatisfactory, therefore, to restrain a victim state
from resorting to force purely by reference to current assessments of
a potential enemy's weapon capability.

The lawyer, it is submitted, must search for a workable and practicable doctrine of self-defense which takes proper account of developments in naval weapon technology and associated systems. Whatever the
merits of precision and objective verification provided by inflicting
an initial casualty or the delivery of physical blow in ascertaining
the occurrence of an "armed attack" within Article 51 of the Charter,
the fact remains that this simplistic concept of the trigger of self-
defense is no longer sufficient, if it ever was. The writer would,
therefore, submit that the requirement of effective self-defense must
be given sufficient weight. A warship should, therefore, be entitled to
activate its weapon systems in self-defense in face of any number of
indicators of hostile action at a time of high tension, even at a stage
short of the actual firing of a missile by the other side, if it would
be militarily unacceptable to sustain an initial casualty.

The search for the "occurrence" of the "armed attack" required
by those who interpret Article 51 of the Charter literally, may seem
sterile and academic to those concerned with the practical implementation of naval policy and with the need to draw up Rules of Engagement
which are both consistent with the law, easily understood and militarily
effective. The need for such a search purely arises from the employment
by the draftsmen of the Charter of a particularly obscure form of words
-- "if an armed attack occurs" -- for which no explanation exists
in the *travaux preparatoires*.[27] It is submitted, however, that what
the draftsmen undoubtedly had in mind was an armed attack on national
territory, *i.e.*, the invasion of another state. The need in 1985 adequately to secure the safety of warships on the high seas from other
warships equipped with sophisticated weapons of mass destruction at a
time of tension, weapons to which there is no response, was obviously
something for which not even the most enlightened draftsman in 1945
could cater.

There is no public servant with such means of involving his government in international complications as the naval officer, and his responsibility is commensurate with the facilities at his disposal.[28]

The average commanding officer of a warship will not be an international lawyer. He is unlikely to have a detailed grasp of the doctrinal controversies of international lawyers with regard to the content and application of the law of self-defense. It will not help him to know of these differences if he is faced with a situation in which he might possibly have to use force. What he then needs to have is clear-cut guidance as to the legal constraints imposed on him in this context by the UN Convention, by treaty rules of general or particular application and by rules of customary international law. He will particularly need this guidance when he comes into contact with the warships of a potential enemy on the high seas or where he is the subject of unjustified hostile attention in the territorial sea of another state, or in an international strait.

If we take as an example of a warship commander for this examination the commanding officer of a missile destroyer or an anti-submarine frigate belonging to a navy of a significant maritime power, we are envisaging an officer whose operational tasks may well bring him even in peacetime into close contact with the warships of a potential enemy on the high seas, especially where he is engaged in surveillance or harassment or an intelligence-gathering role. Alternatively, while minding his own business, he may be the subject of unwelcome attention from the other side. This attention may stem from the fact that he is engaged in a particular operational activity of interest to the other side (such as operating new carrier aircraft), or from the fact that he is deployed in a particular area of the oceans, say, for intelligence gathering. Alternatively, he may be there simply as a projection of the military policy of his state, deployed to stop a potential enemy from asserting that such an area of high seas is its particular preserve. One thinks in this context particularly of NATO deployments in the North Norwegian Sea and of United States deployments into the Black Sea.

In such a situation, a commanding officer needs to know precisely how he is to respond in a range of potentially threatening situations. How, for example, is he to respond to ships of a potential enemy steering on collision courses or otherwise impeding his navigation? What is he to do if a warship of a potential enemy obviously aims a weapon at him or locks its missile fire control radar on him?

This is where *Rules of Engagement* come in, on the assumption that there is not a general state of hostilities and that the broad dictates of the traditional law of peace are observed. This picturesque term has superseded the old term *Fighting Instructions* and is used as a general term to define the operational instructions given to a commander, not only designed to constrain his initiation of the use of force and to accommodate it to suit the requirements of the particular policy his state, but also to assist him to react to provocation by a warship of a potential enemy in a way which is consistent with national policy requirements.[29]

The political advantages of Rules of Engagement are obvious in the sense that they enable a government, first, to assess the national political requirement, and then to translate that requirement into a military course of action. The bounds of that action can be set in precise military instructions to an on-scene commander as to the extent to which, and the manner in which, he may use force. Naturally the primary task must be to advise the on-scene commander whether it is national policy in a situation of tension to maintain the *status quo* or to increase or decrease the level of tension by careful adjustments to a level of force authorized.

To the lawyer, Rules of Engagement as operational rules and practices must be embraced and constrained by international law. Given that rules of Engagement are of particular importance in the context of maritime operations, they must in that field of operation be constrained by the UN Convention and by the general rules and principles left aside under the Preamble to the Convention. To that extent Rules of Engagement which purport to authorize a maritime commander to break or ignore rules of international law in order to achieve a particular political objective are obviously illegal. Adherence to such rules by a warship commander might involve his government in just the sort of international complications to which O'Connell referred. It is obviously that on-scene commanders should not be put by their governments in such a predicament.

Where the principles of international law are clear, Rules of Engagement can transmit the content of those principles into instructions which the on-scene commander can understand. For example, a commander may be advised in a particular case that he has discretion to use a particular weapon in order to destroy hostile forces. Alternatively, he may be told that the political objective is to be achieved without the actual firing of weapons. All too often, however, the rules of customary international law are open to interpretation: as we have seen, the law of self-defense is no exception. In such a case, Rules of Engagement can embody that interpretation of the law favored, for example, by the flag-state of a warship as a matter of national policy. Where lethal weapons are to be used to protect the defense security or territorial integrity of the state, then, on general principles, the. use of those weapons must be within the scope of the law of self-defense. And so the Rules of Engagement applicable to the particular situation must reflect the legal constraints of the law of self-defense. Inevitably these rules will in turn tend to reflect the policy approach of the state with regard to the attributes of the right of self-defense. Thus the Rules of Engagement will indicate whether live weapons can be first used in self-defense or only in response to another state's first use. The Rules of Engagement will thus reflect the particular government's interpretation, at the end of the day, of the *Caroline* formula, allowing the use of pre-emptive force in situations of exigency.[30]

Traditionally Rules of Engagement approach the problems of classification for an on-scene maritime commander by characterizing the activities of the warships and military aircraft of a potential enemy which might trigger the use of force in self-defense as either *hostile acts* or acts demonstrative of *hostile intent*. A typical instruction in a set of Rules of Engagement might, for example, inform the commanding officer of a warship that he *may* in times of high tension or rising tension regard a particular act as being a hostile act, that is to say the instruction will be couched in permissive terms. In my view the hostile act must be synonymous and synchronous with the *armed attack* as that term is used in Article 51 of the UN Charter. The act in question must, according to the point of view of the particular state, either constitute a military appreciation of what represents the onset of an armed attack or be the trigger which entitles the on-scene commander to use the *Caroline* type of pre-emptive action. Either way the response -- that is, the response to the other side's illegal use of force, actual or immediately threatened -- must be proportionate. That at least is clear as a matter of law. O'Connell, indeed, suggested that the concept of the hostile act must be broader than the armed attack as formulated in the Charter.[31] In my view, however, it is essential that the terms *hostile act* and *armed attack* should have exactly the same connotation. Then, if both states engaged in the confrontation which gives rise to the application of Rules of Engagement are conversant with general principles of customary international law, they will form the same appreciation of what constitutes a hostile act or an armed attack. They will, in effect, be on the same wavelength and can instruct their maritime commanders accordingly.

Typical Rules of Engagement also provide for the characterization of certain acts as demonstrating *hostile intent*. As we have seen in the case of a state which takes the broader view of the right of self-defense and holds that pre-emptive action is permissible, the stage of hostile intent may, indeed, be that at which the actual use of force may be triggered. Belief in the existence of an anticipatory right of self-defense leads inevitably to the conclusion that force may be used whenever there is evidence that a warship or military aircraft of a potential enemy is unmistakably preparing to fire or launch a weapon against one's own national forces, warships or military aircraft. Even if the narrower interpretation of self-defense is taken by a government -- the view which suggests that an initial casualty has to be sustained before a live weapon can be activated by the victim state's warship or military aircraft -- it seems sensible to be able to identify or classify activities of potential enemy forces as posing a threat at an earlier stage. This will serve to alert the on-scene commander of the unit which may thereafter have to respond to a hostile act or an armed attack (assuming these expressions are synonymous) by resort to self-defense.

Where hostile intent is concerned, in particular in the context of naval operations on the high seas, the activities alleged in Rules of Engagement to constitute such a threat will take on that color from the degree of political and military tension between the two or more states engaged in what may be termed a confrontation. To that extent the categorization of activities in Rules of Engagement as showing the degree of hostile intent will undoubtedly be subjective. It is, therefore, particularly important in this context to give precise guidance to the commanding officer of a warship to enable him to distinguish between acts on the part of a potential enemy demonstrating hostile intent and those which are designed merely to harass or inconvenience but not to pose any greater threat. What always has to be borne in mind, moreover, in drafting Rules of Engagement is that apparently threatening navigation by a warship of a potential enemy (say, when it continues on a collision course) may well be the result of negligence or incompetence. It is a sad feature of maritime life generally that vessels of whatever type operating in close formation or close proximity to one another are vulnerable to the risk of collision. This vulnerability is acute even in the cases of friendly warships operating in concert on in close formation.[32] To that extent, Rules of Engagement must have the necessary tolerances built into them to enable the maritime commander to identify a threatening situation with precision. The concept of hostile intent is, therefore, of particular importance in the context of naval operations in that it plugs for the benefit of the maritime commander the information gap between the rules and principles governing normal usages of navigation on the high seas and the situation in which force can be used lawfully in self-defense and assists him to identify the latter.

In drawing up Rules of Engagement, it may be expedient or necessary to provide for circumstances in which one's own warships or naval aircraft initiate provocative action themselves rather than merely react to "triggers" from a potential enemy. In the context of sophisticated naval operations on the high seas conducted by the principal maritime powers, for example, it may be expedient to probe or stimulate one's potential enemy in order to achieve a particular political objective. It may be militarily advantageous to engage in close surveillance of ships of a potential enemy, or, indeed, to harass or ride off those forces when they seek to engage in surveillance themselves. Jamming of the communication systems of a potential enemy force, or use of other methods of electronic warfare, may be envisaged. The political objective may even be seen as requiring provocative or aggressive maneuvering, the steering of collision courses, the misuse of the collision regulations, or the preparation of one's own weapons system. Yet these objectives must, it is submitted, be subject to the overriding considerations of long-established principles of customary law. If this is ignored, the result is chaos and unpredictability.

The draftsmen of Rules of Engagement would also do well to bear in mind that, in all the cases cited, the potential enemy will also have *his* Rules of Engagement. The other side's classification of "hostile intent" may well be broader than one's own. One cannot assume that even at the lower levels of activity in naval confrontation there will be an identity of view, even as between major maritime powers, as to whether or not particular activities pose threats. There is, then, a strong case for formalizing and publicizing at least some of the basic Rules of Engagement, which are, presumably, common to all major navies of the world. This is certainly true in so far as Rules of Engagement seek to avoid the use of force and to prevent unfortunate and potential lethal misunderstandings.

There is agreement as between the major naval powers as to the need for such publication and notification of Rules of Engagement.[33] Ideally this notification should be provided for under a treaty regime binding important naval states. But any form of general notification should suffice. Notifications by way of diplomatic notes to other states is one alternative, although doubts may arise as to whether this notification will percolate to that state's national merchant shipping generally. Publication through Notices to Mariners (NOTMARS) has the merit of circulation through established maritime circles. The United States government, for example, favored this method in 1984 of notifying other states of the defensive Rules of Engagement adopted by United States naval units in the Straits of Hormuz and the Persian Gulf.[34] These Rules had as a particular feature the creation of a five-mile security zone around such units. While it adopted Rules of Engagement in that case, which seemed a bold approach to the right of self-defense, to put it mildly, at least the United States government made a welcome acknowledgement of the need to publicize Rules of Engagement insofar as they related to likely responses by warships to unconventional activities of other vessels or aircraft.

The Rules and Principles of General International Law and Multilateral Treaties

Our analysis so far has not taken into account those general rules of international law which supplement the UN Convention. The intention of the draftsmen was that the Convention should be supplemented by reference, for example, to *other rules of international law* (Article 87(1)); *applicable international instruments* (Article 94(3)(b)); *applicable international regulations* (Article 94(4)(c)); and *generally accepted international regulations, procedures and practices* (Article 94(5)). The inference for the purposes of the present paper is that the supplementation should embrace both rules of customary international law and rules contained in relevant multilateral treaties which are capable of being applied to warships, particularly when there is any risk of the use of force in conditions of non-armed conflict. Rules appertaining to safe navigation and general safety at sea are obviously relevant.

The UN Convention is basically concerned to promote good order on the high seas and to secure the peaceful uses of the seas and oceans by enhancing safety at sea. Consequently the Convention, by Article 94, enjoins every state party to the Convention to take necessary measures to ensure safety at sea, particularly specifying measures relating to

> 3(c) the use of signals, the maintenance of communications and the prevention of collisions.

Article 94(4) and (5) make it clear that in these respects the measures must conform to the "applicable international regulations" or "generally accepted international regulations, procedures and practices."

The obligations of states parties to the Convention in this regard obviously extend to warships flying their flag. It seems clear, therefore, that an obligation is laid on those who draft Rules of Engagement for warships to have due regard for provisions of such applicable international regulations.

In the context of naval operations on the high seas in peacetime, the relevant international regulations are those relating to signals and communications under the general umbrella of the SOLAS Convention of 1974[35] and those relating to prevention of collisions under the Convention on the International Regulations for Preventing Collisions at Sea of 1972.[36] The SOLAS Convention and its related annexes only exceptionally provide for their application to warships. The Regulations with regard to radio telegraphy and radio telephony communications, for example, specifically exclude warships,[37] as do the Regulations relating to safety of navigation.[38] It is submitted, however, that insofar as the obligations of the SOLAS Convention represent basic and internationally agreed safety standards, a state party to the Convention which does not insist on the maintenance for its own warships of safety standards equivalent to those applied to its merchant ships may well incur international responsibility for any damage resulting therefrom. The fact that Chapter V of the Annex to SOLAS (dealing with safety of navigation) does not technically apply to warships should not, it is submitted, free a government from responsibility if there is a departure from the internationally agreed standards by warships of that state in such matters as the use of signals (especially distress and life-saving signals) and the requirements of the International Code of Signals.

31

The basic instrument in general use in international law governing the conduct of naval operations and seeking to prevent the risk of close contact between warships, just like other ships, is the Collisions Convention of 1972, and the Regulations attached thereto. This Convention is clearly within the ambit of Article 87(1) of the UN Convention insofar as the latter article subjects the freedom of the high seas not only to the UN Convention but to "other rules of international law." The Collision Regulations are, at least, applied expressly and squarely to warships, contracting states having additionally the discretion to have rules with regard to additional lights and signals for warships, provided that such additional signals cannot be confused with other signals provided for under the Rules.[39]

What is perfectly clear from the Collision Regulations is that warships have no license to depart from the Rules. They must be scrupulously obeyed. If, then, Rules of Engagement (like those mentioned by O'Connell) instruct a maritime commander to ignore the constraints of the Collision Regulations, any injury caused thereby would clearly sound in damages in terms of the international responsibility of the flag-state of the warship concerned. The whole philosophy of the Collision Regulations is designed to ensure that vessels keep safely clear of one another in all circumstances which might result in a collision.

This is not to say that the Collision Regulations are not concerned with the special problems associated with naval operations. Leaving aside the general saving clause as to the need to have due regard for any special circumstances "including the limitations of the vessels involved,"[40] the Rules make a significant contribution to the avoidance of the sort of misunderstandings which lead to an acrimonious exchange between the governments of the United Kingdom and the USSR in 1970 after a collision in the Mediterranean between HMS *Ark Royal* and a Soviet DDG *Kotlin*.[41] There were, indeed, ambiguities in the old 1960 Collision Regulations which preceded the 1972 Convention as to the precedence given to hampered vessels, that is, vessels restricted in their ability to maneuver. An aircraft carrier launching aircraft (as was HMS *Ark Royal* at the time of the incident in question) was a typical case of a hampered vessel. Such vessels were defined in the "Lights and Shapes" sections of the 1960 Regulations but were not referred to specifically in the "Steering and Sailing" rules. Consequently there was an obvious risk of collision if one vessel believed it had priority and the other vessel did not adhere to the same principle.

The 1972 Collision Regulations make it clear that certain types of naval operations at sea do command precedence in the sense that vessels should keep out of the way of warships engaged in such operations and not interfere with them. Thus Rule 18 provides that, except where there is a narrow channel situation, a traffic separation scheme or an overtaking situation:

(a) A power driven vessel under way shall keep out of the way of: ...
(ii) a vessel restricted in her ability to manoeuvre ...

By rule 3(g), a vessel "restricted in her ability to manoeuvre" includes:

(iii) a vessel engaged in replenishment or transferring persons, provisions or cargo while underway;

(iv) a vessel engaged in the launching or recovery of aircraft;
(v) a vessel engaged in minesweeping operations;

Rule 27 supplements this by providing that such vessels should exhibit specific lights and shapes in addition to those required of them in any event as power-driven vessels underway.

It is, then, apparent that as far as, say, strike aircraft carrier operations on the high seas are concerned, or replenishment underway of warships by fleet auxiliaries, Rule 18 for basic safety reasons, if for no other, protects the vessel engaged in the particular activity. By inference, at least, the Collision Regulations of 1972 put a seal of approval on the identified types of naval operations in peacetime, and suggest that these activities at least are within the ambit of freedom of navigation on the high seas as the term is used in the UN Convention.

On the face of it, Rule 18 should eradicate in the enumerated cases cases the risk of collision leading to possible confrontations as between naval units of potential enemies. Whether the Rule will in *all* cases be sufficient is less certain. No doubt there may be occasions in which vessels protected by Rule 18 could themselves be hampered by other warships, occasions in which it will be alleged that the vessel ostensibly protected by Rule 18 was not in fact at the moment of collision, or whatever, "engaged" in the protected work. In the case of the HMS *Ark Royal* mentioned above, for example, there was much discussion as to whether or not the aircraft carrier was in any event to be given precedence by the Soviet destroyer at a time when the carrier was merely turning into the wind and working up speed preparatory to launching aircraft.[42]

Expressio unius, exclusio alterius. One is reminded of the old maxim when considering the protected naval activity spelled out in Rules 3 and 18 of the Collision Regulations. The clear inference from these Rules is that any other type of naval operation on the high seas is intended to be subjected to the general rules. Thus naval units engaged in, say, anti-submarine warfare exercises, or steaming in close formation, or engaged in surveillance must abide by the Rules at large. This is so even if they are (as is common in the case of vessels engaged in electronic intelligence-gathering) lying stopped in the water. In such a case they are classified under the Rules as being underway in any event.

The Preamble to the Collisions Convention of 1972 stresses the contracting parties' desire to maintain a high level of safety at sea. It is then legitimate to infer that their intention was that the Rules should be applied in an honest and *bona fide* fashion and that those Rules which provide in certain cases for one vessel to have a preferred status, or right of way, should not be abused. Rule 15, the crossing rule, is just such a provision. It has been all too common in the past for warships of states engaged in low-level confrontation on the high seas to seek to put a warship of the other side in a give-way situation. This is done by creating a crossing situation under Rule 15. A typical example of this is where a warship proceeding on the starboard bow of another warship on a parallel course then alters course to port to cross the head of the other ship, at the same time slowing down. In this situation the other vessel is obliged to give way under the Rule. The first ship's action is within the letter, but not, it is suggested, within the spirit of the Collision Regulations.

The truth of the matter is that the Collision Regulations were never intended to deal with the activities of naval forces engaged in low-level confrontation with a potential enemy on the high seas in peacetime. This is especially the case where the confrontation requires as a matter of military policy close contact between one's own warships and those of the potential enemy. The Collision Regulations were, in short, purely designed to cater to those vessels which wished to proceed on their lawful business on the high seas as far as possible without hindering, or being hindered by, other vessels. If, however, naval operations are to involve close physical contact between warships, the 1972 Collision Regulations require to be supplemented. Possible methods of supplementation will be discussed in the next section.

Special Rules and Principles Applicable Under Bilateral Treaties

By 1972 the governments of the United States and the USSR had decided that the risks of conflict and of unintended use of force on the high seas had become so great that it was necessary to take bilateral action to ensure the safety of their respective maritime forces while operating on the high seas in proximity to one another. While the Collision Regulations, if enforced strictly, should have prevented any risk of collision, there had been a series of collisions and close-quarters situations involving the Soviet Navy and the U.S. Sixth Fleet in the Mediterranean and the Soviet Navy and the U.S. Seventh Fleet in the Far East, particularly in the Sea of Japan. During the course of the diplomatic negotiations which led to the SALT I Treaty, therefore, the opportunity was taken to draw up a suitable bilateral agreement which would, it was hoped, substantially reduce the risks of unhealthy contacts between the naval forces of the signatory states on the high seas -- the sort of contacts which might result from provocative and aggressive maneuvering. The treaty was entitled *The Agreement on the Prevention of Incidents On and Over the Seas* and was signed on May 25, 1972.[43] It has become known as *the INCSEA Agreement*. A Protocol extending the ambit of the agreement was signed on May 25, 1973 during the course of the first review of the Agreement.[44]

The INCSEA Agreement is applied to the high seas and is "in effect, a set of international Rules of Engagement"[45] and, in my opinion, constitutes an express acknowledgment on the part of the signatory states that such operational instructions in situations of non-armed conflict must be subject to the constraints of the general law in relation to the peaceful uses of the seas and oceans. Article II of the INCSEA Agreement puts the matter squarely:

> The Parties shall take measures to instruct the commanding officers of their respective ships to observe strictly the letter and spirit of the International Regulations for Preventing Collisions at Sea, hereinafter referred to as The Rules of the Road. The Parties recognize that their freedom to conduct operations on the high seas is based on the principles established under recognized international law and codified in the 1958 Geneva Convention on the High Seas.

Given that the signatories are both parties to the later Collisions Convention of 1972, the reference to the "Rules of the Road" is, presumably, to be construed as a reference to those Rules described in the preceding section of this paper. Insofar as reference is made to the "freedom to conduct operations on the high seas" codified in the

Geneva Convention on the High Seas of 1958, it must be presumed that the Agreement reflects the wording of Article 2 of that Convention which is, on the face of it, more generous in its formulation of such freedoms than the 1982 UN Convention in that, as stated above, the 1958 Convention states that in addition to the enumerated freedoms there are "others which are recognized by the general principles of international law," whereas Article 87(1) of the 1982 Convention suggests that the list of freedoms there given (which does not include naval "operations on the high seas") is exhaustive. Provided that both parties to the INCSEA Agreement are at one as to the content of the freedoms of the high seas, the difference between the two texts should not matter.

The core of the INCSEA Agreement is to be found in Article III. The basic principle provided there is that the warships of the parties shall remain well clear of one another when operating in proximity to each other so as to avoid the risk of collision. Certain naval operations are tacitly permitted: surveillance by warships of one party of the other; exercises with submerged submarines; simulated attacks; carrier operations; replenishment at sea. The crucial principle laid down is that if (or when) these activities are carried out on the high seas, they should not be conducted so close to the warships of the other party as to create a risk of collision or otherwise to cause embarrassment or to endanger. Further, the warships of the parties should communicate their intentions to one another. Three to five days' notice, for example, is to be given by radio and Notices to Mariners (NOTMARS) of actions "which represent a danger to navigation or to aircraft in flight." When in sight of one another, the warships of both parties shall use such signals as are provided for in the Collision Regulations, the International Code of Signals and any other mutually agreed signals. Special emphasis is laid on the need for the "proper signals" concerning the intention to begin launching or recovering carrier aircraft.

Again and again in the Agreement, stress is laid on signalling and communication of intention by the warships of one party to the warships of the other. Pursuant to the Agreement, the parties adopted on a trial basis a set of some 45 Supplementary Signals -- supplementary, that is, to the signals provided for in the Collision Regulations and the International Code of Signals. These signals were transmitted to the International Maritime Organization (IMO) which has circulated them to member-states.[46]

The Supplementary Signals enable one party to give the other basic information as to the type of naval operation which is being conducted at the particular time. Some signals directly supplement special signals under the Collision Regulations in relation to vessels restricted in their ability to maneuver. Some signals give an additional, early indication by a warship that will pass or overtake another warship on a particular side, or conduct particular maneuvers. Other signals give warning of any intention to approach the other party's ships to a given distance. Most significant of all, some signals give warning of military intentions, whether it be the testing of gun or missile systems or the conducting of exercises involving missiles, guns, explosive charges, torpedoes, helicopters or even amphibious training operations.

Consistent with its policy of trying to ensure safety, the INCSEA Agreement provides specifically that neither warships nor military aircraft of the parties shall make simulated attacks "by aiming guns, missile launchers, torpedo tubes and other weapons in the direction of passing ships of the other Party."[47] The Protocol to INCSEA rather curiously forbade the simulation of attacks against non-military ships of the other party, at least where such simulations might be hazardous to the ship or be a hazard to navigation, but made no provision for simulated attacks against non-military aircraft.[48] Nor did the Protocol apply to non-military ships the prohibitions on particular embarrassing maneuvers prohibited against warships in the Agreement -- the launching of objects in the direction of passing ships of the other party, or the use of search lights and the like to illuminate the navigation bridges of such passing ships.[49]

There are curious omissions from the INCSEA Agreement. Distances are never stated. The *practical workability of concrete fixed distances* to be observed in encounters between ships was left over to a committee of the parties set up under Article X of the Agreement. No distances have apparently been agreed upon. To be worthwhile from a military point of view -- that is, from the point of view of alerting the other party's warships to problems or to the development of hazardous situations -- a minimum separation between vessels would, presumably, have to be of the order of five nautical miles. This is the distance specified by the United States government with regard to naval operations on the high seas in the area of the Persian Gulf.[50] Maintenance of such a separation might not, indeed, be feasible in the course of ordinary navigation. Undoubtedly, if distances were to be introduced in the Agreement, there might be considerable difficulty in laying down whose primary duty it was to maintain the fixed distance from the other party's ships at a particular time. There would have to be exceptions to the minimum distance rule and some indication as to what was to happen if the minimum distance requirement was ignored. Traditional exceptions such as *force majeure* and distress would have to be built into the Agreement. Above all it has to be remembered that there may well be operational reasons (such as those related to close surveillance) why the parties might well wish their warships to be rather close to the other party's vessels. The present writer would submit that the introduction of fixed distances would add little to the substance of the Agreement, provided that the Parties ensure in any event that their vessels remain "well clear" of the other side so as to avoid the risk of collision. If the letter and spirit of INCSEA are followed, it should automatically prevent problems arising.

The question arises as to how far the INCSEA Agreement limits particular types of naval operations. On the face of it, activities such as shadowing and marking the warships of the other side would be brought under the general heading of *Surveillance*. The INCSEA Agreement has, however, been heralded as an anti-harassment measure. If harassment is defined as the deliberate and wanton initiation of aggressive or provocative maneuvers or those maneuvers which are plainly dangerous, then the Agreement seems to exclude it. The problem is one of definition. If, however, naval forces of a state are confronted with extra-close surveillance of particularly sensitive activities and they take counter-surveillance measures such as riding off the surveillant, is that harassment? If they jam electronically the communications equipment of a marking vessel, is this harassment? In the opinion of the present writer, in the event of any breach of the terms of the INCSEA Agreement (particularly Articles III and IV), appropriate counter-measures are legitimate. Provided that the Agreement is operated *bona fide* by the parties, they should be able to make maximum use of the high seas for operational purposes without inconveniencing each other too much and will have ample opportunity to examine each other's operations from a discreet distance.

The INCSEA Agreement has undoubtedly resulted in a drop in the number of potentially hazardous confrontations since it came into force, if one has regard for the statistics of reported incidents alone. Its success may be measured by the fact that the principles contained therein have apparently been adopted by NATO member-states in their Rules of Engagement, if one is to go by press reports.

Imitation is the sincerest form of flattery. The USSR has now entered into an INCSEA Agreement with the third major naval power in the world, the United Kingdom. An Agreement signed on 15 July 1986 followed the text of the U.S.A.-USSR Agreement of 1972 and the 1973 Protocol thereto very closely, but with some significant variations and improvements.[51] These include the following. First, the U.K.-USSR Agreement deals with activities "beyond the territorial sea," thereby indicating that the EEZ is to be assimilated for the purposes of the Agreement to the high seas. Second, express reference is made to the application of the Collision Regulations made under the Collisions Convention of 1972. Third, the prohibition on the making of simulated attacks, the launching of objects, and the use of searchlights against navigating bridges of passing vessels of the other party is extended to cover non-military ships without qualification. As in the U.S.A.-USSR Agreement, simulated attacks against non-military aircraft are not mentioned. Other felicitous improvements in the U.K.-USSR Agreement include the use of VHF as alternative to flashing lights for communication purposes. Fourthly, there is provision for timely exchange of information with regard to incidents. No fixed distances are specified in the new Agreement, and there is no provision for a standing committee to be set up. The annual review mechanism of the U.S.A.-USSR Agreement is, however, preserved. Finally, there is an Annex to the Agreement containing a Table of Special Signals which are to be used in addition to those provided under the Collision Regulations and the International Code of Signals. These Special Signals follow the U.S.A.-USSR list of signals with some minor additions and refinements.

The two INCSEA Agreements undoubtedly represent a major contribution to safety in the context of naval operations in peacetime. They contain so much common sense that one wonders why the philosophy of the 1972 U.S.A.-USSR Agreement was not built into Part VII of the United Nations Convention, either wholly or partially. The two INCSEA Agreements in effect acknowledge that the present-day relations between the super-powers and the long-standing, low-level confrontation between the military forces of NATO and the Warsaw Pact are characterized by the deployment of naval forces on a global basis, and that military and political requirements may result in some basic muscle-flexing and putting-down of markers. Above all, the two INCSEA Agreements indicate that, in the belief of the respective signatories, the freedoms of the high seas include the freedom to conduct a wide range of naval activities -- weapons-testing, exercises with submarines, formation work and just plain hanging around on patrol for intelligence-gathering purposes. This writer suggests that there is nothing, in principle, in the INCSEA Agreements which could not be embodied in multilateral treaty form and included, say, in an extended version of Part VII of the UN Convention. But that would, presumably, not be welcome to those states which resist and resent the worldwide deployment of maritime forces for policy projection purposes.

Conclusions

Parturient montes, nascetur ridiculus mus.[52] Ten years of negotiation, and nothing worthwhile said about national defense security in the context of the law of the sea. To those who believe that naval operations in peacetime, on the high seas at least, should be regulated by a multilateral treaty regime so as to ensure that the high seas are genuinely reserved for peaceful (in the sense of non-aggressive) purposes, the failure of the Third UN Conference to evolve any specific rules at all came as a great disappointment. National defense security considerations clearly influenced states in their global approach to the work of this UN Conference, like its predecessors. Yet these factors were only given expression in the Convention of 1982 in the very limited context of the security of the coastal state in its territorial sea where non-innocent passage is concerned and that of the littoral state in event of the infringement of transit passage rights through through international straits. Even then it is debatable whether the legal constraints on foreign vessels imposed in these respective contexts by Articles 19 and 39 of the Convention in fact enlarge upon the customary rights of the coastal or littoral states, as the case may be, to use force by way of self-defense.

Thus it is that the warship, the potent symbol of a state's mili tary power, makes only fleeting appearances in the UN Convention, particularly cast in the role of a rather special, limited policeman on the high seas. The warship's primary function, to project the military and political influence of its flag-state on the high seas, is not touched upon. No attempt is made to harmonize traditonal naval operations with other equally traditional uses of the high seas. The most that can be said is that the Third UN Conference seems, by implication, to have accepted that the deployment of maritime forces on the high seas in peacetime is consistent with the reservation of the high seas for peaceful purposes within the meaning of the UN Convention. The warship, in short, has an accepted, if unspecified, general function over and above its special policing function.

At times of high tension between states, in the phase which used to be described as *transition to war*, the conduct of naval forces on the high seas is, of course, likely to be dictated by the customary principles of self-defense, buttressed and (it is hoped) clarified by Rules of Engagement. There is little that a multilateral treaty can do to assist in the resolution of a confrontation at that stage. But at more mundane levels of confrontation on the high seas between rival navies, when their respective national policies call for jousting, or boisterousness, there is surely a case for clearly expressing in a suitable multilateral treaty framework the parameters of naval operations, if for no other reason than to prevent the outbreak of the Third World War. The two INCSEA Agreements point the way, agreements of enormous significance in that they have the support of the three major maritime powers in the world. The INCSEA Agreements focus on the basic truth that conflict between warships and the use of force at sea can often be avoided by the removal of the other's uncertainty as to one's intentions, particularly through agreed communications procedures. As a well-known eighteenth-century poet put it:

> In full, fair tide, let information flow,
> That evil is half cur'd, whose cause we know.[53]

NOTES

1. UN Document A/CONF.62/122: 7 October 1982.
2. For a comprehensive (if inevitably dated) general account of the traditional law, see *Tucker (R.W.)*, The Law of War and Neutrality at Sea (1955), a publication under the auspices of the U.S. Naval War College, Newport, Rhode Island.
3. The literature on the *Pueblo* incident is voluminous. See, in particular, *Rubin (A.P.)*; Some legal implications of the *Pueblo* incident, 18 I.C.L.O. 691 (1969); *Bucher (L.M.) and Rascovich (M)*; Bucher -- My Story (1970); *Harris (D.J.)*, Cases and Materials on International Law (3rd Ed. 1983), pp. 332-333. For documents, see 62 A.J.I.L. 756 (1968) and 8 I.L.M. 199 (1969).
4. *Kelsen (H.)*, The Law of the United Nations (1950) p. 791 *et seq.*; *Bowett (D.W.)*, Self-Defence in International Law (1958), pp. 182-189; *Brownlie (I.)*, International Law and the Use of Force by States (1963), pp. 264-265, 269-275.
5. *Bowett, op. cit.*, pp. 58-60, 187-193. Cf. *Brownlie, op. cit.*, pp. 257-264.
6. I.C.J. Reports, 1949, p. 4.
7. *Oxman (B.H.)*, The Regime of Warships under the UN Convention on the Law of the Sea, 24 Virginia Journal of International Law 809 (1984).
8. Chicago Convention on International Civil Aviation 1944: 15 U.N.T.S. 295.
9. See, generally, *Harris, op. cit.*, pp. 322-323.
10. See, *e.g.*, the statement of policy of the United Kingdom Government in 1957 quoted by *Harris, op. cit.*, p. 321.
11. *Bowett, op. cit.*, Ch. 1; *Brownlie, op. cit. passim* (especially Ch. XIII).
12. See, in addition to general accounts of the Falklands/Malvinas dispute, *British Year Book of International Law 1982*, p. 538 *et. seq.*; *Coll (A.R.) and Arend (A.C.)*, The Falklands War: Lessons for Strategy, Diplomacy and International Law (1985), Part One.
13. *Kelsen, op. cit.*, p. 791 *et. seq.; Waldock (C.H.M.)*, The Regulation of the Use of Force by Individual States in International Law, Hague Recueil des Cours 1952, II, pp. 451-517; *Bowett, op. cit.*, Part I; *Stone (J.)*, Legal Controls of International Conflict (Second impression, 1959), pp. 243-281; *Brownlie, op. cit.*, Ch. XIII.
14. *Brownlie, op. cit.*, p. 274.
15. *O'Connell (D.P.)*, The Influence of Law on Sea Power (1975), p. 71. See, generally, the same writer's exhaustive article "International Law and Contemporary Naval Operations"; 44 British Year Book of International Law 1970, p. 19.
16. North Atlantic Treaty 1949, Art. 5: 34 UNT.S. 243; 43 A.J.I.L. Supp. 159 (1949).
17. *Brownlie, op. cit.*, pp. 275-278; *Akehurst (M.)*, A Modern Introduction to International Law, (4th ed. 1982), p. 223.
18. *Kelsen, op. cit.*, pp. 797-798; *Waldock, op. cit.*, p. 496; *Bowett, op. cit.*, p. 184; *Brownlie, op. cit.*, pp. 278-279.
19. *Akehurst, op. cit.*, p. 223.
20. *Waldock, op. cit.*, p. 498.
21. *O'Connell, op. cit.*, pp. 70-72.
22. See *infra*, Part V.

23. *O'Connell, op. cit.*, p. 82.
24. *Ibid.*
25. *Ibid.*
26. *O'Connell, op. cit.*, p. 83.
27. See *ante*, note 18.
28. *O'Connell, op. cit.*, p. 179.
29. *O'Connell, op. cit.*, Ch. XIII.
30. *Moore (J.B.)*, Digest of International Law, Vol. 2, pp. 409-414; *Jennings (R.Y.)*, The Caroline and McLeod Cases, 32 A.J.I.L. 82 (1938); *Harris, op. cit.*, pp. 655-656.
31. *O'Connell, op. cit.*, p. 71.
32. On three recent occasions there have been collisions between warships operating together resulting in a serious loss of life:

    (i) the collision between H.M.A.S. *Melbourne* and H.M.A.S. *Voyager* in 1964 (*The Times* (London) 12-13 February 1964);
    (ii) the collision between H.M.A.S. *Melbourne* and U.S.S. *Frank E. Evans* in 1969 (*The Times* (London) 4-7 June 1969);
    (iii) the collision between H.M.S. *Mermaid* and H.M.S. *Fittleton* in 1976 (*The Times* (London) 21-22 September 1976).

33. *I.e.*, the INCSEA Agreements: Part V, *infra*.
34. U.S. Notice to Mariners: Hydropac 78/84(62) Persian Gulf, Strait of Hormuz and Gulf of Oman.
35. International Convention for the Safety of Life at Sea, London, 1974 (SOLAS): for full text, see *Nagendra Singh*, International Maritime Law Conventions (1983), Vol. 2, pp. 1052-1253.
36. Convention on the International Regulations for Preventing Collisions at Sea 1972: for full text, see *Nagendra Singh, op. cit.*, Vol. 1, pp. 3-35.
37. SOLAS Convention, Annex, Ch. IV, Part A, Reg. 1 read together with Ch. I, Part A, Reg. 3 which excludes "Ships of War and Warships": *Nagendra Singh, op. cit.*, Vol. 2, pp. 1067, 1185.
38. SOLAS Convention, Annex, Ch. V, Reg. 1: *Nagendra Singh, op. cit.*, Vol. 2, p. 1201.
39. International Regulations for Preventing Collisions at Sea 1972, Rule 1(c): *Nagendra Singh, op. cit.*, Vol. I, p. 14.
40. *Ibid.*, Rule 2(b): *Nagendra Singh, op. cit.*, Vol. I, p. 15.
41. *O'Connell, op. cit.*, p. 178; *The Times* (London) 11th-14th November 1970.
42. International Regulations for Preventing Collisions at Sea 1960, Rule 4(c)-(g).
43. For text, see *Churchill and Lay* (eds.), New Directions in the Law of the Sea, Vol. II, p. 529 (1973).
44. *Churchill and Lay, op. cit.*, Vol. IV, p. 285 (1975).
45. *O'Connell, op. cit.*, pp. 178-179.
46. Inter-governmental Maritime Consultative Organisation (IMCO) circulars COM/Cir. 68, 7 April 1975; COM/Cir. 69, 29th July 1976.
47. INCSEA Agreement, Art. III.6.
48. Protocol to INCSEA Agreement, Art. II.
49. INCSEA Agreement, Art. III.6.
50. See note 44 *supra*.
51. This has not yet been published in the U.K. Treaty Series. See *The Times* (London), 16 July 1986.
52. *Horace*, Ars Poetica 139.
53. *Churchill (Charles)*, Gotham, III, 651-652 (1764).

NAVAL WEAPONRY AND THE LAW OF THE SEA

David L. Larson
Department of Political Science
University of New Hampshire

Introduction*

This topic is a rather daunting assignment for several reasons. First, the definition of the phrase *naval weaponry* is so broad that it includes almost any instrument or weapons system that might be used to exercise influence, pressure or control over an actual or potential opponent. That is, the concept of naval weaponry includes a range of things from a small offshore patrol vessel (OPV) up to and including a large attack aircraft carrier (CVAN) on the surface; from a small sonar sensing device (SOSUS) to a large underwater mine (CAPTOR) on the seabed; from a small one- or two-man crawling submarine to a large Typhoon-class or Ohio-class nuclear ballistic missile submarine (SSBN) in the water column; from coastal patrol and anti-submarine (ASW) helicopters up to fixed-wing maritime reconnaissance (MR) aircraft of various types; from communication (COMSAT), navigation (NAVSTAR), weather and various intelligence satellites (OSUS) to a possible strategic defense (SDI) system; from conventional guns of all types up to various water-skimmming, anti-ship missiles such as the Harpoon, Otomat and Exocet on up to the SS-N-20 and Trident D-5 sub-launched ballistic missiles (SLBM). In sum, the range and variety of things that can be included within the phrase *naval weaponry* is almost infinite. However, what the phrase leaves out are the intangibles which give to weapons and weapons systems some purpose, meaning and direction. That is, the political culture, the national leadership, the foreign policy, the strategic doctrine and the quality of the manpower in whose hands these weapons are placed. The interplay of these national considerations on the international level are some of the factors that contribute to that complex and intricate field known as international relations.

Second, the phrase *naval weaponry* has to be applied to a specific area or mission to be comprehensible, and therefore intelligible and useful. That is, the mission or purpose of naval weaponry has to be made relatively clear: is it coastal patrol, sea lanes control, protection of power, naval presence/diplomacy (both coercive and supportive), protection of commercial shipping, naval superiority, strategic deterrence, or some combination thereof? Also, the area or region to which this naval weaponry is to be applied has relevance. Is it a geographic region such as the North Atlantic Ocean, the North Pacific Ocean, the Arctic Ocean, the Indian Ocean, the Mediterranean Sea, the Persian Gulf, or where? Or, is it some political/legal zone such as the territorial sea, the contiguous zone, the exclusive economic zone, the continental shelf, international straits, the deep seabed, the high seas, or air space and outer space?

Third, the phrase *naval weaponry* has to be related to specific nation-states in order to give it some utility and credibility. In this sense, the mass of data in regard to naval weaponry and information on national strategy have been compressed into five main categories for the purpose of discussion:

1. *The superpowers* (the United States and the Soviet Union), which have global interests and global capability in terms of naval weaponry,

2. *The major powers* (United Kingdom, France and China), which have some global interests and limited capability in terms of naval weaponry,
3. *The regional powers* (such as Canada, Brazil, India and Japan, *inter alia*), which have regional interests and regional capabilities,
4. *The minor powers* (such as Norway, Indonesia, the Philippines and Mexico, *inter alia*) which have local interests and local capabilities,
5. *The embryonic or developing powers*, which are in the process of acquiring naval weaponry. (Refer to *Appendix A* for chart.)

Fourth, the field of international relations may be divided into five main sub-fields:

1. *International politics* - the struggle for power, prestige, prosperity and ideology,
2. *International law* - international custom, convention and conflict resolution,
3. *International organization* - the struggle for world order,
4. *Area studies* - geographic/cultural regions, and
5. *Topical studies* - arms control, international economics, etc.

The concept of naval weaponry falls primarily within the sub-field of international politics, but clearly relates to and is dependent upon the other four sub-fields. Now, having tried to define the phrase *naval weaponry* and place it in some perspective, let us turn our attention to the second part of the topic, *the law of the sea*.

International law has been divided by such publicists as Hugo Grotius and Lassa Oppenheim into two broad sub-divisions, *the laws of war* and *the laws of peace*.[1] Up until the mid-twentieth century, much of the discourse in international law had to do with conflict, conflict resolution and war. However, this emphasis on the laws of war began to change under the League of Nations and the Hague Conference on the Codification of International Law in 1930, where the Second Committee specifically dealt with the territorial sea and related issues. This trend continued under the United Nations with the establishment of the International Law Commission and the convening of the First, Second and Third United Nations Conferences on the Law of the Sea (*UNCLOS I, II* and *III*). From its conception to conclusion, UNCLOS III was primarily concerned with the *peaceful uses* of the seas and oceans beyond the limits of national jurisdiction, in accordance with United Nations General Assembly Resolutions 2340 (XXII), 2467 (XXIII), 2574 (XXIV), 2749 (XXV) and 2750C (XXV), which was reiterated in the preamble to the United Nations Convention on the Law of the Sea (hereafter, *the UN Convention*). And yet, one of the primary motivations for the convening of UNCLOS III was the concern of the superpowers for the creeping jurisdiction of coastal and straits states out into the high seas and international straits.[2] This concern about creeping jurisdiction by coastal states was justified at the start of UNCLOS III and has increased since that time with expanding claims. (See *Chart 1*.[3]) If all coastal states were to extend their territorial seas out to the twelve nm permitted under the UN Convention, that would overlap 135 international straits.[4] (Refer to *Appendix C* for a *Summary Table of Extent of Maritime Zones*.)

Chart 1

Territorial Sea Claims

Year	Coastal State	Under 12 nm.	Over 12 nm.	12 nm.
1967	86	48	26	12
1974	118	40	56	22
1984	140	32	78	30
1985	140	25	87	28

Chart 2

Summary of Naval Weaponry and the Law of the Sea
(UN Convention on the Law of the Sea)

Area	Legal Status	Naval Weaponry
Internal waters Inside baseline	Complete sovereignty of coastal state over waters, air space, seabed and sub-soil subject to Article 8.	Coastal state permitted anything allowed under international agreement; including shore batteries, missiles, aircraft, bases, submarines, surface vessels, mines, etc.
Territorial seas 12 nm.	Sovereignty of coastal state over waters, air space, seabed and subsoil subject to Article 17 - right of innocent passage of ships, limited by Articles 18-32.	Same as above except that warships are limited by Articles 29-32; no right of innocent passage through airspace.
Contiguous zone 24 nm.	Coastal state control to the extent necessary to regulate customs, fiscal, immigration, or sanitary laws.	No nuclear weapons or weapons of mass destruction in accordance with SACT or testing of nuclear weapons under LTBT; conventional weapons permitted subject to UN Convention.
International straits 24 nm. or less	Coastal/straits state control as in territorial seas, subject to rights of innocent passage under Article 38.	Same as territorial seas; modified by Article 39; right of unimpeded transit passage.

Chart 2 (continued)

Area	Legal Status	Naval Weaponry
Archipelagic waters Inside baseline	Sovereignty of archipelagic state over waters, seabed and subsoil subject to rights of innocent passage under Article 17 and archipelagic sea lanes under Article 53.	Same as internal waters; modified by Article 53; right of innocent passage through internal waters; archipelagic sea lanes and air routes permitted; right of unimpeded archipelagic sealanes passage.
Exclusive economic zone 200 nm.	Limited sovereign rights of coastal state for exploration and exploitation as defined by Article 56, otherwise a high seas regime under Article 87.	Same as for contiguous zone.
Continental shelf 350 nm.	Limited sovereign rights of coastal state for exploration and exploitation as defined by Article 77, otherwise a high seas regime under Articles 78 and 87.	Same as for contiguous zone.
Deep seabed Abyssal plain	The area beyond national jurisdiction regarded as the common heritage of mankind under Articles 136 and 137; no state may claim sovereignty in this area.	Same as for contiguous zone.
High seas Beyond national jurisdiction	Open to all states; usage subject to Article 87, reserved for peaceful purposes under Article 88.	Anything permitted under international agreement.
Antarctic 60 degrees south	*Sui generis* consortium of signatory states (12), and acceding states (11); reserved for peaceful purposes in accordance with Antarctic Treaty.	No military usage, bases, fortifications, maneuvers, testing, nuclear explosions or disposal of radioactive waste.
Air space Up to 100 nm.	Overflight permitted in all areas except for internal and territorial waters which require permission.	Anything permitted under international agreement.

Chart 2 (continued)

Area	Legal Status	Naval Weaponry
Outer space	The area above national jurisdiction is the province of all mankind under Article 1, OST.	No nuclear weapons or weapons of mass destruction in accordance with OST; no military installations, bases, fortifications, testing or maneuvers under OST.
Beyond 100 nm.		

SACT- Seabed Arms Control Treaty
LTBT- Limited Test Ban Treaty
AT   - Antarctic Treaty
OST - Outer Space Treaty

Freedom of navigation for both commercial and naval vessels, then, became one of the underlying themes of UNCLOS III, and was an important part of the package deal, or trade-off, of continued, customary freedom of navigation for the superpowers and major maritime powers in return for some participation by the developing countries in deep seabed mining.[5] This was especially the case for superpower and major power SSBN navigation through international straits, archipelagic waters and the exclusive economic zone. This problem was dealt with in several articles of the UN Convention noted for their brevity and ambiguity -- such as Article 39, Paragraph 1c, pertaining to transit passage through international straits; Article 53, Paragraph 2, pertaining to archipelagic sealanes passage; and Article 58, Paragraph 1, pertaining to navigation and other rights in the exclusive economic zone. Other than these few articles and some related passages, the bulk of the UN Convention deals with peaceful purposes such as deep seabed mining, fishing, scientific research, transfer of technology, pollution and the settlement of disputes. Nonetheless, the major undercurrent of the Conference was international politics -- the struggles for power, prestige, prosperity, and ideology,[6] or, more simply stated, the allocation of resources and the determination of rights. However, "the progressive development of international law and its codification"[7] since 1945 under the International Law Commission and the three United Nations Conferences on the Law of the Sea have emphasized the peaceful purposes or uses of the seas and have largely neglected or purposefully suppressed the non-peaceful purposes or military uses of the seas. The paradox is that, since 1945, there has been an extraordinary revolution in naval weaponry, naval strategy and the concern for national security; yet, international law and law of the sea have suffered a relative blackout with the notable exceptions of a series of arms control treaties or agreements including the Antarctic Treaty, the Limited Test Ban Treaty, the Seabed Arms Control Treaty, SALT I, SALT II and others.

The main purpose of this paper is to outline some of the major naval weapons and weapons systems as they relate to naval strategy and the law of the sea. The basic working hypothesis is that although there are some limitations on the deployment of nuclear weapons and weapons of mass destruction on the seabed, in the Antarctic and in nuclear-free zones such as Latin America, the development and deployment of naval weapons and weapons systems are largely unrestricted and unrestrained by international law and law of the sea. In fact, international law and law of the sea look upon naval weaponry with a blind eye, something like Lord Nelson supposedly did at the Battle of Trafalgar, when he lifted a telescope to his blind eye and failed to see the Spanish and French striking their colors. That is, few naval weapons or weapons systems are restricted, restrained or made illegal by customary or conventional international law. For example, the ultimate weapon system may well be the strategic ballistic missile submarine (SSBN) such as the Ohio class for the United States and the Typhoon class for the Soviet Union, and it is essentially unrestricted and unrestrained by international law and the law of the sea. In that sense, international law and the law of the sea may well be reflections of the current status of international relations.

The scope of this paper is to focus primarily upon those areas of the ocean newly created by customary and/or conventional international law, and the weapons systems most relevant to them. (Refer to *Appendix A* for *General Force Levels*.) The areas of the world ocean that relate to naval weapons and the law of the sea cover the full spectrum; that is, internal waters, territorial seas, international straits, exclusive economic zones, continental shelves, high seas and the deep seabed. The weapons systems developed relate to a particular area and the assigned mission. For example, Offshore Patrol Vessels (OPV) relate primarily to the territorial sea and the exclusive economic zone, and they usually have specific missions assigned to them, such as traffic control, fishery regulation, pollution control, drug traffic interdiction, border control, etc. While strategic ballistic missile submarines (SSBN) have basically two missions assigned to them: one, to deter nuclear war, and two, if that fails, to retaliate with such force as to inflict unacceptable damage upon an aggressor. The main point to be made with these illustrations is that, to some extent, naval weaponry seems to have influenced, if not determined, the new law of the sea in regard to navigation through straits, archipelagic waters and the exclusive economic zone. While the economic zone. While the other hand, the new permissive limits of twelve nm for the territorial sea, twenty-four nm for the contiguous zone, 200 nm or the exclusive economic zone, and up to 350 nm for the continental shelf have clearly influenced the development and deployment of offshore patrol vessels (OPV) to police these new maritime zones. The zones have also spawned such budding developments as regional cooperation between small states' coast guards in order to provide effective enforcement.[8]

The Baseline

The most fundamental aspect of the law of the sea is the *baseline* -- everything is measured from it both internally and externally. Under the new offshore limits permitted by the UN Convention, the potential for national encroachment upon the world ocean is substantial and the full extent of the exclusive economic zone could absorb as much as forty percent of the world ocean. As coastal nations move their baselines and boundaries seaward, the potential for conflict is increased. For example, since 1951 ten major cases have made their way to the International Court of Justice in regard to offshore boundary disputes, and more are sure to come.[9]

The importance of the baseline to the law of the sea is illustrated by two quotations:

46

The key to all zonation of water and seabed off the coast of a state is the *baseline*. It forms the inner limit of the territorial sea, and from it is measured the outer limit. The same baseline forms the maximum seaward margin of a state's internal waters, such as bays, inlets, estuaries and other bodies of water associated with the shore line.[10]

... The delimitation of the sea areas has always an international aspect; it cannot be dependent merely upon the will of the coastal state as expressed in its municipal law. Although it is true that the act of delimitation is necessarily a unilateral act because only the coastal state is competent to undertake it, the validity of delimitation with regard to other states depends upon international law.[11]

The UN Convention endeavors to regulate the drawing of baselines in accordance with the decision of the *Anglo-Norwegian Fisheries* Case in Articles 5 and 7, and refers to the baseline throughout the Convention. However, most coastal states have drawn their baselines in the most advantageous manner possible using whatever method is most suitable to their coastline and national interests. Coastal states and archipelagic states using straight baselines have included substantial bodies of water within these baselines such as historic bays. The drawing of the baseline, therefore, is of fundamental importance to the national interests and national security of the coastal state and other states.

Internal Waters
The internal waters of the coastal state are those waters inside of the baseline, and may include harbors, inlets, port facilities, legal bays, historic bays, mouths of rivers and various land features. The legal status of internal waters is that they are under the complete sovereignty of the coastal state and therefore under its absolute control. This is important for national security and for several other reasons. First, the coastal or port state may exclude any non-national ship or vessel from its internal waters, the air space above and the seabed below. No state has an automatic right to enter these internal waters, the air space above or the seabed below without the explicit or implicit permission of the coastal state, although we know now that such penetrations of Swedish and Norwegian internal waters have been done on a regular basis by the Soviet Union.[12] The most famous case of Soviet penetration of internal waters occurred in October 1981, when a Soviet Whiskey-class submarine, armed with nuclear weapons, ran aground in a militarily restricted area outside of the Karlskrona naval base in southern Sweden.[13] It has been estimated that in the timespan between 1969 and 1982, both Norway and Sweden each had a possible 122 underwater penetrations/incursions by various submersibles, ranging from midget submarines with bottom-crawling capabilities to Whiskey-class submarines. These coastal incursions are not limited to underwater penetrations but also include the penetration of the air space above.[14] These are serious violations of national security, not to mention national security.
Coastal states have a clear legal right to protect their internal waters, subjacent seabed and superjacent air space by whatever means that they deem necessary. Defensive measures can include a wide variety of measures, from offshore patrol vessels to coastal patrol aircraft,

47

the full range of anti-submarine warfare systems (ASW), the full range of anti-aircraft systems (AA), coastal mines, submarine nets and other systems. In addition, the superpowers and major powers have highly sophisticated electronic detection, passive defense systems for early warning. As the cost drops and the technology becomes available, the other coastal states are also expected to acquire more and better defensive systems.

Coastal states also have the clear legal right to emplant or emplace in their internal waters active or offensive weapons and weapons systems, which might be less detectable from offshore, air space or outer space. For example, it would be possible to deploy SSBN in relatively safe and secure coastal waters, such as deep *fjords*, in a stationary position, or in a mobile configuration. With the substantially increased ranges of the Soviet SS-N-20 and the American Trident C-4 and D-5 SLBM, this might become a viable strategic option. In fact, this seems to be what the Soviet Union is doing in the Murmansk/ Arkangelsk region, and the Arctic Ocean.[15] In addition, it would certainly be technologically feasible to deploy large SLBM or ICBM missiles such as the D-5 or MX in fixed underwater locations. Such a deployment would provide a degree of security from detection and protection from attack, but could be destabilizing in that they might prevent identification and verification by national technical means (NTM).

In summary, internal waters, the subjacent seafloor and the superjacent air space are essentially the exclusive jurisdiction of the coastal state. As such, they are unrestricted by international law except as general, regional or bilateral disarmament agreements might mitigate against certain defensive or offensive weapons systems. Insofar as the customary or conventional law of the sea is concerned, there are few if any mitigating circumstances except in so far as international comity and reciprocity might require and rationality might suggest.

Territorial Seas
The territorial seas are those waters outside of the baseline and normally extend to a legal maximum of twelve nm under Article 3 of the UN Convention. The legal status of the territorial sea, the air space above, the seabed and the subsoil is that, in accordance with Article 2 of the UN Convention, the sovereignty of the coastal state extends over this area except for the international servitude of the right of innocent passage through the territorial sea. There are other rights and rules of innocent passage outlined in Articles 17 through 45 of the UN Convention; however, the main thrust is that the coastal state has the basic right to regulate and control the territorial sea and innocent passage. It should be noted, however, that there is no right of innocent passage for aircraft in the air space above the territorial sea. This latter point became rather important in the Yom Kippur War of 1973, when the United States had to resupply Israel and was denied air passage by coastal states adjacent to the Mediterranean Sea. Such a situation could conceivably arise again. However, it would be more serious today since 108 coastal states claim twelve or more nautical miles as the breadth of the territorial sea.

Innocent passage through the territorial sea or internal waters which had previously been defined as territorial seas under Article 8 of the UN Convention is permissible just so long as the passage is not prejudicial to the peace, good order or security of the coastal state.

The determination of what constitutes innocent passage is largely, if not exclusively, left to the discretion of the coastal state despite the duties of the coastal state outlined in Article 24 of the UN Convention. If the coastal state decides to prevent passage through the territorial sea which it deems not to be innocent, it may take the necessary steps in accordance with Article 25 of the UN Convention. Today, these necessary steps may include the full array of naval weaponry, from mines of all types to a wide variety of anti-ship missiles and torpedoes, not to mention shore-based aircraft. Many of these weapons and weapons systems are within the financial and technological reach of most coastal states. The significant point is that today, with the rapid improvement in technology and capability of naval weaponry, most coastal states could deter or forcibly prevent passage through territorial seas except possibly for the superpowers.

In August 1979, the United States issued a policy directive to the effect that it would challenge territorial sea claims that exceeded three nautical miles.[16] Two years later, elements of the Sixth Fleet were maneuvering in the Gulf of Sidra, which Libya claimed as an historic bay, and were approached by two Libyan jets.[17] The Libyan jets were shot down, and the United States effectively asserted its right to maneuver 60 nm offshore in an area that it regarded as high seas. Such an effective defense and assertion of the right might no longer be feasible given the new naval weaponry.

In the fact sheet on *United States Ocean Policy* accompanying President Reagan's *Proclamation on a 200 nm Exclusive Economic Zone for the United States of America*, the White House stated that:

> The President has not changed the breadth of the United States territorial sea. It remains at three nautical miles. The United States will respect only those territorial sea claims of others in excess of three nautical miles, to a maximum of twelve nautical miles, which accord to the U.S. its full rights under international law in the territorial sea. Unimpeded commercial and military tary navigation and over-flight are critical to the national interest of the United States. The United States will act to ensure the retention of the necessary rights and freedoms.[18]

There are several important dimensions to this statement. First, it is an effort to adjust to and yet take advantage of the new UN Convention. That is, the United States explicitly recognizes the norm of twelve nm as the breadth of the territorial sea in accordance with Article 2 of the UN Convention, but no further claims. Second, the United States is implicitly taking advantage of Article 8 of the UN Convention, which states that upon drawing straight baselines (as in the Gulf of Sidra) which has "the effect of enclosing as internal waters waters areas which had not previously been considered as such, a right of innocent passage as provided in this convention shall exist in those waters." Third, the United States is clearly asserting the full rights of innocent passage through the territorial seas of other states for both commercial and naval vessels. That is, there should be no interference with the right of innocent passage through territorial waters by coastal or straits states. Fourth, the United States also seems to be asserting a right of overflight in the territorial seas of other states beyond three nautical miles. Such a claim is rather ambiguous at best and does not clearly exist in international law or the law of the sea. Fifth, the United States asserts that it "will continue to act to ensure the retention of the necessary rights and freedoms." In the context of the Gulf of Sidra incident, this clearly means the force of arms and is consistent with the directive issued in August 1979. Sixth, given the statements of participants at the Law of the Sea Institute in September 1984, it seems that the United States intends to rely upon customary international law and the force of arms for the evolution and development of the law of the sea.[19] In summary, the position of the United States in regard to the territorial sea from 1966 to date seems to be a prime example of the naval weaponry, in the broad sense that we defined it at the beginning of this discussion, shaping if not determining the law of the sea. That is, if the United States persists in this national policy, it is difficult to imagine any coastal or straits state, except possibly the Soviet Union, effectively resisting the United States' interpretation and application of international law and the law of the sea. However, the future action, reaction and interaction of national policies and strategies will inform us better as to what the generally accepted norms of international law will be in regard to the territorial sea.

It should also be noted that in accordance with the *Seabed Arms Control Treaty* (SACT) of 1972, the coastal state may emplace or emplant weapons of virtually any type or dimension out to a limit of twelve nm.[20] Beyond twelve nm, the signatory states have agreed not to emplant or emplace any nuclear weapons or "weapons of mass destruction as well as structures, launching installations or any other facilities specifically designed for storing, testing or using such weapons."[21] The significance of the permissive nature of the Seabed Arms Control Treaty is that the coastal state may do virtually whatever it wants to do in terms of naval weaponry within the territorial sea just so long as it does not significantly interfere with the rights of innocent passage of other states. As with internal waters, this presents a fairly broad opportunity for the coastal state to deploy a vast array of offensive, defensive and passive weapons and weapons systems. Again, the effectiveness of many of these weapons and weapons systems is such that even small states like Libya could deploy them and possibly deny innocent passage to the United States. Whether or not such an acquisition, deployment and utilization would actually occur remains to be seen. However, one year ago there was a rash of underwater mines dropped in the Red Sea by unknown agents, which seriously inconvenienced international navigation for a period of time.[22] Also, in 1983 the United States was accused in the International Court of Justice of aiding and assisting in the laying of mines off the coast of Nicaragua.[23] The main point is that naval mines are still formidable weapons in the arsenal of any state, coastal or not, and may be effectively deployed for either offensive or defensive purposes.[24] Advanced mine systems such as the American Captor, Quickstrike and MK 67 SLMM, the British Sea Urchin and Stonefish, and the Soviet Cluster Bay and Cluster Gulf are capable of interdicting and damaging if not destroying most submarines and surface vessels.[25] The great advantages of mines are that they are cheap, easy to deploy, and fairly effective.

International Straits
International straits are relatively narrow geographic sealanes used for international navigation which connect the high seas and/or exclusive economic zones. The legal status of international straits is that they are subject to the sovereignty or jurisdiction of the straits states with some specific rights granted to the non-straits states.

If all the straits states extended their territorial seas out to twelve nm, it is estimated that 135 international straits would be overlapped. If this had occurred without some form of international guarantee for unimpeded passage through these international straits, then one or more of several things might have happened. First, it is possible that some of these international straits could have been closed to military and/ or commercial vessels by the straits states. Second, the major maritime powers would have to force their way through the straits. Third, chaos, conflict, and even war might result. All of these are worse case scenarios, which fortunately did not come to pass. UNCLOS III developed a special regime for international straits described as transit passage in Articles 37 through 44 of the UN Convention. The essence of this regime is that ships and aircraft shall have the right of unimpeded transit passage through and over such overlapped international straits. Transit passage is different and distinct from innocent passage in several important respects. First, as already noted, it may not be impeded by coastal or straits states. Second, submarines may effect transit passage without prior notification or identification and may remain submerged. Third, aircraft may benefit from the right of transit passage. However, straits states may designate sea lanes and traffic separation schemes do not apply to submarines, or their security would be compromised. The importance of transit passage to the superpowers and major powers can hardly be overestimated. This was the one non-negotiable item at UNCLOS III without which there would have been no Convention. Transit passage was deemed to be essential to the national security and economic well-being of the major maritime powers as well as to the lesser maritime powers. The formula of transit passage seems to have mitigated against the worst possible effects of creeping jurisdiction. Although the United States is not a signatory to the UN Convention, it has tried to assert unilaterally its rights of transit passage as outlined in the *Fact Sheet on United States Ocean Policy* of March 10, 1983. This seems to have been rather unsuccessful, and one view is that the failure to sign the UN Convention jeopardizes United States national security especially in regard to transit passage through international straits.[26] The new regime of transit passage seems to be a generally recognized principle of international law with 159 states and other entities which have signed the UN Convention. However, only nineteen relatively minor states have ratified the Convention. Furthermore, 108 of the 149 coastal states claim territorial seas of twelve or more nautical miles. Given both the fragility of the new legal regime and the vulnerability of international straits to constriction, constraint and interdiction, there is an understandable sensitivity of the major maritime powers as to the safety and security of international straits. For example, a fairly recent article indicates that, in the wake of the Falklands/Malvinas conflict, with the loss of the *Sheffield*, *Ardent*, *Antelope* and *Coventry* to Exocet missiles,[27] several major straits states including Indonesia, Malaysia, Singapore, Morocco, Spain, Algeria and Libya[28] have acquired or ordered Exocet or similar anti-ship missiles. These new anti-ship missiles, including Exocet, Otomat, Harpoon, Seawolf and others[29] (Refer to *Appendix B* for *Summary of Naval Missiles*), in combination with the new sophisticated mines and possibly backed up by shore batteries and land-based aircraft, could certainly provide the weaponry to choke off almost any international strait if the coastal or straits state chose to do so and take the necessary consequences.

Also, some concern has been expressed by a member of this panel that the legal overlay of the UN Convention in regard to transit passage through international straits creates some ambiguity and confusion in relation to "The Rights and Duties of Neutral Powers in Naval War" under the Hague Convention of 1907.[30] He submits that there are several principles of customary and conventional law that should govern the behavior of states in straits in time of conflict:

1. The principle that the use of force is governed by military necessity, and constrained by considerations of proportionality and humanitarian concern;

2. The principle that hostilities must be limited in scope and nature to the participants themselves, and that non-participants must remain unaffected to the maximum extent possible.[31]

These principles seem to be self-evident, but in time of conflict such rational, legal norms get lost in the fog of war. However, what is significant here is the extreme sensitivity and vulnerability of international straits to military conflict. Several efforts to clarify the international legal status of straits and their relationship to national security have been made by leading publicists but thus far do not seem to have met with general acceptance.[32] The discussion of these and other publicists clearly points up the need to update the laws of war in general and as they pertain to the law of the sea in particular.

Archipelagic Waters
Archipelagic waters are one of the newer concepts of the law of the sea and are all the waters included within an archipelagic baseline drawn from outermost point to outermost point by means of straight baselines along a coastal archipelago or mid-ocean archipelago. Examples of a coastal archipelago include Canada and Norway, and examples of mid-ocean archipelagoes include Indonesia and the Philippines. The legal status of these archipelagic waters is *sui generis* and somewhere between that of internal waters and territorial seas. The sovereignty of the archipelagic state extends over the subsoil, the seabed, the surface and the airspace over archipelagic waters. Non-archipelagic states enjoy the right of innocent passage through archipelagic waters, which may be suspended if it is essential to the security of the archipelagic state in accordance with Article 52 of the UN Convention. In addition, non-archipelagic states enjoy unimpeded archipelagic sealanes passage through and over archipelagic waters, and submarines may proceed in their normal mode of operation, *i.e.*, submerged. Thus archipelagic sea lanes passage is in many ways similar to transit passage through international straits. Again, this right is extremely important to the superpowers for the deployment of their strategic ballistic missile submarines. The United States has a forward strategic ballistic missile submarine base at Guam, and to deploy its SSBN in the Indian Ocean it is reported that these SSBNs pass through the archipelagic waters of both the Philippines and Indonesia. The utilization of these archipelagic waters and deep water straits is also important for the supertankers plying between the Persian Gulf and Japan. However, archipelagic sea lanes and air routes are regulated and designated by the archipelagic state in accordance with Article 53 of the UN Convention. This would channel such air and sea traffic through relatively narrow sections of archipelagic waters and air space, making the air and sea

traffic more vulnerable to constriction, constraint and interdiction. The military necessity of using archipelagic sea lanes may no longer be extant given the development of the Trident C-4 and D-5 missiles as well as the SS-N-20.

The Contiguous/Exclusive Economic Zone

The contiguous zone beyond the territorial zone may extend up to twenty-four nm from the baseline and is designed to prevent infringement of customs, fiscal, immigration or sanitary laws and regulations of the coastal state in accordance with Article 33 of the UN Convention. Thus far, only thirteen coastal states have claimed a contiguous zone of twenty-four nm. Eight other states have claimed lesser widths up to eighteen nm. The United States, for example, claims a contiguous zone of twelve nm, which is nine nm beyond the territorial sea. While fifty-four states claim a 200 nm exclusive economic zone, twenty-three states claim a 200 nm fishing zone, and nineteen states claim a 200 nm continental shelf.[33] Obviously, many of these 200-mile offshore claims overlap, as is the case with the United States. In terms of state practice or customary international law, what seems to be developing is that the contiguous zone is being subsumed as part of or being absorbed into the exclusive economic zone. Therefore, for the purposes of this discussion, the contiguous zone will be assumed to be part of the exclusive economic zone along with the 200-mile fishery zone and 200-mile continental shelf.

The legal status of the exclusive economic zone is that the coastal state has sovereign rights for the purpose of exploring, exploiting, conserving and managing the natural resources in the subsoil, seabed or superjacent waters of the zone in accordance with Article 56 of the UN Convention. In addition, the coastal state has jurisdiction over artificial islands, installations, structures, scientific research and the environment as well as other rights and duties. All other states are supposed to retain the various high seas freedoms in the exclusive economic zone in accordance with the 1958 Convention on the High Seas, and/or Article 87 of the UN Convention. Also, land-locked states are supposed to share on an equitable basis the living resources of the zone in accordance with Article 69 of the UN Convention. The enforcement of the rights of the coastal state in the zone is largely left up to the coastal state in accordance with Article 73 of the UN Convention. And, therefore, the interpretation and application of Articles 55 through 75 of the UN Convention pertaining to the exclusive economic zone is largely left up to the determination of the coastal state. As Cardinal Richelieu was reported to have said, "I do not care so much who makes the laws or what the laws are, so much as who interprets and applies the laws."

The process of creeping jurisdiction seaward by the coastal state, from the time of the Truman Proclamation in 1945 down to the present, has led to what several writers have variously described as the *territorialist movement*. That is, the tendency on the part of coastal states to *territorialize* the offshore areas beyond the territorial sea, including the contiguous zone, the exclusive economic zone and the continental shelf as being merely extensions of the territorial sea by another name.[34] The leading territorialist states have been Chile, Ecuador, Peru, Iceland, and Brazil, and now the superpowers seem to be joining in the movement. The national motivations for this creeping jurisdiction vary widely -- from national prestige to protection of fisheries, to exploitation of oil and gas, to national security. However, the net effect is similar -- the partial or complete exclusion of non-coastal states from the zone, and a gradual reduction of non-coastal states' rights in this zone.

The implications of this territorialization of offshore areas for naval weaponry has been rather substantial. Peter Tarpgaard recently wrote to me:

> It seems to me that the most immediate and obvious effect of the Law of the Sea is the sudden increase in coastal patrol responsibilities. The expansion of the old 3 nm territorial zone to 12 nm and the establishment of the 200 nm Exclusive Economic Zone has brought about changes in the way coastal states regard the ocean areas around them. Having been given suzerainty over vast new ocean areas, coastal states have acquired immediate policing responsibilities along with their potential economic benefits. This has resulted in the construction of over 140 offshore Patrol Vessels (OPV) by various nations around the world in the 10 years since the Exclusive Economic Zone was established. We can expect that demand for OPV's will continue in the future and they may take more unusual forms as time goes by. Ultimately, OPV's might not even be ships but rather airships which are now being actively considered by the U.S. Navy and Coast Guard. Also in the offing is the possible appearance of small coastal submarines in navies that have not previously used submarines. At least part of the growing interest in submarines around the world can be attributed to Exclusive Economic Zone defense. As more vehicles and equipment for patrolling offshore are accumulated, there may be more incidents and the need for well-functioning machinery for settling international disputes may become more acute.[35]

The effects of this rapid increase in the numbers, size and capability of offshore patrol vehicles for the territorialization of the offshore areas are rather important. What is occurring is the *leap frog effect*. That is, the territorialization of the offshore areas requires more offshore patrol vehicles, and then the newly acquired offshore patrol vehicles encourage the further territorialization of the offshore areas, etc. This is a clear example of the law of the sea encouraging weapons development, and vice versa, and of the interdependent relationship between the two.

There are also the militarily important issues of high seas freedoms for navigation, overflight, the laying of submarine cables and pipelines, and other internationally lawful uses of the sea in accordance with Articles 58 and 87 of the UN Convention. The generality of these rights contributes in part to the ambiguity. For example, are these high seas freedoms unrestricted and unrestrained? Clearly, they are not. The rights of the coastal state under Article 56 take precedence over the rights of the non-coastal state mentioned in Article 58. Paragraph 3 of Article 58 states that non-coastal states *shall have due regard to the rights and duties of the coastal state and shall comply with the laws and regulations adopted by the coastal state*. Again, the point here is that the coastal state could adopt, interpret, apply and enforce certain rules and regulations that would have the net effect of excluding naval vessels from the exclusive economic zone in time of peace or war -- for example, the exclusion of nuclear-powered or nuclear-armed vessels from the exclusive economic zone in time of peace as a nuclear-free zone. The recent exclusion of United States naval vessels that may have had nuclear weapons from the territorial waters and ports of New Zealand is a case in point.[36] Also, in time of war, coastal states might declare the exclusive economic zone as a zone of peace and exclude all naval vessels and military aircraft of belligerent powers. This might be more difficult to enforce, but with the rapid development of offshore patrol vessels, anti-ship missiles and modern mines, this might be a feasible course of action. Needless to say, the belligerents and the major maritime powers would probably object to such a zone of peace and breach it by force of arms if necessary. (There will be further discussion of this point under *the High Seas*.)

One of the more sensitive military issues is whether or not it is legally permissible for another state to emplant or emplace sonic detection devices within the exclusive economic zone of a coastal state in accordance with the 1958 Convention. The permissive position is argued by Tullio Treves and the restrictive position is argued by Rex Zedalis in the *American Journal of International Law.*[37] On balance, it is difficult to conclude that one position is legally better than the other. However, from a practical political perspective, it is rather doubtful that the state desiring to emplant or emplace sonic listening devices within the exclusive economic zone of another state would do so without the permission of that state. Such seems to be the case of the two sonic detection systems of the United States and the Soviet Union off the North Cape of Norway.[38]

The Continental Shelf

The continental shelf is a natural prolongation of the land mass and all coastal states may claim out to 200 nm. If the continental shelf naturally extends beyond that point, all coastal states may claim out to a maximum extent of 350 nm in accordance with Article 76 of the UN Convention. The coastal state exercises sovereign rights over the continental shelf for the purpose of exploring and exploiting it for natural resources and other states may not exploit the shelf without the express consent of the coastal state in accordance with Article 77 of the UN Convention. Furthermore, the exercise of these sovereign rights over the continental shelf must not infringe upon or result in any unjustifiable interference with the navigation and other rights of other state including the right to lay submarine cables and pipelines. However, the course of such pipelines and submarine cables may be designated by the coastal state in accordance with Article 79 of the UN Convention.

The continental shelf and especially the continental slope are optimal areas for the emplacement of electronic, acoustical and magnetic anomaly detection devices.[39] The principal question is whether the emplacement of such devices is legally permissible under the UN Convention, and if so, does it require the express approval of the coastal state? Again, as in the exclusive economic zone, there is no clear answer. However, it would seem that the deployment of these various detection devices beyond 200 nm is legally permissible with or without the consent of the coastal state.

The deployment of sound surveillance systems (SOSUS) off the Kurile and Aleutian Islands in the North Pacific Ocean and off the North Cape and between Greenland and Iceland, and Iceland and the United Kingdom (the GIUK gap) in the North Atlantic Ocean, are extremely important to the tactical and strategic anti-submarine warfare program (ASW) of the United States and NATO.[40] Once a Soviet strategic ballistic missile submarine gets past these arrays, it is more difficult to detect and track. Although these various underwater detection systems are passive, they are an extremely important element in the arsenal of naval weaponry. (More will be discussed in the next section on *the Deep Seabed and High Seas*.)

The Deep Seabed and the High Seas

As mentioned earlier, the Seabed Arms Control Treaty of 1972 precludes the emplanting or emplacing of nuclear weapons and weapons of mass destruction twelve nm beyond the coastal baseline.[41] The treaty also precludes structures, launching installations or any other facilities specifically designed for storing, testing, or using such weapons. Interestingly enough, the Soviet draft of the treaty would have banned all military uses of the seabed including submarine surveillance systems.[42] However, the United States did not agree. As a result, all military uses of the seabed are permitted except those specifically excluded by the treaty. Verification of compliance with the treaty beyond the twelve-nm zone is permitted through national observation and should not infringe upon the high seas freedoms of other states or the rights of coastal states to explore and exploit their continental shelves.

The Antarctic Treaty of 1959, the Outer Space Treaty of 1967 and the Latin American Treaty on a Nuclear Free Zone of 1967 also preclude the introduction of nuclear weapons. Since the area that is geographically described as Antarctica is everything sixty degrees south to the Pole, it is logical to assume that everything within that area will be a nuclear-free and peaceful zone. Exactly what is outer space and where it begins is difficult to say. However, it is generally regarded as that region about 100 miles or more above earth where a satellite can orbit. The Latin American Treaty on a Nuclear Free Zone specifically covers the land area, territorial sea and superjacent air space. Does that mean that all the Latin American states which claim a territorial sea in excess of twelve nautical miles are to maintain a nuclear-free zone to the full extent and require all other states to comply? If so, that would set an interesting precedent and might possibly infringe upon the high seas rights of other states to navigate nuclear-armed warships through that zone. For example, in 1970 the UN General Assembly passed Resolution 2660 (XXV) which declared the Indian Ocean a zone of peace; in 1971 the General Assembly passed Resolution 2832 (XXVI) which called for the establishment of a nuclear weapon-free zone in the South Pacific; in 1975 the General Assembly passed Resolution 3477 (XXX) which called for the establishment of similar zones in other parts of the world ocean.[43] However, thus far the superpowers and some of the major powers have chosen not to abide by these resolutions, especially in the Indian Ocean where the United States has a major naval base at Diego Garcia. The Indian Ocean has also been a major patrol area for the United States' strategic ballistic missile nuclear submarines (SSBN), because it provides better targeting for the mid-section of the Soviet Union.

Beyond the general statement in the Preamble of the UN Convention about the peaceful uses of the seas and oceans, very little is said about military warships and aircraft, except in regard to innocent passage, transit passage, and archipelagic sealanes passage. What this means or implies is that, generally speaking, everything of a military character or purpose is virtually unrestricted and unrestrained by international law and the law of the sea. To be sure, there are some broad limitations set forth by the SALT I Treaty and the SALT II Agreement, and some specific exclusions such as poison gases and bacteriological toxins under the Geneva Protocol of 1925, and nuclear testing is precluded underwater in the territorial or high seas by the Limited Test Ban Treaty of 1963. However, again generally speaking everything else is permitted -- strategic nuclear ballistic missile submarines (SSBN), strategic nuclear attack submarines (SSN) and a host of other naval weaponry.

Therefore, it can probably be reasonably concluded that the UN Convention has had little or no effect on curbing or limiting naval weapons and activity on the high seas. In point of fact, during the fourteen-year period from 1968 to 1982 when the Third United Nations Conference on the Law of the Sea (UNCLOS III) was in process, both the Soviet Union and the United States substantially increased the size and capabilities of their respective navies.[44] The growth of the Soviet Navy during this period was more dramatic than that of the United States in quantitative terms, but the growth of the United States Navy seems to have been substantial in qualitative terms. That is, the United States seems to be keeping its technological lead, especially in sub-launched ballistic missiles (SLBM), sub-launched cruise missiles (SLCM), strategic ballistic missile submarines (SSBN), strategic nuclear attack submarines (SSN), and a wide variety of associated anti-submarine warfare (ASW) systems.[45] However, the Soviet Union is reportedly closing the technological gap.[46] For example, although the new Soviet Alfa-class strategic nuclear attack submarine (SSN) is probably the fastest submarine at an estimated forty-two knots, and can dive the deepest to an estimated 3,000 feet because of its titanium hull, it is also one of the noisiest and therefore not very effective.[47] When the first Alfa-class went on sea trials off Norway in 1980, the United States picked it up on ASW acoustical equipment in Bermuda -- 4,000 nautical miles away.[48]

In order to maintain its technological lead, and therefore its strategic superiority and relative invulnerability of the strategic nuclear ballistic missile submarine (SSBN), the United States reportedly budgeted $13 billion for ASW in FY 1983, which is expected to rise to $26.8 billion in fiscal year 1986.[49] This is the largest share allocated to a single mission in the Navy's budget. The importance of ASW to the Navy was recently highlighted by the Walkers' spy case because their expertise and experience was largely in ASW, and it was that intelligence which was allegedly compromised to the Soviet Union.[50]

Back in 1979 there was a minor controversy in regard to United States' ASW capability.[51] Owen Wilkes of the Stockholm International Peace Research Institute (SIPRI) argued that if global real-time pinpoint submarine detection and tracking had been achieved by the United States, then the almost-simultaneous destruction of all enemy submarines became a distinct possibility.[52] Wilkes contended that if this was the case, the United States was near achieving or had achieved first-strike capability, which would be fundamentally asymmetric and destabilizing to the overall strategic equation of nuclear deterrence.[53] A United States Navy spokesman denied this and said that,

> The basic premise of the [SIPRI] article, that the United States will soon be able to effectively eliminate the Soviet submarine-based retaliatory capability in so short a period of time as to be destabilizing from a nuclear deterrent standpoint, has no basis in fact.[54]

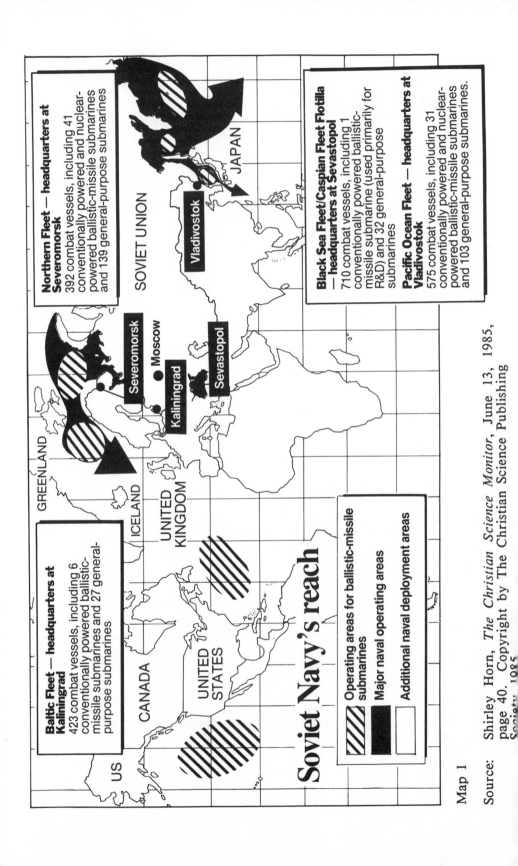

Soviet Navy's reach

Northern Fleet — headquarters at Severomorsk
392 combat vessels, including 41 conventionally powered and nuclear-powered ballistic-missile submarines and 139 general-purpose submarines

Black Sea Fleet/Caspian Fleet Flotilla — headquarters at Sevastopol
710 combat vessels, including 1 conventionally powered ballistic-missile submarine (used primarily for R&D) and 32 general-purpose submarines

Pacific Ocean Fleet — headquarters at Vladivostok
575 combat vessels, including 31 conventionally powered and nuclear-powered ballistic-missile submarines and 103 general-purpose submarines.

Baltic Fleet — headquarters at Kaliningrad
423 combat vessels, including 6 conventionally powered ballistic-missile submarines and 27 general-purpose submarines

Severomorsk
Moscow
Kaliningrad
Sevastopol
Vladivostok

SOVIET UNION
JAPAN
GREENLAND
ICELAND
UNITED KINGDOM
UNITED STATES
CANADA
US

Operating areas for ballistic-missile submarines

Major naval operating areas

Additional naval deployment areas

Map 1

Source: Shirley Horn, *The Christian Science Monitor*, June 13, 1985, page 40. Copyright by The Christian Science Publishing Society, 1985.

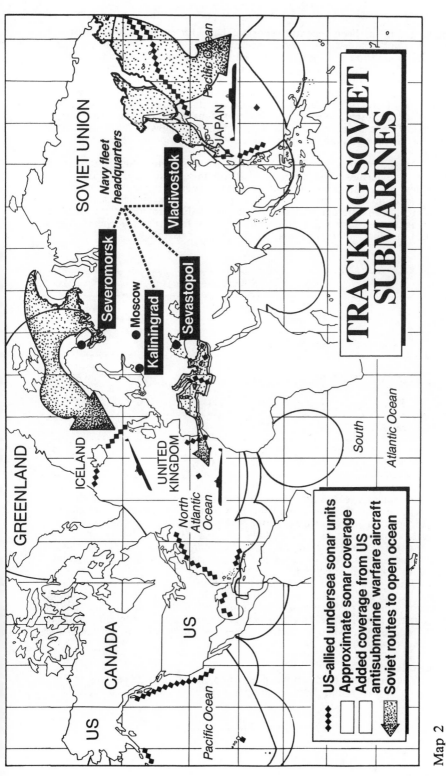

Map 2

Source: Shirley Horn, *The Christian Science Monitor*, June 14, 1985, page 40. Copyright by The Christian Science Publishing Society, 1985.

However, it has been recently reported that with major improvements in the sound underwater surveillance system (SOSUS), the "position and type of submarine will now be flashed in real time to ASW ships via a satellite data link, ensuring a response within three minutes to target location."[55] If the newly upgraded SOSUS system does in fact have a three-minute real time capability, that may be more important than the "Strategic Defense Initiative," because it does raise again the possibility of total destruction of the Soviet sea-based deterrent. However, the significant point is that these new breakthroughs in electronic ASW may make the ultimate deterrent more vulnerable in the foreseeable future.

On the other side of the equation are the United States and Soviet combat submarines. The strategic ballistic missile submarine (SSBN) provides the strategic deterrent or nuclear counter-punch. The strategic guided missile submarine (SSGN) provides both tactical and strategic force. The strategic attack submarine (SSN) provides both tactical force against surface ships and strategic ASW force against enemy SSBN. A brief summary of this submarine capability is as follows:

Chart 3.

Superpower Submarine Forces[56]

Type	United States		Soviet Union	
	Diesel	Nuclear	Diesel	Nuclear
SSB	0	35	14	65
SSG	0	4	18	49
SS	4	91	136	75
Subtotals	4	130	168	189
Totals	134		357	

Although the United States is quantitatively outnumbered, it compensates for this deficiency through more ships days at sea, much quieter running submarines, better navigation systems, greater technological competence, and better ASW systems. However, to retain a credible and effective deterrent only one Typhoon class or one Ohio class SSBN needs to survive in order to inflict unacceptable damage upon an actual or potential opponent.[57]

What does all this underwater capability, not to mention surface capability, mean for the law of the sea? In a sense, it means nothing, because all this naval weaponry is unrestricted and unrestrained on the high seas. That is, the world ocean is largely a legal vacuum, with the noted exceptions, when it comes to the laws of naval warfare, arms control and disarmament.

Conclusion
The problems of naval weaponry and the law of the sea are not so much military and legal as they are political and psychological.

Therefore, they must first be addressed at those levels. In order to start addressing some of these problems, I have two general observations:

First, that there is an urgent need to hold another Hague Conference on the laws of war in general, and naval warfare in particular.

Second, that there is an urgent need to actively and effectively address arms control and disarmament issues as they relate to the world ocean.

However, given the current state of international relations, it is rather doubtful that the superpowers would be willing to sit down at the table and start discussing these issues in the foreseeable future. In the meantime, specialized groups such as the International Law Commission, the Law of the Sea Institute, and the various Naval War Colleges might begin the preparatory work and start drafting new codes of naval warfare and arms limitation agreements for the world ocean.

NOTES

* The author wishes to acknowledge and express his appreciation to Christopher Cole and Michael W. Roth of the Department of Political Science, University of New Hampshire, for their research assistance. The author also wishes to express his appreciation to Prof. Wendell S. Brown, Acting Director of the Marine Program at the University of New Hampshire, and to Dean Stuart H. Palmer of the College of Liberal Arts at the University of New Hampshire for their financial assistance and research support.

1. a. Hugo Grotius, *De Jure Belli ac Pacis Libri Tres*, edited by James Brown Scott (Oxford: The Clarendon Press, 1925).
b. Lassa Oppenheim, *International Law: A Treatise, Volume 1 -- Peace, Volume 2 Disputes, War and Neutrality*, edited by Hersh Lauterpacht, eighth edition (New York: David McKay Company Inc., 1963).

2. a. Richard G. Darman, "The Law of the Sea: Rethinking U.S. Interests," *Foreign Affairs*, Volume 56, no. 2, January 1978, p. 375.
b. United States, House of Representatives, Committee on Foreign Affairs, Ninety-Seventh Congress, Second Session, *U.S. Foreign Policy and the Law of the Sea*, Hearings, June 17, August 12 and September 16, 1982, pp. 92-93. Testimony of Elliot L. Richardson.
c. United Nations, *A Quiet Revolution: The United Nations Convention on the Law of the Sea* (New York: United Nations, 1984), p. 6.
d. Bernard H. Oxman, "From Cooperation to Conflict: The Soviet Union and the United States at the Third UN Conference on the Law of the Sea," Donald L. McKernan Lectures in Marine Affairs, University of Washington, Seattle, Washington, 1985, pp. 4-8.

3. a. United States Department of State, *Limits of the Seas*, April 1, 1974.
b. Robert W. Smith, editor, Office of the Geographer, United States, Department of State, "National Maritime Claims," mimeo, January 6, 1984.
c. Robert W. Smith, editor, Office of the Geographer, United States Department of State, *Limits in the Seas: National Claims to Maritime Jurisdiction*, no. 36 -- 5th Revision, March 1985 (Washington, D.C.: Department of State, 1985).

   d. United Nations, Office of the Special Representative of the Secretary General for Law of the Sea Negotiations, *Law of the Sea Bulletin*, no. 2, March 1985.

4. David L. Larson, "Security, Disarmament and the Law of the Sea," *Marine Policy*, vol. 3, no. 1, January 1979, pp. 40-58.

5. United Nations, *A Quiet Revolution... op. cit.* pp. 12, 18.

6. Larson, "Security, Disarmament and the Law of the Sea," *op. cit.*, p. 40.

7. United Nations, Office of Public Information, *Charter of the United Nations and Statute of the International Court of Justice* (New York: United Nations, n.d.), Article 13, paragraph 1a.

8. a. David E. Simcox, "The Regional Coast Guards," *Proceedings of the United States Naval Institute*, July 1985, p. 44.
   b. Michael R. Adams, "Caribbean Coast Guard," *Proceedings of the United States Naval Institute*, July 1985, p. 52.

9. Norwegian Fisheries Case 1951, North Sea Continental Shelf Cases 1969, Icelandic Fisheries Cases 1972, Anglo-French Continental Shelf Case 1977, Aegean Sea Case 1981, Libya-Tunisia Continental Shelf Case 1982, Gulf of Maine Case 1984, Beagle Channel Case (arbitral settlement by Pope John Paul II) 1984, Libya-Malta Continental Shelf Case 1985.

10. G. Etzel Pearcy, "Geographical Aspects of the Law of the Sea," *Annals of the Association of American Geographers*, Volume 49, 1959, p. 1.

11. International Court of Justice, "Fisheries Case" (United Kingdom v. Norway), *I.C.J. Reports*, 1951, p. 132.

12. Carl Bildt, "Sweden and the Soviet Submarines," *Survival*, vol. XXV, no. 4, July/August 1983, pp. 165-169.

13. *Ibid.*

14. a. Anders Sjaastad, *Time* magazine, vol. 112, August 7, 1978, p. 48.
   b. *The New York Times*, July 30, August 4, 5, 6, 1978.

15. Orr Kelly, "Sub Duels Under Polar Ice: How Ready is the U.S.?", *U.S. News and World Report*, vol. 96, no. 9 (5 March 1984), p. 35.

16. *The New York Times*, August 10, 1979. "The Carter Administration has Ordered the Navy and Air Force to Undertake a Policy of Deliberately Sending Ships and Planes into and over the Disputed Waters of Nations that Claim a Territorial Limit of More than the Three Miles Accepted by the U.S. and 21 Other Nations."

17. a. *The Christian Science Monitor*, August 21, 1981.
   b. John Lehman, "The Law of the Sea," *Defense*, March 1982.

18. Office of the Press Secretary, The White House, "Fact Sheet: United States Ocean Policy," mimeo, March 10, 1983.

19. a. Bruce A. Harlow, "UNCLOS III and Conflict Management in Straits," *The Developing Order of the Oceans*, Proceedings of the 18th Annual Conference of the Law of the Sea Institute, eds. Robert B. Krueger and Stefan A. Riesenfeld, (Honolulu: Law of the Sea Institute, 1985, p. 682).
   b. James L. Malone, "Freedom and Opportunity Foundation for a Dynamic Oceans Policy." *Department of State Bulletin*, vol. 84, no. 2093 December 1984, p. 78.

20. United States, Arms Control and Disarmament Agency, *Arms Control and Disarmament Agreements, 1982 Edition* (Washington, D.C.: U.S. Government Printing Office, 1982) p. 102.

21. *Ibid.*

22. *The New York Times*, August 2, 6, 7, 8, 1984.

23. International Court of Justice, "Case Concerning Military and Paramilitary Activities in and Against Nicaragua." (Nicaragua v. United States of America.) *I.C.J. Reports*, 1984 p. 215 ff.
24. Ted Hooton, "Naval Mines: The Hidden Menace," *Military Technology*, vol. VIII, no. 9, 1984, pp. 27-33.
25. a. *Ibid.*
    b. Roy McLeavy, "U.S.A. Gives New Priority to Mine Warfare," *Jane's Defence Weekly*, vol. 2, no. 1, July 14, 1984, p. 21.
    c. John Cristy, "Danger Beneath the Sea," *International Combat Arms*, March 1985, p. 78.
    d. (no author), "The Soviet Fleet: Minesweepers, Mine Hunters and Mine Layers," *Strategy and Defense*, vol. XIII, no. 93, March 1985, p. 36.
26. Jon Van Dyke, "Law of the Sea: A Lost Opportunity," *The Washington Post National Weekly Edition*, June 10, 1985, p. 25.
27. a. Brenda Ralph Lewis, "The Loss of HMS Coventry: The Falklands War 1982," *Defense Update*, no. 47, 1984, p. 25.
    b. Martin Douglas, "Naval Lessons from the South Atlantic," *Jane's Defence Weekly*, April 17, 1984, p. 519.
28. James A. Hazlett, "Strait Shooting," *Proceedings of the United States Naval Institute*, June 1982, p. 70.
29. a. "Matra/Otomelara Otomat," *Aviation and Marine International*, no. 70, February 1980, p. 81.
    b. John Cristy, "Sea-Going Missiles," *International Combat Arms*, vol. 2, no. 43, September 1984, p. 78.
    c. "Seawolf v. Exocet," *Strategy and Defense*, September 1984, p. 73.
    d. Damian Housman, "The Deadly Harpoon," *International Combat Arms*, May 1985, p. 32.
30. Bruce A. Harlow, "UNCLOS III and Conflict Management in Straits," p. 683.
31. *Ibid*, p. 682.
32. a. Elizabeth Young, "New Laws for Old Navies," *Survival*, vol. XVI, 1974, p. 262.
    b. W. Michael Reisman, "The Regime of Straits and National Security: An Appraisal of Lawmaking," *American Journal of International Law*, vol. 74, no. 1, January 1980, p. 48.
    c. John Norton Moore, "The Regime of Straits and the Third United Nations Conference on the Law of the Sea," *American Journal of International Law*, vol. 74, no. 1, January 1980, p. 77.
33. United Nations, Office of the Special Representative of the Secretary General for the Law of the Sea, *Law of the Sea Bulletin*, no. 2, March 1985, p. v.
34. a. Richard G. Darman, "The Law of the Sea: Rethinking U.S. Interests," *op. cit.* p. 375.
    b. Ken Booth, "Naval Strategy and the Spread of Psycho-Legal Boundaries at Sea," *International Journal*, vol. 38, no. 3, 1983, pp. 373-396.
    An interesting variation of this territorialization occurred during the Falklands/Malvinas conflict when Great Britain imposed a 200 nm "war zone" around the islands. *The New York Times*, April 8, 1982, p. 1.
    Of course, this is not the first war zone to have been asserted. There are various precedents in World War I and World War II. At the present time, thirteen coastal states claim a territorial sea of

200 nm., including Argentina, Brazil, Congo, Panama, Ecuador, Nicaragua, Somalia, and Uruguay.

35. a. Peter Tarpgaard, Captain USN (Ret.) Principal Security Analyst, Congressional Budget Office, Letter dated May 9, 1985. The expanding literature in the field supports the contention of Dr. Tapgaard:

b. (no author), "A Missile Armed Fast Attack Craft of Wood," *Aviation and Marine International*, no. 50, February/March 1978, p. 35.

c. (no author), "New Combat Hovercraft," *Aviation and Marine International*, no. 51, April 1978, p. 32.

d. (no author), "Nigeria: A New Naval Power," *Aviation and Marine International*, no. 53, June 1978, p. 17.

e. (no author), "CMN Proposal for an off-shore," *Aviation and Marine International*, no. 62, April 1979, p. 33.

f. (no author), "Air and Maritime Patrol," *Aviation and Marine International*, no. 69, January 1980, p. 35.

g. (no author), "Something New for the U.S. Coast Guard," *Aviation and Marine International*, no. 70, February 1980, p. 27.

h. (no author), "Wadi Mragh," *Aviation and Marine International*, no. 73, May 1980, p. 55.

36. David Lange, "New Zealand's Security Policy." *Foreign Policy*, vol. 63, no. 5 (Summer 1985), p. 1009.

37. a. Tullio Treves, "Military Installations, Structures, and Devices on the Seabed," *American Journal of International Law*, vol. 74, no. 4, October 1980, p. 808.

b. Rex Zedalis, "Military Installations, Structures, and Devices on the Continental Shelf: A Response," *American Journal of International Law*, vol. 75, no. 1, January 1981, p. 926.

38. *Time* magazine, vol. 112, August 7, 1978, p. 48.

39. The continental slope is normally a gradual decline from the continental shelf edge to the abyssal plain or seabed. It is advantageous to deploy detection devices on the slope because then a larger range of water depths and temperature layers, such as the thermoclime, and sound waves are more readily transmitted within each layer.

40. David Larson and Peter Tarpgaard, "Law of the Sea and ASW: National Security versus Arms Control," *Marine Policy*, Volume 6, no. 2, April 1982, p. 90.

41. a. United States, Arms Control and Disarmament Agency, *Arms Control and Disarmament Agreements, 1982 Edition*, *op. cit.*, p. 102.

b. Larson and Tarpgaard, "Law of the Sea and ASW," *op. cit.*, pp. 93-94.

42. United States, Arms Control and Disarmament Agency, *Arms Control and Disarmament Agreements*, *op. cit.*, p. 100.

43. United Nations, *Third United Nations Conference on the Law of the Sea*, Official Records, Volume V, Fourth Session, New York, March 15-May 7, 1976, p. 54.

It is interesting to note that this debate on zones of peace includes the only discussion of military uses of the world ocean at UNCLOS III, and the debate lasted only four days. Needless to say the discussion was inconclusive.

44. United States, Department of Defense, *Soviet Military Power 1985*, (Washington, D.C.: U.S. Government Printing Office, 1985).

45. Jonathan B. Tucker, "Cold War in the Ocean Depths," *High Technology*, vol. 5, no. 7, July 1985, p. 29.

46. *The Christian Science Monitor*, June 13, 14, 1985.

47. Tucker, "Cold War in the Ocean Depths," *op. cit.*.
48. *Ibid.*
49. *Ibid.*
50. a. *The New York Times*
 b. *The Christian Science Monitor*, June 5, 12, 1985.
 c. *Time* magazine, vol. 125, no. 24, June 17, 1985 p. 18 ff.
51. Larson and Tarpgaard, "Law of the Sea and ASW," *op. cit.*, p. 101.
52. Stockholm International Peace Research Institute, *SIPRI Yearbook 1979* (New York: Crane, Russak, 1979), p. 430.
53. *Ibid.*
54. Drew Middleton, "Expert Predicts a Big Gain in Sub Warfare," *The New York Times*, July 18, 1979, p. A5.
55. a. Anthony Preston, "SOSUS Update Aims to Keep Track of Alfa," *Jane's Defence Weekly*, January 21, 1984, p. 60.
 b. Tucker, "Cold War in the Ocean Depths," *op. cit.*, p. 32.
 c. Norman Friedman, "Real-time Ocean Surveillance," *Military Technology*, vol. VIII, no. 9, September 1984, p. 76.
 d. Geoffrey Till, "Strategic Aspects of ASW," *Naval Forces*, vol. V, no. IV, p. 14.
 e. B.W. Lythall, "Underwater Detection -- Active or Passive?" *Naval Forces*, vol. V, no. V, 1984, p. 66.
56. a. IISS, *The Military Balance, 1984-1985* (London: International Institute for Strategic Studies, 1984), pp. 8-22.
 b. *The Christian Science Monitor*, June 14, 1985, p. 40.
57. The new Trident D-5 SLBM is scheduled to be operational in 1989, and it will have 10 to 14 warheads, each with silo-busting capability. This will significantly change the strategic equation. Roy Hane III, "Super Underwater Warriors," *International Combat Arms*, vol. 3, no. 3, May 1985, p. 15 ff.

NOTES ON APPENDICES

1. Sources for Glossary and Appendices A and B:
 a. Moore, John, editor. *Jane's Fighting Ships, 1984-85*. London: Jane's Publishing Co., Ltd., 1984.
 b. IISS. *Military Balance, 1984-85*. London: International Institute for Strategic Studies, 1984.
2. For the charts in *Appendix A* on *General Force Levels*, the power levels used should be translated into the more common descriptions according to the following chart:

Power Level	Description
1	Superpower
2	Major Power
3, 4	Regional Power
5, 6, 7, 8	Minor Power
9, 10	Developing Power

3. The above power levels are used in the charts in *Appendix A* to compare the relative strengths of the various navies of the world in terms of the ships and aircraft that each possesses. The charts do not attempt to account for a nation's capacity to produce any or all of its own weapons. Thus, in power level 3 you will find Italy, a major producer of naval weapons, grouped with countries that do not have the same level of production capacity.

Glossary of Acronyms

AAM	Air to Air Missile
ASM	Air to Surface Missile
ASW	Anti-Submarine Warfare
BB	Battleship
CB	Battle Cruiser
CG	Missile Cruiser, Conventionally Powered
CGN	Missile Cruiser, Nuclear Powered
CT	Corvette, Gun
CTG	Corvette, Missile
CVA	Aircraft Carrier, Conventionally Powered
CVAN	Aircraft Carrier, Nuclear Powered
CVL	Aircraft Carrier, Light
DC	Depth Charge
DD	Destroyer, Gun
DDG	Destroyer, Missile
EW	Electronic Warfare
ECM	Electronic Counter-Measures
FAC(G)	Fast Attack Craft, Gun
FAC(M)	Fast Attack Craft, Missile
FAC(T)	Fast Attack Craft, Torpedo
FF	Frigate, Gun
FFG	Frigate Missile
HE	High Explosive
KT	Kiloton
LAMPS	Light Airborne Multi-Purpose System (Light Helicopter)
LHA	Amphibious General Assault Ship
LPH	Landing Platform, Helicopter
MCM	Mine Counter-Measures
MR	Maritime Reconnaissance
MT	Megaton
RECCE	Reconnaissance
SAM	Surface to Air Missile
SLBM	Submarine Launched Ballistic Missile
SLCM	Submarine Launched Cruise Missile
SS	Submarine, Attack, Diesel
SSBN	Submarine, Ballistic Missile, Nuclear
SSG	Submarine, Cruise Missile
SSGN	Submarine, Cruise Missile, Nuclear
SSM	Surface to Surface Missile
SSN	Submarine, Attack, Nuclear
TN	Thermonuclear
USM	Underwater to Surface Missile

Appendix A: General Force Levels

Power Level	Countries	SSBN SSGN SSG	SSN	SS
1	United States	38	91	4
	Soviet Union	146	65	150
2	Great Britain	4	13	15
	France	5	2	15
	China	1	2	100
3	Argentina	---	---	3
	Brazil	---	---	7
	India	---	---	8
	Italy	---	---	10
	Spain	---	---	8
4	Australia	---	---	6
	Canada	---	---	3
	Chile	---	---	3
	Columbia	---	---	2
	Ecuador	---	---	2
	Egypt	---	---	12
	West Germany	---	---	24
	Greece	---	---	10
	Japan	---	---	14
	Pakistan	---	---	11
	Peru	---	---	12
	Taiwan	---	---	2
	Turkey	---	---	16
5	Algeria	---	---	2
	Bulgaria	---	---	2
	Cuba	---	---	4
	Denmark	---	---	5
	Indonesia	---	---	3
	North Korea	---	---	21
	Libya	---	---	6
	Netherlands	---	---	6
	Norway	---	---	14
	Poland	---	---	3
	Portugal	---	---	3
	South Africa	---	---	3
	Sweden	---	---	12
	Venezuela	---	---	3
	Yugoslavia	---	---	7

Submarines (continued)

Power Level	Countries	Submarines SSBN SSGN SSG	SSN	SS
6				
7	Albania	---	---	3
	Israel	---	---	3
8				
9				
10				

Power Level	Countries	Aircraft Carriers CVAN CVA	CVL CVE LHA/LPH
1	United States	14	12
	Soviet Union	---	5
2	Great Britain	---	3
	France	1	2
	China	---	---
3	Argentina	---	1
	Brazil	---	1
	India	---	1
	Italy	---	1
	Spain	---	1
4			
5			
6			
7			
8			
9			
10			

Power Level	Countries	Major Warships		
		BB CB CG/CGN	DD DDG	FF FFG
1	United States	30	49	119
	Soviet Union	36	69	185
2	Great Britain	---	12	43
	France	1	19	25
	China	---	14	22
3	Argentina	---	10	---
	Brazil	---	10	6
	India	1	3	26
	Italy	2	4	15
	Spain	---	11	11
4	Australia	---	3	10
	Canada	---	20	---
	Chile	2	4	2
	Colombia	---	2	4
	Ecuador	---	2	---
	Egypt	---	5	5
	West Germany	---	7	8
	Greece	---	14	7
	Japan	---	32	18
	Pakistan	---	8	---
	Peru	2	10	2
	Taiwan	---	23	9
	Turkey	---	13	2
5	Algeria	---	---	2
	Bulgaria	---	---	2
	Cuba	---	---	2
	Denmark	---	---	5
	Indonesia	---	---	9
	North Korea	---	---	4
	Libya	---	---	1
	Netherlands	---	2	16
	Norway	---	---	5
	Poland	---	1	---
	Portugal	---	---	17
	South Africa	---	---	1
	Sweden	---	2	---
	Venezuela	---	---	8
	Yugoslavia	---	---	2

Major Warships (continued)

Power Level	Countries	Major Warships BB CB CG/CGN	DD DDG	FF FFG
6	Bangladesh	---	---	3
	Belgium	---	---	4
	East Germany	---	---	2
	Iran	---	3	3
	Iraq	---	---	1
	South Korea	---	11	8
	Malaysia	---	---	2
	Mexico	---	3	6
	Nigeria	---	---	2
	Philippines	---	---	7
	Romania	---	---	1
	Saudi Arabia	---	---	1
	Syria	---	---	2
	Thailand	---	---	6
	Vietnam	---	---	6
7				
8	Dominican Rep.	---	---	1
	Ethiopia	---	---	2
	Morocco	---	---	1
	New Zealand	---	---	4
	Tunisia	---	---	1
	Uruguay	---	---	3
9				
10				

Power Level	Countries	CT CTG	FAC(M) FAC(G) FAC(T)	Minor Warships Patrol Vessels Large	Small	Special
1	United States	28	---	76	80	16
	Soviet Union	30	396	103	---	484
2	Great Britain	---	---	35	---	12
	France	---	6	4	---	4
	China	8	847	48	60	7
3	Argentina	6	8	26	19	---
	Brazil	---	---	15	---	---
	India	3	16	7	---	---
	Italy	8	2	---	---	---
	Spain	4	12	18	64	---
4	Australia	---	---	21	---	---
	Canada	---	---	---	12	41
	Chile	---	6	4	22	---
	Colombia	---	---	9	2	---
	Ecuador	6	6	---	7	---
	Egypt	---	52	22	---	---
	West Germany	5	39	---	---	---
	Greece	---	29	---	11	---
	Japan	---	5	4	9	---
	Pakistan	---	24	---	49	---
	Peru	---	6	---	---	---
	Taiwan	3	28	---	30	---
	Turkey	---	18	25	4	---
5	Algeria	3	16	---	---	---
	Bulgaria	3	20	---	13	---
	Cuba	---	74	11	12	---
	Denmark	---	16	22	5	5
	Indonesia	---	6	14	6	---
	North Korea	---	361	33	30	---
	Libya	8	27	7	1	3
	Netherlands	4	---	3	3	---
	Norway	2	46	6	1	7
	Poland	---	31	8	---	---
	Portugal	---	---	10	13	---
	South Africa	---	9	6	---	2
	Sweden	---	34	6	10	69
	Venezuela	---	6	---	---	---
	Yugoslavia	3	31	24	---	---

Power Level	Countries	CT CTG	FAC(M) FAC(G) FAC(T)	Minor Warships Patrol Vessels Large	Small	Special
6	Bangladesh	---	22	4	5	---
	Finland	2	10	5	1	---
	East Germany	10	64	19	---	---
	Iran	2	6	2	---	---
	Iraq	---	17	2	5	---
	South Korea	3	8	23	4	---
	Malaysia	---	14	21	---	---
	Mexico	6	---	66	14	---
	Nigeria	4	6	8	48	---
	Philippines	10	3	16	62	---
	Romania	3	43	3	---	---
	Saudi Arabia	4	12	1	---	---
	Syria	---	28	1	3	---
	Thailand	---	9	19	31	---
	Vietnam	---	49	6	9	---
7	Albania	---	18	12	---	---
	Israel	4	20	---	45	---
8	Burma	4	---	---	15	---
	Dominican Republic	5	---	5	11	---
	Ethiopia	---	7	9	3	---
	Ghana	2	4	4	4	---
	Morocco	---	8	4	9	---
	New Zealand	---	---	4	2	---
	Tunisia	---	6	4	12	---
	Uruguay	1	---	4	4	---
	South Yemen	1	12	2	---	---
9	Angola	---	8	5	8	---
	Brunei	---	3	---	3	---
	Cameroon	---	5	---	9	---
	Cape Verde	---	2	---	2	---
	Congo	---	4	5	3	---
	Equatorial Guinea	---	1	1	4	---
	Gabon	---	5	---	2	---
	Guinea	---	8	---	7	---
	Guinea-Bissau	---	6	---	6	---
	Kenya	---	4	3	---	---
	Kuwait	---	8	---	47	---
	Oman	---	8	4	---	---
	Qatar	---	3	6	38	---
	Singapore	---	12	2	12	---

Minor Warships (continued)

Power Level	Countries	CT CTG	FAC(M) FAC(G) FAC(T)	Patrol Vessels Large	Small	Special
(9)	Somalia	---	10	5	---	---
	Sri Lanka	---	8	---	26	---
	U.A.E.	---	6	6	3	---
	North Yemen	---	4	---	6	---
	Zaire	---	4	---	47	---
10	Bahrain	---	4	---	---	---
	Benin	---	---	---	4	---
	Costa Rica	---	---	---	9	---
	Cyprus	---	---	2	---	---
	Djibouti	---	---	---	3	---
	El Salvador	---	---	---	4	---
	Fiji	---	---	---	3	---
	Guatemala	---	---	---	15	---
	Guyana	---	---	1	7	---
	Haiti	---	---	---	15	---
	Honduras	---	---	4	5	---
	Ireland	---	---	5	---	2
	Ivory Coast	---	---	6	4	---
	Jamaica	---	---	1	3	---
	Jordan	---	---	9	---	---
	Liberia	---	---	---	6	---
	Lebanon	---	---	4	---	---
	Madagascar	---	---	1	---	---
	Mauritania	---	---	---	8	---
	Mozambique	---	---	---	14	---
	Nicaragua	---	---	---	14	---
	Panama	---	---	6	---	---
	Papua New Guinea	---	---	5	---	---
	Senegambia	---	---	4	7	---
	Seychelles	---	---	4	1	---
	Sierra Leone	---	---	---	1	---
	Sudan	---	---	5	3	---
	Suriname	---	---	3	4	---
	Togo	---	---	---	2	---
	Trinidad & Tobago	---	---	6	7	---

Power Level	Countries	Mine Warfare		Hydrofoil & Air Cushion	Amphib-ious Warfare	Support & Others
		Layers	Sweepers			
1	United States	---	21	6	105	259
	Soviet Union	3	354	97	45	269
2	Great Britain	---	37	1	6	25
	France	---	24	---	48	13
	China	---	23	---	59	576
3	Argentina	---	6	---	1	3
	Brazil	---	6	---	2	78
	India	---	16	---	---	---
	Italy	---	24	7	2	2
	Spain	---	12	---	2	2
4	Australia	---	1	---	---	5
	Canada	---	---	---	---	3
	Chile	---	---	---	8	69
	Colombia	---	---	---	---	8
	Ecuador	---	---	---	4	---
	Egypt	---	12	3	---	---
	West Germany	---	57	---	---	31
	Greece	2	14	---	13	---
	Japan	---	39	---	6	---
	Pakistan	---	3	---	---	2
	Peru	---	---	---	4	14
	Taiwan	---	14	---	29	10
	Turkey	---	33	---	7	56
5	Algeria	---	1	---	---	1
	Bulgaria	---	30	---	---	28
	Cuba	---	12	---	2	7
	Denmark	7	6	---	---	---
	Indonesia	---	2	---	---	30
	North Korea	---	---	3	---	104
	Libya	---	6	---	2	8
	Netherlands	---	19	---	---	12
	Norway	2	10	---	---	15
	Poland	---	50	---	---	45
	Portugal	---	4	---	---	13
	South Africa	---	6	---	---	31
	Sweden	19	27	---	---	284
	Venezuela	---	---	---	2	15
	Yugoslavia	13	31	---	---	22

Power Level	Countries	Specialized Warfare and Support				
		Mine Warfare		Hydrofoil & Air Cushion	Amphib- ious Warfare	Support & Others
		Layers	Sweepers			
6	Bangladesh	---	---	---	1	---
	Belgium	---	27	---	---	6
	Finland	3	13	---	---	29
	East Germany	---	46	---	---	20
	Iran	---	3	10	---	5
	Iraq	---	5	---	---	4
	South Korea	---	9	17	---	16
	Malaysia	---	2	---	2	31
	Mexico	---	---	---	3	1
	Nigeria	---	2	---	---	---
	Philippines	---	---	---	31	61
	Romania	---	46	21	---	46
	Saudi Arabia	---	4	16	---	16
	Syria	---	4	---	---	---
	Thailand	---	9	8	---	98
	Vietnam	---	---	---	6	---
7	Albania	---	5	32	---	---
	Israel	---	---	2	3	9
8	Burma	---	---	---	---	56
	Dominican Rep.	---	---	---	1	2
	Ethiopia	---	---	---	---	1
	Morocco	---	1	---	---	4
	Tunisia	---	2	---	---	---
	Uruguay	---	---	---	---	4
	South Yemen	---	---	---	---	7
9	Angola	---	---	---	---	9
	Brunei	---	---	---	---	29
	Cameroon	---	---	---	---	14
	Cape Verde	---	---	---	---	2
	Congo	---	---	---	---	4
	Eq. Guinea	---	---	---	---	4
	Gabon	---	---	---	1	3
	Guinea	---	---	---	---	3
	Guinea-Bissau	---	---	---	---	2
	Kuwait	---	---	---	---	6
	Oman	---	---	---	---	9
	Singapore	---	2	---	6	6
	Somalia	---	---	---	---	5
	U.A.E.	---	---	---	---	2
	North Yemen	---	---	---	---	2
	Zaire	---	---	4	---	---

Specialized Warfare and Support (continued)

Power Level	Countries	Specialized Warfare and Support				
		Mine Warfare		Hydrofoil & Air Cushion	Amphib- ious Warfare	Support & Others
		Layers	Sweepers			
10	Benin	---	---	---	---	4
	Costa Rica	---	---	---	---	1
	Djibouti	---	---	---	---	3
	El Salvador	---	---	---	---	2
	Fiji	---	3	---	---	---
	Guatemala	---	---	---	---	23
	Ivory Coast	---	---	---	---	5
	Madagascar	---	---	---	---	8
	Mozambique	---	---	---	---	1
	Nicaragua	---	---	---	---	1
	Panama	---	---	---	2	6
	Papua New Guinea	---	---	---	---	2
	Senegambia	---	---	---	---	3
	Seychelles	---	---	---	---	1
	Sudan	---	---	---	---	3
	Suriname	---	---	---	---	3

Power Level	Countries	Fixed Wing Aircraft				
		Fighter & Attack	EW ECM RECCE	ASW	Maritime Patrol	Support & Others
1	United States	1,229	211	110	369	1,095
	Soviet Union	415	80	190	55	325
2	Great Britain	16	---	---	28	60
	France	50	8	16	30	109
	China	750	---	---	8	60
3	Argentina	36	---	9	7	66
	Brazil	---	---	15	31	---
	India	23	---	5	7	26
	Italy	---	---	---	14	---
	Spain	11	---	---	6	4
4	Australia	---	2	---	26	---
	Canada	---	---	---	33	12
	Chile	---	---	---	5	16
	Colombia	---	---	---	---	1
	Ecuador	---	---	---	---	5
	Egypt	---	---	---	5	---
	West Germany	77	32	---	14	19
	Greece	---	---	---	8	---
	Japan	---	---	---	81	104
	Pakistan	---	---	---	3	---
	Peru	---	---	7	2	12
	Taiwan	---	---	---	29	---
	Turkey	---	---	18	---	---
5	Algeria	---	---	---	7	---
	Indonesia	---	---	---	17	3
	Netherlands	---	---	---	13	---
	Poland	34	10	---	---	---
	Portugal	---	---	---	---	6
	South Africa	---	---	---	18	---
	Venezuela	---	---	6	3	7
6	Iran	---	---	---	2	9
	South Korea	---	---	22	---	---
	Malaysia	---	---	---	3	---
	Mexico	---	---	---	8	25
	Philippines	---	---	---	9	---
	Thailand	---	---	10	19	32
7	Israel	---	---	---	13	---
8	New Zealand	---	---	---	5	---
	Uruguay	---	---	6	1	20
9	Angola	---	---	---	1	---

Fixed Wing Aircraft (continued)

Power Level	Countries	Fixed Wing Aircraft				
		Fighter & Attack	EW ECM RECCE	ASW	Maritime Patrol	Support & Others
10	Cyprus	---	---	---	---	1
	Ireland	---	---	---	2	---
	Papua New Guinea	---	---	---	4	---
	Senegambia	---	---	---	2	---

Power Level	Countries	Helicopters		
		ASW & LAMPS	MCM	Support & Others
1	United States	174	17	874
	Soviet Union	255	10	100
2	Great Britain	130	---	113
	France	64	---	16
	China	52	---	---
3	Argentina	6	---	18
	Brazil	17	---	30
	India	23	---	17
	Italy	95	---	---
	Spain	25	---	26
4	Australia	8	---	26
	Canada	32	---	2
	Chile	4	---	9
	Colombia	---	---	30
	Ecuador	---	---	2
	Egypt	6	---	---
	West Germany	12	---	22
	Greece	12	---	---
	Japan	56	7	33
	Pakistan	10	---	---
	Peru	10	---	9
	Taiwan	12	---	---
	Turkey	9	---	14
5	Bulgaria	3	8	---
	Denmark	8	---	8
	Indonesia	10	---	5
	Netherlands	17	---	5
	Norway	---	---	16
	Poland	---	---	35
	Portugal	---	---	12

Helicopters (continued)

Power Level	Countries	Helicopters ASW & LAMPS	MCM	Support & Others
(5)	South Africa	---	---	10
	Sweden	---	10	13
	Venezuela	6	---	6
	Yugoslavia	10	---	20
6	Belgium	---	---	3
	East Germany	13	5	---
	Iran	10	2	7
	South Korea	10	---	21
	Mexico	---	---	14
	Nigeria	---	---	3
	Philippines	---	---	5
	Romania	---	---	8
	Saudi Arabia	20	---	4
	Thailand	---	---	11
	Vietnam	---	---	10
7				
8	New Zealand	---	---	7
	Uruguay	---	---	7
9				
10				

Appendix B: Summary of Naval Missiles

Class	Missile	Max. Range (N.M.)	Speed	Warhead
		United States		
SLBM	Polaris A-3	2500.0	10.0 Mach	3 x 200KT/TN
	Poseidon C-3	2500.0	--	10 x 50KT/TN
	Trident I C-4	4350.0	--	8 x 100KT/TN
	Trident II D-5	6000.0	--	12?x 100+KT/TN
SLCM	Tomahawk	1500.0	475 Kts	HE or nuclear
SSM	Harpoon RGM84A	50.0	0.9 Mach	500 lb/HE
USM	Harpoon RGM84C	60.0	0.9 Mach	500 lb/HE
ASM	Harpoon AGM84A	120.0	0.9 Mach	?/HE
	Bullpup A	7.0	2.0 Mach	250 lb/HE
	Bullpup B	10.0	2.0 Mach	HE or nuclear
	Maverick	--	--	--
	HARM	--	--	--
	Bulldog	35.0	--	
	Shrike	10.0	2.0 Mach	?/HE
	Walleye I	16.0	--	HE or nuclear
	Walleye II	35.0	2.0 Mach	HE or nuclear
	Standard Arm	35.0	--	?/HE
SAM	Standard SM1	10.0	--	?/HE
	Standard SM2	10.0	--	?/HE
	Standard SM1ER	30.0	--	--
	Standard SM2ER	30.0	--	--
	Ram	--	--	--
	Seasparrow	8.0	--	?/HE
	Tartar	14.0	2.0 Mach	?/HE
	Terrier	20.0	2.5 Mach	HE or nuclear
AAM	Agile	2.0	--	?/HE
	Phoenix	60.0	2.0 Mach	?/HE
	Sideswider-1B	8.0	2.0 Mach	?/HE
	Sparrow 3/AIM7E	12.0	3.5 Mach	?/HE
	Sparrow 3/AIM7F	25.0	3.5 Mach	?/HE
A/SW	ASROC	6.0	--	torpedo or DC
	SUBROC	30.0	1.0 Mach	nuclear

Class	Missile	Max. Range (N.M.)	Speed	Warhead

Class	Missile	Max. Range (N.M.)	Speed	Warhead
SLBM	SS-N-5 Serb	850.0	--	800 KT/ N
	SS-N-6 MK1	1300.0	--	1 MT/ N
	SS-N-6 MK2	1600.0	--	1 MT/ N
	SS-N-6 MK3	1800.0	--	3 x ?/ N
	SS-N-8 MK1	4200.0	--	800 KT/ N
	SS-N-8 MK2	4900.0	--	800 KT/ N
	SS-N-17	2400.0	--	?/N
	SS-N-18 MK1	3500.0	--	3 x ?/ N
	SS-N-18 MK2	4100.0	--	1 x 450 KT/ N
	SS-N-18 MK3	3500.0	--	7 x 200 KT/ N
	SS-N-20	5000.0	--	7 x ?/ N
SCLM	SS-N-7	35.0	0.9 Mach	200 KT/ N or 1100 lb/ HE
	SS-N-9 Siren	70.0	1.4 Mach	HE or nuclear
SSM	SS-N-2A Styx	25.0	0.9 Mach	900 lb/ HE
	SS-N-2B Styx	25.0	0.9 Mach	900 lb/ HE
	SS-N-2C Styx	45.0	0.9 Mach	1000 lb/ HE
	SS-N-3A Shaddock	250.0	1.4 Mach	1100 lb/ HE or
	SS-N-3B Sepal	250.0	1.4 Mach	350 KT/ N
	SS-N-9 Siren	70.0	0.9 Mach	HE or nuclear
	SS-N-12	300.0	2.5 Mach	HE or nuclear
	SS-N-19	300.0	--	HE or nuclear
	SS-N-21	1600.0	0.7 Mach	nuclear
	SS-N-22	80.0	2.5 Mach	HE
SAM	SA-N-1 Goa	17.0	3.0+Mach	160 lb/ HE
	SA-N-2 Guideline	25.0	1.0+Mach	290 lb/ HE
	SA-N-3 Golbet	30.0	3.0+Mach	450 lb/ HE
	SA-N-4	6.0	2.0 Mach	27 lb/ HE
	SA-N-5	5.6	1.5 Mach	HE
	SA-N-6	42.0	3 Mach	HE
	SA-N-7	19.0	3 Mach	HE
	SA-N-8	--	--	HE
ASM	AS-2 Kipper	115.0	1.4 Mach	HE or nuclear
	AS-3 Kangaroo	350.0	1.8 Mach	500 KT/ N
	AS-4 Kitchen	250.0	3.0+Mach	HE or nuclear
	AS-5 Kelt	125.0	1.2 Mach	2200 lb/ HE
	AS-6 Kingfish	150.0	3 Mach	HE or nuclear
	AS-7	6.0	0.6 Mach	220 lb/ HE

Class	Missile	Max. Range (N.M.)	Speed	Warhead
(ASM)	AS-9	60.0	3 Mach	330 lb/ HE
	AS-10	6.0	1.0 Mach	220 lb/ HE
	AS-11	500.0	3.5 Mach	--
A/SW	SUW-N-1	16.0	--	Nuclear
	SS-N-14	30.0	0.9 Mach	torpedo or /N
	SS-N-15	25.0	--	nuclear

Great Britain

Class	Missile	Max. Range (N.M.)	Speed	Warhead
SSM/	Sea Dart	40.0	--	?/HE
SAM	Sea Dart/ LW	40.0	--	?/HE
	Seacat	3.2	--	?/HE
SAM	Sea Slug	26.0	2.0+Mach	?/HE
	Sea Wolf	3.0	2.0+Mach	?/HE
	SLAM	--	--	4.8 lb/ HE
ASM	Sea Eagle	--	--	--
	Sea Skua	8.0	--	45 lb/ HE

France

Class	Missile	Max. Range (N.M.)	Speed	Warhead
SLBM	MSBS M1	1350.0	--	1 x 500 KT/ N
	MSBS M2	1860.0	--	1 x 500 KT/ N
	MSBS M20	1860.0	--	1 x 1 MT/ TN
	MSBS M4	2160.0	--	7 x 150 KT/TN
	MSB M5	3500.0	--	? x MIRV
SSM	RP14	9.0	--	?/HE
	Otomat MK2	100.0	0.9 Mach	132 lb/ HE
	Exocet MM38	23.0	0.9 Mach	363 lb/ HE
	Exocet AM39	27.4	--	363 lb/ HE
	Exocet MM40	38.0	--	363 lb/ HE
	SS11	2.0	330 Kts	Torpedo or HE
	SS12	4.4	--	66 lb/ HE
SAM	Masurca	30.0	3.0 Mach	105 lb/ HE
	Hirondelle	--	--	--
	Catulle	--	--	--
	Crotale	10.0	0.9-1.2 Mach	31 lb/ HE
	Mistrel	--	--	6.6 lb/ HE
ASM	AS37 Martel	30.0	0.8-2 Mach	?/HE
	AS20	4.0	--	66 lb/ HE
	AS30	6.2	1.5 Mach	506 lb/ HE
	AS15TT	8.0	--	--

France (continued)

Class	Missile	Max. Range (N.M.)	Speed	Warhead
AAM	R550 Magic	3.0	--	?/HE
	R530	6.0	2.7 Mach	56 lb/ HE
A/SW	Malafon MK2	8.1	530 Kts	torpedo

Italy

Class	Missile	Max. Range (N.M.)	Speed	Warhead
SSM	Seakiller I	6.0	1.9 Mach	77 lb/ HE
	Seakiller II	13.5	0.8 Mach	156 lb/ HE
	Otomat MK 1	50.0	--	440 lb/ HE
ASM	Seakiller MK2	11.0	0.8 Mach	156 lb/ HE
SAM	Aspide	10.5	3.0 Mach	--

Australia

Class	Missile	Max. Range (N.M.)	Speed	Warhead
A/SW	Ikara	13.0	--	torpedo/HE

West Germany

Class	Missile	Max. Range (N.M.)	Speed	Warhead
SSM/	Kormoran	21.0	0.95 Mach	350 lb/ HE
ASM	ANS	55.0	1.0+Mach	--
SAM	SM-1MR	--	--	--

Norway

Class	Missile	Max. Range (N.M.)	Speed	Warhead
SSM	Penguin 1 & 2	18.7	0.7 Mach	264 lb/ HE
ASM	Penguin MK2	18.7	--	--
A/SW	Terne MK3	1.5	--	110 lb/ HE

Sweden

Class	Missile	Max. Range (N.M.)	Speed	Warhead
SSM	RB 08A	110.0	0.85 Mach	?/HE
	RBS 15	62.0	0.8 Mach	440 lb/ HE
A/SW	Type 375	0.5-2.2	--	?/HE

Israel

Class	Missile	Max. Range (N.M.)	Speed	Warhead
SSM	Gabriel I	11.0	0.7 Mach	400 lb/ HE
	Gabriel II	18.0	0.7 Mach	400 lb/ HE
	Gabriel III	22.0	0.7 Mach	400 lb/ HE

Appendix C: Summary of Maritime Zones

Summary Table of Extent of Maritime Zones[*]

Territorial Sea		Exclusive Economic Zone	
Breadth (NM.)	No. of States	Breadth (NM.)	No. of States
3	18	150	1
4	2	200	54
6	5		
12	84		
15	1		
20	1		
30	2		
35	1		
50	3		
70	1		
100	1		
150	1		
200	13		

Fishery Zone		Contiguous Zone	
Breadth (NM.)	No. of States	Breadth (NM.)	No. of States
12	1	3	1
25	1	12	2
50	1	18	5
200	23	24	13

Continental Shelf

Criteria	No. of States
Depth (100 fathoms)	1
Depth (200 fathoms)	1
Exploitability	1
Depth (200 fathoms) plus exploitability	51
Breadth (150 nm.)	1
Breadth (200 nm.)	3
Outer edge of the continental margin or breadth of 200 nm	16

Source: United Nations, Office of the Special Representative of the Secretary-General for the Law of of the Sea, *Law of the Sea Bulletin*, No. 2, March 1985, p. v.

[*]This issue of the *Bulletin* gives maritime legislation for 137 of the 141 coastal States tabulated, as information was unavailable for the remaining four States. The table is, therefore, a summary listing of the various maritime zones legislated by those 137 States specifying either the breadth of the zone or the criteria to determine it.

Bibliographies
United Nations, Third United Nations Conference on the Law of the Sea, *Current Bibliography on Selected Topics of the Law of the Sea*, mimeo. New York: United Nations, 1980.
United Nations, Third United Nations Conference on the Law of the Sea, *List of Books and Monographs on the Law of the Sea*, mimeo. New York: United Nations, 1976.
United Nations, Special Representative of the Secretary-General for the Law of the Sea, *Law of the Sea: A Select Bibliography*. New York: United Nations, 1985.
United Nations, *The Sea: Economic and Technological Aspects, A Select Bibliography*. New York: United Nations, 1974.
United Nations, *The Sea: Legal and Political Aspects, A Select Bibliography*. New York: United Nations, 1974.
United Nations, *The Sea: A Select Bibliography on the Legal, Political, Economic and Technological Aspects, 1974-75*. New York: United Nations, 1975.
United Nations, *The Sea: A Select Bibliography on the Legal, Political, Economic and Technological Aspects, 1975-76*. New York: United Nations, 1976.
United Nations, *The Sea: Economic and Technological Aspects, A Select Bibliography*. New York: United Nations, 1974.

Books and Monographs
Berman, Robert P. and John C. Baker. *Soviet Strategic Forces: Requirements and Responses*. Washington, D.C.: Brookings Institution, 1982.
Booth, Ken. *Law, Force and Diplomacy at Sea*. London: Allen and Unwin, Ltd., 1985.
Booth, Ken. *Navies and Foreign Policy*. London: Allen and Unwin, Ltd., 1977.
Butler, William E. *The Soviet Union and the Law of the Sea*. Baltimore: Johns Hopkins University Press, 1971.
Clingan, Thomas A., editor. *Law of the Sea: State Practice in Zones of Special Jurisdiction*. Honolulu: Law of the Sea Institute, 1982.
Collins, John M. *U.S.-Soviet Military Balance: Concepts and Capabilities 1960-1980*. New York: McGraw-Hill Publications, 1980.
Colombos, C. John. *The International Law of the Sea*. London: Longmans, 1967.
Gamble, John King. *Law of the Sea: Neglected Issues*. Proceedings of the Annual Conference on the Law of the Sea, 1979. Honolulu: Law of the Sea Institute, 1979.
George, James L. *Problems of Sea Power As We Approach the Twenty-First Century*. Washington, D.C.: American Enterprise Institute, 1978.
Gorshkov, Sergi G. *Red Star Rising at Sea*. Annapolis, Maryland: United States Naval Institute, 1974.
Janis, Mark W. *Sea Power and the Law of the Sea*. Lexington, Mass.: Lexington Books, 1976.
Juda, Lawrence, editor. *The United States Without the Law of the Sea Treaty: Opportunities and Costs*. Wakefield, R.I.: Times Press, 1983.
Knight, H. Gary. *The Law of the Sea: Cases, Documents, and Readings*. Baton Rouge, La.: Claitor's Publishing Division, 1980.

Larson, David L. *Major Issues of the Law of the Sea*. Durham, N.H.: University of New Hampshire, 1976.

Laursen, Finn. *Superpower at Sea: U.S. Ocean Policy*. New York: Praeger Publishers, 1983.

MccGwire, Michael, editor. *Soviet Naval Developments Context and Capability*, New York: Praeger Publishers, 1973.

MccGwire, Michael and John McDonnell. *Soviet Naval Influence: Domestic and Foreign Dimensions*. New York: Praeger Publishers, 1977.

MccGwire, Michael, Ken Booth, and John McDonald. *Soviet Naval Policy: Objectives and Constraints*. New York: Praeger Publishers, 1975.

McCoy, Dennis F. *International Law and Naval Operations*. Newport, R.I.: Center for Advanced Research, Naval War College, 1977.

McDonald, John. *Strategy in Poker, Business and War*. New York: W.W. Norton and Co., 1950.

McGeehan, Robert. *Strategic and Security Implications of a New Ocean Regime*. Toronto: International Studies Association, February 25-29, 1976.

Nitze, Paul H. and Leonard Sullivan. *Securing the Seas*. Boulder, Colorado: Westview Press, 1979.

O'Connell, Daniel P. *The Influence of Law on Seapower*. Annapolis, Maryland: The United States Naval Institute Press, 1975.

Osgood, Robert E. and Others. *Toward a National Ocean Policy: 1976 and Beyond*. Ocean Policy Project, The Johns Hopkins University. Washington, D.C.: U.S. Government Printing Office, 1975.

SIPRI. *Tactical and Strategic Antisubmarine Warfare*. Cambridge, Mass.: MIT Press, 1974.

Tsipis, Kosta, editor. *The Future of the Sea-Based Deterrent*. Cambridge, Mass.: MIT Press, 1973.

Articles

Ackley, Richard T. "The Wartime Role of Soviet SSBNs." *U.S. Naval Institute Proceedings*, vol. 104, no. 6 (June 1983): 34-43.

Adam, John A. "Probing beneath the Sea." *Spectrum*, vol. 22, no. 4 (April 1985): 55-64.

Adams, Michael R. "Caribbean Coast Guard." *Proceedings of the United States Naval Institute*, vol. 111, no. 7 (July 1985): 52-55.

Alford, Jonathan. "Some Reflections on Technology and Seapower." *International Journal*, vol. 38, no. 3 (1983): 397-408.

Anonymous. "H.M.S. S-107 Trafalgar." *Strategy and Defense*, vol. 93, (March 1985): 59-66.

Anonymous. "HU-24A Delivery Forecast in February 1981." *Aviation Week and Space Technology*, vol. 112, no. 15 (14 April 1980): 22.

Anonymous. "KH-11 Recon Satellite, NAVSTAR Launched from Vandenburg." *Aviation Week and Space Technology*, vol. 112, no. 7 (18 February 1980): 23.

Anonymous. "Seawolf v. Exocet." *Strategy and Defense*, vol. 88 (September 1984): 73.

Anonymous. "Soviet SSN's (II)." *Strategy and Defense*, vol. 90 (November 1984): 35-42.

Anonymous. "Soviet SSN's (III)." *Strategy and Defense*, vol. 91 (December 1984): 35-42.

Anonymous. "Soviet SSN's (IV)." *Strategy and Defense*, vol. 92 (February 1985): 51-58.

Anonymous. "Soviet Undersea Forces." *Strategy and Defense*, vol. 89 (October 1984): 61-69.

Anonymous. "Space Maritime Capacity Expected to Double Soon." *Aviation Week and Space Technology*, vol. 116, no. 7 (15 February 1982): 132-135.

Anonymous. "The Soviet Fleet: Mine Sweepers, Mine Hunters and Mine Layers (1)." *Strategy and Defense*, vol. 93 (March 1985): 36-42.

Anonymous. "Trident Missile Capabilities Advance." *Aviation Week and Space Technology*, vol. 112, no. 24 (16 June 1980): 91-99.

Anonymous. "Naval Electronic Reconnaissance -- Part I." *Jane's Defence Weekly*, vol. 1, no. 18 (12 May 1984): 726-728.

Anonymous. "Naval Electronic Reconnaissance -- Part II." *Jane's Defence Weekly*, vol. 1, no. 19 (19 May 1984): 778-779.

Ashmore, Edward. "The Possible Effects on Maritime Operations of any Future Convention of the Law of the Sea." *Naval War College Review*, vol. 29, no. 2 (Fall 1976): 3-11, or *International Law Studies*, vol. 61 (1980): 119-207.

Barry, James A., Jr. "The Seabed Arms Control Issue 1967-71: A Super-power Symbiosis." *Naval War College Review*, vol. 25, no. 2 (November-December 1972): 87-101, or *International Law Studies*, vol. 61 (1980): 572-585.

Bellany, Ian. "Sea Power and the Soviet Submarine Forces." *Survival*, vol. 24, no. 1 (1982): 2-8.

Bildt, Carl. "Sweden and the Soviet Submarines." *Survival*, vol. 25, no. 4 (1983): 165-167.

Bjol, Erling. "Nordic Security." *Adelphi Papers*, no. 181, Spring 1983.

Blake, Bernard. "NAVSTAR Global Positioning System." *Jane's Defence Weekly*, vol. 1, no. 4 (4 February 1984): 169-170.

Bland, Raymond D. "Controlling the EEZ: Implications for Naval Force Planning." *Naval War College Review*, vol. 37, no. 4 (1984): 23-30.

Booth, Ken. "Foreign Policies at Risk: Some Problems of Managing Naval Power." *Naval War College Review*, vol. 37, no. 4 (1976): 23-30.

Booth, Ken. "Law and Strategy in Northern Waters." *Naval War College Review*, vol. 34, no. 4 (1981): 3-21.

Booth, Ken. "Naval Strategy and the Spread of Psycho-Legal Boundaries at Sea." *International Journal*, vol. 38, no. 3 (1983): 373-396.

Booth, Ken. "U.S. Naval Strategy: Problems of Survivability, Usability, and Credibility." *Naval War College Review*, vol. 31, no. 1 (Summer 1978): 12-20.

Broadbent, Stephen. "Talking to Submarines." *Jane's Defence Weekly*, vol. 1, no. 9 (10 March 1984): 370-372.

Brown, Andrew. "No Answer to the Soviet Subs." *Jane's Defence Weekly*, vol. 1, no. 19 (19 May 1984): 765.

Brown, David A. "British Affirm Decision to Buy Trident SLBM's." *Aviation Week and Space Technology*, vol. 113, no. 3 (21 July 1980): 23-25.

Brown, E.D. "The Legal Regimes of Inner Space: Military Aspects." *Current Legal Problems*, vol. 22 (1971): 181-205.

Caldwell, Hamlin. "The Empty Silo-Strategic ASW." *Naval War College Review*, vol. 34, no. 4 (1981): 4-14.

Charney, Jonathan I. "Law of the Sea: Breaking the Deadlock." *Foreign Affairs*, vol. 55, no. 3 (1977): 598-629.

Christy, John. "Countering the Sea Missile Threat." *International Combat Arms*, vol. 3, no. 1 (1985): 64-79.

Christy, John. "Danger Beneath the Sea." *International Combat Arms*, vol. 3, no. 2 (1985): 78-85.

Clawson, Carl H. "The Wartime Role of Soviet SSBN's -- Round Two." *U.S. Naval Institute Proceedings*, vol. 106, no. 3 (1980): 64-71.

Cohen, Paul. "New Roles for the Submarine." *U.S. Naval Institute Proceedings*, vol. 98, no. 9 (1972): 31-37.

Darman, Richard G. "The Law of the Sea: Rethinking U.S. Interests." *Foreign Affairs*, vol. 56, no. 2 (1978): 373-395.

Dehaven, Oren E. "Strategic Mobility: Shortfalls and Solutions." *Defense '82* (March 1982): 11-15.

Douglas, Martin. "Naval Lessons from the South Atlantic." *Jane's Defence Weekly*, vol. 1, no. 13 (7 April 1984): 519-523.

Easter, David T. "ASW Strategy: Issues for the 1980's." *U.S. Naval Institute Proceedings*, vol. 106, no. 3 (March 1980): 34-41.

Edwards, Mickey. "Soviet Expansion and Control of the Sea Lanes." *U.S. Naval Institute Proceedings*, vol. 106, no. 9 (September 1980): 46-51.

Feld, B.T. and G.W. Rathjens. "ASW and the Sea-Based Deterrent -- Opportunities for Arms Control." *Survival*, vol. 15, no. 6 (1973): 268-274.

Fink, Donald E. "Workload for Pilot Reduced in SH-60B." *Aviation Week and Space Technology*, vol. 113, no. 22 (1 December 1980): 111-114.

Friedman, Norman. "SOSUS and U.S. ASW Tactics." *U.S. Naval Institute Proceedings*, vol. 106, no. 3 (March 1980): 72-76.

Gasteyger, Curt. "Soviet Global Strategy." *Survival*, vol. 20, no. 4 (1978): 159-162.

George, Bruce and Michael Coughlin. "British Defense Policy after the Falklands." *Survival*, vol. 24, no. 5 (1982): 201-210.

Giorgi, Giovanni. "Helicopters at Sea." *NATO's Sixteen Nations*, vol. 29, no. 6 (1984): 67-75.

Gorshkov, S.G. "The Sea Power of the State." *Survival*, vol. 19, no. 1 (1977): 24-29.

Griffiths, David R. "Readiness Rate of RH-53 Key Issue." *Aviation Week and Space Technology*, vol. 112, no. 18 (5 May 1980): 2-23.

Griffiths, David R. "Turbulence Factor Cited in RH-53 Iran Mission." *Aviation Week and Space Technology*, vol. 112, no. 19 (12 May 1980): 16-18.

Groning, H.W. "A New Concept in Mine Countermeasures." *Naval Forces*, vol. 5, no. 6 (1984): 66-75.

Haass, Richard. "Naval Arms Limitation in the Indian Ocean." *Survival*, vol. 20, no. 2 (March/April 1978): 50-57.

Hane, Ray. "Super Underwater Warriors." *International Combat Arms*, vol. 3, no. 3 (May 1985): 15-22.

Harlow, Bruce. "Legal Aspect of Claims to Jurisdiction in Coastal Waters." *JAG Journal*, vol. 23, no. 3 (1968-69): 81-96. Heaton, Joel B. "A New Law of the Sea: Why Not Both Ways." *U.S. Naval Institute Proceedings*, vol. 105, no. 11 (November 1979): 62-65.

Hellyer, Joel B. "Hormuz Straits Defense Global Responsibility." *Jane's Defence Weekly*, vol. 1, no. 8 (3 March 1984): 310.

Hickman, William F. "Soviet Naval Policy in the Indian Ocean." *U.S. Naval Institute Proceedings*, vol. 94, no. 8 (August 1971): 42-52.

Holme, Thomas T. "The Soviet Submarine Threat -- Past, Present and Future." *U.S. Naval Institute Proceedings*, vol. 97, no. 8 (August 1971): 60-63.

Hooton, Ted. "Naval Mines: the Hidden Menace." *Military Technology*, vol. 8, no. 9 (1984): 27-33.

Hull, Andrew W. "Potential Soviet Responses to the U.S. Submarine Threat." *U.S. Naval Institute Proceedings*, vol. 104, no. 7 (July 1978): 24-30.

IISS. "Power at Sea." *Adelphi Papers*, no. 112, 123, & 124. London: International Institute for Strategic Studies, 1976.

IISS. "The Indian Ocean in Soviet Naval Policy." *Adelphi Papers*, no. 87. London: International Institute for Strategic Studies, 1972.

Isby, David. "One MCM could clear Hormuz Strait -- Study." *Jane's Defence Weekly*, vol. 1, no. 17 (5 May 1984): 680.

Jacobson, Jon L. "Law of the Sea -- What Now?" *Naval War College Review* vol. 37, no. 2 (1984): 82-99.

Janis, Mark W. "Dispute Settlement in the Law of the Sea Convention: the Military Activities Exception." *Ocean Development and International Law* vol. 4 (1977): 51-66.

Janis, Mark W. "The Soviet Navy and Oceans Law." *Naval War College Review*, vol. 26, no. 5 (March-April 1974): 52-58. Or *International Law Studies*, vol. 61 (1980): 609-615.

Jordan, John. "Soviet Ballistic Missile Submarines: Part I." *Jane's Defence Weekly*, vol. 1, no. 2 (21 January 1984): 85-88.

Jordan, John. "Soviet Ballistic Missile Submarines: Part II." *Jane's Defence Weekly*, vol. 1, no. 3 (28 January 1984): 122-125.

Jordan, John. "Soviet Ballistic Missile Submarines: Part III." *Jane's Defence Weekly*, vol. 1, no. 5 (11 February 1984): 202-205.

Jordan, John. "Soviet Cruise Missile Submarines: Part I." *Jane's Defence Weekly*, vol. 1, no. 20 (26 May 1984): 841-844.

Jordan, John. "Soviet Cruise Missile Submarines: Part II." *Jane's Defence Weekly*, vol. 1, no. 21 (2 June 1984): 882-884.

Jordan, John. "Soviet Cruise Missile Submarines: Part III." *Jane's Defence Weekly*, vol. 1, no. 25 (30 June 1984): 1077-1080.

Jordan, John. "Soviet Torpedo Attack Submarines: Part I." *Jane's Defence Weekly*, vol. 2, no. 11 (22 September 1984): 500-504.

Jordan, John. "Soviet Torpedo Attack Submarines: Part II." *Jane's Defence Weekly*, vol. 2, no. 14 (13 October 1984): 630-637.

Jordan, John. "Soviet Torpedo Attack Submarines: Part III." *Jane's Defence Weekly*, vol. 2, no. 15 (20 October 1984): 686-689.

Jordan, John. "Soviet Torpedo Attack Submarines: Part IV." *Jane's Defence Weekly*, vol. 2, no. 17 (3 November 1984): 786-793.

Joyner, Christopher. "Antarctica and the Law of the Sea: Rethinking the Current Legal Dilemmas." *San Diego Law Review*, vol. 18, no. 3 (1981): 415-442.

Kaye, Lawrence W. "The Innocent Passage of Warships in Foreign Territorial Seas: A Threatened Freedom." *San Diego Law Review*, vol. 15, (1978): 573-602.

Kelly, Orr. "Sub Duels Under Polar Ice: How Ready is the U.S.?" *U.S. News and World Report*, vol. 96, no. 9 (5 March 1984): 35-36.

Kissinger, Henry A. "The Admiral Raymond A. Spruance Lecture." *Naval War College Review*, vol. 31, no. 1 (Summer 1978): 4-10.

Knight H. Gary. "The Law of the Sea and Naval Missions." *U.S. Naval Institute Proceedings*, vol. 13, no. 6 (June 1977): 32-39.

Knott, Richard C. "Who Owns the Oceans?" *U.S. Naval Institute Proceedings*, vol. 99, no. 3 (March 1973): 65-71.

Krepon, Michael. "A Navy to Match National Purposes." *Foreign Affairs*, vol. 55, no. 2 (1977): 355-367.

Lacouture, John E. "Seapower in the Indian Ocean: A Requirement for Western Security." *U.S. Naval Institute Proceedings*, vol. 105, no. 8 (August 1979): 30-41.

Lange, David. "New Zealand's Security Policy." *Foreign Affairs*, vol. 63, no. 5 (1985): 1009-1019.

Larson, David L. "Security, Disarmament and the Law of the Sea." *Marine Policy*, vol. 3, no. 1 (1979): 40-58.

Larson, David L. "The Reagan Administration and the Law of the Sea." *Ocean Development and International Law*, vol. 11, no. 3-4 (1982): 297-320.

Larson, David L. "The Reagan Rejection of the UN Convention." *Ocean Development and International Law*, vol. 14, no. 4 (1985): 337-361.

Larson, David L. "The United States Position on the Deep Seabed." *Suffolk Transnational Law Journal*, vol. 3, no. 2 (January 1979): 1-34.

Larson, David L., and Peter Tarpgaard. "The Law of the Sea and ASW: National Security vs. Arms Control." *Marine Policy*, vol. 6, no. 2 (April 1982): 90-102.

Lawrence, Keith D. "Military-Legal Considerations in the Extension of Territorial Seas." *Military Law Review*, vol. 29 (1965): 47-95.

Lawyer, John E., Jr. "International Straits and the Law of the Sea Conference." *Air University Review*, vol. 25, no. 6 (September-October 1974): 36-41.

Lehman, John. "The Law of the Sea." *Defense '82* (March 1982): 1-9.

Leifer, Michael. "The Security of the Sea Lanes of South-East Asia." *Survival*, vol. 25, no. 1 (1983): 16-24.

Leonard, Alan T. "Ixtoc I: A Test for the Emerging Concept of the Patrimonial Sea." *San Diego Law Review*, vol. 17, no. 3 (1980): 617-627.

Lenorvitz, Jeffrey M. "French to Build Two Nuclear Carriers." *Aviation Week and Space Technology*, vol. 113, no. 15 (13 October 1980): 67-68.

Levie, Howard. "Mine Warfare and International Law." *Naval War College Review*, vol. 24, no. 8 (April 1972): 27-35, or *International Law Studies*, vol. 62 (1980): 271-279.

Lissitzyn, Oliver J. "Electronic Reconnaissance from the High Seas and International Law." *Naval War College Review*, vol. 22, no. 2 (1970): 26-34, or *International Law Studies*, vol. 61 (1980): 563-571.

Lonsdale, P. Taylor. "ASW's Passive Trap." *U.S. Naval Institute Proceedings*, vol. 105, no. 7 (July 1979): 34-40.

Lucas, Hugh. "U.S. Engineers Working on ASW Component Snag." *Jane's Defence Weekly*, vol. 1, no. 2 (21 January 1984): 65.

Lucas, Hugh. "U.S. Navy Bid for New Deep Water Technology." *Jane's Defence Weekly*, vol. 1, no. 15 (21 April 1984): 558.

Lucas, Hugh. "U.S. Navy Plans Trident Force of 20 Subs." *Jane's Defence Weekly*, vol. 1, no. 22 (9 June 1984): 904.

Lucas, Hugh. "U.S. Navy's Sub-Launched Cruise Now Operational." *Jane's Defence Weekly*, vol. 1, no. 26 (14 July 1984): 1091.

Lucas, Hugh. "U.S. Radio Link to Submarines at 400-ft. Depth in Mediterranean." *Jane's Defence Weekly*, vol. 2, no. 2 (21 July 1984): 52.

Lythall, B.W. "Underwater Detection -- Active or Passive?" *Naval Forces*, vol. 5, no. 1 (1984): 66-73.

MccGwire, Michael. "Changing Naval Operations and Military Intervention." *Naval War College Review*, vol. 29, no. 4 (Spring 1977): 3-25.

MccGwire, Michael. "The Geopolitical Importance of Strategic Waterways In the Asian Pacific Region." *Orbis*, vol. 19, no. 3 (Fall 1975): 1058-1076.

McGwire, Michael. "The Rationale for the Development of Seapower." *U.S. Naval Institute Proceedings*, vol. 106, no. 5 (May 1980): 154-184.

MccGwire, Michael. "Soviet Naval Programmes." *Survival*, vol. 15, no. 5 (1973): 218-227.

McDougal, Myers S. "The Law of the High Seas in Time of Peace." *Naval War College Review*, vol. 25, no. 3 (1967): 35-47, or *International Law Studies*, vol. 61 (1980): 551-562.

McLeavy, Roy. "USA Gives New Priority to Mine Warfare." *Jane's Defense Weekly*, vol. 2, no. 1 (14 July 1984): 21.

Mellin, William F. "ASW for the Amphibious Task Group." *U.S. Naval Institute Proceedings*, vol. 104, no. 3 (March 1978): 96-101.

Moore, John Norton. "The Regime of Straits and the Third United Nations Conference on the Law of the Sea." *American Journal of International Law*, vol. 74, no. 1 (January 1980): 77-121.

Murphy, Frank B. "Ocean Surveillance: New Weapon of Naval Warfare." *U.S. Naval Institute Proceedings*, vol. 97, no. 2 (February 1971): 38-41.

Neutze, Dennis R. "Whose Law of the Sea." *U.S. Naval Institute Proceedings*, vol. 109, no. 1 (January 1983): 43-48.

Neutze, Dennis R. "Bluejacket Diplomacy: A Juridical Examination of the Use of Naval Forces in Support of United States Foreign Policy." *JAG Journal*, vol. 32, no. 1 (1982): 81-158.

Neutze, Dennis R. "The Gulf of Sidra Incident: A Legal Perspective." *U.S. Naval Institute Proceedings*, vol. 108, no. 1 (January 1982): 26-31.

Nolta, Frank. "Passage Through International Straits: Free or Innocent? The Interests at Stake." *San Diego Law Review*, vol. 11, no. 3 (1974): 815-833.

North, David M. "Survivability Key to Trident Program." *Aviation Week and Space Technology*, vol. 112, no. 24 (16 June 1980): 101-106.

O'Connell, D.P. "The Influence of Modern International Law on Naval and Civil Operations at Sea." *U.S. Naval Institute Proceedings*, vol. 103, no. 5 (May 1977): 156-169.

O'Connell, D.P. "The Juridical Nature of the Territorial Sea." *British Yearbook of International Law*, vol. 45 (1971): 303-383.

Osgood, Robert E. "U.S. Security Interests in Ocean Law." *Survival*, vol. 171 (1975): 122-128, or *Ocean Development and International Law*, vol. 2 (1974): 1-36.

Pariseau, Richard R. "The Role of the Submarine in Chinese Naval Strategy." *U.S. Naval Institute Proceedings*, vol. 105, no. 10 (October 1979):66-69.

Park, Choon-Ho. "The 50-mile Military Boundary Zone of North Korea." *American Journal of International Law*, vol. 72 (1978): 866-875.

Patterson, Andrew Jr. "Mining: A Naval Strategy." *Naval War College Review*, vol. 23, no. 9 (1971): 52-66.

Polmar, Norman. "Thinking About Soviet ASW." *U.S. Naval Institute Proceedings*, vol. 102, no. 5 (May 1976): 108-129.

Preston, Anthony. "SOSUS Update Plans to Keep Track of Alfa." *Jane's Defence Weekly*, vol. 1, no. 2 (21 January 1984): 60.

Preston, Anthony. "Stopping the Anti-Ship Missile." *Jane's Defence Weekly*, vol. 1, no. 14 (14 April 1984): 564-570.

Preston, Anthony. "The PLA Navy's Underwater Deterrent." *Jane's Defence Weekly*, vol. 1, no. 16 (28 April 1984): 659-660.

Preston, Anthony. "The U.S. Navy's New Mine Countermeasures." *Jane's Defence Weekly*, vol. 2, no. 6 (18 August 1984): 232-259.

Preston, Anthony and Nick Childs. "Submarine Developments: World Wide Review." *Jane's Defence Weekly*, vol. 2, no. 6 (18 August 1984): 232-239.

"Power at Sea, I: The New Environment." *Adelphi Papers*, no. 122, (1976).

"Power at Sea, II: Superpowers and Navies." *Adelphi Papers*, no. 123, (1976).

"Power at Sea, III: Competition and Conflict." *Adelphi Papers*, no. 124 (1976).

Purver, Ron. "The Control of Strategic Anti-Submarine Warfare." *International Journal*, vol. 38, no. 3 (1983): 409-431.

Ratiner, Leigh S. "The Law of the Sea: A Crossroads for American Foreign Policy." *Foreign Affairs*, vol. 60, no. 5 (1982): 1006-1021.

Reisman, W. Michael. "The Regime of the Straits and National Security: An Appraisal of International Lawmaking." *American Journal of International Law*, vol. 74 (1980): 48-76.

Richardson, Elliot P. "Law of the Sea: Navigation and Other Traditional National Security Considerations." *San Diego Law Review*, vol. 19, no. 3 (1982): 553-576.

Richardson, Elliot P. "Power, Mobility and the Law of the Sea." *Foreign Affairs* vol. 58, no. 4 (1980): 902-919.

Robinson, Clarence A. "Egypt's Technology Shift: Navy Gives Missiles, Aircraft Priority." *Aviation Week and Space Technology*, vol. 116, no. 6 (8 February 1982): 61-64.

Rubin, Alfred P. "Sunken Soviet Submarines and Central Intelligence: Laws of Property and the Agency." 69 *American Journal of International Law* 855-858 (1975).

Ruhe, William J. "Missiles Make ASW a New Game." *U.S. Naval Institute Proceedings*, vol. 106, no. 3 (March 1980): 72-75.

Ruhe, William J. "The Nuclear Submarine: Riding High." *U.S. Naval Institute Proceedings*, vol. 101, no. 2 (February 1975): 55-62.

Schratz, Paul. "The Nuclear Carrier and Modern War." *U.S. Naval Institute Proceedings*, vol. 98, no. 8 (August 1972): 16-25.

Selzer, Steven. "The Seabed Arms Limitation Treaty." *Journal of International Law and Economics*, vol. 6, no. 1 (1971): 157-174.

Silverstein, Harvey B. "Ocean Surveillance Technologies and International Payoffs." *Ocean Development and International Law*, vol. 10, no. 1-2 (1981): 187-198.

Simcox, David E. "The Regional Coast Guards." *Proceedings of the United States Naval Institute*, vol. 111, no. 7 (July 1985): 44-53.

Sisco, Eric A. "Comment: Hot Pursuit from a Contiguous Fisheries Zone -- An Assault on the Freedom of the Seas." *San Diego Law Review*, vol. 14, no. 3 (1977): 656-680.

Sreenivasa Rao, P. "Legal Regulation of Maritime Military Uses." *Indian Journal of International Law*, vol. 13, no. 3 (1973): 425-454.

Sreenivasa Rao, P. "The Seabeds Arms Control Treaty: A Study in the Contemporary Law of the Military Uses of the Seas." 4 *Journal of Maritime Law and Commerce* 67-92 (1972).

Stavridis, James. "Marine Technology Transfer and the Law of the Sea." *Naval War College Review*, vol. 36, no. 4 (1983): 38-49.

Stevenson, John R. and Bernard H. Oxman. "The Third United Nations Conference on the Law of the Sea." *American Journal of International Law*, vol. 69 (1975): 1-30.

Stubbs, Bruce B. and Richard R. Kelly. "Technology, ASW and the Coast Guard." *U.S. Naval Institute Proceedings*, vol. 106, no. 10 (October 1980): 29-35.

Swayze, Frank B. "Negotiating a Law of the Sea." *U.S. Naval Institute Proceedings*, vol. 106, no. 5 (May 1980): 82-93.

Swing, John T. "Who Will Own the Oceans." *Foreign Affairs*, vol. 54, no. 3 (1976): 527-546.

Taylor, William D. "Surface Warships Against Submarines." *U.S. Naval Institute Proceedings*, vol. 105, no. 5 (May 1980): 168-181.

Teplinsky, B. "America's Naval Programmes." *Survival*, vol. 15 (1973): 75-80.

Till, Geoffrey. "Strategic Aspects of ASW." *Naval Forces*, vol. 6, no. 4 (1984): 14-21.

Tomilin, Iu. "Keeping the Sea-Bed out of the Arms Race." *International Affairs*, vol. 1 (1970): 41-45.

Travik, Kim and Willy Ostreng. "Security and Ocean Law: Norway and the Soviet Union in the Barents Sea." *Ocean Development and International Law*, vol. 4 (1977): 343-368.

Treves, Tullio. "Military Installations, Structures, and Devices on the Seabed." *American Journal of International Law*, vol. 74 (1980): 808-857.

Tucker, Johnathan B. "Cold War in the Ocean Depths." *High Technology*, vol. 5, no. 7 (July 1985): 29-38.

Truver, Scott C. "New International Constraints on Military Power: Navies in the Political Role." *Naval War College Review*, vol. 34, no. 4 (1981): 99-104.

Turner, Stansfield. "The Naval Balance: Not Just a Numbers Game." *Foreign Affairs*, vol. 55, no. 2 (1977): 339-354.

Ullman, Harlan K. "The Cuban Missile Crisis and Soviet Naval Development -- Myths and Realities." *Naval War College Review*, vol. 28, no. 3 (1976): 45-56.

Vego, Milan. "Submarine Surveillance Soviet Style." *Jane's Defence Weekly*, vol. 2, no. 3 (28 July 1984): 117-121.

Vego, Milan. "The Soviet Navy's ASW Capabilities: Part I." *Jane's Defence Weekly*, vol. 1, no. 7 (25 February 1984): 282-288.

Vego, Milan. "The Soviet Navy's ASW Capabilities: Part II." *Jane's Defence Weekly*, vol. 1, no. 9 (10 March 1984): 360-363.

Vego, Milan. "The Soviet Navy's ASW Capabilities: Part III." *Jane's Defence Weekly*, vol. 1, no. 15 (21 April 1984): 619-622.

Vego, Milan. "The Soviet Navy's ASW Capabilities: Part IV." *Jane's Defence Weekly*, vol. 1, no. 16 (28 April 1984): 656-658.

Walker, Peter B. "What Is Innocent Passage?" *Naval War College Review*, vol. 21, no. 5 (January 1969): 53-76.

Weinland, Robert G. "The Evolution of Soviet Requirements for Naval Forces: Solving the Problems of the Early 1960's." *Survival*, vol. 26 (1984): 16-25.

Wiegley, Roger D. "Law and Conflict at Sea." *Naval War College Review*, vol. 33, no. 1 (1980): 68-77.

Winnifield, James A. and Carl H. Builder. "ASW -- Now or Never." *U.S. Naval Institute Proceedings*, vol. 97, no. 9 (1971): 18-25.

Wit, Joel S. "Advances in ASW." *Scientific American*, vol. 244 (February 1981): 31-41.

Wit, Joel S. "American SLBM: Counterforce Options and Strategic Implications." *Survival*, vol. 24, no. 4 (July 1982): 163-174.

Wit, Joel S. "Are Our Boomers Vulnerable?" *U.S. Naval Institute Proceedings*, vol. 107, no. 11 (November 1981): 62-70.

Wit, Joel S. "Soviet Cruise Missiles." *Survival*, vol. 25, no. 6 (1983): 249-26.

Wright, Sherman E. "ASW and the Modern Submarine." *U.S. Naval Institute Proceedings*, vol. 99, no. 4 (1973): 62-70.

Wrixon, Tim. "Sweden Strengthens ASW Capacity." *Jane's Defence Weekly*, vol. 1, no. 2 (21 Janurary 1984): 60.

Young, Elizabeth. "Jurisdiction at Sea." *World Today*, vol. 34, no. 6 (1978): 199-201.

Young, Elizabeth. "New Laws for Old Navies: Military Implications of the Law of the Sea." *Survival*, vol. 16, no. 6 (1974): 262-267.

Young, Elizabeth and Sebek, Viktor. "Red Seas and Blue Seas: Soviet Uses of Ocean Law," *Survival*, vol. 20, no. 6 (November 1978): 255-262.

Zakheim, Dov S. "Towards a Western Approach to the Indian Ocean." *Survival*, vol. 22, no. 1 (1980): 7-14.

Zedalis, Rex J. "Military Installations, Structures and Devices on the Continental Shelf." *American Journal of International Law*, vol. 75 (1981): 926-933.

Zedalis, Rex. J. "Military Uses of Ocean Space and Developing International Law of the Sea: An Analysis in the Context of Peacetime ASW." *San Diego Law Review*, vol. 16, no. 3 (1979): 575-664.

Documents

IISS. *The Military Balance, 1984-1985*. London: International Institute for Strategic Studies, 1984.

IISS. *The Military Balance, 1983-1984*. London: International Institute for Strategic Studies, 1983.

IISS. *The Military Balance, 1982-1983*. London: International Institute for Strategic Studies, 1982.

IISS. *The Military Balance, 1981-1982*. London: International Institute for Strategic Studies, 1981.

IISS. *The Military Balance, 1980-1981*. London: International Institute for Strategic Studies, 1980.

IISS. *Strategic Survey, 1984-1985*. London: International Institute for Strategic Studies, 1985.

IISS. *Strategic Survey, 1983-1984*. London: International Institute for Strategic Studies, 1984.

United Nations. *The Law of the Sea: United Nations Convention on the Law of the Sea*. New York: United Nations, 1983.

United States, Arms Control and Disarmament Agency. *Arms Control and Disarmament Agreements, 1982 Edition*. Washington, D.C.: U.S. Government Printing Office, 1982.

United States, House, Committee on Interior and Insular Affairs. *Deep Seabed Hard Minerals Act*. Report on 94-754, Ninety-First Congress, Second Session, April 1976, Doc. #68-329-76-1. Washington, D.C.: U.S. Government Printing Office, 1976.

United States, Senate, Committee on Foreign Relations. *Law of the Sea Negotiations*, Hearings, 97th Congress, 2nd Session, September 15, 1982. Washington, D.C.: U.S. Government Printing Office, 1982.

United States, House, Committee on Foreign Affairs. *Proposed Expansion of U.S. Military Facilities in the Indian Ocean*, Hearings, 93rd Congress, 2nd Session, February-March, 1974. Washington, D.C.: U.S. Government Printing Office, 1974.

United States, Senate, Committee on Foreign Relations. *Two-Hundred-Mile Fishing Zone*, Hearings, 94th Congress, 1st Session, October 1975. Doc. # 61-003. Washington, D.C.: U.S. Government Printing Office, 1975.

United States, House, Committee on Foreign Affairs. *U.S. Foreign Policy and the Law of the Sea*, Hearings, 97th Congress, 2nd Session, June 17,

August 12, and September 16, 1982. Washington, D.C.: U.S. Government Printing Office, 1982.

United States, Department of Defense, *Soviet Military Power*, 1st edition, Washington, D.C.: U.S. Government Printing Office, 1981.

United States, Department of Defense, *Soviet Military Power*, 2nd edition, Washington, D.C.: U.S. Government Printing Office, 1982.

United States, Department of Defense, *Soviet Military Power*, 3rd edition, Washington, D.C.: U.S. Government Printing Office, 1983.

United States, Department of Defense, *Soviet Military Power*, 4th edition, Washington, D.C.: U.S. Government Printing Office, 1984.

Papers

Harlow, Bruce A. "UNCLOS III and Conflict Management in Straits," Paper, Eighteenth Law of the Sea Institute, San Francisco, September 1984.

Larson, David L. "Deep Seabed Mining: A Definition of the Problem." Paper, 26th Annual Meeting, International Studies Association, March 1985.

Laursen, Finn. "Norway and the New International Marine Order." Paper, 26th Annual Convention, International Studies Association, March 1985.

Miles, Edward L. "U.S. National Interests in the Oceans and their Priorities: A Scorecard for the UNCLOS Treaty." Paper, Annual Meeting, American Bar Association, August 9, 1982.

Ostreng, Willy. "Delimitation Arrangements in Arctic Seas: Cases of Precedence or Securing of Strategic/Economic Interests." Paper, 18th Annual Law of the Sea Institute, September 1984.

A.G.Y. Thorpe: Let me give you some thoughts on the technology of the future generation of mines. If you draw comfort from the laws of war, the principle of the rather weak Hague Convention VIII, the *Corfu Channel* case and subsequent state practice is that a mine is a nondiscriminatory weapon, basically likely to attack innocent shipping, and therefore you should give warning of danger as soon as it is placed in the waters. We are now light-years away from that; we are talking about bottom-placed mines which are rocket-propelled, which could be remotely activated from very long distances by acoustic pulses by technology which already exists in the off-shore oil rigs. The fail-safe mechanism is better than one in ten million, so you can be sure that the thing will not be switched on until you wish it, which gives you tremendous military advantages in laying your mines, but with the follow-on that you would have to notify once the weapons had been activated. That has been state practice in relation to the U.S. mining of Hai-Phong and the Argentine mining of the waters around Stanley in the Falklands. We have also built into these weapons highly discriminatory sensors; these mines will not only not attack surface ships but will attack only specified submarines. You can actually lay down a system which is in place; you give notice of activation, and it will only attack adversary submarines. If you act on the scale of tension to which I referred at the outset of this discussion, you can see that you might wish to not lay at all in times of low tension; as tension rose, you might wish to lay in your territorial sea and activate or not, giving notice if you do, and work further out as the tension went up. It is hoped that if you went down the scale, you would go the other way, and you could recover the weapons. That is the future and a problem that lawyers are going to have to think about.

In answer to Professor Larson's point about the nuclear weapons on the seabed, everybody ratified that treaty because nobody wants to put nuclear mines on the seabed. The problem with acoustic capture through the water is that, by the time you can actually capture the target, it is so close that you do not need a nuclear weapon. So, being a total cynic, I am saying people ratify that because there is no reason not to. Finally I must say that the views in my paper are my own views and those of some of the U.S. Navy's lawyers; they are not the views of our respective governments.

The following paper was first delivered at a meeting of the British Institute of International and Comparative Law on July 22, 1985.

MINE WARFARE AT SEA: SOME LEGAL ASPECTS OF THE FUTURE

Captain A.G.Y. Thorpe
Chief Naval Judge Advocate
Royal Navy, United Kingdom

I would like to address the problems that new weapons technology at sea are posing to traditional concepts, and to illustrate this I have taken the topical weapon: the sea mine. However, I would like to look to future weapons in the field rather than to traditional mines and would remind you that the mine is a very cheap weapon and one therefore attractive to many nations, particularly in view of its devastating effect on maritime trade.

When considering any aspect of the use of armed force at sea, it is important to bear in mind that there are two complementary principles that govern the conduct of both parties to the conflict or potential conflict and of third parties. On the one hand, belligerents have power to wage war on the seas; on the other hand, neutrals have the right to navigate the seas despite the conflict. These principles emerge clearly clearly from the notes of the German and Dutch governments concerning the existence of German minefields in 1939, of which no notice had been given.[1] The major discussion leading up to the compromise text of the Hague Convention No. VIII of 1907, relative to the laying of Automatic Submarine Contact Mines, centered on the opposing interests reflected in the formulation of these principles, which is so well described in Pearce Higgins' commentaries on the Hague Peace Conference.[2] The difficulty in reconciling these two principles is undoubtedly the main reason for the Hague Convention No. VIII of 1907 being so restrictive that it has been described as worthless.[3] This Convention is the only multilateral treaty specifically dealing with mines and is discussed later.

There is a tendency among some writers to consider that a nation is either at peace or at war, and if it is not at war, then the Law of War can have no application.[4] In the light of the development of the law since the Hague Peace Conferences of 1907, through the Covenant of the League of Nations and the Paris Treaty of 1928 renouncing war as an instrument of national policy, and up to the situation after the Charter of the United Nations, it is improbable that any nation will ever again declare war. This would mean on the extremist view that we can derive no assistance from the law in addressing the problems that the all-too-obvious use of armed force poses, not only to the parties to the dispute but to the rest of the world who need guidance in regulating their affairs in the light of the dispute. I consider that this is neither a constructive approach nor one that accords with the actual practice of of states, which has taken effective if not overt cognizance of what Schwarzenberger called *status mixtus* -- the intermediate state between peace and war often known to the services as *transition to war*. It is very important to remember that the actual practice of states, if generally accepted or even tolerated, is a most potent force in shaping the law, and in the twilight area between the traditional concept of peace and war it is clearly sensible to draw assistance where one can from the traditional Law of War, and I suggest that states have done this.

In the absence of declared war, it is probably most helpful to categorize the threat or use of armed force as either a delict, a sanction or self-defense.[5] In general, states who use or threaten to use force will plead self-defense under Article 51 of the UN Charter. Alternatively or additionally, states will justify their actions as measures taken under regional arrangements relating to the maintenance of international peace and security under Article 52 of the UN Charter. A good example of this approach was the quarantine imposed by the United States during the Cuban Missile Crisis in 1962.

States do in fact predicate their practice on some of the traditional Law of War suitably adapted to modern situations. In support of this contention, I cite two examples: the *West Breeze* and the Cuban Missile Crisis. The facts of both are well known, the former being particularly well described by Van Zwanenburg.[6] They show that the Law of War will be imported into modern situations, and also that states not involved will probably accept a reasonable exercise of wartime-type belligerent rights, even if they make some protest at the time. They also tend to support the proposition that the Geneva Convention on the High Seas 1958

> is not against reasonable restriction on the free use of the seas by all states where this restriction is grounded on a valid peace, security or self-defense basis and the responsive action is necessary and proportional to the threat[7]

-- a reminder that the freedom of the seas is not an absolute right.

It should perhaps be observed that a state's own assessment of whether a state of war exists at any time is unlikely to be conclusive in the situation that now obtains in the post-Charter world. Brownlie takes the view that states reserve the right to look at the facts and to determine that "war" exists for purposes of general international law irrespective of the characterization by the parties to a conflict.[8] This may support the contention that belligerent rights will be accorded based on the reality of the actual situation at any given time. The other general proposition that may be advanced in considering the justification for any contemplated course of action is that one should first look to see if there is a rule of treaty or customary international law that actually prohibits the contemplated action. If there is not, there is a sound arguable basis for the action, assuming that the state actually wishes to do it. This is not entirely predicated on the principle *expressio unius est exclusio alterius*, described by Professor Bowett as "dubious,"[9] but rather a recognition of the reality that if a conduct is not expressly forbidden, a state by undertaking it will, if it is accepted by other states without widespread protest, in fact produce a precedent that may in time ripen into a right in customary law. In other words, state practice will push out the boundaries of the law. I would place defensive exclusion zones of the type operated in the Falkland Islands dispute in this category. Security interdiction zones with an attendant right of visit and search of the type employed in the Cuban Missile Crisis are another example. There is, however, the need to remember that both the preamble to and Article 88 of the 1982 United Nations Convention on the Law of the Sea declare the high seas to be reserved for peaceful purposes. So all measures taken on the high seas in peacetime by a state that appear to conflict with these declarations will be carefully scrutinized by other states and will need justification on the actual facts of the situation. Sometimes the restriction on the use of the high seas may be in an area where not many important states have interests, so the absence of protest may be less persuasive as an indication of tacit acceptance. It is the quality as well as the quantity of protest or acceptance that is important in molding international legal opinion. It was the general toleration by the international community of Norway's use of straight baselines to establish the breadth of her territorial sea that caused the International Court of Justice to decide that her case against the United Kingdom was unanswerable.

With these general propositions in mind, I now turn to the use of sea mines and the legal aspects of mine warfare. The use of mines in any context gives rise to two fundamental questions:

a. Is the mine a lawful weapon?
b. If it is a lawful weapon, what are the legal restraints, if any, on its use?

Hague Convention (See *Appendix*)

The Hague Convention nowhere prohibits the mine as then known. It is clear that the Convention reflected the views of the contracting parties (it is only binding on contracting parties and if all belligerents are parties -- Article 7) that the mine was not an illegal weapon, but one whose propensity for destroying innocent merchant shipping or non-combatants generally had to be controlled. The British were very dissatisfied with the compromise text with its inherent defects, such as the escape clause in Article 2 which effectively allowed enemy coasts and ports to be mined, provided it was not for the sole object of intercepting commercial shipping. Little ingenuity is required to avail oneself of the obvious justification for wholesale mining of enemy coasts. Indeed, when the British plenipotentiaries signed the Convention, they entered the following reservation:

> The mere fact that the said Convention does not prohibit a particular act or proceeding must not be held to debar His Britannic Majesty's Government from contesting its legitimacy,[10]

a forceful plea that not in every case is an act allowed merely because it is not expressly prohibited by a rule of treaty or customary law. This argument came to the fore during the world wars. The attempt by the British in 1907 to limit mining activities to territorial seas had failed, but worse, if a belligerent did mine the high seas, he was only under an obligation "to notify the danger zones as soon as military exigencies permit" (Article 3).

Although the Convention does not prohibit mines as such, it only concerned itself with contact mines (command mines were not considered dangerous[11]); does this therefore mean that modern mines are outside the provision of the Convention and should therefore be regarded differently? The better view is advanced by Professor O'Connell:

> General considerations tend towards extending the principles of the Hague Convention to cover all types of mine, whether or not moored. This is because the technology of mine warfare requires a tactical doctrine that is not easily accommodated to the policy of proportionality and necessity and can only with difficulty be reconciled with the requirements of immediate self-defence.[12]

Although O'Connell is here concerned with the classic elements of self-defense in accordance with the *Caroline* doctrine, he did not argue to outlaw current mines of the magnetic, acoustic or pressure type. However, one must look to the next generation of mine to see if this is likely to pose a new problem to the application of the principles of the Hague Convention. Here I am assuming the final choice of the new continental shelf mine is to be of the tethered version, perhaps with a rocket-propelled large warhead. The fact that it is likely to be tethered at depths where it is genuinely an ASW weapon, particularly in view of its discriminatory sensors, does not alter the basic question, still less its possible ability to operate an arming/disarming mechanism at considerable ranges with some form of acoustic link using North Sea oil technology. The mine will become sterilized on breaking loose or after a predetermined time lapse. If the general principles of the Hague Convention No. VIII are extended to this type of mine it cannot be realistically said to be so different in overall effect either from the mines contemplated in the Convention or now to be considered as included in O'Connell's proposition, merely because of the sophistication of the delivery system; *a fortiori* the various discriminatory sensors that may be included would only help to support the applicability of the Convention, which was aimed at limiting the inherent problems arising from the use of a non-discriminatory type of weapon which is inevitably likely to harm innocent third party ships.

However, there have been developments in the law affecting weapons since the Hague Convention, and it is necessary to consider how they affect the tentative conclusion that the mine, whether contact or influence type, of current or planned future design, is not a weapon illegal *per se*. The first multilateral treaty to be considered is Additional Protocol 1 to the Geneva Convention.[13] The United Kingdom has signed the Treaty with several reservations, including a statement that the new rules are not intended to have any effect on and do not regulate or prohibit the use of nuclear weapons, but the United Kingdom has yet to ratify it, and may well not do so if the U.S. does not do so. However, this Protocol probably reflects the customary international law position on conventional weapons, amplifying as it does Articles 22 and 23 of and 23 of Hague Rules Annexed to Convention No. IV of 1907 Respecting the Laws and Customs of War on Land which read, in the normally used English translation of the official French text,

> a. *Article 22.* The right of belligerents to adopt means of injuring the enemy is not unlimited.
> b. *Article 23e.* It is equally prohibited to employ arms, projectiles or material calculated to cause unnecessary suffering.
> (Pearce Higgins in fact translates the French text probably more aptly as *material of a nature to cause superfluous injury*.)

The distinction between weapons *calculated to cause unnecessary suffering* in Article 23e of the Hague Rules and weapons *of a nature to cause superfluous injury or unnecessary suffering* in Protocol 1 is not such as to render the sea mine illegal, since even looking to effect rather than to any possible interpretation of Article 23e as denoting intention, no maritime state will accept that this long-established weapon is now outlawed. The Hague Peace Conference did not succeed in codifying the law of all aspects of maritime warfare but expressed the wish that "the powers may apply, as far as possible, to war by sea the principles of the Convention relative to the laws and customs of the war on land."[14]

The Hague Convention No. VIII did not outlaw the mines then in use and, even when extended to modern and planned future types, it cannot be argued that Article 35(1) of the Protocol makes the mine illegal. Equally, it would be impossible to contend seriously that a mine of the likely charge is caught by Article 35(2) any more than a 1000-lb bomb used by an aircraft. Finally, Article 35(3) must be aimed at chemical weapons rather than at traditional conventional charge weapons. It is for that reason that the United Kingdom and America entered reservations over the applicability of the Protocol to nuclear weapons. I would conclude therefore that this Protocol has not made the mine illegal and suggest that Article 36 will not pose any problem for planned future conventional charge mines such as the continental shelf mine.

The Convention on the Prohibitions of Certain Conventional Weapons of 1981 dealt in Protocol II, Article 1, with mines, but specifically did not cover the use of anti-ship mines at sea.[15]

I now turn to the use of nuclear weapons in the sea which may affect the legality of any nuclear mines such as those held by the Soviet Union. In the light of reservations that will clearly be entered by the United Kingdom and the United States to the Geneva Protocol 1, to the effect that nuclear weapons are not caught by Article 35, it is probable that other nuclear powers will take the same view, so the Protocol will be ineffective to make nuclear mines illegal. However, a more relevant multilateral treaty is on the prohibition of emplacement of nuclear weapons or other weapons of mass destruction on the seabed.[16] O'Connell has taken the view that tactical nuclear mines of very low-yield for ASW purposes might fall into a different category and would not be prohibited.[17] This appears hard to sustain in the face of Article 1, which reads:

> The State Parties to this Treaty undertake not to emplant or emplace on the sea bed and the ocean floor and in the subsoil thereof beyond the outer limits of a sea bed zone, as defined in Article II, any nuclear weapon *or* any other types of weapons of mass destruction or structures, launching installations or any other facilities specifically designed for storing, testing or using such weapons.

Only if a tethered nuclear mine could not be said to be emplanted or emplaced could it appear to escape the provisions of this article, since it must clearly be a nuclear weapon. It would be possible but implausible to contend that only a device which is both a nuclear weapon *and* a weapon of mass destruction is prohibited by the treaty *i.e.*, that the *or* in Article 1 is conjunctive. The area referred to in Article II is defined as being coterminous with the twelve-mile outer limit of the zone referred to in Part II of the Convention of the Territorial Sea and the Contiguous Zone.

The provision of the Treaty, which has been extensively ratified and may be a new legal norm, therefore appears to mean that nuclear mines inside internal waters or the territorial sea of the coastal state laying them, up to a twelve-mile limit from the baseline used for measurement of the width of the territorial sea, are not prohibited but nuclear mines beyond that limit are prohibited whether ground or tethered. The Treaty can have no application to conventional mines, a view supported by the United States official naval position.[18]

It is therefore permissible to argue that the Hague Convention No. VIII should be extended to modern and planned conventional charge sea mines, whether contact or influence, and that such weapons are not illegal *per se* under treaty or customary international law. The legality of the weapons is unaffected by the different aspects of law pertaining in time of peace, declared war or tension of varying degrees. Nuclear mines positioned outside the twelve-mile limit from a coastal state's baseline are prohibited as against states party to the Treaty and it appears to be irrelevant whether or not they are armed. (This is now possibly a new norm of customary law.)

The Legal Restraints on the Use of Mines

It is easiest to consider the restraints on the use of mines imposed by the law in time of war and peace, and then go on to extrapolate to the twilight periods of tension in between. This is in accordance with my introductory contention that the Law of War will, in a modified form, provide guidance to permissible action in times other

101

than that of declared war -- in other words, during the period of *status mixtus* or transition to war.

It is important to remember that the restraints imposed by both customary law and convention were aimed at restricting the danger to which neutrals were exposed when the mine, basically an indiscriminate weapon, was used. The historical approach to mine warfare has been based on the assumption that, as soon as a mine is laid, it is a danger. The technological innovations associated with the continental shelf mine are a major new factor that requires a revision of legal thinking. It is therefore worth recalling what those technological innovations are. I am assuming that the continental shelf mine will be a short-tethered, rocket-propelled warhead. The mine could have a long bottom life and, most importantly, can be remotely activated and deactivated by acoustic link telemetry from a considerable range. Modern technology allows for the possibility of interrogating the weapon remotely to ascertain its state of arming. If the weapon breaks loose, it will become sterilized. The mine will have sensors, and these sensors could have discriminatory devices built in. The remote-arming device is to have a planned high reliability factor; it is this innovation that transforms the mine into a highly discriminatory weapon, and if designed as an Anti-Submarine Warfare weapon, it will pose no dangers to non-belligerent surface shipping which has traditionally been the source of concern, since it does allow a safe field of uncultivated mines to be laid. These will pose no danger to shipping until armed. The historic danger of laid fields with which the law has been concerned is is therefore now altered dramatically, and caution must be exercised in deciding from precedent what future restraints there may be. Indeed, the mine will become a more flexible weapon and more likely to be used in the future.

It is also important to remember that a state's perception of its interests may change with time, so that whereas in 1907 the United Kingdom was concerned with safe passage on the high seas for its large merchant fleet, defense interests that need protection may now loom larger and indicate a different view of mining in general. When considering the effects of relevant treaties, I am assuming that although the 1982 United Nations Convention of the Law of the Sea is not yet in force, the navigational provisions are likely to become generally accepted.

War

The overriding restraining principle that appears to be supported by the practice in both World Wars, and the reaction of other states, is that for minefields, irrespective of the type of mine, to be legal they must not be sown indiscriminately, and their presence must be notified together with safe routes neutrals can use or areas they enter at their own risk, without an unreasonable degree of hardship or inconvenience being thereby caused to them. Failure to notify until "military considerations permit" will be scrutinized very strictly by the international community to see if the claim is genuine. The result of this approach is that, during wars, the belligerents may mine their internal waters, territorial seas and those of their adversary, subject to notification to safeguard neutral rights of innocent passage in territorial seas and internal waters, if enclosed behind straight baselines[19] (this may be suspended temporarily, except for international straits, or controlled by the use of traffic schemes in line with the 1982 Convention, Article 22). High seas may only be mined with conventional charge mines and these can only be laid in zones that can be reasonably termed *theaters of operations*, and notification will again be required. Neutrals may mine their own waters, subject again to notification, but it is likely that any attempt by belligerents to mine a neutral's waters as a reprisal or for any other reason will violate the neutral's sovereignty and attract grave protests.

The discriminatory package that can be built into a continental shelf mine will mean that it will be a genuine Anti-Submarine Warfare weapon and therefore less likely to attract protest from neutrals, whether used in territorial seas or in defensive fields on the high seas -- for example, in the north-western approaches to the Clyde out to the 200-meter depth line or in the south-western approaches to similar depths. Remote arming or disarming is unlikely to alter the perception of other states provided the field is declared before the mines are armed. They could, however, be laid and not notified until armed, provided the planned reliability factor can really be achieved, unless they would be argued to be a realistic danger to navigation by being laid in areas where ships legitimately anchor; this seems unlikely. The mines can be remotely interrogated to check the state of arming and should have a long bottom life.

Peace

Before looking at the restrictions placed on mining by treaty and customary law in peacetime, it is instructive to consider the very important case that was brought before the International Court of Justice: the *Corfu Channel* case. The facts of the case are well known.

The judgment of the Court was extensive, covering several interesting aspects of law, but the relevant points for this subject were the right of innocent passage of warships through international straits and the duty of the coastal state with regard to mines in its territorial seas. The Court found that it was generally recognized and in accordance with international custom that states in time of peace have a right to send their warships through straits used for international navigation between two parts of the high seas, without the previous authorization of a coastal state, provided that the passage is innocent. Unless otherwise prescribed in international convention, there is no right for a coastal state to prohibit such passage through straits in time of peace. The Court found the mines were of the moored contact and that, in view of Albania's surveillance of the water, she must be presumed to have had knowledge of their presence. The Court then said she had failed in her obligation in law:

> Obligations incumbent upon the Albanian authorities consisted in notifying for the benefit of shipping in general, the existence of a minefield in Albanian territorial waters and in warning the approaching British warships of the imminent danger to which the minefield exposed them. Such obligations are based not on the Hague Convention of 1907, No. VIII which is applicable in time of war but to certain general and well recognized principles, namely: elementary considerations of humanity, even more exacting in peace than in war; the principle of the freedom of maritime communications and every State's obligation not to allow knowingly its territory to be used for acts contrary to the right of other States.[20]

The Court reinforced again in this judgment the right to mine in the territorial sea, but not to the extent of a field that would close off an international strait, provided always that notification was given of the field to avoid unnecessary risk to other states' ships and subjects. This judgment was based on the implicit finding that there may have been a *status mixtus* existing between Greece and Albania, but that it should be approached on the basis that the peacetime law applied, although it did allow that Albania might have issued regulations of a general character to control innocent passage in light of the state of tension. The obligation identified by the Court was said to be more exacting than those in the Hague Convention, particularly the duty of notification of mines laid in the territorial sea.

Turning now to applicable treaty law, there is nothing in the Geneva Convention on the Territorial Sea of 1958 or the 1982 Convention that prevents a state from mining its internal or territorial sea in time of peace. Both treaties were essentially concerned with peaceful navigation on the sea. However, if the field is armed, it would be necessary to give due warning under Article 15 of the Geneva Convention or Article 24 of the 1982 Convention and the general precepts already postulated.

Outside the territorial sea it is probable that for the purposes of this subject it is better to consider the waters as assimilated to the high seas. Although the exclusive economic zone, which is likely to be claimed eventually out to 200 miles by all states in accordance with Article 55 of the 1982 Convention, is specifically designated not to be high seas (Article 86 of the 1982 Convention), Article 58 specifically reserves the freedom of navigation to other states. Coastal states may establish security zones around any artificial islands they construct, but these may not exceed 500 meters and are similar to those allowed by the Geneva Convention on the Continental Shelf of 1958, Article 5(3). It may be justifiable to mine these zones with notification. On the high seas, states do enjoy freedom of navigation, of laying submarine pipelines and cables, and subject to the regime of the exclusive fishing zone, of the right to fish. Moreover, the high seas are reserved for peaceful purposes (Article 88 of the 1982 Convention). The various rights are all to be exercised by states with reasonable regard to interests of other states in their exercise of the freedom of the high seas (Article 2 of the Geneva Convention).

Looking at the various principles stated in the treaty articles above, it is clear that laying active mines in the high seas in peacetime would be very severely scrutinized and would in any event provoke strong protest. It is likely that the only acceptable justification would be based on self-defense under Article 51 of the UN Charter. This would accord with Bowett's view that

> It can scarcely be contemplated that a state must remain passive while a serious menace to its security mounts on the high seas beyond its territorial sea. It is accordingly maintained that it is still permissible for a state to assume a protective jurisdiction, within the limits circumscribing every exercise of the right of self-defense on the high seas in order to protect its ships, its aircraft and its right of territorial integrity and political independence from an imminent danger or actual attack."[21]

It would clearly be very difficult, but not impossible, to satisfy the tests of justifiable self-defense in peacetime, with an armed minefield laid covering the approach to highly sensitive defense areas, such as the approaches to the strategic deterrent base or even the Falklands, unless there were some quantifiable threat. It would have to be stressed that the field was a preparation for self-defense[22] akin to the moat around the castle. It is more likely that the existence of a quantifiable threat would have arisen after a period of increasing tension, which means that the situation would fall into the next major category for the purpose of this paper.

I have, however, been considering armed mines to date, and it can be forcefully argued that the laying of a field of mines not yet armed would not be illegal. It would require a certainty of technological reliability of the planned order for the continental shelf mine, and a sound reason for the laying of the field to justify the political repercussions if an accident occurred. There would be no need to notify of the existence of the field since it should not pose a risk to other ships unless likely to prove an obstacle to navigation (including anchoring), fishing, research or ocean mining.

The laying of mines, armed or not, in another state's territorial sea or internal waters without permission would be a direct interference with sovereignty. It would therefore be considered a hostile act and certainly illegal in peacetime, unless justified as a legitimate act of self-defense under the United Nations Charter.

The conclusions that I have drawn from the foregoing discussion are that the mining of a state's own internal waters and territorial sea in peacetime is permissible, but if the mines are active they should be declared together with safe routes, and this is likely to provoke protests -- although in the case of Swedish high command as in peacetime is a very high-risk policy, justifiable in the case of armed mines only by sound, pressing reasons of self-defense or a similar need, and then only if notified. An unarmed field could be laid in the high seas for defensive reasons and would not require notification, provided the technical advances assumed are in fact achieved, but it would attract significant protest if discovered by the international community.

Period of Tension: *Status Mixtus*
The most difficult area in which to be able to predict the legality of actions is during the periods of tension. The degree to which rights and obligations will be imported from the Law of War will vary considerably with the perception of the degree of tension. Naturally, perception of the degree of tension will vary with the perceived amount of threat to a state's important interests or the interference with its day-to-day operations. This is why it is now generally accepted that states may close off areas of the high seas for training or defense exercises,[23] because they invariably try to do so in areas where there is little disruption to other states' shipping. The practice of states is therefore of supreme importance in trying to determine what the limits are on a state's action. Purists may dislike the mining of Hai-Phong being cited as a precedent, but it was action taken by a major maritime state which would undoubtedly be repeated in similar circumstances in the future, particularly in view of its effectiveness. To that extent, it can be used as an argument to show the parameters of legal self-defense, and it will undoubtedly be thus used in the future. The view that we are still testing the limits of the changing post-Charter situation may be supported by contrasting O'Connell's conclusion on modern local disputes in 1970 with what happened in the Falklands. O'Connell said:

The experience of the last 20 years tends to verify the hypothesis that, except on occasions when the balance of deterrence which

105

exists between the Great Powers is threatened, as at the time of the Cuba quarantine operation, hostilities not amounting to war must be confined to the territorial sea or at least to the contiguous zone. Hence it must not be carried into the high seas, where international interests are directly engaged.[24]

If states really feel their interests are threatened and it is necessary to take defensive action, they will not abstain from action on the high seas -- as the recent Falklands and Iran/Iraq conflict demonstrated.

The minefields laid by the United States to block Hai-Phong and other North Vietnamese ports in 1972 is the most interesting case since 1945. The policy was first considered in 1968 and initially rejected. The overt reasons given were the risks to international shipping and the uncertainty that would be caused by moving to a new and uncertain mode of warfare. In fact, the Americans at that time had political reasons for ensuring that Russian aid could get through in some form and had no great military need to close the route. The apparent unwillingness to escalate the war was given a legal reference and the Director of the International Law Division of the Office of the U.S. Navy Judge Advocate General said:

> If a legal state of war existed between the United States and North Vietnam we could immediately blockade the port of Hai-Phong as a belligerent right of warfare. Without a state or war, such a blockade would be of doubtful legality. A similar analysis could be made with respect to mining harbors, contraband, neutrality, and the right of visit and search on the high seas.[25]

It is interesting to note that the author of this advice clearly took the view that I suggest no longer represents the law evidenced by the practice of states; that is, there is either peace or war, and the Law of War has no application except in a legal state of war.[26] By 1972, the military assessment of the need to mine the harbors and effectively blockade them had intensified and was in tune with the political will to undertake the risks of aggravating relations with Russia and China. The major assault taking place against South Vietnam, supported by accelerated imports of military material through Hai-Phong, had to be stemmed. The movement towards a ceasefire and release of prisoners of war all required continued support to South Vietnam. The interference with shipping that mining caused was not sufficiently proportional to the defense of South Vietnam in 1968 but by 1972 had become so mainly in view of the major attack taking place. By 1972, the United States clearly felt that self-defense required this action in the face of the flow of military material directly in support of the major offensive in the south.[27]

The solution to the tactical problems of the mining had to allow the objectives to be achieved without unnecessary risk to international shipping. If Hague Convention No. VIII applied to unmoored influence mines and instant notification was required, the minelaying aircraft in subsequent waves would be at risk. In fact, the decision was taken to lay in the internal waters and territorial seas of North Vietnam inactive mines that would become active after a period of three days, and to give warning to all shipping once the aircraft had all returned. Of the thirty-six ships in harbor at Hai-Phong[28] at the time of the announcement, over one quarter were under way within three hours.[29] No ships were lost, the traffic to and from Hai-Phong was effectively disrupted and, of course, the departures from Vietnam and release of prisoners of war followed shortly thereafter. The mining was justified and reported in accordance with Article 51 of the UN Charter by the United States as an exercise of the right of self-defense in view of the attack against South Vietnam and the need to protect the 60,000 remaining United States troops. Russia and China protested the United States action (Russia in relatively mild terms), but made no mention of the Hague Convention No. VIII (which neither had ratified) nor of international minelaying in general, but placed reliance on the freedom of navigation on the *high seas* under the Geneva Convention. They also denied that the American action could be justified by Article 51 of the UN Charter. The United States agreed in the peace agreement to remove the mines (something only they had the expertise to undertake), which exceeded the duty arising under Hague Convention No. VIII.

The Argentines did, of course, mine the waters around Stanley with contact mines, giving notice on April 15 they had done so. Their justification was, no doubt, that it was a defensive measure; they had complied with both Hague Convention No. VIII and the principles in the *Corfu Channel* case. This argument is obviously open to challenge on the ground of the whole illegality of their presence, but nonetheless, it is noteworthy that they saw the need to assuage world opinion by notification of the danger to shipping.

Turning to the North Atlantic area as the most likely area of tension where NATO might wish to mine as an Anti-Submarine Warfare measure, it is clear that both United Kingdom internal waters and territorial sea could be mined at any time in the period of tension, just as in time of peace, but international straits could not be closed. The minefields could be laid unarmed and therefore unnoticed in the same way as already discussed, assuming the technological reliability of the planned continental shelf mine, or they could be laid armed with notification. In the latter case, it would be advisable to lay down controlled sea lanes in accordance with Article 22 of the 1982 Convention to minimize the risk to international shipping.

Mining of the high seas in a period of tension will be easier to justify militarily than similar action in time of peace (see Paragraph 27 above). As tension mounts, Bowett's view quoted above, that a state may take positive action to defend itself against a serious menace being mounted on the high seas, is clearly more likely to gain international acceptance. Any field would have to be justified as a defensive measure or preparation for self-defense.

Mining of another neutral state's territorial sea or internal waters in the North Atlantic area without permission would be a major step in escalating tension whether or not the field was armed. It would therefore only be justifiable once actual hostilities had broken out and then only when self-defense could be seriously advanced as a justification for such action.

Conclusions

The law on the use of mines is not entirely free from ambiguity, and there are differences of opinion in some respects over the restraints on their use. It is, however, clear that the conventional charge mine of the planned continental shelf mine type is not an illegal weapon *per se* and that the restraints are on its deployment. It is the major technological innovations associated with the continental shelf mine that have made that have made many of the restrictions imposed by the law hitherto on the use of mines less necessary and therefore less likely to be demanded in the future. The whole concept of laying a minefield that is, in fact, safe until activated remotely obviates the need to notify the presence of mines as a danger to non-belligerent shipping as soon as they are laid. Legal opinion will, in the future, have to take cognizance of the changes which mean that, operationally, the mine becomes a more flexible method of defense than in the immediate post-world war situation. The nuclear charge mine used outside a twelve-mile limit is, on the other hand, illegal. Although war is most unlikely to be declared again in the post-United Nations Charter world, the practice of states shows that the law of war, where relevant, including Hague Convention No. VIII, will be imported in varying degrees to resolve the conflicting objectives of belligerents and other states. The parameters of the law are still being established, and it is here that the actual practice of states as in the Hai-Phong case is so relevant and cannot be swept aside by those academics who prefer to regard such examples as unfortunate aberrations unlikely to recur; they will undoubtedly recur.

The general principles that can be extracted are that, if armed minefields are laid, they must be declared with safe routes where applicable. The fields must be justifiable as a genuine measure of self-defense, and their acceptability will depend on the state of tension existing, the degree of interference with and danger to other states and the area that is effectively closed to shipping and for how long. The larger the area in a low period of tension, the less likely it is that it will be generally accepted. The new technology allows profit to be taken of the considerable advantage in laying unarmed fields and notifying, as they are armed, as tension actually mounts. In the end, it is a question of weighing the reasonableness of a state's action in the genuine self-defense against the degree of protest that all interference with the freedom of navigation will probably provoke. This protest will depend on how other states view the case that a state mining the seas really is defending its vital interests.

APPENDIX

HAGUE CONVENTION VIII
RELATIVE TO THE LAYING OF
AUTOMATIC SUBMARINE CONTACT MINES (1907)

His Majesty the German Emperor, King of Prussia; [etc.]:

Inspired by the principle of the freedom of sea routes, the common highway of all nations;

Seeing that, although the existing position of affairs makes it impossible to forbid the employment of automatic submarine contact mines, it is nevertheless desirable to restrict and regulate their employment in order to mitigate the severity of war and to ensure, as far as possible, to peaceful navigation the security to which it is entitled, despite the existence of war;

Until such time as it is found possible to formulate rules on the subject which shall ensure the interests involved all the guarantees desirable;

Have resolved to conclude a Convention for this purpose, and have appointed the following as their plenipotentiaries:

[Here follow the names of plenipotentiaries.]

Who, after having deposited their full powers, found in good and due form, have agreed upon the following provisions:

Article 1
It is forbidden --
1. To lay unanchored automatic contact mines, except when they are so constructed as to become harmless one hour at most after the person who laid them ceases to control them;
2. To lay anchored automatic contact mines which do not become harmless as soon as they have broken loose from their moorings;
3. To use torpedoes which do not become harmless when they have missed their mark.

Article 2
It is forbidden to lay automatic contact mines off the coast and ports of the enemy, with the sole object of intercepting commercial shipping.

Article 3
When anchored automatic contact mines are employed, every possible precaution must be taken for the security of peaceful shipping.

The belligerents undertake to do their utmost to render these mines harmless within a limited time, and, should they cease to be under surveillance, to notify the danger zones as soon as military exigencies permit, by a notice addressed to ship owners, which must also be communicated to the Governments through the diplomatic channel.

Article 4
Neutral Powers which lay automatic contact mines off their coasts must observe the same rules and take the same precautions as are imposed on belligerents.

The neutral Power must inform ship owners, by a notice issued in advance, where automatic contact mines have been laid. This notice must be communicated at once to the Governments through the diplomatic channel.

Article 5
At the close of the war, the contracting Powers undertake to do their utmost to remove the mines which they have laid, each Power removing its own mines.

As regards anchored automatic contact mines laid by one of the belligerents off the coast of the other, their position must be notified to the other party by the Power which laid them, and each Power must proceed with the least possible delay to remove the mines in its own waters.

Article 6
The contracting Powers which do not at present own perfected mines of the pattern contemplated in the present Convention, and which, consequently, could not at present carry out the rules laid down in Articles 1 and 3, undertake to convert the materiel of their mines as soon as possible, so as to bring it into conformity with the foregoing requirements.

Article 7

The provisions of the present Convention do not apply except between contracting Powers, and then only if all the belligerents are parties to the Convention.

Article 8

The present Convention shall be ratified as soon as possible.

The ratification shall be deposited at the Hague.

The first deposit of ratifications shall be recorded in a *proces-verbal* signed by the representatives of the Powers which take part therein and by the Netherlands Minister of Foreign Affairs.

The subsequent deposits of ratifications shall be made by means of a written notification addressed to the Netherlands Government and accompanied by the instrument of ratification.

A duly certified copy of the *proces-verbal* relative to the first deposit of ratifications, of the notifications mentioned in the preceding paragraph, as well as of the instruments of ratification, shall be at once sent, by the Netherlands Government, through the diplomatic channel, to the Powers invited to the Second Peace Conference, as well as to the other Powers which have adhered to the Convention. In the cases contemplated in the preceding paragraph, the said Government shall inform them at the same time of the date on which it has received the notification.

Article 9

Non-signatory Powers may adhere to the present Convention.

The Power which desires to adhere notifies in writing its intention to the Netherlands Government, transmitting to it the act of adhesion, which shall be deposited in the archives of the said Government.

This Government shall at once transmit to all other Powers a duly certified copy of the notification as well as of the act of adhesion, stating the date on which it received the notification.

Article 10

The present Convention shall come into force, in the case of the Powers which were a party to the first deposit of ratifications, sixty days after the date of the *proces-verbal* of this deposit, and, in the case of the Powers which ratify subsequently or adhere, sixty days after the notification of their ratification or of their adhesion has been received by the Netherlands Government.

Article 11

The present Convention shall remain in force for seven years, dating from the sixtieth day after the date of the first deposit of ratifications.

Unless denounced, it shall continue in force after the expiration of this period.

The denunciation shall be notified in writing to the Netherlands Government, which shall at once communicate a duly certified copy of the notification to all the Powers, informing them of the date on which it was received.

The denunciation shall only have effect in regard to the notifying Power, and six months after the notification has reached the Netherlands Government.

Article 12

The contracting Powers undertake to reopen the question of the employment of automatic contact mines six months before the expiration of the period contemplated in the first paragraph of the preceding article, in the event of the question not having already reopened and settled by the Third Peace Conference.

If the contracting Powers conclude a fresh Convention relative to the employment of mines, the present Convention shall cease to be applicable from the moment it comes into force.

Article 13

A register kept by the Netherlands Ministry for Foreign Affairs shall give the date of the deposit of ratifications made in virtue of Article 8, paragraphs 3 and 4 as well as the date on which the notifications of adhesion (Article 9, paragraph 2) or of denunciation (Article 11, paragraph 3) have been received.

Each contracting Power is entitled to have access to this register and to be supplied with duly certified extracts from it.

In faith whereof the plenipotentiaries have appended their signatures to the present Convention.

Done at The Hague, the 18th October, 1907, in a single copy, which shall remain deposited in the archives of the Netherlands Government, and duly certified copies of which shall be sent, through the diplomatic channel, to the Powers which have been invited to the Second Peace Conference.

NOTES

1. Kalshoven, *Belligerent Reprisals* at 136.
2. Pearce Higgins, *The Hague Peace Conference*, at p. 335.
3. Tucker, *The Law of War and Neutrality at Sea*, at p. 303.
4. O'Connell, *Contemporary Naval Operations*, 44 BYIL (1970), at p. 24.
5. Bowett, *Self Defence in International Law*, at p. 155.
6. Van Zwanenberg, *Interference with Ships on the High Seas*, 10 ICLQ (1961), p. 785.
7. Christol and Davis, *Maritime Quarantine: Naval Interdiction of Offensive Weapons and Associated Material to Cuba*, 57 AJIL (1963), p. 525.
8. Brownlie, *International Law and the Use of Force by States*, at p. 401.
9. Bowett, *op. cit.* at p. 122.
10. *Parliamentary Papers*, Misc. No. 5 (1909).
11. Command mines posed no danger to neutral shipping because they were not indiscriminate weapons but controlled defensive weapons usually deployed on the territorial sea.
12. O'Connell, *The Influence of Law on Seapower*, at p. 157.
13. Protocol Addition to the Geneva Conventions of 12 August 1949 and Relating to the Protection of Victims of International Armed Conflicts (Protocol 1).
14. Final Act of the Second International Peace Conference of 1907.
15. Convention on the Prohibitions or Restrictions on the Use of Certain Conventional Weapons which may be deemed to be Excessively Injurious or to have Indiscriminate Effect: Protocol on Prohibi-

tions or Restrictions on the Use of Mines, Booby Traps and other Devices (Protocol II).

16. Treaty on the Prohibition of the Emplacement of Nuclear Weapons and other Weapons of Mass Destruction on the Ocean Floor and in the Subsoil Thereof, 1971.
17. O'Connell, *The Influence of Law on Seapower*, at p. 157.
18. *Department of State Bulletin*, 3 November 1969, at p. 365.
19. Geneva Convention on Territorial Sea 1958, Art. 5(2).
20. *ICJ Reports 1949*, at p. 71.
21. Bowett, *op. cit.*, at p. 71.
22. Schwarzenberger, *International Law*, Vol. II: *The Law of Armed Conflict*, 1968, at p. 35.
23. Van Zwanenberg, *op. cit.*, at p. 797.
24. O'Connell, *Contemporary Naval Operations*, 44 BYIL (1970), at p. 27.
25. Carlisle, 22 *JAG Journal of USN* (1967), at p. 11.
26. State practice shows the Law of War suitably modified will be imported to give assistance in time of *status mixtus*.
27. Discussion with JAG Department of United States Navy of 7 March 1984.
28. Swayze, *United States Mining of Internal and Territorial Waters of North Vietnam -- JAG Journal of USN* (1977), at p. 163.
29. O'Connell, *The Influence of Law on Sea Power*, at p. 95.

A.G.Y. Thorpe: Before I ask our commentators to add their weight to what you've heard, I'd say this, that there may be jurisdictive doubt about the right of pre-emptive self defense. There is no naval doubt whatsoever. Given modern weapon systems, which not only do not require fire control radar, but don't require radar at all -- it can be line of sight -- don't require any missile doors to open, the first thing you know is when it's actually left the mounting, you can see why we need the ROE.

COMMENTARY

Bruce A. Harlow
Rear Admiral, United States Navy (Retired)

Professor Kinley had a difficult subject because it was on law of self-defense and contemporary naval operations, while the panel is on the impact of UNCLOS on contemporary naval operations. He handled it very well. He, in one sense, said the impact was negligible; on the other hand, the impact was significant.

In terms of contemporary naval operations, one has to think in terms of two categories. The first is the normal peacetime operations. If you look at the number of hours the U.S. Navy units have been at sea for the last forty years, 99 percent of those hours were in peacetime operations not involving the use or threat of force. The United States Navy was very interested in the 1982 Convention for that category. The United States Navy views its responsibilities as abiding by the normal rules applicable to all ships and aircraft, with a safety valve and exemption for extraordinary circumstances. But in normal peacetime operations we deploy and navigate our ships and aircraft in a way entirely consistent with the requirements and provisions of the 1982 Convention. The category of self-defense or exercise of an extraordinary right was left untouched by the negotiations.

On the first category, it is important to put the situation in perspective. Although there have been some bumps and rough seas along the way, basically in the last forty years the peacetime deployment of warships throughout the world has been incident-free. Coastal nations have not been threatened and if you talk to the foreign offices of most coastal nations with certain exceptions -- whiskey on the rocks, etc., -- the general pattern has been that the maritime nations of the world have deployed their naval forces in a non-confrontational, law-abiding manner which has been relatively incident-free. I feel certain that, under the provisions of the 1982 Convention, they would remain so.

The law of self-defense raises many interesting issues. I have the courage now after having been a quasi-practitioner in the law of war and law of the sea for over twenty years to confess to you for the first time in public that I do not know the difference between peace and war. It sounds extraordinary, but the truth is that in the last forty years the issue has been blurred by the United Nations Charter, by the practice of nations and certainly by the internal policies of the United States of America. Largely the issue need not concern us because it is not particularly relevant to the issues raised by Professor Kinley.

Rather than talk in terms of peace and war and when war breaks out or when peace breaks out, we should ask whether or not our armed forces are engaged in armed conflict. I am not talking about the United Nations Law of the Sea Convention, but about the other arena that was left untouched and undiscussed in the negotiations. It is useful to think in terms of three situations. The first is, are our naval forces engaged in armed conflict and if the answer is no, they probably fit within the peacetime category. If they are involved in armed conflict, then rules of self-defense, proportionality, humanity, and necessity all come into play. It does not matter whether there is a declared war or not -- the question is, are your forces engaged in armed conflict? The Professor mentioned that students often look at the Charter as rendering war illegal and are reluctant to attribute to nations engaged in armed conflict any of the rights of belligerency. That has an ominous side to it. In my experience, nations have not taken that outcome as limiting their rights in the circumstances. Indeed, they have taken that outcome as opening the door to further levels of violence. In other words, if you argue to a nation involved in armed conflict that the laws of war are not applicable, you run the danger of not having the Geneva Conventions applied and not involving the rules of necessity and proportionality in warfare.

Professor Kinley raised an extremely important point on pre-emptive attack. He asked when armed attack commences, *i.e.*, when is there an immediate and overwhelming threat that would warrant a reaction? I believe the law permits a nation to pre-emptively attack under appropriate circumstances, *i.e.*, if there is an immediate and overwhelming threat or certainly if armed attack has commenced. But the problem is a practical one. Very seldom, in very few circumstances at two o'clock in the morning in the command center, can you determine with assurance that an armed attack is about to occur. There are intelligence-gathering and identification problems. There are friction problems with regard to communications and other issues all of which prevent you from knowing precisely what is going on and the nature of the threat you face. There are problems in positive identification of the assailant or potential assailant. The best you can hope for is that you have men acting prudently with the best judgment they can, employing the best information they have and using the standard of reasonableness to determine whether or not armed force should be resorted to. I think that would be a fair summary of what the law actually is.

The other problem that faces nations today in this difficult arena of self-defense is the time that is available for decision-making. Reference was made to new weapons and missiles and the fact that they can be armed and utilized very quickly. We are dealing not in hours or days but in minutes or seconds. It is important to educate our commanding officers of ships on the intricacies of the law of war. We may be getting to the point where we will have to educate our computers on the intricacy of the laws of war -- which is an ominous development indeed.

Reference was made to terrorism and the response of the United States in the Persian area with regard to the safety of our ships -- a standoff requirement. One can argue that that is not consistent with historic utilizations of the right of self-defense. While I agree with that, I would emphasize that the law should be viewed as one that permits an intelligent application of the needs of the nation under the circumstances that obtain at the time. We were dealing with a new and unique threat -- government-sponsored and ominous levels of terrorism in the area -- and, in my judgment, the response of the United States to publish a standoff distance not only was legal -- it was prudent and grounded on common sense. I cannot prove a negative but I consider that action may have tended to defuse what otherwise could have been an explosive situation. I would argue that such a measure that did not contemplate the direct use or threat of force is not an exercise of the extraordinary right of self-defense but simply a prudent peacetime measure that was demanded under the extraordinary circumstances faced by our forces. I would hope such measures would be unnecessary in the future but that may not be the case.

My final point is on the submerged submarine problem in territorial seas -- the intractable issue which Professor Kinley mentioned of dealing with an unidentified submerged object in your territorial sea. As with the measures contemplated *vis-a-vis* terrorism, one has to look at the circumstances surrounding the particular case. It may be appropriate to view the circumstances as a law enforcement problem -- ultimately authorizing the use of force as a law enforcement measure and not an extraordinary right of national self-defense. So under those circumstances, I think submerged objects in your territorial sea could be dealt with in many ways, either as law enforcement or as an extraordinary right of self-defense.

COMMENTARY

Glen Plant
Office of the Special Representative of the
Secretary-General for the Law of the Sea

I would like to emphasize that the views that I am about to express are my own and not those of the Secretariat of the United Nations.

I find myself in a potentially embarrassing situation for a commentator of being very largely in agreement with most of what Mr. Kinley has said, but I would like to discuss two matters further.

Concerning the U.S.-USSR Agreement on the Prevention of Incidents on and over the High Seas (INCSEA) 1972, Mr. Kinley omitted to mention the existence of a Protocol of 1973 extending the provisions to merchant ships of the parties. It is true that the International Regulations for the Avoidance of Collisions of 1972 do improve the position of certain types of naval vessels from the point of view of collision-avoidance, but INCSEA goes beyond this and is a potential model for global agreement aimed to reduce collisions involving warships. Essentially, it establishes a system of priorities, with formations of warships being the most privileged vessels, single vessels having to keep out of their way and, in turn, shadowing vessels having to keep out of *their* way. Unfortunately, it does not go further by establishing, as originally contemplated, fixed distances to be kept between vessels.

As far as the anti-harassment provisions of INCSEA are concerned, discrepancies between the texts of the Agreement and the Protocol have led to certain acts of harassment which should be prohibited from being impliedly permitted in some situations.

The second issue concerns self-defense of ships. I am assuming, as does Mr. Kinley, the existence of anticipatory rights of self-defense of naval units and the difficulty in some modern circumstances of distinguishing between acts of governments and of terrorist organizations. I certainly agree that it is vital to break the concept of an armed attack down into its constituent elements, such as "identification," presence with "hostile intent" and "hostile act."

The title emphasizes "contemporary" naval operations, and to my mind the contemporary practice which should cause most concern is the declaration by the U.S.A. of five-mile security zones around its naval units in the Persian Gulf. It may be argued that the terrorist threats, against a background of powerful weapons capable of destroying naval platforms instantaneously, present a threat of a new order justifying anticipatory measures against any unidentified craft entering the zone. The better view, however, is that it is important to identify such a vessel before attacking it, lest an innocent ship be attacked, that there is no basis in state practice for such zones and that there has never been any suggestion that they were permissible even in factually similar situations, such as the Spanish Civil War.

Among all the past examples of war zones or security zones only two possible precedents exist for the U.S. action. These, however, can be explained as the product of unique sets of circumstances not present here. The first is the Admiralty Instruction, dated 18 August 1937, issued during the Spanish Civil War, authorizing HM warships to hunt and destroy any foreign submarine found within five miles of a torpedoed merchant ships or an unidentified submarine found diving in such a place. Despite a superficial similarity, however, the circumstances were quite different from the modern example: successful attacks had occurred over a long period and were likely to continue, and, up to that time, all attacks on non-Spanish ships were against merchant shipping. *Most importantly*, those attacks were clearly by government vessels, but vessels for which no government was prepared to accept responsibility, and no response was forthcoming from a warship until an armed attack had been perpetrated on a non-Spanish merchant ship. A "hostile act" was required and not mere presence within the zone or area with a "hostile intent."

It is true that the following month the Nyon Agreement authorized the warships of States parties to hunt and destroy unidentified submarines believed to be attacking or in the vicinity of non-Spanish merchant ships, which were advised to follow designated routes. Since exercise areas were established for submarines of the States parties and the merchant shipping lanes were publicized, the mere presence of an unidentified vessel with hostile intent was considered a sufficient basis for action. The lanes were similar in conception to our modern zones. This was not, however, a collective exercise of the right of self-defense. The treaty was designed to remove the restraints surrounding that right by designating the presence of submarines in such circumstances *piratical*. In their discussion of the matter in 1955 all twelve members of the International Law Commission accepted these measures as a legal reaction to one form of piracy; a majority of ten, however, considered this to be the result of a unique set of circumstances, namely, the avoidance of acceptance of responsibility for the continuing acts by all states. The earlier British self-defense measure was not discussed at all.

Modern parallels may be found. Several Israel-bound U.S. merchant ships have been attacked in the Straits of Bab-el-Mandeb by anonymous, fast-moving, missile-firing vessels, for which no government has claimed responsibility. Upon a recurrence of such a threat, the U.S. might be justified in declaring a stand-off distance around its vessels in the region and in taking measures against unidentified craft with an apparent "hostile intent." No such clandestine attacks have, however, yet taken place against U.S. ships, naval or merchant, in the Gulf, so that these conditions do not exist. No similar precedent exists in the Gulf, except the PLO threats in 1973 to sink tankers in the Straits of Hormuz, which were never carried out.

The second possible precedent is the U.K. Maritime Exclusion Zone (later, the Total Exclusion Zone) declared around the Falkland Islands in 1982. At an early stage in the "crisis" this was essentially a device to enhance the protection of elements of HM task force from Argentine attack. Based, initially at least, on the right of self-defense, it served as a notice that that right would be enforced with heightened vigilance within the declared zone. Unfortunately its value as a precedent is diminished, because the legal situation is complicated by three things: the course of events appears to have brought into operation the laws of war; the defense of land territory as well as of ships was tied up with the zone's declaration; and, whether the laws of war applied or not, the rights of the disputants were qualified by Security Council Resolutions 502 and 505. In addition all vessels, not merely Argentine, were warned to keep clear from the TEZ. It thus appears to have been more a means to limit the field of operations of "limited war" than a security zone for the protection of ships.

There are many points in Professor Larson's paper with which one might take issue. I shall list a few and emphasize one:

1. I do not agree with his ideas that the extension of territorial waters and establishment of the EEZ necessarily lead to further creeping jurisdiction." The EEZ regime is clearly a fine balance between coastal and non-coastal state interests and not a zone of sovereignty.

2. Nuclear weapon-free or peace zones cannot, as he suggests, affect the legal status of the high seas without the consent of the naval states whose activities they aim to restrict.

3. He is incorrect in suggesting that the Law of the Sea Convention imposes no restrictions on naval weaponry. It may well be that there are no or very few restrictions on the *possession* of naval weaponry, but there are certainly many on the *use* of such weaponry.

Since the Convention is primarily aimed at regulating peacetime uses of the sea, one of the most important issues which he should have discussed is the position under the Convention of peacetime uses of weaponry in exercises and tests. The provisions concerning this are good examples of one of the major flaws in the Convention.

It is generally assumed in the West that, despite heavy Third World pressure in the Sea-Bed Committee and at UNCLOS III, the UN Convention on the Law of the Sea has had little impact on traditional naval uses of the seas. This is often described in terms of a "package deal" in which economic concessions have been made in order to preserve communications and military interests. The provisions of the Convention which touch upon uses of naval weaponry in tests or exercises are a good example to suggest that there may be much self-deception in this.

The tactic used by the maritime powers, put simply, was to minimize opposition to proposals with potential military implications by avoiding direct references to military issues. They secured the acceptance in the Second Committee of UNCLOS III of "compromise proposals" containing provisions ensuring liberal rights of navigation and then asserted that these provisions and the vague language surrounding them secured the traditional rights of warships too. If other states objected too strongly, the threats to have nothing further to do with the Convention were revived. This approach resulted in a text with which Western military interests appear to be quite happy, but this satisfaction is based on dubious interpretations of some very vague formulae.

Having said that, the position in the UN Convention on such uses of weaponry in peacetime in or over territorial and archipelagic waters and straits used for international navigation is clear. Coastal or archipelagic states may only employ them (other than in self-defense) if their use does not hamper or endanger passage or transit of foreign vessels. Such foreign vessels must refrain from their use entirely, except in self-defense. A coastal state may temporarily suspend the innocent passage of foreign vessels in designated areas of its territorial waters (other than in straits used for international navigation) in order to conduct weapons exercises there, if such suspension is essential for its security. This addition to Article 25(3) is based on an informal proposal of Belgium of 1977. Those who assume that the regimes of territorial and archipelagic waters are identical should note that the identical proposal made by Papua New Guinea in March 1982 in relation to archipelagic waters was not adopted.

The position with the EEZs, which presumably will cover most traditional naval exercise areas, is much less clear. This is particularly serious since the UN Convention provisions on the EEZ are presently widely considered to serve as the best guide to what is permitted in customary law, and any lack of clarity will encourage unilateral claims by coastal states to control military activities in their EEZs. Maritime powers insist that the position is the same as on the high seas with the additional restraint incumbent on non-coastal-states of having to have due regard for the interests of the coastal state. To reach such a conclusion on the basis of the UN Convention, one of the three initial assumptions must be made.

First, a maritime power might assume the EEZ to be a high seas zone in which it enjoys residual rights not allocated to the coastal state; these would include traditional high seas military activities, whether designated as incidental to another freedom or as a separate freedom. This, however, would be to ignore the overwhelming evidence, reflected in the text, that the zone is *sui generis* in nature.

Alternatively, it might assume that the freedoms allocated to it in Article 58(1), of navigation and overflight, are akin to high seas freedoms and comprehend traditional high seas military activities. That many military activities have traditionally been carried out and are regarded as legal under the freedoms regime cannot be denied, but it is generally considered a matter of taste whether one describes these as part of or incidental to the freedom of navigation (or overflight) or as a separate freedom. In the case of Article 58, one has to make an additional assumption that they are part of the freedoms of navigation or overflight. The value of any examples of state practice apparently supporting such an assumption is diminished when one considers that no practical need to make such a distinction previously existed. In addition, if one did make this assumption, one would have to distinguish between activities incidental to navigation and overflight and those not; the latter must stand, if at all, as separate freedoms. The wish to avoid a decision on the legality of one controversial use, that of nuclear tests, was the reason for the decision to leave the list of freedoms in Article 2 of the Geneva High Seas Convention (now Article 87, UN Convention) inexhaustive, by the use of the words *inter alia*. Nuclear and ballistic missile tests and the establishment of warning zones around them cannot realistically be described as incidental to navigation or overflight. I was interested by Professor Larson's mention of bottom-crawling submarine vehicles. Are these navigating or exercising a separate freedom?

Finally, a maritime state might argue that military uses fall within the description in Article 58 of "other internationally lawful uses of the sea related to these freedoms, such as those associated with the operation of ships and aircraft ... and compatible with the other provisions of this Convention." The term "related to" is vague. In what way is the testing of a weapon or other actions other than actual maneuvers necessarily "related" to navigation or overflight? The simple answer is to say that a use is "related" if it is a reflection of the very role of warships; warships, it is said, operate in part as weapons platforms which must for effective use be navigated, in part to protect the navigation of other flag vessels. This is true, but warships (especially now that the definition in Article 29 of the UN Convention effectively extends to cover certain vessels in civil departments of government and does not necessarily require a warship to be armed) have many other roles besides. Is each of these roles or activities necessarily "related" to navigation? Some, such as establishing nuclear or ballistic missile test warning zones, clearly are not. Others are more controversial and might be argued to fall under Article 59 rather than Article 58.

There is talk of an UNCLOS IV to come up with a workable seabed mining regime. Perhaps it should also deal with clarification of all of the provisions concerning military activities. I understand that there are political and ideological difficulties involved in this, but is it really honest to talk of a "package deal" when one side of the trade-off is so open to misinterpretation?

Indeed, if such a Conference did take place, I would urge consideration of an entirely new approach to the matter, namely, the separate treatment of the freedom of navigation of war and merchant ships. Given the uncertain state of the law with the present status of the Convention, states legislating to control naval activities off their coasts may also be tempted to try to restrict navigation, too, to the quite unnecessary disadvantage of merchant shipping. To separate the two might save merchant ship navigation from undue risks involved in the defense of the rights covering naval activities against such encroachment.

Alternatively, one could clearly distinguish between the freedom of navigation and a freedom to conduct military activities. In any event, it would be necessary to come up with a better definition of warship than either the Geneva Convention on the High Seas (Article 8(2)) or the UN Convention (Article 29) provides.

DISCUSSION AND QUESTIONS

Myron H. Nordquist: I am an attorney in Washington, D.C. My question relates to the potential for mischief when there is a disparity between what states say and what they do -- or the potential for conflict or confrontation when there is a substantial discrepancy between conventional law and state practice. For example, under the 1982 Convention, there is no requirement that a warship give notice when passing through the territorial sea of a country that is not of that same flag. However, the great preponderance of municipal legislation on that issue requires warships to give notice. The United States, while not a signatory to the 1982 Convention, certainly took the position at the Conference that the warship had no obligation to give notice or to identify itself going through a territorial sea; yet the panel noted that on the high seas proper, there was a recent Notice to Mariners that the United States would require a foreign military vessel approaching within five miles of a warship of the United States to identify itself. What is the likely prevailing norm when there is an apparent discrepancy between what states have agreed at the 1982 Conference and what they have in their own laws?

David L. Larson: Under Article 20 of the UN Convention, submarines must surface and show the flag, which is a form of identification of the warships. Ken Booth has suggested that there ought to be maritime identification zones similar to the Air Defense Identification Zone that the United States has around its continental land mass. For example, the Atlantic Air Defense Identification Zone extends 500 to 700 nautical miles offshore, depending where you measure from, and we require all incoming aircraft, civilian and military, to identify themselves and be recognized. Ken Booth suggested that we ought to have analogous maritime identification zones in the interests of international peace and stability, but he did not specify what the width should be.

A.G.Y. Thorpe: One of the problems is straits. The practice of navies is to go submerged through straits and fly over them. Whether or not they have ratified the Convention and therefore gained what might be regarded as a new right, they will go on arguing that it is a customary right. In other words, they will do it anyway. Whether they say it is a customary right or derived from the Convention, it is really not going to matter in the end. No modern submarine is going to surface to go through an international strait. It is more difficult with overflight.

Bruce Harlow: There is an expression in the United States Army that when the map varies from the terrain, you have to go with the terrain, so I think the best evidence of international law would be the state practice. It has been my observation over the years that you do not look at the law to determine what civilized nations do; you look at what civilized nations do to determine the law. With regard to the 1958 and 1960 Conferences, the history of the negotiations is clear: there was no agreement at the Conferences or in the provisions or language of the Geneva Convention that required notification or authorization for the exercise of innocent passage for warships. That issue continued into the decade of negotiations leading up to the 1982 Conference, and indeed it even came to a vote at the last flurry of negotiations. The vote would sustain the argument that there is no requirement for prior authorization or notification for warships. It is an issue that will be of some importance, but it should be viewed as separate and distinguishable from the current situation in international straits.

A.G.Y. Thorpe: That was one of the points of the *Corfu Channel* case -- not having prior notification.

D. Cameron Watt: I'm from the London School of Economics. The discussion so far seems to be ignoring the context in which the law actually has been interpreted, which is by naval officers or by those who are responsible for directing naval officers in a moment of emergency. This is particularly the case with the use of naval force because, in most cases since 1945 between the major powers, naval force has been used not as an instrument of war, but as part of the negotiating process -- either as a threat of naval force or its actual use as in the Cuban crisis and many other cases. It is therefore a bit distressing to find that some of the discussion is based on false statements of the context. Mr. Kinley, in commenting on the Falklands, talked about it as though it were a case of war; it was not, as neither side declared war and indeed took great care not to.

I thought that Mr. Harlow's comments were obsessed with the American view of Pearl Harbor, *i.e.*, the preoccupation with the idea that it was a bolt from the blue. Pearl Harbor was *not* a bolt from the blue; it was only a bolt from the blue because the American bureaucracy could not get its act in order, and one side could not tell another side what was on the way. It is an example of bad history being applied to current legal discussions.

I would like to invite Professor Larson to discuss some of the issues faced by a medium-ranking naval power which wishes to use its power in pursuit of its overall policy or finds itself threatened with the use of power by another major power in similar circumstances.

The case that Professor Larson cited of Nelson is a very good example of both bad history and of naval officers in a legal position. It was not Trafalgar but Copenhagen; it was not the Spanish signals Admiral Nelson ignored but instructions from his own government, and he ignored them to launch an attack as a pre-emptive strike on the Danish ships that were in the position of partial neutrality. It was orders from his own government that he turned a blind eye to.

Speaking as a non-naval officer but as a possible sufferer from naval officers who might misinterpret or ignore their orders in similar processes today, I feel that discussions of this sort must be directed toward the actual state of the law in the kinds of states of tension which, in every case, have anticipated the use of force. It is very important that academic lawyers, even those employed by government, and still more, political scientists, should discuss the use of force in the context of what is likely to occur, and not spend their time talking either in purely academic terms as to what might or might not happen or what might or might not be the interpretation. That is not going to be much use to a naval officer who finds himself in a difficult position -- even with instant satellite communication. It it also important that they discuss these questions in terms of control over naval officers by governments, because it is out of the Nelsonian kind of action that greater crises and larger things may very well come. As an example: if the deep sea mining should occur under two separate regimes, one under the UN Law of the Sea Convention and the other under the legislation of those who are non-signatories, what action should be taken, and what kind of protective zones can legitimately be enforced around the mining operations? Presumably there will have to be some sort of protective zones around them; otherwise, the financial hazards to any operator might be prohibitive.

David L. Larson: I stand corrected on Nelson, because we do not study the battle of Trafalgar as well as you do. If I understand your first question, namely, what do you do about middle-sized powers, medium powers, regional powers, and developing powers in regard to naval warfare, the law of the sea, and so forth, the basic point is made in my paper, which I could not go over in detail, as follows. Given what I regard as the legal vacuum, state practice seems to be developing in an unrestricted, unrestrained fashion, and the states are doing whatever they deem necessary to protect their interests, their coastlines, the straits, etc., and this is involving a wide panoply of weapons. Given the weapons market now, as for example, the naval missiles listed in Appendix B that are available commercially to any state, and the fact that most of these weapons and weapons systems are now within financial and technological range of most coastal states, I suggest that, rather than allow this naval weaponry to continue to develop and proliferate, some form of international conference should try to regulate and control both straits passage, archipelagic sealanes passage, and, to a certain extent, innocent passage for both belligerent and neutral states. In my judgement, that time is now.

David Colson: I'm from the Legal Adviser's Office of the Department of State in Washington, D.C. The panel has sold short the 1982 Law of the Sea Convention in this context: if we had this discussion ten years ago, those of us representing foreign ministries from various parts of the world would have had a very different view of the geographic scope of national jurisdiction. Regardless of what our national positions might be with respect to signature of the instrument itself, the Law of the Sea Treaty and the Conference have clarified the scope of national jurisdiction in the ocean.

Professor Larson was not correct when he interpreted the President's Ocean Policy Statement the way he did. The United States said that we will abide by the coastal state rights as set forth in the Convention and recognize those rights so long as our rights are also recognized in international law. That means that now we have an agreed set of rules which, in this context, invariably becomes part of the rules of engagement that naval officers have. Those rules do refer to territorial seas, they refer to economic zones, and we now know what those rules are and generally where those areas are.

In any national crisis, the first group of people that come to the forefront are the geographers in foreign ministries because, invariably, people must plot where an incident occurred. We then extrapolate from that and learn what the rules are. The 1982 Convention is what we look to.

We will always have situations like the Gulf of Sidra, where the claim by the coastal state is so egregious in other states' views that there are challenges. That is a situation where a baseline is drawn across a large portion of the Mediterranean which is claimed not as territorial sea but as the internal waters of Libya. In that instance the United States did not assert a right of innocent passage; we were engaged in the freedom of navigation in the area when we were approached by the aircraft. I believe that the Law of the Sea Convention has done a great deal in this area, and that we ought to give a little more credit to the Convention and to the Conference in this context.

A.G.Y. Thorpe: Irrespective of one's government's position, I do not think that you will find a naval officer who would not rather have the Convention. The clarification that was in it and the advantages on the naval side were seen by all navies to be a tremendous step forward.

Bruce Harlow: I agree with Dave Colson and Captain Thorpe that the importance of the Convention lies in the willingness of the nations to incorporate those balances envisioned therein into their national practice. It is easy for lawyers to stand on the formality of signature and ratification and give too much weight to the dynamics of what others would characterize as technicalities. Whether or not it is going to work -- and it does have the potential to do a great deal by way of clarification -- will depend on the willingness of nations to incorporate those. Certainly the United States has indicated a willingness to work toward that end, so that we could take what many of us had as a dream for a viable blueprint and convert it into a meaningful, workable regime.

Daniel Cheever: I am from Boston University. I have three questions. The first is to Captain Thorpe. Would you repeat your first intervention about radar?

For Professor Kinley, may I ask if the difficulties he mentioned with respect to the law and custom of self-defense are so very difficult? Is it not almost inevitable that coastal states will increasingly establish zones of peace? It seems to me that the incredible difficulties of identification and the unlikelihood that "sailing orders" from governments to skippers will be published produces a degree of uncertainty that will inevitably give rise to increased pressure for zones of peace which legally would further restrict naval movement.

For Professor Larson: perhaps I did not hear correctly, but I thought I heard him say that the UN Convention provided no restriction whatsoever for the exercise of naval weaponry. I wonder if he meant "provided no *practical*," as opposed to legal, restriction on the exercise of naval weaponry.

A.G.Y. Thorpe: I was saying that one of the arguments about "hostile intent" or "hostile act" was that you were illuminated by a fire control radar. With modern missile systems, you don't need a fire control radar or necessarily even a navigational radar. If you're in line of sight, you can actually have no idea that missiles have acquired you or anything until they come straight off the mounting. You may have a matter of seconds to make up your mind what to do. That is why Professor Kinley's point about identification of an enemy coupled with the intelligence of a threat assessment was so important; the first thing you, left in a bald situation, would actually know is the missile coming straight in.

David L. Larson: I find nothing in the UN Convention which explicitly or implicitly restricts and restrains the utilization of almost the total range of naval weapons and weaponry in the ocean. Now, there are other restrictions and restraints -- the Seabed Arms Control Treaty, etc., -- that I mentioned in the paper, but not the UN Convention *per se*.

To David Colson I shall merely ask a question rhetorically and we can argue about it later. If what he says is so, then why does the United States claim only three nautical miles of territorial sea?

G. D. Kinley: Professor Cheever, could you repeat your question to me?

Daniel Cheever: Should I not infer from your presentation that there will be mounting pressure for coastal nations, particularly the less prominent maritime powers, to declare zones of peace, precisely to reduce the danger, the ambiguity, the possibility of force being exercised against them?

G. D. Kinley: The answer to that question is yes; alternatively, no!

Max Morris: I am Max Morris from the United States, a foundation president and an ex-carrier aviator. My question is directed primarily to Professor Kinley, and it has to do with the thorny identification problem, particularly the question of identification, the case of the mounting attempts at unconventional warfare and conventional attacks. In the Persian Gulf case, one of the precursors was an authenticated document that came out of Teheran discussing the formation of the 110th Special Brigade, specifically talking about training people for light plane and commercial vessel attacks, with suicide attacks. How do you think that identification and the problem of suicide attacks by light aircraft or by unidentified or other types of commercial vessels can be dealt with?

G. D. Kinley: Insofar as governments of an extreme character have made statements as to intention beforehand, I thought such statements were part of the circumstances which could be taken into account in deciding whether you could use pre-emptive action or not. There is one classic example of this -- not in the context of the sea, but in the context of air law -- and that was that tragic incident in February 1973, when a Libyan civil airliner intruded into Israeli-controlled airspace in the Sinai. After being challenged in the appropriate manner, dictated by ICAO, and after having initially followed the direction of Israeli interceptor aircraft, that Libyan aircraft attempted to escape, was ultimately fired on, and made a "crash landing" in which many people were killed. The Israeli government was initially criticized severely, but one of the factors that the Israeli government raised and which was taken into account by the subsequent ICAO Commission of Inquiry was the fact that President Gaddafi had, on several occasions, announced that he was going to load explosives onto aircraft and get *kamikaze* pilots to fly them into Israel and crash them on Israeli cities. So it is part of the build-up.

Louise Doswald-Beck: What is the effect of the Law of the Sea Convention on the area of naval operations, in particular the exclusive economic zone? Although it is supposed still to have the character of high seas as far as other states' rights are concerned, I am thinking in terms of belligerent actions and possibly the creation of an exclusion zone for naval operations. Could this be done in an EEZ? Would it not somewhat affect the states' attempts to use that area for economic purposes?

Bruce Harlow: No; they cannot use the economic zone jurisdiction, which is really directed to the resources of the area, with the limited proviso that if military operations unreasonably interfered with those resource rights, then they would have an ability to regulate it to that extent. However, the exclusive economic zone or the regime of the continental shelf is resource-oriented and the crucial task is to try and reasonably divide those areas functionally so as to have a win-win situation; that is, the coastal state can enjoy exclusive jurisdiction over the resources, and, at the same time, the historic maritime rights can be reasonably preserved.

LUNCHEON SPEECH

THE LAW OF THE SEA AND THE UN CONVENTION OF 1982 --
A UNITED KINGDOM VIEW

H.G. Darwin
Foreign Commonwealth Office
United Kingdom

The organizers of this Conference thought it appropriate that, at this early stage, someone should offer a few remarks to the Conference reflecting the position of the Government of the state where the Conference is taking place; and I shall attempt to do so. If therefore I make little mention of the positions of other countries, I hope I may be forgiven; the rest of the program will redress the balance.

May I also say what pleasure it has given that the distinguished institute, the Centre for Marine Law and Policy established in Cardiff, has been chosen by the distinguished Law of the Sea Institute as its partner in holding this Conference. I cannot resist mentioning that one of the leading cases on maritime jurisdiction in this country arose in Penarth Roads, a roadstead just a few miles from this spot.[1] It is good to think that this large and learned group will be able to make a better acquaintance with Wales, this famous and beautiful part of the United Kingdom. I hope that everyone will leave it with memories as happy as mine.

Returning now to my subject, I shall refer to some positions which the United Kingdom Government has taken in public statements -- but adding a number of personal comments, which will, I hope, be distinguished sufficiently clearly.

I would like to begin by recalling the relationship, as I see it, between state practice and legal texts in this field.

All international law is made up of state practice and legal texts of various kinds. The interplay of these two is particularly complex in the Law of the Sea, which regulates the most important international area used by man. The earliest legal texts, recognized as the starting point for present day international law, namely, the "Rhodian Sea Laws" and the "Consolato del Mar" were legal texts setting down practice. More recently, the 1930 League of Nations Codification Conference failed on the territorial sea principally because of major differences in state practice on limits, customs enforcement and fisheries. The 1958 Geneva Conference crystallized state practice on the High Seas, built on state practice and other material, particularly from 1930 and from the International Court, on the Territorial Sea, and set out usefully for the first time continental shelf practice which had already developed; but it, as well as the Second Conference of the United Nations in 1960, failed on the limit of the territorial sea, and the Conference of 1958 failed in its work on fisheries, which did not attract sufficient support to become viable.

The United Nations Conference of 1973 to 1982 -- an astonishing span of years -- shows this interplay in even more complex form. It drew on past state practice from before the Conference; for example, 200-mile limits established for economic reasons by Latin American states, which became acceptable when the navigational and other rights were satisfactorily defined. It led to state practice during the Conference when many countries established EEZs. It is only to be expected that the Conference will be followed by further relevant state practice after the Conference.

The United Kingdom Government, in a statement to Parliament in December 1984, said that much of the Convention is valuable,[2] as it had said in December 1982 that parts are helpful;[3] but that is not immediately relevant since, as the Government also then said, the deep sea mining regime, as envisaged, is unacceptable. The United Kingdom has not signed the Convention and is not contemplating accession with the present deep sea mining regime; and indeed the Convention is a long way from being in force, even for the few states which have ratified it. In short, the 1982 Convention is not a legal text of the same character as the three successful Conventions of 1958. Thought it collected many signatures in the enthusiasm of the Conference, the number of ratifications is not yet large and it has a long way to go. It may be that the financial cost for all ratifying parties of the extravagant seabed mining regime will become a significant discouragement to ratifications, if states decide that they have better ways of spending their money.

Therefore, it is not necessary to comment on all the provisions or answer all the questions which can be extracted from the text of the Convention. Any country can, like the United Kingdom, watch to see how far the concepts in the Convention are continuing to advance and how far, after the Conference states are carrying the generally agreed regimes in it into state practice.

I will discuss the main maritime regimes recognized in the Law of the Sea or envisaged in the Convention under three headings: navigation, resources and pollution.

The balance of interests between a coastal state and other states whose vessels pass close to its coast is seen at its sharpest in the waters adjacent to its shores or baselines assimilated to its shores, namely, the territorial sea. But the regime in the Convention mostly follows closely that of 1958 -- indeed more than appears on its face. For example, Article 19 of the Convention of 1982 appears to be new but is in fact based on a list in the ILC Commentary which underlies the 1958 Territorial Sea Convention.[4]

The principal novelty of this part of the text lies in its solution for a point which baffled the First UN Conference of 1958 and the Second UN Conference of 1960, namely, the breadth of the territorial sea. The main problem lies in the question of straits, which was discussed at great length at the Conference and which led to the drafting of the transit passage regime.[5] An extension to twelve miles brings into the territorial sea many major straits for which no alternative route exists. Navigation in these straits is of vital interest to many countries in the world. State practice shows very many instances of recognition of the special status of straits. Some of the most important straits are subject to a special regime, such as those applying to the Danish and Turkish Straits. This is reinforced by some recent state practice; in certain straits of Japan and in parts of the Baltic outside the traditional Danish straits, the limit of the territorial sea has not been extended to twelve miles. A solution to this problem in the framework of a generally accepted Convention is preferable, as was made clear when the Government first commented on this question. But the Conference did not go that way; though much of the Convention was generally accepted in the Conference, a regime for deep sea mining was forced through which was not acceptable to countries having a major interest and significant investments in this field. The United Kingdom did not sign the Convention in 1982 and in December 1984[6] confirmed its decision not to sign before the closing date.

Straits are a problem of particular delicacy for the United Kingom since we have one of the most travelled straits on our doorstep, namely, the straits of Dover. But equally we and our allies are vitally depend ent on use of straits in other parts of the world for our shipboard trade and necessary resources. The problem remains how best to reconcile navi gational and other interests in straits with a twelve-mile territorial sea.

The contiguous zone calls for less comment. In principle, it is accepted by the United Kingdom since it figures in the 1958 Convention. But it is of limited importance since it gives rights only where offenses have been or are about to be committed in the territorial sea. It increases the zone in which enforcement measures may have to be taken taken and paid for. Successive United Kingdom Governments have never seen an attraction in it for the United Kingdom. The maximum limit of twelve miles for a contiguous zone in the 1958 Convention was extended to twenty-four miles in the 1982 text; but this change is, of course, closely linked to the twelve-mile breadth of the territorial sea and must be considered in connection in it. This position was made clear in a Parliamentary answer in June last year.[7]

A regime for waters within archipelagic states was not expressed in international legal texts before the 1982 Convention. Acceptance of such a regime was widespread at the Conference; it involved a careful balance between the rights of coastal states having this character and those of states requiring transit through the archipelago. Indeed, archipelagic sealanes passage, with its close resemblance to transit passage through straits, constitutes a further acknowledgement of the need for special regimes in especially important and necessary navigational routes. Fiji has now established an archipelagic regime including archipelagic sea-lanes passage along the routes normally used for international naviga-tion as envisaged in Article 53(12). The Philippines also made a declaration in connection with signature which seems to imply acceptance of the regime envisaged in UNCLOS for archipelagic waters; it excludes the right of transit passage explicitly, but presumably, in place of transit passage, will be recognizing the right of archipelagic sealanes passage, since, under Article 310, declarations made on signature cannot modify the legal effect of the Convention.

Turning to resources, the first great novelty of the Convention is the Exclusive Economic Zone. It too has a certain basis in state prac-tice before the Conference in that the Latin American states made claim to a 200-mile zone long ago primarily to protect their fishery inter-ests. Here again a balance must be struck with the navigational and other interests of other states; a solution was with some difficulty hammered out at the Conference. Even during the Conference a number of states declared EEZs. Indeed one of the problems in this field is that some of this legislation is based on earlier texts which did not even-tually command general support in the second half of the Conference. The Government made clear in a Parliamentary answer in March 1983 that it recognized EEZs provided the navigational and other rights of other states are respected.[8]

The principal resources in the waters and seabed around the United Kingdom are fisheries and continental shelf minerals. We have a 200-mile fishery zone which is administered in accordance with the Common Fisheries Policy of the European Community. I do not propose to go further into fisheries, but it is a fully developed regime. Similarly, for our continental shelf minerals, we have a complete and detailed regime for oil and gas resources as well as other minerals. Our legislation is largely based on the continental shelf regime of the 1958 Convention on this subject, most of which was carried into the 1982 Convention. In connection with these, an EEZ of wider scope would not help.

The third element in the field of resources within the concept of an EEZ, given as an example in Article 56 of the 1982 Convention, is the production of energy from water, currents and winds. The production of wave energy as well as energy from ocean thermal devices was extensively examined during the last decade. This was done in an atmosphere of optimism about these resources and pessimism about alternative, more conventional sources of energy. The United Kingdom is favorably placed for the production of wave energy if this is economically feasible. But the practical economics of such devices as well as developments in the availability of other resources have much discouraged work in this field. There seems little point in adopting legislation for a non-existent industry. If such devices became practicable, this country, like others, would no doubt take the necessary steps. But in the interests of freedom, apart from any other reasons, this country tends not to legislate in the absence of a sufficient need -- and there is no such apparent need in connection with this third element of the EEZ. It is not therefore surprising that the United Kingdom has not declared an EEZ.

What then of resources outside the continental shelf? For the sake of completeness, though this is not the topic of these meetings, I should add some words on deep sea mining. Here the Conference failed to achieve the general acceptance which it reached on so many other topics. To summarize what was said of it by the Government in December 1982, the seabed regime voted in at the closing stages of the Conference was based on undesirable regulatory principles and amounted to unsatisfactory precedents. The wording of the Convention, if imposed through the international seabed authority, could result in an unwieldy bureaucratic and possibly unworkable system which would deter, rather than encourage, investment and cooperation. Since then we have tried to obtain improvements through our action in the Preparatory Commission. Before the final stages of the Conference, it was widely recognized that working out detailed arrangements on deep sea mining was an essential element for the assessment of the deep sea mining regime as a whole. But, as was said in Parliament in December 1984, "We have put forward proposals and ideas in attempts to improve the Convention. However, that has not pro duced the results for which we hoped."[9]

This is not only our view. As was recalled in the statement made by the European Community on its signature in December 1984, "several Member States of the Community have already expressed their position that Part XI of the Convention contains considerable deficiencies and flaws which require rectification."[10]

Part of the difficulty here again is that the companies which have provided the only state practice in the field are not at present investing much further money in the deep sea mining; there is a certain unreality in drafting a mining code without real mines or talking about an Enterprise when the practitioners in the industry cannot see how to conduct it on an economic basis. But perhaps the recent signs of realism, which I have mentioned, are a bud from which there may be growth in the future.

I turn now to the very important question of marine pollution. Certainly the Government of the United Kingdom recognized the importance of this problem.

The practice and the formulations of the Convention on pollution are somewhat different from those of which I have spoken so far. Pollution is not like piracy. It cannot be eliminated entirely at our present standard of living with its related industry and extensive transport activities. The questions are how much, of what kinds and where. This is recognized by the 1982 Convention. Article 197 of the 1982 Convention envisages the need for cooperation "on a global basis and, as appropriate, on a regional basis, directly or through competent international organizations, in formulating and elaborating standards..." These organizations specialize in the practical aspects of specific types of pollution. The Convention itself, where it provides substantive rules, necessarily divides its provisions in dealing with the different types of pollution.

The United Kingdom is active in all the relevant organizations. The Convention refers first to land-based pollution, which is perhaps the least close to our discussion here. The creation of pollution from our seabed activities is closely regulated. For dumping, the United Kingdom is a party to the worldwide London Dumping Convention and to the Oslo Convention for regional aspects. The latter in particular provides a regime which takes account of circumstances in the region where this country lies. But the Government has strengthened its control over dumping through the Food and Environment Protection Bill discussed earlier this year in Parliament.[11] Similarly, it has actively pursued strengthening of control of vessel source pollution through Conventions negotiated in IMO. The importance of this work is recognized in the 1982 Convention through the frequent references to "generally acceptable standards." These specialized Conventions and institutions seem at present the best route for consideration of the appropriateness and practical consequence of any additional measures on marine pollution. Every effort is made to try to deal with each of the problems on their merits and as they really are, in a practical way.

I have not dealt with by any means all interesting and important aspects of Law of the Sea or the Convention. For example, scientific research, in which this country is in the forefront, has been regulated here for many years as concerns fisheries and oil production. We expect appropriate notifications from other countries. Equally, our scientific cruises to distant waters are notified to the coastal states as appropriate. We are active in the Intergovernmental Oceanographic Commission trying to advance the cause of scientific research and its contribution to the advancement of the world. Furthermore I have made no comment on the interesting matters which were discussed this morning.

But I could not, of course, discuss all aspects of this enormous subject in the time allotted; so I must ask your indulgence if I have not mentioned or dealt with a topic of particular interest to you. It seemed to me best to deal, however summarily, with the major regimes which are the subject of discussion in contemporary international law.

How can one draw together the threads of this vast and varied tapestry -- if I may be allowed such a metaphor? Few countries, perhaps no country, is touched so widely and so profoundly as the United Kingdom by the law of the sea in all its many aspects. We have one -- or half of one -- of the most important straits in the world and we have worldwide trading and political interests. We have a massive offshore oil industry; and the industrialized community to which we belong -- on both sides of the Atlantic and further away -- has a massive dependence on oil brought across the sea. We have a significant tanker fleet, successors to the many vessels which carried "best Welsh steam coal" all over

133

the world -- but equally there was one of the worst tanker disasters in the Seven Stones passage, just a little way southwest from here off Cornwall. Everywhere complicated and delicate balances must be struck.

In these circumstances the policy of the Government on the law of the sea has not been and, I believe, cannot be expressed in a single phrase or slogan of a sweeping character. If I had, on a personal basis, to try to identify very summarily some tendencies which can be seen in its positions taken together, they would be the following: a tendency not to restrict and regulate until the need for restriction and regulation is sufficiently shown; a tendency to examine problems pragmatically in the light of state practice, including practice based on or reflecting the generally accepted parts of the Convention; and then, in the light of its examination of all aspects of these difficult questions, to take initiatives and establish positions, as and when this becomes useful. These are limited conclusions -- which you could have drawn yourselves, you may say -- but perhaps not out of line with the tradition of this country in other fields as in international law.

NOTES

1. *R. v. Cunningham* (1859) Bell's Cr. Cas. 72.
2. Hansard, H.C., 6 December 1984, col. 643.
3. Hansard, H.C., 2 December 1982, col. 410.
4. Report of the ILC to the General Assembly, *Yearbook of International Law Commission*; 1956, vol. II, p. 274.
5. Articles 37 to 44, UN Convention 1982.
6. Hansard, H.C., 6 December 1984, col. 643.
7. Hansard, H.L., 18 June 1984, W. Ans., col. 136.
8. Hansard, H.L., 21 March 1983, W. Ans., col. 995.
9. Hansard, H.C., 6 December 1984, col. 643.
10. UN Publication, "Status of the United Nations Law of the Sea Convention," 1985, E.85.V.5., p. 30.
11. The Food and Environment Protection Act 1985.

PART II:

THE IMPACT OF UNCLOS III ON FISHERIES

INTRODUCTION

Lee G. Anderson, Chairman
Professor of Economics and Marine Studies
College of Marine Studies
University of Delaware

The general theme of this Conference is "The UN Convention on the Law of the Sea: Impact and Implementation." In this session a well-qualified and distinguished panel of experts will discuss the impacts and implementation effects of fisheries utilization and fisheries management. The debates on fisheries issues at the UNCLOS sessions and the unilateral proclamations of extended fisheries zones which occurred at the same time contained many explicit and implicit arguments about what would and should occur under particular regimes. These arguments boil down to positions on who should catch the fish and hence who should reap the economic benefits from that activity. Some also argued that exclusive fisheries zones provided the opportunity for rational utilization because management authority was placed in a single entity: that is, over and above issues of distribution of catch, there was a potential for increasing the efficiency of harvest. Our purpose today is to take a preliminary look at how things have actually turned out with respect to the distribution of harvest and the potential for rational management.

Professor Giulio Pontecorvo of Columbia University, will describe some of the problems of quantitatively identifying the winners and losers in the fisheries access game and he will provide us with a rough measure of how this has occurred using the limited data available.

Mr. William Edeson of the Australian National University will discuss how various nations are choosing to use their newly acquired fisheries zones as evidenced by the types of bilateral and multilateral agreements which are being developed for fisheries exploitation.

Mr. Philip Major of the New Zealand Fishing Industry Board will describe how one nation, New Zealand, is using the potential to improve management efficiency offered by extended fisheries zones. New Zealand is a very good choice for a case study because at the time of implementation it had both an underdeveloped deep sea fishery and a heavily exploited in-shore fishery. There are many lessons to be learned from its handling of these two basic problems in fisheries exploitation.

Professor Gordon Munro of the University of British Columbia and Professor Rognvaldur Hannesson of the Norwegian Business School will then comment on the papers. Professor Munro will focus primarily on Professor Pontecorvo's paper, while Professor Hannesson will focus on Mr. Major's paper. Both commentators will discuss Mr. Edeson's paper.

THE IMPACT OF THE LAW OF THE SEA TREATY ON THE ORGANIZATION OF WORLD FISHERIES: SOME PRELIMINARY OBSERVATIONS ON PRODUCTION

Giulio Pontecorvo
Graduate School of Business
Columbia University

Introduction

Historians with a long view of twentieth century development will have to grapple with the problem of what was the substantive impact (if any) of the LOS negotiations and subsequent treaty on the new regime of the oceans -- a regime, in contrast to the previous one, characterized by limited freedom of access and dominated by coastal state preference.

In attempting to link the law of the sea negotiations to the structure of the new order of the oceans, one may draw an analogy between the worldwide economic and political trauma that accompanied the sharp rise in energy prices in the 1970s and the emergence of the new order of the oceans. Today, in retrospect, many economists believe that the long-run increase in the demand for energy, against known supply constraints, that took place in the 1950s and 1960s, had more to do with the subsequent rapid increase in energy prices than did OPEC. Similarly, the underlying developments in technology, economic growth and political organization may have preordained the new order of the oceans.

The question is whether or not the Law of the Sea Treaty simply ratified what had become or was about to become generally accepted state practice. As yet, we do not have a careful analysis of the historical development of the forces that, throughout the twentieth century and especially since the Second World War, underlie the several political attempts at rationalizing a new order of the oceans. Historical evaluation of the place of the new regime of the oceans in world development is necessary to provide the perspective that will enable use to judge whether or not the LOS impact on the emergence and structure of the new order extends beyond the short run issues of timing and focus.

In the case of fisheries there is considerable evidence -- the Alaskan political agitation for an extended fisheries zone for salmon in the 1930s, the Truman Proclamation relating to fisheries in 1945, the economic zones of Chile, Ecuador and Peru in the 1950s, the British-Icelandic disputes, etc. -- that extended fishery zones would have come into existence *sui generis* without the worldwide treaty negotiations that took place in the 1970s and early 1980s.

Also, it is possible that today's regime is a halfway house. The line drawn by the LOS Treaty between zones that provide for national authority over fisheries but not complete sovereignty may, under the pressure of national interests, not be sustainable; *i.e.*, creeping jurisdiction may ultimately prevail. In the case of fisheries we see pressure from domestic fishing interests for the elimination of foreigners. In those cases where domestic agents cannot directly and immediately substitute their own for foreign fishing effort, we see joint ventures and other indirect attempts at control of foreign fishing activity.[1] Accordingly, at the beginning of the new order of the oceans it is appropriate to be cautious and to reserve judgment on the impact, if any, of the treaty on the structure of world fisheries.

A second difficulty in an attempt to evaluate the impact of extended fishery zones and the Law of the Sea Treaty on world fisheries lies in the bioeconomic complexity of fisheries themselves and in the inadequate data produced by the process of fisheries management throughout the world. The unique source of worldwide data on fisheries is the United Nations Food and Agricultural Organization's (FAO) annual report on the physical volume of output.[2] This report gives output but not price data. In market-oriented economies, fishing activity is primarily driven by the relationship of price minus cost. Therefore, for those countries, a key element is missing in the data set. Even in non-market economies or in those that for several reasons may highly subsidize the fishing industry, the absence of price/cost data removes the crucial issue of the value of the catch from the calculations.

A second, less important data problem involves the classification system utilized by FAO. The FAO divides the world's marine fishing zones into nineteen sub-parts (Northeast Atlantic, Northwest Atlantic, etc.).[3]

While this division is of much greater utility to the analyst than the division proposed by Pope Alexander VI in 1493, it nonetheless raises analytical problems in assigning catch by countries and it also presents difficulties in the case of migratory species (tunas, etc.).[4]

Finally, the FAO species classification must be taken at a reasonable level of aggregation. This leaves one with groupings such as #31 -- Flounders, Halibuts, Soles, or #32 -- Cods, Hakes, Haddocks, etc. Halibut and haddock tend to be higher valued than the other species included with them, therefore the data (metric tons) on output may conceal important value changes; *e.g.*, variation in the physical amount of the c atch of haddock may be offset by changes in the catch of hake, etc.

However, the most substantive problems involved in measuring the impact of extended economic zones on fisheries area, as noted, rooted in the bioeconomic structure of fisheries. This includes: the variation in the separate elements of the biomass that constitute a large marine ecosystem (LME); variation in the aggregate biomass that constitutes an LME; and the ability of the fishermen to change the location, amount and the focus of fishing effort as economic conditions (prices and costs), biological conditions (variance in individual stocks and the aggregate biomass) and institutional parameters (national regulation of fishing effort and changes in boundaries such as the International Court of Justice decision in the *Gulf of Maine* case) alter.[5]

However, at the moment we are limited, in our analysis of the impact of extended fishing zones on the income and wealth of nations, to the data on physical quantity of fish caught. There may be a high variance in the quantity of an individual species of fish available in the fishery; *e.g.*, the U.S. catch of haddock on Georges Bank was at the level of 10,000 tons in the period 1904-1910, peaked at 150,000 tons in 1929, sank to a low of 2,000 tons in 1974, and more recently has recovered to about 20,000 tons.

This observed variation in the catch of haddock in one limited fishery involves the preferred economic position of haddock in the fresh fish market, variation in the stock of haddock due both to "overfishing" and exogenous biological events, significant variation in the aggregate biomass perhaps caused by heavy fishing by foreign fleets in the 1950s and 1960s, and two changes in the institutional rules of the game -- the extensions of fisheries zones by the U.S. and Canada, and the concomitant substitution of coastal state authority for the authority of the international fisheries commission, ICNAF, in the management of the fishery.

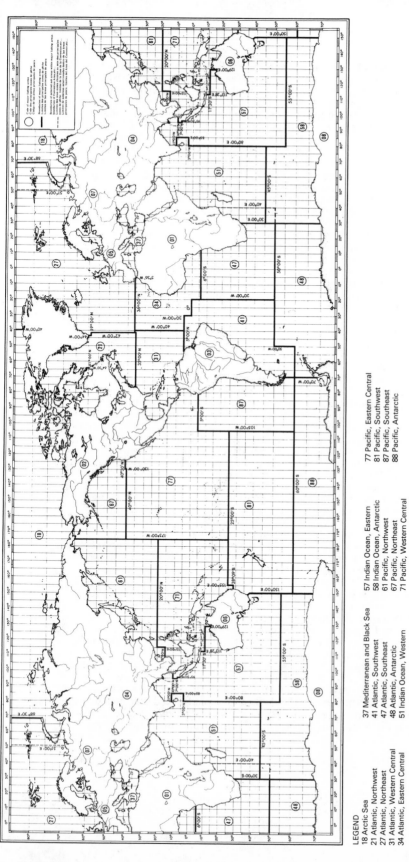

Map 1: Major Fishing Areas for Statistical Purposes

LEGEND

18 Arctic Sea	37 Mediterranean and Black Sea	77 Pacific, Eastern Central
21 Atlantic, Northwest	41 Atlantic, Southwest	81 Pacific, Southwest
27 Atlantic, Northeast	47 Atlantic, Southeast	87 Pacific, Southeast
31 Atlantic, Western Central	48 Atlantic, Antarctic	88 Pacific, Antarctic
34 Atlantic, Eastern Central	51 Indian Ocean, Western	
	57 Indian Ocean, Eastern	
	58 Indian Ocean, Antarctic	
	61 Pacific, Northwest	
	67 Pacific, Northeast	
	71 Pacific, Western Central	

Source: *1982 Yearbook of Fisheries Statistics, Catches and Landings,* v. 54, Rome: Food and Agricultural Organization of the United Nations, 1984. pp.57-58.

Finally, the most recent development is the institution of the legal suit and the settlement rendered by the World Court in the U.S.-Canadian east coast boundary dispute.

This brief enumeration of factors that influence the composition and the volume of the catch, does not include subsidization by governments of new entrants or the expansion of capital and labor in the fishery that result from the expectations of the industry. An additional and perhaps most important source of variance in the catch is a combination of the others -- the voluntary action taken by fishermen (fishing fleets) in response to biological supply changes, foreign (or domestic) competition for that supply, regulation and institutional changes, changes in expectations, and changes in economic (market) conditions; *e.g.*, in the 1960s the Canadians partially subsidized the entry of vessels in the Georges Bank scallop fishery. The response of the New Bedford fleet was to shift fishing effort from the Georges Bank population of scallops to populations offshore in the mid-Atlantic. When these latter populations subsequently declined, the New Bedford fleet again shifted its effort back to Georges Bank.

Note also that this shift of fishing effort may affect the catch statistics across FAO area designations; *e.g.*, while the catch made on Georges Bank was reported properly by New Bedford fishermen as northwest Atlantic catch, the catch made in the west central Atlantic may have been reported in New England. Similar problems involving proper location and attribution of the catch may also occur across national boundaries.

At this point, it is appropriate to ask what are the information requirements that would permit accurate analysis of the establishment of extended fishery zones on the wealth and income of nations? The basic information set required is the same set that is required for bioeconomic modeling of a fishery for the purposes of economically efficient management. However, with the possible exception of a very few limited areas in the world -- *e.g.*, certain fisheries in the northwest Atlantic, northeast Pacific, North Sea -- the necessary data is not available and even if it were, its analysis on a worldwide basis would present major statistical problems.

What can be done, given the known biological and economic measurement problems in fisheries within the framework of the limited data on the production that is available? The approach utilized here is a process of averaging to reduce the observed variance in the catch data. Two periods were selected: the average catch for each country in 1973, 1974, 1975, and for 1981, 1982, and 1983. The former period is intended to provide a benchmark for the level of catch prior to the establishment of most extended fishery zones. For purposes of comparison, the most recent period for which complete FAO data is available, 1981-1982-1983, is used. It is hoped that this latter period reflects some of the adjustments that have taken place under extended fisheries zones (EFZs), but clearly, not enough time has elapsed for these adjustments to have fully worked themselves out.

This paper is limited to comparison of production (catch) data for these two periods. We consider:

1. The change in total catch by country.
2. The "winners" and the "losers" (winners and losers solely in terms of catch, *i.e.*, until we add price and cost to the calculation we cannot ascertain economic impact) over this time frame. Examination of this categorization will point up the several different patterns of

development that are present in world fisheries today. Inspection of this categorization will also allow a comment on the implications of developments in fisheries for the ideological division between the Group of 77 and the developed states at the Conference.

3. Examination of changes in the geographic pattern of production, *i.e.*, changes in catch by FAO areas. This will illustrate the increases in fishing effort by certain coastal states and also some of the impact of EFZs on long distance fleets.

4. Examination of changes in the catch by country by geographic area.

Finally, as part of the conclusions there will be suggestions as to how the analyses may be extended beyond just enumeration of observed changes in catch.

Aggregate Change in Catch by Country

Table 1 (on following page) presents catch date in millions of metric tons for all countries reported separately averaged over the base years 1973-1974-1975 (Mean 1) and ordered on the basis of the 1981-1982-1983 average (Mean 2).

Total catch for all countries rose from 57.1 million metric tons to 66.4, an increase of 16 percent. This increase in output results from a combination of increased demand for fish and the impact of extended fishery zones on both of the extension and intensity of fishing effort. On the basis of current information this latter level of catch is close to the sustainable biological yield of the current mix of the catch of ocean fish.

Perhaps contrary to preliminary expectations about the impact of EEZs on catch, the catch by those most actively engaged in distant water fishing, Japan and the USSR, increased by 8 percent and 6 percent, respectively.

As shown in *Table 2*, if we limit our list to those countries catching 1,000,000 tons or more in either period we reduce the number of countries to nineteen. In the period 1973-1975, these nineteen accounted for 79 percent of the catch and in the period 1981-1983 for 80 percent, so that fewer than 20 nations account for 80 percent of the catch of ocean fish.

In fact, the concentration of the total catch in the hands of a few countries and geographic areas is a key characteristic of world fisheries. Based on the 1981-1983 average catch the leaders, Japan and the USSR, caught almost 30 percent of the world total, while the eight leading fishing nations -- Japan, the USSR, the U.S.A., Chile, China, Norway, Peru and the Republic of Korea -- accounted for 57 percent of the total. Since the FAO reports individually on sixty-five nations with a catch of at least 46,000 metric tons, we find 3 percent of the fishing nations reported on accounting for 30 percent of the landings and 12 percent providing 57 percent of the catch.

Tables 3 and *4* provide a complete list of winners and losers for the period examined. The five leading "winners," in order of gains in catch over the period, are Chile, the U.S.A., Mexico, Japan, and the Republic of Korea. Total increases for all countries including this group were approximately 12,000,000 metric tons, and these five countries accounted for over half (52%) of the increase. It is also of interest that seven of the first ten "winners" were developing countries: Chile, Mexico, the Republic of Korea, Indonesia, Thailand,

142

Table 1

Mean Catch by Country 1973-1975/1981-1983
in descending order based on 1981-1983 Mean Catch

Country	Mean 1	Mean 2	M2-M1	% Change
Japan	9,844,049	10,679,185	835,136	8
USSR	8,422,942	8,950,821	527,879	6
USA	2,746,360	3,894,632	1,148,271	42
Chile	898,310	3,678,637	2,780,327	310
China	3,020,467	3,246,898	226,431	7
Norway	2,656,697	2,607,610	(49,087)	-2
Peru	3,300,800	2,551,087	(749,712)	-23
Korea R.	1,674,352	2,305,251	630,899	38
Thailand	1,429,215	1,970,338	541,124	38
Denmark	1,674,411	1,857,985	183,574	11
Indonesia	939,063	1,490,731	551,669	59
India	1,388,166	1,482,350	94,184	7
Korea D.R.	931,667	1,465,000	533,333	57
Canada	984,641	1,333,018	348,377	35
Mexico	423,528	1,292,357	868,829	205
Spain	1,512,003	1,266,518	(245,484)	-16
Philippines	1,161,947	1,248,273	86,326	7
Iceland	946,650	1,022,797	76,148	8
U.K.	1,058,042	874,131	(183,912)	-17
Other N.E.I.	830,229	852,202	21,973	3
France	790,305	770,546	(19,759)	-3
Malaysia	477,888	728,330	250,442	52
Brazil	583,970	632,775	48,804	8
Poland	663,955	630,963	(32,991)	-5
South Africa	617,724	609,865	(7,859)	-1
Ecuador	184,013	564,141	380,128	207
Turkey	116,631	478,368	361,737	310
Netherlands	336,470	477,641	141,171	42
Vietnam	536,400	457,333	(79,067)	-15
Burma	333,613	446,330	112,717	34
Italy	393,074	428,872	35,797	9
Argentina	245,149	404,425	159,276	65
Morocco	302,262	396,288	94,026	31
Nigeria	231,326	342,270	110,944	48
Germany F.R.	446,938	294,783	(172,155)	-37
Pakistan	180,078	274,244	94,166	52

Table 1 (continued)

Country	Mean 1	Mean 2	M2-M1	% Change
Faero Is.	259,428	273,535	14,106	5
Namibia	770,300	265,617	(504,683)	-66
Sweden	208,838	253,212	44,374	21
Portugal	428,972	253,172	(175,800)	-41
Germany D.R.	354,248	221,715	(132,533)	-37
Senegal	318,442	210,839	(107,603)	-34
Ireland	89,487	202,142	112,655	126
Venezuela	145,012	194,300	49,288	34
Ghana	192,394	191,571	(824)	0
Sri Lanka	102,686	182,897	80,211	78
Hong Kong	136,577	176,815	40,239	29
Cuba	151,101	173,483	22,381	15
Romania	79,410	168,030	88,620	112
Australia	121,277	160,227	38,950	32
Panama	99,588	142,811	43,224	43
Bangladesh	90,667	138,333	47,667	53
New Zealand	65,998	122,716	56,718	86
Finland	85,656	112,023	26,367	31
Angola	339,613	110,762	(228,851)	-67
Greenland	47,718	106,905	59,187	124
Bulgaria	118,754	100,298	(18,455)	-16
Oman	186,283	93,931	(92,353)	-50
Greece	86,700	89,874	3,174	4
Yemen D.R.	36,551	73,943	37,392	102
Ivory Coast	63,740	73,876	10,136	16
UAE	59,667	70,397	10,730	18
Tunisia	39,359	62,489	23,130	59
Belgium	49,361	48,567	(794)	-2
Sierra Leone	66,645	36,139	(30,507)	-46
Iran	46,667	35,045	(11,621)	-25
TOTAL	57,144,473	66,352,658	9,208,186	16

Source: Food and Agriculture Organization of the United Nations, *Yearbook of Fishery Statistics: Catches and Landings*, Rome (several issues).

Table 2

Mean Catch of Countries > 1 million metric tons
(in descending order based on Mean 2 - Mean 1 Catch)
1973-75/1981-83

Country	Mean 1	Mean 2	M2-M1	% Change
Chile	898,310	3,678,637	2,780,327	310
USA	2,746,360	3,894,276	1,147,916	42
Mexico	423,528	1,292,357	868,829	205
Japan	9,844,049	10,679,185	835,136	8
Korea R.	1,674,352	2,303,635	629,283	38
Indonesia	939,063	1,490,731	551,669	59
Thailand	1,429,215	1,970,338	541,124	38
Korea D.R.	931,667	1,465,000	533,333	57
USSR	8,418,576	8,950,821	532,245	6
Canada	984,641	1,333,018	348,377	35
China	3,020,467	3,246,898	226,431	7
Denmark	1,674,411	1,857,985	183,574	11
India	1,388,166	1,482,350	94,184	7
Philippines	1,161,947	1,248,273	86,326	7
Iceland	941,378	1,022,797	81,419	9
Norway	2,656,697	2,607,610	(49,087)	-2
UK	1,058,042	874,131	(183,912)	-17
Spain	1,512,003	1,266,518	(245,484)	-16
Peru	3,300,800	2,551,087	(749,712)	-23
TOTAL 19 Countries	45,003,669	53,215,647	8,211,978	18
TOTAL All Countries (as per Table 1)	57,144,473	66,352,658	9,208,186	16
19 Countries as % of all Countries	79%	80%	89%	

Source: Food and Agriculture Organization of the United Nations,
Yearbook of Fishery Statistics: Catches and Landings,
Rome (several issues).

Table 3

Country Winners and Losers 1973-75/1981-83
Catch in descending order based on M2-M1 (In Metric Tons)

Winning Countries		Mean 1	Mean 2	M2-M1	% Change
Chile	1	898,310	3,678,637	2,780,327	310
USA	2	2,746,360	3,894,632	1,148,271	42
Mexico	3	423,528	1,292,357	868,829	205
Japan	4	9,844,049	10,679,185	835,136	8
Korea R.	5	1,674,352	2,305,251	630,899	38
Indonesia	6	939,063	1,490,731	551,669	59
Thailand	7	1,429,215	1,970,338	541,124	38
Korea D.R.	8	931,667	1,465,000	533,333	57
USSR	9	8,422,942	8,950,821	527,879	6
Ecuador	10	184,013	564,141	380,128	207
Turkey	11	116,631	478,368	361,737	310
Canada	12	984,641	1,333,018	348,377	35
Malaysia	13	477,888	728,330	250,442	52
China	14	3,020,467	3,246,898	226,431	7
Denmark	15	1,674,411	1,857,985	183,574	11
Argentina	16	245,149	404,425	159,276	65
Netherlands	17	336,470	477,641	141,171	42
Burma	18	333,613	446,330	112,717	34
Ireland	19	89,487	202,142	112,655	126
Nigeria	20	231,326	342,270	110,944	48
India	21	1,388,166	1,482,350	94,184	7
Pakistan	22	180,078	274,244	94,166	52
Morocco	23	302,262	396,288	94,026	31
Romania	24	79,410	168,030	88,620	112
Philippines	25	1,161,947	1,248,273	86,326	7
Sri Lanka	26	102,686	182,897	80,211	78
Iceland	27	946,650	1,022,797	76,148	8
Greenland	28	47,718	106,905	59,187	124
New Zealand	29	65,998	122,716	56,718	86
Venezuela	30	145,012	194,300	49,288	34
Brazil	31	583,970	632,775	48,804	8
Bangladesh	32	90,667	138,333	47,667	53
Sweden	33	208,838	253,212	44,374	21
Panama	34	99,588	142,811	43,224	43
Hong Kong	35	136,577	176,815	40,239	29
Australia	36	121,277	160,227	38,950	32
Yemen D.R.	37	36,551	73,943	37,392	102
Italy	38	393,074	428,872	35,797	9
Finland	39	85,656	112,023	26,367	31
Tunisia	40	39,359	62,489	23,130	59
Cuba	41	151,101	173,483	22,381	15
Other N.E.I.	42	830,229	852,202	21,973	3

Winning Countries		Mean 1	Mean 2	M2-M1	Change
Faero Is.	43	259,428	273,535	14,106	5
UAE	44	59,667	70,397	10,730	18
Ivory Coast	45	63,740	73,876	10,136	16
Greece	46	86,700	89,874	3,174	4
TOTAL WINNERS				12,052,237	28

Losing Countries		Mean 1	Mean 2	M2-M1	Change
Belgium	1	49,361	48,567	(794)	-2
Ghana	2	192,394	191,571	(824)	0
South Africa	3	617,724	609,865	(7,859)	-1
Iran	4	46,667	35,045	(11,621)	-25
Bulgaria	5	118,754	100,298	(18,455)	-16
France	6	790,305	770,546	(19,759)	-3
Sierra Leone	7	66,645	36,139	(30,507)	-46
Poland	8	663,955	630,963	(32,991)	-5
Norway	9	2,656,697	2,607,610	(49,087)	-2
Vietnam	10	536,400	457,333	(79,067)	-15
Oman	11	186,283	93,931	(92,353)	-50
Senegal	12	318,442	210,839	(107,603)	-34
Germany D.R.	13	354,248	221,715	(132,533)	-37
Germany F.R.	14	466,938	294,783	(172,155)	-37
Portugal	15	428,972	253,172	(175,800)	-41
UK	16	1,058,042	874,131	(183,912)	-17
Angola	17	339,613	110,762	(228,851)	-67
Spain	18	1,512,003	1,266,518	(245,484)	-16
Namibia	19	770,300	265,617	(504,683)	-66
Peru	20	3,300,800	2,551,087	(749,712)	-23
TOTAL LOSERS				(2,844,051)	-20
GRAND TOTAL		57,144,473	66,352,658	9,208,186	16

Source: Food and Agriculture Organization of the United Nations, *Yearbook of Fishery Statistics: Catches and Landings*, Rome (several issues).

Table 4

Mean Catch of Countries > 1 Million Metric Tons
(in descending order based on Mean 2 - Mean 1 Catch)
1973-75/1981-83

Country	Mean 1	Mean 2	M2-M1	% Change
Chile	898,310	3,678,637	2,780,327	310
USA	2,746,360	3,894,276	1,147,916	42
Mexico	423,528	1,292,357	868,829	205
Japan	9,844,049	10,679,185	835,136	8
Korea R.	1,674,352	2,303,635	629,283	38
Indonesia	939,063	1,490,731	551,669	59
Thailand	1,429,215	1,970,338	541,124	38
Korea D.R.	931,667	1,465,000	533,333	57
USSR	8,418,576	8,950,821	532,245	6
Canada	984,641	1,333,018	348,377	35
China	3,020,467	3,246,898	226,431	7
Denmark	1,674,411	1,857,985	183,574	11
India	1,388,166	1,482,350	94,184	7
Philippines	1,161,947	1,248,273	86,326	7
Iceland	941,378	1,022,797	81,419	9
Selected Winners	36,476,128	45,916,301	9,440,173	26
Norway	2,656,697	2,607,610	(49,087)	-2
UK	1,058,042	874,131	(183,912)	-17
Spain	1,512,003	1,266,518	(245,484)	-16
Peru	3,300,800	2,551,087	(749,712)	-23
Selected Losers	8,527,541	7,299,346	(1,228,195)	-14
TOTAL 19 Countries	45,003,669	53,215,647	8,211,978	18
TOTAL All Countries (as per Table 1)	57,144,473	66,352,658	9,208,186	16
19 Countries as % of all Countries	79%	80%	89%	

Source: *Yearbook of Fishery Statistics: Catches and Landings*,
Rome (several issues).

148

Table 5

Change in Countries' Catch in All Regions
During the Period 1973-75/1983-83
(In Metric Tons)

	NNA21	NEA27	WCA31	ECA34	M&BS37	SWA41	SEA47	AA48	WIO51
Canada	334,365	0	0	0	0	0	0	0	0
USA	239,987	0	443,686	(19,835)	0	0	166	0	0
Denmark	614	182,960	0	0	0	0	0	0	0
UK	(7,786)	(176,126)	0	0	0	0	(79,427)	0	0
Japan	(18,393)	(999)	432	(68,301)	(530)	34,265	0	5,035	(6,248)
Norway	(57,969)	82,819	0	(73,937)	0	0	0	0	0
Spain	(122,711)	(148,685)	0	3,042	30,684	0	(3,961)	0	(3,853)
USSR	(1,124,341)	(410,349)	(34,515)	(193,738)	58,516	26,502	302,162	348,166	3,160
Iceland	0	85,051	0	(3,632)	0	0	0	0	0
Mexico	0	0	168,388	0	0	0	0	0	0
Korea R.	0	0	(268)	2,406	0	1,698	592	0	0
India	0	0	0	0	0	0	0	0	10,792
Thailand	0	0	0	0	0	0	0	0	(40,846)
Indonesia	0	0	0	0	0	0	0	0	0
Korea D.R.	0	0	0	0	0	0	0	0	0
China	0	0	0	0	0	0	0	0	0
Philippines	0	0	0	0	0	0	0	0	0
Chile	0	0	0	0	0	0	0	0	0
Peru	0	0	0	0	0	0	0	0	0
Total	(756,233)	(385,330)	577,722	(353,995)	88,670	62,465	218,348	353,201	(36,995)

Table 5 (continued)

	EIO57	AIO58	NWP61	NEP67	WCP71	ECP77	SWP81	SEP87	AP88	TOTAL
Canada	0	0	0	22,151	0	(8,139)	0	0	0	348,377
USA	0	0	0	529,900	34,829	(88,538)	3,143	4,577	0	1,147,916
Denmark	0	0	0	0	0	0	0	0	0	183,574
UK	0	0	0	0	0	0	0	0	0	(183,912)
Japan	(8,399)	26,758	971,705	(160,135)	41,631	39,772	50,957	4,199	2,815	835,136
Norway	0	0	0	0	0	0	0	0	0	(49,087)
Spain	0	0	0	0	0	0	0	0	0	(245,484)
USSR	(193)	80,309	1,473,078	(547,269)	7,465	(62,367)	4,311	596,250	5,099	532,246
Iceland	0	0	0	0	0	0	0	0	0	81,419
Mexico	0	0	0	0	0	700,441	0	0	0	868,829
Korea R.	(906)	1,129	303,905	295,346	13,509	15,625	(13,975)	614	0	629,283
India	135,030	0	0	0	0	0	0	0	0	94,184
Thailand	267,132	0	0	0	273,991	0	0	0	0	541,124
Indonesia	76,637	0	0	0	475,032	0	0	0	0	551,669
Korea D.R.	0	0	533,333	0	0	0	0	0	0	533,333
China	0	0	226,431	0	0	0	0	0	0	226,431
Philippines	0	0	0	0	86,326	0	0	0	0	86,326
Chile	0	0	0	0	0	0	0	2,780,327	0	2,780,327
Peru	0	0	0	0	0	0	0	(749,712)	0	(749,712)
Total	469,300	108,197	3,508,453	139,993	932,783	596,793	44,437	2,636,255	7,914	8,211,978

Source: Food and Agriculture Organization of the United Nations, *Yearbook of Fishery Statistics: Catches and Landings*, Rome (several issues).

Note: Countries included are those with annual catches > 1 million tons only.

the Democratic Republic of Korea and Ecuador. This set includes three Latin American and four Asian states.

Chile, the leading "winner" was, through fortunate circumstances, able to expand its fisheries within its EEZ (*Table 5*). This expansion was not only within a single (FAO) geographic area (the southwest Pacific), but it was essentially directed toward a single species.[6] Since this species represents potentially unstable population unless, and perhaps even if, there is very careful management, the Chilean catch may experience ups and downs similar to the recent history of the Peruvian anchoveta fishery.

The Mexican expansion in fisheries is similar to Chile's in that it takes place within Mexico's EEZ. But Mexico's EEZ is in two ocean areas (western central Atlantic, eastern central Pacific). Furthermore, while there is some concentration by species in the expansion of Mexican landings, the stocks of fish exploited by Mexico are more widely distributed and are perhaps more stable biologically than Chile's and therefore -- again assuming the usual heroic assumption of competent biological management -- Mexico's landings are on a sounder biological basis than Chile's.

The case of the U.S.A. is essentially an illustration of the national benefits of a policy of protectionism, *i.e.*, the U.S. expansion is within its several fishing areas at the expense of foreign fishermen. However, the U.S. policy is really more than just protectionism. In normal economic usage the term "protectionism" refers to some technique (tariff, quota, etc.) used to exclude others from or raise the cost to them of selling in the domestic market. The objective of the protectionist policy is to "protect" domestic producers from foreign competitors. Currently, U.S. fisheries policy certainly shows evidence of traditional protectionism.[7] However, the policy is dualistic; *i.e.*, the U.S. allows certain fish products in duty-free, but it behaves toward the fishery resources within U.S. EFZs as if they were under complete U.S. sovereignty. The assumption of complete U.S. hegemony in its EFZs is widespread and is suggestive of how the problem of creeping jurisdiction conflicts with the LOS concept of the legal position of EEZs. In essence, the U.S.A. has just followed a policy of driving the rascals out -- primarily the USSR, but more recently to an increasing extent, Japan -- and U.S. fishermen have reaped the advantage in several geographic areas utilizing a variety of species.[8]

Finally, U.S. exclusive fisheries policy and the fishery policies of many other states raise a question about the theoretical worldwide commitment to the full utilization of stocks, but that is another story.

In many ways Japan and the USSR are the most interesting of winners. Despite a worldwide adoption of EFZs and exclusive policies, Japan and the USSR have managed to adjust the activities of their long-distance fleets, and by their adroit response to changed conditions, they have maintained their level of catch. They have accompanied this by a combination of expansion of the geographic areas fished, more intensive fishing effort within their own EEZs as well as elsewhere, and by negotiation of a variety of institutional arrangements, *e.g.*, joint ventures, etc., that permits them to maintain some level of catch in the EEZ of others.

The losers exhibit characteristics that are mirror images of the winners. The decline in the catch of the largest loser, Peru, was primarily a decline in the catch of the same single species classification within Peru's EFZ. Results in Peru may be considered as the reverse of the results in Chile, although the rise and decline of the Peruvian anchoveta fishery has a long history as well as a linkage in the early 1980s with the geophysical phenomena of *El Nino*.

The losses suffered by Spain, the U.K., the two Germanies, Norway and Poland are linked both to biological phenomena, especially the decline in the herring population, and to the problems encountered by their fleets under extended jurisdiction.

Charts 1 and *2* indicate the change in catch by FAO area. *Chart 3* shows the distribution of catch by region in the period 1981-1983. For reasons noted below the heavy increases in catch were in the Pacific, with the northwest Pacific producing the greatest increase in catch. Conversely, the northwest Atlantic, dominated by the fisheries policies of Canada and the U.S.A., experienced the largest decline in catch.

Table 5 presents the changes in catch in metric tons by country by region. The changes in pattern of fishing effort by the USSR and Japan suggest the pressure imposed in these countries by the new regime. As noted above, the USSR managed an overall increase in catch of 6 percent, or approximately 500,000 metric tons. This increase was achieved despite pressure from the United States that essentially eliminated the Russian catch in U.S. EFZs. The Russians lost 1,100,000 tons in the northwest Atlantic, 410,000 in the northeast Atlantic, and 547,000 in the northeast Pacific. Total Russian losses in all regions were 2,373 million tons. The Russian response to this catastrophic decline in catch (a loss of almost 4 percent of the entire world catch) was worldwide. Significant gains were made in the southeast Atlantic, in the Antarctic Atlantic region and in the southeast Pacific. But the bulk of the the loss, 1,500,000 tons, was made up in the Russian EFZ, the northwest Pacific. What these massive shifts in fishing effort mean for the condition of the resource in the northwest Pacific remains to be seen.

CHART 1

INCREASES BY REGION 1973-75/1981-83

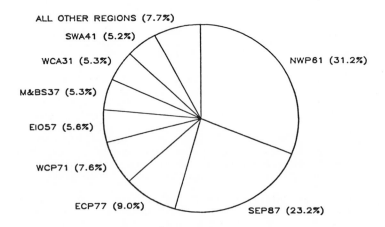

CHART 2

DECREASES BY REGION 1973-75/1981-83

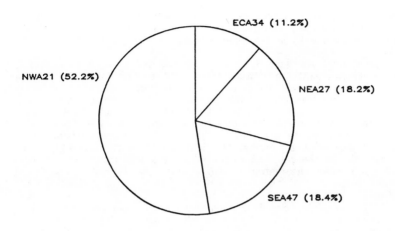

ECA34 (11.2%)

NWA21 (52.2%)

NEA27 (18.2%)

SEA47 (18.4%)

CHART 3

MEAN CATCH BY REGION 1981-83

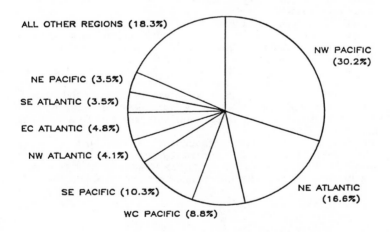

ALL OTHER REGIONS (18.3%)

NW PACIFIC (30.2%)

NE PACIFIC (3.5%)

SE ATLANTIC (3.5%)

EC ATLANTIC (4.8%)

NW ATLANTIC (4.1%)

SE PACIFIC (10.3%)

WC PACIFIC (8.8%)

NE ATLANTIC (16.6%)

The northwest Atlantic, controlled by two countries -- Canada and the U.S.A. -- experienced the largest decline in the catch. This decline came about primarily for three reasons: a decline in the aggregate biomass as a result of overfishing in the 1950s and the 1960s, a tendency by those countries to limit their fishing effort to catching species with a high market value, and a reduction of foreign fishing to benefit their own nationals. Conversely, great pressure has been applied to the stocks in the northwest Pacific by the USSR, the two Koreas and China.

It is much too early to know what the conservation effects of this worldwide shift in fishing effort will be. However, it is unlikely, given the very limited resources devoted to stock assessment throughout the world, that we will see the imposition of effective conservation measures prior to observed changes (declines) in catch. Furthermore, given the complexity of the bioeconomic structure of fisheries, it is extremely difficult to pinpoint the source of observed variance in stocks or aggregate biomasses. The inability to point knowingly and emphatically to the cause of changes in the stocks makes the imposition of effective conservation measures politically very difficult.

Unfinished Business

The Law of the Sea Treaty marks a period in which there has been a massive reallocation of the resources, primarily fish stocks hydrocarbons, from the international commons to the control of the coastal state.

This paper has presented evidence based on the geographic pattern of the physical volume of catch of fish that suggests how the extension of fishery zones has begun to influence the distribution of the catch. However, the observed shifting of the aggregate catch just hints at the more substantive questions that underlie this worldwide redistribution of assets, the resources of the continental shelves.

We need to examine the composition of the catch to note changes in the species caught. This will permit exploration of several issues, among them: how is the changing pattern of the catch affecting the conservation of the stocks?

Further, if we examine the catch by species can we, by utilizing proxy prices, develop a series that will provide approximate measures of the value of the catch by country? If, as is suggested, it is possible to transform the physical output data into reasonable data on values, we can then begin to compute the value of the fish stocks. These fish stocks are assets -- assets that have been, by the creation of EFZs,[9] internalized into the national asset structure of the coastal state.[10] Finally, given the value of the assets, we can begin to think about the potential flow of income from these assets and how this flow will augment the income of nations.[11]

This flow of income must be thought of as potential since, even though the assets have been internalized by the coastal state in order to optimize the yield from its newly gained wealth, each state must come to grips in some way with the common property problem.

NOTES

1. "The TALFF has decreased progressively in most fisheries as U.S. fishermen's catches have grown. The domestic harvest has increased substantially in some areas with the growth of 'joint ventures,' more correctly described as 'over-the-side sales.' United States fishermen harvest fish, transfer their catches at sea, and are reimbursed according to an agreed contract or on some other basis. The cooperative activity is seen as a means to give U.S. fishermen working experience in fisheries for which there were previously only limited markets. We expect this to decrease, and maybe disappear eventually, as U.S. processors become the purchasers of fish." -- in "Allocation of Fishery Resources in U.S. Fishery Management Plans," Roland Finch, Director, Office of Fisheries Management, NMFS, NOAA, U.S. Dept. of Commerce, OECD, Committee for Fisheries, Paris, 7th May, 1985, FI/260.

2. Food and Agriculture Organization of the United Nations, *Yearbook of Fishery Statistics: Catches and Landings*, Rome.

3. The FAO classification of the major "marine" fishing areas is as follows:

Arctic Sea	18	Western Indian Ocean	51
Northwest Atlantic	21	Eastern Indian Ocean	57
Northeast Atlantic	27	Antarctic Indian Ocean	58
Western Central Atlantic	31	Northwest Pacific	61
Eastern Central Atlantic	34	Northeast Pacific	67
Mediterranean and Black Sea	37	Western Central Pacific	71
Southwest Atlantic	41	Eastern Central Pacific	77
Southeast Atlantic	47	Southwest Pacific	81
Antarctic Atlantic	48	Southeast Pacific	87
		Antarctic Pacific	88

The Arctic Sea marine fishing area, #18, is reported to have no catch in all years and for all practical purposes we can consider the eighteen remaining marine fishing areas as the relevant ones to be studied. In addition, the FAO classification includes eight "inland" waters fishing areas. Source: *Yearbook of Fishery Statistics: Catches and Landings*, 1983, issued by FAO, Rome.

4. See note 1, p. 3.

5. See G. Pontecorvo, "Supply, Demand and Common Property: The Historical Dynamics of the Fisheries of Georges Bank; Some Preliminary Observations," *Crutchfield Festschrift*, forthcoming, G. Pontecorvo, "Cost-Benefit of Measuring Resource Variability in Large Marine Ecosystems," New York, publication forthcoming. J. Donaldson and G. Pontecorvo, "Economic Rationalization of Fisheries: The Problem of Conflicting National Interests on Georges Bank," (1980) 8 *Ocean Development and International Law Journal*, 149-169.

6. These species are entitled, "Herrings, Sardines, Anchovies, etc.," in the FAO *Yearbook on Fishery Statistics: Catches and Landings*, and appears in Table B-35 in the FAO publication.

7. "We expect that domestic fishermen will eventually displace foreign fishermen entirely but whether this will be fully achieved remains to be seen. One obvious limitation is that as foreign fishing allocations are reduced the incentives for foreign nations to assist in developing U.S. industry and trade in fishery products

155

will also tend to diminish. Full displacement of foreign fishermen off U.S. coasts will depend on the growth of the U.S. processing industry, which is likely to be constrained by economic limitations, and the acceptance by the U.S. public of fishery products that were previously ignored." Finch, *op. cit.*, p. 3.

8. "In contrast to the protracted negotiations surrounding the Japanese violation of the IWC sperm whaling ban, when the USSR exceeded its share of the minke whale quota for the Antarctic whaling fleet, it was quickly certified under Packwood-Magnuson on April 3 and had its allocation to fish in the U.S. 200-mile zone cut shortly thereafter." "Ocean Policy News," May 1985, Citizens for Ocean Law, Washington, D.C.

9. They are assets in the same sense as agricultural land, industrial plants, etc., and the necessity for conservation measures is to maintain these assets over time.

10. Giulio Pontecorvo, "Division of the Spoils: Hydrocarbons and Living Resources," Ch. 2, *The New Order of the Oceans: From Abundance and Freedom of the Seas to Scarcity and Management of the Uses of the Seas*, Columbia University Press, forthcoming.

11. "The Contribution of the Ocean Sector to the United States Economy," G. Pontecorvo, M. Wilkinson, R. Anderson and M. Holdowsky, *Science*, vol. 208, May 30, 1980, pp. 1001-1006.

TYPES OF AGREEMENTS
FOR EXPLOITATION OF
EEZ FISHERIES

W.R. Edeson
Faculty of Law
Australian National University

The aim of this paper is to review the types of agreements that are currently being employed to regulate access to 200-mile zones. For this purpose, exclusive economic zones and 200-mile fishing zones proclaimed in the light of developments at UNCLOS III will be regarded as synonymous, except where special features of a particular claim need to be highlighted. Because many countries now treat the territorial sea and the 200-mile zone as parts of the same regime for fisheries management purposes, the territorial sea will also be included where appropriate. The predominant focus will be the use of fishing agreements regulating access to the 200-mile zones of developing countries, including agreements amongst developing countries, and between developing and developed countries.

At the outset, it has to be stressed that the number of fishing agreements is extensive,[1] and it is necessary to be selective even within the limitations referred to. Where possible, the more recent trends in state practice will be considered.

The UN Convention

The provisions of the 1982 UN Convention on the Law of the Sea regarding fisheries have been analyzed elsewhere, and it is not proposed here to canvas them,[2] except to highlight those provisions which contemplate some form of international agreement in the context of the EEZ.

Article 62 requires the coastal state to give access to other states to any declared surplus and refers to "agreements and other arrangements" as being the means by which effect will be given to this obligation. The possibilities that this phrase permits will be discussed later. These are, however, several other contexts in which some form of international agreement is contemplated, both directly, or in some instances indirectly, where the Convention refers to cooperation, whether at the sub-regional, regional or global level. Reference can be made to:

Article 61(2), which, "as appropriate," requires the coastal state and competent international organizations, whether sub-regional, regional or global, to cooperate in the formulation of conservation and management measures to ensure "that the maintenance of the living resources in the exclusive economic zone is not endangered by over-exploitation";

Article 61(3), which requires coastal state conservation measures to take into account, amongst other things, "any generally recommended international minimum standards whether sub-regional, regional or global";

Article 61(5), which requires where appropriate the regular contribution and exchange of "available scientific information, catch and fishing effort statistics, and other data relevant to the conservation of fish stocks" through competent international organizations, whether

157

sub-regional, regional or global, including states whose nationals are allowed to fish in the EEZ;

Article 63, which deals with shared and straddling stocks, refers to cooperation either directly or through appropriate sub-regional or regional organizations, in the case of shared stocks to agree upon the measures necessary to coordinate their conservation and development, in the case of straddling stocks, with respect to their conservation only;

Article 64, dealing with highly migratory species, refers to cooperation between the coastal state and other states whose nationals fish in the region, who are to cooperate *directly* or through appropriate international organizations, and in regions where there is no such organization, to cooperate to establish such an organization and participate in its work;

Article 65 on marine mammals refers to cooperation with a view to the conservation of marine mammals, and in the case of cetaceans to work through the appropriate international organizations for their conservation, management and study;

Article 66, which deals with anadromous stocks, at several points contemplates consultations and agreements -- the state of origin may establish the total allowable catch after consultations with certain specified states; where fishing for anadromous stocks is conducted dis-beyond the outer limits of the EEZ (*i.e.*, where there would be economic location for a state other than the state of origin), in which case the states concerned *shall maintain consultations with a view to achieving agreement*, the state of origin is to "cooperate" in minimizing economic dislocation in such other states fishing these stocks; further, Article 66(3)(c) adds that such states "participating by agreement with the State of origin in measures to renew anadromous stocks, particularly by expenditures for that purpose, shall be given special consideration by the State of origin..."; enforcement of regulations regarding anadromous stocks beyond the EEZ are to be by agreement between the state of origin and the other states concerned; and where anadromous stocks migrate into or through the EEZ of a state other than the state of origin, that state is to "cooperate" with the state of origin regarding their conservation and management. The Article ends by requiring the state of origin and states fishing these stocks to make "arrangements for the implementation" of the article, where appropriate, through *regional* organizations.

With catadromous species (*Article 67*), there is a requirement to "regulate by agreement" the management and harvesting of catadromous fish which migrate through the EEZ of a state other than the coastal state in whose waters they spend the greater part of their life cycle. In addition, the agreement is to "ensure the rational management of the species and take into account the responsibilities" of the coastal state referred to.

Articles 69 and 70 deal with the rights of land-locked and geographically disadvantaged states to participate in the exploitation of part of the surplus of living resources of the EEZ's of coastal states of the same sub-region or region, and where that right is found to exist, Article 69(2) and Article 70(3) require that that participation shall be established through bilateral, sub-regional or regional agreements, taking into account certain specified factors. Likewise, Article 69(3) and Article 70(4) refer to the coastal state and other states concerned *cooperating* in the establishment of equitable arrangements on a bilateral, sub-regional or regional basis for the participation of land-locked and geographically disadvantaged states, where the harvesting capacity of the coastal state is approaching a point where it could harvest the entire allowable catch in its EEZ.[3]

Article 297(3)(e) requires that agreements negotiated pursuant to Articles 69 and 70, unless the parties otherwise agree, are to include a clause on measures which they shall take in order to minimize the possibility of a disagreement concerning the interpretation or application of the agreement, and how to proceed in the event of disagreement.

Finally, *Article 73*, which deals with enforcement of coastal state laws and regulations, stipulates in paragraph (3) the need for agreement of "the States concerned" before imprisonment is imposed on breaches of fisheries laws and regulations.[4]

The question, not easily resolved, is *what obligations are imposed by these various clauses?* It will be obvious that in some instances cooperation, whether or not in treaty form, is all that is contemplated (for example, Article 61(2) and (3)). A more positive obligation to seek agreement is expected in Article 62(2) (granting of access to foreign states to a declared surplus) though clearly, by referring to "agreements or other arrangements," it does not matter whether there exists a formal treaty governing access. Likewise, Article 67(3) imposes an obligation to reach agreement. On the other hand, Article 63(1) and (2) ("seek to agree") and Article 66(3a) ("maintain consultations with a view to achieving agreement") do not seem to impose any binding obligation to reach agreement. Curiously, Article 64, which has generated the most controversy, is less strongly worded than the articles referred to, merely requiring that the coastal state and other states whose nationals fish in the region for highly migratory species "shall cooperate directly or through appropriate international organizations with a view of ensuring" etc., and where there is such a body they "shall cooperate to establish [one] and participate in its work." It does not, in other words, actually refer to the need for agreement, though that is obviously what is intended will happen.

Articles 69(3) and 70(4) are ambiguously worded in that they seem to suggest that the coastal state is under an obligation to grant access in certain situations (*i.e.*, when its harvesting capacity would enable it to harvest the entire allowable catch in its EEZ). The difficulty is that paragraph (1), in referring to the "right" of landlocked and geographically disadvantaged states, is to be exercised in conformity with Articles 61 and 62, the latter in paragraph (3) merely requiring the coastal state to take into account, *inter alia*, Articles 69 and 70.

It may be that not all much turns on the precise terms used to describe how access shall be achieved, the more important question being whether the states in question have fulfilled the broad obligations indicated (*e.g.*, to cooperate with a view to seeking agreement, or to cooperate with a view to ensuring conservation, etc.) in accordance with the fundamental requirement of international law, reflected in Article 300, that "States Parties shall fulfill in good faith the obligations assumed under this Convention and shall exercise the rights, jurisdiction and freedoms recognized in this Convention in a manner which would not constitute an abuse of right."

That said, the question which then arises, assuming that some such broader "right" or "obligation" has been established, is whether it would be justiceable, or would be subject to the exemptions set out in Article 297(3), a question well beyond the scope of this paper.

Agreements and Other Arrangements

So long as the objective of optimum utilization is promoted by the coastal state, and the conservation standards of Article 61 are observed, it is clear that Article 62 is not concerned to regulate the precise method by which the coastal state gives access when it refers to "agreements and other arrangements" as the means by which other states shall be given access to the surplus of the allowable catch. This would be apparent from the use of "other arrangements," but in any event, it is arguable that the reference to "agreements," although covering formal treaties, whether bilateral or multilateral, also covers documents or understandings rather less formal than a treaty.[5]

It is proposed now to review briefly the types of agreements and arrangements most commonly employed to give access to foreigners to the fisheries resources of the EEZ.

First, a common method of granting access is by a direct licensing system. Several national laws applying in 200-mile zones provide for the issuance of licenses to foreigners without the need for the negotiation of a bilateral access agreement.[6] In such circumstances, although the foreign fisherman or vessel is usually subject to greater restrictions and conditions not applicable to local fishermen or local vessels, an application is made directly to the relevant authorities of the coastal state. In practice, of course, the foreign fisherman will often have the assistance of his government in seeking a license, and in some instances, despite the lack of any legal necessity to do so, a bilateral access agreement will nonetheless often be negotiated concerning the issuance of licenses to nationals of a particular state. From the point of view of domestic law, apart from instances where treaties might operate directly in certain municipal legal systems, it will be the legislation which will provide the legal basis for the access granted rather than the agreement.[7]

It is also thought that access to foreign fishermen or vessels will sometimes be granted by means of informal executive authorization. In St. Lucia, for example, it was at one stage the practice to issue licenses to foreign fishermen to fish within territorial waters, without reliance on any particular statutory authority, and to impose certain conservation and management measures on the foreign fishermen.[8] In some instances, furthermore, it is believed that there exist informal understandings that certain laws of the coastal state will not be enforced against particular classes of foreign fishermen or vessels, though documentation of such practices is difficult to obtain. From the international law aspect,[9] it would not seem to matter as the instances referred to above would all seem to come within "other arrangements," provided, of course, the objective of optimum utilization was in consequence promoted, and the conservation standards of Article 61 were satisfied.

The most common method by which access to the fisheries of a 200-mile zone is regulated is a bilateral access agreement between the coastal state and the foreign state whose nationals, or fishing vessels possessing its nationality, are to undertake fishing in the 200-mile zone. A major advantage of such an agreement is that it is often possible for the coastal state to cast some of the administrative and enforcement burden onto the foreign state. This can be done, for example, by specifying in the agreement the number of licenses that will be issued, the number of fishing days allowed, species that may be fished for and in what quantities, and leave to the foreign state the task of distributing the licenses and sharing out the resources allocated. The coastal state may also be able to put some of the enforcement burden onto the foreign state, for example, by making it responsible for punishing breaches of the license conditions, or even more generally, coastal state laws and regulations concerning foreign fishing and by providing the foreign state with the incentive to encourage compliance by in effect allowing one state the right to secure access for its nationals so long as they comply with coastal state requirements.[10] Such an approach could be particularly advantageous to coastal states lacking an effective surveillance capacity.

Despite these advantages, the requirement of a bilateral agreement may entail less flexibility, as the negotiation of the agreement can be a time-consuming and protracted exercise. This could be an important factor for countries lacking in bureaucratic resources. In some situations, protracted negotiations may be regarded as advantageous from the coastal state's point of view, as it may be seen as a means of delaying granting access to particular foreign fishermen and may result in a certain state or states directing their negotiating efforts elsewhere.

So far as the Convention is concerned, there is not much that the foreign state can do, for leaving aside the question whether such a motivation might be covered by the reference in Article 62 to relevant factors including *inter alia* "its other national interests," the situation would seem to be covered by Article 297(3) which exempts, amongst other things, "the allocation of surpluses to other States" from the compulsory procedures entailing binding decisions. It would only be subject to a compulsory conciliation procedure if "a coastal State has arbitrarily refused to allocate to any state, under Articles 62, 69 and 70 and under the terms and conditions established by the coastal State consistent with this Convention, the whole or part of the surplus it has declared to exist." So long as negotiations were taking place, it would be difficult to establish that an arbitrary refusal has occurred.

For many countries, the need to have a bilateral access agreement is written into the domestic law,[11] which may or may not indicate some of the terms which the agreement must contain or the standards it must satisfy.

The types of bilateral agreements are numerous, and the conditions that they may contain vary quite dramatically. In some instances fisheries matters can be included in agreements concerning technical cooperation, friendship agreements, boundary agreements, etc.[12] Others are, in effect, umbrella or framework agreements laying down certain general principles that are often supplemented by more detailed, short-term agreements or protocols.[13]

Where the agreement is directly concerned with fisheries, it may or may not contain specific management clauses, in some cases merely requiring that the foreign fishing vessel or vessels fish in accordance with coastal state licenses issued, the terms and conditions attached thereto, and any applicable laws of the coastal state; in other cases, detailed requirements are set out regarding the area of fishing, the volume of catch, by-catch limitations, number of vessels that may be engaged in fishing, fishing methods, details of the vessel and crew, including navigation facilities, registration, sea worthiness, local representation, and many other details.[14]

One trend emerging is that, whereas in the earlier stages of UNCLOS III access agreements were negotiated often for short periods of time, a year being quite common, there has been an increasing tendency towards longer periods of access being granted, or annual reviews of access rights within the context of framework agreements or at least expectations that particular foreign fishing operations will be allowed to continue for a reasonable period of time. This trend in part would reflect the need to afford a measure of tenure to foreign fishing interests which may have invested capital and effort in developing a particular fishery and which may have made contributions to the development of the fishing industry of the coastal state.

Although multilateral fisheries agreements and regional fisheries bodies have been well established, particularly in the North Atlantic region and more generally through the various regional fisheries commissions established by the FAO well before UNCLOS III, for many other areas their establishment has been considerably slower.[15] The UN Convention envisages an important role for sub-regional and regional cooperation in fisheries matters, and it is proposed now to discuss two recent important regional developments of principal importance to developing countries.

These are, first, moves towards enhanced regional cooperation in fisheries in the Gulf of Guinea and amongst the small island states of the Caribbean; and secondly, in respect of highly migratory species, attempts to provide a regime that will adequately accommodate on the one hand the interests of the United States with its current policy of not recognizing coastal state sovereign rights over tuna within 200-mile zones, and on the other, the coastal states in both the Eastern and Western Pacific regions which both claim and have on occasions exercised those rights with respect to U.S.-registered tuna vessels.

The moves in the Gulf of Guinea and amongst the small island states of the Caribbean are significant for two reasons: first, they are essentially moves towards greater cooperation amongst developing countries in the same sub-region or region; secondly, they reflect a desire to encourage sub-groups for "natural management areas."

In the Gulf of Guinea, there was completed on June 21, 1974, a convention relating to the regional development of fisheries in the Gulf of Guinea, the countries participating being the Congo, Gabon, Equatorial Guinea, Sao Tome e Principe, and Zaire.[15] The Convention will give effect to the exhortation in Article 63 of the UN Convention for states to cooperate with respect to shared and straddling stocks directly or through appropriate sub-regional or regional organizations. The Preamble also refers to the migratory nature of the stocks in the region; however, the Convention will not be confined to these categories. Amongst its actual and potential participants are geographically disadvantaged states; thus, this Convention could be the first practical expression of the objectives in Article 70 of the UN Convention also.[17]

The Convention covers in the south the Congo and Zaire and extends North to include the Cameroons. Angola is eligible to participate, but Nigeria and Ghana, geographically part of the Gulf, are not. The reason for this appears to be that the latter two are regarded as too large in relation to the members.[18] It only applies to the EEZs of the member states and is not intended to compete with other regional bodies such as CECAF or ICCAT.

The aim of the agreement is to allow member states to coordinate, harmonize and develop the exploitation of the fisheries, having regard to common stocks found throughout their EEZ s. The agreement also refers to the protection of the marine environment and to development of research. It also aims to develop a unified attitude towards third state fishing vessels, and non-discriminatory priority to fishing vessels from Gulf states. It also envisages a single regime covering conditions of capture and control of fishing operations.

A regional committee on fisheries in the Gulf is also established which has a Council of Ministers (its policy organ) and a Secretariat (its executive organ), and which is to be based in Libreville, Gabon. Amongst the objectives of the Committee referred to are:

Harmonization of national management policies for fisheries and of technical and administrative relations in fisheries matters; cooperation in relations with foreign states fishing in the zone, as well as in surveillance and the respect for fishing regulations. Likewise, the Committee has as its task developing cooperation among member states with a view to facilitating reciprocal rights of access in each other's EEZs and industrial development relating to fisheries and the commercialization of fisheries. Another of the Committee's functions concerns the professional training of fishermen, fisheries research and protection of the marine environment.

The Council of Ministers (one state equals one vote -- an absolute majority is required) is empowered to make recommendations only. Its recommendations will, however, take effect three months after having been notified, and within that period, any government may object to the recommendation, thereby rendering it inapplicable, although it can withdraw the objection and it would then become obligatory for that state.

It is too early to say whether the Convention will be successful. From the brief description above it will, however, provide, like the South Pacific Forum Fisheries Agency and the Nauru Agreement of 1982, a useful model for states of a sub-region or a region to follow. It is understood that these were in fact regarded as sources of inspiration for the Gulf of Guinea states.

Another agreement, signed on March 29, 1985, provides for the establishment of a sub-regional commission on fisheries for the countries of Cape Verde, The Gambia, Guinea-Bissau, Mauretania, and Senegal. The objective, stated in Article 2, is to undertake the long-term harmonization of the member states' policies as regards fisheries resources, and to strengthen cooperation for the benefit of their re spective populations. The Agreement establishes a Conference of Ministers (which is the supreme authority of the Organization), a coordinating committee, and a Permanent Secretariat. The coordinating committee is described (in Article 9) as the intermediate authority between the Commission and the Secretariat, and is to consist of the Directors of Fisheries or any other designated expert of the member states. It is to guide the work of the Permanent Secretary, especially with regard to the organization of meetings and the execution of deci-sions of the Conference of Ministers, and to the formulation of recom-mendations to the Conference of Ministers on all points to be examined. Article 12 establishes the permanent secretariat, headed by a permanent secretary, who, in addition to executing decisions of the Conference of Ministers, also is responsible for preparing documents concerning appropriate management measures to be taken in the interests of the sub-region, and the elaboration of joint research programs for funding.

It is understood that Mauretania is not proposing to ratify the Convention at the present time, and the future of the Agreement is in consequence uncertain.

In the Caribbean region the small island states of the Lesser Antilles comprising the Organization of Eastern Caribbean States (OECS)[19] have participated in workshops organized by the OECS and the FAO on the harmonization and coordination of fishery regimes, regulations and access agreements. In fact, soon after the establishment of the OECS, the Authority of the Organization met to consider which areas covered by the constituent treaty should be looked at where members should coordinate, harmonize, and pursue policies as a matter of urgency. One of the areas referred to in the treaty being matters relating the sea and its resources, the Authority immediately agreed that it should be accorded a very high priority.[20] The first seminar considered, and reached agreement on, the general form of a harmonized fisheries law for OECS members, while a second workshop, in addition to finalizing the draft harmonized fisheries legislation, also considered harmonized fisheries regulations, and discussed policy towards access agreements and the form and content of those agreements. The draft legislation, now adopted by several OECS members, is intended to facilitate cooperation in fisheries matters and, as well as ensuring that the legislation as a whole is compatible with the fisheries laws of member states, it contains along the following lines:

Regional Co-Operation in Fisheries
1. The Minister may enter into arrangements or agreements with other countries in the region or with any competent regional organization, providing for:
a. the harmonization of systems for the collecting of statistics, and the carrying out of surveys and procedures for assessing the state of the fisheries resources;
b. the harmonization of licensing procedures and conditions in respect of foreign fishing vessels;
c. schemes for the issuance of fishing licenses in respect of foreign fishing vessels by a competent regional organization on behalf of the Minister and the recognition of regional licenses issued by such organization, subject to such conditions as may be specified in the agreement or arrangement and to such additional conditions as the Minister may specify from time to time.
d. the taking of joint or harmonized enforcement measures in respect of foreign fishing vessels contravening fisheries laws in the region;
e. the establishment and operation of joint or regional fisheries management bodies where appropriate;
f. where appropriate, the establishment of a regional register of fishing vessels;
g. such other cooperative measures as appropriate including measures for promoting the welfare of fishermen and the insurance of fishing vessels and gear.
2. For the purpose of giving effect to any arrangement or agreement entered into under this Section, the Minister may by Order published in the Gazette:
a. authorize any competent regional organization designated in the Order to issue fishing licenses in respect of foreign fishing vessels on behalf of the Minister, within the limits set out in the Order;
b. exempt from the requirements of Section -- any foreign fishing vessel or class of foreign fishing vessels holding valid regional fishing licenses issued by a competent regional organization designated in the Order; and

164

c. prescribe the conditions to be observed by foreign fishing vessels exempted under paragraph (b) while fishing or navigating in the fishery waters.

Such a clause would enable the adoption, amongst OECS members, of a regional agreement like the Nauru Agreement (between some of the members of the South Pacific Forum Fisheries Agency), and parts of the clause therein are clearly inspired by that agreement.[21] At the present time, the OECS initiative is the most advanced within the region in achieving cooperation in the fisheries sector.

Further, on October 29, 1982, SELA (Systems Economica Latino Americana) established on OLDEPESCA (Organisation Latino Americana de Desarollo Pesquero -- the Latin American Organization for Fishery Development).

The Agreement establishing OLDEPESCA was signed by Bolivia, Costa Rica, Ecuador, El Salvador, Guatemala, Guyana, Haiti, Honduras, Mexico, Nicaragua, Panama and Peru. The areas of action in which OLDEPESCA is to cooperate are: research into fishery resources, exploitation of fishery resources, industrialization, support of infrastructures, aquaculture, technological development, commercialization, training, and international cooperation.[22]

The development of these bodies, particularly amongst smaller states, and the success of the Forum Fisheries Agency of the South Pacific may point the way in which sub-regional and regional cooperation, as envisaged in many of the fisheries provisions of the EEZ articles in the UN Convention, will occur amongst developing countries.

The second category of multilateral cooperation that is certainly undergoing important development is in respect of tuna management in the Western and Eastern Pacific regions. Against the background of the United States refusal to recognize the sovereign rights of the coastal state over tuna, despite an overwhelming body of practice supporting the opening view, with several arrests of U.S. tuna vessels, and the prospect of the Magnuson Act being invoked in the Western Pacific, Papua New Guinea and the Solomon Islands, it is hardly surprising that steps have been taken in the Eastern Pacific region and in the Western Pacific to find a way around the impasse. For many of the island states of the Western Pacific, the right to control the highly migratory species that pass through their 200-mile zones is seen to be vital. Tuna and billfish catches comprise almost 95 percent of total fish catches in the region, and almost 90 percent of that is taken by distant water fishing nations.[23]

To take the Eastern Pacific fleet, an agreement, the Eastern Pacific Ocean Tuna Fishing Agreement, was opened for signature on March 14, 1983, and will come into force thirty days after the deposit of the fifth instrument of ratification or adherence by a coastal state.[24] Although it is doubtful whether the agreement will come into force, it represents an important milestone in accomodating the conflicting viewpoints of coastal states and the U.S. position on tuna. Its principal features are: it covers an enormous area of the Eastern Pacific, stretching from above San Francisco in the United States to above Valparaiso in Chile, though excluding "the areas within the 12-nautical miles of the base line from which the territorial sea is measured and those areas within 200-nautical miles of the baselines of coastal states not signatories to this agreement."[25]

The parties also agree to establish a council, which has *inter alia* the power to issue licenses, to establish license fees within limits indicated in an additional Protocol, to disburse annually the revenues produced by license fees, also in accordance with the Protocol, and to establish regulations for the effective implementation of the Agreement. Contracting parties agree to the issuance of licenses permitting access to fishing in the Agreement Area, with licensing authority vested in the Council, and further agree that in order to fish in the Agreement Area for the species of tuna covered by the Agreement, vessels flying their flags shall be required to have a valid license. Also, the Council, through the Director, or an appointed national authority, shall issue licenses to the owners or their representatives of the Contracting Parties.[26]

It will be apparent that the Agreement is in the nature of a regional licensing arrangement covering tuna in a considerable area of the Eastern Pacific, but its effectiveness will depend on it being accepted by most of the states covered by the Agreement area. It is described in Article 1 of the Agreement as an *interim* regime,[27] and important though it is as an improvement on the conflicts which preceded it, the fact that it does not resolve the basic controversy of coastal state sovereign rights versus international management will probably ensure its interim status. On this point, the treaty is silent except for Article XIII which states that the Agreement does not prejudice the positions of Contracting Parties regarding "internal waters, territorial seas, exclusive economic zones, fishery conservation zones, high seas or sovereign rights or jurisdiction for any other purpose."

In the Western Pacific negotiations are still underway between the United States and the South Pacific Forum Fisheries Agency states (Australia, Federated States of Micronesia, Fiji, Kiribati, Nauru, New Zealand, Palau, Papua New Guinea, Solomon Islands, Tonga, Tuvalu, Vanuatu and Western Samoa).

These talks are aimed at concluding a region-wide fisheries treaty which would govern the access of U.S. tuna vessels to fish in the fishery zones of the member states. At the round of negotiations held in Port Moresby from March 4-8, 1985, the United States announced that the embargo on the importation of tuna from Solomon Islands into the U.S. would be lifted. This announcement removed significant obstacles in the negotiations and it is believed that substantial progress was made at that round of talks. More talks are expected in the near future.

Meanwhile, talks are also continuing between Australia, New Zealand and Japan over management of southern bluefin tuna, and it is hoped that an agreement may be reached next year.

Fisheries and Maritime Boundary Agreements

Bilateral treaties principally concerned with matters other than fisheries may of course impinge on fisheries issues in varying degrees, although it is maritime boundary negotiations that will often have a decisive impact on fisheries arrangements. As maritime boundaries become finalized in treaties, it is increasingly likely that they will deal with fisheries matters, not merely because in many instances, perhaps most, will the boundary line drawn be both the fisheries and the seabed line, or a more general EEZ line, but because in several localities, a more complex set of lines might be required, involving a separation of seabed and fisheries issues, and possibly other issues as well. Even where a single line is drawn, it may nonetheless be appropriate to make special arrangements for granting preferential or exclusive rights to the other party to the agreement. Despite the current enthusiasm of the International Court of Justice in delimiting the continental shelf[28] for a single multipurpose line, it is thought that, especially where the parties choose to continue with negotiations rather than submit the matter to a court or arbitrator, a single multi-purpose line might not be as helpful as the simplicity of the solution it provides would suggest.

The Treaty of Peace and Friendship of 1984 between Argentina and Chile settling the long-standing dispute over the boundary in the Beagle Channel area is one example where the parties, in resolving the long-standing border dispute between them, have agreed to establish a Standing Bilateral Commission "with the purpose of increasing physical integration and economic cooperation." It will undertake "the promotion and development in land links and connections, habilitation of ports and duty free zones, land transport, air transport, electricity connections and telecommunications, exploitation of natural resources, protection of the environment" (Article 12).

An example of a maritime delimitation agreement which involves a substantive provision impinging on fisheries is the Colombia-Dominican Republic-Haiti agreement, which establishes a common scientific research and fishing zone between them.[29]

The Torres Strait Agreement between Australia and Papua New Guinea, ratified by both countries on February 15, 1985, had to contend with a very complex locality. Hardly surprisingly, fisheries and seabed issues were separated, not only as regards the drawing of different lines for those purposes, but also allocations of catches were made for both parties in a manner which came close to integrating the area covered by agreement as a single management area for fisheries purposes.

Amongst the complexities which had to be taken into account in negotiating the Agreement were:

-    three inhabited islands belonging to Australia (Boigu, Dauan, and Saibai) which are only a few hundred meters from the shore of Papua New Guinea, and numerous uninhabited rocks and cays throughout the general locality;
-    navigation by large vessels is effectively restricted to one channel at the present time;
-    the islands of the Torres Strait area are inhabited by the so-called Torres Strait Islanders, who are ethnically distinguishable from both the inhabitants of Papua New Guinea and from the aborigines of the Australian mainland and whose traditional way of life had to be protected;
-    the former colonial relationship of Papua New Guinea to Australia had to be considered;
-    for Australia there was the added constitutional restraint thought to flow from the federal constitution, namely that the cession of any of the islands in the areas that form part of the State of Queensland would require a referendum in that state, as well as the consent of the Parliament of the State.[30]

The Treaty provides for a seabed line which, for most of the area delimited, is also the fisheries line between the two parties.[31] However, in the Torres Strait area itself, the two lines diverge, with the fisheries line extending directly northwards to meet and incorporate the inhabited Australian islands just off the coast of Papua New Guinea, and then proceeding directly southwards to the seabed line. The purpose of this was apparently to ensure that the Australian inhabited islands did not become enclaves within the Papua New Guinea seabed area, as

167

well as reflecting the importance of those islands.[32] On the other hand, the uninhabited islands did become enclaves. In addition to the divergence referred to, the fisheries jurisdiction line terminates in the east before the seabed line does, the point of termination for the fisheries line being the point no longer within a 200-mile zone of either party, whereas the seabed line continues beyond that point.[33] As well as separating the seabed and fisheries line, a third line was drawn, which delimits the Protected Zone.

The Protected Zone is important because within it are special provisions governing the Protected Zone Commercial Fisheries. These will be discussed shortly. These provisions are subject, however, to the provisions on traditional fishing in the Protected Zone. In fact, in Article 10(3) it is stated that

> The principal purpose of the Parties in establishing the Protected Zone, and in determining its northern, southern, eastern and western boundaries, is to acknowledge and protect the traditional way of life and livelihood of the traditional inhabitants including their traditional fishing and free movement.

There are substantive provisions concerning free movement and traditional activities, including traditional fishing, traditional customary rights, protection of the marine environment, and of flora and fauna, a prohibition on mining and drilling of the seabed for ten years after the treaty has entered into force, special provisions concerning the application of immigration, customs, quarantine and health procedures, as well as the creation of liaison arrangements and advisory mechanisms.

These provisions are of wider importance because, in several localities, it is understood that the question of securing of customary fishing rights, especially where they are territorial in character, is being examined in the context of the UN Convention.

Under the Treaty, "Protected Zone Commercial Fisheries" are defined[34] as

> the fisheries resources of present or potential commercial significance within the protected zone and, where a stock of such resources belongs substantially to the Protected Zone but extends into an area outside but near it, the part of that stock found in that area within such limits as are agreed from time to time by the responsible authorities of the Parties.

Because "fisheries resources" is defined elsewhere as including sedentary species, there is no need to distinguish within the Protected Zone between such species and others. It will also be apparent that the Parties have incorporated a "shared stocks" provision into the definition.

Although the fisheries resources within the Protected Zone are shared, and the parties also are to determine jointly the allowable catch (described as the "optimum sustainable yield") of a Protected Zone commercial fishery,[35] there are provisions that apportion that catch between them, which, leaving aside certain transitional entitlements, is as follows: in areas under "Australian" jurisdiction (which would include the territorial sea of Australian islands and its fisheries jurisdiction), Australia is entitled to 75 percent and Papua New Guinea 25 percent of the allowable catch, whereas in areas under "Papua New Guinea's" jurisdiction (including its territorial sea and its fisheries

168

jurisdiction), that allocation is reversed. Two important exceptions exist: first, in the territorial sea around the *un*inhabited Australian rocks and cays, the parties have an equal share of the allowable catch. Secondly, in respect of the commercial barramundi fishery "near the Papua New Guinea coast," Papua New Guinea has the sole entitlement, except within the territorial sea of the Australian islands close to its coast.

There are several other clauses which are important, though space precludes anything other than a brief mention of them here. Reference may be made to detailed liaison arrangements,[36] a Torres Strait Joint Advisory Council[37] provisions concerning the calculation of the allowable catch,[38] cooperation between the parties in licensing arrangements,[39] third state fishing for Protected Zone Commercial Fisheries, and inspection and enforcement procedures.[40]

As regards cooperation in licensing arrangements, in the Protected Zone, each party may issue licenses to fish for any Protected Zone Commercial Fisheries, and is not confined to its jurisdictional area, further each party may request the other to endorse licenses (or by other means) authorizing the holders to fish in the waters under the jurisdiction of the other party. Such persons are required to "comply with the relevant fisheries laws and regulations of the other Party except that they shall be exempt from licensing fees, levies and other charges" imposed.[41]

Third state fishing for Protected Zone Commercial Fisheries is also subject to special requirements. First, there is an obligation to inform and consult concerning proposed fishing where it involves a "joint venture in which there is third state equity participation" or by a "vessel of third state registration or with a crew substantially of the nationality of a third state." The concurrence of the responsible authorities of both parties is required before a license is issued in respect of the "vessels the operations of which are under control of nationals of a third state."[42]

The provisions dealing with inspection and enforcement require the parties to cooperate to prevent violations of the Protected Zone commercial fisheries arrangements and to take appropriate enforcement measures. They are also to ensure that laws adopted for that purpose are mutually consistent, and that each party's fisheries laws and regulations make it an offense for unlicensed or unauthorized fishing to take place, or if licensed or authorized, to act in breach of the other party's laws and regulations. Each party also agrees to investigate suspected offenses against its laws and regulations and to take corrective action when necessary. However, corrective action can only be undertaken by the "authorities of the Party whose nationality is borne by the vessel or person concerned ... and not by the Party in whose area of jurisdiction the offense or suspected offense occurs."[43] Likewise, where an offense has been, or is reasonably considered to have been, committed in the course of traditional fishing, corrective action shall be taken by the authorities of the party of the nationality of the vessel or person concerned, or if detained by the authorities of the other party, they are to be released or handed over to the authorities of the party of the nationality of the vessel. The object of these clauses was, it seems, to ensure so far as possible "that Australian citizens who lived and worked in the Protected Zone did not find themselves suddenly subject to Papua New Guinea jurisdiction because a seabed or fisheries line had arbitrarily been drawn through the Strait."[44]

The Agreement demonstrates what can be achieved through negotiations. The different approaches to seabed delimitation, on the one hand,

and on fisheries jurisdiction, on the other, is perhaps a warning signal that, in localities possessing some of the complexities of the Torres Strait, a single line approach is unlikely to be very helpful, at least as regards fisheries and environmental aspects. In the *Gulf of Maine* case, the International Court was asked, under the Agreement submitting the matter to a Chamber of the Court, to determine "the course of the single maritime boundary that divides the continental shelf and fisheries zones of Canada and the United States of America" in the Gulf of Maine. The Chamber laid down a single line, and acknowledged the trend towards a single line determination on the part of the states with the adoption of exclusive economic zones.[45] It did not, however, rule out altogether the possibility of separate lines being drawn in certain circumstances.[46] In the *Libya/Malta* case (1985), however, the International Court asserted that:

> In view of the Court, even though the present case relates only to the delimitation of the continental shelf and not to that of the exclusive economic zone, the principles and rules underlying the latter concept cannot be left out of consideration. As the 1982 Convention demonstrates, the two institutions -- continental shelf and exclusive economic zone -- are linked together in modern law ... It is in the Court's view incontestable that, apart from those provisions, the institution of the exclusive economic zone, with its rule on entitlement by reason of distance, is shown by the practice of states to have become a part of customary law; ... Although the institutions of the continental shelf and the exclusive economic zone are different and distinct, the rights which the exclusive economic zone entails over the sea-bed of the zone are defined by reference to the regime laid down for the continental shelf. Although there can be a continental shelf where there is no exclusive economic zone, there cannot be an exclusive economic zone without a corresponding continental shelf. It follows that, for juridical and practical reasons, the distance criterion must now apply to the continental shelf as well as to the exclusive economic zone; and this quite apart from the provision as to distance in paragraph 1 of Article 76.[47]

The point of this minor *excursus* into maritime delimitation, however, is to highlight the fact that the clear trend in the Court's decisions towards single multipurpose lines is apt to be a serious oversimplification of the issues that need to be resolved, especially fisheries and environmental issues, in certain complex localities. Arguably, it is necessary to develop, where possible, principles for EEZ delimitation that can deal with those issues in a more sophisticated manner. There is furthermore the risk that the Court's decisions might encourage states to overlook the advantages of more complex solutions, and to assume that the single line approach is the "better" legal solution. However, this is not the occasion to explore this point further.[48]

Umbrella Joint Venture Agreements and Joint Ventures

Space precludes anything but a brief reference to the role of umbrella joint venture agreements and joint venture agreements themselves, which are becoming increasingly important in the development of EEZ fisheries. The umbrella agreement is essentially a bilateral agreement that allows for joint ventures concerning fisheries, fishing gear, fish processing or fish marketing to be entered into between nationals and business organizations of the two states party to the agreement. These agreements usually cover such matters as the extent of local equity to be held by the partner from the state in whose waters fishing will take place, the "seat" of the company, the possibility of favorable fiscal treatment under national law, cooperation in training, and exchange of information (including information on relevant technology).[49] Some countries[50] issue guidelines or minimum requirements as statements of government policy regarding joint ventures with foreign fishing interests, which achieve in a more general way the objectives of the umbrella agreements referred to above.

As to the joint ventures themselves,[51] the joint venture enterprise has become a popular means of developing a particular sector of the economy where the state lacks the necessary skills or manpower or capital, but nonetheless has a resource worth exploiting. As regards fisheries, it is most likely to prove useful in situations where the coastal state has a valuable resource in the waters subject to its jurisdiction, but nonetheless lacks the technical expertise to exploit those resources fully. The joint venture arrangement can be utilized as a means of bringing in foreign capital, or management, or technical skills, or simply the necessary equipment, while the coastal state can, by requiring the inclusion of appropriate clauses in the agreement, provide for local control over the activities of the venture, the transfer of technology, or the training of local personnel. In addition, it may be possible for the same venture, or related ventures, to provide processing expertise in regard to the fish caught, and marketing, either at a local level or in another country or countries.

In theory, therefore, the concept of a joint venture is very attractive, both in relation to the fisheries sector, and as regards other related sectors. It may well provide a solution for certain countries which have a fisheries resource and who wish to have that resource exploited ultimately by their own nationals but, in the interim, are unable to do so.

Despite its apparent advantages, the joint venture system, in fisheries as much as in other sectors, has had a checkered career. In part, this is due to false expectations by one or both parties. The state with the exploitable resource, for example, might expect to gain control over the activities of the venture because it (or its nationals) has a majority holding in the share capital of the venture. Often, however, this control has proved illusory because the overseas partner has important *de facto* controls through its greater management expertise. Sometimes the agreement itself may disguise the real level of foreign control, where, for example, decision making may be vested in foreign managers, under a management agreement, or in an executive committee with, in effect, a veto on the more important decisions. Another difficulty has been differing perceptions about of same agreement -- the coastal state partner often seeing it as an agreement about transfer of technology, training of manpower, etc., while the foreign partner might see the agreement only as a device for gaining access to a particular fishery, while looking on the conditions imposed as irritants, perhaps to be given token observance only.

A complicating factor can occur when the government of the host country may have certain objectives when it permits joint ventures to be set up, but these objectives are not necessarily shared to the same degree by a local private enterprise partner. The government in allowing such a venture might, for example, intend that a transfer of technology should occur, or that local persons should be trained in relevant fisheries skills, while the motive of the local private partner might be simply to make a quick profit.

Not least among the problems that may be encountered is the possibility that very complex business relations can be set up to manipulate profits in such a way that the coastal state partner obtains practically nothing, while the foreign partner, through such techniques as affiliated company transactions and transfer pricing, or through the manipulation of company capital and related loans agreements, maximizes its profits. Woven through these factors are inevitable risks of misunderstandings based on differing cultural assumptions between the parties. Clearly, therefore, if joint ventures are to have any real chance of success, they will need to be planned and negotiated with considerable care.

In addition, it is vital that the government should have a clear idea just what it wants to achieve by a system of joint ventures in fisheries, and that its views are communicated to and clearly understood by all parties. Publication by a government of guidelines or objectives or minimum requirements can be very useful in ensuring that several of the pitfalls mentioned above are avoided.

Finally, it is unlikely that a joint venture will be of much benefit to the country unless there exists in the private or public sector an entity which is able to take an active part in the venture and which can both benefit from and absorb the benefits of participation.

At the risk of overgeneralizing, it does seem that experience over the last ten years in the area of exploiting EEZ fisheries by the use of joint venture mechanisms is doing much to reduce the misunderstandings between the coastal state and the foreign entity, with the result that they are more likely to be negotiated and assembled in a more realistic environment than has always been the case hitherto.[52]

NOTES

1. See, for example, J. Carroz and M. Savini, "The Practice of Coastal States Regarding Foreign Access to Fishery Resources (An analysis of bilateral agreements)" in *Report of the Expert Consultation on the Conditions of Access to the Fish Resources of the Exclusive Economic Zones*, FAO Fisheries Report No. 293, p. 43. In an appendix to the paper, the authors list some 280 "selected" bilateral agreements, entered into between January 1975 and December 1982. For a detailed analysis of fisheries agreements in a particular region, see, by the same authors, "Les Accords de Peche Conclus Par les Etats Africains Riverains de l'Atlantique," (1983) 23 Annuaire Francais de Droit International 675. For a review of fisheries agreements in the Caribbean region, see W. Edeson and J.F. Pulvenis, *The Legal Regime of Fisheries in the Caribbean Region*, p. 93 (Springer Verlag, Berlin 1983).
2. See, for example, R.R. Churchill and A.V. Lowe, *The Law of the Sea*, Ch. XIII; D.P. O'Connell, *The International Law of the Sea*, vol. I, ch. 14, 15, ed. Shearer, 1982; W. Burke, "The Law of the Sea Convention and Fishing Practices of Non-Signatories, with Special Reference to the United States" in J. Van Dyke (ed.) *Consensus and*

Confrontation. The United States and the Law of the Sea Convention, p. 314; W. Burke, "The Law of the Sea Convention Provisions on Conditions of Access to Fisheries Subject to National Jurisdiction" (1984) 63 Ore L. Rev. 73; S. Oda, "Fisheries Under the United Nations Convention on the Law of the Sea," (1983) 77 AJIL 739; and W. Edeson, "Access by Foreign Fishing Vessels to Economic Zones and Problems of Enforcement," Paper presented to the International Law Association, Sydney, June 1982.

3. For a discussion of Arts. 69(3) and 70(4) see W. Burke, in Van Dyke (ed.) *op. cit.* pp. 322-328.
4. For a discussion of the meaning of "violations of fisheries laws and regulations" in Article 73(3), see W. Edeson *op. cit.*, pp. 9-11. Undoubtedly, the flag state of the vessel would be such a state con cerned (N.B. para 4, which refers to the need to notify the flag state), but is it arguable that other states might also be "concerned," such as the state of nationality of the individual, or even where there is a regional or sub-regional arrangement regarding a particular fishery, that those states are all concerned?
5. Contrast, for example, Arts. 110(1) and Arts. 116(a), and note the use of *agreement* in Arts. 66 and 67, and *agree* in Art. 63.
6. For example, Honduras in its Law of June 13, 1980 (Law on the Utilization of Marine Natural Resources), Art. 3 provides that "the State may issue to foreigners licenses or permits to explore or exploit the ... resources ..."
7. For example, this was, and remains, substantially the situation under the Australian Fisheries Act, 1952.
8. For example, no use of dynamite, all fish caught to be sold or otherwise disposed of within St. Lucia, boats to be used for fishing only, no use of trammel nets.
9. The lawfulness of such practices in domestic law will of course vary quite considerably from country to country.
10. For more detailed discussions of these possibilities, see "General Guidelines for Monitoring, Control and Surveillance" p. 153 and "Access Conditions and Compliance Control" by Dean Robb p. 157, *Report of the Expert Consultation on the Conditions of Access to the Fish Resources of the Exclusive Economic Zones*, FAO Fisheries Report No. 293. For some comments on Australian practice, see. W. Edeson, "Access by Foreign Fishing Vessels to Economic Zones and Problems of Enforcement," Paper presented to the International Law Association, Sydney, June 1982.
11. For example, Cuba, Decree No. 2, February 24, 1977: "In order to promote the optimum utilisation of the living resources in the Economic Zone, the Republic of Cuba, through the conclusion of appropriate agreements, shall give other States access to the surplus of the allowable catch ..."; The Bahamas Fisheries Resources (Jurisdiction and Conservation) Act, 1977 Sect. 10(4)(b) requires entry by foreign fishing vessels to be, with minor exceptions, only by means of a bilateral agreement. Likewise, the U.S., in the Fishery Conservation and Management Act, 1976, Sec. 201 (c) provides for a governing international fishery agreement (GIFA) as a condition precedent for foreign fishing in the U.S. fishery zone. The EEC regulations applying in the waters of French Guiana, although not dependent on the negotiation of an agreement, nonetheless states that licenses shall be issued "on request to the authorities of the countries concerned," Regulation 848/81, Art. 2. In the Regional Compendium of Fisheries Legislation (Western Pacific Region) (FAO

Legislative Study No. 35, Rome 1984), p. 13, it is stated that the Federated States of Micronesia, the Marshall Islands, Palau, Vanuatu, and Western Samoa all require the prior negotiation of an umbrella bilateral agreement. In Barbados (the Marine Boundaries and Jurisdiction Act, 1977 Sect. 11) and Grenada (Marine Boundaries Act, 1977), foreign fishing requires either an agreement with the Government or a permit. For other examples, see G. Moore, "Coastal State Requirements for Foreign Fishing" vol. I, *FAO Legislative Study* No. 21, Rev. 1.

12. For a recent example, see the Treaty of Peace and Friendship 1984 between Argentina and Chile, Arts. 12 and 13 of which deal with "Economic Co-operation and Physical Integration." Art. 12 refers to the establishment of a Standing Bilateral Commission to promote and develop initiatives concerning *inter alia* "exploitation of natural resources."

13. For example, the *Australia-Japan Head Agreement* of 17 October 1979, is given practical effect by an annual subsidiary agreement.

14. For details, see J. Carroz and M. Savini, footnote 1 above. In this study, there is a discussion also of the criteria referred to in Art. 62(3), regarding which states ought to be given access. So far as landlocked and geographically disadvantaged states are concerned, no bilateral agreement was noted which referred expressly to these two categories of states, though negotiations amongst Gulf of Guinea states for a regional fisheries treaty would appear to be based on the considerations referred to in Art. 70. Very few agreements were found to refer explicitly to the requirements of developing states in the subregion or region in harvesting part of the surplus, though many were found to refer to the need to minimize economic dislocation in states whose nationals have habitually fished in the zone. Only in a few agreements referred to the factor concerning substantial efforts in research and identification of stocks. See esp. pp. 49-50. For a recent analysis of fisheries agreements in West Africa, see by the same authors the article referred to in note 1 above. For an analysis of fisheries agreements in the Caribbean, see W. Edeson and J. Pulvenis, *op. cit.* Pt. IV.

15. See further J. Carroz, "Institutional Aspects of Fishery Management Under the New Regime of the Oceans" (1984) 21 *San Diego Law Review* 513; A. Koers, "The European Economic Community and International Fisheries Organisations" [1984] *Legal Issues of European Integration*, 113.

16. The Cameroons was also eligible to participate, but owing to a coup at the time of the final draft was completed, did not do so. It is understood that it is now a full participant in the Agreement.

17. J. Carroz and M. Savini report (in 1983) that member countries of the West African Economic Community are negotiating a convention providing for the establishment of a company which will be jointly owned by three landlocked countries (Mali, Niger, Upper Volta) and three coastal states (Ivory Coast, Mauritania, and Senegal), "The Practice of Coastal States Regarding Foreign Access to Fishery Resources," footnote 1 above. See also the Asian Africal Legal Consultative Committee Report (AALC/XXIV/16) "Determination of the Allowable Catch of the Living Resources in the Exclusive Economic Zone in Relation to Land-locked States." At the time of writing, no further information is available on the progress towards completion of the Convention.

18. D. Ruzie, "Une Experience Originale de Co-operation: la Mise en Valeur des Ressouces Halieutiques du Golfe de Guinee" (1984) III *Journal du Droit International* 848. It is also understood that the EEC, which played a part in promoting the development of the Gulf of Guinea proposal, is involved in promoting a similar proposal in the Indian Ocean, though based on tuna.
19. Its members are Antigua and Barbuda, Dominica, Grenada, Montserrat, St. Christopher-Nevis, St. Lucia, St. Vincent and the Grenadines.
20. For an outline of the steps leading to the workshops, see the opening address by Augustus Compton, Director, OECS Secretariat, to the second workshop, held in St. John's, Antigua and Barbuda, September 26 - October 1, 1983.
21. Nauru Agreement Concerning Co-operation in the Management of Fisheries of Common Interest, February 11, 1982. See further, "Economic Development and Management of Fisheries in the Exclusive Economic Zones of Pacific Island States" by L.G. Clark, and A.J. Slatyer. *Developing Order of the Oceans*, Proceedings of the 18th Annual Conference of the Law of the Sea Institute, ed. Robert B. Krueger and Stefan A. Riesenfeld (Honolulu: Law of the Sea Institute, 1985), pp. 608-613.
22. For the sake of completeness mention should be made of two important regional fisheries organizations, whose areas of competence also cover the Caribbean: the Western Central Atlantic Fisheries Commission and the International Commission for the Conservation of Atlantic Tuna. For a brief review of international organizations concerned with fisheries in the region, see W. Edeson and J. Pulvenis, *op. cit.* p. 5. See also J. Carroz, note 15 above.
23. See further, "Ocean Management -- A Regional Perspective. The Prospects for Commonwealth Maritime Co-operation in Asia and the Pacific" p. 92. Report of Commonwealth Expert Study Group, 1984.
24. Art. IX. For a discussion of the Agreement, see G. Carter, (1984) 14 *Georgia Journal of International and Comparative Law* 235.
25. Art. IIA. The Council has the power in Art. III(10) to "adjust" the boundaries of the Agreement Area, in accordance with recommendations by the Director to be appointed under Art. III.
26. Art. IV.
27. This is reaffirmed in Art. XIV, and the parties agree to continue efforts "to establish a new regional regime for the conservation, management, and orderly exploitation of tuna resources in the Eastern Pacific Ocean."
28. *Continental Shelf* (Tunisia/Libyan Arab Jamahiriya) [1982] ICJ Rep. p. 1; *Case Concerning the Delimitation of the Maritime Boundary in the Gulf of Maine Area* (Canada/United States of America) (1984) 18 ILM 1197; *Continental Shelf* (Libyan Arab Jamahiriya/Malta). Decision handed down June 3, 1985, Communique No. 85/11. Note also the Maritime Delimitation Award between Guinea and Guinea-Bissau, February 14, 1985.
29. For a map, see K. Nweihed, "EZ (Uneasy) Delimitation in the Semi-Enclosed Caribbean Sea: Recent Agreements Between Venezuela and her Neighbours" (1979) 8 *Ocean Development and International Law Journal* 1 at 8.
30. Sect. 123, Australian Constitution. Whether this section applies to the cession of part of Australia, even though part of a state, has not been conclusively established, and academic opinion is divided on the point. Three small islands -- Kawa, Mata Kawa, and Kussa -- which are very close to Papua New Guinea and which had been thought

to be Australian were, after the original documents and maps incorporating the islands of the Torres Strait into Queensland were carefully examined, found not to have been included, and were therefore already part of Papua New Guinea.

31. For a comprehensive discussion of the Treaty, see H. Burmester, "The Torres Strait Treaty: Boundary Delimitation by Agreement" (1982) 76 AJIL 321.
32. *Ibid*. p. 337.
33. For a fuller description of the seabed line beyond the fisheries jurisdiction line, see H. Burmester, *ibid*. p. 333.
34. Art. I.
35. Art. 23 paras (1) and (2).
36. Art. 18.
37. Art. 19.
38. Art. 23(6), (7) and (8).
39. Art. 26.
40. Art. 27.
41. Art. 26(2).
42. Art. 27(2).
43. Art. 28(6).
44. H. Burmester, *op. cit.* p. 347.
45. See para. 194 of the Chamber's judgment: (1984) 18 ILM at p. 1238.
46. See, for example, para. 193: (1984) ILM at p. 1238.
47. Paras. 33 and 34 of the judgment of the majority.
48. For a maritime delimitation which, while utilizing a single line, nonetheless contains an area subject to cooperative seabed arrangements and cooperative fisheries arrangements, see the Iceland/Norway agreement concerning the Jan Mayen area, discussed in R. Churchill, "Maritime Delimitation in the Jan Mayen Area" (1985) 9 *Marine Policy* 16.
49. See, for example, the Agreements between Brazil and Barbados (1978), and Brazil and Trinidad (1978), discussed in Edeson and Pulvenis, *op. cit.* pp. 126-127. Carroz and Savini, "The Practice of Coastal States Regarding Foreign Access to Fishing Resources," 43 at pp. 54-55 also discuss agreements of this kind. For an overview of the legal considerations of a coastal state might consider when formulating a policy of joint ventures, see L.C. Christy and G. Moore, "Forms of Foreign Participation in Fisheries: Coastal State Practice," *Report of the Expert Consultation on the Conditions of Access to the Fish Resources of the Exclusive Economic Zone*, p. 95.
50. For example, Brazil and Mexico, discussed in W. Edeson and J. Pulvenis, *op. cit.*, pp. 124-125; Australia, discussed in W. Edeson, "Legal Aspects of the Management of Foreign Fishermen in the AFZ," paper presented to the Regional Sciences Seminar, Canberra, 1982.
51. The following discussion draws in part from Edeson and Pulvenis, *op. cit.*, pp. 127-129.
52. See further P. Appleyard, "Joint Ventures: A Changing Scene," (1983) 7 *Marine Policy* 313; L. Christy and G. Moore, *op. cit.*, pp. 97-99. For a table that lists certain joint ventures in West Africa, see Carroz and Savini, "Les Accords de Peche Conclus Par Les Etats Africains Riverains de l'Atlantique" (1983) 21 *Annuaire Francais de Droit International* at pp. 707-709.

For other recent discussions of joint ventures in the fisheries sector see: G.K. Moore, "Coastal State Requirements for Foreign Fishing" (F.A.O. Legis. Study no. 21, rev. 1, 1983) vol I; S.K. Meltzoff rand E. Lipuma, "A Japanese Fishing Joint Venture: Worker

Experience and National Development in the Solomon Islands" (ICLARM Technical Report 1983, 63 pp); D. Shieh, "Expansion of Taiwan Distant-Water Fishing Industry" (1981) 8(1) J Fish Soc of Taiwan 12-22; M.Y. Puzon and R.T. Lao, "Are Joint Ventures in Fisheries a Bane or a Boost?" (1982) 4(1) Fisheries Today 29-34; R. Anderson "Off the Pacific Coast -- a Soviet/American Joint Fisheries Venture. An Experiment in Peaceful Co-Existence Between Rival Nations" (1982) 99(12) *Fisheries Gazette* [NY] 26-29; V. Kaczynski and D. Le Vieil, "International Joint Ventures in World Fisheries" (1981) 10(1) J of Contemporary Business 75-89; W.T. Pereyra, "Some Preliminary Results of U.S.-Soviet Joint Fishing Venture" in *ibid.* 1-19; C.C. Hufflett, "Joint Ventures and Charters: Do They Provide a Short Cut for Fishing Advancement?" in *Prospects and Problems for New Zealand's Demersal Fisheries: Proceedings of the Demersal Fisheries Conference,* October 1978 (Occ. Publ. of the Fish. Res. Div., Min. of Agri. and Fish. [NZ], no. 19, 1979) pp. 61-63; B. Hobson, "Conditions for Joint Ventures" (1979) 6(11) Catch '79 [NZ] 6-7; A. Paz-Andrade, "Joint Ventures in the Development of the Fishing Industry" in Proceedings of the 2nd Annual International Seafood Conference, held at Marabella (Spain) November 11-14 1979 (Chicago: Int Seafood Conf, 1979) 105-110 (Focuses on Spanish joint ventures in South Africa, Argentina, Uruguay, Mexico and Chile); "Joint Ventures: Their Future Role" (1979) 6(6) Catch '79 3, 5-6 (1980) 10; "Policy on Joint Ventures Defended" (1979) 18(6) Comm. Fish., Akld 5; D.R. Christie, "Regulation of International Joint Ventures in the Fishery Conservation Zone" (1980) 10 Georgia J of I and Comp L 85-100; P. Ridlings, "Resource Use Arrangements in South West Pacific Fisheries," East-West Center, Jan. 1983.

FISHERIES DEVELOPMENT IN NEW ZEALAND SINCE UNCLOS III: A CASE STUDY

Philip Major
Assistant General Manager
New Zealand Fishing Industry Board

Introduction

New Zealand is a small island nation with a temperate climate, situated in the South Pacific Ocean between 30 and 50 degrees south and at approximately 170 degrees east. The country includes a number of small outlying islands and, as a consequence, its 200-mile exclusive economic zone is 1,300,000 square nautical miles in area, more than fifteen times its land mass.

As indicated on the map in *Figure 1*, there are two small enclaves east and southeast of the South Island which remain high seas. Also note that to the northwest and southwest there is a slight overlap with waters claimed by Australia.

Although New Zealand's waters are substantial, there is very little continental shelf, so much of the area is not biologically productive. In fact, 72 percent of the zone has waters deeper than 1,000 meters. 22 percent is between 200 and 1,000 meters and only 6 percent is less than 200 meters in depth. It can also be noted from the map that one of the areas of the continental slope, the Challenger Plateau, projects beyond the 200-mile zone. It is, however, a relatively unproductive area.

Fish Stocks

The productivity of the waters around New Zealand is not high by international standards, because of insufficient nutrients in the top layers to support high levels of phytoplankton. The FAO has established a productivity scale ranging from 5 (highly productive) to 0. On this scale, New Zealand's waters rank about 2.5 because of its slight continental shelf, its small land mass and the lack of upwelling currents to bring nutrients from the sea bottom. As a consequence, the fish stocks in the zone, although allowing room for considerable expansion of New Zealand's effort, are not large compared with those found in the northern hemisphere. The biological estimate of the sustainable yield from all fisheries is approximately 600,000 tons. In comparison, Japan catches 6,000,000 tons (live weight) from a zone which is half the size of New Zealand's and the EEC takes approximately 13,000,000 tons from a zone with the same area.

In 1976, just prior to the declaration of the New Zealand 200-mile zone, Japan caught 160,000 tons, the USSR 100,000 tons and Korea 60,000 tons from waters outside the New Zealand twelve-mile territorial sea. In the same year, New Zealand caught 80,000 tons, of which 60,000 tons were finfish, within the territorial sea. In 1977, the Japanese reportedly caught in excess of 250,000 tons, and the total catch from our waters was around 500,000 tons. Because of concern over this heavy foreign fishing pressure, efforts were made to estimate the New Zealand deepwater demersal fishery potential. As well as estimates of maximum sustainable yields (MSY), other physical and biological parameters of the New Zealand deepwater fishery were obtained and compared with similar measures from the other major temperate demersal fishing areas around the world, such as the North Sea, Bering Sea and Southeast Atlantic.

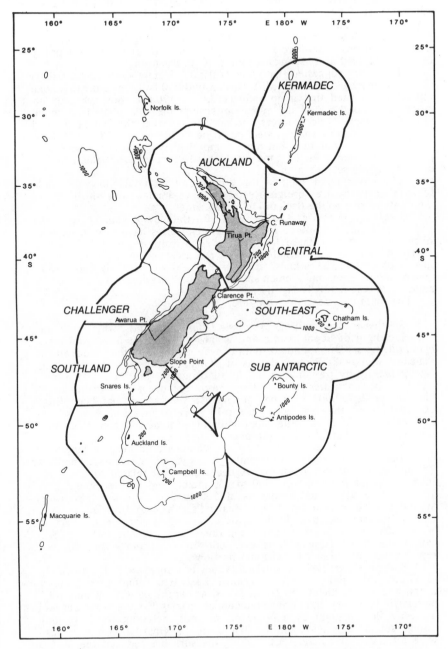

Figure 1: The New Zealand 200 Mile Exclusive Economic Zone (EEZ)

The estimates of the maximum sustainable yield relied heavily on the detailed trawl records of the *Shinkai Maru*, which operated in New Zealand waters from November 1975 to February 1977 (300 fishing days, 1,086 trawls, 9,047 tons of catch). The vessel did an extensive and comprehensive survey of most of the deepwater fishing grounds of the EEZ, fishing each ground over several seasons whenever possible. Detailed Japanese commercial catch and effort data for the overlapping period were used as a secondary source of information.

This work suggested that New Zealand's deepwater demersal fishery should be managed as if the MSY was around 250,000 tons annually. Some sources interpreted this as an annual TAC of 170,000 tons, whereby no more than two-thirds of the maximum sustainable yield should be taken from any stock. Other sources further advised that the potential yield from New Zealand fishery waters could be in the range of 600,000 to 1,400,000 tons per annum, but more comprehensive surveys and some practical experience in the zone would be necessary before the TAC could be safely set this high.

The government adopted this advice and set total allowable catches for the participating foreign fleets at approximately one-third of their catch prior to the declaration of the zone.

Table 1 summarizes TAC estimates for the New Zealand zone in 1977 and 1985. Note that orange roughy and orea dories have been discovered since 1978 and that there has been a significant decrease in the estimated yield from the coastal demersal resource. There are over 700 species of marine fishes known in New Zealand waters. Only about 150 are commonly seen, and a much smaller number, between seventy and eighty, are commercially significant.

The main commercial species are:

Southern blue whiting (*Micromesistius australia*), which has an average length of about 40 cm and weighs 400 gms. It is a deepwater, mainly demersal fish abundant south of New Zealand on the Campbell Plateau and Pukaki Rise at depths of 300 to 600 meters. Whiting is caught mainly by trawling during its spawning season August to early October. It constitutes a very large resource, probably capable of yielding up to 50,000 tons per annum. To date, there has been little exploitation of the resource, except by foreign licensed vessels. The fish itself produces a white fillet with low fat and firmer flesh than that of the Northern Hemisphere blue whiting.

Hoki (*Macruronus novaezelandiae*) which has an average length of 60 to 100 cm and weighs approximately 1.5 kgs, which occurs around New Zealand and Southern Australia. A deepwater fish related to hake, it inhabits depths ranging from 500 to 900 meters and is most abundant around the South Island at depths of 200 to 800 meters. It also occurs around the North Island and New Zealand's sub-antarctic islands. Caught mainly by trawling, hoki is the basis of a major winter fishery on the West coast of the South Island from June to September. It has a delicate white moist flesh that is excellent for fillet block and for reprocessing into breaded sticks and portions.

Snapper (*Chrysophrys auratus*) which has an average length of 30 to 50 cm and weighs between 0.5 and 2.5 kg. It is found around the North Island and the north of the South Island at depths between 5 and 100 meters. It is a very important commercial species for the New Zealand domestic fleet, caught by a range of methods including trawling, long lining, set netting and seining. While the original allowable yields were estimated at 15,000 tons, fishing pressure has reduced the TAC to

180

Table 1

Estimated Annual Yield (tons) of All Resources from the New Zealand EEZ

Species	1977 Case I	1977 Case II	1985
Shellfish			
Rock Lobster, Octopus, Oysters, Mussels, Crabs (excluding Squid)	20,000	20,000	20,000
Finfish (Coastal Pelagic)			
Barracouta, Jack Mackerel [*T declivis*], & Trevally	See Coastal Demersal		
Sprat	10,000	10,000	10,000
Pilchard	4,000	5,000	5,000
Anchovy	10,000	10,000	10,000
Mackerel [*T novae zealandiae*]	15,800	15,000	---
Blue Mackerel	5,000	10,000	10,000
Others: Case I Kahawai 5000,# Yellowtail 200	5,200	10,000	10,000
	50,000	60,000	45,000
Migratory Pelagic			
Skipjack	15,000	23,000	23,000
Albacore	9,000	10,000	10,000
Southern Bluefin	2,000	5,000	5,000
Others	---	2,000	2,000
	26,000	40,000	40,000
Coastal Demersal			
Snapper	14,000	14,000	6,000
Tarakihi	6,000	6,000	3,500
Red Cod*	5,000	5,000	8,800
Gurnard	4,000	4,000	3,000
Warehou*	3,000	3,000	5,100
Grouper	1,000	1,000	1,700
Flounder	1,000	1,000	1,000
Sole	1,000	1,000	1,000
Trevally	8,000+	5,000+	2,100
Barracouta*	17,000+	30,000+	31,000
Jack Mackerel [*T delvis*]	17,000+	20,000+	45,000
Spiky Dogfish	5,000	10,000	---
Others	7,000	20,000	8,335
	89,000	120,000	116,535

Table 1 (continued)

Species	1977 Case I	1977 Case II	1985
Deepwater Demersal			
Orange Roughy			39,000
Oreo Dory			23,000
Hoki	50,000	80,000	100,000
Southern Blue Whiting	50,000	100,000	100,000
Ling**	19,000	25,000	11,500
Silverside	---	20,000	20,000
Silver Warehou	10,000	13,000	9,000
Hake	2,000	3,000	4,500
Others	19,000	39,000	23,665
	150,000	280,000	330,665
TOTAL FINFISH	315,000	500,000	552,200
Squid	80,000	100,000	100,000
GRAND TOTAL	415,000	620,000	652,200

+ Also in coastal pelagic
** demersal fishery
Also taken in coastal
demersal fishery

* Also taken in deepwater
demersal fishery
Also taken in coastal
demersal by netting

a safe estimate of 6,000 tons. In New Zealand it is a very popular fish which is suitable for most cooking methods, including smoking. It also produces a roe which is used for smoking.

Arrow squid (*Nototodarus sloanii*) is the main commercial squid species in New Zealand and has a mantle length of between 15 and 35 cms and grows to a weight of approximately 18 gms. There are fishable stocks on the southern plateau and on both coasts of the South Island, where it is found at depths of 50 to 300 meters, but it is more abundant at the edge of the continental shelf. It is caught mainly by jigging and trawling between December to May. It constitutes a very large resource, probably capable of yielding up to 100,000 tons, but it is subject to a substantial annual variation due to its short life cycle. It has a white, dense firm flesh with a delicate shellfish flavor. There is a ready market in Asia, where it is dried.

Orange roughy (*Hoplostethus atlanticus*) is currently the "darling" of the New Zealand industry. Its existence was not known when the 200-mile zone was declared, but the catch is now about 39,000 tons a year. It produces a pearly white fillet which is in high demand in North America. The fish itself has an average length of 30 to 40 cm and an average weight of 1.5 kg. It appears to be very common at depths of 700 to 1400 meters.

Oreo dory (*Oreosomatidae*) is another recently discovered species. It has a stock size of 23,000 tons and is found between 600 to 1400 meters. Dories produce a white, dense fillet with a good flavor, but they have not proved to be as popular with the market as orange roughy. Both species are caught by trawling.

Tuna (*Scombridae*) is the main pelagic resource in New Zealand. Albacore and Skipjack are the most prolific, but Southern Bluefin tuna is perhaps the most interesting. It is a big fish, up to 2.20 meters long, and weighing as much as 180 kg. It breeds around Java and is distributed in the southern oceans of the world between 10 degrees and 50 degrees south. It is caught in New Zealand between February and October and the annual catch is estimated to be between 4,000 and 5,000 tons, taken mostly by Japanese longliners for shipment back to Japan. It is related to the Northern Bluefin tuna, which grows up to 600 kg.

Zone Declaration

On April 1, 1978, the Territorial Sea and the Exclusive Economic Zone Act, which had been passed by the New Zealand Parliament on September 26, 1977, came into force. This Act provided, *inter alia*, for the establishment of an exclusive economic zone around New Zealand and its outlying islands. This was a unilateral declaration, but one which followed the pattern adopted by many other countries. The Act closely followed the Informal Composite Negotiating Text of the Third United Nations Law of the Sea Conference, which then represented the world consensus on fishing matters.

From New Zealand's point of view, the most significant element of the text concerned living aquatic resources. While sovereignty over fish stocks is not unlimited, the coastal state has the first right to fish and it can decide who will utilize remaining stocks. In essence, the coastal state is obligated to assess the stocks available and determine the quantity which can be harvested on a continuing basis. It is also necessary to determine the proportion of this catch which its industry can be expected to catch in the immediate future. The remainder must be allocated to foreign fishing nations. New Zealand based its 200-mile zone law on these principles.

When this law was passed, the New Zealand fishing industry comprised some 5,200 commercial fishing vessels valued at approximately $94 million. Most were relatively small; 76 percent were less than nine meters in length and only 1 percent were more than 21 meters long. The vessels operated largely in inshore fisheries, with earnings evenly divided between income from wet fish, crustaceans and molluscs.

In 1977, the total domestic catch was 82,000 tons, valued at NZ$35 million, of which wet fish contributed 60,000 tons (NZ$18 million), and crustaceans and molluscs 22,000 tons (NZ$17 million). Rock lobster was the main species in the latter category, while the wet fish was mainly sold on the domestic market in fresh or semi-processed form.

The consensus at that time was that the 200-mile resource zone would produce an astronomical economic bonanza for New Zealand, a view based on the size of the zone, not on its biological productivity. Nevertheless, the government began to provide incentives for the expansion of the domestic industry, because this was seen as the best way to reap the benefits of the zone. The following incentives were offered:

1. Remission of duty on vessels greater than twenty-one meters imported to fish the zone.
2. The provision of cheap government finance.

3. Provision of suspensory loans (which would be written off if a certain catch target was met) for upgrading fishing vessels to fish the zone.

4. A range of diversification loans for fishermen in stressed inshore fisheries.

5. Taxation incentives for investment in plant and equipment to fish for and process the catch of export.

6. Suspensory loans for plant and machinery to process products and encourage development of fish farms.

7. Price support schemes were also introduced for barracouta (*Thyrsites atun*) and mackerel (*Scombridae*).

8. As a mechanism for encouraging low risk expansion of domestic involvement, the government permitted New Zealand companies to form joint ventures with foreign firms if the foreign involvement component was no greater than 24.9 percent of total investment.

At this stage, the development of New Zealand fisheries started to diverge into four distinct areas, which are considered in detail below.

The Deepwater Trawl Fishery

By 1981 the joint venture component of the deepwater demersal trawl fishery had expanded considerably. (See *Table 2*.) At the same time, the deepwater component of the New Zealand domestic fishery had also expanded. As a result the government faced a range of problems:

1. Increasing numbers of other companies wanted approval for joint ventures.

2. The capacity of existing joint ventures was in excess of that needed to harvest the available resource.

3. It was necessary to restrict foreign licensed vessels in order to give capacity to joint ventures.

4. The government's incentives encouraged expansion by the domestic fleet, but the new vessels fell neither into the coastal category nor into the truly deepwater category. As a result, they fished inshore, to the detriment of the coastal resource, because they did not have the sea-keeping qualities to fish consistently in deepwater. In fact, thirty-nine vessels no longer than 21 meters, representing a total investment of NZ$47 million, were added to the domestic fleet. There were, however, prospects that these vessels might be able to fish in depths of up to 1,000 meters in more sheltered waters for orange roughy, which would make them more profitable. There was also a corresponding increase in investment of between NZ$25 million and NZ$30 million in onshore processing facilities.

5. There was criticism that the joint ventures had slowed down domestic expansion and were, in fact, competing with domestic vessels, where they were expanding into the deepwater. This was not entirely true, however, since most joint ventures had fulfilled the function originally anticipated of them:

a. They had enabled domestic firms to acquire fishing technology and expertise in areas and in vessels which were unfamiliar to domestic fishermen, without a significant initial outlay of capital.

b. They had brought with them knowledge of international markets and access to those markets.

c. They had provided significant volumes of fish for shore processing plants, thus ensuring better utilization of capacity.

Table 2

Total Catch from New Zealand's EEZ

Species	New Zealand		Foreign licensed vessels			Total Catch	Resource Estimates	
	Domestic	Joint Venture	Japan	USSR	South Korea		Case I	Case II
1977								
Finfish								
Tuna	1,590	5,951	2,348	---	---	9,889	21,000	35,000
Other	54,943	---	192,525	96,200	38,512	382,180	294,000	465,000
Squid	556	380	40,942	26,800	1,480	70,140	80,000	100,000
Shellfish	21,741	---	---	---	---	21,741	20,000	20,000
Total	78,830	6,331	245,797	123,000	39,992	493,950	415,000	620,000
1978								
Finfish								
Tuna	4,612	6,593	2,500	---	---	13,705	21,000	35,000
Other	67,144	---	25,712	47,475	24,772	165,003	294,000	465,000
Squid	784	1,683	17,298	7,976	517	28,258	80,000	100,000
Shellfish	18,367	---	---	---	---	18,367	20,000	20,000
Total	90,907	8,276	45,510	55,451	25,289	225,333	415,000	620,000
1979								
Finfish								
Tuna	3,921	5,868	4,231	---	---	14,020	21,000	35,000
Other	76,079	25,000	33,597	48,053	19,808	200,537	294,000	465,000
Squid	414	9,203	19,842	7,976	585	38,020	80,000	100,000
Shellfish	20,886	---	---	---	---	20,886	20,000	20,000
Total	101,300	40,071	57,670	56,029	20,393	275,463	415,000	620,000

Table 2 (continued)

Species	New Zealand		Foreign licensed vessels			Total Catch	Resource Estimate	
	Domestic	Joint Venture	Japan	USSR	South Korea		Case I	Case II

1980
====

Finfish

Species	Domestic	Joint Venture	Japan	USSR	South Korea	Total Catch	Case I	Case II
Tuna	2,934	6,803	7,063	---	---	16,800	21,000	35,000
Other	72,347	88,050	27,025	15,498	1,520	204,000	294,000	465,000
Squid	280	26,180	37,570	4,005	671	68,706	80,000	100,000
Shellfish	21,018	---	---	---	---	21,018	20,000	20,000
Total	96,579	121,033	71,658	19,503	2,191	310,964	415,000	620,000

1981
====

Finfish

Species	Domestic	Joint Venture	Japan	USSR	South Korea	Total Catch	Case I	Case II
Tuna	5,313	4,743*	6,559**	---	---	16,615	21,000	35,000
Other	83,098	92,442	28,842	14,365	1,188	219,935	294,000	465,000
Squid	1,019	21,799	27,660	6,570	1,955	59,003	80,000	100,000
Shellfish & rock lobster	18,507	(excludes farmed mussels & oysters)		---	---	18,507	20,000	20,000
Total	107,937	118,984	63,061	20,935	3,143	314,060	415,000	620,000

*
** figure for 1980/81 season - skipjack only
longline tuna catches mainly sbt

1982
====

Finfish

Species	Domestic	Joint Venture	Japan	USSR	South Korea	Total Catch	Case I	Case II
Tuna	6,437	1,507	5,296	---	---	13,240	21,000	35,000
Other	90,424	75,043	20,957	17,438	6,203	210,065	294,000	465,000
Squid	610	43,269	35,358	8,498	2,729	90,464	80,000	100,000
Shellfish & rock lobster	18,157	---	---	---	---	18,157	20,000	20,000
Total	115,628	119,819	61,611	25,936	8,932	331,926	415,000	620,000

Table 2 (continued)

Species	New Zealand		Foreign licensed vessels			Total Catch	Resource Estimates	
	Domestic	Joint Venture	Japan	USSR	South Korea		Case I	Case II
1983								
Finfish								
Tuna	4,745	4,222	2,729	---	409	12,105	21,000	35,000
Other	111,282	95,521	23,521	26,582	8,984	265,890	294,000	465,000
Squid	1,422	37,148	33,745	9,658	3,605	85,578	80,000	100,000
Shellfish & rock lobster	33,355*	---	---	---	---	33,355	20,000	20,000
Total	150,804	136,891	59,995	36,240	12,998	396,928	415,000	620,000

Includes aquaculture

1984								
Finfish								
Tuna	6,161	91,754	2,554	---	524	9,235	21,000	35,000
Other	113,500		28,289	14,085	13,196	260,824	294,000	465,000
Squid	633	54,983	46,119	8,431	5,536	115,752	80,000	100,000
Shellfish & rock lobster	22,602	---	---	---	---	20,968	20,000	20,000
Total	142,896	146,737	76,962	22,516	19,256	406,779	415,000	620,000

187

In most arrangements the foreign partner was required to bear most of the risk and conduct the fishing. The New Zealand partner's role was to process a portion of the fish and adopt an active marketing role. For the most part, charters were paid for in kind, with the foreign partner taking a percentage of the catch and a percentage of the profits.

Table 2 shows catches of fish foreign nations made from 1977. While these catches were high, they were less than the amounts offered. Foreign nations argued that the difference was a result of area restrictions and bycatch limits that were imposed on some species in some areas. Once a bycatch limit was reached, then fishing in the area was required to cease. Since the New Zealand government did all the decision-making, however, foreign nations had no options but to comply.

Against this background the government determined to review its policy on the deepwater catch. In coming to a judgment about the economic prospects of the deepwater trawl fishery, it analyzed three inter-related aspects:

The Resource
The government concluded that it had sufficient knowledge of the resource to set TACs with confidence. It also concluded that the industry was critically dependent on limited volumes of relatively high value prime species. The catching record of the deepwater fleet during those years has shown that the resource capable of being caught economically is significantly below the biological sustainable yield.

Cost and Earnings
The government and the New Zealand Fishing Industry Board spent considerable time examining deepwater catching operations. Detailed historical figures of returns were obtained from several joint ventures. Domestic companies supplied forecasts in support of applications to import large vessels and thus ensure their position in the fishery. The data related to a wide range of vessel sizes, ages, and varying degrees of processing on board and on shore. Despite the wide variation in types of operation undertaken or proposed, the data revealed a consistent set of conclusions. The economic returns were marginal and in some cases substantial losses were envisaged in the first years of domestic vessel operations.

Some of the domestic budgets projected positive returns, but these were based on the assumption that the fishing management regime would be modified to allow the firms concerned exclusive access to high valued species. It became evident from the development plans that were submitted by the industry that a deepwater fishery with a significant increase in catching effort by New Zealand domestic vessels would leave little room for joint ventures. However, a rapid increase in domestic catching capacity, even with exclusive access, entailed high risks, both for new investments and for existing capital and labor in the industry.

The government was reluctant to jeopardize the economic future of the industry through sudden changes in access conditions, and decided instead to explore strategies which could lead to a more controlled and efficient expansion of New Zealand investment in the fishery. Consequently the duty-free import scheme for vessels was suspended.

Fisheries Management Controls and Regulations
The primary aims of the government's management policies at the time were to conserve the fish resources and promote the efficient

development of the domestic fishing industry. The management program included the following measures:

* limits on the number of vessels allowed into the industry, which applied principally to the joint venture fleet.
* controls on catching efficiency, mainly through gear restrictions.
* limits on catching effort through controls on access to particular species in given fishing zones.

The usual response worldwide of fisheries management authorities, including those of New Zealand, had been to control the quantity of inputs allowed into the fishery initially by restricting the number of vessels. However this was usually only the first step in an ever widening array of controls. If the number of vessels is controlled, fishermen will replace smaller vessels with larger ones. This in turn may result in restrictions on tonnage and length, engine horsepower and units of gear.

The basic weakness in a policy based on restriction of inputs is that the design and structure of the fishery unit is flexible, and so restrictions on one or two elements cannot in the long run prevent investment in other components. In theory, it would be possible to place restrictions on all elements of fishing effort simultaneously covering vessel size, power, crews, fishing time, fishing gear and so on, but the controls would have to be so diverse that they would be virtually impossible to administer and enforce. In addition, they would preclude any technological improvements in the catching sector.

Given the problems that arose in New Zealand and the tendency for these controls to escalate, the government reviewed a number of alternative management regimes. After a considerable amount of investigation and discussion it was concluded that the system that offered the greatest promise of stability and efficiency was one based on company allocations or quota rights to catch specific quantities of fish. New Zealand already had some experience of this system, with an oyster fishery in Foveaux Strait which had procured encouraging results.

This approach has the advantages that:

1. It provides a direct means of controlling the total catch and ensuring that it will stay within the sustained yield targets set for the stocks.
2. It frees the regulatory authorities from many of the problems associated with regulating fishing activity. Most restrictions on vessels, gear and fishing time could be removed.
3. It adds to the security of operation and elimination of much of the risk that the companies would otherwise face under a system of competitive fishing.
4. It can accommodate changes in economic conditions without causing disruption. Notably if fish prices rise or for other reasons the fishery becomes more profitable and earnings increase, there will *not* be an automatic tendency to expand fishing capacity.
5. It lends itself to a variety of methods for raising revenues, in the form of license fees and landing charges.
6. In principle, at least, it is administratively simple. Because it deals directly with the problems of regulating the catch, once licenses are issued the regulatory authorities can concentrate on resource management rather than on regulating the fleet's fishing activities.

Even so, the quota applied to the deepwater fishery also gave rise to a series of problems:

Allocation of Quotas. The government decided not to select tendering as a means of allocating quotas or rights to fish, because tendering involves a high degree of risk for the eligible participants. Effectively, their future in the industry may be decided by their success in the initial tendering allocation. Also, tendering accords no recognition of the historical involvement in the industry of individual fishing enterprises, particularly of substantial investments they have already made.

Consequently, the government adopted an administrative allocation system. The rights to fish would be allocated on the basis of each enterprise's proven record of performance in the fishery to date and on the investment that it had already made in processing and catching facilities.

Each of these factors was weighted and included in a formula. Companies then provided the reviewers with statistical information to which the formula was applied to determine allocations.

A principal advantage of this approach was that it gave due recognition to the proven efforts of New Zealand companies in developing the deepwater fishery in accordance with government policy and to the investments they had made. The system was also based on objectively ascertainable data and so did not involve the government in conjectures on the fishing plans of individual companies.

In the context of a limited resource fishery, the concept of fair shares for those who had already risked capital and effort in its development was considered acceptable.

It was determined that the allocation should be made to those companies that were selected on the basis of the proportion of deep water catch processed on shore in 1980/81 and 1981/82.

The allocation formula valued the following:

* Investment in onshore processing plant at replacement value weighted by commitment to joint venture caught fish.
* Investment in vessels over 20 meters at replacement value.

The criteria were considered reasonable because they were measurable, took into account commitment to the fishing industry, and reflected the extent of existing investments at that stage. No one company was favored more than any other.

Companies were required to submit to the government annual financial reports, which, together with the reports of catch, would allow the system to be monitored.

Resources to be Allocated. The government was prepared to allocate all the TAC of the deepwater species except for:

* A small volume of higher valued species outside Area E. At that time, 11,000 tons were allocated to Japanese and Korean licensed fleets. The government proposed to keep this level of allocation under review.
* These resources found in Area E, it being assumed that the domestic industry would not wish to fish the area for other than squid in the foreseeable future, because of the difficult catching conditions in the area. Although it was not proposed that these resources be included in the company allocations, it was intended that they could be exploited

by any New Zealand company wishing to do so, on a competitive or joint venture basis.
* The premium inshore species which were already fully harvested by the existing inshore fleet.
* The lower value deepwater species such as mackerel and barracouta, which, at the time, were not considered likely to be placed under pressure. *Table 3* lists the species which were made available for allocation, together with their catch. Within twelve months, barracouta (*Thyrsites atun*) was added.

Should the Companies be Allowed to Transfer Quota? The prevailing view at the time was that we were alienating a public resource to private use, and that a fair measure of control should be kept over it. Consequently it was determined that allocations would only be made to New Zealand companies with a greater than 75.1 percent New Zealand shareholding. The government also set a minimum potential catch of 2,000 tons for consideration as a bar to entry. It recognized, however, the existence of other groups who also had some involvement in the deepwater fishery, and it therefore set aside some 13,000 tons for them to fish competitively and establish future claims. In the end, the government accepted that there should be transfer of the quota on the basis that the initial allocations, although recognizing past performance and commitment, would not necessarily reflect future intentions. Indeed, some trading of quotas did take place, to secure a quote mix which best accorded the companies' future plans.

If the result of the administrative allocation proved to be inefficient, then the ability to transfer enabled the market to deal with this problem. There were, however, several restrictions:

* to stop speculation the government determined that the holder must be able to demonstrate genuine use of the quota either by himself or by another holder, or surrender it to the government.
* the concentration of licenses in one hand so that the formation of a monopoly occurred was not to be countenanced, and so only a maximum of 35 percent holding of the total quantity was to be permitted.
* given that true private property rights were being allocated to the individuals, there should be a payment of fees for access to the fishing rights, and the fees were to be paid on allocation rather than catch. This would encourage trading if a company was not catching its quota.

What Terms and Conditions Should be Attached to the Quota? The government was prepared to provide a ten-year term for the initial allocations, with a review to be undertaken after three years to consider utilization by the companies of their quotas. Companies failing to utilize their quotas adequately would be required to surrender them to the government.

A provision was made that quotas must be traded only to companies having 75.1 percent New Zealand ownership. This was designed to ensure that New Zealand industry retained control of exploitation of the resources and retained ownership of the catch, to discourage disruptive marketing and foreign ownership.

Table 3

Deepwater Trawl Catch (tons) of Species Allocated Under the
Deepwater Trawl Policy For the Year Ended December 31, 1983

Species	Allocations			Catches*			Percent of Quota
	Companies	Other	Total	Domestic	Charter	Total	
Hake	2,243	157	2,400	160	1,119	1,279	53.3
Hoki	37,761	2,639*	40,400	7,706	20,693	28,399	70.3
Ling	7,478	522*	8,000	2,706	2,365	5,074	63.4
Orange Roughy	33,047	1,653	34,700	18,099	23,660	41,759	120.3+
Oreo Dories	19,618	982	20,600	1,472	14,554	16,026	77.8
Silver Warehou	5,608	392	6,000	269	2,700	2,969	49.5
TOTAL	105,755	6,345	112,100	30,415	65,091	95,506	85.2

* The data as supplied by MAF did not allow the catch to be compared directly to company and
other allocations.

+ Approximately 7,000 tons of orange roughy was reported as caught outside the EEZ.

Compiled by:
The New Zealand Fishing Industry Board
Source:
MAF Fisheries Statistics Unit (as at August, 1984)

Source:
New Zealand Fishing Industry Board *Annual Report*

The government required that a minimum of 35 percent of the total deepwater catch, *i.e.*, allocated and non-allocated species, be processed in New Zealand. This condition was intended to provide through-put for New Zealand processors and discourage transfer of fish to offshore factories. Allocation holders were permitted to charter vessels from foreign sources, but charter fees had to be denominated in cash rather than kind, and any sale of fish to the foreign vessel owner had to be made at realistic market prices. The failure to meet these terms and conditions was to result in forfeiture or reduction of allocations, which would then be redistributed, either administratively or by tender.

A royalty of $3 a ton was to be paid.

In 1984 royalties being paid under the scheme were: $75 per ton for orange roughy; $25 per ton for hoki; $15 per ton for other species.

What Management Controls Should be Retained? Although the intention behind the scheme was to limit the number of controls on the deepwater fleet, it was considered essential that large vessels should not be permitted to fish in the inshore waters. Accordingly, it was proposed that all vessels of forty meters' length or more would be excluded from the twelve-mile territorial sea, from Area B and from those other areas closed to foreign trawling.

The government intended to seek voluntary agreement from the industry that vessels would also avoid the inner waters of Area C, where smaller inshore vessels were fishing.

Catch Position Reporting. All vessels of over twenty meters' length operating in the deepwater fishery would be required to:

* Report their daily noon positions to the Fisheries Control Centre of the Ministry of Agriculture and Fisheries.
* Complete deepwater trawl catch effort records on a daily basis and submit these regularly to the MAF.
* Report to the Fisheries Control Centre weekly, or at more frequent intervals if required to do so, on aggregate catches and species catches by area for the preceding week.

This was the same reporting procedure that joint venture trawl vessels were required to follow and was necessary so that catches could be monitored and quotas enforced.

This, then, was the system as introduced by the government in April 1983. To date, the scheme has worked effectively and has brought about a reduction in friction between domestic vessels and deepwater vessels, and a reduction in the number of management regulations needed to control the fleets.

There are, however, problems in the following areas:

* Large numbers of other companies are now seeking quotas in the fishery as those who hold them are clearly demonstrating that they are profitable.
* The 13,000 tons made available for competitive fishing is creating a problem because the domestic fleet has expanded its capacity to take more than the quotas allocated in some management areas.

The government is conducting an initial three-year review of the fishery, and listening to submissions from a range of interested parties. Unfortunately, at this stage there are no results available for publication. It is clear, however, that the industry as a whole approves of the idea of the individual transferable quotas provided they can all have a share. As a result of the implementation of the deepwater policy, it now appears that the management of all other sectors of the fishing industry will follow suit, with the establishment of individual transferable quota regimes.

The Tuna Fishery

In the New Zealand zone there are several tuna species -- bluefin, albacore, skipjack, yellowfin and big eye, and several associated bill fishes. All these species migrate from the New Zealand zone into tropical waters, and are usually available for fishing in New Zealand only for a limited period. Although we suspect there may be some resident stocks, we have not been able to demonstrate this at the present time.

The tuna fishery has never got off the ground in New Zealand, mainly because of the dramatic decline in world tuna prices since 1980. New Zealand interests did not attempt to develop tuna fisheries themselves, but complained of harrassment from American vessels. Nevertheless, in 1983 approximately 8,133 tons of skipjack tuna were landed in New Zealand. Some was processed into canned form, and the balance exported to the American cannery in Pago Pago, Western Samoa.

Albacore tuna is fished on the west coast of the South Island by a domestic fleet which fishes inshore species for the rest of the year. Again progress in this fishery is spasmodic, depending on weather conditions and sea temperatures. It also has a relatively short season. The albacore are either canned in New Zealand or Pago Pago.

The bluefin is the most valuable species of tuna in New Zealand waters. Between March and August each year, Japanese longline vessels fishing off the east coast of New Zealand catch about 4,000 tons.

The New Zealand industry has been unsuccessful in its efforts to fish for bluefin tuna off the east coast of the country, although it has developed a small west coast fishery. The fish is either air-freighted to Japan or frozen to -50 degrees centigrade and shipped on specialized carrier boats to Japan, where it sells for up to $38 per kilo. Notwithstanding these high prices, the low catch rate of the fishery makes it a risky one. Prospects for New Zealand expanding its effort in the fishery will be dependent on the ability of New Zealand, Australia and Japan to come to an arrangement on the international management of the resource, which is heavily overfished as a result of past efforts of the Australian and Japanese fleets.

At present, the three countries are discussing the future management of the fishery. The size of the resource has been established, as has the need for a reduction in future catches. Although both New Zealand and Australia have instituted measures to conserve the resource, the Japanese are finding it more difficult to introduce restrictions on their own industry. New Zealand is pursuing the line that quotas to the fishery should be allocated on a fishing zone basis, whereas the Japanese are pursuing the line that they should be allocated on a country/catch basis.

Squid

Management of the squid fishery is complicated by the fact that half the catch is taken by trawling and half by jigging. Having earlier dealt with the part of the allocation which comes under the trawl policy, I shall now discuss that which is dealt with under a jig policy.

Since the institution of the 200-mile zone, New Zealand has been trying to encourage the development of its own domestic jig fishery for squid found around the main islands. Because the resource has for a number of years been fished by the Japanese, Taiwanese and Korean fleets, it was thought desirable to permit joint ventures between New Zealand operations and companies from those nations. Although from these joint ventures we have obtained a great deal of knowledge about fishing methods, seasonality and markets, there has never been a change to domestic exploitation, nor has there been a significant improvement in the net economic benefit that is obtained from the resource.

The primary reason for lack of development is that jig squid is a premium product on the Japanese market where it is used for drying. The price of squid sold for manufactured products for either the American or European markets is uneconomic. Consequently the only profitable way to sell the squid is as sea-frozen direct to the Asian market. However Japan has market access restrictions that mean New Zealand is largely unable to sell there.

Secondly, there are problems with the catching of squid. Squid are attracted by lights at night, particularly to large concentrations of vessels providing not only a great deal of light, but also stable fishing platforms that create shadows for them to retire to. In effect, small New Zealand vessels are not sufficiently stable for the type of fishing that is necessary, and the costs of investment require that larger boats be used all the year round, as are the foreign fleets which fish the Sea of Japan when away from New Zealand.

Finally, as joint venture approvals are only given on a year-by-year basis, there has not been a great deal of security for New Zealand operators wishing to invest in processing facilities or engage in the fishery in a more committed manner. The New Zealand government is currently reviewing its policy with a view to adopting the principle set out in the deepwater fishery. It appears that the jigging resource will be established at some 50,000 tons, a portion of which will be allocated exclusively to New Zealand-owned vessels operating in the fishery on a long-term basis.

A further quantity will be made available to New Zealand-owned companies for exploitation by jigging, probably through tender. This would then allow companies that have held charter arrangements in the past to continue to operate if they wish to tender. The allocation would be short term.

The balance, probably in the order of 30,000 tons, will be made available to foreign nations, either through tender or the paying of a license fee, as at present.

It is clear that the changes envisaged in the squid fishery will eventually lead to the adoption of individual transferable quotas, in line with the policy already established in the deepwater fishery.

Coastal Inshore Fishery

To quote from the proposed policy for the future management of the inshore fin fishery, the problem of the inshore industry is that the major fish stocks are too low as a result of over-fishing. Since March 1982 there has been a moratorium on new entrants to the inshore fishery. During the 1983-1984 fishing year, a number of part-time fishermen were administratively, in line with the provisions of the removed Fisheries Act of 1983. As expected, this had a negligible effect on fishing effort or catch.

The harvesting sector remains overcapitalized by about NZ$28 million. The need, therefore, is to reduce catches to a level that will enable fish stocks to recover to their previous levels and to provide a management regime whereby the sustainable yields are taken by the most efficient means. The objectives of the measures proposed are to achieve a long-term continuing maximum economic benefit from the resources and to preserve a satisfactory recreational fishery.

The benefits of increased fish stocks and improved harvesting efficiency are difficult to measure. However, it is clear that there would be substantially increased returns to the industry and the New Zealand economy, as well as an improved recreational fishery.

The government's new policy for the future management of the inshore fishery provides for:

* management of the fishery by individual transferable catch quotas;
* restructuring assistance provided by the government under a competitive tendering scheme to those who voluntarily offer to reduce their quotas of key species;
* the introduction of a resource rental on the granting of the individual transferable quota property right;
* future adjustments of the total allowable catches by the purchase or sale of quotas by the government by competitive tender;
* the exclusion of the rock lobster and shell fisheries with proposals for them to be included at a later date;
* the retention of a minimum number of biological controls, such as closed areas and mesh net restrictions, to continue.

It is envisaged that the scheme will continue to work as follows:

Each individual fishermen will be allocated a quota based on his historical catch performance. The government will then offer to buy back from him some or all of that allocation, in order to reduce the total catch to the desired level. Fishermen will offer a tender price to the government, which will assess all tenders on a species-by-area basis and purchase accordingly. So that there will be no complaints about the prices paid, the government will pay for each species it buys back at the rate for the highest tender that it accepts.

It is estimated that to buy back the property rights that are necessary to reduce the catch to a sustainable level will cost between NZ$20 million and NZ$30 million. In the event that the Government is unsuccessful in its bid to buy back quotas there will be an administrative reduction made in relation to those species that are under stress. This, in itself, is a good incentive for fishermen to offer tenders.

In addition to the inshore species that have been referred to, the 17,000 tons of species set aside for domestic involvement under the deepwater policy will also be allocated to inshore interests. We will then have a fully integrated management regime for finfish and squid stocks in the whole of the 200-mile economic zone, based on the allocation of individual transferable quotas to participants.

Access of Foreign Nations

Three nations have concluded treaties with New Zealand for access to our zone: the USSR, Japan and Korea. The quotas, conditions and fees for each nation are set annually, following negotiations with each nation. Appendix one contains details of the arrangements for the fishing years commencing October 1, 1982, 1983, and 1984.

Significant aspects of the agreements are:

* For trawl fisheries, foreign nations are restricted primarily to Area E, a difficult fishing ground;
* Fees are set at 5 percent of the estimated gross value of the accepted tonnage, not the caught tonnage;
* Often less fish is caught than countries have in quotas, so the fee is effectively higher per ton of catch;
* Fees are set to cover the cost of managing the zone and not to recover economic rent;
* There is no requirement to land fish in New Zealand and in fact this was prohibited until 1985;
* There is no requirement to carry out research, although offers of assistance from the USSR and Japan are evaluated and accepted from time to time. There is concern over possible arguments about the size of resources, were foreign nations to conduct research.
* In entering into agreements with foreign nations, their historical involvement in the fishery was taken into account.
* Arrangements with states who had not had a presence in the zone have been considered. Spain, Poland and West Germany all received initial approval, but only West Germany fished the zone and only for a short time.
* New Zealand issues a quota of fish and it is up to the foreign country to determine what number of vessels it uses to harvest.
* New Zealand requires observers to be permitted on board for policing purposes but not for training.
* To date, New Zealand has not linked market access to fisheries access.
* Japan has offered a range of assistance for technology transfer, research and technician training, most of which has been accepted.

What Has Been Achieved
The results of exports of fisheries products in *Table 4* are a measure of what has been achieved from the declaration of the zone. While spectacular on the face of it, they do hide a number of anomalies:

* Until 1982, joint venture arrangements for finfish and trawl squid provided that the majority of fish caught by foreign vessels were to be retained by the foreign partner as payment for charter. They were, however, recorded as exports from New Zealand although there was no real economic benefit.
* With the establishment of the individual quotas regime and the requirement that charter fees be paid in cash, the New Zealand operators were placed in a strong negotiating position, with the result that fish caught by chartered vessels is predominantly landed and processed in New Zealand before export. There are substantial economic benefits accruing to New Zealand as real prices are being paid for the charters.
* In relation to squid jigging, joint venture practices still continue. This, however, is being addressed by a government review.
* Although there has been a range of bilateral assistance from Japan, there has also been criticism from the industry and commentators that the government has been too "soft" in negotiating with Japan and Korea in particular, and should have required from them market access for squid and mackerel, in return for rights to New Zealand waters, squid

197

Table 4

Summarized Exports of NZ Fisheries Product 1977 - 1984

Calendar Year	1977		1978		1979		1980	
	Tons	FOB Value $(000)	Tons	FOB Value $(000)	Tons	FOB Value $(000)	Tons	FOB Value $(000)
Finfish	22,480	21,452	29,699	32,130	52,153	53,347	74,726	85,873
Rock Lobster	1,979	23,667	2,174	25,397	2,133	26,937	2,480	29,481
Shellfish	1,592	5,243	2,384	6,098	10,738	17,361	33,262	47,090
GRAND TOTAL	26,051	50,363	34,357	63,625	65,024	97,646	110,468	162,444
JV CONTRIBUTION					27,827	26,056	61,725	64,200

Table 4 (continued)

Calendar Year	1981		1982		1983		1984	
	Tons	FOB Value $(000)	Tons	FOB Value $(000)	Tons	FOB Value $(000)	Tons	FOB Value $(000)
Finfish	92,146	117,217	79,140	135,099	86,842	169,729	85,926	242,965
Rock Lobster	2,276	35,693	2,684	48,119	2,737	53,458	2,623	78,756
Shellfish	33,856	37,311	41,760	69,881	41,063	86,188	52,821	119,265
GRAND TOTAL	128,278	190,221	123,584	253,099	130,642	309,464	141,370	440,986
JV CONTRIBUTION	89,965	76,000	85,000	118,100	78,000	135,000	NA	

and mackerel being under import quotas in both countries. From recent government to government talks, it is clear that New Zealand is now taking this line.

There are, however, several aspects that have mitigated against taking a strong line on market access until now:

* A friendly nation agreement between New Zealand and Japan.
* A desire to ensure that we did not exceed what was considered acceptable under the Law of the Sea Convention bearing in mind that, although not excluded, market access was not a matter specifically mentioned in Article 62.
* Concern at the effect a hard line on fisheries might have on imports of New Zealand primary products into Japan.
* Concern at a possible loss of revenue from license fees.

It has also been argued that New Zealand should have based its license fees on the economic rent generated from the fisheries rather than having set a flat fee covering administration. The former was not done for the following reasons:

* Concern as to whether this was a correct interpretation of the Law of the Sea Convention.
* Difficulty in obtaining data.
* A belief that the economic rent from most fisheries might be less than 5 percent and hence not recover the administration costs.

Policing the Zone

Policing is carried out by Fisheries Patrol Vessels Aerial Survey and by the Observer Placement Programme.

The patrol vessels conduct random inspections and the observers are placed randomly.

To date, several arrests and prosecutions have been made. (See *Table 5*.)

Conclusions

Since the establishment of the zone there have been significant benefits to stock management of New Zealand inshore resources. Although the zone is still heavily fished, it has been possible to devise a management regime that will be effective because we will no longer have to be concerned over lack of control on efforts on stocks outside the twelve-mile territorial sea.

It is clear that the regime of individual quotas has provided a better framework for decision-making by companies. Decisions to import vessels are now being taken on the basis of profitability, rather than on the basis that such investment provides a means of access to the resource.

The program of management now in force is raising sufficient revenue to cover administrative costs. This year the government is budgeting to spend NZ$16 million on research and management and is planning to receive NZ$18 million from all sources. This is the first year that this has occurred.

Finally, the establishment of a 200-mile EEZ for New Zealand has been of tremendous benefit. From a small coastal fishing state we have developed a significant fishing industry that still has room for expansion, and is based on sound biological and economic policy.

Table 5

Major Offenses: 1977 to 1984

Countries	Fines	Confiscations
Japan	4	-
USSR	-	-
Korea	2	1
Taiwan	2	-

Note: Fines and costs up to $130,000.

Minor Offenses: 1977 to 1984

Countries	Fines
Japan	7
USSR	1
Korea	4
Taiwan	-

Note: Penalties between $500 and $3,500.

REFERENCES

Catch, various issues, 1977-1985.

Commercial Fishing, May 1985, pp. 19-20.

Duncan, A.J., "Economics of the Deepwater Fishery," *Commercial Fishing*, April 1983.

Jarman, N.E., "Implications of New Zealand's Declaration of a 200-mile Exclusive Economic Zone, 1977.

New Zealand Fishing Industry Board *Annual Reports* 1977-1984.

New Zealand Fishing Industry Board *Bulletin*, various issues, 1977-1985.

New Zealand Fishing Industry Board, *Guidebook to New Zealand Commercial Fish Species*, 1981.

New Zealand Ministry of Agriculture and Fisheries, *Annual Reports*, 1977-1984.

New Zealand Ministry of Agriculture and Fisheries and New Zealand Fishing Industry, *Inshore Finfish Fisheries Policy for Future Management*.

New Zealand Ministry of Agriculture and Fisheries and New Zealand Fishing Industry Board, *Future Policy for the Deepwater Fishery*, July 1982.

Organization for Economic Cooperation and Development, *Bilateral Arrangements*.

Organization for Economic Cooperation and Development Experiences in the Management of National Fishing Zones, 1984.

TACs, Allocations, FLV Fees and Quotas for 1982-85

	1982-1983	1983-84	1984-85
Squid Jigging			
TAC (tons)	40,000	40,000	49,120
Joint venture vessel approvals (numbers)	78	78	78
Joint venture vessel recruitment (numbers)	63	63	63
FLV approvals: Japan (number)	96	96	92
Korea (number)	6	6	6
FLV fees: per vessel	$15,000	$20,250	$25,350
per ton over 150 tons	$100	$135	$169
Squid Trawling (tons)			
TAC: Southern Islands	30,000	30,000	30,000
Rest of the EEZ	20,000	20,000	25,880
FLVS			
Allocated thus:	22,700	22,700	18,660
Southern Islands - Japan	5,000	5,000	4,000
- Korea	1,500	1,500	1,200
- USSR	9,500	9,500	7,600
Rest of the EEZ - Japan	4,900	4,900	3,920
- Korea	1,300	1,300	1,040
- USSR	500	500	900
Deepwater Allocations Total	27,300	27,300	32,300
Southern Islands	14,000	14,000	14,000
Rest of the EEZ - quota	6,000	13,300	18,300
- competitive	7,300	--	--
FLV fees per ton	$53	$103	$114
Tuna			
Northern albacore			
FLV-fees per vessel	$3,000	$4,500	$7,500
Domestic albacore			
Domestic vessels only, unlimited access and catch	--	--	--
Skipjack:			
Joint venture - vessel approvals	11	11	11
- vessel arrivals	2	--	1
Nominal license fee per ton	--	$72	--
Access for joint venture vessels	Provision to allow inside 12 mile on West Coast to 173E and East Coast to 35S.	(Outside 12 mile limit.)	

Appendix 1 (continued)

	1982–1983	1983–84	1984–85
Southern Bluefin			
West Coast:			
Maximum catch domestic			
industry (number of fish)	5,000	10,000	10,000
East Coast:			
FLV – Japanese approvals			
(number of vessels)	96	93	93
FLV – fee per vessel	$36,000	$59,000	$74,000
Finfish trawl			
TAC Total	340,000	342,000	359,000
Allocated thus: FLVS Japan	66,000	66,100	66,100
Area D	8,000	8,000	8,000
E	40,000	34,000	34,000
F	8,000	14,100	14,100
H	10,000	10,000	10,000
Korea	8,750	20,800	21,000
Area D	800	1,000	1,000
E	6,750	18,000	18,200
F	700	800	800
H	500	1,000	1,000
USSR (all Area E)	23,250	25,000	25,000
FLV Fees (ton): Area E	$21	$25	$40
Others*	$35	$47	$59
Domestic (individual allocations)	228,100	231,000	246,900
Finfish, bottom longline			
TAC (tons)	23,000	23,000	10,000*
FLV licence fee (per ton)	$40	$67	$84
Other fees:			
Fish carriers (per ton carrying			
capacity each voyage)	$2	$3	$5
Support craft (gross reg.			
tonnage each voyage)	$1	$1.50	$2.50

* Includes company allocations under deepwater policy. Area D only.

COMMENTARY

Gordon Munro
Professor of Economics
University of British Columbia

I have been asked to comment on the papers by Giulio Pontecorvo and Bill Edeson, but since my fellow commentator, Ron Hanneson, will also be commenting on Edeson's paper, most of my remarks will be on Giulio's paper.

I expect a paper by Giulio to be provocative, and I was not disappointed in this case. A basic theme of Giulio's paper was winners and losers under extended fisheries jurisdiction. It came as no small surprise to me to learn that one of the big winners was Japan, and I suspect that this will also come as no small surprise to the Japanese. The most pertinent and relevant comments really come at the end of the paper where, after looking at different catch levels, he concludes that we cannot yet really make a precise assessment of who the so-called winners and losers are under extended jurisdiction, because there simply is not sufficient evidence.

Where I part company with Giulio is on the use of the raw catch statistics even as a first approximation of winners and losers. We have to remind ourselves what the purpose of extended fisheries jurisdiction is. Giulio has also commented on this. The extension of fisheries jurisdiction has meant a massive transfer to the coastal states of fishery resources that were hitherto international common property. I would go further than Giulio here and say that under the Law of the Sea Convention coastal states have virtual property rights to these resources. It is certainly much more than just management control. The justification was that as international fisheries the resources could not be managed effectively -- the common property problem was simply insuperable; but if the resources were transferred to the coastal state control the common property problem would be mitigated, better management would follow, and the benefits which these resources were capable of yielding would be greatly increased. The winners, of course, were expected to be the coastal states; the losers, the distant-water fishing nations who might be able to recoup partly in their role as coastal states as well. It was certainly anticipated that the gains to the winners would far exceed the losses that might be experienced by the losers. But what were the additional benefits that we are talking about that were supposed to flow from this superior management? It is not just or even primarily additional fish to be caught. Giulio refers to these fishery resources as assets, as indeed they are, and like other assets we see them capable of yielding a stream of income through time -- something that Giulio stressed at the very end -- basically capable of making a contribution to somebody's gross national product, so that the benefits that we are talking about are economic. If we take this approach, which is correct, then one has to treat the unvarnished catch statistics with extreme care because they can be easily misleading. I want to take two examples.

Economists such as Giulio and I have said over and over again that extended fisheries jurisdiction promises potential benefits, but these potential benefits are going to be realized only if the resources acquired by the coastal states are effectively managed. If they are not effectively managed, then it is quite possible that extended fisheries jurisidiction will bring negative benefits to coastal states once we take into account the additional administrative burdens. I want to cite the case of Canada. If we look at Giulio's table of winners and losers based on the catch statistics, we find that Canada is down there as a winner -- not a dramatic winner, to be sure, but nonetheless a winner. If we compare the growth in catches experienced by Canada, we see that they increase by a very satisfying 35 percent. Most of this increase was concentrated off Canada's Atlantic coasts in spite of what Giulio said about the decline generally in Northwest Atlantic catches, and much of it reflected catches of ground fish, *e.g.*, cod, flounder, etc. In the 1973-1975 period, Giulio's base period, the Canadian Atlantic coast groundfish industry was close to bankruptcy and had to be bailed out by the Canadian federal government. The root cause lay with over-exploitation by distant-water fishing nations off Canada's shores, so a 200-mile fishing zone was implemented by Canada, the stock-restoration program was undertaken, and Canada's Atlantic harvest grew appreciably. By 1981-82, the end period in Giulio's tables, the groundfish catches were up, and what was the state of the Canadian-Atlantic groundfish industry? It is in a state of bankruptcy even worse than the state that it was in in 1973-75, and once again the federal government had to mount a bail-out operation. What went wrong? The catches had been increased, but this had been accompanied by an ineffectively restrained over-expansion of both the harvesting and processing sectors in Canada. The common property syndrome had re-emerged to dissipate the potential benefits of extended jurisdiction. Once the enhanced administrative costs imposed by Canada are taken into account, we in Canada would be lucky if we did not find that so far the benefits from extended fisheries jurisdiction are negative, so that the apparent winner may in fact at this stage be a loser.

Secondly, the catch statistics as presented seem to imply that the only way that a coastal state can win is by catching the fish itself. Many coastal states have acted as if this were the case, but the economics of fisheries do not always support this approach. While it is unpopular to say so, in some instances it may make far more sense for the coastal states to hire the services of distant-water fishing nations rather than trying to harvest and process the resource with its own capital.

One of the groups of coastal states that have had the most to gain in terms of their national economies have been the Pacific island nations, for many of which fisheries are the prime economic resource, as Bill Edeson stressed in his paper. What evidence we do have, while it suggests that certainly much can be done to enhance the management and the gain, does appear to show that they are definitely one of the winners. But while they have been expanding their harvesting activity, it is likely to remain the case on good economic grounds that the bulk of the harvest, most of their rich offshore tuna resources, will continue to be taken by distant-water fishing nations for the foreseeable future. The Pacific island nations are certainly winners, but one searches in vain for the list of winners in the tables that we have been presented with for any reference to these states. Catch-statistics alone can be therefore very misleading -- either by grossly overstating or understating the coastal state gains from resources acquired. We have to repeat, in-season and out-, the point that Giulio made right at the very end of his paper: the benefits for the coastal states from extended fisheries jurisdiction are potential; they can be easily lost if the acquired resources are not accompanied by effective management.

I turn now to Bill Edeson's paper. He is concerned primarily with small developing coastal and island states, and especially those in the South Pacific and the Caribbean. He emphasizes the cooperative activities that have developed among these states, using the Forum Fisheries Agency as a model case. From my perspective as an economist, the paper points out two major additional management problems that have to be faced by coastal states -- developed as well as developing -- in addition to the common property problem. First is the management of transboundary stocks, or what Bill refers to as "straddling stocks." This arises because fish are highly mobile, and consequently a coastal state is likely to find that it is sharing its resources with other coastal states. Obviously effective joint management is required, and if this is not forthcoming, then once again the benefits of Extended Fisheries Jurisdiction can be easily dissipated. The other problem is the development of effective cooperative arrangements between coastal states and distant-water fishing nations; among many of the developing coastal states Bill refers to this is critical, and if it is not done effectively, once again many of the benefits can easily be lost. What can we say about it at this stage? Not very much, except that the problems are relatively new -- they require a great deal of study and examination through time. There is one benefit from this: it will provide employment for practitioners and academics for some time.

I want to conclude with one comment on the most interesting and the most difficult cooperative arrangement, namely the arrangements between the United States with respect to tuna fishing and developing coastal states in the eastern and the western Pacific. Bill invited a comment on where the negotiations lay with respect to the United States and the member states of the Forum Fisheries Agency. I had the pleasure of meeting with the Deputy Director of the Forum Fisheries Agency a couple of weeks ago, and I am authorized to tell you that the negotiations are poised, that there are going to be one or two critical meetings forthcoming; if things go well, then all the unpleasantness that has occurred will fade into the past. If they are not successful, then the future does not bear thinking about.

COMMENTARY

Professor Rognvaldur Hannesson
The Norwegian School of Economics and Business Administration
Bergen

I would like to begin by re-emphasizing something that Professor Pontecorvo says in his paper, namely that the new order of the oceans may have been preordained by an underlying development in technology, economic growth, and political organization. Some of us will recall that the 1950s and 1960s were a period of rapid improvement in fishing technology. Fishing vessels became larger and ranged further afield, and the pressure on the limited productivity of fish stocks increased. So-called coastal states increasingly saw their interests being threatened by distant water fleets and sought protection through enlarged national fishing zones.

There is little doubt that the enlarged exclusive fishing zones are the result of coastal states' arrogating to themselves whatever value fish stocks in their adjacent waters may have. Exclusive fishing zones, or economic zones, are thus just another milestone in the development of exclusive rights, or property rights. But even if the purpose of property rights is to confer benefits upon the holders of such rights, it is a fact that economic organization based on such rights can be beneficial for a much wider community, and more so than economic organization based on communal or common property. This comes about through a better husbandry of resources. Ironically, the forces of competition are prone to transfer a part of the gain from a better husbandry of resources from those who own the resources to those who buy the derived products.

Exclusive fishing zones represent an opportunity for a better husbandry of fish resources, an opportunity, that is, because the coastal states that now have acquired fish stocks as an exclusive or shared property would seem to have much to gain from making the best possible use of them. Most states presently seem to have failed to do so, one of the exceptions being New Zealand. Why they have failed to do so takes us into the subject of public choice that is, why governments fail in their management of the economy, which I shall not pursue here.

What, then, are the gains which could be derived from a better husbandry of fish resources? Here we may distinguish between two types of gains. First, the reduction of excessive fishing may result in a larger yield of fish. Secondly, the curtailment of excessive fishing capacity means that more resources will be available for other kinds of production, and so more goods will become available to satisfy our needs. There is hardly any presumption which of these will prevail. If the world's fish resources can be taken to have been grossly over-exploited prior to the establishment of the 200-mile limit, then we would expect it to result in a larger world catch. But if the world catch fails to increase, this cannot by itself be taken as a sign of the 200-mile limit having failed to improve the utilization of fish stocks. To pass judgment on this we must look into what has happened with fishing effort and capacity.

Professor Pontecorvo has focussed his attention on the first type of gain, the increase in world catch after the new law of the sea regime came into being. He finds an increase of 16 percent, from the three-year period 1973-75 to the three year period 1981-83. This would seem to count in favor of the new regime. We do not know, however, what has happened to fishing effort and fleet capacity, or even which fish stocks are responsible for the increase in yield. It is just possible that what we witness here is an unsustainable increase due to overfishing of yet more fish stocks.

The fishery policy of New Zealand is one of the few cases in which a country aims at utilizing its fish resources in an economically efficient manner and has shown a willingness to use the means necessary to accomplish this. This raises the question why New Zealand is such a special case. The answer is to be sought in political economy; the management of fish stocks is, by its nature, very much a matter of government policy, and how well or badly governments do this depends on how they perceive that their interests will be served. In countries with a long tradition of fishing, the fishing industry is often economically depressed, due to overexploitation of common property stocks. Governments have, for reasons of incomes policy, tried to bail out the fishing industry by throwing money at it. This has been self-defeating, encouraging further overfishing and excessive capacity, and governments have ended up throwing good money after bad. This policy is often made easier by the fact that the fishery is only a small part of the gross national product and located in geographically disadvantaged areas considered to need economic support of some kind.

In New Zealand, by contrast, fishing is a relatively new industry. This is particularly true of the deep water fishery, in which the system of individual transferable quotas was first implemented. The accepted rules of the game appear to have been that the fishing industry would prevail or perish according to its own profitability. This attitude, it would seem, accounts for the industry's acceptance of the quota scheme and its promise of enhanced profitability. On the government's side, what accounts for the interest in having the fishing industry as efficiently run as possible is its role as a new export industry and the concern to improve the overall performance of the economy. Although the fishing industry is not a large part of New Zealand's economy, it is a rapidly developing export industry in a country which has suffered severe setbacks in its traditional trade because of protectionism with respect to agricultural products. Furthermore, the prevailing mood in the country seems to be one of acute awarness that New Zealand has been lagging behind other so-called western nations in economic growth. There seems, at the present time, to be a willingness in New Zealand to rely more heavily on market oriented solutions, rather than controls and regulations, to improve the performance of the economy. The individual quota scheme can be seen as a part of this process. Everybody recognizes that the fishery is an example of an industry which must be regulated if economic efficiency is to be attained, but the scheme of the individual transferable quotas is probably the method that best emulates a perfect market solution.

A management system based on individual transferable quotas implies that there is an overall quota, or a total allowable catch, for each particular year. A point worth noting about the system in New Zealand is that it was put in place before the yield potential of the fish stocks involved was very well known. This is, at any rate, true for the deep sea fishery, where the individual quotas were first implemented. The fishery biologists that I have talked to in New Zealand readily acknowledged that their estimates of maximum sustainable yields might err by as much as 50 percent. An example is the orange roughy that was virtually unknown less than a decade ago. One might ask whether the

208

implementation of catch quotas under such uncertainty might not be ill-conceived and be an unjustifiable limit to an otherwise possible further development of the fishing industry. I think the New Zealanders have erred on the safe side. The experience of other fishing nations shows how difficult it is to end overfishing and eliminate excessive fishing capacity once they get entangled in that type of mess. The New Zealanders appear to have taken care to avoid that trap. The New Zealanders cite falling catch rates and profitability as a sign of diminishing fish stocks and a proof that the total allowable catch is not being set too conservatively.

This last point raises the issue of how the optimal catch from a given fish stock depends on economic parameters. This comes about in two ways. First, the discount rate affects the trade-off between the present and the future and thereby the optimal standing stock and catch. Secondly, the cost of catching a ton of fish may increase as the stock from which it is taken is depleted. The New Zealanders refer to the latter when they say that a higher catch quota and a further depletion of the fish stocks is not economically justifiable. So, if the discount rates or fishing costs differ between any two nations, their views on optimal standing stocks and catches will also differ. Nevertheless, Articles 61 and 62 of the Law of the Sea Treaty seem to be based on the idea that the optimal allowable catch from a fish stock is a uniquely determined quantity. The Treaty vests the coastal state with the right to determine the allowable catch and any surplus thereof, and a potential low cost foreign harvester does not seem to have any recourse in case he desires a greater total allowable catch. The only case in which a coastal state would be expected to set the allowable catch on the basis of a foreign harvester's low cost would be the one in which the coastal state rents the harvesting rights of its fish to a foreign harvester. This could be in the coastal state's own interest, and does take place to some extent.

This takes us to the subject of Mr. Edeson's paper: international fishery agreements. He reminds us how the Law of the Sea Treaty urges nations to cooperate in using the fish resources of the world. The teeth of these urgings will, however, be provided by nations finding it in their self-interest to do so. That a forceful self-interest exists need not be doubted, and international fisheries agreements have indeed become prolific since the 200-mile limit became universal. A useful way of classifying fishery agreements would be to distinguish between agreements that allow foreign fleets to harvest "surplus" allowable catch and agreements on the use of shared fish stocks. Since surplus allowable catch is a consequence either of the coastal state's insufficient fishing capacity or high fishing costs, both of which are likely to be of a temporary nature, there is reason to expect this type of agreement to be short term and *ad hoc*. The so-called joint venture agreements belong to this category. By contrast, the sharing of fish stocks is dictated by geography, and so we would expect agreements on such matters to be long term and based on principle. Most of the agreements that Mr. Edeson mentions are of this kind, but there are many more. We have yet to learn what principles, if any, are common to such agreements.

DISCUSSION AND QUESTIONS

Unidentified Woman: *The Guardian* recently carried an article on the Soviet Union negotiating with Kiribati on fishing agreements. What is the impact of this on the U.S. and the South Pacific islands negotiations?

W.R. Edeson: I am no better informed than you are, but I have heard of the Kiribati-proposed agreèment and my feeling is that it probably reflects what we could expect to happen if the tuna problem is not settled in the South Pacific fairly quickly.

M.G. Jennings: The papers have reflected largely upon the economics of the implementation of the UNCLOS in relation to fisheries. There are also significant costs for coastal states as well as potential benefits. Would the panel hazard any indication of the likely costs, particularly in enforcement terms, for coastal states in relation to the potential benefits which actually apply? I have in mind Mr. Major's reference to 1,300,000 square miles, admittedly not all of it fished, but representing a substantial area to patrol and a potential for considerable illegal fishing within it. When you are declaring limits on legal foreign fishing, the pressure not only from your own state's fishermen but from those legal foreign fishermen for effective enforcement against any other illegals becomes increasingly greater. Would the panel comment on this aspect of fisheries?

Philip Major: Certainly we are concerned with the policing of our zone. We police our extended zone with flyovers by Nimrod aircraft with radar monitoring. We also have naval patrols and fisheries patrols. We have, on at least two occasions, arrested foreign vessels fishing illegally for tuna in the northern area of our zone. Currently, the total cost of managing our zone -- for doing fisheries research, for policing by our Ministry of Agriculture and Fisheries -- is $16 million. This year for the first time we are going to recover $18 million from unlicensed vessels, New Zealand deepwater operators and New Zealand domestic operators -- so we are actually making a contribution there. The $16 million does not include the cost of the military operations, which would take us over that amount. For some budgeting reason, the government does not want to assign these costs to fisheries; it treats the military's role in the protection mechanism as practice military maneuvers. I suspect that in the not too distant future when our fisheries royalties increase, those additional costs will be covered as well.

Gordon Munro: When I made my comments on Giulio Pontecorvo's paper and Bill Edeson's paper, I stressed the importance of effective management by the coastal state if the potential benefits from extended fisheries jurisdiction were going to be realized. If the management is not effective, the coastal state could quite easily end up enjoying negative benefits from extended fisheries jurisdiction once one took into account the additional administrative cost in which I include surveillance and enforcement. We have not, in this panel, addressed the question of surveillance and enforcement, but clearly it is an extremely important aspect of management under extended fisheries jurisdiction. That would lead us into the question of the types of agreements with distant-water fishing nations that would tend to minimize illegal activities. One area of the world where this is of extreme importance is the South Pacific. The fisheries resources acquired in the South Pacific have potentially immense value but are held by very small and rather poor island states that are attempting to manage really vast ocean areas. Perhaps that would serve as a good panel for the next Law of the Sea Institute conference.

Kazuo Sumi: My question concerns the more fundamental and broader aspects of the fisheries programs. There are three main problems in the impact of UNCLOS on fisheries. They involve conservation, distribution of resources, and delimitation. We have had, in the past, good international cooperation for conserving fishery resources, but this regime is rather fragmented, and it is very difficult to achieve cooperation among states. So how can we overcome the practice of military action by each coastal state? Coastal states arbitrarily determine the allowable catch, their harvesting capacity and the surplus. Is this a good way to conserve living resources, especially in enclosed or semi-enclosed seas?

My second question concerns the reduction of the economic gap between developed and developing countries. One speaker referred to "winners" and "losers." In a sense, Japan is a loser, but in another sense Japan is a winner, because Japan can enclose very vast sea areas. On the other hand, landlocked countries such as Nepal, Bhutan, Afghanistan, Mali, and Swaziland are among the poorest in the world, and they can get nothing. Many speakers referred to the increase of fish production, but there are many serious hunger and starvation problems, so it does not contribute to the improvement of nutrition in the world. Most of the developing countries are more concerned about the cash profit from fish for export, and they do not contribute to the local people's health improvement. What is the impact of UNCLOS on the distribution of resources in the world?

My third question is related to the delimitation problem. There are very serious potential sources of conflict among members of the international community in terms of unresolved delimitation of overlapping zones.

Giulio Pontecorvo: The Convention calls for the full utilization of the resource and Mr. Major's paper referred to it. The problem is that full utilization is a totally unworkable concept, just as the maximum sustainable yield is an unworkable concept. If you have two countries (Country One and Country Two) and two species of fish (A is a high-valued fish and B is a low-valued fish), the coastal state, Country One, will only catch Species A because it can only sell that in its markets. Country Two, which fishes in those waters, will catch both species A and B, high-valued and low-valued. If you transfer control over the resource to the coastal state, the coastal state will catch only species A, the high-valued species, and the low-valued species will go unutilized. That, nevertheless, represents to Country One, and Country One has jurisdiction in this instance, full utilization of the resource, which is the Species A. Since there is no agency that can define the full extent of the resources, since there is no really adequate stock assessment across the board, you find that the question of full utilization comes down to coastal state preference. This result may be unfortunate, but I see no easy way out of it. If you have a well-managed fishery with no real entry pressures and if the industry is profitable and has an interest in conservation, you may have an allowable surplus. However, the problem is more complicated than that. In the Georges Bank fishery, for example, the low-value species were the squid and the hake. When the Russians and the other foreign fleets were catching large quantities of squid and hake, they were affecting the entire biomass, so that questions of what constitutes real conservation and what constitutes a set of preferences for the coastal state are very difficult to define.

Philip Major: There was a point Professor Sumi made as to whether Japan or the USSR were winners or losers, and I agree that you have to be careful about the effects of the catch. Certainly, foreign nations are paying significant sums of money for access to the New Zealand zone. While we do not specifically know whether those sums are justified by their catches or whether they are just reserving a position there, there is a real economic cost to them, and I would imagine that to be the case in a lot of other zones around the world.

Ellen Hey: I'm from the Netherlands Institute of the Law of the Sea. I have a question on transboundary stocks. Several of the speakers referred to the fact that these stocks require effective and specific management systems. In temperate waters, we have traditionally thought of one stock or several interdependent stocks that have to be identified and subsequently regulated. Examples would be the halibut fishery in the Pacific or the capelin fishery in the Jan Mayen area. My understanding is that the tuna fishery would be the only fishery that could be regulated in a similar way in tropical waters. Most other fisheries are multispecies fisheries and therefore not subject to this type of regulatory system. It seems that a joint fisheries zone as in the Torres Strait Agreement would be the type of mechanism needed to regulate these fisheries. Is there any evidence of a movement there is a movement towards the creation of more joint fisheries zones in tropical waters?

W.R. Edeson: I understand that there has been discussion in the FAO context for promoting "natural management areas" to deal with the type of questions you raise. It recognizes that 200-mile zones do not always provide the complete answers to the situation. I have heard it discussed in the Caribbean context. The Torres Strait Agreement certainly tries to deal with that situation by fusing the two zones as far as possible to come up with one regime. But I am not aware of other areas unless you include the tuna agreements.

Giulio Pontecorvo: There is a theoretical model on which the management of large marine ecosystems could be conducted, but it has no real practical basis. You can think of Georges Bank as a large marine ecosystem, but the ability to manage the ecosystem to achieve a preferred biomass is clearly beyond us at this point in terms of fisheries management.

PART III:

DELIMITATION OF MARITIME SPACES:
RECENT PRACTICE AND CURRENT PROBLEMS

INTRODUCTION

Bernard Oxman
School of Law
University of Miami

The rules of international law that now permit quite extensive coastal state jurisdiction make it necessary for neighboring coastal states to resolve problems with each other of overlapping jurisdiction. Because of the size of the zones and the importance of the resources involved, the most important of these delimitation questions are those of the 200-mile exclusive economic zone and the continental shelf. The text of the 1982 Convention does not offer much guidance. It says that the delimitation of the exclusive economic zone and the delimitation of the continental shelf are to be effected by agreement between the states concerned in accordance with international law in order to achieve an equitable solution. Therefore, what is the international law on this subject? Court decisions offer us little explicit guidance either; they tend to refer to the application of equitable principles taking into account relevant circumstances. None of this seems very determinate on its face. Thus, in order to figure out what to do under those kinds of rules, the emergence of the boundary issues has made its own contribution to ameliorating the underlying world problem of unemployment. Batteries of lawyers, geographers, geologists, oceanographers, marine biologists, and economists have been assembled by governments for three purposes: first, to help each government formulate its own national positions and claims; second, to help the government negotiate the issue with its neighbors; and third, if necessary, to help the government present its case to tribunals authorized to decide the issue where negotiations have not succeeded. There is no doubt that the employment opportunities for the first two purposes will continue well into the future. When states negotiate with each other, they can generally consider any factors that they wish, and the International Court of Justice recently made that quite clear. However, where the boundary is submitted to a legal tribunal for determination, the field may be narrowing a bit. In its most recent decision in the case between Libya and Malta on delimitation of their continental shelves, the International Court of Justice had some rather interesting things to say about the relevance of certain geological and economic considerations. The Court said,

> Since the development of the law enables a State to claim that the continental shelf appertaining to it extends up to as far as 200 miles from its coast, whatever the geological characteristics of the corresponding sea-bed and subsoil, there is no reason to ascribe any role to geological or geophysical factors within that distance, either in verifying the legal title of the States concerned or in proceeding to a delimitation as between their claims.

So much for the geologists. The Court went on to say that, insofar as geological facts are disputed -- which they were, in that case --

> The Court is unable to accept the position that in order to decide this case, it must first make a determination upon a disagreement

between scientists of distinction as to the more plausibly correct interpretation of apparently incomplete scientific data.

In other words, if it is necessary for us to decide disputed scientific questions in order to resolve legal cases, we will decide that the scientific questions are irrelevant.

Finally, on economics, the Court says, "there can be no question of distributive justice"; and continues,

> the Court does not, however, consider that the delimitation should be influenced by the relative economic position of the two States in question.

In light of these remarks, which are from the most recent judgment of the Court, any of you who feel that you could be more profitably employed elsewhere should feel free to leave the room right now. But I should tell you that if you do leave the room, you will miss some very stimulating presentations from a very distinguished panel of experts from three continents.

Our first panelist is David Colson, Assistant Legal Adviser of the United States Department of State. He has worked on oceans and boundary questions for many years, and he served as Deputy-Agent of the United States in the presentation of its recent case before the Chamber of the International Court of Justice with respect to the Gulf of Maine.

The Legal Adviser of the Canadian Department of External Affairs, Ambassador Leonard Legault, has for a long time been a friend and supporter of this Institute and an imaginative architect of the international law of the sea. He was looking forward to being with us today, but unfortunately he was prevented from doing so by his other responsibilities. Please join me in expressing our particular gratitude to our next speaker for agreeing to be with us today on relatively short notice. Donald McRae is a Professor of Law at the University of British Columbia. He has served as an academic visitor in the Legal Bureau of the Canadian Department of External Affairs and participated in the preparation of the Canadian arguments in the *Gulf of Maine* case. He is the author of many learned studies by no means limited to questions of international law or the law of the sea.

Any discussion of delimitation at this meeting would be incomplete without a presentation on some of the unresolved delimitation problems in the very waters that are washing these shores. Dr. Clive Symmons is a Senior Lecturer in Law at the University of Bristol, and he will be speaking on "The Outstanding Maritime Boundary Problems between Ireland and the U.K." These are not necessarily limited to the Irish Sea.

The regimes of the continental shelf and the EEZ are very much concerned with natural resources. From this one might conclude that economic considerations lie at the heart of the delimitation question, and that this would be particularly true in the case of developing countries attempting to build their economies through the development of natural resources, as well as for other states that are dependent upon the consumption of such resources. These factors may indeed explain the existence of maritime boundary disputes, but their relevance to the settlement of such disputes by a court of law is much less clear. The Dean of the Faculty of Law of the University of Kurukshetra in India, Surya P. Sharma, is a highly respected and thoughtful observer of this process who has come a very considerable distance to be with us today.

Our commentator, Robert Krueger, is a private attorney in Los Angeles with a great deal of experience in the law of the sea and in coastal zone management.

ENVIRONMENTAL FACTORS:
ARE THEY RELEVANT TO DELIMITATION?

David A. Colson
Assistant Legal Adviser
U.S. Department of State

If one had asked a group of international lawyers a few years ago if they thought that the first delimitation of a 200 nautical mile maritime boundary would stress new elements of legal relevance for delimitation, I feel safe in asserting that most persons would have answered *yes*. And I believe that they would have said that environmental factors would attain such a role. Most of those lawyers probably would not have said more, but they would have been comfortable with their prediction. It would have been based upon the logical assumption that if factual characteristics of the seabed, such as geology and geomorphology, might be relevant to a continental shelf delimitation, certainly characteristics of the marine environment might be legally relevant to the delimitation of the water column.

The international judicial process has now produced a delimitation of the 200 nautical mile zone -- the maritime boundary between the United States and Canada in the Gulf of Maine area, decided by a Chamber of the International Court of Justice on October 12, 1984. We find that environmental factors play no identifiable role in the decision -- despite being strongly urged upon the Court by at least one of the parties.

It is fair then for us to ask:

(a) whether the preliminary prediction was faulty; or
(b) whether the Gulf of Maine court erred; or
(c) whether the *Gulf of Maine* case and its decision is distinguishable, either in fact or law, so that the preliminary prediction might still hold -- that is, environmental factors may yet play a legal role in the delimitation of maritime boundaries?

For those of us who will admit to assuming that environmental factors would stand out in the first 200 nautical mile zone delimitation case, it is important for our own self-esteem to address the three questions stated above. Even those of you perceptive enough not to have so predicted may nonetheless find such an examination of interest, if for no other reason than to see your foresight confirmed.

Thus, I propose to examine these three questions in the light of my experience as Deputy-Agent for the United States in the *Gulf of Maine* case. At this point I must note that the views I am about to express are my own and do not constitute the views of the United States government.

Was It Reasonable to have Predicted that Environmental Factors Would be Legally Relevant to the Delimitation of a 200 Nautical Mile Zone Boundary?

The acceptance in international law and practice of the 200 nautical mile fishing zones or exclusive economic zones established in the mid-1970s resulted in the need to delimit those zones of jurisdiction between neighboring states. In the 1970s, the general establishment of the 200 nautical mile zone as an international fact was first and foremost in the thinking of most persons participating in that legal process. Just as had been true for the continental shelf, the boundaries of those zones between neighboring countries were secondary to the fundamental definition of the nature and scope of the coastal state's jurisdiction outward toward the open sea. As in the case of the continental shelf, at the time the zones became an international fact of life, the analysis of the factors that might be relevant to their delimitation was sparse to non-existent. Most persons participating in this process perceived that the delimitation of the zones would be dealt with as the delimitation of the continental shelf had been -- with some states oriented toward application of the equidistance method while others argued for boundaries that gave them more than strict application of the equidistance method could achieve.

Nevertheless, in the 1980s, as the first decision of a tribunal approached on the question of a water column delimitation, the legal guidance available indicated that a broad range of factors might have legal relevance. This was so whatever the perspective from which one approached the law: from the perspective embodied in Article 6 of the 1958 Geneva Convention on the Continental Shelf -- the equidistance-special circumstance rule; or from a perspective based upon the formulation stated by the International Court of Justice in the *North Sea Continental Shelf* cases -- equitable principles and relevant circumstances; or, from a perspective along the lines of the equitable solution referred to in Articles 74 of the 1982 LOS Treaty. In each case there was room to identify a broad range of factors, including environmental factors, that could be legally relevant to a delimitation.

This perception was certainly encouraged by the International Court of Justice. In 1969, in its judgement in the *North Sea Continental Shelf* cases, the Court's statements concerning natural prolongation led many international boundary lawyers into the scientific realms of geology and geomorphology. Furthermore, the Court also spoke of the concept of the unity of resource deposits as a factor to be taken into account in delimitation.

Both of these elements, endorsed and perhaps propagated by the Court in delimitation of the continental shelf, call upon scientific fact for their determination. They are, in the case of natural prolongation, based upon a natural boundary concept, and, in the case of unity of deposit, a concern for conservation and efficient resource management.

These quasi-legal/quasi-factual general concepts are readily transferable by analogy to a water column delimitation. Scientists tell us of natural boundaries in the water, and resource conservation is clearly a matter of concern.

Besides these analogies found in the *North Sea Continental Shelf* cases, other developments seemed to open up the law to new considerations rather than narrowing it down: the two subsequent continental shelf cases, the *Anglo-French* case and the *Tunisia-Libya* case; and, the delimitation negotiations in the Third United Nations Law of the Sea Conference. The Court of Arbitration in the *Anglo-French* case indicated that there was no particular limitation on the special circumstances that might require deviation from the equidistance method under Article 6 of the Continental Shelf Convention. The International Court of Justice in the *Tunisia-Libya* case also indicated that the relevant circumstances referred to in the equitable principles formulation of customary law were not limited to geographical factors. At the Law of the Sea Conference, moreover, efforts to promote the equidistance method failed. With this background one can only be left with the conclusion that the legal debate concerning the location of a maritime boundary was open to any factor that might help achieve, or identify, an equitable solution.

Thus, I believe one was on firm ground if one made the prediction that environmental factors would be relevant to a delimitation of the water column. The trend was to expand the relevant considerations applicable in a maritime boundary delimitation.

But having said this, it is important to ask what are the environmental factors that might be relevant and how are they said to affect a delimitation. Here we begin to get the real question. For the Chamber of the International Court of Justice in the *Gulf of Maine* case did not say that environmental factors were irrelevant; it just did not find them to be relevant in that case.

Did the Chamber of the International Court of Justice Err in the *Gulf of Maine* Case by not Finding Environmental Factors to be Relevant in that Delimitation?

The *Gulf of Maine* case was principally about whether the United States was entitled to jurisdiction over 100% of Georges Bank, a rich fishing ground in the Northwest Atlantic Ocean, or whether Canada was entitled to jurisdiction over some significant portion of the Bank, up to about 35% to 40% of the Bank that it claimed. A boundary that would have given the United States what it claimed would have run northeast of Georges Bank through something called the *Northeast Channel* -- a shallow geomorphological trough that divides the Scotian Shelf from Georges Bank.

The United States believed that if ever there was a case where environmental factors were legally relevant, this was it. The world community knew a great deal about the oceanography of the delimitation area, including its flora and fauna. The United States asserted that the marine environment in this area might have been the subject of more intense scientific study than any other major ocean area in the world. The Georges Bank ecosystem was an established scientific fact. For decades, international organizations and domestic institutions of both the United States and Canada had managed the fisheries in the area relying upon certain common environmental assumptions, including the division of fishery stocks at the Northeast Channel. But although the United States believed that these facts concerning the marine environment were relevant to the delimitation, it became a bit more difficult to explain precisely how they were relevant to delimitation.

The marine environment is relevant in one sense, of course, as being part of the area in which the delimitation takes place. It is no doubt useful for a court to understand something about the marine environment of the area being delimited. The depth of water, the currents, the water temperature, the plants and animals that live in the water, are all matters of general interest. But the fact that environmental factors are interesting and descriptive of the delimitation setting does not necessarily mean they are actually legally relevant.

As the United States sought to determine how environmental factors might be legally relevant in the *Gulf of Maine* case, it found little to guide it. There is little of note on this subject in the legal literature. The United States legal team had to develop its own theories in this respect, and were perhaps the first to do so.

In a general sense, the United States decided that environmental factors might be relevant to delimitation in three basic ways. I shall describe each of our arguments together with the Chamber's treatment of them.

The first approach was to argue that there was a natural boundary in the marine environment along which the Chamber ought to establish the international legal boundary. In continental shelf terms, this was akin to arguing that there was a natural division in the seabed creating two separate legal continental shelves in the delimitation area. In other words, the natural boundary in the marine environment argument was analogized to the physical natural prolongation argument put forward by the parties in both the *Anglo-French* case and the *Tunisia-Libya* case and never rejected in principle by either the Court of Arbitration or the International Court of Justice. The United States supported this argument by reference to the land boundary cases which have often looked to natural boundaries in the terrain for a legal boundary. Indeed, it is fair to say that courts have always felt free to use a natural feature to mark a boundary when it seemed appropriate to do so.

It is beyond the scope of this paper to describe the factual arguments put forward in proof of the existence of a natural boundary in the marine environment at the Northeast Channel. Suffice it to say that the United States argued vigorously to prove the point, and Canada just as vigorously denied the existence of any such natural boundary, at least in the location proposed by the United States.

As a matter of law, the Chamber dealt with this argument much as the Court dealt with the natural prolongation arguments in the *Tunisia-Libya* case. The Chamber did not expressly state that there was no such thing as a natural boundary in the marine environment which might constitute a legal boundary. But the Chamber indicated more than considerable doubt on the point.

First, the Chamber seems to have found it difficult conceptually to handle the relationship between the marine environment and continental shelf, almost as if the Chamber did not fully appreciate that the exclusive economic zone includes the seabed and the water column. The Chamber decided that it had to find both a natural boundary on the continental shelf, a geological break which the United States admitted did not exist, and a natural boundary in the water column, before a natural boundary might govern the case. This finding, of course, completely negated the United States' natural boundary argument and was the only ruling the Chamber had to make to dispose of this issue. Nonetheless, the Chamber went on to say that even if there had been a natural division in the seabed, the facts did not show a natural boundary in the water column. The Chamber held the United States' argument to an extraordinarily high standard of proof, stating that "the result was not such as to clear away all doubt, at least as regards certain of the technical aspects debated" (para. 53). Besides this, however, the Chamber went even further. It cast doubt on the whole notion of natural boundaries in the marine environment, stating, "The Chamber is not however convinced of the possibility of discerning any genuine, sure and stable 'natural boundaries' in so fluctuating an environment as the waters of the ocean, their flora and fauna" (para. 54). And, it indicated that the legal boundary need not follow a natural boundary if the location of the natural boundary is inequitable (para. 56).

The second way that the United States argued that environmental factors were legally relevant was by proposing that the boundary ought to be based upon two equitable principles which called upon environmental factors in their application. This argument drew upon the concept of unity of deposit identified by the Court in the *North Sea Continental Shelf* cases. The first of these principles was that the delimitation should facilitate the conservation and management of the resources. The second was that the delimitation should minimize the potential for international disputes. The facts which were drawn upon were those designed to show that Georges Bank is an integrated ocean ecosystem and that the living resources of Georges Bank are common pool resources in economic terms. Any delimitation dividing the Bank, the United States argued, would thus result in wasteful competition and harm to the resources that international law was designed to protect. Application of these principles in this factual context, of course, strongly supported the United States' position that it was entitled to 100% of Georges Bank.

Canada responded that these principles were not delimitation principles *per se*, but standards of responsible international conduct. In Canada's view, even if the marine environment facts were as stated by the United States, which Canada did not concede, these principles could not be applied to those facts to establish in law the boundary proposed by the United States.

The Court clearly sided with Canada on these points. It said that there was no rule of international law that the "boundary should make it possible to ensure the optimum conservation of and management of living resources and at the same time reduce the potential for international disputes" (para. 110).

On its face this holding does not seem reasonable. Why should not a court seek a boundary that promotes these goals? The Chamber gives us no real reason. It says that this is still "a new and unconsolidated field" (para. 111) and that it is "unrewarding ... to look to general international law to provide a ready-made set of rules that can be used for solving any delimitation problems that arise" (para. 111). One in my position can only feel that the Chamber shied away from these arguments due to their strength. The Chamber was confronted with two eminently reasonable principles to which it would have subscribed in almost any other context. Here, however, application of these principles pointed one way, and thus, ironically, to a delimitation that the Chamber did not find equitable, since it would seem to be characteristic of the international boundary adjudication process that neither party's claims are ever deemed equitable by the court.

The third way in which the United States argued that environmental factors were legally relevant was in the more classic sense that the facts of the marine environment were relevant circumstances to be taken into account in the delimitation.

In its formulation of the law, the Chamber found that there was a three-step legal process: choice of equitable criteria, choice of method, and examination of the resulting line to ensure an equitable result. This is a useful way of thinking about the law of maritime boundaries. However, it does not clarify at what stage "relevant circumstances" are to be taken into account.

In the *Gulf of Maine* case, the Chamber looked only to geographical facts, relationships, and principles in deciding upon and applying the equitable criteria and choice of method. In its third step, examination of the equitableness of the line so determined, the Chamber avoided any examination of the marine environment considerations. The only conclusion reached in its third step was that socio-economic considerations might have caused it to adjust the result it reached by application of criteria and method, if that result had led to disastrous economic

222

consequences for one country or the other. In this respect the Chamber indicated that a line reflecting the United States position might have had such an impact upon Canada. It did not indicate that disastrous environmental consequences could have had the same impact on its consideration.

It is not for me to say whether the Chamber erred in the treatment of the environmental factors in the *Gulf of Maine* case. I do note, however, that I do not find the treatment, on balance, unreasonable, particularly from the perspective of judicial policy. The Chamber dealt with the United States' natural boundary argument as if to say that it did not want to open up this new area of the law to the same type of inconclusive scientific debate that had come out of the Court's reference to natural prolongation in 1969. The Chamber did not appreciate the U.S.'s environmental principles because they left no room for maneuver. And, the Chamber found the environmental facts not to be so compelling as to cause it to change a geographically induced line it otherwise considered equitable. Yet, those of us on the U.S. team found it disappointing that the Chamber regarded the resource and marine environment issues in this case so lightly. In its judgment, the Chamber brushes aside our environmental concerns which will arise out of having to share jurisdiction over Georges Bank between the United States and Canada. The Chamber seems to discount these concerns, noting that the United States and Canada are friendly nations with a record of cooperation. Would the Chamber have considered the environmental issue differently had the political relationship between the United States and Canada been different? Probably not; thus, one can only take the Chamber's treatment of these issues with a grain of salt. As a matter of judicial policy, it was simply unwilling to entertain them.

Is the Chamber's Treatment of the Environmental Factors in the *Gulf of Maine* Case Distinguishable on the Facts or on the Law?

I submit that this case is distinguishable on both the facts and the law from the cases that will follow. I also submit that lawyers will try to distinguish their cases, but that they will be no more successful with environmental arguments than the United States was in the *Gulf of Maine* case.

On the facts, I believe that it is unlikely that any other country in any other boundary situation will be able to marshal the marine environment evidence that the United States was able to marshal in this case. What was particularly compelling was the fact that the domestic fisheries management institutions of both countries, as well as international conventions, had operated on the environmental assumptions that the United States advanced in its case.

But each boundary situation is different. The facts are always going to be distinguishable. That is the nature of the marine environment. The ability of lawyers to distinguish facts keeps them in business. In my view, however, no matter how good a job a lawyer does in distinguishing the facts of his case from the *Gulf of Maine* case, I do not believe that a court will look at the marine environment issues much differently than the Chamber did in the *Gulf of Maine* case.

There are two legal and two tactical considerations for this viewpoint. The legal reasons are, first, that the legal relevance of marine environment facts is hard to judge and weigh, and, second, that the standard of evidence that must be met before a court is willing to rely on factual evidence of this character is likely to be very high. Against the background of these legal concerns come into play the two tactical considerations which can negate even the most solid scientific assertions with devastating effect.

One tactic is not to argue with the facts presented but to approach the same factual issue on a different level of scientific understanding. Thus, if one side seeks to prove a break in the submarine geology by drawing upon facts associated with the Pleistocene era, the other may counter effectively with facts identifying a different break in the geological structure during the Miocene era. Or, if one side shows that the commercially most important species of fish in the relevant area do not swim across a proposed boundary, the other side argues that the proper level of analysis, if the matter is legally relevant, is to examine the entire body of flora and fauna in the region -- which shows no preponderant species division at that point. By the time this sort of debate is over, a judge can only be saying to himself that scientists know a lot of interesting facts and have some interesting ideas, but why should a judge choose between them in delimiting a boundary between nation states in the twentieth century?

The other tactic for negating a scientific argument is to focus upon the exceptions to the rule. There is, for example, always a stray lobster that some scientist has identified that does not do what all the other lobsters do. This means that no categorical positions may be taken and that all assertions must be tempered. The stray lobster, thus, introduces a degree of uncertainty in the court's search for the boundary, and says to the judge that he or she is on uncertain ground in relying too heavily upon such facts as basis for decision.

On the law, the *Gulf of Maine* case is clearly distinguishable. The Chamber found the phrase *single maritime boundary*, which the parties had asked it to determine, to be the vehicle for stressing the legal uniqueness of the case. This was not intended by the parties. In my view, the Chamber adopted this stand so as not to prejudice the full Court's opportunity to be the first to speak to the law relating to the delimitation of the exclusive economic zone. The full Court is thus free to deal with environmental factors as it so chooses in its first EEZ delimitation case.

Yet I can only anticipate that the full Court's treatment of environmental factors will be similar to that of the Chamber. The marine environment is an interesting setting for delimitation, but it is too complex for international courts to come to grips with.

THE SINGLE MARITIME BOUNDARY:
PROBLEMS IN THEORY AND PRACTICE

Donald M. McRae[*]
Professor of Law
University of British Columbia
Academic-in-Residence
Department of External Affairs
Ottawa[**]

When Canada and the United States agreed in 1979 to ask a Chamber of the International Court of Justice to delimit a *single maritime boundary* dividing the continental shelf and fisheries zones of the two parties in the Gulf of Maine area, probably neither side realized the full implications of a request for a single maritime boundary; nor did they realize that this aspect of the request would so preoccupy the Chamber.

The two states were responding to practical considerations. Although the dispute in the Gulf of Maine area had originally concerned the continental shelf, the advent of 200-mile fishing zones for the two states in early 1977 brought the boundary dispute to a head. The negotiations for a boundary had always presupposed that any agreement reached would be for a single line even though neither side claimed an exclusive economic zone (EEZ).[1] For obvious reasons the two states did not want to go through the long and trying process of litigation twice, once for the continental shelf and once for the fishing zone, and they did not want the administrative inconvenience of separate boundaries for the shelf and the water column. Thus the pragmatic solution was to request the Chamber to draw a single maritime boundary that would govern *both* the continental shelf and fishing zones and any other forms of jurisdiction that either might claim or exercise on its side of the boundary.[2]

Thus, the Chamber in the *Gulf of Maine* case was requested to perform a single operation -- draw a single line -- and the two parties were free to make their own arguments about the considerations that should govern the drawing of such a "single" line and the relative importance of the considerations relating to the one form of jurisdiction (the shelf) or to the other form of jurisdiction (the water column or the fishing zone).[3]

Perhaps surprisingly, neither party devoted much attention in their written pleadings to whether such a thing as a *single maritime boundary* existed in law. Canada sought to show that the single maritime boundary was the logical outgrowth of the extension of coastal state jurisdiction over the resources of the water column and the amalgamation of that jurisdiction with pre-existing rights over the continental shelf.[4] In effect, Canada assimilated the single maritime boundary to an EEZ boundary. Although the United States argued that the continental shelf regime was distinct from the 200-mile resource zone,[5] like Canada, it treated the single maritime boundary as approximating an EEZ boundary. Thus the United States proclamation of a 200-mile EEZ during the course of the written phase of the case posed no difficulty.

Both parties, however, devoted a considerable amount of effort to show what body of law should govern the delimitation of a single maritime boundary and how it differed from a continental shelf delimitation -- for example, the role of Article 6 of the 1958 Convention of the

Continental Shelf, and the relevance of environmental or ecological factors concerning the water column. But the two states were directed specifically to the issue of the existence in law of a concept of a single maritime boundary by a question put by the President of the Chamber, Judge Ago, to both parties at the end of the first round of the oral proceedings. The question was as follows:

> In the event that one particular method, or set of methods, should appear appropriate for the delimitation of the continental shelf, and another for that of the exclusive fishing zones, what do the Parties consider to be the legal grounds that might be invoked for preferring one or the other in seeking to determine a single line?[6]

Judging by its response, the United States had as much difficulty as Canada did in formulating an answer to that question!

The United States said that in the event that there were different methods for the shelf and for the fisheries zone there were no legal grounds that could be invoked *a priori* for preferring one method over the other, but that the matter should be considered as an integrated whole and there should be a balancing of the relevant circumstances.[7] Canada said that if there were different methods for the shelf and fisheries zone the preference as to the method should be dictated by the circumstances relating to each particular sector of the line,[8] thus recognizing implicitly that there was a balancing process involved. These answers did not satisfy Judge Gros at least. He took the view that the parties had simply referred the problem back to the Chamber itself.[9]

In a sense the question posed by Judge Ago is unanswerable, for it goes to the issue of whether there is a *single regime* of the shelf and the water column out to 200 miles, or in other words, whether there is an autonomous legal regime of the exclusive economic zone. It is true that the 1982 Convention on the Law of the Sea provides for such a regime, but the Convention does not provide answers to many questions about the nature of that regime. The loose ends were never tied together as the nature of the UNCLOS process was to strive for consensus rather than for clarity.

In short, I do not think that we have yet thought through, or perhaps even perceived, all of the implications of a single maritime boundary nor have we considered all of the implications, at least for maritime delimitation, of the EEZ regime. Problems exist at both theoretical and practical levels.

Problems of Theory with the Single Maritime Boundary Concept

The fundamental problem is itself quite simple; it derives from the fact that continental shelves and fishing zones developed separately, both historically and in terms of the nature of the rights over them. When you combine the two regimes, as a request for a single maritime boundary does or as the exclusive economic zone appears to have done, how are these differences to be reconciled? Which takes priority?

An important question that was dwelt on by Canada in both the written and oral pleadings in the *Gulf of Maine* case concerns the legal basis of title to the "unified" regime. In the case of the continental shelf the basis of title has generally been perceived to rest (at least since the *North Case* cases[10]) in the concept of natural prolongation.

In the case of the 200-mile economic zone the basis of title appears to rest not on any geological or geomorphological concept of prolongation but rather on geographical adjacency measured in terms of distance. This view is expressed in the *Tunisia-Libya* case[11] and developed in *Libya-Malta.*[12] What then is the relative significance of "natural prolongation" or the "distance principle" in the delimitation of a single maritime boundary or of an EEZ? In the *Gulf of Maine* case Canada sought to attach significance to this "trend towards the distance principle" because, Canada argued, if distance is the basis of title, equidistance takes on greater importance as a method of delimitation. The United States sought to shift "natural prolongation" from its geological and geomorphological association towards geography. Thus, in the United States' view "natural prolongation" was to be viewed in the sense of a notional *geographical* extension of the land seaward -- the United States termed it "coastal front extension."[13] Both approaches (although neither was adopted by the Chamber) represented a search for concepts adequate to a single maritime boundary delimitation, as opposed to the more traditional continental shelf delimitation. Ironically, it was in the *Libya-Malta* case, which concerned the continental shelf and not a single maritime boundary, that the Court accepted the view that distance is the basis of title to the new 200-mile zone.[14]

The 1982 Convention does not really assist in clarifying the issue. Although the rule for the delimitation of the continental shelf is expressed in terms identical to those in the rule for the delimitation of the EEZ, the concept of a continental shelf within 200 miles of the coast seems to remain intact, certainly for those states that do not claim an EEZ. In *Libya-Malta*, moreover, the Court considered that although they are linked, the two regimes remain separate.[15] The obvious reason for maintaining a separate continental shelf regime in the Convention was to allay the fears of the "wide-margin" states that the EEZ regime would eliminate their rights beyond 200 miles. But in important respects the two regimes differ even within 200 miles -- for example, continental shelf rights exist *ipso facto* and *ab initio*, while EEZ rights must be claimed; obligations exist to allocate surplus fishery resources within the EEZ, but no comparable obligation exists under the continental shelf regime.

Thus, the fundamental problem remains. In the delimitation of a single maritime boundary, or of an EEZ boundary, how are considerations (equities) relating to the continental shelf to be compared against and balanced up with those relating to the fishing zone? Or, as Judge Ago put it in the *Gulf of Maine* case, if the method for the delimitation of the continental shelf differs from the method for the delimitation of the fishing zone, on what basis is the one to be preferred over the other?

In the *Gulf of Maine* case, Judge Gros appeared to consider that the resolution of this theoretical question was a precondition to effecting *any* delimitation of a single maritime boundary, and he criticized the parties for assuming that such a boundary could be delimited simply because they had asked for one.[16] The majority, on the other hand, took the pragmatic view that there was no rule prohibiting the Chamber from complying with the parties' request for a single maritime boundary. The request itself provided a sufficient mandate for effecting the delimitation.[17] Moreover, by giving primacy to the "neutral" element of geography and putting aside considerations that were relevant to one element alone (continental shelf or fishing zone), the Chamber avoided the potential problem of having to choose between the equities of the shelf and the equities of the fishing zone. In effect, the Chamber's approach to the law renders the theoretical problem one of pure theory only.

In the light of the prominence that this issue took in the *Gulf of Maine* case as a consequence of Judge Ago's question, and particularly in the dissenting judgment of Judge Gros, it is intriguing to note that the arbitral tribunal in *Guinea v Guinea Bissau*[18] did not appear to be troubled by these theoretical considerations at all. The tribunal was asked to determine whether the "maritime boundary" between the two states had been fixed by a Convention of 1986 and, if not, to identify the course of the line "delimiting the maritime territories" of the parties. Although the term *single* was not used in the *compromis*,[19] the boundary was to divide both continental shelf and fisheries jurisdiction, and the tribunal characterized the request as one for a "single" line.[20] The tribunal did not appear to consider that this request posed any difficult conceptual problems and delimited the boundary without reference to the separate nature of the regimes of the continental shelf and fishing zones or of any fusion of them. Like the Chamber in the *Gulf of Maine* case the tribunal gave overriding significance to geographical factors, which are common to both regimes, and discounted the relevance of other factors. Thus, it too avoided any need to weigh or balance the equities of the shelf against the equities of the fishing zone.

Practical Problems with the Single Maritime Boundary Concept

There is no doubt that states are free to negotiate whatever boundaries they wish -- if they consider that separate boundaries for the continental shelf and for the fishing zones serve their interests, then there is certainly no rule of law requiring them to delimit a "single" maritime boundary. Indeed, there are those who would argue that from a functional point of view single boundaries can ignore the real interests at stake. A single maritime boundary, according to this view, reflects a convenient political solution that may not, and probably does not, take into account the biological or ecological factors or of the resource management considerations that should be of paramount concern. Moreover, the delimitation of a maritime boundary involves a complex of issues. A willingness on both sides to negotiate separate boundaries or to enter into joint exploitation agreements, reciprocal access agreements and joint management arrangements will introduce much more flexibility into the negotiations.

This view was certainly not ignored in the Gulf of Maine. It was the belief of the Canadian and United States negotiators in 1977 that if they could conclude a comprehensive fisheries treaty for the east coast, then the delimitation of the boundary would be much less contentious. Such an agreement was concluded by the negotiators but it failed for political reasons to achieve ratification in the United States Senate. A single line was the only alternative. By the time any dispute is referred to a tribunal, the position will generally be the same -- all alternatives will have been exhausted and the only option left will be to draw a single line.

It is precisely the existence of political factors that will make the negotiation of separate boundaries for the continental shelf and the fishing zone extremely difficult. In principle, cooperative schemes can be devised to share jurisdiction or to grant access by one country to an area subject to the jurisdiction of another. The *Torres Strait* treaty between Australia and Papua New Guinea is a good example of how flexibility on separate boundaries facilitated the resolution of the boundary problems and of related jurisdictional issues.[21] In part, this was apparently achieved by leaving certain questions (relating to "residual jurisdiction") for "future resolution by mutual agreement."[22] Moreover, the definition of "residual jurisdiction" was sufficiently broad that, in effect, the parties "had foregone certain rights that otherwise, in the light of developments in international law, would be within their jurisdiction by virtue of their sovereign rights over an area for resource purposes."[23] This was acceptable to the parties concerned but it may not be a result that is acceptable in every boundary delimitation.

A negotiated solution requires the willingness to compromise that was obviously present in the case of the *Torres Strait* treaty. Other boundary problems must be viewed in the light of their own particular circumstances. Are the fishermen of State A prepared to fish alongside the fishermen of State B? Will gear conflicts or differing approaches in the two states to conservation and management make this impossible? Are the parties able to agree upon a scheme to manage overlapping areas? Are there established hydrocarbon concessions or other established interests in the area? Is State B prepared to risk the possibility that State A will erect oil-drilling installations in the center of State B's rich fishing ground -- something that can be a real possibility where there are separate continental shelf and fishing zone boundaries? These are some of the factors that will determine whether the negotiation of separate boundaries is feasible.

I suspect that given the administrative complexity and the potential for continuous and perhaps unresolvable conflict that separate boundaries would entail, in the long run many if not most states will opt for the relative simplicity and certainty of a single line, notwithstanding the advantage in principle of separate boundaries or of functional alternatives to boundaries altogether.

The importance of boundaries to resource management should not, however, be overestimated. A boundary is not an alternative to shared or cooperative management. Once a single boundary is established, there is nothing to stop a state from making whatever reciprocal access arrangements or joint or shared management systems it considers desirable, or even from relinquishing management control or authority over particular uses or particular areas in favor of its neighbor. In fact, resolution of the boundary may get an important political issue out of the way and make it easier to negotiate a cooperative arrangement. The fact that the boundary is there, however, might provide reassurance. It will be a "fall-back" if the other arrangements do not work out.

In addition to the practical problems associated with having separate continental shelf and fishing zone boundaries, there are several considerations relating to the adjudication of single maritime or EEZ boundaries. The first problem concerns the relationship between a new EEZ boundary and an existing continental shelf boundary. In many new cases states will simply agree to utilize their old continental shelf boundaries as their new EEZ boundaries. But if one state is not happy with such a result and the question of an EEZ or single maritime boundary is referred to adjudication, what implications does this have for the old continental shelf boundary? Would the tribunal be required to take the existence of the old continental shelf boundary into account as a relevant factor? Would the delimitation of a new EEZ boundary have the effect, by operation of law, of abrogating the old continental shelf boundary?

An answer to these questions depends in part on a resolution of the theoretical questions raised earlier. If the continental shelf regime out to 200 miles has been fused with the fishing zone to become a juridically new entity -- the EEZ (at least for those states that claim an EEZ) -- then the question arises whether the old continental shelf boundaries can remain at all. Is there an implied revocation of either agreed or adjudicated continental shelf boundaries where two neighboring states both claim an EEZ? Certainly the act of one state in claiming an EEZ could not unilaterally terminate an agreed boundary with a neighboring state that does not claim an EEZ. And it seems even less likely that a boundary established through adjudication would lapse under such circumstances. But does a request for an EEZ delimitation constitute an abrogation of any existing continental shelf boundary in the area? How can a tribunal delimit an EEZ or a single maritime boundary without abrogating the old continental shelf boundary? One can also turn the problem around. Can a tribunal delimit a continental shelf boundary for states that both claim an EEZ? If the continental shelf and fisheries regimes have been fused into the EEZ, then it would appear that a tribunal could not delimit the shelf boundary alone.

The relevance of the EEZ to continental shelf delimitation was raised in the *Libya-Malta* case. The Court concluded that "the legally permissible extent of the exclusive economic zone" was one of the relevant circumstances to be taken into account for the delimitation of the continental shelf.[24] Judge Oda in his dissenting opinion noted that the question "whether the sea-bed -- within 200 miles of the coast -- has been incorporated in the regime of the exclusive economic zone, or whether it should still come under the separate regime of the continental shelf in parallel with the exclusive economic zone" was "far more essential than initially thought."[25] The Court's approach in *Libya-Malta* seems to be that as a matter of law, there has been no fusion of the two regimes.[26] But the issue of a single maritime or EEZ boundary was not before the Court. Thus, I doubt that we have had the final word on this matter.

We probably will not be able to make progress on these questions until there are further decisions of international tribunals and the development of state practice. The whole issue, however, deserves careful attention by those states that have a continental shelf boundary but have yet to resolve the question of a boundary for the water column, or those states that are still contemplating whether to promulgate an EEZ. A *compromis* to submit a boundary dispute to arbitration or to the International Court of Justice will also have to take careful account of these questions and endeavor to resolve the problem of pre-existing boundaries. Nevertheless, it will not always be possible to do so, in which case the matter will have to be passed on to the tribunal to decide.

Another problem that arises in the adjudication of a single maritime or EEZ boundary concerns the designation of the outer limit of the boundary. In principle a 200-mile zone boundary should extend to 200 miles. But the only point that is within 200 miles of the coasts of *both* parties is the intersection of the outer limits of their 200-mile zones at the equidistance point. This is illustrated by line A-B in *Diagram A*. Obviously the party that opposes an equidistance line will not want the equidistance point specified as the termination of the boundary. But if the boundary does not terminate when it first meets the 200-mile zone of one party (line A-C in *Diagram A*), it will extend more than 200 miles beyond the coast of that party. The use of a depth contour as the limit for the tribunal is one alternative, but even that may not be acceptable as the configuration of the seabed might work to the detriment of one of the parties.

In the *Gulf of Maine* case, the parties passed the problem on to the Chamber. Rather than specifying a particular limit, the Special Agreement asked the Chamber to terminate the boundary anywhere within a triangle that encompassed the intersection of the 200-mile zones of the two parties and the end points of their claims on their respective 200-mile zones. In fact the Chamber terminated its line at the outer limit of the 200-mile zone of the United States, which was the first intersection with the 200-mile zone of one of the parties.

Part of the difficulty surrounding the means of designating the terminus of the line in the Special Agreement in the *Gulf of Maine* case resulted from the fact that the continental shelf of Canada and the United States on the east coast extends beyond the 200-mile limit. The parties wanted the Chamber to delimit the boundary within 200 miles but to leave the extension of the line beyond 200 miles to the outer limit of the continental shelf to be negotiated after the decision of the Chamber.[27]

The problem that arises where the continental shelf extends beyond the 200-mile limit is one that requires particular attention. In the *Gulf of Maine* case this was described as the "grey area" problem. Its nature was outlined long ago by Whittemore Boggs when dealing with the outer limit of the territorial sea.[28] But it is of even greater importance today because a 200-mile zone boundary involves considerably larger areas.

The problem is this: unless the boundary intersects the 200-mile zones of the two parties (that is, unless it goes through the equidistance point -- line A-B in *Diagram B*) any extension of the line beyond 200 miles will take away from one state an area that is within 200 miles of its coast and give it to the other state, even though that area is more than 200 miles from the latter state's coast. (See shaded area in *Diagram B*.) Since this "grey area" is beyond 200 miles from its coast, presumably State Y (*Diagram B*) would have no jurisdiction over the resources of the water column. If the line so extended beyond 200 miles is only a continental shelf boundary, then presumably State X will retain jurisdiction over the water column notwithstanding that it falls on the other side of the boundary. If this approach is correct then there will always be divided jurisdiction -- a "vertical superimposition of rights"[29] whereby one state has jurisdiction over the continental shelf and another state has jursidiction over the water column -- within the grey area.

The only way to avoid a "grey area" problem is to terminate the boundary within 200 miles at the equidistance point. The further from the equidistance point that the boundary intersects the 200-mile limit, the greater the potential grey area problem beyond 200 miles. This matter, which is obviously an argument to support equidistance, did not go unnoticed in the Canadian pleadings in the *Gulf of Maine* case,[30] although the Chamber still rejected the Canadian argument for an equidistance line.

I am not yet aware of any agreements dealing with the "grey area" problem specifically, although the final leg of the boundary in the recent Argentine-Chile agreement (resulting from the Papal Mediation) prevents Chile from exercising jurisdiction in what would otherwise be a grey area.[31] No tribunal has yet been asked to delimit both a single maritime or EEZ boundary out to 200 miles and the continental shelf boundary beyond.[32] There is no guidance in the 1982 Convention, and it is probably safe to say that states faced with this problem have yet to come up with ready solutions.

Conclusion

The problems that have emerged with the single maritime boundary concept in the light of the *Gulf of Maine* experience are a useful precursor to the difficulties to be faced with the delimitation of EEZs. States with existing continental shelf boundaries will save themselves many of these difficulties by simply converting those boundaries into EEZ boundaries. It can be safety predicted, however, that this approach will not be followed universally and that some of the questions outlined here will have to be faced. States that have yet to conclude boundaries for either the continental shelf or the fishing zone will have to weigh carefully whether a single boundary best serves their interests or whether they would be prepared to contemplate separate boundaries, and whether the uncertainties of litigation constitute a better risk than the compromises necessary for a negotiated solution of either a single boundary or of separate boundaries.

In this regard, one might argue that the focus on geography in the *Gulf of Maine* judgement represents an attempt to avoid these difficulties. Although the Chamber justified recourse to geography on the ground of its "neutrality," the real rationale is that geography is constant" whether one is concerned with the continental shelf, a fishing zone, or an EEZ -- the geography is always there. Moreover, the Chamber indicated that there is a hierarchy of relevant factors, an approach that brings more certainty to the law. This development in maritime boundary delimitation law -- the placing of overriding importance on geography and providing a hierarchy of relevant factors -- is to be welcomed. On the other hand, it brings into question what has been fundamental to the whole debate over maritime boundary delimitation: what is more important, *certainty* or *equity*?

NOTES

*Currently Doyen/Dean at the University of Ottawa Faculty of Law, Common Law Section.

** The views expressed are those of the author and do not necessarily reflect the views of the Government of Canada.

1. The United States subsequently claimed a 200-mile EEZ by Presidential Proclamation of 10 March 1983.
2. Special Agreement between the Government of Canada and the Government of the United States of America to Submit to a Chamber of the International Court of Justice the Delimitation of the Maritime Boundary in the Gulf of Maine Area, 29 March 1979, Article III.
3. The Chamber itself took the view that Canada had traditionally perceived the continental shelf to be the dominant consideration in the area while the United States' approach had always been governed by fisheries considerations: [1984] I.C.J. Rep. 246 para. 70.
4. Canadian Counter Memorial, p. 191, para. 459.
5. U.S. Reply, p. 60, paras. 94-99.

6. C1/CR 84/22 pp. 34-39.
7. C1/CR 84/24 pp. 19-26.
8. C1/CR 84/24 pp. 34-39.
9. *Supra*, note 3, pp. 362-363, para. 5.
10. [1969] I.C.J. Rep. 1.
11. *Tunisia-Libya Continental Shelf* Case [1982] I.C.J. Rep. 1 p. 48, para. 48.
12. *Libya-Malta Continental Shelf* Case, Judgement of 3 June 1985, paras. 33-34.
13. U.S. Reply, pp. 63-67, paras. 100-107.
14. *Supra* note 12 at para. 34.
15. *Ibid*, para. 33: "This does not mean that the concept of the continental shelf has been absorbed by that of the exclusive economic zone."
16. *Supra* note 3, pp. 362-364, paras. 5-6.
17. This aspect of the judgment is dealt with L.H. Legault and B.G. Hankey in a forthcoming article in the *American Journal of International Law*.
18. Award of 14 February 1985.
19. The Special Agreement in the *Gulf of Maine Case* described the boundary as a *frontiere maritime unique*, whereas the compromise in the *Guinea Bissau* case simply referred to it as a *frontiere maritime*.
20. *Supra* note 18, para. 42.
21. H. Burmester, "The Torres Strait Treaty: Ocean Boundary Delimitation By Agreement" 76 AJIL 321 (1982).
22. *Ibid*, 340.
23. *Id*.
24. *Supra* note 12, para. 34.
25. *Ibid*. Dissenting opinion of Judge Oda, para. 60.
26. *Supra*, note 15.
27. Special Agreement, Article VII.
28. Boggs, *International Boundaries* (1940) p. 188.
29. Judge *ad hoc* Arechaga in *Tunisia-Libya*, *supra* note 11, p. 130, para. 98.
30. Canadian Counter Memorial, pp. 237-242.
31. Treaty of Peace and Friendship, 29 November 1984, 24 International Legal Materials 11, Article 7.
32. The question of the "grey area" was not dealt with expressly in *Guinea v. Guinea Bissau*, but as neither state can claim any rights on the other side of the boundary then, presumably, no "grey area" problem will arise.

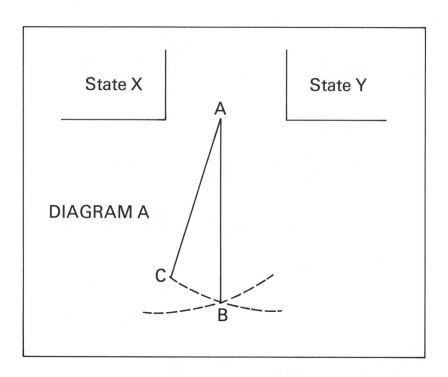

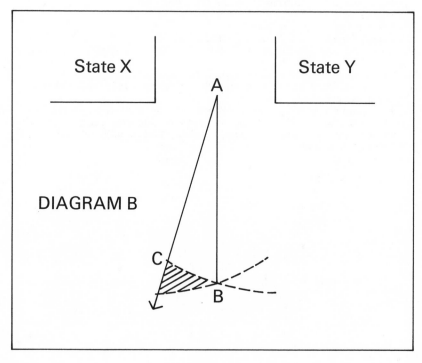

THE OUTSTANDING MARITIME BOUNDARY PROBLEMS BETWEEN IRELAND AND THE UNITED KINGDOM

Clive R. Symmons
Faculty of Law
University of Bristol

Introduction: The Fishery Limits Aspect

Unlike the United Kingdom, Ireland has merely signed, but not ratified, the 1958 Convention on the Continental Shelf. (Ireland has, however, gone one step further than the U.K. by signing the 1982 LOS Convention.) As such, Ireland is not strictly bound by Article 6 of the 1958 Convention, even though the latter Convention received favorable official mention[1] during the passage of the bill resulting in the Continental Shelf Act of 1968,[2] when in the Irish Dail (parliament) the matter of delimitation of the Irish shelf was stated to be "a matter of negotiation" with other coastal states.[3] As in the U.K. Continental Shelf Act (Sibthorp, p. 167) so also in the Irish, there is, however, no reference to a rule to govern the delimitation of continental shelf boundaries in areas of potential overlap, though by way of contrast, in the case of the 200-mile exclusive fishery zones declared by both states in 1976, *both* official decrees do make express provision for the case of overlap in sea areas less than 400 miles wide, the Irish referring to an "equitable equidistant line" in para. 4 of the Maritime Jurisdiction (Exclusive Fishery Limits) Order of 1976,[4] and the British Fishery Limits Act of 1976 (s.1(3)) referring expressly to a "median line" unless an Order in Council should otherwise declare.

As matters stand at the present time on the question on the Anglo-Irish continental shelf boundary situation, there has been, as will be seen, agreement in principle to submit this to arbitration,[5] and no bilateral treaty so far exists to fix any part of this boundary between these two states, or indeed *vis-a-vis* the other interested parties on the northern seaboard, namely Denmark (on behalf of the Faeroes) or Iceland, despite the holding of periodic discussions on the matter.[6] The *de facto* continental shelf situation, therefore, is currently represented by the zig-zag line delimiting the furthest seaward extent of the respective Irish and British *designations* under the legislation referred to *supra*, so that in some areas there exists a significant "no-man's-land" between the two designations, whereas in other areas they touch,[7] and in one exceptional situation, they actually overlap.[8]

It is, of course, desirable to make clear at this early stage that these actual designations of continental shelf do not necessarily represent the extent of the respective *claims* thereto, so that even if by and large the existing designations do not overlap, the existing *claims* of both states certainly do, most especially in the Rockall area (see Symmons, 1979, pp. 725, 726 and Brown, 1978, p. 290). And it may be noted parenthetically that in the broader perspective, recent designations of both Denmark (on behalf of the Faeroe Islands) and Iceland[9] have dramatically overlapped with those of both Ireland and the U.K., so elevating the seabed boundary dispute in the "Atlantic sector" to a complicated pattern of quadripartite dimensions.[10]

In the Anglo-Irish context, the extent of overlap of seabed *claims* is to a large degree evidenced by the boundaries decreed by both states under their respective officially published 200-mile *fishery limits*, effected in the Irish case by statutory instrument of 1976[11] and in the

British case by successive *Notices to Mariners* (see Symmons, 1979, pp. 719, 723, 726, 733). In its fishery limit decree, Ireland has made an opportunistic interpretation of its "equitable equidistant line"[12] (as compared with the U.K.'s strict imposition of a "median line"[13]) largely based, as will be seen, on its down-grading of British islands as basepoints according to its submission at the Caracas session of UNCLOS III that, in determining the median line, "account may be taken of an island only if it is inhabited and if (i) it is situated less than the breadth of the territorial sea from the low-water line of the coast or (ii) it contains at least one-tenth of the land area and population of the state concerned."[14]

By utilization of this individualistic viewpoint on delimitation of maritime zones in international law, Ireland has consequently even ignored (in fixing its 200-mile fishery limits line) British islands in *close* proximity to the U.K. mainland; namely in the southern sector (the Celtic Sea area), the effect of the Scilly islands off the Cornish coast, which lie only twenty-one miles from the British mainland and contain a population of almost 2,500 (see Symmons, 1979, pp. 718, 719), the Smalls off Pembrokeshire (see Symmons, 1979, p. 723), and even more significantly in the "Atlantic sector" (the area north and west of Ireland), most -- if not all -- of the Scottish western Isles such as Islay[15] which is populated and lies *within* the British-proclaimed straight-baseline system of 1964[16] (which appears to have been acquiesced in by Ireland[17]) as well as the Outer Hebrides. In effect, Ireland has selectively chosen in this latter area, as in the others, only the most prominent geographical projections as basepoints on *both* sides of its line (possibly excluding even the truly "inshore" Scottish islands of Skye, Mull and Jura).

Not surprisingly, such cavalier treatment by Ireland of British-claimed insular basepoints has been the subject of criticism within the British Parliament,[18] and has given rise to official British protest, particularly when it has led to existing British *seabed* designations being affected.[19] But the consequential fishery zone overlaps which are evident from this conflict of delimitation policy throughout most of the Celtic Sea to the south and in the Atlantic sector off the Scottish coast (see Symmons, 1979, pp. 719, 725) and which also involve, to a large degree, overlap of existing *continental shelf* designations by the U.K. (see Symmons, 1979, pp. 719, 723) pale into relative insignificance when the more distant part of that Atlantic sector northwest of Ireland -- the *Rockall sector* -- is examined. For here, as the Irish and U.K. fishery limit lines approach 11 degrees west, both radically diverge in a northwesterly and southwesterly direction respectively.

The reason for this boundary divergence is in part based on the Irish insular basepoint policy already discussed, for not only has Ireland ignored the dominant southern Outer Hebrides' islets (used as basepoints by the U.K.) such as Mingulay and Barra lying some fifty-three miles from the Scottish mainland (contained in the 1964 straight baseline system)[20] but also the remote islet group of St. Kilda, now effectively unoccupied (except for Nature Conservancy and M.O.D. personnel) and lying some eighty-four miles from Scotland (so too distant to be included in the straight baseline system) (see Bowett, 1979, p. 86). The island of St. Kilda has been utilized to great effect by the U.K., as it exercises a dominant influence in pushing the median line not only south against Ireland, but also north against Iceland.[21]

Most particularly, though, the overlap is caused by British utilization -- and Irish non-observance -- of Rockall, that freakish phenom-

236

enon of conical rock only some eighty feet in diameter, and seventy feet high and lying in the Atlantic some 256 miles from the nearest Scottish mainland (but 170 miles from the nearest Scottish islet, St. Kilda), which was formally annexed to the U.K. in 1955.[22]

Confirmation that the U.K. had used Rockall under the 1976 Fishery Limits Act for generating an arc of waters 200 miles wide into the Atlantic (or to a median line position around it), was made in the House of Commons on 24 January 1977,[23] and in the ultimately published coordinates in the 1978 *Notice to Mariners*.[24] But it was quickly followed by a protest note from Ireland indicating that this action was "not consistent with applicable principles of international law,"[25] in particular, it appears, because Ireland, like Denmark (on behalf of the Faeroes) (see Symmons, 1979, p. 730), places reliance on the effect of Art. 121(3) of the 1982 LOS Convention which provides that "rocks which cannot sustain human habitation or economic life of their own shall have no EEZ or continental shelf."[26]

The Seabed Boundary Situation

It is useful to sketch in the conflicting Irish and British claimed 200-mile fishery limit boundaries first because, as already stated, they are also indicative of both states' *claims* to seabed rights as well, even if their *present* continental shelf designations do not extend thus far. Furthermore, it is an obvious fact that the claimed 200-mile fishery boundaries of today could easily be converted into the *EEZ* boundaries of tomorrow, and recent developments in the International Court of Justice indicate the intrinsic inter-relationship of both these regimes -- as most recently seen in the *Libya/Malta Continental Shelf* case,[27] where the court has emphasized that for juridical and practical reasons the distance criterion must now apply to the continental shelf as well as to the EEZ.

Apart, though, from the underlying seabed implications, the overlapping fishery limits of both states do not appear to have caused any serious problems in the way of jurisdictional rights and enforcement largely because of the EEC common fisheries policy (See Symmons, 1979, p. 732).

The following are indications from existing Irish actions to justify a conclusion that Ireland considers its "equitable equidistant" fishery limit line to be also a potential continental shelf boundary.

1. The coordinates listed in its 1976 Maritime Jurisdiction Order extend in both the sectors (to the south and north of Ireland) to a distance *exceeding* 200 miles (respectively by about 20 and 36 miles in each direction) from the Irish baselines, an overshoot which, of course, is not necessary for this particular exercise and implies a *dual* role for this particular line, particularly in the area of Rockall, which it passes to the south at a distance of about twelve miles, so also indicating that this rock only merits a nominal territorial sea of this width.[28]

2. The Irish continental shelf designations of 1977 -- both to the north[29] and the far south[30] -- were made essentially for tactical reasons in response to, in the case of the former, a British decision to offer production licenses in blocks 133 and 134 off Scotland in an area that Ireland considered to be *its side* of an "equidistance" line (see Symmons, 1979, p. 724), and in the latter case because the British Continental Shelf designation of the previous year[31] intruded into an area west of 9 degrees west, which Ireland considered to be trespassing on *its* side of an equitable dividing line (See Symmons, 1979, p. 718).

237

It is significant that the sloping top of the first-mentioned Irish rectangular-shaped designation in the Atlantic sector almost exactly coincides with the coordinates in that area issued under its Fishery Limits Order (see Brown, 1978, p. 295); and to the South, the Irish designations both in the Western Approaches and the Celtic Sea, although they do not all touch the already-claimed Irish fishery line, do cross the existing U.K.-claimed 200-mile fishery boundary. In the latter case the U.K.'s 1976 continental shelf designation in turn intrudes over the Irish-claimed fishery limit line imposed at the end of the same year.

British official moves also indicate some co-relation between the 200-mile fishery limit boundary and the *claimed* continental shelf boundary. In 1974, the U.K. made its expansive continental shelf designation,[32] taking in some 52,000 square miles of seabed west of Scotland and around Rockall -- subsequently officially justified by the U.K. as being a natural prolongation of the Scottish landmass or as being generated by the British "island" of Rockall in its own right[33] -- a move strongly protested by Ireland, particularly in regard to the latter rationale (see Symmons, 1975, pp. 66, 67). In retrospect, this U.K. designation marked the beginning of the subsequent successive Irish and British claims and counter-claims. But the trapezium-shaped area does appear to have been carefully designed at the time to parallel -- but still stay well within -- any median line to the north (with the Faeroes),[34] and to the west (with Iceland), albeit modified to the important extent of *not* utilizing Rockall at all; and similarly relative to Ireland it does somewhat reflect the later British 200-mile line to its south, at least as far as 11 degrees west. But even so, early Irish protests played on the fact that the designation included areas which, as a matter of international law, fell within Irish jurisdiction and which were "nearer to the Irish than British coast."[35] And in fact it is true that if one calculates the distance of the designated part of the Rockall Plateau south of Rockall from the nearest Scottish baseline (ignoring St. Kilda), it is 394 miles as compared with 357 to the nearest Irish one.[36]

In comparison, the U.K., as seen, has utilized all possible insular baselines, *including Rockall*, in fixing its 200-mile *fishery* limit boundaries, and in the official British charts which have been published to illustrate the existing continental shelf designations, chart Q.6155 of 1977 "shades off" the north-west corner of the previous Irish designation of 1974 (see Symmons, 1979, p. 727); and the later chart of the same number (published 1979)[37] completes the process by shading off also a large swathe of the 1976 Irish-designated seabed stretching 520 miles from Ireland's coast,[38] this diagonal line exactly coinciding with the published median line south of Rockall for *fishery* limit purposes. Furthermore, the 1977 designation north of Ireland (see *supra*, fn. 29) is depicted by a mere dotted line on the latter chart, and in the Celtic sea area, the Irish-designated blocks protruding across the U.K. fishery limit line are shaded off. The obvious implication from this is that the U.K. views -- as also does Ireland -- its unilaterally decreed fishery limit line as being indicative of its seabed boundary as well.[38a]

A past official Irish viewpoint has in fact been that in any future third-party settlement procedure of a judicial nature, the question of the continental shelf boundary is intrinsically bound up with the 200-mile fishery zone/EEZ issue, so that if a future tribunal should, for example, decide that Rockall has no basepoint value in the context of continental shelf delimitation, the same should apply in the case of the EEZ/fishery limit line.[39] Undoubtedly, in the light of recent case law before the ICJ -- particularly the *Gulf of Maine* case[40] and the *Libya/Malta* case[41] -- such a viewpoint does carry a lot of weight. But, as has been pointed out elsewhere,[42] Ireland is in some dilemma (as also is Denmark for the Faeroes) in denying Rockall's capacity to generate seabed rights, for this principle when applied to the *water column* rights of fisheries could disadvantage the EEC as a whole (including Ireland) by allowing a free-for-all fisheries bonanza to other states in the Rockall region which would not then be the preserve of the shared EEC fishery zone. A similar problem might in fact arise also on the continental shelf aspect if Rockall should prove vital (rather than natural prolongation from mainlands) to generate seabed rights in the region for the four existing claimants to the Rockall Plateau and its environs; and indeed, more generally, Iceland has pointed out to the other three claimants that if quadripartite solidarity fails in the Rockall area, all of these states might be the losers to the international community as the area might be viewed as part of the "common heritage of mankind."[43] The idea that the U.K. and Ireland might jointly agree to vest the seabed around Rockall in the U.N. has, indeed, received isolated mention in the British Parliament.[44]

The Agreement in Principle to Submit to Arbitration

After the controversial 1974 British designation in the Rockall area (see *supra*, fn. 32), there was some pressure from the Irish Government to submit the dispute to arbitration[45] (as early as April, 1976); and on February 21, 1977, the British Government announced that it was willing to refer the *continental shelf* delimitation issue to an independent third party settlement procedure of a judicial nature, subject to reaching agreement with Ireland on the type of tribunal, its composition and its terms of reference.[46] Subsequently, on February 11, 1980, it was announced in the House of Commons that it had been agreed that this delimitation should be submitted to an *ad hoc* arbitral tribunal of five members, subject again to agreement on its composition, terms of reference and related matters.[47]

Unfortunately, the setting up of such a tribunal is still the subject of continuing and protracted Anglo-Irish negotiations.[48] But it has at least been made clear that the terms of reference will be confined to the *continental shelf* boundary between the two states, and along its *whole* extent, that is, in both the Celtic Sea and in the Atlantic sectors. This was clearly affirmed by an Irish spokesman in the Dail on May 21, 1981, when he said:

> The delimitation covers the entire extent of the continental shelf contiguous to Britain and Ireland. It is not concerned solely with delimitation of the Rockall Plateau or exclusively with any single feature in isolation such as Rockall, but involves the whole shelf in the north west and in the Irish and Celtic Sea areas.[49]

It is unfortunate that the potential terms of reference appear to confine the proceedings purely to the seabed issue -- as indeed was also the situation in the previous Anglo-French delimitation arbitral proceedings over the continental shelf boundary in the Western Approaches, 1977, where the Anglo-French 200-mile fishery/economic zone boundary still remains problematical (see Symmons, 1979, pp. 715, 716).

But at least in the Anglo-Irish situation neither party has pushed its claims to the ultimate extent of translating these into *extensively* overlapping seabed *designations*, as has since happened in the "Rockall sector" in the case of Denmark and Iceland.[50]

As seen, the only location where an actual overlapping *designation*[51] exists is in the Atlantic sector, where in 1977 Ireland made a tactical counter-designation, though it has also been affirmed recently in the British Parliament that "substantial areas" designated by Ireland *prior* to 1977 "cut across areas which would fall to the U.K. on a delimitation of the continental shelf by means of a median line."[52]

Thus Ireland in its designations of 1974[53] (in response to the U.K. "Rockall designation") and in 1976[54] appears to have been anxious to stake a claim to the Rockall Trough and beyond onto the Plateau, while at the same time ignoring Rockall as having any influence on the median line. And although it is true that in the *Libya/Tunisia* case, the ICJ did there controversially take some account of the respective parties' existing seabed activities,[55] Ireland's view has been that international law does not allow one state to steal a march over another in this way (see Symmons, 1975, p. 71, 72), a view that has not seemingly been shared since by Denmark and Iceland in the same region who have deemed *positive* counteraction by *designation* to be desirable.[56] Certainly the U.K. claims to have protested to Ireland about all Irish seabed designations which cross a notional median line with the U.K.[57]

One important effect on the past sequence of claim and counter-claim (set out above) resulting from the informal consensus to submit the seabed dispute to a form of arbitral process has been that it has effectively led to a gentleman's agreement for a "stand-off" policy in making further conflicting designations[58] in the *de facto* "no-man's-land" area which exists, and a cautious attitude even towards making licensing awards in any controversial areas already designated. Thus, in the case of the overlapping blocks 132 and 133 (mentioned *supra*), although they were opened up to license for exploration in the fifth U.K. licensing round, little active follow-up by the commercial companies involved has resulted, so as not to prejudice any future settlement procedure.[59] Thus, when a question was asked of the British Secretary of State for Energy in Parliament in 1982 as to what oil exploration activities had taken place in these "overlap" blocks, it was replied that no exploration activities by BP or BNOC (the licensees) had then been carried out, though there had been "some speculative seismic work covering the area."[60]

Even the most recent U.K. licensing (9th round) awards of 1985 -- as those of 1984 -- have in the Rockall-facing area off Scotland kept well clear of Irish seabed claims, even though they enter the "frontier" area of the Rockall Trough;[61] and when the awards were first announced, a spokesman from the Irish Department of Foreign Affairs stated that the awards did not appear at first glance to impinge upon areas in which Ireland had "an interest."[62] In point of fact, though, further south in the Celtic Sea, British ninth round blocks 102/22 and 102/27 do appear to trespass provocatively across the Irish fishery limits line east of Kinsale Head -- the first instance in which this has occurred *since* the agreement to submit to arbitration by the U.K.

Conclusion

It must of course remain a matter of speculation as to precisely what form the *compromis* of an agreement for settlement of the seabed dispute between Ireland and the U.K. will take, and whether the past legal positions of both states will be exactly repeated before the envisaged 5-member tribunal.[63] Ireland has already viewed the downgrading treatment of British islands -- particularly of the Scilly islands -- by the arbitral tribunal in the 1977 Franco-British *Western Approaches* Case[64] as helpful to its legal case, both in the Celtic Sea sector (where the "half-effect" method was adopted to deal with the Scilly Isles[65]), and *a fortiori*, in the case of Rockall[66] in the Atlantic sector. Rockall is certainly destined to loom large in any Anglo-Irish proceedings, even to the extent of British title thereto (which this commentator has viewed elsewhere as being solidly based -- see Symmons, 1975, pp. 68-70) being challenged in the proceedings, as Ireland, while not in the past claiming the rock for itself,[67] has officially reserved its position on British sovereignty there.[68] By way of contrast, both other claimants to the Rockall Plateau -- Denmark and, it seems, Iceland -- have officially accepted British sovereignty over the rock.[69]

As has already been seen,[70] the U.K. has already used Rockall to radiate a 200-mile arc of fishery zone into the Atlantic, and, on its continental shelf claim in the area, has in the past used as a *secondary* justification the fact that this "island" generates seabed ownership for the U.K. in its own right. Apart from Ireland, Denmark[71] and Iceland[72] have disputed the legal capacity for such a rock to generate such expansive maritime zones, and Article 121(3) of LOSC has been much cited to back up this contention.

The U.K. has not, of course, yet signed the 1982 LOS Convention and one of the reasons for this may have been that this provision would weaken its maritime claims presently based on Rockall, and indeed on the "fall-back" insular basepoint of St. Kilda (about 170 miles to the east of Rockall) which is effectively uninhabited: see Brown, 1978, p. 298 (who opines that it would be "highly likely" that an international tribunal would ignore this and the other minor Scottish islets as having a basepoint value).

This "Article 121(3)" aspect has already surfaced in the British parliament in 1982 when the LOS Convention text was finalized. In response to a query[73] as to whether the U.K. could continue to claim a 200-mile fishery zone around Rockall, St. Kilda, and the other uninhabited off-shore islands in the light of the LOS Convention provisions thereon, it was officially replied that the U.K. was examining the texts in the light of all U.K. interests, and that any decision about signing would depend on this examination;[74] and a little later, in response to a question[75] as to whether the U.K.'s signature of the Convention would "prejudice" the U.K.'s position on Rockall's status in any international *arbitration*, it was explicitly confirmed that among the many aspects being then considered by the British Government was whether and how signature *might affect arbitral proceedings* in the Rockall area.[76] Such tactical British maneuvering may, of course, come to naught, if now -- or at least at the time of the future arbitral proceedings -- Article 121(3) of the Convention should be found to form part of customary law.[77]

A further factor to be borne in mind in the Anglo-Irish boundary dispute is the dramatic intervention recently by the other two contenders for the Rockall Plateau (and its environs) seabed, namely Denmark and Iceland which on May 7 and 9, 1985 respectively, designated enormous areas of seabed which vastly overlap with those of Ireland and the U.K.[78] In making these unilateral moves, these two outside contenders have shattered any illusion that the North Atlantic seabed around Rockall is simply a matter for a bilateral carve-up by the U.K. and Ireland, and have truly internationalized the dispute into one of quadrilateral dimensions, as Iceland in particular has emphasized it to be its July 1984 memorandum to the other three parties.[79]

It may well be, therefore, that events have overtaken the existing agreement in principle between the U.K. and Ireland to refer the whole of their seabed dispute to arbitration, albeit only as far as the North Atlantic area around Rockall is concerned,[80] and this is vaguely hinted at in the Danish Ministry of Foreign Affairs press release of May, 1985,[81] following the declaration of the Danish designation. It would now seem artificial in the extreme for any future arbitral tribunal to examine only the Anglo-Irish dimension, not only because the absence from the proceedings of Iceland and Denmark would make it difficult for a tribunal to assess "the effects, actual or prospective, of any other continental shelf delimitation" in the same region,[82] but also because recent delimitation cases before the ICJ have shown up the undesirability of excluding other neighboring states from being joined to an *initially bilateral* judicial proceeding if their maritime claims are likely to be vitally affected. The exclusion of Italy (having applied to intervene under Art. 62) from the *Libya/Malta* case is an excellent example of this.[83] This latter problem features even more prominently in the Rockall Plateau dispute as both Denmark[84] and Iceland[85] have strongly *denied* that this plateau is a "natural prolongation" of the Scottish *or* Irish land-masses,[86] as the U.K. and Ireland claim.

It may well be desirable, therefore, to convert the present bilateral Anglo-Irish agreement in principle for arbitration (as far as the Rockall area is concerned) into a quadrilateral one so that *all* the present conflicting interests may be taken into account together and contemporaneously, except for the trilateral application before the ICJ in the *North Sea Continental Shelf* cases. Unfortunately, the indications are that of the othe two contenders, Iceland has perceived in Denmark's claim some correspondence of interest and thus has viewed the delimitation dispute, as have in the past the U.K. and Ireland, as having some element of bilaterality[87] *inter se*; and it is in the context of *bilateral* contacts that discussions between the four states appear to be continuing.[88]

REFERENCES

Birnie, P., *Rockall: A Problem of the Delimitation of the British Continental Shelf*, a Lecture delivered to the Commonwealth Law Conference on July 28, 1977.

Bowett, D.W., *The Legal Regime of Islands in International Law*, 1979.

Brown, E.D., "Rockall and the Limits of National Jurisdiction of the U.K.," (1978) 2 *Marine Policy*, (Pt.1) 181, (Pt.2), 275.

Sibthorp, M. (ed.) *The North Sea: Challenge and Opportunity. Report of a Study Group of the David Davies Memorial Institute of International Studies*, 1975.

Symmons, C.R., "Legal Aspects of the Anglo-Irish Dispute over Rockall," (1975) 26 *Northern Ireland Legal Quarterly*, 65.

Symmons, C.R., "British Off-Shore Continental Shelf and Fishery Limit Boundaries: An Analysis of Overlapping Zones," (1979) 28 *International and Comparative Law Quarterly*, 703.

Symmons, C.R., "The Rockall Dispute Deepens: An Analysis of Recent Danish and Icelandic Actions," (1986) 35 *International and Comparative Law Quarterly*, 344.

NOTES

1. See *Dail Debates*, vol. 232, cols. 1560, 1572, 1573 (areas "within the limits laid down in the Convention" and "half-way across the Irish Sea).
2. No. 14, 1968.
3. *Supra*, fn. 1 at col. 1573.
4. No. 320 of 1976.
5. See *infra*, fn. 47.
6. See the reply in *Hansard* (HL) vol. 458, col. 635, (*Written Answers*, Dec. 18, 1984) affirming that the continental shelf boundaries to the west of Scotland have yet to be established with other States concerned, but that discussions were continuing with the Irish and Danish Governments concerning parts of the continental shelf "in the general area of Rockall." *Cf.* the bilateral continental shelf delimitation agreements which the U.K. is party to in the *North Sea* area: see Symmons, 1979, pp. 705, 706.
7. As for example in the Celtic Sea in blocks 82 and 102.
8. See *infra*, fns. 29 and 51.
9. *Infra*, fn. 78.
10. See *id.* and accompanying text.
11. Maritime Jurisdiction (Exclusive Fishery Limits) Order No. 320 of 1976.
12. See *infra*, fn. 15 and accompanying text.
13. See Irish Government Information Services Information communique of April 1975 which mentions the British proposition that the continental shelf division should be based on an equidistance line measured from *all* U.K. islands; and see also *Hansard* (HC) vol. 27, col. 271 (*Written Answers*).
14. UN Doc. A/CONF. 62/C2/L.43. See confirmation of this policy in *Dail Debates*, vol. 296, col. 1572 and Symmons, 1979, p. 725, fn. 171.
15. See confirmation of this in *Hansard*, (HL) vol. 380, cols. 7 & 8.
16. Territorial Waters Order in Council, 1964, Art. 3 as amended June
18. 1979.
17. For British official affirmation that Ireland has accepted the U.K. straight baseline system, see the parliamentary reply of Mr. Rifkind: *Hansard*, (HC), vol. 27, col. 271, (*Written Answers*, July 12, 1982). It is doubtful, however, whether Ireland has accepted these under the *treaty* provisions of Art. 6 of the 1964 European Fisheries Convention, because Art. 7 thereof provides that the equidistance line (for 12-mile fishery zone purposes) is to be measured from the "low-water mark"; it is also doubtful whether

Ireland's non-use of its *own* islands in its straight baseline system amounts (as argued by Brown, 1978, p. 301) to *implied* rejection of the British lines. One additional factor in the *Celtic Sea* boundary dispute is that the U.K. seems not to have accepted the *Irish* straight baseline system on the South-East coast. See O'Higgins, (1960) I.C.L.Q. 325, 327-331.

18. See *id.*, (question by Lord Campbell of Croy) and more recently the question of Lord Douglas-Hamilton as to what uninhabited islands the Irish Government considered should not be used as basepoints: *Hansard*, (HC), vol. 27, col. 271.
19. See *infra*, fn. 51.
20. See *infra*, fn. 16.
21. Thus in the Icelandic continental shelf designation of May 9, 1985, Iceland appears to have completely ignored any 200-mile zone from St. Kilda, whereas Denmark in its designation two days earlier does appear to have made allowance for it.
22. For discussion of the *sovereignty* aspect relating to the rock, see *infra*, fn. 69 and accompanying text.
23. *Hansard* (HC), vol. 924, col. 348.
24. Where Rockall is mentioned as having a 200-mile radius of water between points No. 26 and 27.
25. See *Dail Debates*, vol. 296, col. 2572; see also *id.*, vol. 313, col. 1350.
26. For a recent official Irish affirmation of this, see *Irish Times*, May 8, 1985.
27. See (1985) ICJ Rep. 13, at para. 34.
28. *Cf.* the recent Icelandic and Danish continental shelf designations in the Rockall area which also seem to indicate that Rockall merits at most a 12-mile territorial sea (see *infra*, fn. 78 and accompanying text).
29. Continental Shelf (Additional Areas) Order, S.I. No. 22 of 1977.
30. Continental Shelf (Additional Areas) Order, S.I. No. 21 of 1977.
31. Continental Shelf (Designation of Additional Area) Order, 1976.
32. Continental Shelf (Designation of Additional Areas) Order, 1974 (S.I. No. 1489).
33. See *Hansard*, (HC), vol. 884, col. 1467. Reaffirmed by Mr. Rifkind on July 12, 1982: see *Hansard*, (HC), vol. 27, col. 272 (*Written Answers*) (the U.K. Government considered it had "valid claim to the area known as the Rockall Plateau on the basis of the criterion of natural prolongation"); and by Baroness Young: *Hansard*, (HL), vol. 458, col. 635 (*Written Answers*, Dec. 18, 1984).
34. See Symmons 1975, p. 72, fn. 39.
35. See *id.*, at p. 67.
36. But, of course, in the *North Sea Continental Shelf* Cases, (1969) ICJ Rep. 3, 30-31, the Court did emphasize that "adjacency" only implies *proximity* "in a general sense."
37. Neither chart claims to be "definitive" as to continental shelf boundaries.
38. Continental Shelf (Designated Areas) Order, S.I. No. 164 of 1976. For a critical analysis of this Irish designation, see Walsh, "The Changing Offshore Jurisdiction of the Republic of Ireland" (1980) xiii *Irish Geography*, 77, 78 and (sub.nom.P.Breathnach) the same writer's updated comments in his paper of the same title delivered to the Annual Conference of the Institute of British Geographers at Durham on Jan. 6, 1984.

38a. See *Hansard* (HC), vol. 27, col. 271, (*Written Answers*, July 12, 1982).
39. See *Dail Debates*, vol. 296, col. 1573.
40. (1984) ICJ Rep. 4, esp. at para. 194.
41. See *supra*, fn. 27.
42. *Dail Debates*, vol. 296, col. 1574. See Symmons, 1979, p. 778.
43. See the statement of the Icelandic Foreign Minister in *Morgunbladid*, June 21, 1985. Use of Rockall itself by the U.K. -- or indeed the other claimants -- could also be vital for their claim to the potential seabed wealth around the rock in areas *outside* the 200-mile EEZ limits in the light of the *revenue-sharing* obligations contained in Art. 82 of LOSC.
44. By Lord Avebury: see *Hansard*, (HL), vol. 380, col. 7.
45. See *Dail Debates*, vol. 325, col. 591, 325.
46. *Dail Debates*, vol. 296, col. 1573.
47. See Mr. Hurd's statement in *Hansard*, (HC), vol. 978, col. 466. Another serious possibility considered by the two governments seems to have been a submission of the dispute to the ICJ or a panel thereof: see *Dail Debates*, vol. 314, cols. 26 and 27.
48. See, *e.g.*, *Dail Debates*, Vol 325, Cols. 590, 591 and vol. 328, col. 3573; and in the U.K., *Hansard* (HC), vol. 27, col. 271 (*Written Answers*, July 12, 1982; and more recently, reports in *Irish Times*, May 8, and 28, 1985, which indicate that the negotiations are still proceeding.
49. *Dail Debates*, vol. 328, col. 3574 (Mr. Lenihan).
50. See *infra*, fn. 78.
51. As was confirmed on July 12, 1982 in the House of Commons: see *Hansard*, (HC), vol. 27, col. 271. On February 18, 1977, the U.K. protested to the Irish Government about this: see *Hansard*, (HC), vol. 926, col. 1015.
52. *Hansard*, (HC), vol. 27, col. 271, (*Written Answers*, July 12, 1982).
53. See "The Rockall Dispute," (1975) VIII *Irish Geography*, 122, 125.
54. See *supra*, fn. 38.
55. (1982) ICJ Rep., 18, 84 ("it is evident that the court must take into account whatever indicia are available of the line or lines which Parties themselves may have considered equitable or acted upon as such -- if only as an interim solution ..."). But *cf.* the ICJ's attitude to the *modus vivendi* approach in the Gulf of Maine case (1984) ICJ Rep. 246, 304.
56. See *infra*, fn. 78. Compare para. 3 of the Irish submission at UNCLOS III: UN Doc.A/Conf./62/C.2/L.43, Aug. 6, 1974 at p. 4.
57. See *Hansard* (HC), vol. 27, col. 271.
58. See *Dail Debates*, vol. 312, col. 1165.
59. See *Irish Times*, May 13, 1978.
60. *Hansard*, (HC), vol. 27, cols. 306, 307 (*Written Answers*, July 12, 1982); *cf.* the very different reply earlier in the House of Lords: *Hansard*, (HC), vol. 380, Art. 6 (*Written Answers*, Feb. 22, 1977).
61. The nearest to the Irish fishery limit line is in the block 142/28 and 29 due west of Barra and some eighteen miles north from that line.
62. *Irish Times*, May 24, 1985.
63. See, *e.g.*, *Hansard*, (HC), vol. 27, col. 271 (*Written Answers*, July 12, 1982) (Her Majesty's Government "do not know what claims or arguments may be advanced on behalf of the Republic of Ireland in the forthcoming arbitration on the delimitation of the continental shelf").

64. See *Decision* of June 30, 1977.
65. See *id.*, paras. 24-28 for the Court's mention of the potential *Irish* boundary situation in this area; and Symmons, 1979, pp. 720-22.
66. See *Irish Times*, July 28, 1977 and *Dail Debates*, vol. 314, col. 26.
67. Despite encouragement from some of its citizens to do so; see most recently the plea from Mr. O'Halloran (of the Irish National Co-operative Council) that the Irish Government should make an "immediate claim" thereto: *Irish Times*, April 16, 1985.
68. See, *e.g.*, *Dail Debates*, vol. 268, col. 1197 (Nov. 1, 1973); and the Irish Government Information Services Bulletin of April, 1975; and, most recently, *Irish Times*, May 8, 1985. The recent exploits of Mr. McClean -- a former British SAS soldier -- in the landing on Rockall with the intent to make a month's stay there (in May 1985) has aroused suspicion in some Dublin circles that there were political motivations behind the episode; but according to an Irish Department of Foreign Affairs' spokesman, this "visit" had no legal or diplomatic consequence for Ireland ("The fact that someone chooses to sit on a rock does not confer a government with a right to it": *Irish Times*, May 28, 1985). His eventual sojourn of forty days on the rock does not, of course, imply that the rock is now habitable for the purposes of Art. 121(3) of LOSC: see *The Times*, July 11, 1985.
69. See, *e.g.*, the Danish Foreign Affairs Department Press Release of May 7, 1985, ("Denmark does not contest the sovereignty claimed by the U.K. over the Rockall skerry").
70. See *supra*, fn. 23 and most recently *Irish Times*, May 8, 1985.
71. See *supra*, fn. 26 and *Hansard*, (HC), vol. 27, col. 271 (*Written Answers*, July 12, 1982).
72. See, *e.g.*, the "Explanatory Note" attached to the Althing (Icelandic Parliament) Resolution of Dec. 22, 1978 where this is implicit.
73. By Lord Douglas Hamilton.
74. *Hansard* (HC), vol. 27, col. 270 (*Written Answers*, July 12, 1982).
75. By Mr. Deakins.
76. See *Hansard*, (HC), vol. 28, col. 750 (*Written Answers*, July 30, 1982).
77. See, *e.g.*, the dissenting opinion of Judge Evensen in the *Libya/Tunisia* case (1982) ICJ Rep. 18, 283 and the opinion of the Conciliation Commission on the question of the continental shelf of Jan Mayen Island: (1981) XX ILM 797, 803 and E.D. Brown, *Sea-bed Energy and Mineral Resources and the Law of the Sea*: vol. I: *The Areas within National Jurisdiction*, 1984, 424. *Cf.* Churchill, "Marine Delimitation in the Jan Mayen Area," (1985) *Marine Policy* 16, 20 and Dipla, *Le Regime Juridique des Iles dans de Droit International de la Mer*, 1984, at pp. 100, 101.
78. See respectively Communication concerning the Continental Shelf Area Around the Faeroe Islands (1985) *and* Regulations concerning the Delimitation of the Continental Shelf to the West, South and East of Iceland (1985). For more detailed discussion, see Symmons, 1986, p. 344.
79. See the Icelandic Foreign Minister's interview in *Morgunbladid*, June 21, 1985.
80. But not, of course, in the Celtic Sea area where Iceland and the Faeroes have no claims.
81. At p. 3 ("If and when exploration and exploitation of potential resources in the [Rockall] area *should come up for consideration* it

will be important for Denmark to have announced that we consider the right to exercise jurisdiction over the seabed belongs to Denmark" (emphasis added.)

82. *North Sea Continental Shelf Cases*, (1969) ICJ Rep. 4, 54.
83. See *supra*, fn. 27 at p. 4, where the ICJ refused to accede to Malta and Libya's invitation not to limit its judgment to the area in which theirs were the *sole* competing claims, in view of the intervention of Italy and its prior judgment on this of March 21, 1984. Thus the ICJ determined that the geographical scope should be *limited* and confined to the area in which, *according to information supplied by Italy*, Italy had no claims to continental shelf rights. By this means the Court ensured to Italy the protection which it sought to obtain by intervening.
84. See Danish press release *supra*, fn. 81, p. 2.
85. See *News from Iceland*, No. 111, May 1985, p. 1.
86. On the strength of the British, Irish and Faeroese claims in this regard, see Brown, 1978, pp. 279-289.
87. See, *e.g.* the Resolution of the Althing (Icelandic Parliament) on May 19, 1980 which empowered the Icelandic Government "to agree that an *arbitration tribunal* decide on the division of the area between the Icelanders and the Faeroese if the Faeroese so desire" (emphasis added).
88. See the query in the House of Lords by Lord Kenneth (*Hansard* (HL), vol. 458, col. 635, *Written Answers*, December 18, 1984) on the Icelandic suggestion of *quadripartite* discussion.

THE RELEVANCE OF ECONOMIC FACTORS TO
THE LAW OF MARITIME DELIMITATION
BETWEEN NEIGHBORING STATES

Surya P. Sharma
Faculty of Law
Kurukshetra University, India

Introduction

This paper is designed as a clarification of the possible role of economic factors in the process of maritime boundary delimitation between neighboring states. The existing law of delimitation is based on equitable concepts. It demands the application of equitable criteria and methods taking into account all relevant factors. Our enquiry would seek to demonstrate whether economic factors have the independent status of equitable principle or rule, or whether they are just one of the relevant circumstances deemed applicable in conjunction with the main criteria or other relevant factors in the delimitation process. In the latter case, is it possible to quantify or articulate the weight to be accorded to economic factors independently or in relation to other factors?

The principal purpose of an individual maritime boundary settlement is to settle the issue permanently in order to achieve "stability and finality." This assumes the importance of applying in a delimitation process those criteria and methods that are precise, stable, and would lead to equitable delimitation. In actual practice, no criteria, even the ones based on geographic factors, are perfect. There are instances of the criteria borrowed from geography causing varying degrees of inequity. Thus arises the relevance of other factors playing a supplementary, remedial role in the process of boundary delimitation in order to achieve equitable results. Economic factors are just one of them. If economic considerations are of a variable nature, such as data concerning the relative wealth and poverty of the contesting states, they may not serve the purpose of a stable and permanent boundary. Conversely, the existence, over a reasonable period of time, of the potential use and dependency patterns of resources deserves appropriate weight, as they might be manifesting physical realities, or they may help explain the significance of geographic factors. If such economic factors are ignored, they might, in a given situation, cause severe deprivations to the entire social processes of the concerned states. Therefore, if a balanced consideration, based on the reasonableness of the claims of contesting parties, were given to these factors, it would, for sure, promote the goal of "stability and finality" of maritime boundaries.[1]

Sources of the Law of Delimitation

The contemporary world arena, which has undergone a drastic qualitative and quantitative transformation since 1945, is witnessing an unprecedented acceleration in demands for expansion of exclusive authority of states over the seas to secure a variety of interests, particularly of economic content.[2] Also, advances in modern science and technology have made new methods for exploiting the resources of the seas possible and commercially more profitable. This factor has lent strength to coastal state campaigns to gain exclusive authority to manage and exploit the natural resources of the oceans. The overall result is the addition of the two more seaward zones, namely, the continental shelf zone to the existing territorial sea zone.

As the campaign in support of coastal states for extensive jurisdiction in the oceans gained momentum, the international law of the sea was faced with the necessity of devising a set of criteria for delimiting the vast areas of the ocean between no fewer than 132 coastal states. The initial attention was devoted to the formulation of prescriptions and policies regulating the regime of the continental shelf in view of the fact that national claims to continental shelf jurisdiction preceded claims of extended jurisdiction over the water column, and to deriving from these fundamental norms the specific rules that could apply to continental shelf delimitation. Thus, there is already a growing body of state practice applying these rules in concrete cases. On the other hand, due to its later birth, less attention was paid to ascertaining the legal norms applicable to exclusive economic zone boundaries. With the increasing number of states claiming extended jurisdiction both on the continental shelf and the water column, the focus of the sea law appears to be shifting to the delimitation of a single maritime boundary which would serve the purpose of continental shelf as well as economic zone boundaries. A number of emergent single maritime boundary agreements and the decision of the Chamber of the International Court of Justice (ICJ) in the *Gulf of Maine* case bear testimony to this current phenomenon.

The question at this stage arises whether the criteria and methods as well as other considerations of delimitation deemed applicable to the process of delimitation in the aforesaid zones are common. There are significant *inter se* legal differences between the delimitation of a continental shelf boundary, determined by the legal criteria emphasizing geological and geographical features, and an exclusive economic zone boundary, based on criteria that might include the relevance of usage and economic considerations, and also between either of them and a single maritime boundary, which attracts the criteria of a multipurpose boundary. Referring to the *inter se* legal differences between a continental shelf boundary and an exclusive economic zone boundary, a recent collaborative study by Collins and Rogoff, after a thorough analysis of the pertinent legal materials, has concluded that "the process by which an equitable delimitation of exclusive economic zone boundaries is to be achieved is essentially the same as that required for delimitation of continental shelf boundaries."[3] Indeed, the analogous relationship between them can be fortified by the identical wording of Articles 74 and 83 of the new Law of the Sea Convention governing delimitation of each of these zones. Thus, as observed by Collins and Rogoff, "the emerging law that relates to delimitation of economic zone boundaries is, in its essence, the same as the law applicable to delimitation of continental shelf boundaries."[4] Central to this law is the duty to negotiate in good faith on the basis of international law to achieve an equitable solution. According to the aforesaid authors, the various equitable principles and even the consideration of relevant circumstances, including geographic and economic, are essentially the same, inasmuch as the economic zone includes both the seabed and subsoil and the resources of the water column.[5] The state practice, in the form of negotiating several single maritime boundary agreements in recent years, has revealed that the principles and rules, which have been developed in the context of continental shelf, exclusive economic zone and territorial sea boundaries, have provided the legal basis for particular delimitations which were the subject matter of those agreements.[6] Thus, based as it is on equitable concepts, the existing law of delimitation of these three categories of zones provides sources for ascertaining the principles and rules of a single, multipurpose maritime boundary delimitation. The judgment of the Chamber of the International Court in the *Gulf of Maine* case[7] involving a single line boundary is significant in this regard. Inasmuch as the delimitation of a single maritime boundary entails a delimitation of the two distinct elements (continental shelf and the water column) by means of a single line, the Chamber differentiated the *Gulf of Maine* case from the previous decisions involving continental shelf delimitations. Nonetheless, this did not mean, in its view, that the criteria applied in those decisions must *ipso facto* be held inapplicable in the present case.[8] In fact, the tenor of the fundamental norms set out by the Chamber and deemed applicable in this case was no different from the tenor of the law of continental shelf and economic zone delimitation. Once again, the judicial attention was focused on agreement in good faith and delimitation by the application of equitable criteria and by the use of practical methods capable to ensuring, with regard to the geographic configuration of the area and other relevant circumstances, an equitable result. The sole condition the Chamber put was that "the adaptability of those criteria to this essentially different operation should first be verified in relation to its specific requirements."[9]

The aforesaid discussion leads to the conclusion that the sources of delimitation of various maritime zones, taken singly or in combination, are to a great extent common except that the significance of a particular kind of relevant circumstance may be specific to a particular zone and, as such, might warrant special weight to be given to it. In view of this integration of various factors deemed applicable in the maritime delimitation process, the examination of the relevance of economic factors might also require a unified approach. Accordingly, our study of the relevance of economic factors to the process of delimitation is not classified in terms of various maritime zones; rather, it seeks to focus on an approach that would generally apply to all maritime zones.

Relevance of Economic Factors

In the light of national claims and international judicial and arbitral decisions, economic factors can be classified into the following familiar categories: (1) the existence of the natural resources -- the unity of the deposit, (2) considerations relating to relative wealth or general socio-economic data, and (3) usage and economic dependency.

The Existence of the Natural Resources -- The Unity of the Deposit

Issues

If the mineral deposits and other resources were separate and divisible by a geographically identifiable line, no problem would arise. But the same cannot be said about sea areas containing resources where claims overlap. Then the question arises as to what consideration should be given to the mineral deposits in areas of overlapping claims in a process of delimitation. Very often a reference is made to the so-called principles of the unity of the deposit in this context, thereby implying, to use the words of Mouton, "a dividing boundary line should not cross an oil-pool."[10] There are, however, some problems concerning its legal status. Is it an independent element forming part of the equitable criteria? Can it be treated as a *special circumstance* in

250

terms of Article 6 of the 1958 Geneva Convention on the Continental Shelf, forming a basis for delimiting a line that varies from the equidistance line? Or, at any rate, how much weight should be accorded to it, in conjunction with other factors, in a delimitation process?

Policies

There are two competing policy goals: (a) achievement of maximum productivity of resources and avoidance of harmful and uneconomical use and exploitation; (b) equitable distribution of resources. Decision-makers should seek to draw a reasonable accommodation between them. It frequently happens that the same mineral deposit lies on both sides of the line dividing a continental shelf between two states. As there is a possibility that such a deposit may be exploited from either side, one has to face the problem arising from the risk of prejudicial or wasteful exploitation by one or the other of the concerned states. One possible solution is to preserve the essential unity of a mineral deposit by assigning the deposit in entirety to one party through deviation from the delimitation line. But this solution might cause economic deprivation to the states losing the deposit through delimitation. Cooperative arrangements between coastal states containing a variety of solutions have been favored as the more feasible method to resolve these problems with a view to ensuring the most efficient exploitation or apportionment of the products concerned.[11]

Trends

The aforesaid questions and policies have been considered by courts and tribunals, as well as in state practice. Whether the unity of a deposit constitutes a "special circumstance" was considered in the *North Sea Continental Shelf* cases.[12] In view of its finding that the use of the equidistance method of delimitation was not obligatory, the ICJ deemed it legally unnecessary to prove the existence of "special circumstances" in order to justify its not using that method.[13] From this, Professor Lagoni has concluded that the ICJ did not allude to the unity principle as a "special circumstance" and has cited, for authority, the Court's formulation that the unity of a deposit does not constitute "anything more than a factual element which it is reasonable to take into consideration in the course of the negotiations for a delimitation."[14] While agreeing with the general conclusion of Professor Lagoni that the existence of mineral deposits would not constitute a "special circumstance" justifying deviation from the equidistance principle, Professor Brown has interpreted the *North Sea* cases in a slightly different manner.[15] In his opinion, the Court's consideration of the role of equity amounts, in reality, to a consideration of special circumstances as well.[16] This view can be fortified by the statement of the Court that "there is no legal limit to the considerations which states may take account of for the purpose of making sure that they apply equitable procedures"[17] and by the Court's approval of a list of factors which include not only geographical features but others also such as the unity of any deposit[18] that must be taken into account. "Whether one calls this application of equity or of special circumstances is immaterial," adds Professor Brown.[19] He cites at least one situation where reference to natural resources (for example, the existence of a sedentary fishery, which, like oil and gas, is a continental shelf resource) as constituting special circumstances is justified. The test is whether a coastal state has acquired exclusive rights

251

to such resources independently of, and prior to, the development of the continental shelf doctrine.[20]

Specifically, in the context of the facts of this case, the Court was willing to say no more than that the unity of a deposit does not constitute anything more than a factual element deserving consideration in the course of delimitation negotiations. Nonetheless, the Court's judgment, when construed in a broader context, does seem to endorse the relevance of the existence of the natural resources to the process of maritime boundary delimitation. The Court focused its attention on the supportive value of "known or readily ascertainable ... natural resources, of the continental shelf areas involved."[21] It clearly laid down that one of the factors to be taken into consideration in the delimitation of areas of continental shelf is the unity of any deposits,[22] and it is the balancing of all such factors that would produce an equitable delimitation.[23] Although the Court admitted that these criteria were not entirely precise, they nonetheless "provide adequate bases for decision adapted to the factual situation."[24] In short, the Court did not rule out the relevance of the natural resources to reaching an equitable delimitation; it ascribed to this factor the value of supporting the decision adapted to the factual situation. Regarding the question of how much weight should be given to each factor in relation to others, the Court ruled that it would vary with the circumstances of each case.[25]

That the decision-makers must take into account all relevant factors, geographical and others like the unity of a deposit, in order to achieve an equitable delimitation, was strengthened in the subsequent international arbitral and judicial decisions on maritime delimitation. In the *Anglo-French Arbitration* case involving continental shelf delimitation, the ICJ ruled that Article 6 of the 1958 Convention on the Continental Shelf provided a combined equidistance-circumstances rule having the same object as the rules of customary international law, to wit, "the delimitation of the boundary in accordance with equitable principles."[26] The application of equitable principles, as the past practice indicates, requires consideration of all factors that may be relevant in a particular contextual situation and no single factor is, on its own footing, decisive in determining the boundary. In this case, the Court's insistence on taking into account the geographical and other circumstances assured that all the relevant factors including economic shall be taken into account in any particular situation.[27]

The ICJ in yet another case -- the *Tunisia-Libya Continental Shelf* case -- while reiterating the law of maritime delimitation, laid down the general rule that "delimitation is to be effected in accordance with equitable principles, and taking account of all relevant circumstances."[28] Significantly, as the Court did not elaborate equitable principles as such, its attention was focused primarily on identifying and balancing up the various circumstances or considerations that it regarded as relevant "in order to produce an equitable result."[29] The Court also made it clear that while "no rigid rule exists as to the exact weight to be attached to each element in the case," nonetheless "this is very far from being an exercise of discretion or conciliation; nor is it an operation of distributive justice."[30] It went on to say: "...what is reasonable and equitable in a given case must depend on its particular circumstances."[31]

Libya strenuously argued in this case that, in view of its invocation of geology as an indispensable attribute of its view of "natural prolongation," the presence or absence of oil or gas in the oil-wells in the continental shelf areas appertaining to either party should play an important part in the delimitation process. Responding specifically to the presence of oil-wells in an area to be delimited, the Court ruled that "it may, depending on the facts, be an element to be taken into account in the process of weighing all relevant factors to achieve an equitable result."[32] Thus, the Court highlighted the potential relevance of the presence of natural resources to the delimitation process; however, no precise criterion was laid down to assess the degree of weight to be given to this factor independently, or in relation to other factors.

The significance of economic factors for boundary delimitation was invoked on a large scale by both the U.S. and Canada in the *Gulf of Maine* case. Although the thrust of the argument of the parties, as discussed in the later part of the text, centered upon historic usage and economic dependency in respect of fishing activities, they also invoked the potentiality of natural resources, particularly activities in the field of oil exploitation. The reasoning given by the Chamber of the ICJ was predominantly addressed to the significance of fishing resources and activities, but its conclusions apply, in an equally ample measure, to the relevance, in a delimitation process, of activities concerning potential exploitation of oil. The Chamber restated the general, equitable criteria prescribed in the international law of delimitation and added that these criteria are not spelled out, but they are to be determined in relation to what may be properly called the geographical features of the area.[33] Only when, on the basis of these criteria, the drawing of a delimitation line has been envisaged, then the other criteria, still in conformity with a rule of law, may and should be brought in and be taken into account "in order to be sure of reaching an equitable result."[34]

The Chamber, in short, laid down that, as per the requirement of the international law of delimitation demanding the application of equitable criteria, initially the boundary line should be drawn on the basis of geographical features. Thereafter, with a view to ensuring the equitable results of such a delimitation, the Court might take into account, still in conformity with a rule of law, other criteria such as economic factors. The apparent objective of the latter is to correct the possible inequity caused by the geographical factors. The criteria of geography could be decisive, whereas the others are probative only, though still within the framework of a rule of law.

More precisely, the Court ruled that the respective scale of activities regarding natural resources cannot be taken into account as a "relevant circumstance" or "equitable criteria" to be applied in determining the delimitation line.[35] The test laid down was that the overall result, based on equitable criteria, should not lead to catastrophic repercussions for the livelihood and economic wellbeing of the population of the countries concerned.[36] Should it lead to such consequences, an appropriate deviation from the line based on geographical criteria will be permissible.

In this case, the Chamber was convinced that the choice of delimitation line, particularly in reference to its third and final segment, led to equitable results. It observed that the recommended line so divided the main areas in which the subsoil was being explored for its mineral resources as to leave on either side broad expanses in which prospecting had been undertaken in the past and might be resumed to the

253

extent desired by the parties.[37] The conclusion of the Chamber in respect of the division of fish stocks was just about the same.[38]

To conclude: the above discussion demonstrates that the delimitation of maritime boundaries is to be achieved by applying "equitable criteria" which cannot be divorced from consideration of "relevant circumstances". The predominant "relevant circumstance" is undoubtedly geographic features. The world jurisprudence has not alluded to the presence of natural resources such as the unity of a deposit as a "special circumstance" in the sense of Article 6 of the 1958 Geneva Convention on the Continental Shelf, justifying deviation from the delimitation based on geographic features. Nonetheless the requirement of taking into account the presence of physical resources, in the process of weighing all relevant factors in order to produce an equitable result, is now firmly established as a matter of a rule of law. No precise criteria have yet been laid down, however, to measure the weight to be given to each such factor taken independently or in relation to other factors; nor has there been any authoritative clarification on how each factor is to be integrated with other factors in the process of delimitation. From the above, it is also clear that the presence of natural resources cannot be of any decisive value in the delimitation process; at best, it can provide a supportive basis for a decision adapted to the factual situation. Or, in terms of the *Gulf of Maine* decision, it is relevant to assessment of the equitable character of the delimitation drawn on the basis of criteria borrowed from physical and political geography. The contribution of this case is noteworthy. It has enlarged the scope of natural resources that can be covered under relevant circumstances. Prior to this case, the emphasis of the Court was on the presence or exploitation of "known" or "readily" ascertainable resources. But in the *Gulf of Maine* case, the Chamber expressed willingness to consider, if the context so allowed, the potential relevance even of the exploration of mineral resources, or prospecting activities, in the areas of overlapping claims. Moreover, the Chamber provided at least one instance when the delimitation based on geographic factors may be allowed to be modified due to the operation of economic factors; namely, if the application of equitable criteria or the use of appropriate methods should result in serious economic repercussions for the parties.

The reluctance of courts and tribunals to allow major deviations from delimitation lines, based on geographical factors, on the ground of relevant circumstances such as the presence and use of natural resources, has been circumvented in actual state practice by concluding agreements that incorporate "economic solutions." Indeed, the ICJ in the *North Sea* cases hinted that the parties should resolve such problems through agreements.[39] Taking this hint, at the time of implementing the decision of the Court by redelimiting certain areas of the continental shelf in the North Sea, Denmark retained a certain area where drilling operations had been conducted by Danish Concessionaries, although from a strictly geographic point of view Germany should have gotten it.[40] Saudi Arabia and Iran, by an offshore boundary agreement of 1968, agreed to a modification of the geographical equidistance line in the northern part of the area in order to give an equal share of a single oil deposit to both sides.[41] Bahrain and Saudi Arabia, through an agreement in 1958, agreed to the allocation of a hexagonal zone of overlapping claims to the latter on the condition that it would return half of the net revenues derived from exploitation of that zone to the former. The economic solution worked out in this case was independent

of any geographic considerations.[42] Apart from such agreements, several
other legal arrangements, providing for numerous kinds of bilateral
cooperation in equitably exploiting the natural resources, exist.[43] It
is also significant to note that state practice of boundary delimitations provide suggestions as to how geological and geographic factors
are to be integrated with certain economic considerations.[44]

Relevance of Comparative Socio-Economic Data

Issues
    The issue here is whether general socio-economic data constitute
special circumstances justifying deviation from the delimitation line
based on geographic features. Even if the answer to this question is
no, are they relevant at all in effecting an equitable delimitation,
and if so, how should these data be weighed?
    The most important legal policy here is that of achieving perma-
nency and finality of the boundaries. This goal presupposes the existence of predictable factors. General socio-economic considerations
related to the relative wealth and poverty of states are generally
regarded as variables of an unpredictable nature and hence unhelpful to
boundary delimitation designed to achieve permanency. Conditions of
unpredictable national fortune or calamity "might at any time cause to
tilt the scale one way or the other." Therefore, a very limited considerations should be given to such factors in a boundary delimitation. At
best they can help the decision-makers to grasp the significance of
certain features concerning the delimitation area.

Trends
    General competitive socio-economic data concerning population,
employment, wealth and poverty, and industrial activity were most
clearly invoked, in a domestic context, in the *Mississippi-Louisiana*
case.[45] Mississippi defended its case for a favorable boundary on the
ground that it was a very poor state. It also, in support of the case,
cited statistics on personal income, *per capita* income, tax burden, and
proved recoverable natural gas resources. Louisiana denied these claims
and pleaded that it had a heavy public burden to discharge due to the
fact that it was used as the base for carrying out almost all offshore
hydrocarbon activities. Referring to severance taxes that in the past
had proved to be adequate, it was further argued that the exploitation
of hydrocarbons on and near the shore had reduced this source of income. The NOAA consultants concluded that the data presented by the
parties were not relevant to the delimitation and failed to provide any
significant factual basis for determining the correct locations for the
boundaries in the question.[46] At the international level, in the *Tunisia-Libya* case, Tunisia invoked economic considerations by drawing
attention to its relative poverty in terms of absence of natural resources like agriculture and minerals, compared with the relative
abundance in Libya, especially of oil and gas wealth, as well as agricultural resources.[47] The ICJ ruled that these economic considerations
cannot be taken into account for the delimitation of the continental
shelf areas appertaining to each party. The Court observed:

> They are virtually extraneous factors since they are variables
> which unpredictable national fortune or calamity ... might at any
> time cause to tilt the scale one way or the other.[48]

The *Gulf of Maine* case predominantly concerned itself with the issue of historic usage and economic dependency; nonetheless, general socioeconomic conditions of the disputed areas were also involved. As the Court noted, the disputants, Canada and the U.S., in support of their respective cases, submitted comparative analyses (supported by statistics, tables and graphics) of the respective importance of the resources drawn from fisheries for what was called the one-dimensional economy of Lunenburg County and for the diversified, urbanized economy of Massachusetts.[49] The Chamber refused to make an in-depth assessment of these and similar other aspects. The Court observed that such activities "may require an examination of valid considerations of a political and economic character" resulting possibly in a decision *ex aequo et bono*, which it was not allowed to do by its Statute.[50]

Although the ICJ has rejected the general relevance of economic considerations relating to relative wealth, nonetheless the importance of particular geographic features has been regularly tested by reference to demographic and economic factors. In the *Anglo-French Arbitration*, the United Kingdom argued that the special features of the Channel Island region militated positively in favor of the delimitation it proposed.[51] It laid stress on the particular character of islands as not being rocks or islets, but populous islands of a certain political and economic importance. The Court also recognized that the islands possessed a considerable population and a substantial agriculture and commercial economy. Recognizing the relevance of the size and importance of the Channel Islands, the Court ruled that they might be taken into account in balancing the equities of this region.[52] In actual application of this ruling, the Court neither accepted the suggestion of France for a six-mile enclave around the islands nor the course of the boundary proposed by the United Kingdom and concluded that the specific features of the island region called for an intermediate solution that effected a more appropriate and a more equitable balance between the respective claims and interests of the parties.[53]

Historic Use and Economic Dependency Issues

Issues
Whether circumstances of historic use and economic dependency are relevant to boundary delimitation and would justify deviation from the criteria based on geographic considerations is the main issue here. Moreover, whether the weight to be given to such economic factors can be articulated, and in what manner they can be integrated with other factors require a close examination.

Policies
There are two interrelated policy considerations. The first is that the stability of historical and use patterns of resources producing dependency requires not to be disturbed in the interest of stable boundaries. On the other hand, if such economic considerations which might change over a period of time are allowed to play an overriding role in a delimitation process, the outcome may lead to refashioning of geography. Therefore, a reasonable balance must be achieved. Historical patterns may reveal that certain ocean areas are more closely identified with one land area than another. As a result these patterns may help the decision-maker to assess the significance of the important features of the ocean area and permit the development of a boundary line that reflects those identifications.[54] In the same way, continuous

existence of use patterns and conditions of dependency over a substantial period to the present creates expectations which can be destroyed only at the cost of the well-being of the contesting states and their nationals. Therefore, the highest degree of weight should be attached to such patterns which indicate a relatively clear demarcation of activities, as they are most likely to reflect the physical realities as well. Conversely, where patterns have varied over a time or demarcation of activities is less than clear, less weight should be given. Finally, if the patterns of use have changed significantly over time, no weight need be given to them. As Professor Charney observes: "A permanent boundary based on variable usage patterns would be no more justifiable than one found upon variable economic factors."[55]

Trends

Apart from certain international legal agreements which, in their boundary delimitation provisions, have recognized the significance of historic rights in the water column,[56] decisions of the international courts have also supported the proposition that historic rights and economic dependency might have relevance in maritime boundary delimitation. The judgment in the *Anglo-Norwegian Fisheries* case is one such example.[57] "The novelty of this judgment," in the words of Blum, "lies in the fact that the Court recognized an historic right to certain waters, deriving not from an historic claim to a given area of water -- as is the case with historic claims over bays, for instance -- but from an *historic right to delimit* territorial waters in a given manner.[58] This case upheld the validity of Norway's use of straight baselines, fortified by a constant and sufficiently long practice and attitude of other governments, to determine the outer limits of a portion of its territorial sea. Apart from usage, the Court also attached a certain weight to dependency factors, though only in support of the principal criteria based on geographical factors, namely, the close dependence of the sea on the land domain and the general direction of the coast. The Court took into account the dependence of the Norwegian nationals in certain localities (particularly Lopphavit) on the exploitation of the sea and observed that "in these barren regions the inhabitants of the coastal zone derive their livelihood essentially from fishing."[59] The Court also stated: "There is one consideration not to be overlooked, the scope of which extends beyond purely geographic factors: that of certain economic interests peculiar to a region, the reality and importance of which are clearly evidenced by a long usage."[60] Referring to the Lopphavit area, the United Kingdom argued that in this region the line did not exactly follow the general direction of the coast. The Court, in response, observed that even if there was a pronounced deviation, Norway had relied on "historic title clearly referable to the waters of Lopphavit, namely, the exclusive privilege to fish and hunt whales granted at the end of the 17th century ..."[61] Moreover, in the opinion of the Court, these traditional fishing rights were founded on the vital needs of the population and, in consequence, could legitimately be taken into account.[62] However, as stated earlier, the economic factor was not conclusive; it was deemed to be an element of probative, rather than of constitutive value.[63] It was taken into account in conjunction with more important geographical and other relevant circumstances.

Another illustration of historic use and economic dependency resulting in a slight deviation from a maritime boundary line based solely on geographic considerations is found in the *Grisbadarna* case.[64]

This case entailed a dispute, in the late nineteenth century, between Norway and Sweden regarding the course of boundary in the area of the Grisbadarna banks, which was rich in lobsters. The Permanent Court of Arbitration, which decided the case in 1909, held that the line should be drawn perpendicular to the general direction of the coast. Since such a line would have cut across the Grisbadarna banks, a result unsuitable to both parties, the Tribunal decided to diverge by one degree from the purely geographical perpendicular line in favor of Sweden. To arrive at this decision to deviate from geographical criteria, the Tribunal relied on historic use, economic dependency and acquiescence. The Tribunal made a particular note of the facts that lobster fishing was the most important fishing activity on the Grisbadarna banks; that Swedish fishermen had carried on lobster fishing in the shoals of Grisbadarna for a much longer time and to a much greater extent than had the subjects of Norway[65]; and that fishing in that area was much more important to the inhabitants of Koster, Sweden, than to those of Hvaler, Norway.[66] In light of these facts, the Tribunal ruled that "it is a settled principle of the law of nations that a state of things which actually exists and has existed for a long time should be changed as little as possible.[67] Again, as Collins and Rogoff conclude, the factual circumstances concerned were treated by the Tribunal "as supporting evidence for a slight variation of a line based on purely geographical factors rather than independent sources of rights to maritime territory."[68]

Once again, in the *Fisheries Jurisdiction* case,[69] the ICJ was faced with the issue of historic rights and economic dependency. This case involved a conflict between Iceland's proclaimed fifty-mile exclusive fishing zone and the traditional fishing activities of subjects of the United Kingdom. The Court held that under customary international law, which had emerged since the 1960 Geneva Conference on the law of the sea, a coastal state may claim preferential rights when it is in a situation of dependency on coastal fisheries.[70] In this case, Iceland was deemed to have acquired preferential rights because of its clear dependence on its coastal fisheries and because those fisheries were subjected to intensified exploitation.[71] But the Court made it clear that these rights were not exclusive in nature and scope; they had to be shared with rights of other states to fish in the same area. The coastal state was obligated to give particular regard to the rights of other states, in this case the United Kingdom, which had been engaged in the same fishery over a considerable period of time and which had established economic dependency on the same fishing grounds.[72] Since the rights of the parties were competitive, the Court ruled that "the most appropriate method for the solution of the dispute is clearly that of negotiation."[73]

In the *Tunisia-Libya* case, while invoking the relevance of economic factors in the delimitation process, Tunisia argued that fishing resources derived from its claimed "historic rights" and "historic waters" areas must necessarily be taken into account as supplementing its national economy in eking out its survival as a country.[74] More specifically, it claimed that the delimitation of the continental shelf between itself and Libya must not encroach at any point upon the area within which Tunisia possessed such historic rights.[75] The Court held that only if the method of delimitation chosen by it was such that it will or may encroach upon the historic rights area, then it will have to determine the validity and scope of these rights.[76] Conversely, if the method of delimitation arrived at, independently of the existence

258

of those rights, was such that the delimitation would undoubtedly leave Tunisia in the full and undisturbed exercise of those rights over the claimed area, then a finding by the Court on the subject would be unnecessary.[77] Indeed, the line determined by the Court largely left Tunisia in complete exercise of those rights and hence it declined to give any finding on this beyond stating that its judgment concerned itself with Tunisia's claim to "historic rights" and "fishing zones" only to the extent that it found it necessary to do so for the purpose of equitable delimitation in the case in question.[78] From this it follows that the Court did not completely rule out the consideration of historic rights and economic dependency, if found necessary for equitable delimitation.

By far the most instructive case entailing economic considerations in the form of historic use and dependency is, indeed, that of the *Gulf of Maine* case. The broad issue before the Chamber of the ICJ was: should the Court take into consideration the relevance of the human environment, and more particularly its socio-economic conditions, in the delimitation of a single maritime boundary between the two countries (Canada and the U.S.) as requested?[79] The Chamber divided the delimitation line into three segments. Regarding the first two segments, the parties did not make any special reference to the fishing resources of any explorations carried out in this sector with a view to the discovery and exploration of petroleum resources.[80] Referring to the final segment of the line drawn by the Chamber, it noted that it was one of greatest interest to the parties on account of the presence of Georges Bank, which was the real subject of the dispute between them and the principal stakes in the proceedings, from the view of the potential resources of the subsoil and also, in particular, that of fisheries that were of major economic importance.[81] In support of their respective cases, both Canada and the U.S. presented a mass of data concerning human and economic geography, contending that they constituted a relevant circumstance which the Chamber should take into account for determining a single, multipurpose boundary.

The United States' case was predominantly based on its historic presence in the disputed areas, the activities pursued by it and its nationals -- taking the form especially of fishing, and of the conservation and management of fisheries -- as well as other activities concerning navigational assistance, rescue, research, defense and so forth.[82] According to the United States' pleadings, all these activities, which it thought greatly exceeded in duration and scale the more recent and limited activities of Canada and its nationals, must be regarded as a major relevant circumstance for the purpose of reaching an equitable solution to the delimitation problem.[83] It pleaded, "A boundary will rarely produce an equitable solution if it leaves to one state maritime areas within which its neighbor historically has had the predominant interest -- both in using the area and in exercising international responsibilities there."[84]

Canada, in fact, laid larger emphasis on the alleged decisive importance of socio-economic aspects; however, it did not, like the United States, invoke any historic right. Canada was relying rather on the more recent period, especially of the past fifteen years. It drew the Chamber's attention to (a) the distribution of fish stocks in the various parts of the area, and (b) the fishing practices respectively established and followed by the two parties.[85] Canada argued that any single maritime boundary should ensure the maintenance of the existing fishing patterns that are in its view vital to the coastal communities

259

of the region in question, and it sought to give this idea the status of an equitable principle of determining force for the purpose of delimitation.[86] Additionally, Canada claimed that it is well established in international law that economic dependence associated with established patterns of exploitation of the disputed area constitute legally relevant circumstances which must be given a special weight in the final balancing up, if a truly equitable result is to be achieved.[87] The relevant economic circumstances stressed by Canada in this case included a strong Canadian presence in the fishery of Georges Bank and the established and vitally important economic dependence of Canadian coastal communities in the area upon the resources of the Bank and the lack of comparable dependence on the part of United States coastal communities.[88] In substance, Canada was pleading with the Chamber to avoid in any way harming the economic and social development of the centers of population in Nova Scotia, especially built up during the past fifteen years.

The Chamber refused to ascribe any decisive weight for the purpose of delimitation to the antiquity or continuity of fishing activities carried on in the past within the delimitation area outside the closing line of the Gulf.[90] With special reference to competing fishing activities, and others relating to activities in the field of oil exploration, scientific research, or common defense arrangements, the Chamber was unwilling to make an in-depth assessment of these activities, fearing that it might lead to a decision *ex aequo et bono*, whereas its job was to achieve the result on the basis of law.[91] At the same time, the Chamber could not just ignore them, in view of the past background of the law of delimitation and the potential threat that avoidance of such an issue might result, in some contextual situations, in severe deprivations for the parties and their nationals. Accordingly, it had to choose a middle way.

The Chamber first focused on the *equitable criteria* -- the main criteria -- which were to be determined in relation to the geographical features of the area; and thereafter, it addressed itself to economic considerations such as those involved in this case. Economic considerations, in its opinion, were relevant to the course of the boundary to be determined. Nevertheless, inasmuch as they were of supportive value only, their consideration must be postponed until the main criteria based on geographic factors had been exhausted.

The Chamber observed that "other circumstances" in this case -- the data presented by the parties concerning human and economic geography -- ought to be taken properly into consideration in assessing the equitable character of the result produced by this portion of the line, which was destined to divide the riches of the waters and shelf of Georges Bank between two neighboring countries.[92] The Court held that (a) these circumstances were ineligible for consideration as criteria to be applied in the delimitation process itself; nevertheless, (b) they were relevant to the assessment of the equitable character of a delimitation first established on the basis of criteria borrowed from physical and political geography.[93]

The Court remained unpersuaded, as stated in the earlier part of the text, in accepting that the respective scale of activities connected with fishing, petroleum exploration and exploitation and other matters could be taken into account as a relevant circumstance or as an equitable criterion to be applied in determining the delimitation line.[94] In the opinion of the Chamber, these considerations would become relevant only if the overall result, even though achieved through the application of equitable criteria and the use of appropriate methods for giving them concrete effort, should unexpectedly be revealed as radically inequitable, that is to say, as likely to entail catastrophic repercussions for the livelihood and economic well-being of the population of the countries concerned.[95] What the Court meant was that if the results of the delimitation achieved are radically inequitable, in this case, if they are likely to entail catastrophic repercussions for the livelihood and economic well-being of the population of the countries concerned, they may become relevant or acquire the status of equitable criteria in order to ensure an equitable result. Conditions of an exceptional kind might justify correction of the delimitation line drawn on the basis of geography.[96] In the context of this case, nothing less than a decision which would have assigned the whole of Georges Bank to one of the parties might possibly have entailed serious economic repercussions for the other, as referred to above.[97] There was no such danger in view of the finding of the Chamber that the division of water resulting from the Chamber's choice of delimitation line very nearly met the claims of both parties regarding fishery stocks and other connected activities.[98]

Appraisal
    The international law of maritime boundary delimitation, as recently restated by the Chamber of the ICJ in the *Gulf of Maine* case, prescribes that delimitation is to be effected by the application of equitable criteria and by the use of practical methods capable of ensuring, with regard to the geographic configuration of the area and other relevant circumstances, an equitable result. It follows that equitable criteria cannot be divorced from legal consideration of relevant circumstances which include economic factors. Economic factors have never been given an independent status as the criteria of decisive value. Nonetheless they have been regarded as fundamental in determining a boundary line in the form of supportive criteria which operate in conjunction with the main criteria based on geographic factors. Is it possible to spell out these supportive criteria, especially those based on economic factors, and to articulate and quantify the weight to be attached to various categories of economic factors, and for what purposes? The world jurisprudence has not perfected answers to these questions. Law and practice are still at a formative stage. Nevertheless, the main components of the emerging framework are discernible.
    The significance of economic factors to boundary delimitation has never been questioned. In the *North Sea* cases, the ICJ confirmed the relevance of natural resources of the areas involved "so far known or readily ascertainable." In the *Tunisia-Libya* case, the Court regarded economic considerations relating to the relative wealth or the general socio-economic data as extraneous to the delimitation process. Nonetheless, it restated that the physical presence of natural resources, such as an oil well and by analogy fish and fish stocks, must be taken into consideration. The *Gulf of Maine* case also ruled out consideration of the relevance of general and socio-economic data as it would lead to decision *ex aequo et bono*, but it was held that "other circumstances" concerning human and economic geography ought to be taken properly into consideration as a matter of a rule of law. Even in those cases where the Court had refused to treat economic factors as "special circumstances" in terms of Article 6 of the 1958 Geneva Convention on the Continental Shelf, permitting deviation from a boundary line based on

geographic features, the Court did, in fact, justify taking account of relevant circumstances as a matter of equity.

Regarding the degree of weight to be given to economic factors, independently or in relation to other factors, the guidelines of the Court have been less than precise since the circumstances of each case vary a great deal. In the *North Sea* cases, the ICJ was not willing to regard economic factors in issue as more than "a factual element which it is reasonable to take into consideration in the course of negotiations for delimitation." In its opinion, such considerations at most "can provide adequate bases for decision adapted to the factual situation." The guidelines in the *Tunisia/Libya* case were slightly more clear. In this case, the potential relevance of the physical presence and actual exploitation of known natural resources was alluded to as an element that might be taken into account "in the process of weighing all relevant factors to achieve an equitable result." This means that economic factors must be integrated with other factors, particularly geographic, in a single balancing up in order to achieve equitable results overall. The articulation of the weight to be given to economic factors provided in the *Gulf of Maine* case is instructive. The ICJ laid down that circumstances concerning human and economic geography are ineligible for consideration as independent criteria, but they are relevant to an assessment of the equitable character of a delimitation first established on the basis of criteria borrowed from physical and political geography. The Court spelled out a concrete test. Should the boundary line based on geographic features lead to catastrophic repercussions for the parties and their nationals, consideration of economic factors can be pressed into service as a matter of a rule of law. In certain contexts, the Court was even prepared to give them the status of "equitable criteria."

The above discussion has demonstrated that geographical features are the most relevant circumstances in maritime boundary delimitation and that they play a primary role in delimitation, whereas non-geographic factors such as presence of natural resources, economic use or competitive dependency play a supportive role only, and that too in conditions of an exceptional nature. More concretely, deviations of varying kinds from the delimitation line based on geographical features can be envisaged only when they result in the allocation of an inequitable share of the seabed areas or water columns to a particular state by the use of that line.

State practice has sought to fill in the gaps generated by decided cases. There is an increasing trend to enter into legal arrangements containing numerous forms of bilateral cooperation in the equitable exploitation and sharing of economic resources of the sea.

NOTES

1. The world jurisprudence has not yet laid down the precise criteria of reasonableness in the context of maritime boundary delimitation. It requires "a disciplined multifactoral analysis to avoid arbitrary decision." The basic approach to this is to identify and weigh the relevant factors bearing upon the decision regarding the reasonableness of the alleged claims. See generally, McDougal and Burke, *The Public Order of the Oceans* 579-580 (1962); also at 12-14. See also, Sharma, "Delimitation of Maritime Boundaries between

Adjacent and Opposite States -- Clarification of Basic Community Policies" in *New Directions in International Law* 316 (1982) (Essays in honor of Wolfgang Abendroth -- Festschrift zu seinem 75 Geburstag). A theoretical framework outlined by Charney in a recent study is also useful: "Ocean Boundaries Between Nations: A Theory for Progress," 78 *A.J.I.L.* 582 (1984).

2. Sharma, "Composition of 'Old' and 'New' Public Order of the Oceans -- Some Reflections," 23 *Indian Journal of International Law* 78-79, 83 (1983); Sharma, *op. cit.*, *supra* note 1, at 317-321.

3. Collins and Rogoff, "The International Law of Maritime Boundary Delimitation," 34 *Maine Law Review* 61 (1982).

4. *Id.*, at 53.

5. *Id.*, at 54.

6. *Id.*, at 6.

7. *Case concerning Delimitation of the Maritime Boundary in the Gulf of Maine Area* (Canada/United States of America) I.C.J. Rep. 1984 p. 246.

8. *Id.*, at 326 (para 192).

9. *Id.*

10. Mouton, "The Continental Shelf," 85 *Recueil Des Cours* 422 (1954, I).

11. *Infra*, notes 39-44.

12. *North Sea Continental Shelf Cases* (Federal Republic of Germany/Denmark; Federal Republic of Germany/Netherlands) I.C.J. Rep. 1969, p. 3.

13. *Id.*, para. 82. See also paras. 81, 90, 101.

14. Lagoni, "Oil and Gas Deposits Across National Frontiers," 73 *A.J.I.L.* 241 (1979). Court's statement is at *supra*, note 12, para. 97.

15. Brown, *The Legal Regime of Hydrospace* 63 (1971).

16. *Ibid.*

17. *Supra*, note 1, 2 para. 93.

18. *Id.*, para. 97.

19. *Op. cit.*, *supra* note 15, at 63.

20. *Id.*, at 67. Charney, citing the NOAA Consultants in the Mississippi-Louisiana case, has confirmed that the ICJ ascribed particular weight, among others, to the unity of any deposits in order to avoid uncoordinated exploitation of the continental shelf resources by two states. Charney, "The Delimitation of Lateral Seaward Boundaries Between States in a Domestic Context," 75 *A.J.I.L.* 36 (1981).

21. *Supra*, note 12 para. 101 D(2).

22. *Id.*, para. 22.

23. *Id.*, paras. 93, 94.

24. *Id.*, para. 94.

25. *Id.*, para. 93.

26. Decision of June 30, 1977, by the Court of Arbitration on the Delimitation of the Continental Shelf between the United Kingdom and France, para. 75.

27. Colson, "The United Kingdom-France Continental Shelf Arbitration," 72 *A.J.I.L.* 111 (1978). See also *supra*, note 26, at para. 97.

28. *Case concerning the Continental Shelf* (Tunisia/Libyan Arab Jamahiriya) I.C.J. Rep. 1982, p. 18, para. 133A(1).

29. See Feldman, "The Tunisia-Libya Continental Shelf Case: Geographic Justice or Judicial Compromise?" 77 *A.J.I.L.* 219, 234 (1983).

30. *Id.*, para. 71.

31. *Id.*, para. 72.

32. *Id.*, para. 107.
33. *Supra*, note 7, para. 59.
34. *Id.*, See also para. 110.
35. *Id.*, para. 237.
36. *Id.*
b7. *Id.*, para. 239.
38. *Id.*, para. 238.
39. *Supra*, note 12, paras. 97, 99.
40. Delimitation Agreement between the Federal Republic of Germany and Denmark 1971, U.N. Doc.ST/LEG/SER.B/16, at 424.
41. 696 UNTS 189.
42. U.N. Doc. ST/LEG/SER.B.16, at 409.
43. These arrangements contain the solutions of joint management of or joint benefit from the resource located in the vicinity of the line and the continuance of particular use on the wrong side of the line. Collins and Rogoff, *op. cit.*, supra note 3, at 44, also at 42. See also Lagoni, *op. cit.*, supra note 14, at 242, 243; Jagota, "Maritime Boundary," *Recueil Des Cours*, II 1981, at 85, 195. He has observed that where boundary agreements have been delayed for one reason or another, a common or joint development zone has been established, details of which differ from case to case. A joint development zone may deal with petroleum or fisheries exploitation, or with protection of traditional fishing rights, or merely provide for abstention from exercise of jurisdiction in case of involuntary transgression (*id.*).
44. Collins and Rogoff, *op. cit.*, *supra*, note 3, at 20.
45. "Consultant's Report on the Mississippi/Louisiana CEIP Delimitation Line," dated May 24, 1979 (unpublished).
46. *Id.*, at 24. Charney has observed, however, that such data were found unpersuasive because the states in question were constituent parts of a strong federal union that exercised considerable control over their economic status; furthermore, these cases involved only the right to receive certain revenue-sharing funds and not rights in the resources themselves. Charney, *op. cit.*, *supra*, note 20, at 66; see also at 53.
47. *Supra*, note 28, at para. 106.
48. *Ibid.*
49. *Supra*, note 7, para. 58.
50. *Id.*, para. 59.
51. *Supra*, note 26, para. 197.
52. *Id.*, para. 187, also 184. Charney (*op. cit.*, *supra*, note 20, at 67) has pointed out that consideration of socio-economic factors in this case also provided information from the perspective of the earth sciences on the island's true utility and independence.
53. *Supra*, note 7, para. 198.
54. Charney, *op. cit. supra*, note 1, at 601.
55. *Ibid.*
56. For instance, Art. 12 of the Geneva Convention on the Territorial Sea and Contiguous Zone; Art. 15 of the UN Convention on the Law of the Sea; Art. 7(5) of the Convention on Fishing and Conservation of the Living Resources of the High Seas incorporating the application of Art. 12 of the Convention on the Territorial Sea and Contiguous Zone.
57. I.C.J. Rep. 1951 p. 116.
58. Blum, *Historic Titles in International Law* 284 (1965).
59. *Supra*, note 57, at 128.

60. *Id.*, at 133.
61. *Id.*, at 142.
62. *Ibid.*
63. *Op. cit., supra*, note 58, at 285.
64. Hague Ct. Rep. (Scott) 121 (Perm. Ct. Arb. 1909).
65. *Id.*, at 130.
66. *Id.*, at 131.
67. *Id.*, at 130.
68. *Op. cit. supra*, note 3, at 57-58.
69. I.C.J. Rep. 1974, p. 3.
70. *Id.*, at 23.
71. *Id.*, at 26-27.
72. *Id.*, at 28.
73. *Id.*, at 31. Regarding economic dependency, the Court observed that exclusion of British Vessels would have "very serious adverse consequences with immediate results for the affected vessels and with damage extending over a wide range of supporting and related industries." *Id.*, at 28.
74. *Supra*, note 28, para. 106.
75. *Id.*, para 98; Libya, in counterclaim, argued that insofar as the areas claimed might overlap with the natural prolongation of Libya's land territory, a fishing practice of one state cannot in principle prevail over the inherent and *ab initio* rights of another state in respect of its natural prolongation. *Id.*
76. *Id.*, para. 105.
77. *Id.*
78. *Id.*, para. 132.
79. *Supra*, note 7, para. 57.
80. *Id.*, para. 231.
81. *Id.*, para. 232.
82. *Id.*, para. 233.
83. *Id.*
84. U.S. Memorial, submitted in April 1982, para. 261.
85. *Supra*, note 7, at para. 234.
86. *Ibid.*
87. Canadian Memorial submitted in April 1982, para. 311; Oral Proceedings: Statement of Mr. Binnie CI/CR 84/3, p. 35.
88. *Id.*, Canadian Memorial, para. 229.
89. *Supra*, note 7, para. 234.
90. *Id.*, para. 235.
91. *Id.*, para. 59.
92. *Id.*, para. 232.
93. *Id.*
94. *Id.*, para. 237.
95. *Id.*
96. *Id.*, para. 241.
97. *Id.*, para. 238.
98. *Id.*

COMMENTARY

Robert B. Krueger
Finley, Kumble, Wagner, Heine,
Underberg, Manley & Casey
Los Angeles

At the outset I would note that I am one of the lawyers with some familiarity with the subject who would not have predicted a few years ago that environmental factors or other broadly equitable considerations would be relevant in delimitation determinations, as suggested by David Colson. In an exclusive economic zone delimitation you are, of course, dividing resources -- resources of the seabed, such as oil, and resources of the water column, essentially fish. For one party to suggest that it is entitled to the lion's share of both because it would keep a perceived ecosystem intact seems self-serving at best. In boundary negotiations a party being presented by such a claim would say "So what?" and this appears to be what the Chamber of the ICJ said in the *Gulf of Maine* case.

This position, as noted earlier, has been essentially confirmed by subsequent decisions and is consistent with the history of the doctrine of the exclusive economic zone evidenced by the Convention on the Law of the Sea and existing independent of it. The wellsprings of the doctrine were the 200-mile claims of Chile, Ecuador and Peru which laid claim to the areas encompassed despite, or even because of, the absence of continental shelf in them. The stated justification for such early claims was the nexus between the land mass and the offshore living resources -- an ecosystem type of claim to be sure but one that extended to seabed resources as well. Further, as the doctrine evolved in the LOS Conference and by unilateral national action, it was clear that it was to permit each state to establish unconditionally and exercise sovereign rights over resources in a 200-mile zone, irrespective of geological or geographical features, and this is the clear holding of the *Malta* case.

It is only with respect to delimitation of EEZs between states that such equitable considerations have been suggested. If, however, a state could not claim beyond 200 miles on environmental considerations or other broadly equitable grounds (and I do not think that anyone here would accept such a claim as responsible), why should it be able to resort to such contentions in delimitation deliberations with another state? The realities of bargaining between states on this issue would limit these considerations to directly affected economic aspects of the resources involved. If the parties are unable to forge an agreement, it is predictable that a court or arbitral panel would restrict the issue even further. The *Libya-Malta* case indicates that an essentially mechanical approach starting with equidistance alternatives, regardless of its logic, will be employed to give some semblance of objectivity to the decision.

One may or may not like the decisions of the ICJ in the *Maine* and *Malta* cases, but between allowing more issues and evidence into boundary determinations and allowing less, I find the latter choice to be far preferable. If environmental considerations are allowed in, why not socio-economic impacts or considerations of national security? Note, however, that *security* was cited by the ICJ as a negative consideration to one of the alternative lines on the *Malta* case.

Pragmatically the effect of the decision that we have on the subject suggests that states with EEZ boundary issues had better resolve them voluntarily if they want the full array of what would normally be regarded as equitable considerations to be taken into account. They will be ignored or strictly limited in judicial or arbitral proceedings. The "configurational features" and "unity of resources" elements of the "North Sea Continental Shelf cases" are as noted in the *Malta* case "now belong[ing] to the past." The Pandora's box of other considerations, including Mr. Colson's environmental one, that have tantalizingly been invited in the past appears to have been firmly, and appropriately, closed.

PART IV:

DELIMITATION OF MARITIME LIMITS:
GEOGRAPHICAL AND TECHNICAL ISSUES

INTRODUCTION

Robert W. Smith
Officer of the Geographer
U.S. Department of State

Panel IV is concerned with *The Delimitation of Maritime Limits: Geographical and Technical Issues.* The international community is now at a very crucial time with respect to the law of the sea. Years of negotiations have finally resulted in what most believed to be a very balanced text of carefully chosen words, and many states have implemented the Law of the Sea Convention to various extents by way of passing national legislation and by negotiation or arbitration on maritime boundaries. Implementation of the LOS Convention and national claims in particular will certainly involve an interpretation of the LOS text. A panel of lawyers discussed how the text, and particularly its boundary aspects, have been interpreted. This panel will look at the geographical and technical aspects of the Law of the Sea Convention, and at some of the issues and problems that may arise or have already arisen.

Our first speaker is Lew Alexander, a professor of geography at the University of Rhode Island and a long-time expert on marine geography, who will provide an overview on the technical and geographical aspects of the LOS text. Two important topics will then be addressed in detail. Dr. Victor Prescott, a political geographer from Australia, will speak on straight baselines. Baselines have already been alluded to as one of the first and more important aspects of determining national claims or national zones in the oceans. Then Mr. Peter Beazley, a former United Kingdom Territorial Waters Officer who is very experienced in the law of the sea matters, will address the technical perspective of maritime boundaries. Peter has been involved in the British multilateral and bilateral LOS negotiations; most recently, he has been involved from the technical standpoint in several boundary arbitrations. So he definitely speaks from working experience.

We will then have three commentators. First, Mr. Mario Manansala, who was involved with the Philippine delegation to UNCLOS III -- and who has informed me that he is perhaps more active in his retirement than he was while "working" -- will comment on the three papers. Then, Chungchen Lian, a professor at the University of Jilin Law Department in the People's Republic of China and currently a visiting scholar at the University of Virginia Law School, will present his remarks. Our final commentator is Dr. Joseph Morgan of the University of Hawaii Department of Geography.

271

THE IDENTIFICATION OF
TECHNICAL ISSUES OF MARITIME BOUNDARY DELIMITATION
WITHIN THE LAW OF THE SEA CONVENTION CONTEXT

Lewis M. Alexander
Center for Ocean Management Studies
University of Rhode Island

The 1982 Law of the Sea (LOS) Convention is a remarkable document because it is capable of accounting for a wide variety of geographical conditions existing throughout the marine environment. In ten early articles, for example, the Convention provides for baseline delimitations along practically all categories of coastlines of the world. Later, it distinguishes between archipelagic states and other multi-island systems, between islands and "non-conforming" rocks, between semi-enclosed seas and other large coastal indentations, and between the continental margin and the "Area" of the deep seabed. Yet, as with any comprehensive Convention whose non-seabed provisions reflect the consensus of over 150 delegations, there are both technical and non-technical issues which were never satisfactorily addressed. For example, there is no clear definition of a bay's "natural entrance points," nor what constitutes a legally acceptable historic bay. The criteria for identifying "non-conforming" rocks (that is, rocks which are not entitled to their own exclusive economic zone or continental shelf) are poorly worded, and although the Convention on several occasions addresses questions of nautical charts, it never really comes to grips with problems which may arise in cartographic representations, particularly those of maritime boundaries between opposite and adjacent states.

It is the purpose of this paper to describe some of the technical issues associated with maritime boundaries, as provided in, or omitted from, the Convention, as well as to consider some delimitation questions which have arisen as a result of settlements and agreements during the past several years. In this discussion the material will be divided into the following: (1) interpretation of Convention terms; (2) some techniques of delimitation, based on Court decisions and state practice; and (3) cartographic considerations. Finally, some concluding remarks will be made on future needs.

Interpretation of Convention Terms

Following are some of the Convention terms about which there might be technical uncertainties.

Low-water line

Article 5 of the Convention notes that "...the normal baseline for measuring the breadth of the territorial sea is the low-water line along the coast as marked on large-scale charts officially recognized by the coastal State." But what is the low-water line -- the mean low-water springs, mean lower low waters, vernal equinox spring low water, or some other measure?

The United States uses two low-water datums, one for the Atlantic and Gulf of Mexico coasts, and the other for the Pacific coast and Alaska. Iceland's and Belgium's low-water lines are the mean low-water spring, while Norway's is the vernal equinox spring low-water line. Clearly, when two opposite or adjacent states initiate the process of formally delimiting their mutual maritime boundary, an early consideration must be the establishment of a common vertical datum to be used by both parties. In areas where the tidal range is considerable, the use of different datums can have a noticeable impact on the location of an equidistance boundary.

Low-tide elevation

A low-tide elevation is a naturally formed area of land which is surrounded by and above water at low tide but submerged at high tide. Low-tide elevations may be treated differently from islands and rocks in the delimitation of the baseline for measuring the breadth of the territorial sea.

The key element in determining whether or not a feature is ever completely covered by water is the establishment of its relationship to mean low or lower low water -- that is, the average elevations of all daily low or lower low tides occuring over a period of 18.6 years -- a span which represents a complete tidal cycle. It is clearly impossible to maintain tidal gauge stations on all questionable features for that period of time, and hydrographers, in the preparation of nautical charts, must generally rely on estimates of conditions of submergence or emergence at low tide. It should also be remembered that ocean levels are constantly changing as a result of tides, waves, winds, and conditions of subsidence or uplift of the land and seabed; charts of coastlines periodically need to be updated. United States charts, for example, are scheduled for revision according to set time cycles. The cycles range from once every six months for areas where the coastline frequently shifts, such as along the Mississippi River delta, to once every seven years for stable or remote coastlines, such as along Alaska's north shore. Unfortunately, there are areas of the world where coastal charts are out of date and inaccurate.

Rocks and islands

There is no definition in the Convention for rocks, *per se.* Presumably these features are included within the definition of islands -- that is, naturally formed areas of land, surrounded by water, which are above water at high tide. Each island (or rock) generates its own territorial sea.

Some years ago, the late Dr. Hodgson attempted to distinguish between rocks and islands. He suggested that the term "rocks" be used for above-water features less than .001 square miles in area; "islets" for features between .001 and 1 square miles; "isles" for those greater than 1 square mile but no more than 1,000 square miles; and "islands" for those larger than 1,000 square miles. According to this classification, there would be approximately 123 islands in the world, ranging in size from Greenland down to Choiseul Island in the Solomons. These were in the days when some thought was being given to providing for different weights to be accorded to islands and rocks as basepoints, depending on their size. All that remains of this suggestion of weighted values is the practice of giving half-effect to certain islands and island groups.

Non-conforming rocks

Under the Convention's description of islands appears the statement, "Rocks which cannot sustain human habitation or economic life of their own shall have no exclusive economic zone or continental shelf." The provision presumably refers to islands as well as rocks, and it is these features which are considered here as "non-conforming." All other islands and *conforming* rocks have their own exclusive economic zone and continental shelf.

But how can one describe the distinguishing criteria? In one exercise on this topic, Van Dyke and Brooks have concluded that the key element in determining whether an island or rock should generate its own ocean space beyond territorial limits should depend on the feature's ability to support a stable population "of organized groups of human beings" -- an ability which would seem to imply the presence of potable water and perhaps tillable soil.

Land-locked waters of a juridical bay

The criteria for establishing a juridical bay (capable of being closed off at its mouth by a straight line) are spelled out fairly concisely, but there are nevertheless ambiguities. One is the statement that a bay "is a well-marked indentation whose penetration is in such proportion to the width at its mouth as to contain land-locked waters..." The article goes on to describe certain arithmetic and geometric criteria for determining a juridical bay, and the question might then be asked, if the bay conforms to these mathematical standards, but does not contain land-locked waters, is it still a juridical bay?

The term "land-locked waters" would seem to imply, first, that the waters of the bay are isolated and detached from the sea. Ideally, the opening of the bay should be narrower than the bay's principal lateral axis. One analysis of the term concluded that a semi-circular shape for a bay "represents an absolute minimum condition" for its waters to be considered land-locked. According to this reasoning, inclusion of the term "land-locked" in the Convention merely reinforces the semi-circle test as defined in Article 10.

Natural entrance points of a juridical bay

The term *natural* is one which should be treated with great respect, particularly by lawyers. For some bays an abrupt change of direction of the coast at one or both sides of the mouth is readily discernible; for others, either of several sites along the coast could be seen as "natural entrance points."

Over a decade ago, Dr. Hodgson carried out a study, in which I collaborated, attempting to define more precisely how one could determine a bay's natural entrance points. He suggested that one should look for the points where the two-dimensional character of the bay is replaced by that of the sea or ocean. At what point does the general direction of the shore change from one facing on the bay to one facing on the sea? His answer was to apply a 45-degree angle test, which, although not included in the Convention, has been referred to several times in Court decisions affecting baselines of individual U.S. coastal states.

In this same publication, attention was also given to other uncertainties regarding juridical bays. For example, should the areas of all subsidiary water bodies opening onto a bay be considered in calculating the area of the bay under the semi-circle test? If screening islands at the mouth of the bay extend further seaward than the normal closing line, can the line be recalculated so as to extend along these islands? Can islands themselves constitute one or both of the headlands of the bay? Questions such as these must probably await the records of court decisions and state practice before they are universally resolved.

274

Closing points at the mouths of rivers
Article 9 specifies that if a river flows directly into the sea, "the baseline shall be a straight line across the mouth of the river between points on the low-water line of its banks." This condition prevails, of course, only in the case of estuaries. If the river ends in a delta, the provisions of Article 7, Paragraph 2, apply.

It is at least arguable that the rules for closing off bays should also apply to rivers; indeed, it is sometimes difficult to distinguish bays from estuaries. In some cases, estuaries may expand gradually into very wide indentations, over which a coastal state may claim historic rights. Venezuela has closed off the mouth of the Orinoco River by a ninety-nine mile line, and Burma has closed off the Gulf of Martaban at the mouth of the Sittang River with a 222-mile closing line. In retrospect, the compilers of the 1982 Convention seem to have given up trying to define a "juridical" estuary, but in so doing, they may have contributed to the process whereby all well-marked coastal indentations, bays and gulfs are eventually being closed off as internal waters, under one pretext or another.

Historic bays
The Convention text alludes to historic bays only once: in Article 10 where it is noted that the mathematical provisions for juridical bays do not apply to so-called "historic bays." Much has been written on the topic of historic bays and other historic waters, and this is not the place to dwell on the matter, other than to note that "history" today seems to connote a much shorter time frame than was the case in the past.

General direction of the coast
Article 7, in dealing with the straight baseline regime, provides that the drawing of straight baselines must not depart to any appreciable extent from the general direction of the coast. It is not my intention here to discuss straight baselines, since one of my fellow panel members is prepared to do so, but I would note the term "general direction," which appears only in this one Article of the Convention, has also been used in connection with Court decisions on maritime boundary delimitations.

Permanent harbor works
According to Article 11, "...the outermost permanent harbour works which form an integral part of the harbour system are regarded as forming the part of the coast. Off-shore installations and artificial islands shall not be considered as permanent harbour works." In some ports there are extensive moles, piers, jetties and breakwaters which are "off-shore" in that they are not directly connected with the land. Also, in a number of ports, there are offshore monobuoys, located some distance from the coast, which are used for the loading and unloading of tankers. Whether or not these should all be considered as basepoints for locating the territorial sea may be open to question.

Archipelagoes
The problem of distinguishing archipelagic states whose territory can be closed off by straight baselines from other island groups was a difficult one to resolve at UNCLOS III, and Article 47 is quite precise in its provisions on archipelagic status. But there are borderline situations in which either an "excessive" number of individual baselines

greater than 100 nautical miles in length were seen as necessary by the archipelagic state to enclose all of its "natural" territory, or in which the calculation of a water-to-land ratio of at least 1:1 may be possible only through a certain positioning of baselines.

One unresolved issue for most archipelagoes is the designation of specific archipelagic sea lanes, which "shall include all normal passage routes used as routes for international navigation or overflight, through or over archipelagic waters." To date, agreement has tended to lag between user and archipelagic states on the final designation of sea lanes.

Some Techniques of Delimitation Based on Court Decisions and State Practice

Both Article 74 of the LOS Convention, dealing with boundaries between exclusive economic zones, and Article 83, dealing with continental shelf boundaries, stress the need for reaching agreement on the basis of international law. Such agreement can lead to a direct bilateral settlement, or to the submission of a boundary question to third party settlement.

The various methods for boundary delimitation generally fall into three categories: strict equidistance, modified equidistance, and non-equidistance. Boundaries computed on the basis of strict equidistance are, at every point on the line, equidistant from the nearest point on the baselines from which the breadths of the territorial seas of each of the two opposite or adjacent states is measured. For such boundaries to succeed, it is necessary that the countries reach agreement on the baselines to be employed. In the case of the U.K.-France boundary in the English Channel, for example, disagreement arose over the British use of Eddystone Rock as a basepoint for determining the equidistance or median line. In this case, the Court of Arbitration ruled in favor of the British, arguing that in an earlier fisheries agreement between the two countries, France had acquiesced to Britain's use of the Rock as a basepoint for determining the fisheries limits.

There are a variety of forms of modified equidistance lines. Small coastal islands may be ignored on the grounds that they give a disproportionate effect to the boundary location. Alternatively, they may be given partial effect, as has occurred in the settlement of the U.K.-France boundary in the western approaches to the English Channel, where Britain's Scilly Islands off Cornwall were given half effect by the Court of Arbitration.

Another modification practice is to describe arcs of circles about an island or island group which is located close to the equidistance boundary. The radius of the semi-circle is generally equal to the territorial sea claimed by the state which controls the island. The use of such arcs is particularly prevalent in semi-enclosed seas, such as the Adriatic, the Mediterranean and the Persian Gulf (see *Figure 1*). In the case of the U.K.-France boundary in the English Channel, arcs were described about Britain's Channel Islands off the coast of France, and these islands were ignored in the measurement of the equidistance boundary through the Channel (see *Figure 2*). Among other forms of modification of an equidistance line are the use of artificial coastlines, the modification of turning points along the boundary, and the exchange of small areas in the boundary zone in order to "smooth out" the line and make it easier to administer.

Non-equidistant boundaries are those based on historic title, lines of latitude, perpendiculars to the general direction of the coast, or

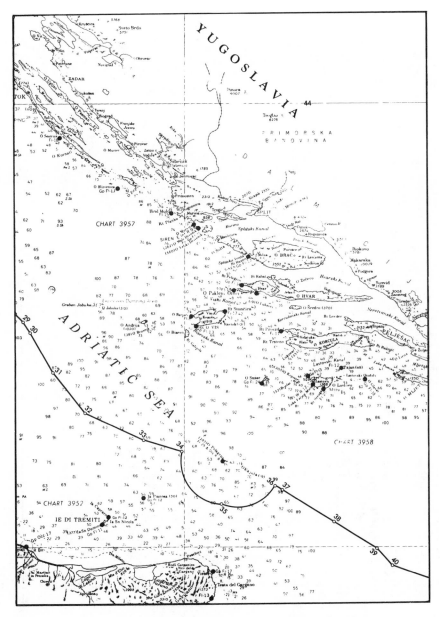

Figure 1: The use of arcs of circles in the Adriatic Sea.

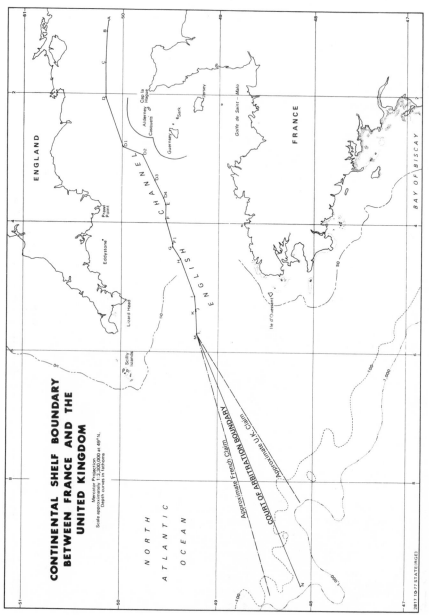

Figure 2

the application of certain equitable principles, often as a result of third-party settlement. Two decisions of the International Court of Justice (ICJ) resulted in non-equidistance boundaries. One of these is related to Germany's maritime boundaries with the Netherlands and Denmark; the other concerned the Tunisia-Libya boundary. In a third judgment, this time by a Chamber of the Court, the U.S.-Canada boundary in the Gulf of Maine/Georges Bank area was based on a modified equidistance formula.

From this brief introduction to maritime boundary types, I shall now turn to consideration of a number of technical problems which have arisen in the course of delimitations. References will be made here to four third-party settlements, three of which involved the ICJ. These are: the 1969 *North Sea Continental Shelf* cases, involving the Federal Republic of Germany, the Netherlands and Denmark; the 1977 *Arbitration between the United Kingdom and France*; the 1982 *Tunisia/Libya Continental Shelf* case; and the 1984 *Canada-U.S.* case, which for the first time concerned not only a continental shelf boundary, but a boundary for all purposes, including the water column. The use of examples, however, is not limited to these four decisions.

Equidistance boundaries based on different baseline regimes
    Article 4 of the 1958 Convention on the Territorial Sea and Contiguous Zone and Article 7 of the 1982 Convention both permit the use of a straight baseline regime in areas where the coastline is deeply indented and cut into or in areas where there is a fringe of islands along the coast in its immediate vicinity. At the present time, some fifty-seven countries have delimited straight baselines along all or a part of their coasts, and twelve others have adopted enabling legislation for the use of straight baselines. But should the situation arise where one country utilizes a straight baseline system and a neighboring one does not, any equidistance line drawn between the two is favorable to the state with the straight baseline regime. Such was the case with the U.S.-Cuba maritime boundary, where Cuba had adopted straight baselines while the U.S. utilized normal baselines. In this case, two equidistant lines were calculated, one based on the Cuban straight baselines and an artificial "straight baseline" construction line which was drawn along the coast of Florida. A second equidistant line was then calculated, based on the low-water lines of Florida and Cuba. From these two, a third line was created, which, although not equidistant, divided equally the area between the two lines.

General direction of the coast
    Calculating the general direction of the coast may be important in the case of states with adjacent coasts, if a final decision is to delimit a boundary which bisects the angle formed by the directions of the two coasts. This was done in the *U.S.-Canada* case by drawing construction lines from the termination of the U.S.-Canada boundary twelve miles from the coast southwestward to Cape Elizabeth on the coast of Maine, and southeastward to Sable Island on the Nova Scotia coast (see *Figure 3*). Since the Court was asked to decide on the boundary starting south of Machias Seal Island and North Rock, rather than at the seaward terminus of the existing boundary, perpendiculars were drawn to the two "general direction" lines; these perpendiculars were joined at the starting point of the boundary to be decided upon by the Court. The larger (seaward) angle formed by the two perpendiculars was then bisected, and

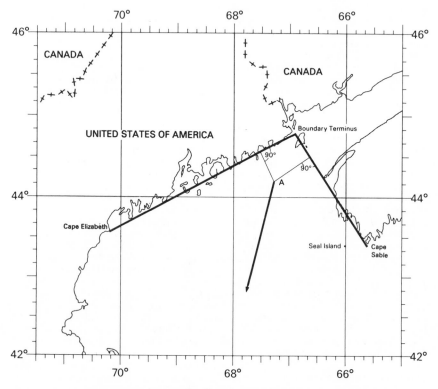

Figure 3:   Construction lines drawn to determine general
            direction of the coast.

Source: *Ocean Development and International Law*, vol. 16,
          no. 1 (1986)

this bisector formed the first segment of the maritime boundary (see *Figure 3*).

In the *Tunisia-Libya* case, however, the Court found "in assessing the direction of the coastline, it is legitimate to disregard the present coastal configurations found at more than a comparatively short distance (from the intersection of the land boundary with the coast)." Specifically, the Court disregarded the Tunisian island of Djerba, located about forty-five miles from the seeward terminus of the land boundary. Having determined what it felt was the general direction of the coast, the Court then felt free to utilize its 26-degree line, which was generally perpendicular to this direction and was, conveniently, also the line agreed upon earlier as one dividing fishing zones and areas for the granting of oil concessions.

Lengths of coastline

In the 1969 *North Sea* decision, the Court noted that account had to be taken of "the element of a reasonable degree of proportionality which a delimitation effected according to equidistance principles ought to bring about between the extent of the Continental Shelf appertaining to the states concerned and the length of their respective coastlines -- these being measured according to their general direction..." This principle of proportionality has figured both in late ICJ decisions and in bilateral agreements.

In delimiting the outer portion of their continental shelf boundary in the Bay of Biscay, France and Spain used artificial baselines and calculated the ratio of the lengths of the respective lines (see *Figure 4*). The same approach was taken in the case of the *U.S.-Canada* decision, with one exception. Although the U.S. "coast" was reduced by the Court to three closing lines for the purpose of measurement, the Canadian "coast," in addition to three closing lines, was taken also to include the northern and southern coasts of the Bay of Fundy, in its western portion (see *Figure 5*).

In *Tunisia-Libya*, however, the Court noted the lengths of the relative portions of the coastlines of the two countries "measured along the coastline without taking account of small inlets, creeks and lagoons." But there is no other reference in the judgment as to exactly how the coastal length measurements were arrived at.

Half-effect given to islands

There are no prescribed methods for applying half-effect to equidistant lines. Commander Beazley has written of half-distance lines, bisector lines, and half-angle lines, and has pointed out that different methods for expressing half-effect may produce very different results.

In three third-party settlements, half effect was given to islands; the computations for two of the three were based on half-angle lines. In the *Anglo-French* case, two median lines were drawn in the western approaches to the English Channel. One of these gave full effect to the Scilly Islands, and the other gave no effect. The angle between the two lines was bisected, giving the half-effect line (see *Figure 2*).

In the *Tunisia-Libya* case, half effect was given to the Kerkannah Islands off the Tunisian coast. This time, the Court suggested that a line be drawn from the westernmost point of the Gulf of Gabes along the southernmost point of the island, thereby giving them full effect. Another line was drawn northeastward to Ras Kaboudia, giving the Kerkannah Islands no effect. The angle formed by these two lines was to be bisected (see *Figure 6*). The court, however, left it to the experts of

281

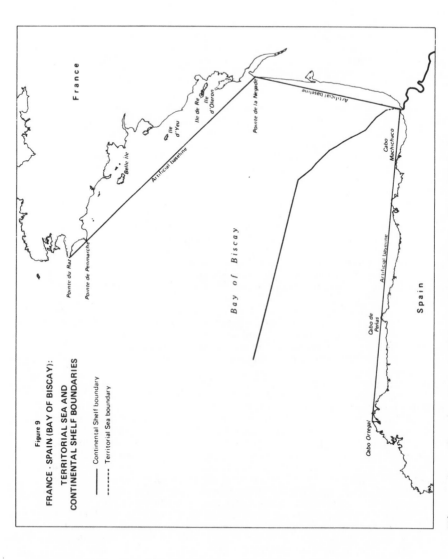

Figure 4:   Continental shelf boundaries in the Bay of Biscay.

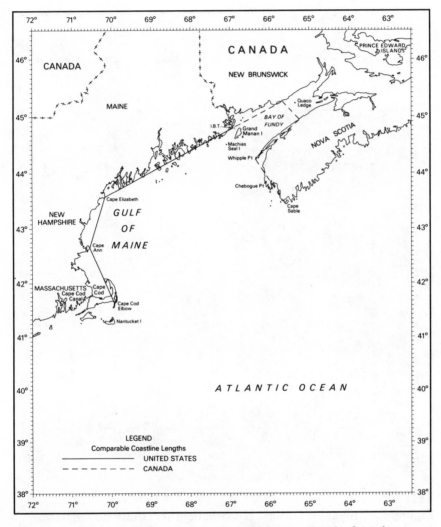

Figure 5: Comparable coastline lengths in the Gulf of Maine.

Source: *Ocean Development and International Law*, vol. 16, no. 1 (1986)

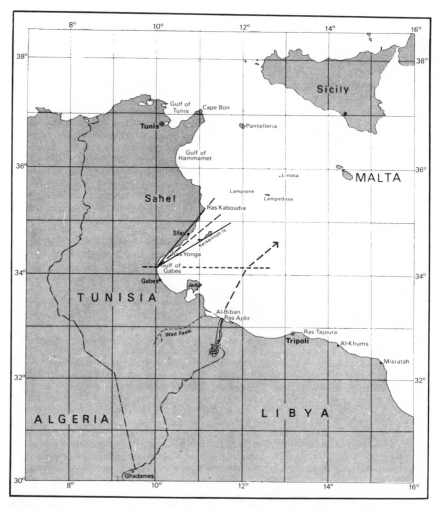

Figure 6: Libya – Tunisia: Hypothetical maritime boundaries.

the two countries to make the final decision on the location of the lines.

Half effect was given to Seal Island, lying off the southwestern coast of Nova Scotia, in the *U.S.-Canada* case. This half effect was a factor in determining the turning point on the location line in the Gulf of Maine which represented what the Court found to be the proportion between the lengths of the U.S. and Canadian coasts facing the relevant areas (see *Figure 7*).

Cartographic Considerations

A number of articles have appeared in recent years on the cartographic representation of maritime boundaries, and on technical aspects of measuring distances. This paper will briefly summarize these issues under the headings of projections, straight lines, spheroids, horizontal datums, and scale.

Projections

It is clearly impossible to reproduce the three-dimensional surface of the globe on a two-dimensional chart, so inevitably some properties must be sacrificed. There may be distortions of area, of shape, or distance and direction, or a combination of these; and the larger the area portrayed on the chart, the greater the distortion becomes. Many navigational charts are plotted on the Mercator scale, where a straight line on the chart is a line of constant direction. Thus the mariner, sailing constantly northeast, can plot his position with little difficulty on the chart. Because of their frequent use for navigation, Mercator-based charts are often the ones on which the greatest detail of coastlines are shown. Here one finds the rocks, drying rocks, reefs, mud flats, and other features portrayed in detail, and it is these features which may figure prominently in calculating equidistance boundaries.

But the Mercator projection uses latitude and longitude lines at right angles to one another; the further one goes away from the equator, the greater is the distortion of scale, since on the globe the longitude lines converge toward each other as one moves poleward. As Hodgson and Cooper have written, " ... Mercator projection charts cannot be relied upon for equidistant boundary delimitations that extend ... farther than the breadth of the territorial sea. They furnish sufficient precision only in very special circumstances -- for example, short boundaries, parallel north-south trending coasts, and lines developed in lower (equatorial) latitudes."

For the middle latitudes, Lambert conformal projection charts are recommended, since representations of both shape and direction show little distortion, particularly in the areas of the standard parallels used to construct the chart. In polar regions the stereographic projection is best, for here there is the true shape and direction at the pole, in the center of the chart, and distortions are not too great within the Arctic and Antarctic Circles.

Straight lines

Lines connecting fixed points on a chart will vary considerably, depending on the projection. For Mercator, a straight line is a rhumb line which makes the same angle with all meridians on the earth's surface, but which is not the shortest distance between any two points. The approximate least distance is a great circle arc, that is, a circle on the surface of the earth whose plane passes through the earth's

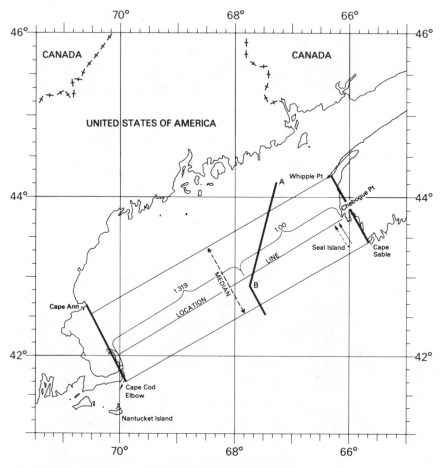

Figure 7: Half effect given to Seal Island.

Source: *Ocean Development and International Law*, vol. 16, no. 1
(1986)

center. Unfortunately, great circle arcs are shown as straight lines only on gnomonic projections, which otherwise greatly distort shape and scale. The shortest distance between two points on the globe is actually shown by a geodesic line, which is a straight line on a mathematically derived surface.

Spheroids

The true shape of the earth approximates that of an oblate spheroid, that is, a sphere flattened slightly at the two poles; there are also several additional southern hemisphere "flattenings." To describe the earth's surface accurately, geodesists have developed several spheroid equations, among them Clarke 1866 for North America, and International 1924 for Europe. Using computers, based on these systems, exact least distances can be measured with great precision. Maritime boundary negotiators should ensure that parties to a settlement are utilizing the same spheroid in their calculations.

Horizontal datums

Locations on the earth's surface, in the interests of accuracy, should be established with reference to some fixed point. For the North American 1927 datum, which, by agreement, was utilized by both parties in the *U.S.-Canada* case, the point of origin is located in southwestern Kansas. The issue of vertical, or tidal, datums has already been covered earlier in this paper.

Scale

The amount of detail which can be shown on a chart increases with scale, so that territorial sea boundaries, or other matters requiring considerable precision, should be calculated on a scale of 1:40,000 or less. But if a full 200-mile zone is to be shown, the scale must be much less. On a 1:1,000,000 scale, 200 miles would cover about twelve inches on the chart. Care must be taken that charts of approximately the same scales are used by boundary negotiators.

Conclusion

Over the past two decades or so, particularly since the appearance of Shalowitz's *Shore and Sea Boundaries*, geographers, hydrographers, geodesists and others have been working on, and writing about, many technical aspects of maritime boundary delimitation, but with little apparent coordination of efforts. We have now a new Law of the Sea Convention and growing record of experience to draw upon in assessing these technical issues; moreover, we are now entering a new phase of boundary delimitation, namely the division of both seabed and water column together.

Since we have upwards of 300 maritime boundaries still to be negotiated, may not the time be ripe for the relatively small community of technical experts to begin increasing their coordinated efforts? Perhaps a new form of *Shore and Sea Boundaries* is called for -- this time by a group of authors. Perhaps some central filing system should be developed for recording the evolving state and judicial practice with respect to technical issues. What we face is an increasingly complex data base, and before long, no single person can be expected to remain current on all of these diverse issues.

STRAIGHT BASELINES: THEORY AND PRACTICE

J.R.V. Prescott
Department of Geography
University of Melbourne

Introduction

The 1982 Convention on the Law of the Sea permits straight lines to be substituted for the low-water mark, which forms the normal baseline, in three different situations. First, there are *closing lines* drawn across the mouths of some rivers and bays. It must be presumed that the mouths of harbors can also be closed by straight lines, although Article 11 is silent on this matter. The presumption is based on the fact that Article 50 empowers archipelagic states to draw closing lines in accordance with Article 11 to delimit internal waters.

Second, there are regional *straight baselines* which are drawn along sections of coast which possess a multitude of specified features which make the use of individual closing lines inappropriate. The rules for drawing such baselines are set out in Article 7. Third, there are *archipelagic baselines* which archipelagic states may draw in certain circumstances.

Articles 14 and 50 respectively allow closing lines to be combined with regional straight baselines and archipelagic baselines. There does not appear to be any prohibition in the 1982 Convention on a single country drawing both archipelagic and straight baselines. That view is based on the following reasoning. Some archipelagic states are unable to draw archipelagic baselines because they cannot satisfy the rules set out in Article 47. Some of these countries, such as Australia, Cuba, Iceland, Madagascar and the United Kingdom, have already drawn straight baselines along sections of their coasts. It is reasonable to assume that all such states will reserve the right to draw straight baselines if they are appropriate. Some archipelagic states, such as Fiji, Papua New Guinea, Seychelles, the Solomon Islands and Tonga can only draw archipelagic baselines around some of their islands. Those islands left outside the archipelagic baselines seem certain to claim the right to draw straight baselines where appropriate in the same fashion as those archipelagic states which cannot draw archipelagic baselines. Since there appears to be no case where an archipelagic state has left a large island outside the archipelagic baselines which it has drawn, the combination of straight and archipelagic baselines has not occurred. Nor does there appear to be any case where archipelagic baselines drawn in the future would create the opportunity for such a combination.

This paper is only concerned with straight baselines drawn in accordance with Article 7 of the 1982 Convention.

Article 7

There are historic cases of countries drawing straight lines around their coasts to define various types of waters, but the concept became an effective part of international law in 1951. In that year, the International Court of Justice gave its decision in the case between the United Kingdom and Norway. The British authorities objected to the use of straight baselines along the Norwegian coast north of parallel 66 degrees 28'48" north. The use of this line since 1937 had caused difficulties for British skippers of trawlers operating close to the Norwegian coast, and some had been arrested and forfeited their boats

(International Court of Justice 1951, 125-5). The Court held that the method employed by Norway for the delimitation of the fisheries zone was not contrary to international law.

Some of the language and most of the concepts expressed in the judgment have found their way into Article 7 of the 1982 Convention. The route they followed was marked by two major landmarks. First, the International Law Commission (United Nations 1956) drafted some articles on the law of the sea in the period of April to June 1956. The Commissioners interpreted the Court's judgment on straight baselines as expressing the law in force and used it as the basis for drafting the Article on that subject. While the Commission's Article contained only three paragraphs, it covered all but one of the points contained in Article 7 of the 1982 Convention.

The second landmark was provided by the 1958 Convention on the Territorial Sea and Contiguous Zone (United Nations 1958). Article 4 of the 1958 Convention was based very firmly on Article 5 of the *Report of the International Law Commission*. All the recommendations of the Commission were adopted and there were two small additions. First, it was stipulated that only low-tide elevations surmounted by lighthouses or similar structures could be used as basepoints; and, second, states were required to show their straight baselines on charts.

Paragraphs 1 and 2 of Article 7 were incorporated without change from Article 4 of the 1958 Convention. Paragraphs 5 and 6 of Article 7 were transferred from Article 4 of the 1958 Convention with only slight changes in expression which did not change the meaning or operation of the 1958 version. Paragraph 4, dealing with the use of low-tide elevations as basepoints, was modified for the 1982 Convention in a manner which makes it easier for such features to be used as basepoints. Paragraph 2 of the 1982 Convention is entirely novel and does not appear to owe anything to the 1956 Commission. In the 1958 Convention, states were required to show only straight baselines on charts. In the 1982 Convention, Article 16 requires countries to show all baselines from which the territorial sea is measured.

The analysis which follows deals with the six paragraphs of Article 7 in turn.

Paragraph 1 of Article 7

> In localities where the coastline is deeply indented and cut into, or if there is a fringe of islands along the coast in its immediate vicinity, the method of straight baselines joining appropriate points may be employed in drawing the baseline from which the breadth of the territorial sea is measured. (United Nations 1983, 4)

The text does not give any indication of the extent of *localities* where the method of straight baselines may be used. Nor is it possible for any commentator to suggest any maximum length of coast which could be described as a locality. One of the longest straight baselines in the world was proclaimed by Denmark on 1 June 1963 on the west coast of Greenland. The coast bordering Davis Strait from Kap Farvel to Kap Alexander extends for 1380 nautical miles, and most of that coast is clearly deeply indented or fringed with islands. It is possible to suggest with some confidence that a locality, for the purposes of this Article, must include more than a single feature, such as a bay or the mouth of a river. Such individual features can be treated without

289

difficulty under Articles 9 and 10. Beazley (1978, 8) has wisely observed that the number of indentations and islands must be such that the application of Articles 5, 9, and 10 would be tedious and largely irrelevant. Unfortunately no one can specify the minimum number of features to which Article 7 can be applied in a single locality.

There is agreement amongst commentators, such as Fitzmaurice (1959), Shalowitz (1962, 214) and Beazley (1978), that it is impermissible for countries to use indentations or fringing islands along one part of their coast to justify straight baselines along the rest of the coast or parts of the coast which do not possess these characteristics.

The phrase *deeply indented and cut into* has survived intact from the 1951 Judgment to the 1982 Convention. The French version has been altered and shortened during the same period and now seems closer to the English phrase than at any other time. The International Law Commission presented the two conditions as alternatives, as the French form of the judgment had done, but that arrangement was not adopted in either the 1958 or 1982 Conventions.

It is difficult to understand why the two descriptions are used either in conjunction or as alternatives, because they appear to have identical meanings. It is inconceivable that an indented coast could not be described as cut into, or that a coast which had been cut into did not possess indentations. There is only one sense in which it is necessary for the two terms to appear, and, curiously, that sense would be appropriate in respect of the Norwegian coast which was the subject of the 1951 Judgment.

The two terms are necessary if the adverb *deeply* applied to both terms and if *indentations* refer to the horizontal plane while *cuts* are deemed to be vertical incisions. By that interpretation, straight baselines could only be drawn along coasts which had deep, linear bays penetrating considerable distances inland. The *fjord* coast of Norway possesses such features in abundance. For example, the Sognefjord, Trondheimsfjord and Hardangerfjord extend for 100, seventy-five, and seventy miles inland respectively, and the Sognefjord scarcely exceeds three miles in width at any point.

There is no evidence that this restrictive interpretation was in the minds of the judges in 1951 or the delegates to the conferences which produced the 1958 and 1982 Conventions. Indeed, there is no suggestion in any of the literature that the depth of the water in the vicinity of the coast had any bearing upon the construction of straight baselines. Shalowitz (1962, 71), in his usual perceptive manners stresses that the members of the International Court of Justice were particularly impressed by the geographic characteristics of Norway's northern coast. After writing the words *where a coast is deeply indented and cut into*, they added the illustration *as is that of Eastern Finnmark*. This coastline is shown in *Figure 1*. There was reference throughout the *Anglo-Norwegian* case to similar coasts in western Scotland, Canada and northern Ireland. It would have been just as appropriate to refer to the United States' coasts of south and west Alaska and Maine; the coast of Chile south of 41 degrees south; Britain's Falkland Islands; Norway's Svalbard; Denmark's east coast and Greenland and the Faeroes; parts of the Swedish, Finnish and Estonian coasts in the Baltic Sea; the west coasts of Brittany and Corsica in France; the west coast of Spain's Galicia; sections of the Greek and Turkish coasts facing the Aegean Sea; regions of the west coast of North Korea and the south and west coasts of South Korea; parts of northeast Honshu and south and west Kyushu in Japan; the east coast of Indonesia's Kalimantan; the coast of China

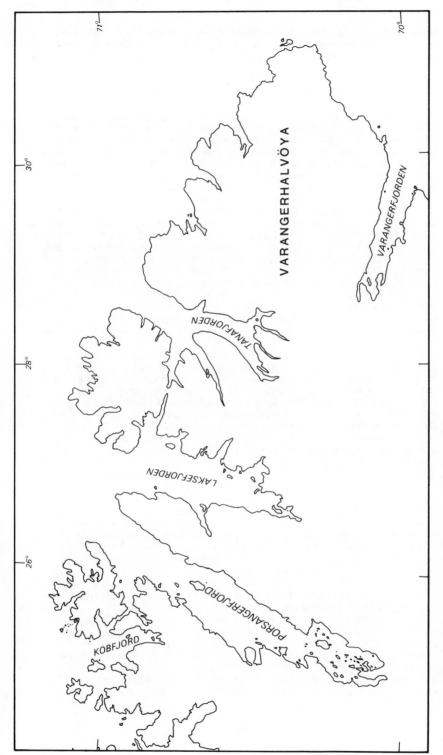

Figure 1: The indented coast of eastern Finnmark.

south of Shanghai; the extreme south coast of Burma and part of its
Arakan coast; sections of the coasts of Taymyrskiy and Novaya Zemlya in
the Soviet Union; the southeast and northwest coasts of New Zealand and
the Australian coast northwest of the Kimberly Plateau. The fact that
others might wish to add different localities to this list of indented
coasts simply emphasizes the subjective nature of the descriptive phrase
deeply indented and cut into.

While most of the coasts listed are in highland regions, those
of eastern Denmark and Kalimantan are lowlands. They are all drowned
coasts, and rising sea-levels have invaded valleys formed by rivers or
glaciers. Many of these regions also possess offshore islands because
the rising seas isolated the highest peaks of an irregular topography
formed from resistant rock or glacial moraine. The west coast of the
Antarctic Peninsula provides an excellent example of a complex coast
with deep indentations and offshore islands.

The word *deeply* can be interpreted in an absolute or relative
sense. For example, in an absolute sense an indentation of 3.4 nautical
miles can hardly be described as *deep* when compared with the lengths of
some Norwegian fjords, but on Nordhoyar Island in the Faeroes an indentation of that length cuts across more than half the island! So there
is no reliable test on which all would agree to determine whether a
coast is deeply indented and cut into or simply indented and cut into.

Table 1 lists ten countries which have proclaimed straight baselines along coasts which can without doubt be described as deeply
indented and cut into. Other countries have drawn straight baselines
along indented coasts, but the basepoints are located almost entirely
on fringing islands.

There are also cases where countries have drawn baselines along
coasts which are not deeply indented and cut into and where there are
no offshore islands. For example, Albania announced straight baselines
in the *Adriatic Pilot* of March 1, 1960 (The *Geographer* 1970). The four
segments which extend from Kep i Rodonit to Kep i Semanit enclose a
smooth coast with shallow embayments. The straight baselines proclaimed
by Cuba on February 26, 1977 include some sections which must be related
to the concept of indented coasts since there are no offshore islands
and no evidence of coastal instability. The southeast coast from Punta
Caleta to Cabo Cruz, a distance of 197 nautical miles, is fairly
straight and is characterized by a series of small bays separated by a
few broad bays with long, gently curved outlines; it has been enclosed
by thirty-five segments of Cuba's continuous straight baseline. The
amended Icelandic straight baselines published on 14 July 1972 border
a deeply indented coast on the northwest and east coasts of the island.
However, the south coast does not share this character and the straight
baseline from Ingolfshofdhi to Lundadrangur encloses a coastline marked
by a smooth outline. This section of the baseline consists of two sections which total seventy-one nautical miles. The two sections are
separated by a short gap two nautical miles wide. It would be possible
to add further examples by reference to sections of the baselines drawn
by Ireland, Italy, Senegal and Spain.

It has proved very difficult to find a good example of a straight
baseline around a coast which is indented in a manner which would
provoke debate between those who thought straight baselines were appropriate and those who were sure this requirement of Article 7 could not
be satisfied. There are some good examples of such coasts, but none
has been enclosed by a baseline. The only example which can be offered
relates to Madagascar, which proclaimed its straight baselines on

292

Table 1

Straight baselines drawn along indented coasts

State	Date	Location
Australia	14 Feb 1983	The northwest coast
Canada	08 Nov 1967	Labrador and Newfoundland
	25 May 1969	Nova Scotia and British Columbia
Chile	14 Jul 1977	The coast south of 41 degrees south
Denmark	21 Feb 1966	The east coast of the mainland
	01 May 1978	Amendments
	01 Jun 1963	Greenland
France	19 Oct 1967	The coast of Brittany and western Sicily
Iceland	22 Apr 1961	The west, north and east coasts
Ireland	01 Oct 1959	The west coast
Norway	12 Jul 1935	The north coast
	18 Jul 1952	The south coast
	25 Sep 1970	Vestspitzbergen
Spain	05 Aug 1977	The coast south of Punta Candelaria
Turkey	15 May 1964	The coast of the Aegean Sea

Source: Author's research

March 9, 1963, more than a year before it became a party to the 1958 Convention on September 10, 1964. In the extreme northeast of the island, there is a segment of baseline measuring sixty-three nautical miles which links Cap d'Ambre, in the north, with Nosy Akao, a small island to the southeast. There are a number of indentations along this section of coast, and although they are not deep in any absolute sense, they invest the coastline with a degree of complexity which is conveniently resolved by using a straight baseline.

When territorial waters are measured from straight baselines drawn along smooth coasts, such as those found in northern Senegal and south Iceland, rather than from the low-water mark, it will usually be found that there is only a negligible extension of the outer limit of those waters. For this reason, there might be a temptation for some countries to ignore this evident breach of the rules. However, if baselines along smooth coasts are tolerated because they do not significantly augment the national maritime claims of the countries concerned, it is harder to argue against baselines drawn along coasts which have a less regular outline without being deeply indented and cut into. Such baselines might add significantly to the extent of internal waters and push the outer limits of territorial waters away from the coast to a marked extent. In short, it seems most sensible to argue against any breach of the rule on principle rather than on the ground that such a breach extends the limits of territorial waters in an unreasonable manner.

The existence of *a fringe islands along the coast in its immediate vicinity* provides the second justification for employing straight baselines. This concept was also derived from the 1951 Judgment when the members of the Court clearly demonstrated the importance they attached to the insular character of the Norwegian coast south of Nord Kapp.

> To the west, the land configuration stretches out into the sea: the large and small islands, mountainous in character, the islets, rocks and reefs, some always above water, others emerging only at low-tide, are in truth but an extension of the Norwegian mainland. (International Court of Justice 1951, 127)

In their counter-memorial, the Norwegian authorities estimated the number of islands to be 120,000. The concept that fringing islands justified the use of straight baselines was expressed in the following terms by the Court.

> Where a coast is deeply indented and cut into, as is that of Eastern Finnmark, or where it is bordered by an archipelago such as the "skjaergaard" along the western sector of the coast here in question, the baseline becomes independent of the low-water mark, and can only be determined by means of geometric construction. (International Court of Justice 1951, 128-9)

The phrase *bordered by an archipelago* was translated into the following terms by the International Law Commission in 1956.

> Where circumstances necessitate a special regime because the coast is deeply indented or cut into, or because there are islands in its immediate vicinity, the baseline may be independent of the low-water mark. (United Nations 1956, 13-14)

Two years later, in the 1958 Convention, the concept had been refined by requiring that the islands should be a fringe along the coast, and this new form was included in the 1982 Convention without change.

The analysis of the phrase *a fringe of islands along the coast in its immediate vicinity* must be divided into two parts. First, it is necessary to consider the various arrangements of islands which might constitute a fringe along the coast, and then some reasonable limits should be sought for the phrase *immediate vicinity*.

The first point that is clear is that there must be more than one island in the fringe. It could reasonably be argued that since the purpose of straight baselines is to avoid complex patterns of maritime jurisdiction, the minimum number of islands which constitute a fringe must be greatly in excess of two. However, it would be open to countries to stick to the letter of the Convention and insist that two islands can form a fringe.

The stipulation that the fringe must be located *along the coast* is not very helpful since fringes always border the feature they decorate or to which they are attached. However, given this explicit condition, it would be hard to argue that islands arranged like stepping-stones, at right angles to the general direction of the coast, should be considered as a fringe. Equally, it would be easy to argue that the line of stepping stones which lay at an angle of 10 degrees to the general direction of the coast constituted a fringe. But no one can say what is the critical angle at which the line of islands ceases to be a fringe within the meaning of Article 7. Beazley (1978, 8) has pointed out that the size of islands should also be taken into account. While three large islands might be taken to be a fringe, three small islands along the same length of coast might not satisfy this requirement. Shalowitz (1962, 214) tries to stay close to the 1951 judgement by asserting that what must be present is a continuous fringe of islands sufficiently solid and close to the mainland to form a unity with it. There can be no doubt that this strictly orthodox view has been replaced by general acceptance of more liberal interpretations in the twenty years since Shalowitz wrote. Indeed, it could be claimed that by using the justification of existing straight baselines, which have apparently been accepted by many governments, any offshore islands around the world could be considered to form a fringe along the coast for the purposes of Article 7.

Today, the case of islands forming a unity with the mainland would be only one of four situations when some would argue that the islands could be considered to form a fringe. The four situations are shown in *Figure 2*. There are many cases along the fjord coasts of Canada, Chile and Norway where large islands appear to be dovetailed into indentations of the mainland. In Castlereagh Bay, off the coast of the Northern Territory, the Howard and Banyan Islands could be mistaken for parts of the Australian mainland when medium-scale satellite aerial photographs are examined. Mariners would certainly assume they were looking at the mainland as they approached from the north.

The second situation occurs when linear islands, aligned in the same direction as the coast, mask the mainland from the sea. While mariners would also see such islands as part of the mainland, navigators in aereoplanes would be able to see the channels which separated the islands and the mainland. The Frisian Islands located along the Dutch coast and Dauphin, Petit Bois, Horn and Ship Islands along the shore of the State of Mississippi provide good examples of linear islands which mask the coast.

The coast can also be masked by a swarm of small islands. A good example of this situation is provided by the myriad of islands which mask the Finnish mainland at the junction of the Gulfs of Bothnia and Finland. Off the south coast of Western Australia, the Archipelago of the Recherche provides another example on a more local scale of many small islands masking the coastline.

The third situation, where some would claim that the concept of fringing islands could be applied, is provided by an arrangement of islands spaced at intervals which ensure that the territorial seas claimed from them overlap. Such a pattern of islands would provide an extended continuous belt of territorial waters seaward of the islands.

Finally, it is possible that some arrangements of islands will create a very complex pattern of territorial seas if the low-water line around each island forms the baseline from which the territorial sea is measured. In such cases it is possible that enclaves of the exclusive economic zone will be surrounded by territorial waters. Such complexities are more likely to occur when the coastal state claims waters three or six nautical miles wide. When the zone claimed is twelve nautical miles, most potential enclaves will be eliminated, providing we are really dealing with islands in the immediate vicinity of the coast. The decision of the Australian government to draw its straight baseline

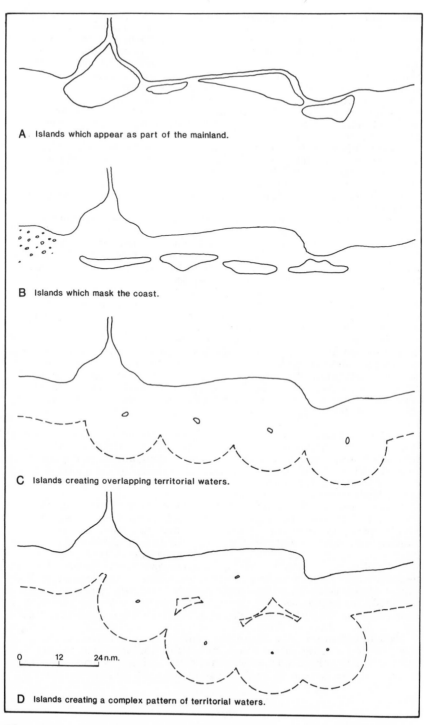

A Islands which appear as part of the mainland.

B Islands which mask the coast.

C Islands creating overlapping territorial waters.

0   12   24 n.m.

D Islands creating a complex pattern of territorial waters.

Figure 2:   Situations in which islands might be considered to fringe the coast.

inside the swarm of islands which form the Great Barrier Reef means that those islands outside the baseline generate a complex pattern of territorial seas interrupted by many convoluted corridors and enclaves of waters belonging to the Australian Fishing Zone.

Table 2 lists seventeen states which have drawn straight baselines around fringing islands which either appear to form part of the mainland or mask the mainland on seaward approaches. The Norwegian and Chilean baselines connect several islands which form a unity with the mainland, while the Yugoslav baseline connects a series of linear islands which mask the coast. The 1966 baseline drawn by the Portuguese around Guinea Bissau provided an excellent example of a straight baseline drawn around the outer edge of a swarm of islands called the Arquipelago dos Bijagos. Unfortunately, the baseline proclaimed in May 1978 adopts an historical basis which cannot be justified by any part of the 1958 or 1982 Conventions.

There are several cases where baselines have been drawn between islands which do not appear to fringe the coast. Iceland's amended straight baseline of July 14, 1972, uses two islands in the southwest region. Geirfuglasker and Eldey Eldeyjardrangur lie seventy-one nautical miles apart, and they have been connected by a straight baseline even though there are no other islands along that sector and even though the line is twenty-three nautical miles from the nearest coast at one point.

While islands are scarce along the coast of Ecuador, the authorities have managed to make the most of Isla la Plata. This small island, which has an area of about three square miles, is connected on the north to Punta Galera, which is 139 nautical miles distant, and on the south to Punta Santa Elena, which is fifty-six nautical miles away.

The straight baseline which Vietnam published on November 12, 1982, extracts maximum advantage from the small Hon Hai Islet which is located at 9 degrees 58' north and 109 degrees 28' east. It is connected northwards to Hon Doi Islet, which is 161 nautical miles distant, and southwestwards to Bay Canh Islet, which is also 161 nautical miles away. Hon Hai Islet is seventy-four nautical miles from the coast.

Table 2

Straight baselines drawn around fringing islands

State	Date	Location
Australia	14 Feb 1983	Archipelago of the Recherche, the Great Barrier Reef and southern Tasmania
Canada	08 Nov 1967	Labrador and Newfoundland
	25 Sep 1969	Nova Scotia and British Columbia
Chile	14 Jul 1977	The coast south of 41 degrees south
Denmark	14 Sep 1978	The Fyn Group bordering the Store Baelt
East Germany	19 Feb 1964	Rogen Group off Straslund

Table 2 (continued)

State	Date	Location
Finland	18 Aug 1956	Gulf of Bothnia
France	19 Oct 1967	Iles d'Hyeres southeast of Toulon
Guinea Bissau	22 Aug 1966	Acquipelago dos Bijagos
Ireland	01 Oct 1959	Coasts of the Counties Mayo and Galway
Mozambique	22 Aug 1966	The coast north of Porto Amelia
Norway	12 Jul 1935	The north coast
	18 Jul 1952	The south coast
South Korea	20 Sep 1978	The west and south coasts
Sweden	03 Jun 1966	The Baltic coast
Tunisia	02 Aug 1973	Iles Kerkenna
United Kingdom	25 Sep 1967	Hebrides
West Germany	1970	Ostfriesische Inseln
Yugoslavia	23 Apr 1965	Adriadit Coast

Source: Author's research

It would be possible to cite less extreme cases of straight baselines drawn around the islands which do not appear to fringe the coast from the proclamations made by Iran and Italy.

It is possible that Mexico relies on the fact that territorial seas drawn from the islands along the west shore of the Golfo de California overlap to justify the straight baseline which connects them. The segment connects Punta Arena with Punta Mangles 196 nautical miles to the northwest and includes six short segments of the low-water line on islands or the mainland. There are only about a dozen islands along this coast, and it would be possible to argue that they do not form a fringe along the coast.

The concept of fringing islands which justifies straight baselines is not difficult to apply if the standard against which claims are measured is Norway's *skjaergaard*, which so impressed the International Court of Justice in 1951. Unfortunately, that standard has not been applied with any consistency, and there is evidently a strong temptation, to which many countries have yielded, to use any offshore islands to justify straight baselines. If baselines such as those drawn by Ecuador, Iran and Vietnam receive general acceptance by the international community, the word *fringe* in Article 7 will become redundant.

Neither Beazley (1978) nor Shalowitz (1962) tackle the phrase *in the immediate vicinity*, perhaps in the reasonable belief that it is an explicit description. There is no doubt about the intended meaning of the phrase if its origins are traced. The International Law Commission was simply interpreting the judgment of the International Court of Justice. Thus an archipelago such as the *skjaergaard* became islands in the immediate vicinity of the coast. A very good editor once challenged the phrase as a tautology, and it had to be explained that both words were important. *Vicinity* suggests the neighborhood and *immediate* indicates a restriction of that area. But the terms have no absolute meaning. Probably everyone would agree that a fringe of islands three nautical miles from the coast was in its immediate vicinity. Equally, everyone would probably concur that a fringe of islands 100 nautical miles from the coast was outside its immediate vicinity. Unfortunately, it would not be possible to predict with confidence what the majority thought of a fringe of islands twenty-five, forty, or sixty-five nautical miles from the coast.

The concept must be applied to the inner edge of the fringe of islands. Providing the islands on the landward side of the fringe are in the immediate vicinity of the coast, there can be no objection to the baseline being drawn around the seaward edge of the fringe. Providing the territorial seas claimed from the fringing islands overlap the waters claimed from the mainland, it would be difficult to argue that the fringe was outside the immediate vicinity of the coast. However, there are some islands which form basepoints in systems of straight baselines which lie more than twenty-four nautical miles from the shore. They include Ko Tao, which is thirty-five nautical miles from the Thai mainland, Scoglio Africa which is forty nautical miles from the Italian coast, and Hon Hai Islet which is seventy-four nautical miles from the shore of Vietnam.

The straight baselines drawn according to this part of Article 7 must connect *appropriate points*. Paragraph 4 deals with the extent to which low-tide elevations might be used as basepoints, and that matter will be considered later. At this stage, it is only necessary to assert two points. First, the appropriate point should be located on or above the low-water mark used as the normal baseline. Second, the termini of the straight baselines must be located on the mainland of the country making the claim.

So far, only one country has extended its baseline to the territory of a neighboring state. On 10 July 1968 Venezuela announced a single straight line across the mouth of the Orinoco River. Since that line extended fifty nautical miles beyond the eastern limit of that river mouth, it cannot be considered simply as a closing line. The eastern terminus of this line is fixed twenty-six nautical miles east of the land boundary with Guyana on the coast of that country. Venezuela claims part of western Guyana and has apparently taken this means of demonstrating this claim. In a note which accompanied the proclamation, Venezuela drew attention to the fact that Guyana claims territorial seas three nautical miles wide while Venezuela's claim is to water twelve nautical miles wide. Thus Venezuela immediately claimed the band of water nine nautical miles wide which is generated from the baseline and which lies outside the claimed waters of Guyana. Venezuela also reserved its claims to the internal and territorial waters along that section of Guyana's coast which is subject to this territorial dispute. Guyana increased its claim to territorial waters to twelve nautical miles on November 4, 1977.

Eleven countries have fixed termini of straight baselines which are either located below the low-water mark or which are not positioned on the mainland. These cases can be grouped into four categories. First, a number of countries, mainly in northern Europe, have adopted common origins for their baselines at points in the sea. The point is fixed in the following manner. A straight line is drawn connecting two islands or headlands, one of which is owned by each country. For example, in the case of West Germany and Denmark, the two islands are Sylt and Romo Flak West. Then the maritime boundary between the adjacent coasts is constructed, and the point at which this boundary intersects the straight line is fixed as the origin of the two straight baselines. This arrangement has been adopted by Denmark and West Germany in the North Sea, by Sweden and Norway in the Skagerrak, and by Finland and Sweden in the Gulf of Bothnia. Vietnam and Cambodia have apparently also adopted the same arrangement, but the point of origin of their baselines will have to await the delimitation of the maritime boundary between their adjacent coasts.

The second category results from a country unilaterally fixing a baseline terminus in the manner already described. There are four cases where this has occurred. On June 28, 1971 Ecuador fixed the southern terminus of its straight baseline at the intersection of the parallel which passes through the terminus of the land boundary and a straight line joining Punta Santa Elena in Ecuador and Cabo Blanco in Peru. The northern terminus has been fixed in a similar manner; in this case, the straight line is drawn between Punta Galera in Ecuador and Punta Manglares in Colombia.

On July 14, 1977 Chile declared that its straight baseline terminated in the south at Point XX of the 1977 Arbitral Award in the Beagle Channel case (The Geographer 1978, 2). The Danish baseline in the Baltic Sea terminates at a point in the sea on the common maritime boundary with West Germany.

By its declaration of July 21, 1973 Iran published straight baselines along two sections of coast. The first segment traversed the northern shore of the Persian Gulf from the mouth of the Shatt el Arab to the Strait of Hormuz; the second occupied Iran's coast in the Gulf of Oman. The northern terminus of the first segment is described as a point situated at the intersection of the thalweg of the Shatt el Arab with a line joining the two banks of the river at its mouth. The boundary between Iran and Iraq was moved to the thalweg of the river in this section by the protocol dated 13 June 1975, which was signed in Baghdad. This agreement was abrogated by Iraq at the beginning of the war between these two states in September 1980. The eastern terminus of Iran's second straight baseline segment is located in the mouth of Gwatar Bay. The point is defined as the intersection of the meridian 61 degrees 37'3" east and a straight line joining the headlands of this bay. The point is shown in *Figure 3*. Gwatar Bay is shared by the two countries, and the meridian nominated by Iran is presumably judged to pass through the terminus of the land boundary. This point lies 2.5 nautical miles east of the point which is equidistant from the nearest land on the Iranian and Pakistan sides of the bay.

The 1958 and 1982 Conventions do not refer to basepoints common to two countries being located in the sea. It is therefore not clear whether such arrangements can be legally opposed by a third state which finds them inconvenient. It might be considered significant that the rules applying to the closure of bays do not apply to bays shared by two or more states.

The third category of states which have not terminated straight baselines on the low-water line includes only Bangladesh. This country proclaimed straight baselines measuring 221 nautical miles in April 1974. None of the eight points which fix this line are located on land, and the line appears to correspond fairly closely to the ten fathom isobath, except in the area west of Cox's Bazar where this isobath trends sharply towards the coast. This remarkable baseline was

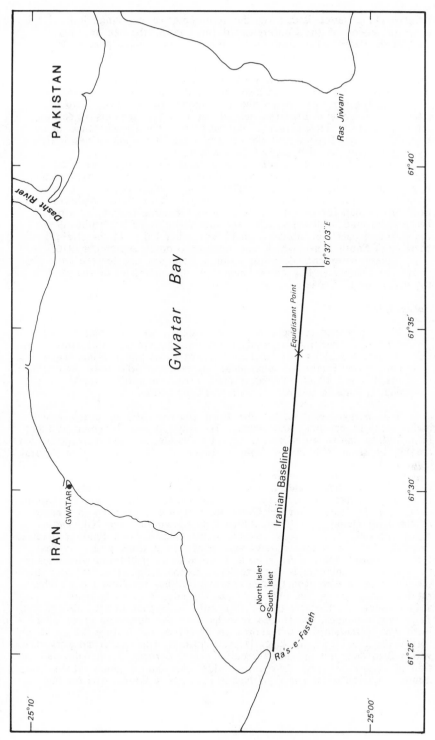

Figure 3: The terminus of the Iranian straight baseline in Gwatar Bay.

justified in a letter issued by the representative of Bangladesh at the eleventh session of the Conference of the Law of the Sea on April 28, 1982. This letter drew attention to the peculiar geomorphological character of the seabed in this zone off the delta of the River Ganges. Special mention was made of wide fluctuations in the low-water mark and the extensive areas of shallow water which meant that the area could not be easily charted. It was also remarked that only the channels leading to the ports of Chalna and Chittagong are navigable. Two days later the Indian and Burmese delegations issued statements rejecting these arguments. This action is not surprising since acceptance of Bangladesh's baselines would deflect any equidistant boundaries with its neighbors to the advantage of Bangladesh.

The final category involves those cases where states have terminated straight baselines on islands and have not provided any indication of how internal waters are defined beyond and landwards of those islands. Examples of this situation are provided by the Danish baselines proclaimed for Greenland on 27 May 1963, the Norwegian straight baselines around Svalbard which were announced on 25 September 1970, the Burmese baseline published on 15 November 1968 and the straight baseline of South Korea which was proclaimed on 20 September 1970.

Unless basepoints defining straight baselines are located on or above the low-water line and terminate on the mainland of the state the definition of the internal waters is incomplete.

Paragraph 2 of Article 7

Where because of the presence of a delta and other natural conditions the coastline is highly unstable, the appropriate points may be selected along the furthest seaward extent of the low-water line and, notwithstanding subsequent regression of the low-water line, the straight baselines shall remain effective until changed by the coastal State in accordance with this Convention.

This paragraph describes the third characteristic of coasts which makes straight baselines appropriate. To coasts deeply indented and cut into, and to coasts which are fringed by islands, are added coasts which are highly unstable because of the presence of a delta and other natural conditions.

Deltas are formed when the sediment deposited at the mouth of a river fills that mouth and then continues the building process so that the newly formed land protrudes into the sea (Samojlov 1956). Herodotus named this landform after the Greek letter which reproduced the shape of the Nile Delta. Bird (1976, 205-9) has shown that the Nile Delta represents only one of four possible shapes which these features assume. The Nile Delta is a lobate delta with a convex outline, and such features are found where there is an abundance of sediment and where scour by waves and currents is not excessive. Cuspate deltas, represented by the Tiber Delta near Roma, have concave outlines resulting from higher rates of scour by waves and currents. Digitate deltas, which other authors such as Whittow (1984, 137) call bird's foot deltas, have a shape which suggest the fingers of a hand or the outspread claws of a bird. The Mississippi Delta represents this type of feature which is formed by the growth of river levees seawards. The fourth category, for which Bird does not provide a specific name, is formed when the deposition of islands in a river's mouth divides the main channel into a number of tributaries. The Fly River in Papua New Guinea and the Rio

Geba in Guinea Bissau offer clear examples of such deltas, which can probably be called island deltas (*Figure 4*).

The presence of a delta alone is not sufficient justification to draw straight baselines around its perimeter. There must also be *other natural conditions*. It is not clear why the word *other* is used in this paragraph. A delta is a landform which could be considered to be a natural condition of the earth's surface although no geomorphologist would use such an expression. The reference to *other natural conditions* cannot apply to additional and different landforms because it is not landforms which create an unstable coast; it is the processes which operate along that coast. Now a coastline can be highly unstable because it is advancing or retreating, but the rest of the paragraph makes it clear that these provisions apply only to retreating coasts.

The form and extent of any delta can be considered as the present answer to an equation which relates the supply of sediment -- mainly by the river but sometimes also from the sea and by the wind -- and the removal of sediment -- mainly by the sea but also sometimes by the wind and human activity. So this paragraph is dealing with those cases where the removal of sediment exceeds the supply and causes the coast to retreat. We must therefore be concerned with those situations where elements in the equation change in such a way that the volume of sediment removed inreases rapidly in relation to the volume of sediment supplied.

This increase could be caused by a reduction in the supply of sediment. Since the load carried by a river is related to the volume of water, the speed at which it flows, the size of the particles and the availability of sediment, a change in any of these elements can reduce the rate at which sediment is delivered to the seaward edge of the delta. For example, the extraction of water for irrigation and industrial or domestic use can reduce the volume of water which reaches the sea. The creation of artificial lakes along with river's course can create still conditions when sediment will settle, causing reduction in load. Reafforestation programs in catchments with many bare slopes will reduce the rate of erosion and therefore the supply of sediment. A prolonged drought would also reduce the volume of water in the river and diminish the rate of erosion by the river in its headwaters.

The removal of material by the sea could be increased by unusually large waves caused by violent storms. The dredging of offshore deposits could change the direction and strength of currents in a way which caused more rapid erosion, or could allow waves to break further inshore with the same consequence.

So far the discussion has been conducted as though the entire coastline of the delta is in retreat. A much more common occurrence will see some sections of the delta advancing while at the same time other sections retreat. Plainly, this paragraph could be applied to any part of the coastline of the delta which was retreating. Differential retreat of deltaic coasts can be caused in a number of ways. The tributaries of deltas sometimes break their banks, especially when they are flowing between levees, and establish new courses which will continue to be followed when the floods subside. In this case the delta coast at the mouth of the abandoned channel will no longer be nourished by a supply of sediment and it might retreat. The coast at the mouth of the new course will receive an increased supply of sediment and may grow seawards.

Human activities can also cause the differential erosion of deltas. For example, Bird and Ongkosongo (1980) have described how the delta

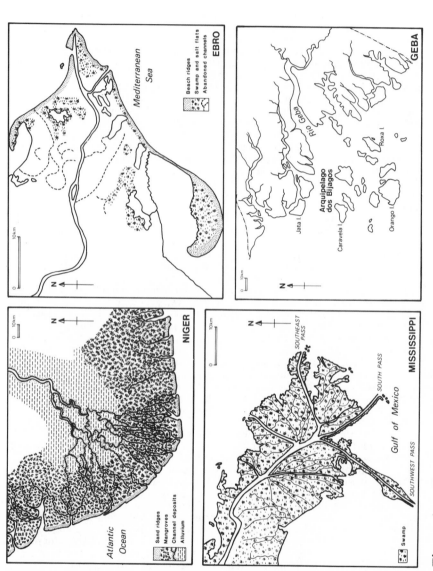

Figure 4: Examples of lobate (Niger), cuspate (Ebro), digitate (Mississippi) and island (Geba) deltas

of the Rambatan River in Indonesia was eroded in one section after the Anyar Canal was built for an irrigation scheme. The removal of sand and gravel from the surface of the delta for construction might lower the surface to a level where it can be invaded by the sea during a major storm. The removal of mangroves along the shore of tropical deltas increases the chance of erosion by waves and currents. The construction of new harbor works might deflect waves and currents to a new section of coast which is more vulnerable to erosion.

Finally, it should be noted that in some cases the great weight of sediment in the delta causes subsidence and allows invasion by the sea. This characteristic has been noted in some of the older sections of the delta of the Mississippi River.

It may be presumed that the phrase *appropriate points* in this paragraph carries the same meaning as the same phrase in the first paragraph. However, it must be noted that the ease with which appropriate points can be selected will depend on the type of delta which is being considered. For example, the outline of the Niger Delta is so smooth and the changes in direction so imperceptible that the selection of appropriate points would be difficult. Unless the segments of straight baseline were very short, it is likely that some segments will leave some parts of the coast seaward of the line. So the selection of points will be hardest on lobate deltas such as those created by the Niger and Yukon Rivers. The task of selecting appropriate points will be much easier on the digitate and island deltas because of the sharp changes in direction of local sections of coast.

Some deltas have already been incorporated within systems of straight baselines, but there is no reason to believe that this has been done because the coastline is considered to be highly unstable. The Po and Rhone Deltas are not surrounded by straight baselines, but they anchor baselines enclosing the coast on either side. Burma has enclosed the Irrawaddy Delta as part of the coast of the Gulf of Martaban. Papua New Guinea has drawn interim archipelagic baselines which connect the outer points of the outermost islands which form the delta of the Fly River. In the same manner, the original Portuguese straight baseline for Portuguese Guinea connected the outer islands of the delta in the mouth of the Corubal River. As noted earlier, these islands were enclosed because they were considered to fringe the coast. That part of the Ganges Delta which belongs to Bangladesh is fronted by a straight baseline which follows the ten fathom isobath.

Because deltas are formed from the deposition of sediment by streams or rivers entering the seas, it is possible that the *furthest seaward extent of the low-water line* will be on a low-tide elevation. Now there can be no question that geomorphologists would consider these low-tide elevations to be an integral part of the delta, and they would argue that it was therefore proper for such features to be the sites for basepoints of straight baselines surrounding the delta. However, a lawyer might argue that these features cannot be used unless they have lighthouses or similar installations in accordance with Paragraph 4 of Article 7.

The phrase *highly unstable* is not capable of any strict mathematical interpretation, but it has the flavor of rapid short-term fluctuations. Orlova and Zenkovich (1974) have recorded retreat of the shore, near the Damietta mouth of the River Nile, at the rate of forty meters each year. Now the width of a line portraying the coast or a baseline on a chart at a scale of 100,000 would represent a distance of 100 meters. This suggests that it would not be worthwhile redrawing the baseline charts unless there was a change in position of at least 300 meters. While that is only the cartographer's viewpoint, it is likely that navigators of surveillance vessels will agree. Even under the best conditions, captains of such vessels will have difficulty in fixing the position of an intruding vessel within 100 meters. Providing that prosecutions are taking place before an independent judiciary, it is likely that they will only be launched when the intrusion is considerably greater than the possible error in fixing the intruder's position. This assumption suggests that there is no reason for countries to worry about the redefinition of their baselines unless the regression of the coast exceeds, say, 250 meters. Even that regression would not have any perceptible effect on the definition of the outer edge of an exclusive economic zone 200 nautical miles wide. However, countries have absolutely nothing to lose by drawing straight baselines around deltas which begin to demonstrate regression. If the regression continues and becomes extensive, then the outer limits of their maritime claims are unaffected. If the regression is only minor, the insurance of drawing baselines will be shown to be unnecessary, but it is very inexpensive insurance since it only costs the work, for a brief time, of a surveyor and a cartographer.

It has been assumed in this analysis that these rules apply to present and future situations. However, it is possible that some countries might feel aggrieved that they are unable to secure relief from coastal erosion which occurred thirty or forty years ago, while countries which are now experiencing coastal retreat can discount that disadvantage. Such aggrieved countries may take the view that the reference to *the furthest seaward extent of the low-water line* is to the outermost low-water line which can be confidently identified in, say, the past fifty years. If that view is ever raised, it should be resisted, because such a concept would open the way to immoderate extensions of maritime claims by recourse to distant and drowned coastlines of earlier periods.

This paragraph concludes with the statement that *the straight baselines shall remain effective until changed by the coastal State in accordance with this Convention.* There is a suggestion that the coastal state should eventually redraw the straight baseline along the new coastline, but there is no absolute instruction to do so; nor is there any indication of the length of time that the original straight baseline can be maintained at sea. If the intention of this paragraph is that states should not be disadvantaged by having to forfeit parts of maritime claims because of coastal erosion, then states would be justified in refusing to redraw their baseline. However, if the intention of this rule is to avoid immediate difficulties created by uncertainties about the extent of territorial seas in zones of rapid coastal erosion, then the international coastal community is entitled to expect adjustment of the straight baseline landwards as soon as the coastal instability ends. Of course, if the termini of the original straight baseline are stranded in the sea by the retreat of the coastline, it will be necessary to extend the straight baseline to the shore to complete the definition of internal waters.

Paragraph 3 of Article 7

The drawing of straight baselines must not depart to any appreciable extent from the general direction of the coast, and the sea areas lying within the lines must be sufficiently closely linked to the land domain to be subject to the regime of internal waters.

The concept that straight baselines must not depart from the general direction of the coast was enunciated by the International Court of Justice (1951, 133) in deciding the *Norwegian Fisheries* case. It was preserved by the International Law Commission (United Nations 1956, 14), and it emerged intact in the 1958 Convention. The 1958 version was included in the 1982 Convention after the phrase *such baselines* was changed to *straight baselines*. The Court noted in its Judgment that the rule about conforming to the general direction of the coast is devoid of any mathematical precision (International Court of Justice 1951, 142). That view is still correct. The only advice which the Court was able to offer was that, except in cases of manifest abuse, it was unsatisfactory to examine one sector alone or to rely on impressions gained from large-scale charts. Beazley (1978) and Shalowitz (1962) consider this problem without being able to provide a solution, although both seem to indicate that the Norwegian straight baseline of 1935 is the standard against which all straight baselines should be tested. An analysis of that baseline demonstrates that very few lines varied from the general direction of the coast by more than fifteen degrees, and that the ratio of water to land in the area between the straight baseline and the mainland is 3.5:1.

It is a hard lesson to learn that not all questions have an answer, but even superficial research into the question of determining appreciable departures from the general direction of the coast would prove convincing to most. While it is an easy task to discover baselines which breach the rules about indented coasts and fringing islands, it is very difficult to discover a straight baseline which the majority of objective commentators would regard as deviating to an appreciable extent from the general direction of the coast.

Where there are no offshore islands and the basepoints are all located on the mainland, it is very difficult to argue that the general direction of the coast has not been preserved. Where offshore islands exist, the matter appears to be complicated beyond hope of a successful conclusion. For example, the segment of baseline which links the mainland to the first fringing island might be drawn perpendicular to the coast and still be a perfectly legitimate line. Further, individual segments along fringing islands might differ from the general direction of the coast by twenty degrees or more, simply because the line has to reflect the alignment of the rampart of islands as closely as possible. As the number of outer basepoints increases it will become more difficult to fix a general direction which most analysts will accept.

It would be possible to plot all the points and produce a line of best fit, but there would have to be agreement about the length of the coast to be considered and the weight given to individual points. These are matters on which it might be difficult to secure consensus.

The best advice is probably to pay little attention to this requirement and to focus instead on the characteristics required for straight baselines to be appropriate. If there are deep indentations or a genuine fringe of islands, there will usually be little scope for cheating by drawing baselines which deviate to a marked extent from the azimuth of the coast.

The test that waters within the straight baseline *must be sufficiently closely linked to the land domain to be subject to the regime of internal waters* originated in the *Norwegian Fisheries* case (Interna-

307

tional Court of Justice 1951, 133). It passed intact via the International Law Commission and the 1958 Convention to the 1982 Convention. Although this rule is incapable of any mathematical definition, the International Court of Justice did give some useful guidance on its application.

> Another fundamental consideration, of particular importance in this case, is the more or less close relationship existing between certain sea areas and the land formations which divide or surround them. The real question raised in the choice of baselines is in effect whether certain sea areas lying within these lines are sufficiently closely linked to the land domain to be subject to the regime of internal waters. This idea, which is at the basis of the determination of the rules relating to bays, should be liberally applied in the case of a coast, the geographical configuration of which is as unusual as that of Norway. (International Court of Justice 1951, 133)

The constant message of this paragraph is that the waters must be in fairly close proximity to the land represented by promontories or islands. This is expressed by the reference to a relationship which is more or less close, to the unusual configuration of the Norwegian coast, and to this concept underlying the rules for closing bays.

The difficulty in finding obvious cases where baselines do not conform to the general direction of the coast does not exist in respect of the second part of Paragraph 3. Some of the internal waters defined by Ecuador, Vietnam and Burma are respectively 50, 71 and 83 nautical miles from the nearest land. It would have been possible to fix a ratio of water to land which could not be exceeded for the zone between the straight baseline and the mainland, although such a rule could only apply to cases where baselines were drawn around fringing islands. The ratio would involve tedious calculations where there are thousands of islands as there are along the Norwegian coast. Even though neither of the requirements in Paragraph 3 has any degree of mathematical exactitude, it will usually be found much easier to attack the propriety of questionable straight baselines by concentrating on the remoteness of some areas of internal waters from the coast rather than by trying to prove that the baseline does not conform to the general direction of the coast.

Navigators will certainly have serious doubts about the legality of straight baselines when they enter internal waters without land being in sight in any direction!

Paragraph 4 of Article 7

> Straight baselines shall not be drawn to and from low-tide elevations, unless lighthouses or similar installations which are permanently above sea level have been built on them or except in cases where the drawing of baselines to and from such elevations has received general international recognition.

This paragraph is less difficult to construe than those which preceded it. There can be no doubt about the meaning of a low-tide elevation which is provided in Article 13.

A low-tide elevation is a naturally formed area of land which is surrounded by and above water at low tide but submerged at high tide.

There is no doubt what a lighthouse is, although it should be noted that there is no requirement that the lighthouse should be either manned or operating. The phrase *similar installations* could be interpreted in two ways. First it could refer to structures, such as towers, which look like lighthouses even though they don't possess lights. It is unlikely that there would be many of such installations on low-tide elevations. Second, and more importantly, the similar installations could consist of navigation aids such as fog horns, radar reflectors and beacons, which, like lighthouses, warn navigators of danger.

Three of the basepoints of the Norwegian straight baseline of 1935 were located on rocks which were covered by the high tide. Although the 1812 Norwegian Decree had proclaimed that the territorial sea was measured from the island or islet farthest from the mainland not covered by water, that had been interpreted by 1935 to mean not covered *continuously* by water! The International Court of Justice (1951, 140) approved the continued use of these three low-tide elevations as basepoints.

This dispensation was rejected by the Law Commission (United Nations 1956, 14) on the ground that at high tide it would not be possible to sight the point of departure of the straight baselines. The 1958 Convention overcame this objection by adding the requirement about lighthouses or similar installations in the form which was copied directly in the 1982 Convention.

The later Convention also had received general international recognition. It is not known which countries other than Norway can take advantage of this qualification. It is possible that some countries will use low-tide elevations as basepoints even though they lack lighthouses and similar installations, and then claim after some years without being challenged that this practice has received general international recognition. This means that such irregularities should be challenged as soon as the straight baseline is proclaimed.

The requirement that low-tide elevations used as basepoints must have a lighthouse or similar installation frees them from the restriction of Article 13.

> Where a low-tide elevation is wholly situated at a distance exceeding the breadth of the territorial sea from the mainland or an island, it has no territorial sea of its own. (United Nations 1983, 5)

since basepoints may not be established on low-tide elevations lacking lighthouses or similar installations there can be no question of basepoints being fixed in the sea as Bangladesh and other countries have done.

Paragraph 5 of Article 7

> Where the method of straight baselines is applicable under paragraph 1, account may be taken, in determining particular baselines, of economic interests peculiar to the region concerned, the reality and importance of which are clearly evidenced by long usage.

Once again some of the words in this paragraph can be traced directly to the Judgment in the *Norwegian Fisheries* case (International Court of Justice 1951, 133). The Law Commission incorporated these phrases into its proposals (United Nations 1956, 14). In both these sources this provision was linked with the requirements that baselines should conform to the general direction of the coast and that waters should be closely linked to the land. In effect the operation of this provision enabled countries to relax the requirements contained in Paragraph 3. This nexus was broken in the 1958 Convention by the insertion of the paragraph dealing with low-tide elevations; the 1958 arrangement was preserved in the 1982 Convention.

The Law Commission made it clear that economic considerations could not justify the use of straight baselines; they could only be used to justify the particular alignment of a baseline.

> The application of the straight baseline system should be justified in principle on other grounds before purely local economic considerations could justify a particular way of drawing the lines. (United Nations 1956, 14)

Beazley (1978, 9) and Shalowitz (1962, 214) have emphasized this point, and there can be no doubt that the correct application of this concept is as follows. Once it has been established that the nature of the coastline merits the use of a straight baseline, it is permissible to consider economic matters in deciding the alignment of particular segments of the baseline. If such analysis reveals economic interests of long standing, then it would be permissible to select a line which deviated from the general direction of the coast to a greater extent than the international community would usually accept.

All that the paragraph tells about these economic interests is that they must be peculiar to the area and possess a reality and importance evidenced by long usage. It does not seem reasonable to interpret the word *peculiar* to mean that a unique economic activity must be carried on in the area in question. There would be more general agreement that there must be a particular activity which is carried on in the region under consideration. To describe the economic interests as *important* is to use a relative term which could apply to a country, a port community or a family. It is therefore unlikely that resort to this rule would be challenged on the ground that the economic interest was unimportant.

The economic interests which attracted the attention of the International Court of Justice in 1951 had existed for centuries. It would be unfair to apply this standard to countries which have only existed for twenty or thirty years. It is safe to predict that there would be no general agreement on a minimum time which economic interests must have existed to allow the use of this rule. Indeed, it may be reasonably guessed that the majority of countries which have achieved their independence in this century would regard a decade of activity as evidence of real and important economic interests.

It seems likely that there would be three kinds of economic interests. First and most frequently, fishing for both swimming and sedentary species would be involved. Second, there could be mining of sand and gravel from the seabed for the building industry. In some areas shell beds might be exploited for lime. The third activity would be connected with tourism, although such an activity would probably be fairly recent. Off some coasts there might be scenic sports which can only be visited

310

by boat, or there may be colonies of birds and seals which attract visitors.

In some cases along the coast of northern Australia, aboriginal communities have a long-standing interest in subsistence hunting and fishing in the sea. Such an activity would surely be considered to be economic. However, the spiritual association which some of these communities have with the sea would not be covered by this paragraph. That must be regretted because these spiritual associations are both real and important to these communities, and they are recognized in Australian legislation.

In no case where a straight baseline has been proclaimed is there any evidence that countries have relied on this paragraph in fixing the alignment of any segment. That does not mean these provisions have not been taken into account. It is precisely this lack of firm information which makes it risky to criticize baselines because they do not conform to the general direction of the coast. It is possible that the disparity is explained by peculiar economic interests.

Paragraph 6 of Article 7

> The system of straight baselines may not be applied by a State in such a manner as to cut off the territorial sea of another State from the high seas or an exclusive economic zone.

This paragraph owes nothing to the 1951 Judgment of the International Court of Justice and first appeared in a slightly different form in the 1958 Convention.

> The system of straight baselines may not be applied by a State in such a manner as to cut off from the high seas the territorial sea of another State.

The meaning of this paragraph is plain. No country can construct a straight baseline which leaves another state or part of that state on the landward side.

It follows that the country or part of a country which might be isolated by a straight baseline must be small, that this territory must be enclosed by the land of one other country, and that the coast of this other country is either deeply indented or fringed with islands. There are two situations where this can occur. First, there are mainland countries such as the Gambia and Brunei which are imbedded in the coast of the larger territories of Senegal and Malaysia. Second, there are small islands belonging to one country which are close to the coast of another state, such as Karaman Island, which belongs to Yemen Aden but which is hard against the coast of Yemen San'a. A list of some situations where this rule might apply is provided in *Table 3*.

It does not seem possible that straight baselines drawn on a highly unstable deltaic coast could ever cut off one state from the high seas or an exclusive economic zone.

This rule also applies implicitly in respect of the closing lines of bays. Such closing lines cannot be drawn if the coast of the bay belongs to more than one state. In the case of South Africa's Penguin and Seal Islands in Luderitz Bay on the coast of Nambia, it is proper to assume that the coast of an island in a bay forms part of the coast of that bay.

311

Table 3

Countries and territories which could be surrounded by
the straight baselines of other states

Country or territory	Surrounding state
The Gambia	Senegal
Penguin Island (South Africa)	Namibia
Monaco	France
Karaman Island (Yemen Aden)	Yemen San'a
Mellila (Spain)	Morocco
Ceuta (Spain)	Morocco
Macau (Portugal)	China
Hong Kong (Britain)	China
United Arab Emirates	Oman
Quemoy and Amoy (Taiwan)	China
Brunei	Malaysia

Source: Author's research

The Representation of Straight Baselines

The Law Commission and the 1958 Convention included a provision in the Article dealing with straight baselines which required due publicity to be given to their location. The 1958 Convention insisted that *the coastal State must clearly indicate straight baselines on charts, to which due publicity must be given.* That requirement has been removed from Article 7 in the 1982 Convention and incorporated in Article 16, which requires all straight baselines and closing lines or the limits derived from them to be shown on charts (United Nations 1983, 6).

The baselines for measuring the breadth of the territorial sea determined in accordance with Articles 7, 9, and 10, or the limits derived therefrom, and the lines of delimitation drawn in accordance with Articles 12 and 15 shall be shown on charts of a scale or scales adequate for ascertaining their position. Alternatively, a list of geographical coordinates of points, specifying the geodetic datum, may be substituted.

The coastal State shall give due publicity to such charts or lists of geographical coordinates and shall deposit a copy of each such chart or list with the Secretary-General of the United Nations.

Since the word *chart* is used, it must be presumed that a map will not do. Charts are used for navigation at sea or in the air. Nautical charts have much important information marked in the sea showing depth of water, prohibited anchorages, lights, dredged channels and reefs. While some offshore information might be provided on a map, a navigator would usually prefer to have the latest chart.

312

It is not possible to describe the specific scale at which the baselines should be shown, and indeed, most countries with long coastlines would probably wish to use a variety of scales. In the case of Australia, for example, it would be satisfactory to show the baselines around the Bonaparte Archipelago in the northwest on charts of a medium scale, because in such areas there is little coastal traffic. The straight baselines at the mouth of Spencer Gulf should be shown on larger-scale charts because of the considerable traffic to and from Adelaide, Whyalla, Port Augusta and Port Pirie. The straight baselines in the vicinity of Fremantle should be shown on large scale-charts, because the entry to Cockburn Sound is much narrower than the entry to Spencer Gulf and Investigator Strait.

When deciding on the appropriate scale for charts, it is necessary to remember a warning given by Shalowitz (1962, 289). He observed that charts have to be kept alive if they are to serve their purpose properly. This means that they must be revised on a regular basis so that the information for navigators is current. The larger the scale of the chart, the greater the burden of revision.

Potential Problems Connected With Article 7

The foregoing analysis has already identified a number of problems which might be experienced in applying the rules set out in Article 7; this section looks at three additional problems, only one of which is evident at present.

Article 7 makes no mention of the possibility of drawing straight baselines along ice-bound coasts. In the northern hemisphere, it appears that only the north coasts of some Canadian islands, such as Ellesmere, and of Greenland are permanently ice-bound. In addition, there are no open waters beyond the ice surrounding these coasts which could be claimed as territorial waters. In the southern hemisphere, most of the coast of Antarctica is permanently ice-bound. If national claims to sovereignty in Antarctica become the basis for claims to the surrounding maritime areas, there would be serious technical problems in deciding which baselines should be used to determine the extent of these claims. Some of the problems have been investigated in a recent study (Prescott 1984).

Coastal instability does not only occur in the vicinity of deltas, and it is surprising that the second paragraph of Article 7 is restricted to deltas. It will not be remarkable if some countries seek to interpret that paragraph in a more general way so that it can apply to coastal instability along shores where there are no deltas.

Coastal instability can be caused by a number of different processes. Volcanic activity can produce coastal instability in at least two ways. First, the extrusion of lava and ash from vents near the sea can create extensions of the coast. Sometimes the protrusion could be considered as the delta of a river of lava. Such features are often subject to fairly rapid erosion. The lava masses cool quickly on entering the sea, and cracks and fissures develop. These lines of weakness are attacked by waves, and whole structures may be undermined. The steep cliffs and many arches along the lava coast of southern Hawaii provide an example of this situation. The extensions of mud and ash, which sometimes occurred off Iceland, are usually unconsolidated and offer little resistance to removal and redistribution by waves and currents.

The second way in which volcanic activity can change a coastline is by a major explosion, which either blows away much of the land as at Rakata, better known as Krakatau, or by causing slumping and down-faulting of the coast. These are the most dramatic form of coastal retreat and, fortunately, are comparatively rare.

Some tundra cliffs along the coasts of Siberia and Alaska are subject to rapid coastal erosion. These cliffs, like the adjoining sea, are frozen for many months. When the thaw begins, the cliffs are attacked and reduced in three ways. First, as the sea-ice begins to break, the waves are able to batter floes against the coast as powerful destructive agents. Second, as the ice clears, the waves have direct access to the shore. Third, much of the cliffs, in a frozen condition, consist of water, and as this thaws, so slumping of the cliffs might occur.

If a measure of an unstable coast is that the capacity of the state to make maritime claims from particular points fluctuates with natural processes, then there is another condition which must be mentioned. Some fringing reefs are not exposed at low tide. They continue to be covered by shallow waters, or perhaps waves in rougher conditions. However, it will often be found that these reefs will be surmounted by coral boulders which have been broken off the front of the reef and thrown onto its surface. Such rocks are found along the edge of the Great Barrier Reef of Australia, the reefs surrounding Mauritius, and on the Minerva Reefs which are claimed by Tonga. While such rocks are above the high-water mark, they can be used as basepoints for the delineation of the territorial sea. While some of these rocks survive for a very long time, others are undercut and lowered, and others are rolled along by storm surges and disappear into channels. In such a situation, it could be argued that the coastline, considered as points from which territorial seas can be claimed, is unstable.

Of course there is the difficulty that these rocks could only be used to claim territorial seas; so, if they could be used as basepoints for straight baselines, these lines could not be used as the basis for claims to an exclusive economic zone or the continental shelf.

Also associated with reefs are cays -- sand islands formed from sand produced by the erosion of the reef. Cays may be colonized by vegetation and become permanent islands. Even if plants will not grow there, the unconsolidated sand might be converted to beach rock by the secondary deposition of calcium carbonate in the zone of alternate wetting and drying. But cays may be impermanent features and subject to erosion and total destruction. If the concept of coastal instability was considered to apply even along coasts without deltas, then countries with offshore cays might seek to apply the provisions of Paragraph 2.

The third problem concerns the tendency for some continental states to surround their offshore archipelagoes with straight baselines. In the *Informal Negotiating Text*, Article 131 dealt with this question, but it was removed from subsequent drafts and the final convention, despite the efforts of some countries, including Canada, Ecuador and India, did not deal with this subject.

The Geographer (1981, 57) has recorded that Ethiopia proclaimed straight baselines around the Danlac Archipelago on September 25, 1952. On July 13, 1971, Ecuador announced straight baselines around the Galapagos Islands. Denmark has maintained straight baselines around the Faeroes since 1959; the latest modification was proclaimed on December 21, 1976. Spain has drawn straight baselines around two of its offshore archipelagoes. The decree of 5 August 1977 linked Ibiza and Formentera in the Mediterranean Sea and surrounded the islands in the eastern Islas Canarias in the Atlantic Ocean. On 9 February 1983 Australia announced its straight baselines and enclosed the Furneaux Group in Bass Strait and the Houtman Abrolhos Islands off the coast of Western Australia.

Now Article 10 of the 1958 Convention and Article 121 of the 1982 Convention make it clear that the territorial seas claimed from islands should be determined in accordance with the provisions of the conventions which apply to other territory. The rules for drawing straight baselines set out in Article 7 therefore apply to islands belonging to mainland states. When a group of such islands is surrounded by a straight baseline, it can only be justified because some of the islands are considered to fringe one other island.

In the Furneaux Group in Bass Strait it is a reasonable interpretation to say that Flinders Island, which is the largest in the group, is fringed by islands such as Cape Barren Island, the Chapell Islands, Hummock and Kangaroo Islands and Great Dog Island. Indeed it is surprising that the baseline was not extended northwards to include the West Sister and East Sister Islands which also fringe Flinders Island.

In the Houtman Abrolhos Group, which is shown in *Figure 5*, it is entirely unreasonable to justify the straight baselines according to the concept of fringing islands. The baselines tie together the Wallabi, Pelsart and Easter Groups which extend over a distance of about fifty nautical miles from north to south. The Wallabi Group has the largest area of land and therefore it must be the territory which is fringed with islands. It is difficult to argue that the Easter Group fringes the Wallabi Group and entirely impossible to maintain that the Pelsart Group fringes the Wallabi Group.

While it has not been possible to inspect a chart of sufficiently large scale to pronounce on the fitness of any straight baselines around the Danlac Archipelago, the other straight baselines around offshore archipelagoes appear to be dubious. In the Galapagos Islands it is stretching the concept too far to assert that Isla Darwin, Isla Pinta, Isla San Cristobal and Isla Espanola fringe Isla Isabela, which is the main island in the group. Most observers would have little difficulty in reaching the conclusion that in the Faeroes the islands called Munken, Fleserne, Sudhuroy, Sandoy Stora Dimun and Litla Dimun do not fringe Stremoy. Fuerteventura is the largest island in the eastern Islas Canarias, and it lies at the southern end of a chain of islands which includes Lobos, Lanzarote, Graciosa, Montana Clara and Alegranza, and which stretches for about 100 nautical miles. It is hard to understand how islands arranged in a linear pattern over that distance could be considered to fringe the northern tip of Fuerteventura.

The enclosure of Ibiza and Formentera is a matter which could provoke an inconclusive debate about whether Ibiza is fringed by the other islands.

Conclusions

The spirit of Article 7 can be traced to the 1951 Judgment by the International Court of Justice. It is that when coasts possess a multitude of deep inlets, or when coasts are bordered by a myriad of islands which appear to be an extension of the land, it is appropriate to substitute straight baselines for the normal baseline along the low-water mark. The subject of that Judgment was the Norwegian straight baseline of 1935, and if that provided the model which other countries tried to achieve, we could all be well pleased and Article 7 would be free from controversy. The profile of a straight baseline which preserves the spirit of Article 7 is well known.

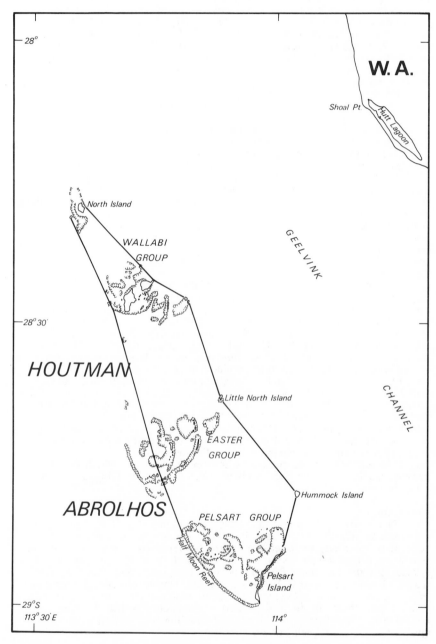

Figure 5: Australian baseline around Houtman Abrolhos.

Proper straight baselines have a number of segments, each of which contains several legs, and the segments are interspersed with sections of the low-water mark of the coasts of mainlands or islands. The length of individual legs is short and thus the entire system conforms closely to the general direction of the coast. The baselines are rarely more than twenty-four nautical miles from the coast, they do not enclose a high proportion of water to land, and they do not extend the outer edge of the territorial sea far beyond the limit which would be established by measurements entirely from the low-water mark.

The letter of Article 7 was mainly fixed by the 1958 Convention, when the delegates had the advantage of the preparatory work done by the International Law Commission in 1956. In its present form, Article 7 contains some imprecise terms which have permitted some countries to interpret the rules in a liberal manner, which is a blatant breach of the spirit of the article. Straight baselines have been drawn along coasts which are neither deeply indented nor fringed with islands. While it is known that the United States of America has been diligent in drawing attention to these infractions, and, where necessary, in asserting their rights of navigation which have been infringed, observers are left with the impression that some countries have cheated with success.

The failure of the civilized nations of the international community to prevent this cheating when it first became apparent has contributed to some of the recent blatant breaches of the rules in Article 7.

My analysis of straight baselines around the world has convinced me that Article 7 is in danger of becoming a dead letter. Such a development will only be avoided if enough members of the international community make a concerted effort to defend the spirit of the rules.

There is no sign that such a campaign will be mounted. Indeed already Cuba, Iceland and Senegal have ratified the Convention although their baselines breach Article 7. This means that the last question I must pose is this. Does it matter if the rules of Article 7 are honored more in the breach than in the observance?

I can only offer the following responses. First, there is no public evidence that the construction of improper straight baselines has created a significant level of international friction. The recent fracas between the air forces of Libya and the United States resulted from disagreement over the closing line of an historic bay rather than a straight baseline drawn in accordance with Article 7.

Second, the most common effect of improper straight baselines is to create extensive internal waters out of what would otherwise have been territorial seas and to push the outer limit of the territorial seas seawards. Now where the internal waters had not previously been considered as such, the right of innocent passage will remain through them. It therefore seems likely that alien states will not be seriously inconvenienced except in respect of overflight. Further, since the additional areas of territorial seas would certainly have fallen within the exclusive economic zone if straight baselines had not been used, alien vessels have again suffered no serious injury, unless they are submarines. However, the question of overflight again arises.

Since the states with powerful navies and air forces will probably ignore claims from straight baselines which are considered to be improper, it seems likely that friction might arise in two distinct situations. First when one of two neighbouring hostile states of equal strength draws an unreasonable straight baseline to put its foe at a disadvantage. Second when excessive claims resulting from illegal baselines impinge upon established commercial air routes.

317

There is one other possible source of friction. If the effect of an improper straight baseline is to push any median line seawards to the disadvantage of a neighboring country, then we have the ingredients for a disagreement. When this happened between the United States and Cuba, the United States drew some construction lines of its own as part of the settlement procedure.

Having invested so much time in studying the provisions of Article 7, I regret the conclusion that it will probably not make much difference to relations between states or to international maritime affairs if Article 7 becomes a dead letter. Perhaps the greatest risk is that such a development will make it harder to defend the spirit and operation of more important articles in the 1982 Convention.

REFERENCES

Beazley, P.B. 1978. *Maritime limits and baselines: a guide to their delineation*. Special publication No. 2. The Hydrographic Society, London.

Bird, E.C.F. 1976. *Coasts*. Second edition, Canberra.

Bird, E.C.F. and Ongkosongo, O.S.R. 1980. *Environmental changes on the coasts of Indonesia*. The United Nations University, Tokyo.

Fitzmaurice, Sir G. 1959. Some results of the Geneva Conference on the Law of the Sea. *International and Comparative Law Quarterly* 8, 73-121. International Court of Justice 1951. *Reports of judgments, advisory opinions and orders*. 116-206. The Hague.

Orlova, G. and Zenkovich, V.P. 1974. Erosion of the shores of the Nile Delta. *Geoforum* 18, 68-72.

Prescott, J.R.V. 1984. Boundaries in Antarctica. In *Australia's Antarctic policy options*, S. Harris (ed.) 83-112, Canberra.

Samojlov, I.V. 1956. *Die Flussmundungen*. Gotha.

Shalowitz, A.L. 1962. *Shore and sea boundaries*. Volume 1 Washington D.C.

The Geographer 1970. Straight baselines: Albania. *Limits in the Seas* No.7. Bureau of Intelligence and Research, Washington D.C.

The Geographer 1978. Straight baselines: Chile. *Limits in the Seas* No. 80. Bureau of Intelligence and Research, Washington D.C.

The Geographer 1980. National claims to maritime jurisdictions *Limits in the Seas* No. 36 (4th revision). Bureau of Intelligence and Research, Washington D.C.

United Nations 1956. *Report of the International Law Commission*. General Assembly, 11th session. Supplement No.9 (A/3159), New York.

United Nations 1958. *Convention on the territorial sea and the contiguous zone*. New York.

United Nations 1983. *The Law of the Sea: United Nations Convention on the Law of the Sea with index and final act of the Third United Nations Conference on the Law of the Sea*. New York.

Whittow, J. 1984. *Dictionary of physical geography*. Bungay, Suffolk.

MARITIME BOUNDARIES:
A GEOGRAPHICAL AND TECHNICAL PERSPECTIVE

Commander Peter B. Beazley
Royal Navy (Retired)
United Kingdom

Introduction

Twenty years ago the task of addressing the question of maritime boundaries would generally have entailed examination of two distinct boundaries: the territorial sea (and perhaps the contiguous zone) and the continental shelf. Ten years ago a third boundary, that between zones of extended fisheries jurisdiction, would have been considered, but still often as being distinct from the other two. Increasingly since then, however, the "single maritime boundary" embracing all zones of jurisdiction at least to a 200-mile limit has been at issue notwithstanding that the states concerned may not claim an exclusive economic zone. Thus in the recent *Gulf of Maine* case, the Court was asked to decide "the course of the single maritime boundary that divides the continental shelf and fisheries zones of Canada and the United States" in the area[1] (although in this instance the area lay wholly outside the limits of the territorial seas).

The 1982 UN Law of the Sea Convention preserves a clear distinction between the provisions governing delimitation of the territorial sea on one hand, and those governing delimitation in the exclusive economic zone or on the continental shelf on the other.[2] Nonetheless this trend towards negotiating a single boundary through the territorial sea and the zones of resource jurisdiction[3] suggests that, whilst such distinctions may still be appropriate in certain circumstances, they are not perceived as being more than one factor to be considered in determining a single line of delimitation through the whole area of the coastal state's jurisdictions. That being so, I do not intend in this paper to discuss the different zones of jurisdiction as presenting separate boundary problems, but as elements governing the approach to a single problem.

State Practice and Judicial Decisions

This paper is concerned with the technical issues that arise in delimitation, but these have to be considered within a juridicial framework without which some of the selfsame issues might not have been identified in a manner that would encourage analysis.

A significant body of state practice has been built up since the 1958 Geneva Convention entered into force. There have been nearly fifty continental shelf agreements and over thirty maritime boundary agreements, although not all are yet in force. These eighty or so agreements involve only sixty sovereign states though, and there are more than 130 possible boundaries that have not yet been negotiated.[4] These would involve at least another seventy countries. So whilst certain conclusions may be drawn from state practice, it is unwise to conclude too much, especially as the very fact that an agreement has been concluded without recourse to arbitration or judgment suggests that the geographical and other conditions were relatively straightforward. Certainly, those areas where agreements have yet to be concluded include a number where considerable goodwill and negotiating skill will be needed to avoid recourse to a dispute settlement procedure.

In the author's view more valuable conclusions are to be drawn from the various judicial awards that have been made since the acceptance in international law of the concept of the continental shelf. The relevant cases are: The 1969 *North Sea Continental Shelf* case; the 1977 *UK/France Continental Shelf Arbitration*; the 1982 *Tunisian/Libyan Arab Jamahiriya Continental Shelf* case; the 1984 *Gulf of Maine Maritime Boundary* case and the 1985 *Guinea/Guinea-Bissau Boundary Arbitration*. Unfortunately, one very important judgment has yet to be announced at the time of writing, that is the *Malta/Libyan Arab Jamahiriya Continental Shelf* Case.

In considering these awards, it must be observed that only two concern maritime boundaries; the others concern continental shelf boundaries. But without making a detailed analysis, it is possible to say that, from a technical point of view, there is little distinction to be made between the cases on that ground.

The Relevant Area and Proportionality

The 1969 *North Sea* cases constitute the first judicial examination of the factors to be taken into account when delimiting a continental shelf and have therefore been the starting point in any argument on the subject. They are also unique in a practical sense because they are the only cases in which the judges were not asked to decide the course of the boundary or at least to specify the practical way in which the principles and rules might be applied to the particular situation. It was left to the Parties to interpret the judgment in the light of the circumstances, and it is not possible to say with any certainty whether the resulting agreed boundaries accurately reflect the Court's views. There are, however, two passages which bear on the question of the role of proportionality and its application.[5]

The first is at Paragraph 93 of the Judgment:

in the present case there are three States whose North Sea coastlines are in fact comparable in length and which, therefore, have been given broadly equal treatment by nature...

The other is at paragraph 98:

A final factor to be taken account of is the element of a reasonable degree of proportionality which a delimitation...ought to bring about between the extent of the continental shelf appertaining to the States concerned and the lengths of their respective coastlines -- these being measured according to their general direction in order to establish the necessary balance between States with straight, and those with markedly concave or convex, coasts, or to reduce very irregular coastlines to their truer proportions ... One method discussed in the course of the proceedings under the name of the principle of the coastal front, consists in drawing a straight baseline between the extreme points at either end of the coast concerned, or in some cases a series of such lines.

The Court did not refer in these cases to a "relevant area," but the first passage cited above can only refer to the whole extent of the North Sea coastlines of the three parties. In considering the equity of the situation, therefore, the Court did not consider some sort of construct that would limit consideration to those areas of continental shelf which could concern only the delimitations with the Federal Republic. The second passage indicates that in applying proportionality, it is not the actual lengths of the coasts with all their indentations and promontories that are to be considered, but rather their actual frontage directly on to the area in question.

The Court of Arbitration in the *UK/France Continental Shelf* case also considered proportionality and concluded that the criteria laid down in the *North Sea* cases were not applicable in all cases, and that "it is disproportion rather than any general principle of proportionality which is the relevant criterion or factor."[6] The question only assumed importance, however, in the Atlantic region (west of a line joining Ushant and the Scilly Isles). Here the Court decided that the Scilly Isles caused a greater projection of the English coast than that of France on to the Atlantic continental shelf. This was a distorting effect to be abated, but not by "any nice calculations of proportionality in regard to the total areas of continental shelf accruing to the parties in the Atlantic region" because in that instance proportionality came "into account only in appreciating whether the Scilly Isles are to be considered a "special circumstance" having distorting effects on the equidistance boundary." The point at issue was "simply whether the geographical situation of the Scilly Isles in relation to the French coast has a distorting effect and is a cause of inequity ..."[7]

Thus in reaching this conclusion the Court eschewed any comparison of coastal lengths with specific area measurements, or any attempts to decide which areas of the UK shelf might be more appropriate for consideration in a delimitation with Ireland than with France (or for that matter, which areas of French shelf might be more appropriate for consideration in a delimitation with Spain). Proportionality became, in effect, a comparison of the westward thrust of the two coasts onto the Atlantic continental shelf.

In the *Tunisia/Libyan Continental Shelf* case, the Court found it necessary to determine what was "the Area in dispute between the Parties and what is the area which is relevant to the delimitation."[8] But the geographical situation with which the Court had to deal was quite different in one important respect from either the *North Sea* or the *Anglo/French* cases (see *Figure 1*). Here there were no third parties in a position of adjacency to either of the states such that the delimitation could affect their rights. The only other states that could be affected were Italy and Malta, both of which stand in a relationship of oppositeness to both Tunisia and Libya and would not be prejudiced by the *direction* of the subsequent boundary.

Furthermore the geographical relationship of the Italian island of Lampedusa and of Malta with the coasts of Tunisia and Libya effectively limited the northern extent of the relevant area. Thus the Court had little difficulty in defining the area as being limited by the coasts of Tunisia and Libya on the west and south, the parallel of latitude through Ras Kaboudia on the north, and the meridian through Ras Tajoura on the east.[9] The choice of Ras Kaboudia and Ras Tajoura specifically depended on the view that the principle of natural prolongation excluded from consideration by the Court "the submarine extension of any part of the coast of one Party which, because of its geographic situation, cannot overlap with the extension of the coast of the other."[10]

Given such a well-defined relevant area, the application of a proportionality rule of the sort envisaged in the *North Sea* cases becomes a relatively simple matter, the one issue to be decided being the precise way in which to measure the coastline lengths. In the event the Court, in the course of specifying the practical way in which the applicable rules and principles applied, considered two measurements: a coastline length omitting small inlets, creeks and lagoons, and a coastal front using straight lines (one in the case of Libya and two for Tunisia).[11] The ratios were approximately

coast lines	Libya:Tunisia	1:2.2
coastal fronts	" "	1:1.9
seabed areas	" "	1:1.5

which are the only indications of what might be considered a *reasonable degree of proportionality* in cases where such a comparison is appropriate.

In the *Gulf of Maine* case (see *Figure 2*), the Chamber was asked to describe the course of a single maritime boundary from a specific point A, agreed by the parties, but lying outside the limits of the territorial sea, to a point to be determined by the Chamber but lying within a triangle embraced with an area of more than 1000 square nautical miles. This triangle embraced significant lengths of 200-mile arcs measured from the Canadian and U.S. coasts, but did not extend as far as the outer limit of the continental shelf defined in Article 76 of the 1982 UN Law of the Sea Convention. The Chamber determined the "delimitation area" to be the whole of the Gulf of Maine, including a substantial part of the Bay of Fundy, and the sea areas "lying seaward of, and over and against the Gulf, between bounds converging towards the outer edges of the triangle."[12] However, the exact limits of this area are not important since the Chamber did not refer to or apply any test of proportionality in the sense discussed in earlier paragraphs.

A geographical situation like that of the Gulf of Maine certainly presents problems in determining a relevant area, for whilst the Gulf itself is well-defined, the area to seaward is not. If the lateral limits are to be, say, perpendicular to a "general direction," a decision must be made as to what general direction. Different choices will affect the limits and so affect the proportionality calculations. Neither is the seaward limit clear-cut for a single maritime boundary which does not extend to its full potential length. These difficulties were well illustrated by the pleadings of the parties.

The Chamber did, however, consider proportionality in relation to the lengths of coastline, not for a comparison of ratios of areas but to correct, on the basis of the inequalities of the coastline lengths, the "untoward consequences" of applying a median line.[13] The ratio of coastline lengths (measured in their general directions) around the Gulf and part of the Bay of Fundy determined the extent to which a median line based also on "general directions" should be moved towards Nova Scotia to abate the cut-off effect that would have disadvantaged the United States.

The last case to be considered is that of the *Guinea/Guinea-Bissau Maritime Boundary* in which the Arbitral Tribunal was also asked to describe the course of the boundary. This case concerned two states with relatively short coastlines of almost the same lengths (154 miles) and shorter than the width of the exclusive economic zone, and each flanked by another State the boundaries with which have yet to be agreed. In such circumstances any determination of the relevant area would be meaningless unless account were to be taken of the possible boundaries with third parties, but any such determination by the Tribunal must have prejudiced negotiations. The approach of the Tribunal reflects the

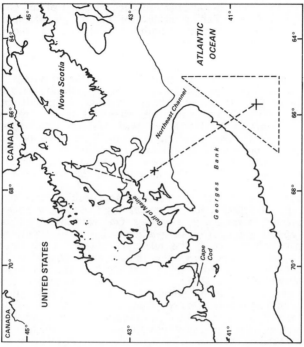

Figure 2.

Source: Delimitation of Maritime Boundaries in the Gulf of Maine Area, Constitution of Chamber, Order of 20 January 1982, *ICJ Reports 1982*, p. 36.

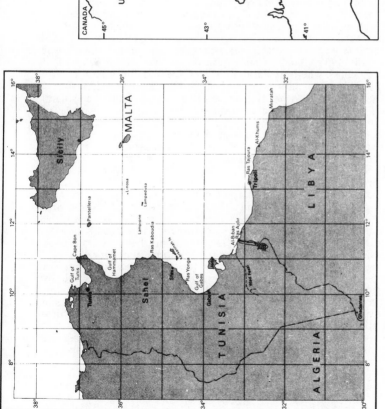

Figure 1

Source: International Court of Justice, *Reports of Judgments, Advisory Opinions, and Orders. Case Concerning Delimitation of the Maritime Boundary in the Gulf of Maine Area.*

approaches of the Court in the *Anglo-French* case and of the Chamber in the *Gulf of Maine* case. Taking account of the Bijagos archipelago of Guinea-Bissau in measuring the lengths of coastlines has the "consequence that the coasts of the two States are considered by the Tribunal to be of the same length. Thus, with regard to proportionality, neither Party can claim an additional advantage."[14]

Proportionality has figured prominently in the Pleadings of the Parties in the *Malta/Libya* case, both as to the relevant area and as to its application. This is particularly interesting because it concerns states which are clearly opposite each other and so in a relationship in which the Court in the North Sea cases has stated that "the continental shelf area off, and dividing, opposite States, can be claimed by each of them to be a natural prolongation of its territory. These prolongations meet and overlap, and can therefore only be delimited by means of a median line ..."[15] The judgment in the *Malta/Libya* case is awaited with interest.

It can be seen that in the cases so far decided, the role of proportionality in an actual delimitation has been used only once in the manner expressed in the *North Sea* cases. One may infer that such a method of applying proportionality is generally possible only where specific limits can be set to the relevant area and those limits are set largely by the geography without bringing into question the effects they may have on third parties.[16] In the *Gulf of Maine* case, proportionality, determined in a slightly different way, was used as a means of locating one sector of the boundary. This use of proportionality partly as a technical tool is discussed later.

The term "general direction" in relation to coastal delineation has been in juridicial use for many years, generally in relation to baselines. It was used in that specific sense in the Judgment in the 1951 *Anglo-Norwegian Fisheries* case.[17] It was taken up in the same sense in Article 4 of the 1958 Geneva Convention on the Territorial Sea and Contiguous Zone,[18] where at Paragraph 2 of the Article, which deals with the use of a system of straight baselines, it states that such baselines "must not depart to any appreciable extent from the general direction of the coast." It occurs again in the equivalent Article of the 1982 Convention.[19]

As we have seen, the term was used by the Court in the *North Sea* cases in relation to determining lengths for application of proportionality. The term is used in the *Tunisia/Libya* judgment in a similar sense.[20] It was also used by both parties in the *Gulf of Maine* case to illustrate the macro-geography of the Atlantic seaboard,[21] to derive a direction from which to take a perpendicular as the direction of the boundary,[22] and as a method of measuring coastline lengths for a proportionality test.[23] The *Guinea/Guinea-Bissau* case used the term "general direction" both in comparing the coastline of the parties and for a line extending over a significantly greater extent than the coasts of the two parties to derive a direction for the maritime boundary.[24]

The term "coastal front" was used in the *North Sea* judgment[25] in a manner implying a rather broader treatment than "general direction" with less regard to changes in direction, at least along the coast of any one country. On the other hand it has been used in the *Gulf of Maine* case[26] in exactly the same way as Canada used the term "general direction" for testing proportionality.

Two questions present themselves: is there a distinction between the two terms, and are there any indications of the lengths of coasts to be considered? Unfortunately the short review above does not give any real guidance.

As to the use of terms, it seems that "coastal front" properly describes a line that is more generalized than the term "general direction" alone might suggest, but is really relevant only to measurement of distance and seems to the writer to be closely linked to the concept of the natural prolongation of the land territory of a state. The term "general direction," which cannot be interpreted with any greater precision, is the only proper term that can be used when actual direction rather than distance is required.

It is not then surprising that, if it were possible to determine any guidelines for the actual lengths of coasts to be considered, such an exercise would require an analysis of breadth that lies beyond the scope of a paper of this length. Such an analysis, furthermore, would need to take into account the use of the term in relation to baselines.

Adjacent and Opposite Coasts

The 1958 Conventions on the Territorial Sea and Contiguous Zone[27] and on the Continental Shelf,[28] in the articles concerning delimitation between states, considered the two cases of states that are opposite and of those that are adjacent to each other. In the *North Sea* cases, the Court considered the relationship of the Netherlands and Denmark to be neither that of "opposite" nor of "adjacent" states,[29] which suggested a third category of relationship. The Court also noted that a given equidistance line might "partake in varying degree of the nature both of a median and of a lateral line";[30] in other words, the coasts of the two states might at one point be *opposite* and at another *adjacent*.

A real significance was attached to the distinction particularly because of the conclusion drawn from the judgment that, in the case of opposite coasts, an equidistance line would in general be held to produce an equitable result, whilst it would not necessarily do so in the case of adjacent coasts.[31] The Court of Arbitration in the *Anglo-French* case, in rejecting a French argument that the Atlantic region of the area of dispute was neither an opposite nor an adjacent states situation, affirmed that in principle all situations fall into one or the other category.[32] But later, at paragraph 239, the Court stated that the appropriateness or otherwise of any method used to effect an equitable delimitation is always "a function or reflection of the geographical and other relevant circumstances of the particular case," and went on to say:

In a situation where the coasts of two States are opposite each other, the median line will normally effect a broadly equal and equitable delimitation. But this is simply because of the geometrical effects of applying the equidistance principle to an area of continental shelf which, in fact, lies between coasts that, in fact, face each other across that continental shelf. In short, the equitable character of the delimitation results not from the *legal* designation of the situation as one of "opposite" States *but from its actual geographical character as such.* Similarly, in the case of "adjacent" States it is the lateral geographical relationship of the two coasts, when combined with a large extension of the continental shelf seawards from those coasts, which makes individual geographical features on either coast more prone to render the geometrical effects of applying the equidistance principle inequitable than in the case of "opposite" States. The greater risk in these cases that the equidistance method may produce an inequitable delimitation thus also results not from the *legal* designation of the situation as one of "adjacent" States but from its *actual geographical character as one involving laterally related coasts.*

This general approach was not contradicted by the Court in the *Tunisia/Libya* case, but the Court identified a situation where the coastal configuration could go a long way to transforming the relationship from adjacency to oppositeness without going the whole way, and so making equidistance a factor to be given more weight than would otherwise be the case.[33] The reason for this opinion can perhaps be seen from the coastal configuration (see *Figure 1*). The Court proposed a line running approximately north-northeast from the land boundary terminus at Ras Ajdir to just north of the 34th parallel. Because of the pronounced change of direction at the westernmost point of the Gulf of Gabes the coasts do then appear to be opposite, with the Kerkennah Islands and Ras Kaboudia opposite Ras Tajoura and the coast immediately west of it. At this point, then, an equidistance line between those sections of coast would be oriented to the northeast, and if continued for any distance in that direction, it would soon again become a lateral line. It was perhaps for this reason that the Court was unable to accept a complete transformation of the relationship.

In the *Gulf of Maine* case (see *Figure 2*), the Chamber identified sectors of the coasts which were clearly either adjacent -- the coast of Maine at the back of the Gulf and the coast of Nova Scotia extended by an imaginary line across the entrance to the Bay of Fundy -- and those which were clearly opposite -- the coasts of Massachusetts and the coast of Nova Scotia southeast from near Yarmouth.[34] The Chamber apparently did not believe it necessary to classify the third sector of the line southeast from the closing line of the Gulf. At Paragraph 206 the Chamber says that

it is only in the northeastern sector of the Gulf that the prevailing relationship of the coasts of the United States and Canada is that of lateral adjacency as between parts of the coast of Maine and part of the Nova Scotian coast.

In the writer's view, this can only be read as a reference to coastal relationships within the Gulf, and it should not be interpreted as meaning that the third sector of the line must result from considerations of a third, but unspecified, coastal relationship. Everything in fact points to this sector being in a situation involving laterally related coasts, as described by the Court of Arbitration.[35]

In the *Guinea/Guinea-Bissau* case, the Tribunal considered that the coasts were partially adjacent and partially opposite, but that it was not necessary to dwell on the point. It was more important in the Tribunal's view that there should be no unusual features in the relevant maritime zones.[36] Although the Court of Arbitration has suggested the proper approach to the question, it is not, from a purely technical point of view, always possible to state unequivocally that one or another situation prevails.

This is well illustrated by comparison of the *Tunisia/Libya* and *Gulf of Maine* cases. *Figures 1* and *2* show a striking similarity between the relationship of the coasts of Tunisia and Libya and the relationship of the coasts of Nova Scotia and Maine. If a line is drawn from Ras

Kaboudia to the southern entrance point of the Gulf of Gabes, it forms an angle of only a little more than 90 degrees with a line from Ras Tajoura to the same point. This situation compares with a line from Cape Sable to the international boundary between the U.S. and Canada (thereby ignoring the Bay of Fundy) and a straight line representing the general direction of the back of the Gulf of Maine. There is a difference in this comparison, but not a significant one, in the relative positions of the international boundaries. In the Gulf of Maine case the sectors of coast (those just mentioned) which governed the first segment of the line extended to a position about 120 miles from the international boundary, but still well within the arms of the Gulf. In the *Tunisia/Libya* case, however, at a point only a little over sixty miles from the boundary, the relationship is seen to change from adjacency to something approaching oppositeness. One is thus faced with a problem. It is clear that where two more or less straight but extensive coasts meet at a pronounced angle, they are at that point undoubtedly in a relationship of adjacency. At what point does that relationship change? This may seem to be no more than a semantic point which is irrelevant from a technical point of view. It may, however, be of considerable conceptual importance if the relevant area of delimitation is to be divided into sectors in the manner used to some extent in the *Tunisia/Libya* Judgment and even more markedly in the *Gulf of Maine* Judgment. One possible answer -- which does not however fit the *Gulf of Maine* decision -- is to distinguish between the territorial sea and the wider maritime zones of jurisdiction beyond. In the situation postulated above, there may be features which would produce a distorting effect within the narrow band of the territorial sea, whilst further seaward their effects may be eliminated by counterbalancing features as is frequently the case where the coasts are opposite. Thus outside the territorial sea these coasts might be considered to have entered into an "opposite" relationship. It must be emphasized that, in discussing cases where an opposite coast relationship was determined as existing, it did not follow that equidistance lines as described in Article 6 of the Continental Shelf Convention were adopted. This will be discussed later.

Finally, it is necessary to revert briefly to the Court's conclusion in the *North Sea* case that the Netherlands and Denmark were neither opposite nor adjacent.[37] This suggested, in the light of the claims of those states at that time, that there was some third category of relationship. But that is ruled out by the Court of Arbitration. In fact, because of the presence of a third state lying between them, and the unacceptability of boundaries that would cut off the natural prolongation of a state in that situation, the Netherlands and Denmark simply did not lie in a relationship that permitted a delimitation between them.[38]

Geology and Geomorphology

In the *North Sea* cases, the Court said that it can be useful to consider the geology of the shelf "in order to find out whether the direction taken by certain configurational features should influence delimitation because, in certain localities, they point up the whole notion of the appurtenance of the continental shelf to the State whose territory it does in fact prolong."[39] Later it listed the physical and geological structure of the shelf as one of the factors to be taken into account in a delimitation.[40] The Court noted that in the continental shelf boundary agreement between Norway and U.K., in the North Sea the existence of the Norwegian Trough with water depths of considerably more than 200 meters was ignored when constructing the equidistance boundary.[41]

In the *Anglo-French* case the United Kingdom put forward an alternative submission that the Hurd Deep and the Hurd Deep Fault Zone interrupted the continuity of the continental shelf.[42] The Deep itself is about eighty miles long but only between one and three miles wide with water depths about forty-five meters greater than those of the surrounding seabed. But the Court considered that these features were not "capable of exercising a material influence on the delimitation of the boundary" and that they did not "disrupt the essential unity of the continental shelf."[43] In the *Tunisia/Libya* case, Tunisia contended that the Tripolitanian Furrow formed a natural submarine frontier (it runs roughly parallel to the coast of Libya between longitudes 13 degrees and 15 degrees east approximately). It was regarded by Tunisia as prolonging the Gulf of Gabes.[44] But the Court rejected the contention and concluded that since both Libya and Tunisia "derive continental shelf title from a natural prolongation common to both territories, the ascertainment of the extent of the areas of shelf apertaining to each state must be governed by criteria of international law other than those taken from physical features."[45]

In the *Gulf of Maine* case the Chamber stated, with regard to various submarine features, that: "Even the most accentuated of these features, namely the Northeast Channel, does not have the characteristics of a real trough marking the dividing line between two geomorphologically distinct units. It is quite simply a natural feature of the area."[46] This channel is about twenty miles wide with water depths of about 230 meters. It separates the important fishing grounds of Georges Bank from Browns Bank.

The Chamber also examined the relevance of another element that had to be taken account of: the "water column." The United States, in its pleadings, identified three different oceanographic and ecological regimes in the waters of the Gulf area and submitted that they were divided by natural boundaries of which the Northeast Channel was one. On that ground it could form the basis for drawing the boundary which would be valid both for the exclusive fishery zone and the seabed and subsoil. The Chamber was not convinced of the "possibility of discerning any genuine, sure and stable 'natural boundaries' in so fluctuating an environment as the waters of the ocean, their flora and fauna."[47]

In the *Guinea/Guinea-Bissau* case, the Tribunal declined to accept that features like the Fosse du rio Grande and the Fosse du rio Cacine, which are from three to ten kilometers wide but only some meters below the surrounding seabed, could detract from the unity of the shelf.[48]

It is clear that for a submarine feature to be of sufficient importance to be regarded as constituting a discontinuity, such as to bound a state's natural prolongation or to form a natural frontier, it must be of major geomorphological or geological significance. There are examples in state practice where even such major features as tectonic plate boundaries appear to have been disregarded in delimitation agreements,[49] but the question has again been raised in the *Malta/Libya Continental Shelf* case with regard to more significant features than those considered in earlier cases. Until that Judgment is read, it is too early to draw further conclusions.

Relationship of EEZ and Continental Shelf
The 1982 Law of the Sea Convention Article 76(1) defined the
continental shelf as comprising:

> the seabed and subsoil of the submarine areas that extend
> beyond its territorial sea throughout the natural prolongation of
> its land territory to the outer edge of the continental margin, or
> to a distance of 200 nautical miles from the baselines from which
> the breadth of the territorial sea is measured where the outer
> edge of the continental margin does not extend up to that dis-
> tance.

It is important to know whether this Article expresses customary
law and is thus applicable to all states whether or not they are signatories and whether or not the Convention is in force. It is equally
important to know which is the main criterion of the two given: "distance" or "natural prolongation." These questions may be of great importance, particularly in the case of opposite states where, for instance,
the natural prolongation of one state might extend beyond 200 miles to
a distance of less than 200 miles from another state. Alternatively, it
would be important where two states lie at a distance, say, of less
than 200 miles from each other, but separated by a geological discontinuity such as to halt the natural prolongation of one state so that it
does not extend to the equidistance line (that this situation exists is
one of the contentions of Libya in the *Malta/Libya* case).
This is essentially a legal question that has not yet -- at the
time of writing -- been addressed by the courts, although in his separate opinion in the *Tunisia/Libya* case, Judge Jimenez de Arechaga considered the distance criterion to be paramount.[50] It is beyond the
competence of the writer to attempt a legal analysis of this point, so
he must content himself with pointing to the problem without suggesting
an answer.

Economic Considerations
The Judgment in the *North Sea* cases took no account of economic
considerations as such, but listed the natural resources of the continental shelf areas involved -- so far as known or readily ascertainable
-- as one of the factors to be taken into account in a delimitation.[51]
It was more specific, however, in an earlier passage where it said that,
in relation to delimitation between adjacent states, a factor to be
taken into consideration was "the unity of any deposits."[52] But from
the remainder of the paragraph just cited, it seems clear to the writer
that the Court was addressing the specific situation that had arisen
over exploration or exploitation licenses granted by the parties in the
area under dispute; it also made clear that it saw agreements for the
exploitation of cross-boundary deposits, such as had been negotiated by
the U.K., Norway and the Netherlands as a perfectly satisfactory way of
dealing with the problem.
In the *Tunisia/Libya* case, both parties pleaded economic factors
to be taken into account. Tunisia invoked her relative poverty in terms
of natural resources and claimed that fishing resources deriving from
historic rights and "historic waters" must be taken into account as
supplementing its national economy. Libya argued that the presence or
absence of oil or gas in the oil wells in the shelf areas appertaining
to either party should be taken into account. The Court, however, took
the view that such economic factors could not be taken into account;

that they were variables which unpredictable factors might at any time cause to change. The presence of oil wells in the area to be delimited might "be an element to be taken into account in the process of weighing all relevant factors to achieve an equitable result."[53]

The Chamber in the *Gulf of Maine* case also considered that socio-economic factors could not be used to determine the course of the line. The Chamber was bound to achieve a result on the basis of law, and, in an operation of the type entrusted to it, that required the use of criteria essentially to be determined in relation to the geographical features of the area. Only after the Chamber had envisaged the drawing of a delimitaution line should other criteria be taken into account to ensure an equitable result.[54]

The Arbitral Tribunal in the *Guinea/Guinea-Bissau* case also rejected economics as a factor to be taken into account. Both states were developing countries faced with immense economic and financial difficulties which an increase in the resources of the sea could mitigate. It also took the view that it would be unsafe to base a delimitation on such variable factors.[55] The authorities have thus far, then, rejected economic factors in general as a matter to be taken into account in drawing an equitable boundary, but, as with proportionality, they may be used to test whether the boundary is equitable. Account may, however, be taken of certain, more concrete factors like the existence of an oil well. Perhaps that might also include an area that was habitually fished by only one of the parties, or other similar factors.

Equidistance and Equitable Principles

If application of the equidistance principle in the strict sense was ever widely regarded as a mandatory rule of customary international law, neither judicial pronouncements from 1969 onwards nor state practice has supported the view. Without further call upon the authorities, it is clear that in practice any delimitation agreed upon between parties will have had regard to equitable principles. To that extent, Articles 74 and 83 of the 1982 Convention do not, in the writer's view, change anything. It is where the parties' conceptions of what constitutes equitable principles differ that problems arise, and this paper does not set out to provide answers to philosophical questions. But studying existing agreements and judgments does give some concept of how states have viewed the matter.

An absolutely strict application of equidistance is very likely to produce a line that has by far too many twists and turns to make it suitable for use as a practical boundary, and there is only a handful of agreements in which such a strict line has been adopted. Almost invariably, it will have been simplified. The extent of this simplification may vary widely, but in general it takes two forms: either it is arranged so that approximately equal areas are exchanged in the process, or the line or segments of the line are simply straightened whilst maintaining the general orientation and direction of the original. Analysis of a given boundary will normally provide convincing evidence whether either method has been employed. Sometimes the agreement states that the boundary is based on equidistance. By analyzing existing agreements in that way, it can be shown that equidistance in the above sense has been used as the basis from which to work in over 70% of cases, but that the effect of distorting features like islands may have been modified by ignoring them, giving them partial effect, or enclaving them. Most of the agreements not based on equidistance concern adjacent states.

330

The Anglo-French Case

The Court decided that, although Article 6 of the 1958 Continental Shelf Convention was applicable between the parties, both the Channel Islands and the Scilly Isles constituted special circumstances. Within the English Channel the boundary should be an equidistance line (simplified by agreement between the parties) which took no account of the Channel Islands; they were enclaved within a twelve-mile limit. Account was taken of the Eddystone Rock for reasons of estoppel but the Court expressed no view on its legal status. In the Atlantic sector westward of the Channel the Court awarded an equidistance line which gave half effect to the Scilly Isles -- achieved in theory by taking a line half way between, one giving full effect to those islands and one giving no effect to them. The manner in which this was actually carried out resulted in a request for interpretation of the Decision by the Court, but that hinged on a purely technical question.

The Tunisia-Libya Case

In this case, the Court made a more pronounced use of a division of the area into sectors. Since the coasts were adjacent at the land frontier, the Court, for this "adjacency" segment, adopted what it had identified as a *de facto* line which was "the result of the manner in which both parties initially granted concessions for offshore exploration and exploitation of oil and gas."[56] The direction (026 degrees) was also considered to approximate to a line perpendicular to the coast at the frontier point. A true perpendicular in *plane* geometry is, of course, equidistant in relation to its baseline.

The second sector, where the relationship of the coasts had nearly been transformed to oppositeness,[57] was held to hinge on the marked change of direction of the Tunisian coast at the head of the Gulf of Gabes. The latitude of this point was chosen as marking the division between the two sectors, and hence the seaward terminus of the first sector line.

In the second sector, the Court recognized that an equidistance line, which by its nature takes account of the variations in the relevant coastlines, would follow a more easterly direction than the line decided upon for the first sector. Acknowledging that in this sector the coasts were to some extent "opposite," the Court considered that the change of direction in the line resulting from application of equidistance should be reflected to some extent in the Court's line. To determine that direction, however, it did not use equidistance but selected a line of bearing halfway between lines from the head of the Gulf to, on one hand, Ras Kaboudia, and, on the other, the seaward coast of the Kerkennah Islands. This line of bearing (052 degrees) was the direction that the second segment of the line was to take from the seaward terminus of the first sector.

It is seen that in this case equidistance as such was not used by the Court but that in both sectors account was in fact taken of it. Moreover, in the second sector the Kerkennah Islands were seen as being features of which some, but not full, account should be taken, so they were given a form of half effect. But whilst the methodology for the first sector is readily understandable, it is difficult to see in the line as a whole any sort of geometrical rule that can be taken as guidance for similar cases elsewhere. This is made the more difficult because any sort of equidistance line in the second sector would run in a markedly more easterly direction (even if the Kerkennah Islands were disregarded entirely). The actual line suggests that greater weight has

331

been given to the natural prolongation of Libya's landmass northwards than to Tunisia's natural prolongation eastwards; an idea which perhaps inspired the United States' theory of primary and secondary coasts put forward in the *Gulf of Maine* case (see text below at note 57).

The Gulf of Maine Case

The Gulf of Maine (see *Figure 2*) can be described as an open rectangle roughly twice as wide as it is deep, with its entrance facing southeast and the general direction of the coast being northeast/southwest. At the northeast corner is the very considerable arm of the Bay of Fundy adding a sizeable area to that of the main part of the Gulf. The international boundary previously agreed between the U.S. and Canada meets the shores of the Gulf at the northeast corner of the rectangle and on the northwestern shore of the entrance to the Bay of Fundy. As described above, the Chamber divided the area into three sectors. As in the *Tunisia/Libya* case, the Chamber rejected the strict equidistance line which would form a continuum throughout the area of delimitation. Instead, it examined each sector separately. In the first sector a constraint had been imposed by the parties in requiring that the boundary should start at a specific Point A -- a location which corresponded with an intersection of the lines representing the fishing zones claimed by the parties in 1976 when they decided on extensions of their fishery jurisdictions.

In order to arrive at the course of the boundary, the Chamber took the general directions of the back of the Gulf and the two wings. Although not described as such, or directly derived in that manner, the first segment of the line is a line from A parallel to the bisector of the general directions of the back of the Gulf and the northeast wing (Nova Scotia). So this line can be seen as a line of equidistance determined from lines of general direction which ignore all the various ins and outs of the coast, individual islands, rocks and so on.

The second segment of the line is a median line between the two general direction lines representing the wings of the Gulf, with the line moved towards the Canadian coast by an amount determined by the ratio of U.S. coast to Canadian coast (including a part of the Bay of Fundy). A small correction to that ratio was made in order to give half effect to the Canadian Seal Island in the entrance to the Gulf. The third segment of the line begins at the point where the second segment intersects the closing line of the Gulf, which was agreed as running from Cape Sable to Nantucket Island, and consists of a perpendicular to that closing line.

A strict equidistance line which took no account of Seal Island would, at some point outside the Gulf and over Georges Bank, become the perpendicular bisector of the line Cape Sable-Nantucket. That being so, the two last segments of the line can be seen as simplified equidistance lines displaced to abate, first, the cut-off effect that would otherwise disadvantage the United States by reason of the position of the international boundary, and, second, to give partial effect to Seal Island. In its pleadings the U.S. advanced the theory of primary and secondary coasts; thus those coasts which faced the Atlantic Ocean were primary coasts. The short length of Canadian coastline formed by the southwest end of Nova Scotia was a secondary coast constituting a special feature which should not be used in the delimitation "to deprive the United States of the extension of its primary coastal front into the sea."[58] This theory was rejected by the Chamber as arising from premises and deductions of an *a priori* nature.[59]

332

The Guinea/Guinea-Bissau Case

The boundary award in this case can be divided into two sectors. The inshore sector adopted, in effect, a part of the southern limit of the Treaty of 1886 between Portugal and France which delimited the area within which any land territory was agreed to be Portuguese. In this sector a strict equidistance line would have been unduly complicated. The Tribunal noted that the 1886 limit, whilst not intended as a maritime boundary, had a more equitable character than an equidistance line, and that until 1958 it had not been crossed by either France or Portugal for matters concerning construction of navigational aids, laying of cables and so on. It also noted that the Court in the *Tunisia/Libya* case stated that the position of the intersection of the land frontier with the coastline was a circumstance to be taken into account.[60] In the instant case a short stretch of land frontier was coincidental with the southern Treaty limit, and the southern limit for a further twenty miles seaward followed the Passe des Pilots which was a geographical extension of, and followed the same direction as, the land frontier which corresponded broadly to the perpendicular to the coast.[61] This exposition requires neither elaboration nor comment.

The second sector is approximately a perpendicular to the line from Almadies Point in Senegal to Cape Shilling in Sierra Leone which the Tribunal considered best to represent the overall configuration of that region of the west coast of Africa.[62] In selecting a line which rejected strict equidistance the Tribunal avoided the danger of producing a cut-off effect for one or the other party by interplay with the boundaries of the states flanking the parties on either side.

It is worth noting at this point that this macro-geographical approach has been adopted over greater distances. The west coast of South America lies in a generally north-south direction. Chile, Peru, Ecuador and Columbia have all agreed boundaries that are parallels of latitude. In the case of the Gambia, which has a very short coastline lying in a north-south direction and flanked on either side by Senegal, Gambia and Senegal agreed in 1975 that the maritime boundaries between the two states should be parallels of latitude. The strict equidistance lines would have converged at a distance of about 140 miles from the coast and cut off the Gambia's natural prolongation.

As has been seen above, the criteria for constructing a maritime boundary are essentially to be determined in relation to the geographical features of the area. These are seen to be the configuration of the coast and the existence, size and location of the off-lying islands and rocks. To those may be added features like low-tide elevations. Existing structures like oil wells may also be taken into consideration. General economic considerations if relevant should be used only as one of the tests of equity after the course of the line has been determined. In the *Gulf of Maine* case the Chamber in approaching the technical task of delimitation, and having rejected the use of equidistance, went on to say that "the practical method to be applied must be a geometrical one based on respect for the geographical situation of the coasts between which the delimitation is to be effected."[63] Both the weight of the state practice and of judicial opinion bears out these requirements.

Equidistance may be modified in many ways, some of which have been mentioned above. Those were all modifications to the strict concept of equidistance. Furthermore, in the case of opposite coasts it is generally acknowledged that the method normally provides an equitable result. The actual geographical conditions in areas where delimitation is to be carried out vary enormously, and it has been demonstrated that

333

there are other ways than strict equidistance by which an equitable delimitation may be achieved. For instance, to achieve an equitable balance between disparate coastlines it may be necessary to use notional baselines or general directions of the coast from which to construct an equidistance line. A perpendicular to a general direction line will often provide a simple solution to the problem of the lateral line, and as was seen above (text at note 61), a similar solution may facilitate matters when there are three or more adjacent states with relatively short coastlines; a perpendicular is also a form of equidistance. Taking the concept or principle of equidistance in the broader sense considered above, and not in the strict sense of the 1958 Convention, state practice shows that the concept has been adopted in over 50% of the adjacent-state agreements not based on "strict" equidistance. Thus it can be seen that the weight of opinion falls heavily on the side of the principle of equidistance as providing the best basis for determining an equitable boundary. The *Tunisia/Libya* Judgment unfortunately provides only slight support for this view, but it is again seen to predominate in the *Gulf of Maine* case. That is not to say that strict equidistance is necessarily acceptable -- particularly for adjacent states -- although in practice it is generally the best point from which to start in order to gauge what specific features or configurations produce a distorting effect that must be corrected.

In both the *Tunisia/Libya* and the *Gulf of Maine* cases, different sectors of the areas of delimitation were classified as to the coastal relationships, and the different segments of the single maritime boundary were independently determined accordingly. The particular merit of this approach, in the writer's opinion, is that it may facilitate application of corrections designed to abate particular distorting features. Because of the way in which a strict equidistance line is generated by the base-points, the transition from one relationship to another is not clear cut, although the final result of each method may be very similar if there are no corrections required to compensate for distorting features.

What if, having applied geometry to the actual geographical features of the area, the resulting boundary line is tested by other criteria, such as proportionality or economic factors, and found to be inequitable? In practice this is unlikely to arise since the relevant factors will have been taken into account when deciding on the appropriate geometry. But looking at the theory one can only conclude either that the tests are wrong -- proportionality has been applied in a manner inappropriate to the circumstances, for instance -- or incorrect methods have been used to determine the line in the particular geographical circumstances. At all events there is now a body of practice and judicial decisions which allows a reasonable assessment to be made in a wide range of differing conditions.

Special Circumstances

Given the infinite variety of geographical circumstances that exist, it must be assumed that there is an almost infinite variety -- or at least degree -- of special circumstances that may exist. The most common are the presence of islands or rocks, and the position of the land frontier in relation to the topography of the coastline. Islands which, if given full effect in constructing a boundary, would cause an inequity, have been treated in four ways:

* ignored entirely, generally where they are very small and do not lie in a position where the boundary would pass close to them;[64]
* semi-enclaved by deviating the boundary around them at a set distance such as the breadth of the territorial sea;[65]
* completely enclaved -- usually within a 12-mile limit -- when they lie too far on the "wrong" side of the boundary;[66]
* given partial effect.[67]

The method of giving partial effect has usually been to determine the course of two strict equidistance lines, one of which takes the island or feature into account and the other of which does not. The partial effect line divides the area between the two lines in the desired proportion.[68] Where the coasts are opposite each other, this usually results in a limited deviation of the boundary, but with adjacent coasts it results in an angular deviation which produces an increasing separation with distance.

Attempts have been made to formulate objective criteria by which to assess the weight to be given to different islands in a delimitation. Unfortunately none has been successful because there are too many variables -- size, location, population, economic importance and so on -- all of which have to be gauged in relation to the states themselves rather than by absolute criteria. It is this lack of any objective test coupled with a very wide divergence in state practice that have defeated any attempt to provide firm guidelines.

Special circumstances arising from the relationship of the land frontier to the topography are typically due to relatively local coastal features like headlands or near-shore islands. The effect of such features can be abated by generalizing the coastline in that locality, or similar treatment. Where, as in the *North Sea* cases, it is the relationship of the land frontier to the land mass as a whole that causes a distorting effect, similar methods to those suggested by the Court may be used but would not have solved the problem that arose in the *Gulf of Maine* case. In that instance the Chamber moved the second and third segments of the line by an amount determined by the ratios of the respective coastal lengths.[69] The half effect given to Seal Island was also achieved by moving the same segments of the line. As the Chamber pointed out,[70] these corrections made a lateral and not an angular displacement to the line, which resulted in a constant ratio of length of line to areal displacement.

A note of caution should be sounded. The result achieved by proportionality in the *Gulf of Maine* case resulted from the particular configuration of the coast -- where the Gulf can be seen as being nearly a rectangle twice as wide as it is deep -- the position of the land frontier, inclusion of some part of the Bay of Fundy in the calculation of the ratio, and from the fact that the ratio was applied across the narrowest part of the Gulf and not across the full width of the "rectangle." An unconsidered application of this method in other approximately similar circumstances might not give an equitable result.[71] For instance, given the same configuration but with dimensions reduced to a tenth, it is not clear that such a solution would be appropriate, since the imperatives of territorial sea delimitation would be paramount. Conversely, were the dimensions to be doubled, the relationship of the "opposite" coasts would be too remote to be taken into account. The method provides no guidance in a situation where there is no opposite coast such as that provided by Massachusetts. Neither is it certain that an equitable result would be achieved if the land frontier was at a different relative position -- say, along the wing of the indentation.

Technical Problems

There are many technical problems that arise in delimitation. Each particular case is likely to give rise to its own particular difficulties, and the solutions require a technical knowledge beyond the scope of this paper to address. Many of these have been dealt with elsewhere.[72] It is perhaps worth mentioning, however, the more obvious points to bear in mind in delimitation.

There is an obvious need for as accurate information as possible on the existence and location of any relevant features -- islands, rocks, etc. -- as well as of the coastline itself. A common geodetic datum must be agreed upon, and sometimes a vertical datum also, since the latter governs the location of the low water line. There must also be an awareness of the significance of the way in which a particular map projection depicts terrestrial features.

The importance of this last point has a particular relevance to one aspect of delimitation dealt with in this paper. The properties of the Mercator projection which is so widely used for nautical charts have been discussed in other works. Just as a "straight line" on the earth's surface cannot normally be depicted by a "straight line" on that projection, so also two straight lines that are perpendicular to each other on that projection do not represent straight lines perpendicular to each other on the earth's surface. These points have significance when considering terms like *general direction* or *perpendicular to a general direction*. The *Gulf of Maine* and *Guinea/Guinea-Bissau* cases illustrate two approaches to the problem. There are difficulties in either approach because very frequently irreconcilable inconsistencies tend to intrude as a result of the various conceptual or semantic approaches to the problem of delimitation over a long period. This is mainly because the *corpus* of authoritative juristic writing has inevitably perpetuated what are now, from a technical viewpoint, outdated and inadequate terms.

Conclusions

Attempts to condense into a paper of this length all the arguments and rationales that contribute to the technical aspects of delimitation give rise to charges of over-simplification, or that it has concentrated too much on legal rather than technical matters. But unless the legalities are reduced to a set of relatively simple conclusions, and unless some of the reasoning is given, it will be difficult to apply technical knowledge effectively, or perhaps for lawyers, to appreciate the technical issues. The techniques of delimitation should not be allowed to suffer the ills that arise from specialized compartmentalization -- ills that have already been experienced. Lack of space has prevented any examination of the purely technical questions touched on in the last section.

The paper has not touched on the place of Article 6 of the 1958 Continental Shelf Convention, although mention has been made of the provisions of that Article in regard to the strict equidistance line and "special circumstances." The Article is not applicable to a single maritime boundary, but even where it is applicable, it is governed by the special circumstances rule, and it was just because special circumstances are perceived as existing in so many places and guises that the strict equidistance rule was called into question. It is that very variability of special circumstances that makes it impossible to determine a set of objective criteria to cover all situations.

If no clear rules emerge from this review, some useful guidelines are seen. Although application of strict equidistance has been called into question, one finds a widespread acceptance of the principle of equidistance being basically equitable. Proportionality is seen as having a more flexible application than that propounded in the *North Sea* Judgment. A major judgment has yet to be read, however. The *Malta/Libya* Judgment will be of great importance with regard to all the aspects of delimitation discussed in this paper. The writer is acutely and uncomfortably aware that he is a hostage to fortune.

Postscript

By the time this paper was presented the Judgment in the *Malta/Libya* case had been delivered. It does not change the main conclusions of the paper, but it does clarify the relationship of the EEZ to the continental shelf mentioned above (text preceding note 50). At Paragraph 34 of the Judgment, the Court states that:

> the institution of the exclusive economic zone, with its rules of entitlement by reason of distance, is shown by the practice of States to have become a part of customary law.

and at paragraph 39:

> since the development of the law enables a State to claim that the continental shelf appertaining to it extends up as far as 200 miles from its coast...there is no reason to ascribe any role to geological or geophysical factors within that distance either in verifying the legal title...or in proceeding to a delimitation...

Light is also shed on the role of proportionality in a delimitation between opposite states. Because Libya's coastline is considerably longer than Malta's, the equidistance boundary that would otherwise have been deemed appropriate is to be moved eighteen miles northward towards Malta. The relationship between coastline lengths and area ratios was not quantified by the Court, and the distance of eighteen miles is not related to any specific proportionality figures.

NOTES

1. Special Agreement of 29 March 1979 between Canada and the U.S. See ICJ Judgment of 12.10.84, p 11. The U.S. in 1983, subsequent to entry into force of the Agreement, proclaimed an economic zone.
2. UN Doc.A/CONF 62/122(1982), Arts. 15, 74 and 83.
3. See, *e.g.*, Uruguay/Brazil, 1972; Senegal/Gambia and Colombia/Ecuador, 1975; India/Sri Lanka and Colombia/Panama, 1976; Venezuela/Netherlands, 1978; Costa Rica/Panama and Burma/Thailand, 1980; France/Brazil and St. Lucia/France, 1981; Guinea/Guinea-Bissau Award, 1985.
4. The U.S. states that agreements are in force respecting less than 25% of potential maritime boundaries. *Gulf of Maine* Case; U.S. Counter Memorial at 217.
5. Judgment, at pp. 50 and 52.

6. Decision at p. 101.
7. *Ibid.*, at p. 250.
8. Judgment at p. 72.
9. *Ibid.*, at p. 133 B[1].
10. *Ibid.*, at p. 75.
11. *Ibid.*, at p. 131.
12. Judgment at pp. 28-39.
13. *Ibid.*, at p. 218.
14. Award at p. 120 (unofficial translation).
15. *North Sea* Judgment, at p. 57.
16. See text above, following note 5.
17. ICJ Judgment, 1951, at p. 133.
18. UNTS, vol. 516(1958), pp. 208-214.
19. *Op.cit.*, p. 4, art. 7[3].
20. Judgment at p. 133 B[5].
21. Canadian Memorial at p. 19.
22. U.S. Memorial, at p. 283.
23. Canadian Counter Memorial, Fig. 51.
24. Award at pp. 97 and 110. The latter line is taken from a point in Senegal (north of Guinea-Bissau to a point in Sierra Leone (south of Guinea)).
25. See text above, following note 5.
26. Judgment, at p. 221.
27. *Op.cit.*, Art. 12.
28. UNTS, vol. 499(1958): Art 6.
29. Judgment at p. 36.
30. *Ibid.*, at p. 6.
31. Above, text preceding note 15.
32. Decision, at p. 94.
33. Judgment, at p. 126.
34. Judgment, at pp. 188 and 189.
35. Above, text following note 32.
36. Award, at p. 91.
37. Text above, at note 29.
38. Award at pp. 92 and 94.
39. Judgment at p. 95.
40. *Ibid.*, at p.101 D[2].
41. *Ibid.*, at p. 45.
42. Decision, at p. 106.
43. *Ibid.*, at p. 107.
44. Judgment, at pp. 32 and 63.
45. *Ibid.*, at p. 67.
46. Judgment, at p. 46.
47. *Ibid.*, at pp. 51-55.
48. Award, at pp. 22 and 117.
49. See, *e.g.*, Cuba/Haiti Maritime Boundary Agreement, 1977, which ignores the Cayman Trench.
50. Separate Opinion, at p. 51.
51. Judgment, at p. 101 D[2].
52. *Ibid.*, at p. 97.
53. Judgment, at p. 106 and 107.
54. Judgment, at p. 59.
55. Award, at pp. 121 and 122.
56. Judgment, at p. 96.
57. Text above, at note 33.
58. U.S. Memorial, at pp. 308 and 309.

59. Judgment, at p. 109.
60. Judgment, at p. 81.
61. Award at pp. 105 and 106.
62. *Ibid.*, at p. 110.
63. Judgment, at p. 212.
64. *E.g.*, the Italian island of Pianosa or the Yugoslav island of Jabuka: Italy/Yugoslavia C S Boundary Agreement (1968).
65. *E.g.*, the Yugoslav islands of Pelagruz and Kajola in the 1968 Agreement.
66. *E.g.*, the Channel Islands in the Anglo-French Decision of 1977.
67. *E.g.*, the Scilly Isles in the 1977 Decision.
68. The writer has dealt with this in more detail in an article "Half-Effect applied to Equidistance Lines" -- *IH Review*, LVI[1] January 1979.
69. Above, text following note 16.
70. Judgment, at p. 337.
71. See also the Judgment, at p. 218.
72. E.J. Cooper and R.D. Hodgson, "The Technical Delimitation of a Modern Equidistance Boundary", (1976) 3 *Ocean Development and International Law* 361, or P. Beazley, "Maritime Boundaries", (1982) LIX(1) *IH Review*.

COMMENTARY

Mario C. Manansala
Consultant, Law of the Sea Secretariat
Philippine Ministry of Foreign Affairs

The 1982 Convention on the Law of the Sea, in its Preamble, asserts its intent ... "to settle, in a spirit of mutual understanding and cooperation, all issues relating to the law of the sea..." This unique and comprehensive treaty is designed to establish a new international legal order for the seas and oceans that should contribute to the strengthening of peace, security, cooperation and friendly relations among all nations.

Introduction
This is a unique document, for three principal reasons:

1. It seeks to balance the rights of coastal (mostly developing) states and those of maritime (mostly highly industrialized) powers.
2. It enunciates the concept of the common heritage of mankind.
3. It attempts to establish a new United Nations organization with a specific mandate and definite administrative and regulatory powers.

The Convention is a comprehensive treaty. Its 320 articles include provisions dealing with the territorial sea, the contiguous zone, innocent passage, enclosed and semi-enclosed seas, islands, archipelagoes, straits used for international navigation, marine pollution, marine scientific research, the new concept of the exclusive economic zone and deep-seabed mining.

The articles on maritime delimitation provide some of the most complex issues in their geographical and technical aspects.

It is remarkable that while the objectives and goals of the LOS Convention are certainly noble and praiseworthy, the problems of maritime boundary delimitation are among the most intractable and contentious issues in the Convention. Indeed, one may recall that these problems were identified at the Seventh Session in 1978, among seven outstanding hard core issues whose solution was specially entrusted to seven Negotiating Groups. It may also be recalled that after three years and six sessions of intensive debate and discussion, Negotiating Group 7 on maritime boundary delimitation between opposite or adjacent states failed to reach a consensus on the criteria to be used in solving delimitation problems. These reminiscences are intended solely to emphasize the magnitude and complexities of maritime boundary delimitation.

The three speakers this afternoon have dealt with the geographic and technical aspects of delimitation in a most admirable, most objective way. Lew Alexander identified some Convention terms which are either ambiguous or could be the subject of "technical uncertainties." He then went briefly into some techniques of delimitation, and finally, referred to certain cartographic considerations.

Commander Beazley analyzed five judicial awards starting with the 1969 *North Sea Continental Shelf* case through the *Gulf of Maine Maritime Boundary* decision last year, and the 1985 *Guinea/Guinea-Bissau Boundary Arbitration*. The analysis of these five judicial decisions forms the basis of an examination of the factors taken into account in boundary delimitation, such as relevant area and proportionality, coastal frontage, geology and geomorphology, economic considerations, equidistance and equitable principles, etc.

Vic Prescott confined his dissertation to only one aspect of delimitation -- straight baselines. But his analysis was so exhaustive that it took almost forty pages to deal adequately with the six paragraphs of the article on straight baselines.

I cannot add much more to the geographical and technical aspects of maritime delimitation under the LOS Convention presented this afternoon by these three distinguished speakers. My role could be most fruitfully utilized by focusing on certain issues brought out in the papers presented.

Equidistance and Equitable Principles

Commander Beazley dwelt on equidistance and equitable principles as criteria for maritime delimitation. Much has been written about the subject, and it has been debated *ad nauseam* at the sessions of the Third UN Conference on the Law of the Sea. One cannot but admire the intrepidity of the good commander when he joins in this highly controversial issue. However, he analyzed the problem with the utmost objectivity, and no one can dispute his assertion that over fifty percent of state agreements now existing use the principle of equidistance in some form or another. But he wisely concluded that special circumstances, (which could only be properly addressed by other equitable principles) could call the strict equidistance rule into question.

Baselines

Now, turning to baselines -- normal, straight or archipelagic -- there seems to be no doubt, as provided in Article 14, that a coastal state may utilize any method or combination of methods to determine its baselines to suit different conditions. However, Dr. Prescott's assertion that a single country may draw both archipelagic and straight baselines is perhaps debatable. It could be reasoned that a coastal state may draw straight baselines if the criteria enumerated in Article 7 are satisfied, but for the coastal state to exercise the right to draw archipelagic baselines, it not only has to satisfy the conditions cited in Article 47, but it must, first of all, be an archipelagic state as stated in the first three words of Paragraph 1 of Article 47. This brings in Article 46 which defines an archipelagic state. No nation has so far drawn both straight and archipelagic baselines, and the problem is still academic.

Juridical Bays

Under Article 50, an archipelagic state may draw, within its archipelagic waters, closing lines for delimiting its internal waters in such geographic features as rivers, bays, ports and other permanent harbor works. An ordinary oceanographic or hydrographic glossary will give a clear and simple definition of "bay," a common geographic feature. But, as pointed out by Dr. Alexander, such terms as "land-locked waters," "juridicial bays," "natural entrance points," etc., have entered into the legal definition under the LOS Convention, which to a poor geographer may have made the meaning less clear. It is comforting to know that Manila Bay passes all those criteria, so there can be no doubt that its waters fall under the regime of internal waters. It can even qualify as a "historic bay," since an American admiral became a national hero by winning a historic naval engagement in the waters inside the bay, about the turn of the last century. It is the application of the legal criteria to certain well-marked indentations in the Philippine coasts like Linga-yen Gulf, Batangas Bay, Bauan Bay, Moro Gulf, etc., that now furnishes an intellectual exercise to some technical men and cartographers in the country.

Low Water Datum

In any maritime delimitation, whether intended to fix the maritime boundary between adjacent or opposite states or simply to delineate a coastal state's maritime space under the LOS Convention, the inner and outer boundaries are essential. The inner boundary is the low-water line -- the normal baseline. The low-water line has been mentioned in all three papers, but Dr. Alexander correctly pointed out some techni-cal aspects of the datum of mean low water. The definition in Article 5 mentions large-scale charts officially recognized by the coastal state. Consider the wording of this requirement. In the delimitation Articles 16, 47, 75 and 84, while charts were mentioned, it was deemed sufficient to specify "...of a scale or scales adequate for ascertaining their position." But in this Article 5 on the low-water line (the normal base-line), the charts must be large-scale charts.

Nautical Charts

All three speakers mentioned nautical charts, but Vic Prescott specifically stated the presumption that a map will not do. A map ordi-narily shows land topography such as valleys, mountains, hills, and cultural features such as buildings, highways, roads, etc., but it is in a nautical chart where depths of water, anchorages, lights, reefs, shoals, rocks, islets, etc., are delineated. The National Geographic Society of Washington, D.C., has published a beautiful map of the ocean floor, but this is a special map showing submarine topography.

Dr. Prescott devoted several pages of his paper to coastal insta-bility. The geologic processes of erosion and deposition are forever taking place; so also, as he pointed out, are coral reef formations, tundra cliff thawing, and even volcanic activity. Now, volcanic activ-ity that blows the top off a volcano or even a portion of an island is a normal crustal phenomenon. But an unusual occurrence has been recorded where an island has emerged from submarine depths after a series of violent volcanic eruptions.

The EEZ and the Continental Shelf

In his discussion on the relationship between the exclusive eco-nomic zone and the continental shelf, Commander Beazley posed two ques-tions. The first relates to the definition of the continental shelf, as provided in Article 76 of the Convention: which of the two criteria -- natural prolongation or 200 miles distance -- should be given greater weight? His illustrative examples are particularly relevant.

Customary International Law

The second question is one that now confronts the international community as well as legal and judicial bodies -- do the articles embodied in the Convention express customary international law and are they thus applicable to all states whether signatories or not and also whether the Convention is in force or not? These are deep legal ques-tions on which I will not venture an opinion.

I conclude with a reservation to the concluding paragraph of Vic Prescott's paper wherein he advised that countries which have straight baselines not conforming with the rules set out in Article 7 should be prevented from ratifying or acceding to the Convention until the offending baselines have been amended. I advance two reasons for my reservation: (a) the Convention was intended to be universally acceptable -- the more states participating, the nearer the attainment of its universality; (b) for countries with domestic legislation not in conformity with some provisions of the Convention, Article 310, which provides a certain period within which domestic laws and regulations could be harmonized with the Convention, was specifically included.

COMMENTARY

Chungcheng Lian
Department of Law, Jilin University
Changchung, China

The 1982 Convention on the Law of the Sea provides a new definition of the continental shelf and establishes the regime of the exclusive economic zone (EEZ). The development of the law brings a series of new issues to maritime delimitation, including two remarkable issues: (1) the relationship between the new definition of the continental shelf and maritime delimitation; and (2) the relationship of EEZ to the continental shelf. This comment is concerned with these issues.

The Relationship Between the New Definition of the Continental Shelf and Maritime Delimitation

Two criteria in Article 76
Article 76(1) of the 1982 Convention defines the continental shelf as follows:

> The continental shelf of a coastal State comprises the seabed and subsoil of the submarine areas that extend beyond its territorial sea throughout the natural prolongation of its land territory to the outer edge of the continental margin, or to a distance of 200 nautical miles from the baselines from which the breadth of the territorial sea is measured where the outer edge of the continental margin does not extend up to that distance.

Paragraph 3 of this Article defines the continental margin as comprising the submerged prolongation of the land mass of the coastal state and consisting of the seabed and subsoil of the shelf, the slope and the rise.

Regarding the maritime delimitation, it is very important to know which is the main criterion of the two given in the definition: distance or natural prolongation? The question may be of great importance, particularly in the case of opposite states, where the natural prolongation of one state might extend beyond 200 miles to a distance of less than 200 miles from another state; or, say, where two states lie at a distance from each other of less than the maximum allowed by law but are separated by a geological and geomorphological discontinuity such as to halt the natural prolongation of one state in such a way that it does not extend to the limit otherwise permitted by law. Considering that the maximum breadth of the continental shelf of one state is 350 nautical miles, theoretically, if the distance between two states were less than 550 nautical miles, and there were some geographical features constituting a discontinuity of natural prolongation between them, it would be possible to raise this issue between them unless the features were located beyond 200 miles from each coast. In other words, if such a feature were within a distance of 200 miles from the coast of either state, the issue might possibly arise unless the distance between the coasts was more than 550 miles. Thus the answer to the above question seems critically important.

Commander Beazley mentioned Judge Jimenez de Arechaga's opinion in the *Tunisia-Libya* case that the distance criterion should be paramount.

In his Separate Opinion, Judge Jimenez de Arechaga said that the criterion of distance had done away with the requirement of geological or geomorphological continental shelf and thus destroyed the conception of the "natural prolongation."[1]

The International Court of Justice expressed a similar opinion in the *Libya-Malta* case. The Court stated: "...since the development of the law enables a state to claim that the continental shelf appertaining to it extends up to as far as 200 miles from its coast, whatever the geological characteristics of the corresponding sea-bed and subsoil, there is no reason to ascribe any role to geological or geophysical factors within that distance either in verifying the legal title of the states concerned or in proceeding to a delimitation as between their claims."[2]

However, given the history of the legal system of the continental shelf, it will be found that either Judge Jiminez de Arechaga's opinion or the Court's above conclusion is questionable.

It is well known that the criterion of 200 miles in Article 76 was a result of the compromise in the Conference, considering the interests of states with a narrow continental margin. Basically, it exists as a supplementary and secondary criterion for the definition of the continental shelf. As a further explanation of Paragraph 1, Paragraph 3 does not even mention the criterion of distance. In the light of the provisions of Paragraph 10, that "the provisions of this Article are without prejudice to the question of delimitation of the continental shelf between states with opposite or adjacent coasts," it seems that the 200 miles criterion can be used only in the case when a state determines the outward limit of its continental shelf, namely the limit between the continental shelf of the state and deep seabed. In a case of maritime delimitation, it should in no way be used to oppose the criterion of the natural prolongation and justify the use of equidistance so as to encroach upon the natural prolongation of another state.

As opposed to the criterion of 200 miles, the criterion of the natural prolongation came from customary international law. It emerged in the Truman Proclamation and has been stressed in the subsequent judicial decisions.

In the *North Sea* case, the International Court of Justice considered it as "the most fundamental of all rules of law relating to the continental shelf,"[3] thus giving it great importance in delimitation.

The *Anglo-French Arbitration* of 1977 followed the 1969 decision of the ICJ in most points and also repeatedly emphasized the importance of the principle of natural prolongation in the delimitation of the continental shelf.

It was on this legal basis that the Third United Nations Conference on the Law of the Sea introduced the concept of natural prolongation into the Law of the Sea Convention. And in all the Negotiating Texts and the final text of the Convention, the concept of natural prolongation has stood as a major criterion of the continental shelf. Its position has never been challenged. Although the definition of the continental shelf has several elements -- for example, it extends beyond the territorial sea, it consists of three geomorphological units, namely the shelf, slope and rise, the determination of its outer limit follows certain standards, and so on -- its basic element and character is that the continental shelf of a coastal state is a natural prolongation of its land territory into and under the sea. Obviously, the criterion of the natural prolongation stands as a predominant feature of the continental shelf in the definition laid down by Article 76. It is paramount

345

over all other elements in the definition including, of course, the criterion of 200 miles. It is this basic character that expresses the inherent link between the geographical and legal concepts of the continental shelf and makes it different from other regimes of the sea.

Actually, the issue relating to the relationship between the criterion of natural prolongation and that of distance is not a new one. The argument of Denmark and the Netherlands, based on "proximity," in the *North Sea* cases, has some similarity to that based on the criterion of distance. Rejecting this argument, the Court pointed out:

> it is this idea of extension which is, in the Court's opinion, determinant. Submarine areas do not really appertain to the coastal State because -- or not only because -- they are near it...whenever a given submarine area does not constitute a natural -- or the most natural -- extension of the land territory of a coastal State, even though that area may be closer to it than it is to the territory of any other State, it cannot be regarded as appertaining to that State; -- or at least it cannot be so regarded in the face of a competing claim by a State of whose land territory the submarine area concerned is to be regarded as a natural extension, even if it is less close to it.[4]

It is plain that the Court considered the criterion of natural prolongation more important than the criterion of either "proximity" or distance.

In the *Tunisia-Libya* case, the Court confirmed:

> While the term "natural prolongation" may have been novel in 1969, the idea to which it gave expression was already a part of existing customary law as the basis of the title of the coastal State. The Court also attributed to that concept a certain role in the delimitation of shelf areas, in cases in which the geographical situation made it appropriate to do so.[5]

With regard to the relationship of the two criteria in Article 76, the Court considered that "...the natural prolongation of the land territory is the main criterion....the distance of 200 nautical miles is in certain circumstances the basis of the title of a coastal State."[6]

In view of the above analysis, it seems logical and reasonable to conclude that the rule of natural prolongation is the "only rule of customary international law retained" by Article 76 of the Convention on the Law of the Sea;[7] it is the "main criterion" in the Article and thus paramount to that of distance; it must be taken into account in the delimitation of the continental shelf if the geological and geographical features so require, whether the distance between two opposite states exceeds 400 miles or not. Being a supplementary and secondary criterion, as Judge Sette-Camara pointed out in his Separate Opinion in the *Libya-Malta* case, the distance criterion of Article 76 is difficult to accept at this time as a rule of customary international law.[8] Its role is only to take "care of the situation of states possessing a continental margin with an outer edge not extending to the distance of 200 nautical miles."[9] In maritime delimitation, it cannot be used to oppose the criterion of natural prolongation. Therefore, there is no doubt that Judge Jimenez de Arechaga's conclusion and the Court's opinion cited at the beginning of this paper are a misinterpretation of Article 76.

It is worth noting that there is still something correct in the Court's Judgment dealing with the relationship between the two criteria in Article 76. For instance, the Court has correctly pointed out that the idea of natural prolongation is not superseded by that of distance, and concepts of natural prolongation and distance are not opposed but complementary.[10] The mistaken idea, in its opinion, is that it improperly gave the criterion of distance a superior status, which it never enjoyed, in the delimitation of the continental shelf, even if the status given by it was only limited to the situation in which two opposite states were apart from each other less than 400 miles. So it is easy to mislead one into reaching the same arbitrary conclusion as Judge Jimenez de Arechaga's.[11] By comparison with previous judicial decisions, the opinion seems too strange to be accepted. Undoubtedly, it is open to challenge and criticism.

Consideration to be Given to the Criterion of Natural Prolongation

Since the criterion of natural prolongation is a rule of customary international law and should be taken into account in delimitation, another question follows: what geographical features should be considered, and what consideration should be given to them in the delimitation of the continental shelf?

Commander Beazley said: "It is clear that for a submarine feature to be of sufficient importance to be regarded as constituting a discontinuity such as to bound a State's natural prolongation or to form a natural frontier it must be of major geomorphological or geological significance." The comment seems reasonable and logical. However, what geographical feature should be regarded as being of "major significance"? The question would be more practical in a particular case.

In the *North Sea* cases, the Court pointed out that various aspects of the situation, such as geological and geomorphological aspects and the idea of the unity of any deposits, must be taken into account in the delimitation.[12]

In the *Anglo-French Arbitration* case, even though both parties recognized that the continental shelf throughout the arbitration area is characterized by its essential geological continuity, the United Kingdom put forward an alternative submission that the Hurd Deep and the Hurd Deep Fault Zone interrupted the continuity of the shelf. However, the Court considered that these features do not "disrupt the essential unity of the continental shelf."[13]

In the *Tunisia-Libya* case, after carefully examining the evidence and arguments put forward by the parties, the Court concluded:

> the area relevant for the delimitation constitutes a single continental shelf as the natural prolongation of the land territory of both Parties, so that in the present case, no criterion for delimitation of shelf areas can be derived from the principle of natural prolongation as such.[14]

However, it also stated:

> The conclusion that the physical structure of the sea-bed ... as the natural prolongation common to both Parties does not contain any element which interrupts the continuity of the continental shelf does not necessarily exclude the possibility that certain geomorphological configurations of the sea-bed, which do not amount to such an interruption of the natural prolongation of one

347

Party with regard to that of the other, may be taken into account for the delimitation, as relevant circumstances characterising the area ...[15]

In the *Gulf of Maine* case, both parties recognized that the geological structure of the strata underlying the whole of the continental shelf of North America, including the Gulf of Maine area, is essentially continuous. As regards the geomorphological aspects, neither party disputed the fact that there is nothing in the single seabed, lacking any marked elevations or depressions, to distinguish one part which might be considered as constituting the natural prolongation of the coast of the United States from another part which could be regarded as the natural prolongation of the coast of Canada. And the Chamber considered that the Northeast Channel "is quite simply a natural feature of the area" and "does not have the characteristics of a real trough marking the dividing-line between two geomorphologically distinct units."[16]

In the *Libya-Malta* case, Libya posed an argument relying on the principle of natural prolongation. It contended that the "rift zone" constituted a discontinuity of the natural prolongation, but because it is not a line but a zone, there still remained a problem of delimitation confined to the "rift zone." The argument was rejected by the Court mainly on the ground that the area to be delimited does not extend more than 200 miles. However, the Court still made the comment that: "Having carefully studied that evidence, the Court is not satisfied that it would be able to draw any sufficiently cogent conclusions from it as to the existence or not of the 'fundamental discontinuity.'"[17]

Unfortunately, it is not possible to provide a straight answer to the above questions. However, it seems still appropriate to draw the following conclusions:

1. Since the features discussed in the above cases were not taken into consideration in the delimitation just because they do not constitute discontinuities of the natural prolongation, then if there were some geographical features which did have such characteristics, they should be regarded as being of major significance and taken into account as the criteria of delimitation.

2. Some geographical features, even if they do not constitute discontinuities of the natural prolongation, can be taken into account in the delimitation as relevant circumstances.

3. Some geographical features, either minor faults in the geological structure of the shelf, or "simply natural features," or "non-real troughs" should be ignored in the delimitation.

4. The idea of the unity of any deposits in the area of delimitation should be taken into consideration.

The Relationship of the EEZ and the Continental Shelf

Since the establishment of the regime of the exclusive economic zone (EEZ), the relation of EEZ and continental shelf has become a serious issue. There is a divergence of opinion between jurists and scholars. For example, Judge Oda maintains that the seabed area to 200 miles from the coast would be incorporated in the regime of the 200-mile economic zone in spite of the geological or geomorphological features of the sea-bed.[18] But Judge Sette-Camara disagrees with this view. He considers that, though the right and jurisdiction of states over the continental shelf and the EEZ overlap to a considerable degree, they differ in many ways:[19] "There are substantial differences in the jurisdiction of the coastal State in the two cases."[20]

Obviously, the EEZ and the continental shelf appear in the 1982 Convention as two different legal regimes. By and large, their differences are as follows:

1. The regime of the continental shelf is one of the seabed and subsoil of submarine areas and designed for the exploitation of mineral resources in the areas; but the EEZ is essentially a regime of the coastal waters and intended to exploit the fishery resource in the water column. Although the 1982 Convention provides that the EEZ contains the seabed and subsoil within the areas, it seems that the provision of Article 56(3), which provides that the rights with respect to the seabed and subsoil shall be exercised in accordance with Part VI on the continental shelf, almost amounts to an exclusion of them from the regime of the EEZ.

2. The determination of the outer limit of the EEZ only follows the test of distance; but the continental shelf has some geographical tests to determine its outer limit. Even though in the regime of the continental shelf there is also a reference to 200 miles, as seen above, it should be construed that it can only apply to the case where an oceanic state determines the outer limits of its continental shelf. Basically the continental shelf should be the natural prolongation of its land territory.

3. The widest extent of the EEZ is 200 nautical miles from the coast; but the continental shelf can extend to 350 nautical miles or 100 nautical miles from the 2500 meters isobath.

4. From the viewpoint of practice, it seems that the establishment of the EEZ must be declared by coastal states, and states have a choice between the EEZ and an exclusive fishery zone. But the continental shelf belongs to the "inherent right," "Its existence can be declared...but does not need to be constituted."[21]

In view of the above basic differences, it is reasonable to conclude that although the conventional provisions applicable to the delimitation of the continental shelf and that of the EEZ are the same, their practical application in each case and the test of equity would be quite different. In a case of the delimitation of the EEZ, exploitation of the living resource, proportionality of the coastlines, status of islands and so on should be mainly considered. Even if the geological structure, geomorphological features and mineral resource may be regarded as relevant circumstances, the question of the natural prolongation need not be considered at all. However, in a case of the delimitation of continental shelf, besides the above elements, it is also necessary to take into account the physical structure of seabed and mineral resources, especially the question of the natural prolongation. Equitable principles should be deemed to have a different meaning and different tests in each case from the other.

However, the differences between the two regimes do not necessarily exclude states from drawing a single boundary. On the contrary, a number of states prefer to do so and they did draw the single boundaries representing both the continental shelf and EEZ, when the practical situation allowed them to do so. But such a practice also does not mean that a state has to draw a single boundary with its neighbor. There is no law to require states to do so. It is supposed to give the states a choice.

349

The above two issues are related, but basically, they are two different questions. The inapplicability of the criterion of 200 miles in the delimitation of the continental shelf does not exclude its application in that of the EEZ. And the criterion of the 200 miles in the definition of the EEZ cannot derogate from the value of the concept of the natural prolongation.

These two issues are very important and sensitive in East Asia because of this area's particular geographical characteristics: (1) the fact that almost all countries surround semi-enclosed seas (marginal seas); (2) the existence of troughs and trenches; (3) the existence of a great number of islands; and (4) the lack of any continental rise.

NOTES

1. Jimenez de Arechaga, Separate Opinion, para. 51, *I.C.J. Reports 1982*, p. 114.
2. *I.C.J. Reports 1985*, p. 35, para. 39.
3. *I.C.J. Reports 1969*, p. 22, para. 19.
4. *Ibid.*, p. 31, para. 43.
5. *I.C.J. Reports 1982*, p. 46, para. 43.
6. *Ibid.*, p. 48, para. 47.
7. Sette-Camara, Separate Opinion, *I.C.J. Reports 1985*, p. 69.
8. *Ibid.*
9. *Ibid.*, p. 68.
10. *Ibid.*, p. 33, para. 34.
11. *Supra*, note 1.
12. *I.C.J. Reports 1969*, p. 50, para. 94.
13. *Anglo-French Delimitation Arbitration*, Decision of 30 June 1977, paras. 106-107.
14. *I.C.J. Reports 1982*, p. 92, para. 133.
15. *Ibid.*, p. 58, para. 68.
16. *I.C.J. Reports 1984*, pp. 273-274, paras. 44-46.
17. *I.C.J. Reports 1985*, p. 36, para. 41.
18. See: Shigeru Oda, *International Law of the Resource of the Sea*, 1979, p. 128; and Oda's Dissenting Opinion, *I.C.J. Reports 1982*, pp. 231-236, paras. 126-131.
19. Sette-Camara, Separate Opinion, *I.C.J. Reports 1985*, p. 71.
20. *Ibid.*, p. 69.
21. *I.C.J. Reports 1969*, p. 22, para. 19.

COMMENTARY

Joseph Morgan
Department of Geography
University of Hawaii

My comments concern subjects with which I have some actual experience, either through visits to the geographic areas used as examples or because I happen to be currently working on studies of the same or related subjects.

The idea of a single maritime boundary embracing all zones of jurisdiction can be construed as a tendency on the part of tribunals to change the intent of the writers of the Convention. Many criticized the evolving Law of the Sea as an enclosure movement, once the EEZ, enlarged territorial sea and continental shelf provisions began to be accepted by the negotiators. Others feared that "creeping jurisdictions" would replace the age-old concept of freedom of the seas. The counter arguments were that each new or enlarged zone of jurisdiction would have carefully limited degrees of sovereignty, and that by keeping the territorial sea, contiguous zone, exclusive economic zone, archipelagic waters, straits used for international navigation, etc., separately defined, the Convention would still preserve the former freedoms. Bodies of law, however, are what the courts make of them, and the substitution of a "single maritime boundary" such as was done in the Canada-U.S. *Gulf of Maine* case now becomes a precedent which might be later used by other tribunals. We now have the serious question to consider: what are the rules and degrees of sovereignty within that single maritime boundary?

The Convention creates the need for boundary negotiations, since the areas where 200-nm EEZs overlap are numerous. While some of the overlaps are of territorial seas, most entail EEZs and continental shelves, or both. Perhaps it was inevitable that the idea of a single maritime boundary would evolve, if for no other reason than to reduce the number of boundary negotiations required.

Many of the technical problems of boundary delimitation arise from the fact that in the majority of cases the contesting states are neither opposite nor adjacent, the two categories envisioned in the Convention. The actual geography of the world abounds in political boundaries and coastal configurations which have the result of making nations whose marine jurisdictional claims overlap neither purely adjacent nor simply opposite; almost all are somewhere in between. Commander Beazley quotes the Court of Arbitration in the *Anglo-French* case, which forcefully brings out the fact that in most cases it is *actual geographic character* of the coasts rather than some categorization by the states as opposite or adjacent that must be considered if an equitable delimitation is to be arrived at. The whole idea of geographic boundaries -- not just the obvious political ones -- is intriguing, and it is a fruitful field for those who believe in the regional method as a useful construct in analyzing both legal and geographic problems. Although the Chamber which decided the U.S.-Canada *Gulf of Maine* case was not convinced of the "possibility of discerning any genuine, sure and stable 'natural boundaries' in so fluctuating an environment as the waters of the ocean, their flora and fauna," many marine geographers and oceanographers rightfully maintain that the western edge of the Gulf Stream forms a stable, natural boundary in the northwest Atlantic Ocean. Gulf

351

Stream waters have discernibly different temperatures, salinities, flora, and fauna than the adjacent coastal waters. The Antarctic Ocean is frequently delineated by the position of the Antarctic Convergence. Admittedly, the position of the Convergence shifts seasonally, and for that reason it would make a poor political boundary, but nevertheless the question of boundaries between physical or natural regions in the oceans needs further examination.

Dr. Alexander points out the deficiencies of the Convention in not defining rocks, as opposed to islands, as basepoints for delimiting exclusive economic zones and territorial seas. Islands are entitled to exclusive economic zones, while "rocks which cannot sustain human habitation or economic life of their own shall have no exclusive economic zone or continental shelf" (UN Convention, Article 121). Since the Convention does not define a "rock," we are presumably expected to use ordinary dictionary definitions. Webster's Third International defined a rock as a "barren islet," in addition to providing a number of other meanings. If we accept the barren islet definition there is no need to distinguish between rocks and islands. Only the question of habitability is applicable. In the State of Hawaii the exclusive economic zone will have to be delineated around the Northwestern Hawaiian Islands, many of which are rocks -- what Dr. Alexander usefully calls "non-conforming" rocks -- and some of which are inhabited islands. Midway and Kure are inhabited islands; the former is a naval base and the latter contains a manned Loran station. All others in the chain are either islands or non-conforming rocks depending on what definitions are accepted and how persuasive the arguments for habitability are.

A study of the *Northwestern Hawaiian Islands and the Law of the Sea* has revealed some interesting things. Necker and Nihoa are rocky, barren, and without water. It is almost impossible to conceive of them ever having supported a human population; yet, there is ample evidence of a former Polynesian habitation of some size. There are archaeological remains of house sites, taro terraces, and *heiaus* (religious temples). Laysan and Lisianski are flat islands with very little water and "millions of flies" according to the U.S. Coast Pilot for the area. Although currently uninhabited and presumably incapable of supporting human habitation or an economic life of their own, they were formerly inhabited by guano harvesters and were economically viable. The absence of a definition of a "rock" creates numerous problems in delineating EEZs around the Pacific, where rocks, islands, islets, reefs, shoals, and atolls abound. The definitions suggested by the late Dr. Hodgson would certainly have been helpful had they been considered by the delegates who wrote the Convention.

Another defect in the Convention, according to Dr. Alexander, is the failure of the compilers to define a "juridical" estuary, a failing that will probably lead to the closing off as internal waters of all coastal indentations that are well marked, under one pretext or another. Physical geographers interested in coastal processes and landforms and oceanographers understand the processes that go on in estuaries and probably could have helped the writers of the Convention to establish a useful definition of estuary for the purpose of drawing straight baselines. It is apparent, however, that the services of qualified earth scientists either were not sought or, if so, their advice was not taken.

Where man has altered the coastal landforms, as he has done in developing port facilities, the Convention recognized that extensions of the land in the form of piers, moles, breakwaters, etc., are part of the coast as long as they are physically attached to the natural coast.

352

Where they are not, for example offshore breakwaters and the large mooring buoys for loading and unloading supertankers, they are not to be considered as integral parts of the harbor system. The number of offshore buoys for oil tankers in Southeast Asia alone is increasing greatly, and virtually all large ports in the region have in effect been extended by these offshore oil handling facilities. It seems appropriate that port facilities -- and offshore mooring buoys for tankers certainly fall in that category -- should be defined as inland waters. There is one such installation in the South China Sea, however, which handles much of Malaysia's crude oil exports, that is some 100 miles off the east coast of the Malaysian peninsula. Perhaps it should be considered an enclave and treated as such, while buoys that are within a reasonable distance of the coast, perhaps twelve nautical miles, could be considered as points on the coastal baseline.

Dr. Alexander makes some very interesting and valid points concerning the cartographic aspects of the many technical issues arising from the Convention. The problem of projections is a very real one, and it is certainly true that the widely used Mercator projection provides sufficient precision in only a few special circumstances. The use of Lambert conformal projections for delineating baselines and maritime boundaries in mid-latitudes and stereographic projections for the same purpose in polar regions will indeed eliminate much of the distortion in scale of the Mercator projection. A real problem, however, is that mariners are the people who must obey the rules and must know the positions of their vessels relative to the various boundary lines. Seagoing navigators use Mercator charts, and boundary delineations shown on Lambert conformal or stereographic projections have to be redrawn onto the Mercator charts in common use. The transfer of points and lines from one projection to another is tedious and leads to errors.

Horizontal datums are another problem, since on a single nautical chart two separate datums might appear. In the Strait of Gibraltar, for instance, the charts in use in the late 1950s showed lighthouses on the African coast on one datum, while the European coast was shown on another datum. Navigational fixes were not as accurate when a combination of European and North African landmarks was used, as when the navigator used either European landmarks exclusively or North African navigational aids and not European ones. Navigation in the Straits of Malacca and Singapore suffered from the same problem of different datums. When the Straits were resurveyed in order to produce improved charts for the use of supertankers a common datum was specified, and the positions of land features and soundings are all related to this datum. These Common Datum Charts are now in use, and from all reports large tankers are better able to determine their positions in the long, navigationally ticklish transit of the straits.

Dr. Prescott has provided us with a thorough, detailed, and carefully analyzed review of the subject of straight baselines in the context of the 1982 Convention on the Law of the Sea as well as in historical perspective. He touches on two geographic areas with which I am quite familiar. In the case of the Antarctic continent, much of the coast terminates in virtually vertical ice cliffs, as the continental ice sheets form ice shelves which calve tabular icebergs. The process of calving can remove very large coastal sections in a short period of time, since the largest icebergs have been of the order of 100 or more miles in length and tens of miles wide. The technical question of how to draw baselines along a rapidly changing coastal configuration either was not envisioned by the writers of the Convention or was not seriously

353

considered since the whole problem of Antarctica in the context of the law of the sea was left for subsequent resolution.

In the case of volcanic areas, such as Hawaii, the technical problem is similar in that volcanic activity both creates and destroys land rapidly. There have been a number of cases where volcanic flows have created new coastal land, and in at least one case the courts had to decide whether the new land was under state or private ownership. Volcanic eruptions also destroy or remove land, creating new coastlines. Although volcanic activity on the island of Oahu has long been dormant, it is possible that a rebirth of volcanic activity such as formed cones like Diamond Head and Hanauma Bay will occur. Both of these tuff cones erupted at the shoreline through an existing coral reef. In the case of Hanauma Bay the seaward side of the cone slumped into the ocean and was subsequently breached by the sea to form a picturesque bay. Eventually corals colonized the waters of the filled crater, creating the popular swimming and snorkeling attraction that draws so many visitors. Lava flows entering the ocean terminate in easily erodable sea cliffs, and, as Dr. Prescott points out, features such as caves, arches, and stacks are common on recent lava coasts. These are indicative of changing landforms, which pose a problem for those attempting to draw baselines which will have some degree of permanence.

While few argue that lava flows are not really land, there are many who feel that the real land of Antarctica lies thousands of feet below the ice cap. Some would map the continent as if the ice were not there, while most cartographers find it difficult enough to map the surface of the continent, whether ice-covered or not, as it appears now. To some ice is a form of rock, especially at the very cold temperatures in Antarctica. The arguments might seem to be more or less philosophical and without relevance, but if the law of the sea is to apply to Antarctica it seems clear that the ice cover must be considered to be the continent and the seaward edge of the ice shelves the true coastline. The fact that it changes shape relatively rapidly must be accepted and the technical problems of drawing coastal baselines somehow solved.

Dr. Prescott has suggested that official protests concerning patently illegal straight baselines be made promptly by all countries, even though the offending baselines have little practical effect. In other words, the law of the sea should be "enforced" to whatever extent it is possible. He further recommends that nations with baselines which contravene the provisions of Article 7 of the Convention should be prevented from ratifying the Convention or acceding to it. Those who take the view that the law of the sea is in general a good law should agree, but I fear that if other provisions of the Convention were to be "enforced" in a similar way, we might find that we truly do not have the consensus that seems to be indicated by the great number of countries that have signed. If all states with stated or implied reservations to various provisions of the Convention and which took actions contrary to any of the law's provisions were to be forbidden to be ratifiers it is possible that the required sixty ratifications would not be met. In that case we would have no Convention and might have to return to lengthy negotiations or rely exclusively on customary international law.

DISCUSSION AND QUESTIONS

Robert W. Smith: I am sure that Dr. Morgan's use of Antarctica was just illustrative, because we all know that no one would put straight baselines around Antarctica. However, one might face this problem at the other end of the earth if one were to draw straight baselines in the Arctic polar region. What happens when the coastline does change? Who gets cheated, the coastal state or the international community? There definitely needs to be a mechanism within the coastal state itself to deal with this problem. In the United States we have an Inter-agency Coastline Committee that reviews the charts as they come up for their normal schedule of publication, and we look at the coastline on set time periods. So, if coastlines do change, we make appropriate changes, be it extending the territorial sea or other zones or bringing it back.

Kaldone Nweihed: I would like to comment on Commander Beazley's reference to our Aves Island in the Caribbean. Aves Island is Venezuelan not because Venezuela went over to occupy the island; it accrued to the Republic through historic processes which were recognized by an international arbitration award in 1856. In negotiations and under the treaty concluded with the United States on maritime delimitation on March 28, 1978, Aves Island was given full effect of maritime jurisdiction. The gist of the conversation between the American delegation and ours was approximately as follows:

The Americans said, "Aves Island does not sustain any economic life of its own; it is not populated, and therefore it is not entitled to any economic zone or continental shelf."

Our delegation rebutted, "Do you remember what happened in 1854?"

"What was that?"

"In 1854 Aves Island was visited by a U.S. ship that had sailed from Boston with a gentlemen named Sheldon who, without any permission, installed a guano-gathering company which gathered and sold guano for along time before he was discovered. If that is not enough proof that the island does sustain economic life of its own, what other proof do you need? Furthermore, as regards the island being inhabited, you yourselves inhabited it without obtaining any visas!"

The scientific and historic information on the Aves Island episode is contained in a thesis submitted to the University of Tennessee in Nashville in 1963 by William Lane Harris.

Robert W. Smith: This audience did not realize how much it was going to learn about such large areas as Rockall and Aves Island.

Tullio Scovazzi: I would like to ask Dr. Prescott two questions. First, what is the difference between the bay and the deep indentation? Deep indentations are regulated by Article 7 of the Montego Bay Convention, which refers to the coastline deeply indented and cut into, and on the other hand bays are regulated by Article 10 of the same Convention, which defines the bay as a well-marked indentation with a mouth not exceeding twenty-four nautical miles. A few years ago, Australia closed two bays along its coast with straight baselines longer than twenty-four nautical miles by qualifying the bays as deep indentations. Can Professor Prescott suggest a clear distinction between a bay and a deep indentation?

355

Second, on the 1983 Australian legislation on straight baselines, did Australia apply the new provision on reefs? How is the problem of the Great Australian Barrier Reef regulated by straight baselines?

Victor Prescott: You can only close indentations with straight baselines when a number of features are in association. I prefer to refer to straight baselines as "regional baselines" to distinguish them from single closing lines. The provision for the semi-circle, when it was added by the Law Commission in 1956, was specifically put in to make quite sure that people could not use a whole series of bay closing lines to get around the problem of a coast that was not deeply indented, but along which they wanted to draw straight baselines. My answer is that a bay is a single feature; and indentations are relevant only where there are a number of indentations all together. Usually they would have offshore islands as well.

I am not sure which two bays you are thinking of along the Australian coastlines that are being closed by more than twenty-four nautical miles. One of them is Hardy Bay, which is on the Queensland coast. It is formed by an island. I used to think that an island could not form a bay; it could be in the mouth of a bay, but it could not form a bay. That view is now not only no longer fashionable, but I think it is probably unreasonable. The United States Supreme Court has certainly indicated very clearly that in certain circumstances islands can form bays, and I think that Great Sandy Island, which forms the eastern part of Hardy Bay, in fact is quite appropriate. But that is part of our straight baseline. It is not closed as a bay; it is closed as an indentation, and indeed it would be possible to argue that Great Frazier Island or Great Sandy Island is in fact a fringing island.

In terms of drawing maritime boundaries along the Great Barrier Reef, we have made a mess of it, because the Great Barrier reef fronts the coast of Queensland, which is presently governed by the most conservative government in Australia. There was a coalition conservative government at the time that the straight baselines were drawn. My own view -- and I understand it was the view of other delegations at the Law of the Sea Conference who spoke to the Australians -- is that the proper, sensible baseline would have been drawn on the outer edge of the Great Barrier Reef, and I have written a paper justifying that particular view. The government decided that it was politically impossible to do that, because it would have been seen by the public as delivering into the hands of a conservative government a great natural resource, perhaps one of the great common heritages. So instead they drew baselines that were inside some of the outer islands of the Great Barrier Reef. The result is a very complex pattern of maritime areas. It really is a terrible mess, and lawyers will make a fortune one day if somebody is murdered on a boat in the Great Barrier Reef because they will not know in which court to try it. But it was done entirely for political reasons. It is a very inconvenient solution, and it would have been just as easy to say "All right, we are going to draw the baseline down the outer edge of the reef, but we are also going to say that we will not, under the terms of the Great Barrier Reef Marine Park Act, which is in existence, allow any drilling for oil within that area."

John A. Knauss: Professor Morgan's picture of how one changes a rock into an island if it is sufficiently important, such as those converted during World War II, leads me to ask the following question. Given the distinction in the LOS Convention between rocks and islands, does any member of the panel think there is any theoretical or practical reason why any rock could not be made into an island and therefore have its continental shelf and exclusive economic zone if a state felt it was important enough to do so?

Victor Prescott: I take the view that if your particular feature is a sand, it cannot possibly be a rock. Therefore, it must be an island, and therefore it does not have to be habitable or have an economic life of its own. If the feature is surrounded by water and is above high water, then it is an island if it is sand. Even if that sand is completely bare, even if there is no vegetation, it has got to be an island.

Joseph Morgan: Victor, I am not sure I agree. "Rock" is never defined in the Convention, and although Lew Alexander's use of the term "non-conforming" is very helpful, I do not know that it has any validity in international law. My view is that since "rock" is not defined in the Convention, we have got to look at ordinary dictionary definitions of what the term "rock" is. One of them, according to *Webster's Third International*, is "a barren island." If we accept the barren island definition of rock, we are not required to first distinguish between rocks and islands and then to distinguish between which rocks are habitable and which are not. That is one of the vagaries of the wording of the Convention which is going to plague us. The view that all islands that are flat, sandy, and have an island appearance can be considered separately from rocks might be valid, but the alternative view is also valid.

Robert Smith: This "man-made" versus "natural" question may be a real problem in the future. What if, in the course of building a harborwork or pier, you change the physical action around that man-made feature so as to cause a build-up or a decretion of the coastline? Is that change man-made or is it natural? We have interpreted it as natural. That example perhaps is microgeography, perhaps, but I envision the day that some man-made construction causes such a substantial change in the coastline that it creates an expansion of the territorial sea.

Scott Sigman: With regard to Article 76, specifying sediments as well as slope of continental shelves, to what degree will submersibles or satellites be used in the future, or perhaps even currently, with regard to technical delimitations?

Lewis Alexander: Not much will be done until there is some economic or strategic reason for wondering where the lines are that far out. But the Continental Shelf Commission, which is called for in the Convention, may someday have to check the lines that countries bring in. I wondered, when they were setting this Commission up, who was going to pay for its operations, because they may be very expensive. But it is going to be some years before there will be an economic or political reason to determine, 300 or 400 miles out, this outer limit.

Peter Beazley: To some extent, this is being done now. Satellite position fixing is extensively used for all offshore determination. The boundary is defined normally by reference to geographical coordinates, and those coordinates can be located on the ground by use of satellites. That is the normal method for determining positions of all platforms and rigs, and in the North Sea it was the method used to determine the exact division of the shelf between Norway and the United Kingdom.

Kazuo Sumi: My question is how to avoid conflict and dispute in the delimitation programs. Dr. Alexander referred to the Continental Shelf Commission, but according to the Convention, Annex II, the Continental Shelf Commission will be established within eighteen months after the date of entry into force of the Convention. There are no objective criteria to determine the outer limit of the continental shelf. After the entry of the Convention, the Commission can review the past delimitations of the outer limits of the continental shelf. Is it possible or not?

I also have a question concerning Article 76, Paragraph 8. The Commission can make recommendations about the determination of the coastal state, and the limit of the shelf established by a coastal state on the basis of these recommendations shall be final and binding. If a coastal state determined the outer limit of the continental shelf in a different way, how would we interpret the expression "on the basis of these recommendations"? I have very serious doubts about provisions of this kind.

I would like to ask about the dispute settlement mechanism under Article 298. A coastal state can make a declaration excluding the application of the dispute settlement procedure. But there is no guarantee of final settlement of the dispute. If the coastal state cannot accept the recommendations of the conciliation commission, what happens? We cannot solve the problem. What can we do?

Lew Alexander: Speaking as a private citizen, I am not sure what the United States' policy is right now. It is my understanding that as a non-signatory to the Convention the U.S. probably would not participate in the Commission activities, nor at this point in the dispute settlement activities. But it may be years before the Commission begins to operate. There was a considerable discussion during the negotiations as to what term should be used; should it be "in accordance with," "on the basis of," or "taking into account"? We got it as strong as possible; that is, the Commission's recommendations would have considerable impact upon what the final decision would be.

Peter Beazley: I think this provision was seen not as a confrontational issue between a coastal state and the Commission so much as a dialog between the state and the Commission. It was hoped that since the Commission would largely consist of experts, the matter would be thrashed out on a technical basis and not on a purely legal or political one, so that, ultimately, the case would perhaps never arise.

Dolliver Nelson: I would like to make two points. Article 121, Paragraph 3, says "rocks which cannot sustain human habitation or economic life of their own shall have no exclusive economic zone or continental shelf." First, there is no attempt to define "rocks," clearly a great weakness of this provision. It defines which rock-like formation would not generate exclusive economic zones or continental shelves. "Cannot sustain," I presume, must mean that we are dealing with the present. Whatever may have happened centuries ago would not be relevant to the notion of what a rock is not able to sustain today. So one has to look at what is happening today, the capability of that rock-like formation at the present time.

Second, I should like to underline the words "of their own." It will clearly mean that any attempt to create an artificial situation by helping the particular rock to sustain human habitation or an economic life would certainly fall under Article 60, Paragraph 8, which says "Artificial islands, installations and structures do not possess the status of islands. They have no territorial sea of their own, and their presence does not affect the delimitation --" etc. In other words, they do not even have a territorial sea.

PART V:

SCIENCE, LAW AND THE SEA

INTRODUCTION

R.J.H. Beverton
Department of Applied Biology
University of Wales Institute of Science and Technology

This panel is about science, law and the sea. I think those scientists who, over many decades, have sought to explore and understand the secrets of the oceans have always been a truly international community. There has always been a degree of fellowship among the marine science community, both as people and as institutions and organizations, that is rivalled perhaps only by our friends in the meteorological world, and the reasons for this are not far to seek. First of all, scientific knowledge of the world, in general, pays little regard to how we mere mortals have chosen to draw boundaries on maps and make rules and regulations about crossing them, and that is especially true of our fluid environment -- whether it be the sea or the atmosphere. Secondly, the the scale of the problem of trying to comprehend synoptically the secrets of the oceans and especially our realization now at the profound influence that the oceans have on so many aspects of the life on this planet means that even the strongest countries with the strongest marine science capability find it a daunting task to attack alone; so, the natural tendency is to get together. In addition, the natural affinity among seafarers of all nations to think of themselves as a community, especially when in distress, adds a special dimension to the marine science integration. So it is perhaps not surprising that many of us in the marine science community have watched with some misgivings the events over the last nearly twenty years now with, as far as the evolution of the law of the sea is concerned, feelings that ranged from resignation even to despair. On the other hand, it is equally clear that the whole way in which the evolution of this new order has gone and the natural aspirations of the coastal states should change the way things are done, and so the task facing the marine science community now is to see how best to maintain the thrust and cooperation necessary to continue the understanding of the oceans within the new framework -- but it cannot do it alone; it needs the help of many other people in many other walks of life. If we can explore that general theme during this morning, it will have been a useful and an interesting exercise.

Now, I would like to introduce my panel. We are doing things a bit differently in that we are not having speakers and then commentators. We have asked a small number of people to speak this morning who have direct experience in various aspects of marine scientific search. It seems to me that, since most of the speakers this morning are scientists, we should get ourselves straight with guidance from the lawyers.

My first panel speaker is Fred Soons who is Deputy Legal Counsel in the Dutch Ministry of Transport. Fred is an appropriate speaker not only because he has written one of the definitive texts on marine science and the law of the sea but also because he comes from the Netherlands, the home of Grotius back in 1605 when he wrote *Mare Liberum* and was instrumental in negotiating with James I of England and Scotland about the conditions governing the freedom of access to fishing rights around the the British Isles.

My second panelist is Professor John Knauss from the Graduate School of Oceanography of the University of Rhode Island, who is one of the founding members of the Institute. He will be talking about the recent United States experience on the operation of the consent regime.

Next is Chris Adams, our operations officer at the Research Vessel base in Barry, only a few miles from here, where he handles the transfer of requests for consent and receives requests from other countries to do research within the U.K. consent regime. He is very much at the forefront of the practical problems that arise in trying to work the new system.

Then Tony Laughton, who is Director of the Institute of Oceanographic Sciences, our largest and only really major research Institute in this country that is concerned with oceanography of the deep oceans, will tell us how he sees the future of oceanography and how it can best be advanced given the framework set by the Convention on the Law of the Sea.

We must not forget fisheries science because it is not all that easily distinguished from basic oceanography. For example, the *El Nino* phenomenon has not only a major impact on the day-to-day fisheries problems of the countries on the west coast of South America but is also a fundamental consequence of major atmospheric oscillations affecting sea levels and long wavelengths right across the Pacific, and illustrates how fisheries science and basic oceanography are inseparable. Our speaker Rowena Lawson, who is a consultant on fisheries with a lot of experience overseas, will speak of the situation arising from the new Convention, and especially in the developing world.

My last panelist is Nic Flemming, also from the Institute of Oceanographic Sciences. He is in charge of the Marine Information Service and will speak about the significance of the Law of the Sea Convention in relation to the fundamental point of understanding information about the oceans. Nic Flemming came with me back in 1967 to the Sea-bed Committee. We were there right from the very beginning, when Henry Darwin, our lunchtime speaker, was trying to map out a logical approach to the very early stages of the final law of the sea discussions. Nic has been closely in touch with what has been happening ever since.

MARINE SCIENTIFIC RESEARCH
PROVISIONS IN THE CONVENTION ON THE LAW OF THE SEA:
ISSUES OF INTERPRETATION

Alfred H.A. Soons
Netherlands Ministry of Transport

Introductory Remarks

This conference is supposed to deal with the impact and implementation of the Law of the Sea Convention, and this morning we will be discussing its science provisions. Being the only lawyer on this panel, I understand that I am expected to deal with the legal aspects. Now I must confess it is not always altogether clear to me what are the legal aspects of a social phenomenon such as an international legal regime, as contrasted with the non-legal aspects. For our purpose, however, I propose to look at the science provisions of the Law of the Sea Convention from the perspective of their *interpretation*. I think it is necessary, in order to be able to implement these provisions or to assess their (future) impact, to know what they mean. In other words, it is important to know what the law *is*, or will be.

What I would like to convey to you is that, although we now have a very comprehensive and detailed regime in the new Law of the Sea Convention -- comprehensive and detailed as compared to the regime under the 1958 Geneva Conventions, which contained only two paragraphs dealing with scientific research (paragraphs 1 and 8 of Article 5 of the Continental Shelf Convention) whereas Part XIII of the Law of the Sea Convention contains 27 articles -- there are still many outstanding questions on what precisely the law is. In legal terms, the meaning of these provisions is often ambiguous or obscure.

While I concentrate on questions of interpretation, the other papers I understand will concentrate on impact and implementation issues. By focusing on interpretation questions, I will be dealing with what one might call the "extrinsic quality" of the provisions. The extrinsic quality refers to the way in which the substantive provisions have been phrased (their clarity, consistency, etc.), whereas the "intrinsic quality" refers to the content of the substantive provisions as such: is it desirable law, policywise, or not? Comments on the "intrinsic quality" of the provisions are political statements and should be identified as such (although I have to admit that the distinction is not always as clear as I now perhaps seem to indicate).

I say this because much has already been said in the past about the "intrinsic quality" of the marine scientific research regime of the (drafts for the) Law of the Sea Convention. We should now consider it a fact, and take it as it is, whether we like it or not. Part XIII of the Law of the Sea Convention is a typical product of UNCLOS III. It is a result of the package deal approach and the consensus procedure, which means that it is very much a compromise regime. As a conventional regime it will not be changed, and I don't think the science part of the Law of the Sea Convention will play any significant role in discussions in any state on whether or not to ratify the Convention. What might happen, of course, is that states which do not intend to ratify the Law of the Sea Convention will try to prevent certain of the main features of the science regime from becoming part of customary international law. I will come back to this issue at the end of my presentation.

Before turning to discussing some interpretation questions, I would like to make two preliminary remarks. First, I will only be dealing in my presentation with provisions concerning marine scientific research conducted in the exclusive economic zone or on the continental shelf, since these areas are most important for marine scientific research and at the same time are subject to a complex regime. Marine scientific research in the internal waters, archipelagic waters and territorial sea, high seas and international seabed area is subject to a much more simple regime: in the internal waters, archipelagic waters and territorial sea, research is under complete coastal state jurisdiction, whereas in the high seas and on the international seabed area it is essentially free.

My second preliminary remark concerns the very meaning of the term "marine scientific research." It is important at the outset to try to indicate as precisely as possible the meaning of the term "marine scientific research" as used in the Law of the Sea Convention; or, in other words, to indicate exactly which activities are governed by the provisions on marine scientific research laid down in Part XIII of the Convention (the scope *ratione materiae* of the regime).

Marine scientific research is only one category of activities undertaken at sea to gather information/obtain knowledge, although sometimes other such activities are also referred to as "marine scientific research." The Law of the Sea Convention uses several terms for such activities, which should be clearly distinguished because different legal regimes apply to them. Careless use of terms will result in confusion about the legal regime that applies to a certain activity.

The Law of the Sea Convention does not contain a definition of marine scientific research. In earlier negotiating texts of the Law of the Sea Conference, a provision had been included defining marine scientific research as "any study or related experimental work designed to increase mankind's knowledge of the marine environment." Although this definition was supported by many delegations to the Conference, it was not retained in the final drafts for the Convention. Apparently there was a consensus at the Conference that a definition of the term "marine scientific research" in the Convention would not be necessary, since the substantive provisions of the Convention would clearly establish the meaning intended.

When attempting to define more precisely the meaning of the term "marine scientific research" as used in the Convention, two categories of factors are involved. The first category concerns the ordinary meaning of the words "marine scientific research"; the second category concerns the significance, for this purpose, of the substantive provisions of the Convention (the "context").

The term "marine scientific research" seems to have a clear ordinary meaning. Scientific research commonly being regarded as an investigation of a question, problem or phenomenon conducted according to the rules and principles of science, *marine* scientific research may be regarded as such investigation concerned with the marine environment or its natural phenomena. The marine environment is commonly understood as covering the water column, the seabed and the subsoil, and the atmosphere immediately above the sea. Thus, the term "marine scientific research" covers any scientific investigation, however and wherever conducted, having the marine environment as object. The Convention's provisions on marine scientific research are mainly concerned with the conduct of research in the marine environment itself; however, some provisions also cover marine scientific research activities conducted in laboratories on land (for example, Article 249).

The significance of the adjective "marine" in the term "marine scientific research" is illustrated by the fact that the provisions of the Convention in some instances refer to "scientific research" generally (as distinct from *marine* scientific research; cf., (Articles 87, 123 and 258-262). It should also be noted that Articles 19 and 40 even refer to any "research." This clearly implies that the legal regime of marine scientific research under the Convention in principle does not apply to scientific research activities *not* concerning the marine environment (*e.g.*, astronomical observations carried out at sea).

Although the term "marine scientific research," in its ordinary meaning, would cover any scientific investigation of the marine environment, both fundamental and applied, it appears from the provisions of the Convention that for the purpose of the application of the Convention certain applied scientific research activities are excluded from its scope. The Convention provides for a separate regime for resource exploration. Resources exploration in all areas under coastal state jurisdiction is subject to the sovereign rights of the coastal state; resource exploration in the international seabed area is governed by the international regime for that area. Exploration may be defined as data-collecting activities (scientific research) concerning natural resources, whether living or non-living, conducted specifically in view of the exploitation (*i.e.*, economic utilization) of those natural resources. Such research is *not* covered by the term "marine scientific research" as used in the Convention. However, as will be seen later, scientific research which is of direct significance for the exploration and exploitation of natural resources but which is not aimed at the utilization of such resources still qualifies as marine scientific research.

Similarly, the Convention provides for a separate regime for hydrographic surveying. I deliberately use the term "hydrographic surveying," and not "hydrography." since the term "hydrography" is still used sometimes to refer to oceanography or at least physical oceanography, which of course is marine scientific research. Hydrographic surveying may be defined as the measurement of the bathymetry of the ocean and the study of waves, currents and tidal phenomena, surveying of underwater rocks, shoals and other hidden dangers for the purpose of the preparation of nautical publications such as charts, sailing directions, tide tables, and current charts. From Articles 19, 21, and 40, which use the term "hydrographic surveying" separately from "research," it follows that the term "marine scientific research," for the purposes of the Convention, does not cover hydrographic surveying activities.

Issues of Interpretation

I now turn to a discussion of some interpretation questions.

An institution wishing to conduct marine scientific research in the exclusive economic zone of another coastal state should, according to Article 248 of the Convention, at least six months before the expected starting date of the marine scientific research project" provide that coastal state with certain information concerning the research project as specified in the Article.

What should be regarded for this purpose as the "expected starting date" of the research project? Several moments can be regarded as such, for example:

367

- the date on which the detailed planning of the research project is started; or
- the date on which the research vessel involved leaves the researching state; or
- the first day of the actual research operations in the exclusive economic zone of the coastal state involved.

I would submit that the last-mentioned date is the date intended in Article 248, although it could be argued that an earlier moment would be more appropriate in view of the possibility for the coastal state to participate in the project. For this participation to be meaningful it might in certain cases be extended to [include] also the preparatory stage of a research cruise.

Article 250 of the Convention requires the notification to the coastal state of the intention to do research in its exclusive economic zone, and indeed all communications between researching states and coastal states concerning marine scientific research projects, [are] to be made through "appropriate official channels," unless otherwise agreed.

What is meant by "appropriate official channels"? I think in principle the coastal state may determine what it considers to be the appropriate official channels, but in the absence of such a determination it will not be clear if, for instance, the notification can be done by a governmental research institution in the researching state to a similar institution in the coastal state, or if diplomatic channels must be used. The latter are undoubtedly "official channels" but not always the most efficient ones.

The communication to the coastal state informing it of the intention to conduct a research object in its exclusive economic zone (or on its continental shelf) can be regarded as the request for consent as required under paragraph 2 of Article 246.

The coastal state can react in several ways to this communication. The first one is to *refuse* consent. According to Paragraph 5 of Article 246 a coastal state *may*, in its discretion, refuse consent if the research project is "of direct significance for the exploration and exploitation of natural resources, whether living or non-living."

When must marine scientific research be considered to be "of direct significance for the exploration and exploitation of natural resources"? It could very well be that this phrase will constitute in the future the main source of disputes relating to the marine scientific research provisions of the Law of the Sea Convention. It will be up to the marine scientists, the real experts in this matter, to indicate how exactly this issue can be handled in practice. However, I would still like to make a few comments as a non-scientist.

As I already indicated, the concept of marine scientific research as used in the Law of the Sea Convention is to be distinguished from the concept of exploration. The term "exploration" is nowhere defined in the Convention, but from the context in which the term is consistently used ("exploration and exploitation of natural resources") it is clear that it is used to denote data-collecting activities concerning natural resources conducted specifically in view of the exploitation (meaning the economic utilization) of those natural resources. This implies that the term "marine scientific research" refers to those data-collecting activities (irrespective of their object, as long as that object is part of the marine environment) which are *not* conducted specifically in view of the exploitation of natural resources.

The objects of both data-collecting activities can be the same. Marine scientific research is concerned with natural phenomena of the marine environment. Exploration can be concerned with the same phenomena, which, because of their economic significance, then are called "natural resources." Thus, the motivations for undertaking the activities (their objectives) differ. Also in most cases the instruments, techniques and methods will differ, although sometimes they are similar.

Since marine scientific research can be concerned with the same object as exploration (natural phenomena which can be considered natural resources), it is obvious that the results of such marine scientific research can be relevant, or significant, for exploration activities. Marine scientific research can also be directly relevant for the *exploitation* of natural resources, particularly living resources.

The phrase "marine scientific research of direct significance for the exploration and exploitation of natural resources" thus is concerned with marine scientific research, the results of which are relevant for the exploration or exploitation of natural resources, and therefore have a certain economic (commercial) value. This relevance, or significance, must however be direct. This would seem to imply that the results of the research in question must have their own, intrinsic value from the point of view of exploration or exploitation and that it is not enough that the research results are only remotely significant (for example, research results which can *become* useful from this point of view when they are combined with other data to be collected).

In conclusion: As research of direct significance for the exploration or exploitation of natural resources should be considered that research which can reasonably be expected to produce results permitting researchers to locate resources, to assess them, or to monitor their status and availability for commercial exploitation. It should be noted that such research could also be significant in a negative sense: it could indicate those areas where it is (probably) not worth looking for resources.

In this connection I should finally mention that Article 251 invites states to promote through competent international organizations the establishment of general criteria and guidelines to assist states (and I assume: particularly developing coastal states) in ascertaining the nature and implications of marine scientific research. Here lies a task for IOC and FAO.

There are two other, less important, cases in which a coastal state is entitled to withhold consent at its discretion, namely if the research project

- involves drilling, the use of explosives or the introduction of harmful substances into the marine environment; or if it
- involves the construction, operation or use of artificial islands, installations and structures.

Apart from reacting to the communication by the researching state by *refusing* consent, a coastal state can also react by *postponing* a decision whether or not to grant consent.

Article 252 entitles a coastal state to require supplementary information when this is necessary to adequately assess the notification by the researching state. This raises the question what the consequences of such a request for supplementary information are for the eventual starting date of the research project. I would submit that the right to request supplementary information must be exercised reasonably;

it may not be abused to delay or prevent altogether the execution of a research project. The coastal state must therefore clearly specify which additional information it requires to make a definitive decision on whether or not to grant consent. It will have to react to the communication from the researching state containing the additional information within a reasonable period of time. This period may vary according to the nature of the supplementary information, but in any case may not last longer than four months.

When the coastal state does react within four months by granting consent, the field work may be started six months after the supplementary information was received by the coastal state, unless the latter agrees to an earlier starting date.

Another possibility to *postpone* a decision occurs for the coastal state when, also according to Article 252, outstanding obligations exist with respect to a previous marine scientific research project carried out by the researching state in question. As a result of this provision, research institutions in one state can be confronted with the consequences of a record of non-compliance of another research institution in the same state: the coastal state is entitled to with-hold consent for the conduct of research projects by institutions from a particular state as long as there is one institution in that state which has not complied with all relevant conditions. The coastal state is only obliged to take a decision on the research project after the outstanding obligations have been fulfilled. This provision raises a number of interpretation questions which I will not go into.

Apart from the situation in which a coastal state may refuse consent or delay a decision, which I have just discussed, in all other cases coastal states should, according to Paragraph 3 of Article 246, "in normal circumstances *grant* their consent for marine scientific research projects by other States or competent international organizations in their exclusive economic zone or on their continental shelf to be carried out exclusively for peaceful purposes and in order to increase scientific knowledge of the marine environment for the benefit of all mankind."

The consent of the coastal state can be given explicitly, or implicitly. Article 252 provides that, if the coastal state has not reacted within four months of the receipt of the communication informing it of the proposed research project, the researching state may proceed with the project six months after the coastal state was informed.

The formulation of the duty to grant consent I just referred to raises a number of interpretation questions. I will only say a few words about the phrase "in normal circumstances" and leave aside phrases such as "peaceful purposes" and "benefit of all mankind." What are to be considered normal circumstances for this purpose? Some guidance can be found in Article 246 itself. Paragraph 4 provides that normal circumstances may exist in spite of the absence of diplomatic relations between the coastal state and the researching state. From this paragraph, it follows that in those situations where the coastal state and the researching state do not maintain diplomatic relations (which could cover even the situation where the two governments involved do not accord each other recognition), the coastal state is not entitled to invoke automatically the existence of abnormal circumstances: the absence of diplomatic relations should be a reflection of the existence between the two states involved of political relations of such a nature that the coastal state could not reasonably be expected to grant consent. An obvious example would be a situation of imminent danger of armed conflict although lesser stages of tension could also qualify as such. It would seem that "normal circumstances" for this purpose not only concern the relations between the coastal state and the researching state, but may also concern the general political situation in the coastal state or within the region of which the coastal state is part. Again, (imminent) armed conflict could be an example of non-normal circumstances for this purpose.

A very special feature of the Law of the Sea Convention regime for marine scientific research concerns the rights of neighbouring land-locked and geographically disadvantaged states.

According to Article 254, not only the coastal state, but also the "neighbouring land-locked and geographically disadvantaged States" should be notified of the intention to conduct marine scientific research, and, when the coastal state has granted consent, these states are also entitled to receive certain information on the project and its results, and may (when feasible), even participate in it. The main question arising here is: which states are the beneficiaries of the rights this article creates? What, for this purpose, are "neighbouring States"; and what are "geographically disadvantaged States"? Land-locked states can, of course, be more easily identified.

A lot can be said about the various possible answers to these questions, but I will not do so now. However, if I may venture a comment relating also to the intrinsic quality of this Article: it would not surprise me if it were never implemented even after the entry into force of the Convention, and I certainly doubt that it will ever become part of customary international law.

The other marine scientific research provisions of the Law of the Sea Convention also raise a number of interpretation questions. For example, the provisions frequently refer to marine scientific research "on the continental shelf." Does this mean marine scientific research conducted physically on the continental shelf (in other words, research involving physical contact with the seabed or subsoil), or any research concerning the seabed and subsoil, however conducted? I think there are convincing arguments supporting the latter interpretation, but the text itself is not completely clear.

Other interpretation questions concern the exact scope and extent of the right of the coastal state to participate, or be represented, in research projects conducted in its exclusive economic zone or on its continental shelf, the right of the coastal state to order suspension or cessation of research in progress, its right of access to data and samples collected and the results, its right to receive assistance from the researching state in the assessment or interpretation of research results; the obligation of the researching state to inform the coastal state immediately of any *major* change in the research program (what is a "major change", and what are its consequences?); the extent of the duty of the researching state to remove scientific research installations or equipment after completion of the research, etc.

Concluding Remarks

The examples I have just discussed of science provisions in the Law of the Sea Convention, the exact meaning of which still has to be determined, are, of course, not all of equal importance, and not all will prove to be controversial. But the point I wanted to make is that they will have to be settled in the near future, and that some of them are of crucial importance for an effective implementation of the regime. How will this be done?

In the first place, state practice will establish the exact meaning. Although one could argue that formally speaking only state practice *after* the entry into force of the Convention should be considered to establish the meaning intended by the parties, I submit that in practice present state practice will already be highly relevant for this purpose.

Of course one should be very careful when drawing conclusions from the practice of states in an area covered by a convention which is not yet in force. Only the practice of states which take the position that they are acting in accordance with the provisions of the Law of the Sea Convention would be relevant. This would also be important in the case the Law of the Sea Convention never enters into force, because in that case certain of its provisions could still become customary international law. Other states may be deliberately acting *not* in accordance with these provisions, because they do not wish them to become rules of customary international law. This means that governments are *now* already faced with important decisions on how they wish that certain provisions should be generally interpreted, and should act accordingly to try to achieve that purpose.

Apart from by state practice, the exact meaning could also be established by judicial or other decisions if disputes between states arise and are submitted to dispute settlement procedures. I expect, however, that this will not happen frequently.

In view of the fact that the Law of the Sea Convention's provisions are often such that their exact meaning can be the subject of a dispute, it would seem extremely important to have adequate compulsory procedures for settling such disputes. It is therefore disappointing that for this purpose, the Convention's provisions on the procedures for the settlement of disputes relating to marine scientific research are totally inadequate.

Those provisions subject the most important disputes relating to marine scientific research activities, *viz.*, disputes arising out of the coastal state's exercise of a right or discretion in accordance with Article 246 (decisions whether or not to grant consent), and disputes arising out of a decision by the coastal state to order suspension or cessation of a research project in progress in accordance with Article 253, only to a conciliation procedure. Other disputes relating to marine scientific research activities are subject to compulsory procedures entailing binding decisions. The absence of compulsory procedures entailing binding decisions for the settlement of disputes concerning the interpretation or application of Articles 246 and 253 must be regarded as a serious deficiency of the Convention regime for marine scientific research.

REFERENCE

A.H.A. Soons, *Marine Scientific Research and the Law of the Sea*, Kluwer (Deventer, the Netherlands) (1982).

R.J.H. Beverton: The range of possible interpretation can be wide if you work too closely to the letter of the Convention, so perhaps the test is how it is working out in practice. And you may say of course that it is early days from the time when the Convention was signed in 1982 -- especially as it is still far from entering into force. On the other hand, arrangements for marine scientific research have been operating for some years in many areas. So we do have a body of experience already being accumulated. The next panel member, Dr. John Knauss, will describe the United States experience in operating the consent regime.

THE EFFECT OF THE LAW OF THE SEA ON MARINE SCIENTIFIC RESEARCH IN THE UNITED STATES: RECENT TRENDS

John A. Knauss
Graduate School of Oceanography
University of Rhode Island

and

Mary Hope Katsouros
National Research Council
National Academy of Science

Introduction

Coincident with the seaward extension of national jurisdiction is the interest of coastal states in being informed about the research taking place off their shores and in exercising some control over it. Much of this interest is generated by the economic importance of their offshore resources, that is, fish and oil. Another important reason is military security. This trend began after World War II with the Truman Proclamation of 1945, which marked the start of the recent movement toward seaward extension of coastal state jurisdiction. The present manifestation of that movement is the 1982 United Nations Convention on the Law of the Sea. Although the Convention is far from receiving the necessary support to enter into force, the concept of some form of coastal state jurisdiction out to 200 nautical miles is widely accepted. As of June 1985, some 103 of the world's 139 coastal nations claim jurisdiction over a 200-mile zone, fifteen claim a 200-mile territorial sea, twenty-four claim a 200-mile fisheries zone, and sixty-four claim a 200-mile exclusive economic zone. It can be anticipated that the remaining 26 percent of the coastal states will make comparable claims.

The United States Proclamation of an Exclusive Economic Zone (EEZ) was made March 10, 1983. In it the President proclaimed:

> sovereign rights for the purpose of exploring, exploiting, conserving and managing natural resources, both living and nonliving, of the seabed and subsoil and superadjacent waters and with regard to other activities for economic exploitation and exploration of the zone.

373

Nowhere in the ten-paragraph proclamation is marine scientific research mentioned. However, in the accompanying statement to the Proclamation, the President said the following:

> While international law provides for a right of jurisdiction over marine scientific research within such a zone, the Proclamation does not assert this right. I have elected not to do so because of the United States interests in encouraging marine scientific research and avoiding any unnecessary burdens. The United States will nevertheless recognize the right of the other coastal States to exercise jurisdiction over marine scientific research within 200 nautical miles of their coasts, if that jurisdiction is exercised reasonably in a manner consistent with international law.

We are unaware of any other coastal state that has made an explicit exemption of marine scientific research from at least some form of jurisdiction within its 200-mile zone.

Any jurisdictional restrictions on marine scientific research carry additional costs to those whose goal is the effective and efficient prosecution of such research. At the minimum these costs are the necessary protocols that must be followed for the research to be allowed, most of which concern providing adequate advance notice of the proposed research, opportunities for coastal state participation, and timely sharing of data and results. At the other extreme, the cost is outright refusal of the coastal state to allow the proposed research in its area of claimed jurisdiction. In between are the missed opportunities, program delays, and time-consuming efforts of both scientist and government officials to ensure the research program is carried out as planned.

The rules under which marine scientific research has operated in claimed coastal state jurisdictions have been in a continuing state of flux since at least the 1964 entrance into force of the 1958 Continental Shelf Convention. Some of the difficulties of the marine scientific community can be laid to misunderstandings, misinformation, and differing interpretations of the law. Unfortunately, this situation seems likely to prevail until such time as the 1982 Convention, or at least most of it, is widely adopted and generally perceived as customary international law. Given the present position of the United States, as well as the positions of a number of other major maritime powers, one cannot be optimistic about this happening soon. However, the range of interpretations and resultant misunderstandings may lessen if both the researching state and the coastal state use the 1982 Convention as a guide to state practice. The United States National Research Council has recently completed a review of those parts of the 1982 Convention which refer to marine scientific research (National Research Council, 1985). We can expect other such studies in the future.

One example of the narrowing of the range of state practice with respect to marine scientific research is the very significant change in United State policy since the March 1983 Presidential Proclamation on the EEZ. This Proclamation implies that the United States will accept all provisions of the 1982 Convention except those pertaining to the exploitation of the resources of the deep seabed, subject of course to its own interpretation of the Convention; for example, its imaginative reading of the Articles of Part V on the Exclusive Economic Zone allows it to continue its present practice of denying coastal state jurisdiction over tuna.

374

Before the Proclamation, the United States did not recognize the right of a coastal state to exercise its jurisdiction over marine scientific research beyond a three-mile territorial sea and on the continental shelf, as defined in the 1958 Convention to which it is a party. Those of us who wished to do research off the shores of such nations as Chile or Peru, both of which claimed jurisdiction to 200 miles but have narrow continental shelves were faced with a dilemma. The United States would not forward our requests for permission since it did not recognize these extended claims. However, if we were to work in these waters without permission, we ran the risk of being apprehended. The usual solution was to design a research program that included at least a minimum amount of work within a few miles of shore. As part of its request to the coastal state for the research vessel to work close to shore, the United States State Department would forward the plan for the total research program, including all the work planned within 200 miles of the coastal state. Assuming there were no other difficulties with the request, the coastal state would approve the entire program. In this way, both the United States and the coastal state preserved their different juridicial positions, and the scientists could carry on their work with confidence that its problems were scientific, not diplomatic.

Most of the distant water marine scientific research in the United States is conducted from ships either owned or operated by universities, although in most cases the funds to support the research, including the operation of the ships, come from the federal government. At times the operating university would bypass the State Department completely. Rather than rearrange its work plan to include a nearshore program, it would use its own coastal state contacts to secure permission. Since such discussions and requests were not at a government-to-government level, the official United States position was not compromised.

As noted, the March 10, 1983 statement of the President accompanying his Exclusive Economic Zone Proclamation "recognizes the right of other coastal states to exercise jurisdiction over marine scientific research within 200 nautical miles of their coast." Since the Proclamation, the United States has forwarded to the coastal state all requests for permission to do marine scientific research within 200 miles.

Results

Previous authors have reviewed the problems of United States researchers in conducting marine scientific research in areas where other states have claimed jurisdiction. Kildow (1973) reviewed a number of problems prior to 1972, and Wooster (1981) reviewed problems in the period 1972 to 1978. We have reviewed recent problems of the United States scientific community in conducting marine scientific research for the six-year period 1979 to 1984 as a result of the ever-changing law of the sea. The statistical data are drawn entirely from the Department of State, whose files in the Bureau of Oceans and International Environmental and Scientific Affairs were made available.

The usual path of a clearance transaction includes the following steps:

1) A plan for marine scientific research is developed to a sufficient extent that a request for permission to work in foreign waters is justified. At the time of the request, which according to the 1982 Convention should be at least six months prior to the start of the work, one can assume that the ship and operating institution have been

chosen, as has the chief scientist. Funding for the program has been "promised," but may not be in hand. Not all members of the scientific party have been chosen, nor have all details of the scientific work plan been developed. As in nearly all scientific research, the program is under continuing modification up to the start of the program, and, of course, is subject to modification during the program as a result of information developed.

2) The appropriate institution initiates a request for clearance to work and provides the State Department with the required information. Article 248 of the 1982 Convention codifies the kinds of information that have been traditionally provided. It includes the nature and objectives of the project, name of vessel, persons and institution responsible, where and when the work will be done, and the extent to which the coastal state may be expected to participate in the project. The Convention accepts the reality of modifications as the program develops, but Article 253 gives the coastal state the right to require the cessation of a previously approved project in the case of a major change in the research project as approved.

3) The Department of State forwards the clearance request to the coastal state through the United States embassy. As previously noted, United States university-based researchers have in the past sometimes made private arrangements for clearances, particularly before the Presidential EEZ Proclamation. Article 250 requires [that] all communications be made through appropriate official channels unless otherwise agreed. However, there is no United States requirement that the researching institution must make its arrangements through the federal government.

4) The coastal state now has several options. It can respond, it can request further information, it can approve the request, it can approve the request subject to modification or it can disapprove the request. If and when the 1982 Convention is widely accepted, Article 252 carries an implied consent clause. A failure of the coastal state to respond to the request in some manner within four months of receiving it implies that consent has been received.

Sometimes the program is not carried out even though the coastal state gives permission. For example, sometimes the project is cancelled because the researching state is not prepared to modify the program as requested by the coastal state. Sometimes the project is cancelled for reasons having nothing to do with the clearance; for example, a major change in ship schedule because of unforeseen funding problems or unforeseen technical problems including a breakdown on the ship. Sometimes the project is cancelled because permission comes too late to reschedule the program.

The number of requests to the United States State Department for clearance to do research in waters of coastal state jurisdiction have steadily increased since 1972. The data for 1979 to 1984 are given in *Table 1*. By comparison there were thirty-seven requests in 1972. The average number of requests from 1973 to 1982, while UNCLOS was being negotiated, was seventy-two with more in the last five years (80) than in the first five (64). There were 109 requests in 1983 and 162 in 1984. We do not believe the increase in clearance requests is because of increased research activity. If anything the number of United States research vessels capable of operating in distant waters is fewer now than it was a decade ago. In the absence of further analysis we assume the slow increase in requests is because of the steady increase in the number of coastal states that claimed extended jurisdictions during

Table 1

Summary of Clearance Experience

	Requests						Total Requests	Total "Denials"
	1979	1980	1981	1982	1983	1984		
Antigua					1	1	2	0
Argentina	1	3				3	7	0
Australia	2					1	3	0
Bahamas	3	4	5	4	5	7	28	0
Bahrain					1		1	1
Barbados	1	1	3	1	5	5	16	1
Belize			1			1	2	0
Brazil	4			5	3	4	16	2
Canada	14	22	14	16	27	35	128	0
Chile	4	1	2	2	5	6	20	0
China		1					1	0
Costa Rica	1	1	1	1		1	5	1
Colombia					1		1	1
Cuba	3	1					4	4
Denmark			1		3	1	5	0
Dominica	2		1			2	5	0
Dominican Republic	2	4		1		6	13	1
Ecuador				3	3	1	7	0
Egypt					1	4	5	0
Fiji							3	0
France	2	2	1	3	4		12	0
French Guiana					1		1	0
Granada	1					2	3	0
Guatemala			2			1	3	0
Guyana	1					1	2	0
Haiti	1	1	2	2	2	5	13	1
Honduras			1	1	1	3	6	0
Iceland					3		3	0
Indonesia	1	1					2	1
Ivory Coast					1		1	0
Jamaica	1	1	1	1	3	1	8	0
Japan						3	3	0
Kiribati					1		1	0
Mexico	33	19	26	12	11	13	114	28
Morocco	1		1	1	2		5	0
Netherlands	1			1	1		3	0
New Zealand	1				1	1	3	0
Nicaragua	1		1				2	1
Norway					5	3	8	0
Panama	2				2	3	7	1
Papua New Guinea	1					2	3	0
Peru	1	1	2	4	4	3	17	0
Philippines	2	2					4	0
Portugal						6	6	0
Romania						1	1	0
Saudi Arabia					2	2	4	1

Table 1 (continued)

	Requests						Total Requests	Total "Denials"
	1979	1980	1981	1982	1983	1984		
St. Lucia	2	1	2	2		3	10	0
St. Vincent	1	1	2	1		4	9	0
Solomon Islands				2		1	3	0
Somalia	1		1			1	3	0
South Africa					1	1	2	0
Spain			2	2	2		6	2
Suriname	1					1	2	0
Tonga				1		1	2	0
Trinidad & Tobago	1					1	2	1
Turkey						1	1	0
U. A. E.					1		1	1
United Kingdom	3	3	2	3	5	10	26	0
Uruguay						2	2	0
U.S.S.R.	2					2	4	3
Vanuatu				1		1	2	0
Venezuela	2	1	1	1	2	2	9	2
No. of requests	100	68	78	72	109	162	589	53
No. of countries	34	19	24	25	31	48	62	18

this period. The sharp rise in 1984 may be for the same reason but could also be related to the change in United States policy affecting requests in the 200-mile zones of other states.

In all, 589 clearance events were identified covering sixty-two different coastal states. Of those 589 clearances, 242 or 41% were for work in the waters of our large neighbors to the north and south, Canada and Mexico. Proportionately large numbers of clearances were requested from other near neighbors including the Bahamas, Barbados, the Dominican Republic and Haiti. Nearly all of the clearance requests for France, the Netherlands, and the United Kingdom are for North American territories. Frequency of requests is not simply a function of distance from the United States. Along the west coast of South America the number of requests were Chile twenty; Peru, fifteen; Ecuador, one; and Columbia, seven.

The coastal state response to fifty-three of the 589 requests for clearance was such that the research did not take place. The distribution by coastal state is listed in Table 1. Not all were simple denials. Our preliminary analysis of the data breaks down into four categories: (1) the request for clearance was denied; (2) the request for clearance was granted but permission came too late (either permission was granted after the scheduled start of the program or such a short time before the start that it was not possible to rearrange the ship schedule to carry out the planned program); (3) no answer was received at all to the request, and as a result the program was cancelled; and (4) permission was granted but under terms unacceptable to the research group planning the program. The breakdown of the fifty-three instances is given in Table 2.

Table 2

Denial	24
Delay	14
No Response	10
Unacceptable Conditions	5
Total	53

A number of observers have argued that the research clearance problem would ease once the law of the sea negotiations ended. There may be some slight evidence for that position based on data up until 1984.

Table 3

	79	80	81	82	83	84	Total
Lost Research Programs	12	10	9	4	7	11	53
Total Requests	100	68	78	72	109	162	589
Percent Lost	12	15	12	6	6	7	9

By comparison Wooster reported for the period 1972 to 1978 that:

> 7 percent of clearance requests had been effectively denied and 21 percent had been approved at such a late date as to damage operations...these numbers may be underestimated since both denials and delays have been screened to eliminate those where there is reasonable doubt about coastal-state responsibility.

We have carried out no such screening in this analysis. We concluded, after a preliminary attempt to do so, that the results would be heavily influenced by the nature of the screen applied. Thus, we include as lost opportunities denials of clearances when the United States was late in processing the request, denials resulting from a last-minute change in plans by the research group, and similar reasons. The only lost research opportunities we excluded were those where the problem was not related to the law of the sea; for example, programs cancelled because of lack of funding or equipment malfunctions. On the other hand, we counted as successes all programs that were carried out, even if delayed permission or coastal state restrictions resulted in a lesser program than originally planned. If the delay in granting permission resulted in program cancellation, it was a lost opportunity. If the program was conducted, even though permission was slow in arriving, it was counted as a successful research opportunity. We agree with Wooster, however, that program inefficiencies can, and do, occur if permission is not granted in a timely fashion. Given the difference in our two approaches it is not clear if there is any trend in the data between 1972 and 1984.

We have also examined those coastal states who have effectively denied access to their water for marine scientific research. Of the sixty-two coastal states to which the United States has requested permission to do marine scientific research during the period of this study, eighteen have effectively denied permission on at least one occasion. Six have done so more than once. They are listed in *Table 4*.

Table 4

	Requests Denied	Total Requests	Percent Denied
Cuba	4	4	100
U.S.S.R.	3	4	75
Spain	2	6	33
Mexico	28	114	24
Venezuela	2	9	22
Brazil	2	16	12

Fifty percent of the fifty-three lost research opportunities between 1979 and 1984 were in Mexican waters. Most were not outright denials. Permission was actually granted in nearly half of the twenty-eight cases, but came too late. The project had already been cancelled.

Discussion

Are there patterns or trends one can discern in the matrix of clearance events of the past six years? Given the large number of variables and the limited information available to us, we are hesitant to draw conclusions. Furthermore, it may be unwise to generalize from the experience of the United States about experiences of other researching states. The following examples may be suggestive but are certainly not definitive.

1) Sometimes the denials are predictable. Given the state of relations between the United States and Cuba, it is not surprising that the United States has received four denials in four attempts to do research within 200 miles of Cuba. A 1981 request to do research off Nicaragua was cancelled because the research group was not prepared to accept the Nicaraguan conditions, conditions that may have been imposed because of concerns about national security. Two of the Mexican denials concerned fisheries research related to tuna. Given the strong difference of opinion between Mexico and the United States on international law governing highly migratory species like tuna, such denials are perhaps not surprising.

2) Sometimes the problems develop out of insufficient notice. Because of a communications breakdown within the United States, clearance requests were not made until almost the last minute for a university research program in 1983 that planned to work along the coast of South America within 200 miles of Panama, Colombia, Ecuador, and Peru. Clearance was received from only two of the four countries. Can a western European nation expect to do as well or better faced with a similar problem? The United States is a strong presence in Central and South America with well-mannered embassies. On the other hand, it may

380

be easier for internal political reasons for a coastal state to forgive a late request from a western European research vessel.

3) More often the problem of short request-time is not an internal communications problem, but simply a change in plans. In 1984, a program approved by seven different states in the Caribbean underwent major scheduling changes because of a ship breakdown. Two of the amended requests were cancelled and one was never answered. On the other hand, the files also show last-minute approvals from the Bahamas, Canada, Mexico, and the United Kingdom, amongst others, for different research programs. The best one can conclude is that a late request stands a good chance of being denied, but there is no inevitability about it.

4) At times, the failure to receive timely approval appears to be caused by disagreements internal to the coastal state. On two occasions recently, United States university vessels were cleared to work in Venezuelan waters by the foreign office only to have the permission rescinded before the start of the work because the Venezuelan Navy insisted the ship make a very inconvenient port stop. Both programs were cancelled.

Permission was received for almost fifty percent of the twenty-eight programs that did not take place off Mexico, but permission came so late the programs were cancelled. Some of the late acceptances were probably caused by late requests on the part of the United States, but some would appear to be the result of problems internal to Mexico. It is perhaps understandable for a state receiving less than one request a year not to have a well-oiled procedure for handling requests, but Mexico has been receiving well over ten requests a year recently. One must assume that their inability to process such requests promptly is not due to inexperience. An equal number of requests have gone to Canada from the United States in recent years (*Table 1*). Timely approval has been received in every case.

5) Sometimes clearance problems result in biased work programs that may not be obvious to the casual observer. A university research vessel received clearance from both Egypt and Saudi Arabia for work in the Red Sea, but ended up working entirely in the Egyptian sector because Saudi Arabia required a departure from the proposed schedule for a port stop and ship inspection.

6) To end on a positive note: for a number of years, Trinidad and Tobago have required that the government must approve the publication of any research results from work undertaken in their waters. Because of the personal effort of a United States scientist with a long record of successful cooperative work with Caribbean scientists, the first research program by a United States vessel has recently been completed in waters off Trinidad and Tobago since the publication restriction was promulgated more than a decade ago. There is reason to hope that the rule that was waived for this one program will be permanently amended.

In summary, some fifty-three of the 589 programs proposed by United States research vessels in coastal states' 200-mile zones have not taken place in the past six years because of "law of the sea" problems. A significant number of these problems are a result of the United States not submitting clearance requests early enough or because of major modifications in the timing of the program after the initial request was submitted. However, some of the unsuccessful attempts are a result of coastal state imposition of regulations and controls that are more stringent than those agreed to in the 1982 Convention.

The nine percent denial figure is artificially low. Because of the past position of such coastal states as Cuba and Trinidad and Tobago, a significant self-selection process must occur in the planning by United States scientists. Given the fact that the Gulf Stream sweeps by Cuba, it is inconceivable that there would be only four requests in six years to work in Cuban waters if scientists had any reason to hope their requests would be approved. One can only speculate about what the denial rate would be if scientists made their research plans in ignorance of local state practice, but it would certainly be significantly higher than the current nine percent.

It is too early to judge whether or not the conclusion of the 1982 Convention will ease the problems of research clearances as some have predicted. The 1983 Presidential Proclamation on the Exclusive Economic Zone and the accompanying statement does ease the problem of the United States State Department in requesting clearances, and the number of clearance requests have steadily risen. There is, however, no indication yet that the problems have significantly lessened. On the other hand, neither do they seem to have significantly worsened.

Acknowledgements

The assistance of William Erb and Thomas Cocke of the Bureau of Oceans and International Environmental and Scientific Affairs of the United States State Department is gratefully acknowledged.

REFERENCES

National Research Council, 1985, "Marine Scientific Research -- Law of the Sea Constraints and Emerging State Practices"; Report of the International Ocean Science Policy Group of the Board of Ocean Science Policy, National Research Council, Washington, D.C.: National Academy Press.

Kildow, Judith A.T., 1973, "Nature of the Present Restrictions on Oceanic Research," in *Freedom of Oceanic Research*, W.S. Wooster, ed. New York: Crane and Rusak, pp. 5-28.

Wooster, Warren S., 1981, "Research in Troubled Waters: U.S. Research Vessel Clearance Experience, 1972-78," *Ocean Development and International Law Journal*, Vol. 9, pp. 219-239.

R.J.H. Beverton: For a more detailed look at the process of seeking and obtaining consent, it would be interesting now to hear from Chris Adams on the U.K. experience.

MARINE SCIENCE RESEARCH:
OPERATING THE CONSENT REGIME

C.M.G. Adams
NERC Research Vessel Services
Barry, South Wales

I propose to summarize some of the problems that occur when undertaking marine scientific research in a consent regime, as seen from my viewpoint as Operations Officer for the Research Vessel Base at Barry -- some eleven miles west of Cardiff.

I am going to refer to the operations of research cruises allocated to various scientific groups on the Natural Environment Research Council's own ships. The Council grants shiptime to scientific users in an annual program normally twelve months ahead, and the users and ourselves, as ship operators, then proceed to plan and expedite the practical side of the cruise for each of our four ships and certain chartered-in tonnage.

We are distinct from the two main fishery organizations in this country and from the British Antarctic Survey. Ships from these three bodies are not part of our particular remit, and we operate mainly for other component bodies of the Research Council and United Kingdom University groups which are funded by this Council.

For practical purposes, we treat every cruise application in the same manner -- be they for U.K. waters, international areas, or waters under foreign jurisdiction. I intend to concentrate on foreign waters.

Every user who is allocated shiptime is sent a pack of forms for completion up to eight months before the cruise. These forms include a Notification document, an Aide-Memoire and safety information. The Notification form will describe the proposed cruise in full. The Aide-Memoire is a guide for the Principal Scientist or Cruise Leader and outlines their particular responsibilities to the ship's owners, the Master, current safety legislation and practices, and comments on the desirability of presenting full and accurate information in sufficient time to obtain the proper clearances for the cruise.

The completed forms are returned to us for collation and are then forwarded to all the relevant authorities who need to be advised or notified about the impending cruise. This occurs six to seven months in advance.

For foreign clearance the Notification is initially forwarded to our Foreign Office in London. Here begins a continuous, and occasionally lengthy dialogue between ourselves, the Chief Scientist, various authorities and often the Master designated to the ship.

Because of the differing requirements of foreign states, the many functions of science that will be undertaken, the effects of our own national policy towards recognition of boundaries and the increasing sophistication of data gathering, it is absolutely necessary to ensure that proper explanations of intentions are submitted to a foreign state.

To assist in this aim, and to cut down delays in obtaining concise and realistic explanations of equipment, we have cooperated with our Foreign Office to distribute a detailed brochure to those British Embassies through whom diplomatic clearance is sought.

It has to be remembered that, like most specialized activities, we utilize specific terms and acronyms to describe procedures and equipment. In our own Embassies and in many Ministries of Foreign Affairs the staff are not always aware of the implications, or even meanings, of oceanographic terminology. We have found it advantageous to produce a lay-person's guide and an explanation of terms often used in Notification forms.

In operational terms, we endeavor to centralize the clearance process and the logistic support requirements between two to three months in advance of actual cruise commencement. Copies of clearance requests are sent to both the Cruise Leader and the Ship's Master for comment. Many states apply certain conditions to a cruise and it is in everyone's interest to be seen to comply. This sometimes means modifying a cruise track or program and, consequently, good communication is vital.

There are occasions when it is difficult to obtain copies of written cruise clearance in time to place details on board prior to sailing. We have found in the past that Masters are reluctant to sail without written approval and especially so when the ship is to operate in a sensitive area.

It is not always easy, or even advisable to explain details over an open radio net, particularly when it is necessary to exercise prudence in defining policy reasons to comply with diplomatic advice or conditions.

It has happened that a ship has found it extremely fortuitous to be in possession of the right document in the original language when a foreign naval vessel heaves-to alongside demanding an explanation of the ship's presence.

A great deal of administrative responsibility is placed on the Cruise Leader, and our aim is that the Ship's Master should be fully involved in the process to advise, liaise and generally assist the scientific aims in a practical manner.

One of the most awkward problems arises when a ship has to be diverted due to logistic difficulties, weather or equipment failures. We often wonder why this always seems to occur late on a Friday afternoon!

To a foreign state, the mere fact of a change may create suspicion, and it can even jeopardize future cruises in the area. Therefore it is of great importance at the cruise planning stage to prepare sensible alternative areas or programs and ensure that all parties are aware of why things may change at short notice. It is, nevertheless, an onerous burden to ask a scientist to detail his aims so far in advance.

Research vessels by their nature fall between direct commercial shipping and naval vessels. To the outside world, they may appear to be government ships, and their advanced systems and unusual facilities create suspicion about their true purpose. We endeavor to ensure that in overseas ports the ship is available for visits by interested groups from the scientific and other communities to help allay suspicion and concern. It is not always easy to arrange, but we consider it is an important function to promote not least with our own Embassy representatives.

Likewise, there are difficulties in accommodating observers. Constraints on spare berths and the obvious desire by the Principal Scientist to maximize his scientific staff numbers mean that there is an inevitable conflict in compliance with UNCLOS Article 249 regarding observers. It is often the case that a state does not nominate an observer until just before the cruise commences, or, where research is being undertaken in waters of multiple states, it is not possible to achieve a consensus view whereby one or two neutral observers act for all interests.

Some countries are obviously using the appointment of an observer as a training opportunity for their own scientists and this is where the requirement comes in for a Cruise Leader to develop good contacts in a foreign state.

With the growing requirement to provide technical engineering support for very expensive and complex systems, an excessive number of observers displacing berths for support engineers could have disastrous effects on the science. What is more, it is difficult to explain why a scientific function may have to be curtailed as a result and why a very expensive program, planned over a long period, could well be at risk.

We are endeavoring to plan details further and further ahead -- for example, we are already discussing events proposed for January 1987 -- but we have to accept that the bureaucratic systems of other nations may not move as rapidly in response times as we would wish.

I now come to port calls. Cruises are planned around the scientific objectives and port calls fitted in to avoid long passage steaming; to fulfill logistic support and generally run the ship as economically as possible.

In these days of increasing containerization, much effort goes into the preplacing of equipment and consumables, so choice of ports is also influenced by the facilities and services available. If a port consent is delayed, then future cruises may suffer because equipment is in the wrong place and, given the time scale, it is effectively irretrievable. Should a coastal state be unable to give clearance approval, or worse, not give an early indication of likely refusal, such that alternative arrangements can be made, there are serious problems.

Diplomatic clearances are more and more being influenced by logistic constraints and the costs of short turn-round times, and ship operations generally must be taken into account in the whole clearance procedure.

To inform a foreign country that, regrettably, we intend canceling a port call for logistic reasons could be construed as an indirect snub, and in the longer term that benefits nobody.

Another subject which adds to clearance difficulties is the increasing use of seabed mounted instruments. The definitions of research in the water column and research involving the seabed are construed differently in some areas. Equipment lying on the sea floor may not have any direct seabed monitoring function -- it merely being a suitable and relatively safe place to site instruments for a variety of water column investigations.

Most instrument packages are very expensive and risk damage or removal by other ships if marked by surface bouys.

The move towards remotely interrogated or long term bottom-mounted sensors further blurs the distinction between water column and seabed research.

In the case of long-term moorings, clearance conditions which state that all equipment should be removed by the end of the cruise require considerable explanation and careful monitoring.

I would also mention the topic of data transferral. The advent of satellite communications whereby direct data transfer takes place from a ship's computer direct to its home base will certainly ease the present requirements to trust taped data to someone's baggage. However, a foreign coastal state might consider that a researcher is avoiding obligations under Article 249 -- where a state may request access to all data. Similarly, when instrument packages dump their information direct via a satellite or are accessed by other research ships, the coastal state could then be in the position where information is being obtained without its consent or knowledge, and it is a matter of conjecture as to the reaction this might cause.

It is here that the role of a foreign observer should take on an additional importance both to ensure that clearance conditions are met and to monitor problems that arise because of those conditions. It is unfortunate that some observers are lacking in scientific capability, have insufficient experience to be aware of the problems or even have no idea at all what the research cruise is all about.

In this respect post-cruise follow-up is a serious matter. Countries which request cruise reports as a condition of granting clearance must be sent a meaningful report as soon as possible after the cruise is completed. With the large quantity of data normally requiring analysis, it may not be practical for a scientist to commit anything but simple facts in the short term.

To endeavor to standardize this, we utilize the international Roscop format as a *what, where, when* -type report. Simple to complete, it is an impartial statement of fact and available immediately upon cruise completion. In fact, we request that a scientist hand it to the Master before leaving the ship.

This is not a substitute for a detailed cruise report but does have the effect of showing a coastal state that someone is responding.

In conclusion, I would say that most of the problems arise from lack of communication. Some say that being open about our intentions result in greater restraints being imposed on science; others consider that we operate despite the clearance system.

I would argue that the majority of incidents arising out of clearance difficulties have been due to a paucity of information somewhere.

Operating under a consent regime, one must accept that the coastal state has a right to know what a researcher is undertaking but this must be allied to practical ship operating terms and a realistic appreciation by the diplomatic departments responsible for negotiating clearances that modern oceanographic research is highly technical and very expensive.

THE FUTURE OF OCEANOGRAPHIC RESEARCH
IN THE LIGHT OF THE UN CONVENTION

A.S. Laughton
Institute of Oceanographic Sciences
United Kingdom

My role in this Panel discussing science, law and the sea is to look at the future of oceanographic research, to try to gaze into the crystal ball to see what oceanographers, marine scientists and technologists may be doing in the next decade or two and to try to judge how their programs interact with the possible new regimes that may be in force at that time.

The nature of the new regimes is still in considerable doubt. The UN Convention is not yet ratified and hence does not have the force of international law. Even if and when it becomes ratified there are considerable legal uncertainties about the status of the Convention for those countries that have not ratified it. For the sake of this contribution, I assume that the Convention will come into force in perhaps the next five to ten years. However, even before potential ratification many coastal states will have declared exclusive economic zones or extended continental shelves, basing these claims on customary law rather than conventional law, and these coastal states will exercise jurisdictional control of one form or another. Countries wishing to conduct oceanographic research in regions which fall potentially within national jurisdiction are likely to approach the coastal states about the conduct of this research. Oceanographers can therefore envisage a period of transition between the older regime of free access to coastal or near coastal waters and one in which some 40 percent of the world's oceans will be subject to coastal state control.

Let me now turn to the oceanographic research itself. This research can cover a very wide spectrum of activities ranging from the strictly applied research as it is conducted by industry or by defense interests to research that is generated by the basic curiosity of scientists to discover how the oceans operate. Some of the early understanding of the oceans came from what would now be called *mission-oriented research*. For example, in the last century the laying of transatlantic telephone cables generated research into the nature and depth of the sea floor and required measurements of the temperature of the water in which these cables were laid. Another example of mission-oriented research was the search for gold in the oceanic waters by Germany in the 1920s to pay for the post-World-War debt. This was one of the motives of the early *Meteor* expedition which produced such a wealth of physical and chemical data in the Atlantic.

Other research cruises such as that of the *Challenger* expedition of 1872 to 1876 sponsored by the Royal Society were prompted by the curiosity of scientists to find out about a wide variety of phenomena in the ocean. More recently, in the late 1950s, the International Geophysical Year brought together many countries to study the oceans in a quasi-synoptic way where long sections were made across the oceans to look at the oceanic currents and associated physical conditions. The success of this led to the first major international oceanographic research applied to a single ocean in the International Indian Ocean Expedition of 1959 to 1965, where nearly all oceanographic disciplines were studied. Thirteen countries and some forty-six ships took part and many continuing programs were started. However, the motives even of this expedition were not solely related to scientific curiosity; they were also related to enhancing the capability of the countries surrounding the Indian Ocean in developing their own oceanographic and marine expertise. The progress since then has been quite outstanding.

Most oceanographic research has a complex mixture of motives and funding, sometimes related to the long-term needs of defense, sometimes to the needs of scientific curiosity, sometimes to the assessment of potential resource exploitation, sometimes commissioned by government or industry to achieve defined objectives related to the utilization of the oceans.

To cover this wide spectrum of activities the words used in the 1982 Convention include *marine scientific research, exploration, prospecting, exploitation*. These words are not specifically defined within the Convention, but the differences between *marine scientific research* and *exploration* are fundamental to the restrictions that could be applied to the activities. In his admirable book on *Marine Scientific Research and the Law of the Sea*, Alfred Soons assesses in some detail what is meant by marine scientific research in the Convention. He states that

> Marine Scientific Research may be defined as any study or related experimental work designed to increase man's knowledge of the marine environment. Thus it encompasses any scientific work, wherever carried out, having the marine environment as object.

Marine scientific research in principle covers both fundamental and applied scientific research, and the freedoms and responsibilities associated with marine scientific research have equally broad application.

I will now review some of the scientific problems facing oceanography as it may be conducted under a transition period and under a Convention, giving examples from various different fields of endeavor.

During the past two decades, research into the ocean floor has revolutionized the geological understanding of the earth as a whole. The concepts of plate tectonics were born; continental geology has benefited from the discoveries under the ocean; ophiolite zones on land have been recognized as being upthrust ocean crust; and often with these zones are associated regions of mineralization which have been economically mined. Current ocean floor research is beginning to recognize some of the processes by which these mineral concentrations may have occurred. The observation that seawater can penetrate deep into the crust at spreading centers, thereby leaching out minerals such as copper, silver, zinc, and other sulphides, and depositing them on the sea floor as hydrothermal deposits, has suggested how mineral concentrations might be generated. If indeed deposits such as those in Cyprus have originated at a mid-ocean ridge and have been transported by sea floor spreading, then they should persist under the sediments of the ocean basins, even though they may not be readily accessible as an ore. The search for these is an exciting challenge.

To take another example from the geological side, it is well known that hydrocarbons underlie many of the continental shelves and almost certainly occur on the continental slope. But it is not known whether they are likely to be found in the sediment accumulations at the base of the slope in the deep oceans. This is a critical issue for coastal states whose EEZs extend well into deep water. It is also important in evaluating the global resource of hydrocarbons. Before industry can venture so deep, science must lead the way with models of early ocean basin evolution and understand the warping, fracturing and erosion of rifted continental edges. These models first need to be tested by scientific drilling. The international Ocean Drilling Programme will address these problems amongst others, and cooperation with coastal states in drilling scientific holes on the continental margins is essential.

Everyone is aware of the terrible tragedies and privation caused by climatic change; the failing of the anchovy harvests off Peru, droughts and desertification in Africa, crop failures in Eurasia, flooding in the East Pacific, fires in Australia. No one expects to be able to prevent climatic change or to control it, but some form of prediction could enable countries to plan their economies more effectively.

The World Climate Research Programme (WCRP) -- sponsored by the World Meteorological Organization, IOC and ICSU -- which is expected to last a decade or more, is addressing the problems of climatic prediction and man's impact on the climate. It is recognized that the oceans play a vital role in providing a fly-wheel for the climate; they can absorb carbon dioxide or heat from the atmosphere and can transport it from the equatorial regions towards the pole, thereby influencing the atmospheric circulation and the weather patterns. Two major programs, the Tropical Ocean Global Atmosphere Program (TOGA) and the World Ocean Circulation Experiment (WOCE) will involve the two major developing technologies of satellite remote sensing and modelling using some of the world's largest computers, as well as the more conventional shipborne research. Physical oceanographers worldwide will be heavily involved in the WCRP, which will require the close coordination of its science and management through WMO, SCOR, IOC, etc., and will require the cooperation of coastal states in key areas.

Stimulated by the possibilities of global ocean modelling, chemical and biological oceanographers want to be able to model the production and fate of biogenic materials in the sea well enough to predict their influence and response to global scale perturbations, whether natural or man-made. These perturbations can have a significant impact on human populations and their economies. To achieve this predictive goal, a long-term multi-disciplinary study of the flux of material through the global ocean environment is needed, and a proposal has been made for a substantial program called *The Global Ocean Flux Study* (GOFS). This will address the biogeochemical cycles of carbon, nitrogen, phosphorus, sulphur and oxygen and will build on new technologies developed for measurements of fluxes in the ocean itself and on satellite observations of near-surface primary production. The program will build on existing and past programs of Transient Tracers in the Ocean (TTO) and Geochemical Sections (GEOSECS) as well as being linked to WOCE.

But while these exciting global programs go ahead, the need is also increasing for research into the more immediately practical needs of managing the ocean and its resources, requiring coastal zone management, pollution control, environmental prediction and protection. There are many conflicts of interest which must be resolved on the basis of scientific understanding and not irrational fears, emotion or politics.

The list of possible future oceanographic research projects is endless, and I have not touched on the research related to resource exploitation or to defense needs, which often involve programs of research indistinguishable from "pure research."

389

What will be the impact of the 1982 Convention on future oceanographic research?

It must be recognized that many of these problems -- climate, ocean floor evolution, ocean currents, fish -- know no political boundaries. The cooperation of coastal states is essential to enable these programs to go ahead in 40 percent of the ocean area that may be under their jurisdiction. International programs coordinated by IOC, WMO, FAO, ICES, etc., should facilitate this, but individual countries and even small laboratories can contribute directly to the research aims and should not be inhibited because they are not part of an international program. It is very important that scientists from the researching countries have a close association with scientists from the coastal states.

The uncertainties of research results and the vagaries of weather and equipment at sea make it essential that programs are flexible. In accepting research cruise proposals, coastal states should be liberal in interpreting their rights. Under the Convention, these rights are extensive and detailed, and the demands made on the researching state substantial. If a coastal state acquires a reputation for inflexibility or for imposing unreasonable conditions, researching states will go elsewhere or else abandon the research. No one will benefit from this.

Interesting questions are raised by the advent of satellite remote sensing of the oceans in relation to the rights of coastal states under UNCLOS. These questions must already have been raised in the use of remote sensing over land and yet are not specifically addressed in the Convention. What is certain, however, is that the use of satellites for remote sensing over the oceans will increase not only for oceanographic research but also for applications to measure wind and sea state, for ship routing, weather prediction, coastal pollution monitoring, etc. Remote sensing of sea conditions at great distances from land-based radio and radar systems is now being developed.

Another aspect of the impact of UNCLOS on oceanic research is the desire of coastal states to evaluate the resources that may lie within their newly acquired EEZs or continental shelves. Already, the United States of America has initiated a major program of morphological and geological mapping of its declared EEZ; rapid and cheap initial reconnaissance surveys are being made using a new long-range side-scan sonar. The countries surrounding the Indian Ocean only last week held a First Conference on *Economic, Scientific and Technical Cooperation in the Indian Ocean in the Context of the New Ocean Regime.* The Commonwealth Heads of Governments Regional Meeting in the Asia/Pacific area initiated a study for cooperation amongst Commonwealth countries in the field of marine affairs, ocean management, marine science and technology, living and non-living resources and maritime services.

This increased realization of the potential of the oceans for national economic benefit is stimulating both developed and developing countries to focus research effort in the EEZs and to build up or strengthen their national research and survey capabilities. Developed countries can assist in training, in advising on infrastructure, and in cooperative research programs as well as by financial aid both bilaterally and through international development banks.

If any benefits are to flow from the oceans, they will only be realized through a better understanding of what is going on by applying the most advanced techniques to the problems to obtain data, and models which can be tested by new data. The benefits of this better understanding are seldom confined to one country, but they increase the general store of knowledge, which is of advantage to all. If marine scientific research can be carried on in this spirit within UNCLOS, then marine scientists will have nothing to fear and progress can be made, but if it is "cribbed, cabinned and confined," then the best brains will turn their attention to other problems, and marine science and the world community will be the poorer.

R.J.H. Beverton: That was a fascinating look ahead -- a task which scientists on the whole are not keen to do. But, when they are put on the spot, it is fascinating to hear what they have to say -- especially from a marine geophysicist of international repute who has the responsibility for long-range planning for his Institute's programs, given what is possible with the facilities, the operational aspects, and the best way to cope with the future. Tony Laughton did touch on one or two things which lead to our next speaker. He emphasized the importance of the coastal states' cooperation in solving and exploring some of the major questions of the ocean. But the coastal states have their own problems, especially those in the Third World. They are faced with enormous areas of economic zones of which they know little and about which, at the moment, they have little capacity to do anything. Yet, especially concerning fisheries resources, these areas may be extremely important as a food supply. They have to face problems of finding, in the best economical way, a good scientific basis for developing fisheries. Therefore, it is appropriate at this point, as a sequel to the earlier panel discussion on fisheries legislation, to ask Rowena Lawson if she would tell us how she sees the future of fisheries science in the context of our discussion this morning.

FISHERIES RESEARCH AND THE LAW OF THE SEA

Rowena Lawson
Consultant Fisheries Economist
University of Hull

This paper is entirely concerned with fisheries research as it affects developing countries. In the short space of time allotted, one is obliged to make rather sweeping generalizations, but I hope to put these in a meaningful global perspective.

One can divide the last thirty to thirty-five years of fisheries development into two periods in which critical changes in the international political scene had an effect in altering the objectives of fisheries research.

First was the emergence of nation-states from colonial to self-governing independent states. Second was the substantial extension of economic zones by many coastal states which effectively extended the artificial colonial boundaries into the seas.

The effect of the first event was to change the focus of fisheries research from what previously had largely been regionally organized by the colonial powers and had in many cases mostly concerned fish resource studies. During the colonial period, government involvement in the colonies was mostly confined to supporting a few fisheries officers, most of whom were biologists and whose research, if there were any, was largely concerned with the biology of fish.

Upon the countries' attaining independence, this changed. Newly independent coastal states wanted a rapid development and increased commercialization of their fishing industry and the emphasis of national fisheries research moved away from biology towards problems concerning socio-economics and the transfer of technology, including studies of fish marketing, processing, loan schemes, and co-operatives, all of which were considered to be relevant to the introduction of mechanized vessels and outboard motors to what hitherto had been largely a small-scale, labor-intensive canoe fishery.

Regional studies of fish resources by the colonial powers gradually ceased, though there are a few notable exceptions such as CRODT and OSTROM in Dakar and Abidjan respectively, in the ex-French colonies, which have continued to undertake fisheries research funded by the ex-colonial power. Later, however, regional research by ex-colonial powers became part of an aid package to developing countries.

In a number of countries, the pursuit of rapid fisheries industry development led to the establishment by the newly independent states of State Fishing Corporations which operated largely with commercial objectives and quite separately from, and sometimes in conflict with, the government Fisheries Departments.

The effect of political independence was to create a national status for fish resources which in some countries had been fished by neighboring tribes across borders without let or hindrance. The artificial national boundaries not only cut across tribes on the land but cut across fish stocks and traditional customary fishing areas at sea. The reluctance of small-scale fishermen to accept the new national boundaries at sea enhances the problems of fisheries management at a national level.

The second international event which affected fisheries research came later in the 1970s and was the extension to 200 miles in most cases of exclusive fisheries zones by many developing countries. Where this led to a vast increase in potential resources and wealth for the coastal states, the focus of research and activity moved away from inshore fisheries to distant water fisheries. Attention, which, in the 1960s, had been primarily directed towards inshore small-scale fisheries, was thus redirected. In retrospect, the late 1970s and 1980s have shown a rekindling of fisheries research and development interest in small-scale fisheries, though this has been largely instigated by socio-political needs following the urgency of maintaining a viable rural-based industry.

From the late 1940s to 1973, however, another development took place which greatly affected marine fisheries development in developing countries. This was the emergence of five marine and four inland regional fisheries organizations funded by the Food and Agricultural Organization of the United Nations. The first was the Indo-Pacific Fisheries Council starting in 1948 with nineteen member states. It has indeed been one of the most successful and has outlived most of the others. Its main functions are "To keep fishery resources under review and to recommend conservation and management measures, to keep under review economic and social aspects of fishing ... and to encourage training and research."

Under these regional organizations the emphasis of research moved away from the resource research towards fisheries management and development. For example CECAF (Fishery Commission for the Eastern Central Atlantic), which is currently being run down, has thirty members including such distant water fishing nations as Cuba, Romania and South Korea, reflecting its involvement in off-shore fisheries management.

The underlying objectives of these regional FAO fisheries organizations, however, were directed towards helping the newly independent coastal states to develop their own fishery industries and to come to mutually advantageous terms with distant water fleets. It was hoped that in time the UN funding of these organizations would be replaced by funding from member coastal states who, it was hoped, would by then have realized the benefits of having a regional fisheries organization. Unfortunately, this has not happened and most of the regional fisheries organizations have been disbanded as UN funds have been withdrawn.

All had the potential for making a substantial contribution to fisheries development in coastal member states. For example, the large library of CECAF documents in Dakar is testimony to the very many conferences, workshops, commissioned research and other studies that it has funded. Many of these have been instigated at the express wish of member states and in view of this it may be difficult to understand why the regional organizations have failed to get local funding.

It is essential to evaluate their operations before new institutions for fisheries research, development and regional cooperation are formulated. This is important because Article 63 of the Convention, which emphasizes the role of its regional organizations, says that "...These states shall seek either directly or through appropriate sub-regional or regional organisations ... to agree upon measures necessary to coordinate and insure conservation and development of such stocks." Before one can hold out any hope for a regional approach to resource conservation, one may venture some reasons for the failure of earlier efforts at regional cooperation.

1. For most coastal states the fishing industry, in comparison with other sectors of the national economy, has played a minor role. For example, the contribution of fisheries to GDP (with the exception of those Pacific island-states for which no UN macro-economic data is available) is more than 4% in only six developing countries. Further, in terms of the contribution of fisheries to exports and to nutrition, its significance is negligible with the exception of island states such as the Maldives, Seychelles, Vanuatu and Cape Verde Isles. For many countries fisheries remain a Cinderella industry, and governments are reluctant to give it additional financial support to fund regional organizations.

2. Much of the research, even that commissioned at the request of member states, remains unused and sometimes unread. This is particularly the case with socio-economic studies on which interest focused for many years. For instance, studies of fish marketing and fish processing, of fishermen's credit and loan schemes, of co-operatives, etc., have been made in many countries, yet the same mistakes continue to be made. The boundary between research and adequate project preparation for aid schemes should be very narrow. Yet governments and aid donors continue to find projects which have proved failures in other countries and the causes for failure are well known.

3. The publication of research results does not reach the persons who make executive decisions. This is partly the fault of inadequate publicity on the part of regional organizations and the FAO and partly that the decisions about the fishing industry are frequently made by people outside the industry. Also, sometimes decisions are made irresponsibly and without due care for the consequences.

For those who have not had field experience in fisheries in developing countries, it might help if one or two examples were given to demonstrate the above.

Eighteen months ago, I was appointed by the FAO to undertake a post-evaluation of bilateral and multilateral aid to small-scale fisheries in the CECAF region of Africa. I studied twelve aid projects. In not one of these had either the donor or recipient provided adequate benchmark data upon which to base the project. In not one case had there been any attempt to examine the causes of failures of similar projects in the region. In not one instance was there any attempt to evaluate or measure the success or otherwise of the project, and no achievement indicators were considered.

In all cases donors had given aid without sufficient preparation or forethought, and in some cases aid was given irresponsibly, in a way which would encourage and enhance the dependency syndrome of the recipient state and would involve the recipient government in a level of expenditure which their economies would be unable to bear.

Just a few examples will flesh out these assertions.

a. $10 million in aid directed towards supporting fish marketing co-operatives which would distribute frozen fish in large refrigerated vehicles over very bad roads, 700 km into the fringe of the Sahel to a very small target population which had in any case other sources of protein. One has to assume, to put it kindly, that this was done in ignorance of marketing studies in the region which had severely criticized the use of refrigerated vehicles and the distribution of frozen fish amongst a community whose preference was for the much less heavy, easily transported and preserved, locally smoked or dried fish.

In one country studied, at the "end" of the project, that is, when the expatriate project manager returned home, the refrigerated vans had windows cut into their sides, and they reverted to being passenger lorries.

b. Africa is a mortuary of ice plants, yet ice plants continue to be provided by aid donors regardless of need. One country with one inch of rainfall per year was provided with eight ice plants by eight donors. All were grossly underutilized. One ice plant, with a capacity for a daily throughput of ten tons, had sold a maximum of 3 cwt. in one day.

c. A huge refrigerated processing plant, supposedly producing fish for export, was constructed under both bilateral and multilateral aid in a country with very spasmodic supplies of electricity and an international telephone system which rarely operated. The plant is currently completely vandalized and overrun by rats.

d. The development under aid of aquaculture amongst geographically dispersed peasant farmers which required a level of extension-officer supervision that would be extremely difficult for the government to maintain.

Some projects had increased the financial burden of the state, some had increased its dependency on aid, some had led to distortions of the economy. All failures could have been prevented if donors and recipients had bothered to study the various reports, research documents, etc., relating to other similar projects in the region.

Now, although the above may make one rather skeptical about the future success of regional organizations, one has to admit that there is some evidence, early though it is, that the Pacific island states may be having more success in getting together in the Forum Fisheries Agency and under the Nauru Agreement. Here cooperation between developing coastal (island) states has reached a level not found anywhere else in the world. Why? I would like to venture some answers.

1. These countries are all highly dependent upon fisheries; hence, governments take the industry seriously and the best administrators go into fisheries.

2. These countries have not hitherto experienced rivalry in fisheries between each other. On the contrary, they can identify a common rival or adversary in the distant water fleets from Japan, South Korea, Taiwan and the United States, and this gives them a common target.

3. The objective of fishery management is directed towards one species, tuna, and to tuna-like species. This is unique in regional organizations which have multi-species stocks as well as shared stocks to contend with.

4. The individual members know and understand that they have a lot to learn from each other by their surveillance, operation and reporting systems and can gain by cooperation.

Now there are very few fishing regions in the world where the above conditions exist and so one is not optimistic for the future of the new regional organizations covering the Gulf of Guinea states and the Caribbean states. All the countries concerned have had the opportunity previously of being active members of regional organizations, but they have not been.

Whilst the UN-organized fishery organizations have largely become run down or defunct, other organizations which have had more modest and limited objectives have succeeded. For example, those directed to single species, such as IATTC (Inter-American Tropical Tuna Commission), the IPHC (International Pacific Halibut Commission) and the SPC (South

395

Pacific Commission), have pursued resource research which has been useful. Other research projects, notably under ICLARM (International Center for Living Aquatic Resources Management), BOBP (Bay of Bengal Program), and SCSP (South China Sea Project) have been successful in promoting research into small-scale fisheries with some local benefit.

So what of the future of fisheries research and the law of the sea? Article 63 is concerned with the conservation and development of stock. This involved continuous highly capital-intensive research into fisheries biology and fish resources which require specialized research vessels and scientists. These are areas of research on which, outside the major single-stock resources such as tuna, the proportion of total funds being spent has fallen heavily in recent years. For example, out of total bilateral and multilateral aid going to fisheries in 1981 of about $400 million, only 13% was spent on research in total; not all of this on resource research. In order to support Article 63, much more must be spent on fisheries biology and resources, the research must be continuous since stocks change, and to make the research valid, the law of the sea should consider making participation in funding research on shared stocks compulsory for all nations using the resource. This would, however, conflict with Article 245(5) of the Convention, which states that "Coastal States may however in their discretion withhold consent to the conduct of a marine scientific research project of another State or competent international organization in the exclusive economic zone or on the continental shelf of the coastal State if that project: (a) is of direct significance for the exploration and exploitation of natural resources, whether living or non-living." I should like to suggest that the contrary be the case, and that coastal states should not be allowed to withhold consent. The Convention does not seem to appreciate the great research and administrative differences between managing and conserving a multi-species fishery and a single-stock fishery.

Under Article 61, the coastal state is required to determine total allowable catch and Article 62 requires the coastal state to promote the objectives of optimum utilization of living resources in its zone. Now developing countries have never before undertaken tasks such as these and the supporting research needed to conform to these Articles will place a much heavier burden on these poor states than it will on developed countries, many of which already possess a research organization with suitable vessels, gear, staff and laboratory technology.

The conservation and management requirements imposed by the Convention on coastal states will also hit the developing countries heavily. Many, particularly those island states with large expanded EEZs, will have to weigh very carefully the costs and benefits of developing their own off-shore fishing industries as against renting out fishing rights to foreign vessels. Unfortunately, the aid which is given to developing fisheries is not always properly amortized by the recipient governments who may be faced with expensive maintenance and replacement costs once the aid has ceased. Thus countries which may consider themselves to have gained by the extension of EEZs may, in the long term, prove to be losers.

Even in inshore fisheries, developing countries are already finding the problems of management intractable. Countries such as Indonesia, Malaysia, the Philippines, Senegal and others have had to drastically exclude mechanized vessels from encroaching on grounds fished less efficiently by small-scale labor-intensive canoe fishermen in the interests of maintaining socio-political efficiency.

The fact that socio-political interests dominate in many developing countries is not generally recognized by the international community (and the LOS Convention is no exception), which considers the main criterion of development to be one of economic issues and harmony. Whilst these may be suitable long-term objectives, they may not be crucial in a period of transition when socio-political stability is vital.

R.J.H. Beverton: That does give us a very different view of some areas of marine science. Those of us who have worked with the developing countries and have seen the problems they face, even in knowing how to respond to requests from advanced oceanographic countries to do research, realize just how difficult it is for them. I am sure one of the main tasks for the future is to try and find all possible ways of bringing the competence and the awareness of the marine science dimension into the developing world as fast as we can. Our final paper from Nic Flemming of the Institute of Oceanographic Sciences is a topic that really permeates all this, namely the exchange of information about the sea and how that is to be maintained in the light of the new regime that has evolved.

THE LAW OF THE SEA AND
THE EXCHANGE OF SCIENTIFIC INFORMATION AND DATA

N.C. Flemming
Institute of Oceanographic Sciences
United Kingdom

Summary

The impact of UNCLOS on international oceanographic data transfer is to produce a requirement for a greatly increased flow of data. These data transfers will tend to be mandatory from operators and data originators to coastal states, and discretionary from data originators to the international community. Coastal states could, but need not, request confidentiality for all data obtained within their EEZ, which would preclude transfer to the international system. Implementation of the required data transfers could be either by direct and repeated bilateral transfers to all the organizations concerned, or through an intermediary oceanographic data banking system. Whilst direct bilateral transfers will always be possible and permitted, it seems probable that the increasing volumes of complex data will require a standard international procedure and formats for data transfer, via professionally staffed data banks. This is already the established practice in meteorological data management, and there is a growing system of National Oceanographic Data Centres which can perform the same service for marine research data. Coastal states, oceanographers, and international organizations have a choice as to whether they maximize the flow of data through the international system, or concentrate data into mutually exclusive confidential data sets held by coastal states. Since some of the most important developments and benefits of ocean science in the next decade depend upon the creation of oceanic data sets, this paper recommends strongly that an international system of data management be promoted.

Introduction

The general principles underlying the legal foundations of the proposed new regime for scientific research at sea are discussed by Alexander Yankov (1982, p. 16). I cannot do better than quote one of his concluding paragraphs exactly:

> Perhaps the key problem would be: how to reconcile national claims and priorities with the long-term interests of the international community. An important condition for tackling such a problem would be a viable *modus vivendi* and accommodation between these two seemingly opposing trends. Practical and constructive resolution of the dilemma could require mutual trust between coastal and "researching" States, and common appreciation of the vital role of marine science for the optimum utilization of the oceans and their resources. (*ibid.*, p. 25)

To quote from the report of the XIth Session of the Working Committee for International Oceanographic Data Exchange (WC for IODE) (1984),

> The Member States of the IODE System, whether considered individually or corporately within the IODE System, are presented with a

very wide range of choices. The existence of these choices is quite explicit in the Convention, and is not due to vague principles. The choices fall into the following categories: choice of degree of compliance with the many Articles which are explicitly discretionary or conditional; choice of the use of bilateral or regional, or international channels for data and information transfer; choice of option to enforce confidentiality and penalty clauses; choice of option to transfer data to neighbouring or landlocked States; choice of whether to join regional organizations; freedom to choose all or any practical technical methods and procedures to achieve the objectives within the Principles of the Convention.

However, the extent to which this degree of choice is really open and free is not usually stressed. Journalistic and political commentators, in attempting to describe the culmination of years of debate and seeing a document of over 300 articles, are bound to conclude that matters are much more narrowly defined now than they were before the debate. Many commentators have a vested interest in showing that a "new ocean regime" has been created which gives legal force to this or that principle which they hold dear. Firstly, of course, the Convention is not yet law. Secondly, although many narrowly restrictive, secretive, and nationalistic practices are given the sanction of permission by some articles of UNCLOS, none of them are mandatory upon states. For every restrictive or nationalist practice tending to remove scientific knowledge from the international community, there is an article reinforcing the importance of cooperation and sharing at every level from the local to regional and global. It is not a weakness in UNCLOS that this choice remains to us: it is a strength. Articles recommending internationalist practices are preceded with discretionary phrases such as "States shall endeavour...", "States shall encourage...", "States shall promote," "States shall facilitate...". Articles on nationalist rights describe rights which do not have to be asserted in a negative way.

As Yankov states so clearly, we are therefore left with the legal problem, or free communal choice, as to how we balance the necessary interests of national institutions, science, commerce, etc., against the broader good of the international community. To make a simple analogy with weather forecasts and meteorological research, nobody imagines that their own weather forecasts would be more accurate if they treated meteorological data gathered within their national frontiers as a state secret. Neighboring countries would retaliate in kind, and the first state to behave in this restrictive way would lose prior information on meteorological phenomena moving towards its frontiers. This would be an almost immediate disadvantage to the individual state, as well as to the international community. Thus weather data are handled globally.

Meteorologists are lucky in working in an environment where acceptance of the flow of scientific and operational information is almost unquestioned. But then no one expects to find oil wells or shoals of fish buried in a cloud which happens to be within their national frontiers.

In oceanography there are conflicting benefits to be balanced between national and international priorities, and there is no concealing the fact. What I want to do this morning is to show how the UNCLOS text presents the options on both sides of the argument, and to stress the enormous responsibility which we have, as scientists, in making the choice. As Yankov makes clear, using the words "modus vivendi" and "accommodation." the resolution does not lie through strict legal agreements, but through something like a code of conduct, or agreement on standards and practices which can be constantly under peer review.

So far my comments refer to the conduct of scientific research generally at sea. At this point I wish to be specific about marine data and information, and to narrow the discussion to that topic. Most commentators on UNCLOS assume that the benefits of marine research are minerals, food, marine technology, the ability to exploit resources, and the more intangible assets of tourism, rights of passage, and waste disposal. The value of data *per se* is referred to in several articles in UNCLOS: Articles 244.2; 277(e); 277(f); 249.1(c); 249.1(d); and 200. But the link between data and more material benefits is difficult to see. The rich countries with most of the hard economic benefits from the sea are also those with the most data, the most access to existing data, and are the most likely to acquire new data. Data are transferred easily and cheaply nowadays; they can be copied and duplicated rapidly; and they can form the basis of many programs: educational, technological, economic, or scientific. I suggest that maximizing the international freedom of flow of data within the principles of UNCLOS would be relatively uncontroversial, and that the trust engendered by such free flow would help to encourage cooperation in the more complex areas of marine scientific research.

Information and Data Flow

The impact of UNCLOS on marine information and data flow has been discussed by Kesteven (1982), Miles (1981), Goncalves (1982), and Flemming (1983). Kesteven (*ibid.*, p. 121) provides an excellent series of definitions of the terms: [data, information, knowledge, and understanding.] His definitions are somewhat philosophical, and will not be repeated here. In the Articles of UNCLOS where the term "data" occurs (listed above), the context implies exactly the meaning which would be used by the most scientists, that is, "measured numerical values." This is the sense used within the Working Committee for International Oceanographic Data Exchange (IODE) of IOC. The numerical values may be supplemented by parameters calculated from the raw data, ratios, averages, monthly means, upper or lower limits, and statistical distributions, etc. The data may be presented as tabulated rows and columns of numbers, so-called listings, or as maps, contoured diagrams, statistical plots or graphs etc. All these versions of the original raw measured values may be called data.

By implication data are in such a form that there has been no interpretation or arbitrary processing of the original numbers, and the user is, in some sense, gaining access to some unvarnished representation of reality. This is of course an illusion, since every measuring program, sampling sequence, plotting procedure, or statistical treatment introduces some distortion of reality. As Kesteven (*ibid.*) points out, it follows that mere lists of numbers are meaningless without a set of words describing what was measured, how, where, and when, what errors were detected, how the errors were corrected or allowed for, how the data have been sampled, averaged, processed, etc. These comments are described as "data documentation." Data without documentation are almost entirely useless.

Near synonyms to the word "data" used in UNCLOS are: "scientific knowledge"; "knowledge resulting from a project"; "research results";

"information"; "results of research"; "transfer of technology and scientific knowledge"; "reports of results"; "publication and dissemination of information and knowledge"; "disseminate."

The term "information" is defined by Kesteven (*ibid.*, p. 121) as: "a statement in which one or more data are assembled with such grammatic and syntactic apparatus as may be needed to convey an intelligible message." This is minimal, and one might add that such a message is scarcely information unless it is delivered in such a way that its context and relation to the real world can be appreciated by the recipient.

To reinforce the relation between, and difference between, data and information, one can distinguish the following categories (from Flemming, 1983, p. 6):

(1) *Data* - numerical measured values, parameters, and statistics.
(2) *Data products* - statistics, graphs, maps, inventories, graphic plots, extreme values, etc., derived from numerical data and usually using a computer.
(3) *Catalogues, guides, inventories* - plain language text documents helping potential users to obtain data or data products.
(4) *Information about data* - educational documents, plain language text providing education, instruction, or information about access to, availability of, exchange of data, and the best ways to use data.
(5) *Information* - published scientific papers, books, reports, manuals, bibliographies, etc.

Numerical data nowadays are usually stored on computer and transmitted in the form of magnetic tapes or discs. Small sections of data may be copied from the computer as listings, but these are very difficult to manipulate and may have to be entered into another computer with tedious keyboard work before they can be used. Derived statistics, data products, etc., may be sufficiently compact to be plotted as one or two graphs, or a book of graphs or plots. This is a fairly familiar way of transmitting data to end users.

The term "Data Exchange" occurs in the name of the WC for IODE. In the present paper, I am going to use the term "Data Transfer" in most cases. The term "exchange" originated in the 1960s when National Oceanographic Data Centers (NODCs) were set up to channel oceanographic data between countries on a basis of equal exchange, without financial charges for services provided. In the context of providing data access to developing countries, this implication should be avoided, and it is also not strictly appropriate when describing the transfer of data from the originator to an international data system for public access. The term "transfer" will be used with no implication that any charge is made for the service, and no implication that data are received in exchange.

Volumes of Data and Levels of Data Transfer

The principles of UNCLOS will lead to an increased flow of oceanographic data between states, which pre-supposes a greatly enhanced facility for the acquisition, transfer, and storage of numerical data and data products. The increase in data flow is caused by two factors:

(1) Increase in the promotion of international oceanographic programs (*e.g.*, the World Climate Research Program, TOGA, WOCE, WMO Wave program etc.); and the need to share data more equitably between all countries, regionally and globally.

401

(2) The legal obligation placed on states operating research ships, platforms, or instruments within the jurisdiction of other states to transfer the scientific results and data to the coastal state if requested. The coastal state has the right to refuse permission for future research if the operating organization has neglected or refused to make data available after having been requested to do so.

It might be thought that data transfer can best be achieved bilaterally, where the data originator simply transfers the necessary tapes to the coastal state. However, the volume of data, the number of potential recipients, the different obligations in different regimes (EEZ, International Area, etc.), make this model very cumbersome.

The regimes include the International Area, the EEZ of coastal states, the territorial sea of coastal states, the agreements pertaining to regional seas, and the high seas. Potential originators of data and participants in data flow include sovereign states, scientific organizations (national and international), the International Sea-Bed Authority, individual commercial and industrial operators, and intergovernmental organizations.

Any of the data originators, operating in an EEZ, territorial sea, regional sea, or the International Area, may be required to transfer data to some or most of the following: the coastal state, neighboring disadvantaged and landlocked states, regional data centers, international data exchange authorities, the World Data Center (Oceanography) of the International Sea-Bed Authority. In spite of the absence of mandatory transfer of data to the Authority, Article 143 and several of the subsequent articles of Section 2 define a regime within which data availability, access, and transfer are inherent to the Area.

UNCLOS expresses the desired objectives of greater data transfer and freedom to gain access to data, both for coastal states and for the international community as a whole. UNCLOS does not, and should not, pre-suppose any particular means by which these ends could be obtained. Although frequent reference is made to "appropriate international channels" etc., no international agency is mentioned by name. Nevertheless, the experience of the oceanographic community is that specialist agencies are needed to facilitate data transfers. It is not possible to envisage each data originator being contacted by a potential data user with a request, and the data originator having the time and skill to make the data transfer effective just when the user needs it.

The reasons for the originator-to-user model of data transfer being nearly unworkable are technical, procedural, and logistical. To transfer data from one computer to another requires that the tape format be physically readable by both computers, and that the data on the tape should be meaningful to the recipient. This means that in almost all transfers there has to be a change of tape format, or preferably, the use of a standardized international format. Assuming that the recipient can read the tape, the data documentation, taken with the data themselves, must be sufficient for the user to understand the data fully. There are many analogies here with banks handling money. Conversion of tape formats, storage of data, maintenance and compiling of totally thorough documentation, are all best performed by professionals who work with data in this way all the time. Nobody nowadays would think of taking a chest full of cash from one country to another, exchanging the money physically for money of the second country, and then taking that chest of money to pay for goods. All these transactions would be carried out by banks. Similarly, although the system is still embryonic, a network of national oceanographic data banks is growing up to handle marine data. A Global Telecommuniations System for the transfer of meteorological data already exists and links Meteorological Centers in all major countries.

Assuming that the technical aspect can be settled efficiently, the originator-to-user model would require that the originator actually had the time and effort to handle the enquiry just when the user asked. In practice the originator of data usually resents the time needed to prepare data for transfer, and would certainly resent having to make transfers in different formats to many different potential users. From the user's point of view, a problem requiring data from a wide area of, say the central Atlantic, might require him to discover and contact a dozen or more data owners. This would be a considerable effort in itself, even assuming that each country published an inventory of the data held by its nationals and organizations. Again, as with money, the solution is to channel transactions through a central organization. The data originator transfers the data once to an archive or data bank; the data bank guarantees the integrity and documentation of the data over a long time period; data users, states or organizations with a right to receive data obtain their copies in the formats they prefer from the bank.

Experience with large data sets of oceanographic measurements has shown that there is great value in transferring the responsibility for long-term care of the data, and servicing requests, to specialized oceanographic data banks. Within the worldwide system of NODCs, IOC has approved special responsibility for certain data types to designated NODCs. Thus, the Canadian NODC archives and services drifting buoy data; the U.K. NODC archives and services data from the Joint Air-Sea Interaction Project (JASIN), and wave data. These centers are known as Responsible National Oceanographic Data Centers (RNODCs).

The existence of satellite remote-sensed oceanographic data is not envisaged by UNCLOS, and yet this factor will influence data transfers. Most remote-sensed data are restricted to the sea surface, but some sensors penetrate several tens of meters below the surface, while Synthetic Aperture Radar (SAR) measurements reveal data on the topography of the seabed to depths of several tens of meters. Such data are almost immediately in the public domain, and are (or will be) archived in data banks which are generally accessible. The specific objective of oeanographic remote-sensing satellites is to gather data on a global scale and make them available to the global scientific and technical community. Although a small percentage of these data will refer to the EEZ and territorial seas of coastal states, they are gained without installing or operating any instruments within coastal states' jurisdiction, and there is no restriction on gathering the data, or on the use. I would hope that the existence of these global remote-sensed data archives would encourage coastal states to contribute their data gathered by conventional instrumentation also to the international data community, rather than asserting their right to confidential classification.

The trend in oceanographc data gathering in the next decade will be greatly influenced by the large international programs such as the World Climate Research Program. Data for these programs will consist of data sets describing whole ocean basins from coast to coast, with standard sections and profiles measured at repeated intervals. These programs are funded by international agreements, and organized with the support of international agencies such as WMO or IOC. It would be ironic if oceanic sections could not be completed in international programs because coastal states chose to maximize their rights within the EEZ. Again, one hopes that the international nature of the objective will encourage coastal states to grant rights of access and publication of data automatically, whilst of course always having the option to place an observer on board a vessel, and to obtain direct copies of the data from within the EEZ.

The Mediation of Data Transfer

The use of an international archiving and transfer system for transferring data from the originator to a multiplicity of users has already been outlined. It is not obvious that the same system should be used for the obligatory transfer of data from the data originator to the coastal state under Articles 249.1(b) and 249.1(c). At this level, it might be supposed that a direct bilateral transfer is simpler.

I suspect that if the data transfer between operator and coastal state is left solely as a bilateral matter, there will be many disputes, much disappointment, and eventually bitterness and acrimony. There is scope for confusion and disagreement about quality of data, calibration, corrections, quantity of data, delays in processing, computer compatibility, formats, comprehensibility to the recipient, data products, usefulness of the type of presentation, etc. Suspicion will often exist, in that the coastal state may be a developing country without sufficient skilled staff to interpret or judge the computerized data. Nothing could be worse for the future of international oceanography than a cynical transfer of useless computer tapes to developing countries, thus complying with the letter or UNCLOS but neglecting the spirit.

Raw data listings are very difficult to use, and unless the coastal state has a great deal of expertise and specialist computer software, tapes of raw data will be useless. Notwithstanding Article 249.1(c) requiring the data originator to help assess the data, a great deal more practical help is really needed. An international agency, acting as a mediator, would provide a guarantee of common standards and fair play. If the data originator informs the coastal state directly that the data will be difficult to understand, and that there will be a delay of six months while the data are processed, this would be merely another ground for suspicion. An international banking service could assure the coastal state that necessary work on the data is being done, and that the delays are reasonable. The oceanographic data banking agency would first accept a copy of the raw data, or partially cleaned data from the originator, to show that the data do exist, and are in good order. The agency could then advise both parties on the data processing and data products which would be most useful to the coastal state. At the completion of the exercise the data originator would only have to submit one set of cleaned and processed data to the data bank.

From that point the data bank would provide one copy, with appropriate data products, to the coastal state. Provided that the coastal state did not assert its right of confidentiality (Article 249.2), the data bank would also transmit copies in appropriate formats to neighboring disadvantaged states, Regional Data Centers, and the RNODC and WDC of the ICSU World Data Center System.

As data are processed, reduced, and converted into maps and graphs, they usually become easier and easier to understand and use. However, the most useful data products, covering large areas of sea, require data from numerous sources and gathered over a long time. You cannot predict the highest wave which will strike an oil rig on the basis of one month of measurements of wave height. You cannot plot the fluctuations in the Gulf Stream on the basis of data obtained on one cruise by one ship, or even all the data available from all ships and satellites for one year. Data banks therefore provide the opportunity to integrate data from many sources and generate data products which have a greatly increased information value to all potential users. This is another reason for hoping that all data originators and coastal states will appreciate the value to themselves of contributing the data to which they have a right, and making it available to the international community.

Review and Discussion

The Articles of UNCLOS discussed in this paper establish the principle that the implementation of the Convention requires an exchange of marine scientific data on a greater scale than previously. Such exchange of data is envisaged at an international level whether the project producing the data is conducted in the EEZ of a coastal state, in a sea which is covered by a regional agreement, or in the international area. In every case, the principles of the relevant Articles refer to the possible involvement of a competent international authority to improve the transfer, exchange, or flow of data.

The Convention requires the promotion of the results of marine scientific work in every way, and the enhancement of the transfer of marine scientific data. References to publication, dissemination, and information amount to a strong endorsement for the publication of more easily understood data products, and the publication of more information about the data system, catalogues and guides to data acquisition, or data management.

Articles concerned with education and assistance to developing countries require that one subject of education should be the management of marine scientific data.

States are advised to establish national marine scientific research centers, and these could include national oceanographic data centers. Competent international organizations are required to give assistance in the establishment of such centers, especially in developing countries.

States are recommended to establish regional centers to advance marine scientific research in enclosed and semi-enclosed seas. Assistance is recommended from appropriate international organizations. This objective is totally compatible with the objectives and procedures of the IODE system, and great assistance could be given in the standardization of data exchange, and management of data sets.

States are given the option in many Articles of complying with the requirements of the Convention either by unilateral or bilateral action, or through an appropriate competent international organization. In all matters concerned with the international transfer of marine scientific data, there is a great deal to be gained by standardizing the exchange with a uniform format. This should be the GF-3 format, and its specialized sub-sets. Whilst states always have the option of exchanging data in a working format, either directly between research institutes or between NODCs, every effort should be made to encourage organizations to use the IODE-WDC system. The Convention stresses the overall importance of marine scientific research for the benefit of all mankind, and the marine scientific data will only be of permanent value, and accessible to all peoples, if it is transferred into a fully international system.

The Convention strongly recommends the principle of certain voluntary transfers of data, and makes it possible to enforce other transfers from an operating state to the coastal state whose EEZ has been carried out. No mechanism or channel is proposed in general for the transfer of data under these voluntary or compulsory obligations. However, if an organization for the promotion of exchange of marine scientific data between states did not exist, it is almost certain that one would have to be invented to meet the requirements of UNCLOS. It would be impossible to meet the objectives of the Convention with regard to marine scientific data without a truly international system. By frequent reference to "competent international organizations" the Convention implies the involvement of a system such as the IODE system coordinated by ICO. The Convention describes objectives in terms of the principles and achievements required, and not the mechanism. Thus there is no reference to the need for data quality control, standardized methods of data gathering, accurate calibration of instruments, the gathering of data into national data centers, standardization of exchange formats, etc. The experience of marine scientists generally is that all these procedures and others are essential to ensure the long-term value of marine scientific data, and its usefulness to people other than the originator.

The obligation on operators to deliver data to the coastal state within whose EEZ they have been conducting research is the area within which argument or disagreement is most likely to arise between states. The WC for IODE might take the point of view that it did not wish to be involved in these transfers of data because the obligation was purely for bilateral exchange, and the relationships between states could become one of confrontation. If the WC for IODE adopted this position, it is possible that large quantities of marine scientific data might be transferred to coastal states under conditions of confidentiality, and would be lost completely to the international community. In addition, the transfer of the data might not be carried out to the highest standards, so that the coastal state in the event would not benefit from the exchange. The overall results of this would be of minimal value to mankind as a whole.

It is possible that the WC for IODE could use its experience and neutral unbiased position to establish a Code of Practice for international data exchange between operators and the coastal states within whose EEZ they have been working. The use of such a Code would be voluntary, and coastal states would, at their own discretion, use the Code or not, and could call upon the advice and assistance of experts from the IODE system. On the basis of their requests, coastal states could be advised as to whether confidentiality was necessary, and could be recommended as to whether short or long terms of confidentiality should be applied. On request, and acting purely in a technical, not legal, capacity, experts of the IODE system could advise operating states on the degree of data quality control, data products, data formats, etc., which would be of greatest use to the coastal state. At the same time, with one transfer operation, the operator could make the data available to the coastal state, to neighboring disadvantaged states, to the regional data center -- if it exists -- and to the competent international organization (IOC). This would be an economy for the operator. Through contacts with the coastal state, or publication of guidelines, the IODE system could make it clear that quality control and full documentation of data takes several months, and that it is preferable for the coastal state to receive good quality, well-doc-umented data, and suitable data products, rather than raw data tapes straight off the ship, with the data in a condition which is almost unusable.

The coastal states have to balance their interests between maximizing their rights to possession and confidentiality of data, or benefitting from the increased accuracy, precision, and knowledge of all oceanography in their area, which would arise from contributing data to the international system. This is not a choice between selfish interest and altruism. It is a choice between two types of benefits which may accrue to the coastal state. Since data contributed to the international system would still be available to the coastal state first, the only point in debate is whether the coastal state benefits most from making the data confidential, or would lose from doing this. I think that, on the balance, coastal states would lose. When we add to this the altruistic factor of contributing to international well-being, I think that the case is very strong indeed for the international freedom of oceanographic data transfer.

Acknowledgement

Parts of this paper are modified from a paper presented by the author at Session XI of the Working Committee for International Oceanographic Data exchange, 1984, reference IOC/MIM *ad hoc* 6, and summarized in the IOC report of that Session, reference IOC/IODE-XI/3 rev., pp. 63-64.

Acronyms Used

EEZ	Exclusive Economic Zone
IOC	Intergovernmental Oceanographic Commission
IODE (WC)	InternationalOceanographic DataExchange (Working Committee)
NODC	National Oceanographic Data Center
RNODC	Responsible National Oceanographic Data Center
TOGA	Tropical Ocean Global Atmosphere (experiment)
UNCLOS	United Nations Convention on Law of the Sea
WCRP	World Climate Research Program
WDC	World Data Center
WMO	World Meteorological Organization
WOCE	World Ocean Circulation Experiment
ICSU	International Council of Scientific Unions.

REFERENCES

Flemming, N.C., 1983, *Implications of the UN Convention on the Law of the Sea for the Activities of the Working Committee on International Oceanographic Data Exchange*, (IOC/MIM *ad hoc* 6).

Goncalves, M.E., 1982, "International co-operation in marine scientific research and in the development and transfer of marine science and technology in the Convention on the Law of the Sea with particular reference to the interests of the developing countries," pp. 36-37, in UNESCO-IOC Workshop 32. Supplement. *Development of Marine Science and the Transfer of Technology in the Context of the New Ocean Regime.*

Kesteven, G., 1982, "Flow of scientific data and information and the transfer of knowledge to developing countries," pp.114-129, in UNESCO-

IOC Workshop 32. Supplement. *Development of Marine Science and the Transfer of Technology in the Context of the New Ocean Regime.*

Miles, E., 1981, *Implications of the draft Convention on the Law of the Sea and the New Ocean Regime for scientific data and information exchange programs of the IOC* (IOC/IODE-X/8, Annex 14).

Yankov, A., 1982, "A general review of the New Convention on the Law of the Sea having a bearing on marine science and its application", pp. 3-35, in UNESCO-IOC Workshop 32. Supplement. *Development of Marine Science and the Transfer of Technology in the Context of the New Ocean Regime.*

R.J.H. Beverton: That was a fascinating insight into an area of activity which only those who have a direct, daily need to use oceanographic data realize is going on behind the scenes. It would be useful to have questions on the role of competent international organizations which are mentioned in many places through the text of the Convention.

DISCUSSION AND QUESTIONS

R.J.H. Beverton: We have a few minutes for questions.

Geoffrey O'Sullivan: I'm from the National Board for Science and Technology in Ireland. I am speaking from the point of view of the state in whose waters a number of foreign vessels carry out research, and I am particularly interested in Article 249 on the position of observers. Perhaps Alfred Soons or Chris Adams could answer my question. The Article says that the operator shall ensure the right of the coastal state to participate, if it so desires. I would be very interested in the panel's view of what "participation" means.

Secondly, it says this participation is "when practical." Now Chris Adams has quite rightly pointed out the problems with ship time at a premium, and that therefore it is very sometimes difficult to take an observer on board. But it is also very easy from the cruise operator's point of view to say that, because there is a premium on time, it is difficult to accept an observer. So I would just like you to comment on the meaning of "participation" and "when practical."

Chris Adams: We make it clear on our notification forms that the coastal state does have a right to participate. It is not a question of whether we could give them the right; they have the right and we will facilitate. In fact, we always ask the principal scientist to ensure that the requisite number of berths are left. I think the problems arise when available berths are limited and when the observer may not be a useful member of the scientific party. Perhaps my other colleagues on the panel could add to this.

John Knauss: I think it is quite clear that all of us accept the fact that the coastal state has the right to participate and can put anybody it wishes aboard. We would prefer somebody who is knowledgeable, who can participate, but we will accept any observer -- a military officer, anyone that the coastal state wishes. The problems we have come across are of the following nature: for example, if we are working off the coast of a nation, say 150 miles out, and are not making a port stop in that country, how do you get that person aboard? We are prepared to fly that person to our most recent port stop and also drop him at our next port stop, but sometimes is not convenient for the coastal nation and that is where the negotiations take place. I would say most of our problems have been of that nature.

Daniel Cheever: As I listened to this morning's fascinating discussion, I recognized that the scientist inevitably feels somewhat under unwelcome constraints. My question is: do members of the panel feel that there are more serious constraints affecting their work than the navigational constraints for ordinary commerce and other usages of the seas?

A.S. Laughton: The answer to that must be *yes* because the research vessels are subject to the same constraints of navigation, passage and so forth that the merchant ships must perform under. Yet on top of that, there are the additional constraints which have been well outlined this morning. These constraints very often involve extra port stops which are not necessarily scheduled on a scientific basis and stops which are not necessarily scheduled on a scientific basis and which would ordinarily not be made by a commercial company operating a shipping line.

Nic Flemming: It is very much a question of point of view rather than of interpretation of the Convention. People who practice science are used to working in a very open community -- based on open publication and the absolutely fundamental assumption that science is a moral, ethical, and social good for the benefit of the general community. Against that background, the additional restrictions placed on science seem to be almost irrational. It is almost an emotional reaction but cuts at something intended to be beneficial to the whole community. I appreciate that science can be used for other purposes, but you have to take that factor into account. Because scientific budgets are, as it were, at the margin, if you do not do science, people do not immediately notice the negative effects. If you put obstacles in the way of scientific projects, they simply do not get done; whereas, in other kinds of work of more immediate economic benefit, one may persevere in the face of minor obstacles. Looking at it as a reaction of a community, people do feel that science is, to a certain extent, discriminated against.

Holgar Rotkirch: I am the Deputy Director General of the Legal Department in the Ministry of Foreign Affairs of Finland. Professor Beverton, in your introduction this morning, you referred to the feelings of resignation and despair that are common among marine scientists because of the new provisions in the United Nations Law of the Sea Convention. These feelings are widely shared by the marine scientists in the Baltic Sea. The establishment of fisheries zones and EEZs has already changed the situation regarding the conduct of marine scientific research in this area. And as the Law of the Sea Convention enters into force, the situation will become even more restrictive. Ultimately, there will be no high seas area in the Baltic Sea. It will be wholly covered by resource zones, where the coastal state's consent is required for the conduct of marine scientific research. I thought it might interest this Conference to hear that efforts have therefore been undertaken by the seven Baltic Sea States, seeking to make the procedure easier to get the necessary consents from coastal States for research in the water column of the research zones outside the territorial sea. The Helsinki Commission on the Protection of the Marine Environment of the Baltic Sea Area has been given the task of compiling the legislation on marine scientific research in the Baltic Sea states and, on this basis, will draft a standard application form to be used by the marine scientists. If this work succeeds, a further step might be taken with a view of making certain requirements in the Law of the Sea Convention less cumbersome for the scientists. For instance, one could foresee a separate agreement between the Baltic Sea states on the speeding up of granting necessary consents and so on. It is thought that such an agreement would, to a large extent, reduce the paperwork for the scientists as well as diminish the risk of having applications rejected. It would thus make the lives of Baltic Sea marine scientists much easier.

R.J.H. Beverton: That is very interesting. I was not aware of such moves in the Baltic. The International Council for the Exploration of the Sea, which covers the North Atlantic generally and the North Sea in particular, is trying to work towards agreements between those countries to facilitate the whole process of working in one another's area. I do not think it has reached finality yet.

Alistair Couper: I would like to follow up on Dan Cheever's question about other users of the the sea. This relates to the distinction between the high seas and the EEZ which, for some vessels, is not totally clear. In this respect, a merchant vessel or, indeed, a fishing vessel or warship making its normal passage and exercising its navigational rights in the EEZ is, for all intents and purposes, on the high seas. Now, such vessels very often are engaged in collecting data. They will be collecting data relating to hazards of navigation and these could probably be construed as activities compatible with the ordinary course of navigation. They will be collecting data on meteorological conditions and will be reporting these. Again, this might be construed as part of normal activity associated with high seas rights in navigation. But some of them, under their flag state instructions, are collecting information, say, on the density of other fishing vessels in an EEZ; or the names of ships under particular flags passing through an economic zone or territorial sea; or even the direction and numbers of whales in the area. These activities are being conducted now by merchant ships in territorial seas and high seas, and it is just not clear where and when they require coastal consent, if any. Perhaps we could get some views on this.

R.J.H Beverton: I think you have picked up one of quite a number of grey areas which are not spelled out and which presumably will gradually become clearer as a result of case precedent. Fred, I think this is a matter where a legal view will be appropriate.

Alfred Soons: I fully agree with what you have just said. Of course, any data-collecting activity by vessels passing through the EEZ which is principally for their own safe navigation is permitted because that is part of navigation. If a vessel would steer a course specifically with a view to collecting certain data, that would be entirely different. Then, one might argue that it is conducting research but, even then, it is possible, under international programs, that a vessel is simply collecting data for the Bathymetric Chart of the Oceans Program -- simply collecting information. It has steered its course especially for that purpose over a certain route, but I think that is perfectly acceptable under the provisions as I read them. But of course you also refer to data-collecting activities which probably are not allowed under the new regime.

John Knauss: You picked up a very interesting point, and I believe that is one of the reasons why you will find no definition of marine scientific research in the Convention. It was deliberately left that way, I believe. You also made the other very interesting point that, for military vessels, the EEZ is the high seas, and therefore military vessels can do whatever they wish in the EEZ, including what many of us would call marine scientific research.

Chris Adams: If you use a 10 kHz echo-sounder through a hull transducer in the bottom of the ship, you are navigating, you are getting bathymetric information for navigation purposes. If you use a towed fish overside, and you get photographed, you are doing it for science, and you get into trouble.

Eduardo Ferrero Costa: I am from the Peruvian Center for International Studies. I will give some brief comments from the point of view of a developing country.

Before I begin, I would like to mention an experience in 1972 when I was kindly invited to Scripps in California by Professor Wooster to participate in inter-disciplinary research on scientific research in the sea -- a project which led to a book on freedom of scientific research. I was just beginning in international law and I defended the Latin American position regarding control of scientific research within the 200 miles of the coast. Very kindly and very gently, they told me that I was crazy. It is really interesting how, in only thirteen years, this panel now accepts the reality of the consent regime. I wanted to mention this to put things in historical perspective. It is incredible how things change.

The data given by Professor Knauss are really very interesting and optimistic in the sense that, of the cases that he has analyzed, only in 10 percent has there been denial of permission to conduct research. That means that, in general, permission is given and that in general, the consent regime is working well. I would like to ask the following question of Professor Knauss: in the United States or in other countries where there is scientific marine research, do you know whether this is done within the economic zones of coastal states without asking for permission, or is permission always asked? If permission is always asked or is at least always tried (for instance, they have asked Cuba recently), could that mean that we are now under a consent regime already established under international customary law?

Finally, I would like to comment that Dr. Soons mentioned several things that were negative in the Law of the Sea Convention regarding the regulations established within the economic zones for marine scientific research -- for instance, the conciliation procedures for settlement of disputes. I would like to say, however, that those things that are inconvenient for the states doing the research are convenient for the coastal states in which the research is done. So we must see both positions. In that context, I really believe that with all its imperfections and lack of accurate definitions, the compromise formula established in the Law of the Sea Convention is a good one. It really is a compromise in which consent must be given all the time in normal circumstances.

R.J.H. Beverton: That was a very interesting comment which touched on a number of different matters. I don't know whether we can do justice to all of them. As far as information is concerned for the coastal states which are developing countries, I think, Nic, that is covered in your paper.

Nic Flemming: The full text of my paper does cover the question of carrying data transfer through to complete acceptance and assimilation within the technical community of the coastal state. I did not speak this morning about particular international agencies, but it is quite clear that training in data management and the ability to accept data is the central part of making the system work. It is no good just squirting computer tapes or telemetered data around and hoping people will use it -- they cannot.

R.J.H. Beverton: Now, Fred, would you take up the other question?

Alfred Soons: Two points. Mr. Ferrero asked if we could already say that the consent regime exists under customary international law. It's extremely speculative to make any pronouncement on what customary international law is now or what it will be in the near future. I would say that the main principles of Part XIII of the Law of the Sea Convention and especially the principle of consent are already part of customary international law as far as the EEZ and research on the continental shelf are concerned. But that does not mean, of course, that all the elements of the consent regime -- for instance, the distinction between various kinds of scientific research -- should to the same extent be considered a part of customary international law.

Then, Mr. Ferrero said that I mentioned only negative things about the regime in the EEZ -- well, I am not aware of that, and if I gave that impression, that is a wrong impression. I think that the new regime certainly contains very positive elements also, especially from the point of view of developing countries.

John Knauss: I think the question was, am I aware of any research going on that is not under the consent regime or some words to that effect. Well, of course, all research done off the United States is without consent because the United States does not require consent. So there is no consent for foreign research vessels doing work off our shores within 200 miles. As to research that is done by the United States off other peoples' shores, I can only speak to that which is done by universities which I know about firsthand, and most of the distant water research is done by university research vessels. I believe that all of the research that is done off coastal states that do indeed have a consent regime, at this point namely 102 of the 139, is indeed done following the regulations of those coastal states.

Scott Sigman: I'm from the London School of Economics. I welcome the last question coming from someone from the developing countries -- the panel being primarily made up of northern and western developing states' representatives. I also commend Rowena Lawson for her irreverent view of the status quo. I would like a commentary from the other members of the panel who did not seem to take account adequately of the difference in administrative structure and the nature of government in the developing world.

R.J.H. Beverton: I hope we did not underestimate the very real position of the developing countries. Would any member of the panel like to take up that request?

Anthony Laughton: The needs of a coastal state in the developing world are very substantial in order to address many of the problems faced in the Convention. The conference in the Indian Ocean which took place last week also was very conscious of this need and was seeking ways to strengthen and improve this infrastructure which would involve both the countries' finances and their organization, administration and skills. It will be a long process, but there are many international organizations which are helping these countries to build up this strength and address these problems.

Scott Sigman: You also indicated efforts by the group from the Commonwealth working towards cooperation. The colonialism and neo-colonialism from the past is something nations today are trying to eliminate, and

413

yet there is recognition, I think, of the need to cooperate. Is there a structure beside that colonialism and neo-colonialism that could be utilized?

Anthony Laughton: There are many international groupings of regional or subregional organizations, some of them supported through the UN systems and some will be Commonwealth groupings. One might take as another grouping the European Economic Community. All kinds of groupings internationally will try to address these problems in their various ways and I do not think that you should single out any one particular grouping.

John Knauss: Could I just say a few words on the same subject? It is an extraordinarily difficult question, and there is no simple answer. There are many examples one can give. I would say that about 50 percent of the research we do off South America is done in real cooperation with at least one or two scientists from those countries, and I would say another 50 percent is not. It is not because we are not willing to do so but because we cannot find anyone in the country concerned that is particularly interested in the kinds of research we are doing. On the other hand, there is an awful lot of other research that is done where the concept is not to find out more about the Peruvian current, sea floor spreading, or something of this nature but, say, to try to solve the problems that Dr. Lawson talked about -- namely, helping a country develop its own fisheries and so forth, which has really nothing to do with the kinds of research we talk about, using highly sophisticated research vessels. And that is also going on almost independently of the kind of work that I was concerned with in my talk today.

Nic Flemming: In my talk about data transfer, I concentrated on the technical side, partly because I am not a lawyer, but in my paper I have tried to show how the technical procedures I have suggested are designed to benefit developing countries to the maximum extent. If data transfer is left exclusively in the area of bilateral transfer between an operating ship, laboratory, or state and the coastal states, there is an enormous potential for misunderstanding, disillusionment, and eventually acrimony and bitterness. If data are transmitted in a crude form very rapidly, the coastal state in most cases will not be able to do anything with it. Chris Adams referred to the transfer of the Roscop form that is an internationally recognized document providing a very brief description of the work done. The situation I would like to encourage is one where, with the participation of the coastal state, some initial data transfer takes place whether it is in the form of a summary or a copy of the tapes. The coastal state at least knows that the work has been done properly and it has got the first version of the data. Then, with an international mediator or with the regional representative of a data banking system, the operating state works up the data, does the data processing to agreed standards which are accepted internationally and transfers the data and the interpretation of it progressively to the coastal state. I put forth that proposition entirely with the needs of the developing countries in mind.

Tom Jamir: I am from the University of the Philippines. I liked very much the paper delivered by Dr. Lawson regarding the failures and perhaps mismanagement of most of the aids given to the developing countries, as well as the apparent disbanding of regional organizations after the withdrawal of support. I would like to add some recommendations from a Third World or developing country's point of view. First, who really benefits from the aid or assistance given by these organizations or developed countries? For example, with respect to the United States, there is what we call *U.S. Aid.* Sometimes in the Philippines, in informal circles, we joke with American consultants and ask them, is U.S. Aid aid to the Philippines, or is it aid from the Philippines to the U.S.?

B.J.H. Beverton: I am not quite sure if we're really able to take on this sort of question, because it really is not about science and the law of the sea.

Rowena Lawson: Speaking of the global amount of aid to fisheries, I just happen to have the figures here. In 1981, $400 million in aid were given through bilateral and multilateral agencies to fisheries in the Third World and, of that, only 13 percent have been spent on research. The rest largely went to industrial development -- vessels, socioeconomic studies. But, as I have tried to say in my little talk, the amount going on actual resource research has been declining over the years. I am sorry that does not really answer your question, but I do happen to have these figures, and I thought they might help you.

R.J.H. Beverton: We must now bring this session to a close. I would like to thank all the panel members who contributed such interesting and helpful papers this morning. I hope you will feel that they were knitted together to make an interesting session, as I certainly did.

I am left with the thought that marine science communities can do quite a bit to bring about a greater worldwide awareness of our natural resources, the world around us, and a way of sharing that understanding.

LUNCHEON SPEECH

IMO AND THE LAW OF THE SEA

C.P. Srivastava
Secretary-General
International Maritime Organization (IMO)

It is a great honor to be invited to address this Conference. The International Maritime Organization is the only specialized agency of the United Nations whose mandate is exclusively maritime. As Secretary-General of that agency, I am very much aware of the relevance of the law of the sea to our Organization and the importance of a stable legal regime of the seas to the successful development and operation of international maritime transport. I am, therefore, most grateful indeed to the Law of the Sea Institute and the Organizers of this Conference for inviting me to speak about IMO and the Law of the Sea.

The remit of the Third United Nations Conference on the Law of the Sea, as approved by the General Assembly of the United Nations in Resolution 2750 c (XXV) of December 17, 1970, included consideration of issues which were of direct relevance to the IMO and its work. Of particular interest to IMO were the issues concerning the regime of the high seas, the regulation of shipping in the territorial sea and in international straits, as well as in preservation of the marine environment, especially the prevention, control and reduction of pollution from ships and by dumping. IMO followed closely and actively contributed to the work of the Conference, including the preparatory work undertaken by the Committee on the Peaceful Uses of the Sea-bed and the Ocean Floor beyond the limits of National Jurisdiction, with regard to matters within the competence of IMO as enshrined in its constitutive Convention.

IMO's Role in the Law of the Sea Convention

It is now a source of much satisfaction to IMO, and to me personally, that the Convention on the Law of the Sea of 1982 gives appropriate and generally satisfactory recognition to the competence of the IMO in the areas of interest it namely, matters relating to "navigation and the prevention and control of marine pollution from vessels and by dumping."

The Convention gives legal and political confirmation to the regulatory regimes developed by IMO, and it implicitly recognizes IMO as the legitimate international forum in which states are expected to develop new international standards and regulations or revise existing rules on these subjects. The Convention also adopts and emphasizes the basic approach adopted in IMO's treaties and instruments, *i.e.*, the principle that the primary responsibility for the enforcement of internationally adopted standards and regulations lies with states -- with flag states, coastal states or port states depending on the nature of the regulations or standards concerned.

Furthermore, the Law of the Sea Convention adopts and underpins a number of important maritime principles which are already incorporated in IMO treaty instruments adopted before the drafting of the 1982 Convention. Indeed, in a number of important cases, the provisions of the Law of the Sea Convention are either *verbatim* reproductions of provisions in previous IMO treaties or minor adaptations of the principles in those treaties. For example, Article 221 of the Law of the Sea Convention states that "nothing in this Part shall prejudice the right of States, pursuant to international law, both customary and conventional, to take and enforce measures beyond the territorial sea proportionate to the actual or threatened damage to protect their coastline or related interests, including fishing, from pollution or threat of pollution following upon a maritime casualty or acts relating to such a casualty, which may reasonably be expected to result in major harmful consequences." The principle in this provision was first given formal expression in the 1969 Intervention Convention adopted as part of the response of IMO to the "Torrey Canyon" disaster. Article I of that Convention states that "Parties to the present Convention may take such measures on the high seas as may be necessary to prevent, mitigate or eliminate grave and imminent danger to their coastline or related interests from pollution or threat of pollution of the sea by oil, following upon a maritime casualty or acts related to such a casualty, which may reasonably be expected to result in major harmful consequences."

Another example is the principle, in Articles 218 and 220 of the Law of the Sea Convention, empowering a port or coastal state to take enforcement action against ships voluntarily within its jurisdiction in respect of discharges in violation of international rules and standards. This principle had been accepted as a part of the regime in the MARPOL Convention adopted by IMO in 1973. Article 4 of the MARPOL Convention gives to states parties the right either to take proceedings, in accordance with their laws, against violations of the Convention within their jurisdiction or to furnish information and evidence in respect of the violation to the flag state concerned. Further, Article 6 of MARPOL empowers the port state to take investigative action in respect of violations of the Convention, wherever such violations may have occurred. Another area in which the Law of the Sea Convention adopts principles in IMO's treaties relates to liability and compensation for damage caused by pollution of the marine environment. Article 235 of the 1982 Convention enjoins states to develop *inter alia* "criteria and procedures for payment of adequate compensation, such as compulsory insurance and compensation funds." It will be recalled that the idea in that provision had already been given concrete application by IMO as far back as 1969 and 1971, in the 1969 Civil Liability Convention and the 1971 Fund Convention. Between them, these two Conventions provide an international arrangement for dealing with the question of liability and compensation for pollution damage. Specifically the regime in these Conventions seeks to ensure the availability of appropriate compensation for victims of pollution damage, by means of a system of compulsory insurance and an international compensation fund, which is already in operation. The limits of compensation under the 1969 and 1971 Conventions were increased at a diplomatic conference arranged by IMO in 1984.

It is, therefore, no exaggeration to say that the 1982 Convention on the Law of the Sea provides clear endorsement for several important aspects of the work so far undertaken by IMO in the development of maritime law.

It is now widely recognized that the 1982 Convention on the Law of the Sea provides the general legal framework for the national and international regulation of such matters as navigation and the preservation of the marine environment. As an "umbrella treaty," the Convention establishes on these matters general principles which have to be implemented and supplemented by special regimes developed in the relevant bodies of the United Nations which are charged with sectoral mandates in the respective areas. As far as IMO is concerned, the 1982 Convention establishes general principles relating to navigation, the promotion of safety at sea, the prevention and control of vessel-source pollution, the regulation of pollution by dumping and international cooperation and technical assistance. The specific implementation of these principles is, for the most part, to be carried out through the development of appropriate international standards, rules and regulations by reference to which states may adopt the necessary measures for applying the provisions of the Convention. This is particularly true of the Convention's provisions and principles concerning the rights and obligations of flag states, coastal states and port states in the territorial sea, the high seas and in the newly-established exclusive economic zone; the obligations and rights of states under the newly-established regime of transit passage through straits used for international navigation; the conditions and procedures regarding the establishment and use of artificial islands, installations and structures in various areas of the sea; and the powers of states in respect of the adoption and enforcement of laws and regulations for the prevention, reduction and control of marine pollution.

Although the IMO is mentioned by name only once in the text of the Convention, many of the Articles of the Convention, in their reference to "the competent international organization," implicitly recognize the standard-setting competence of IMO in the fields of navigation and prevention, reduction and control of marine pollution from ships and by dumping. In many areas the 1982 Convention on the Law of the Sea requires states, in exercising their powers under the Convention, to conform to, or take account of, the standards established by IMO, including those resulting from work of general diplomatic conferences convened by IMO.

While there are no explicit statements of what constitutes "generally accepted" or "applicable" international rules and standards in the text of the Convention, it is, I believe, generally agreed that most of the major international regulations and standards developed in IMO in relation to maritime safety and the prevention of marine pollution by ships and by dumping are covered by these terms. The regulations are, therefore, expected to feature prominently in any practical implementation of the Convention's principles by states and other interested bodies. This will also apply to any revised or updated versions of the current standards and regulations -- in IMO's treaty instruments and, in appropriate cases, in non-treaty regulations contained in the major Codes and Guidelines adopted by IMO's organs and bodies. Moreover, as the organization deemed competent in the area of maritime safety and the prevention and control of vessel-source pollution and dumping, IMO is expected to develop or provide the machinery for developing rules in areas where no such rules exist or to review and up-date existing rules where they are deemed to require modification or up-dating. This gives greater authority and wider applicability to such regulations and standards; but it also imposes greater responsibility on IMO to ensure that such regulations are considered and formulated in a way which make them as widely acceptable as possible.

In addition to the recognition it gives to the work already undertaken by IMO, the Law of the Sea Convention envisages, and sometimes specifically assigns, additional responsibilities and functions to IMO for matters in which IMO had not previously been involved. Perhaps the most significant of these new responsibilities is the role given to IMO in Annex VII of the Convention dealing with special Arbitration procedures. Articles 2 of that Annex states that the list of experts to compose special arbitral tribunals to settle disputes in the field of navigation, including pollution from vessels and by dumping, shall be drawn up and maintained by IMO or by the appropriate subsidiary body concerned to which the Organization has delegated that function.

Another new function concerns the establishment of sealanes and traffic separation schemes in various areas of the sea. Under Article 22 of the Convention, states designating sealanes in their territorial sea are required to take into account the recommendations of IMO. In the case of states bordering straits used for international navigation, Article 41 of the Convention provides that their proposals for new or revised sealanes or traffic separation schemes in such straits must be referred to IMO for adoption before they are put into operation.

Another important area in which IMO is expected to undertake new functions relates to the removal of disused or abandoned installations or structures in the EEZs of states. Article 60, paragraph 3, of the Law of the Sea Convention imposes on a coastal state the duty to remove any artificial installations or structures, installed by it in its EEZs, when such installations or structures are abandoned or disused. The removal is to ensure safety of navigation. Article 60 of the Convention on the Law of the Sea further provides that in removing such installations or structures, the coastal State shall take into account any generally accepted international standards established in this regard by IMO. Having regard to the increasing use of larger and more complex structures and equipment in the marine environment in connection with the utilization of marine resources, it is reasonable to expect that appropriate international regulations and uniform procedures for the removal of abandoned or disused structures will be required by the international community. The work of IMO in this regard will have considerable significance not only in relation to the safety of navigation and the prevention of pollution, but also in helping states to organize other legitimate and important activities in the marine environment in a way which enables them to avoid undue complications to their own program or burdensome responsibilities and liabilities towards other states or other users of the sea.

Also of special significance to IMO are the Articles of the Law of the Sea Convention relating to international cooperation and the provision of advice to developing countries. The Convention places great emphasis on cooperation between states and international organizations in promoting the objectives of the Convention and in enabling states to take the necessary measures to exercise their powers or to fulfill their obligations under the Convention. I refer in particular to Article 268 of the Convention on the objectives of cooperation, and Article 269 which itemizes the specific means by which these objectives should be pursued. Among the objectives listed in Article 268 are the development of the necessary "technological infrastructure to facilitate the transfer of marine technology," "the development of human resources through training and education of nationals of developing states and countries" and "international cooperation at all levels, particularly at the regional, sub-regional and bilateral levels." Under Article 269 the Convention requires states, through the competent international organizations to endeavor, *inter alia*, "to establish programs of technical cooperation and assistance to states which may need or request technical assistance, particularly developing land-locked and geographically disadvantaged states as well as other developing states, for the establishment and development of their own technological capacities and infrastructure." Also included in the measures to achieve the basic objectives are the holding of "conferences, seminars and symposia" and "the promotion of bilateral and multi-lateral cooperation."

Technical Assistance

These provisions of the Law of the Sea Convention strike an extremely responsive chord in IMO. The promotion of technical cooperation is one of the principal objectives of IMO, and measures for assisting developing countries constitute a vital component of the overall program of IMO to ensure that shipping operations and related activities all over the world are undertaken in accordance with the highest practicable standards necessary for safety, efficiency and the preservation of the marine environment. The crucial role of technical cooperation in IMO is now clearly and conclusively demonstrated by the inclusion of technical cooperation as one of the objectives enshrined in its Constitution, and by the formal institutionalization of the Technical Cooperation Committee, the inter-governmental body which is responsible for coordinating and overseeing the development and operation of the program. Following the decision of the IMO Assembly that the IMO should concentrate attention on the implementation of international regulations and rules, and in light of the vital role which IMO's technical cooperation program plays in the global implementation of international standards, the provisions of the 1982 Convention on international cooperation and technical assistance to developing countries are likely to have significant implications in the future work of IMO. This is particularly so because of the expected increase both in the extent and scope of assistance required by individual states and in the number of states who may need and require such assistance from IMO in connection with new or enlarged maritime programs.

I am pleased to be able to state that IMO is doing its best, within the limits of available resources, to pursue the very noble and highly essential objectives which have been so clearly set out in the Convention on the Law of the Sea.

Accordingly, IMO has established, systematically developed and enlarged a pragmatic program of technical cooperation which is now a vital and indispensable part of its work in all areas. The aim of the program continues to be to enable the developing countries to make an effective contribution to world-wide efforts to improve maritime safety and to protect the marine environment from pollution through the concerted and coordinated application of accepted international standards and regulations. Activities under the program include assistance with the establishment and running of competent maritime safety administrations; the formulation of maritime legislation; the upgrading, as appropriate, of merchant shipping and ship repair facilities; and, above all, the training of qualified maritime personnel, including the establishment or improvement of suitable training facilities.

Our experience over many years has shown that most developing countries are willing and ready to contribute to international efforts to improve maritime safety and the prevention of marine pollution, through the adoption and implementation of international regulations and standards. However, most of the international regulations in this field are highly technical in nature and their effective implementation involves considerable expertise and resources. Apart from financial problems, the most serious difficulty faced by developing countries is lack of trained and experienced personnel. In some cases these difficulties can be eased by recruiting expatriate personnel, but this is essentially a short-term solution. In the long run, each country must be able to operate independently, with its own personnel. IMO's technical assistance program therefore concentrates on training, with a growing emphasis being placed on the training of senior personnel -- the men and women who will be ultimately responsible for advising governments on maritime policy matters generally and on the effective implementation of international standards for maritime safety and pollution prevention in particular. This involves the training of several categories of personnel.

IMO has thus helped, and is currently helping, with the creation or development of training institutions in many parts of the world. They include regional academies in West Africa and the Arab states as well as national projects in countries in Africa, Asia, Latin America, the Pacific and Europe. Training of this type is of course essential for the personnel on board the world's ships. But in many ways it is even more important for the men and women in more senior posts -- the administrators, teachers, inspectors and other key figures -- upon whom a nation's shipping industry depends. The problem is that many countries, especially in the developing world, lack the trained personnel needed to fill posts at this level. To make matters worse, they often lack the means to train people of the right caliber to fill these posts. It was to fill this much needed gap that IMO decided to establish the World Maritime University.

Thanks to the extremely generous facilities provided by the Government of Sweden and the Municipality of Malmo, and the very kind support from many international and national donors, the World Maritime University was inaugurated in July 1983 at Malmo, Sweden. I am pleased to state that the University is now fully viable and operational. Indeed, the first graduation ceremony of the University was held in July 1985, when the first batch of students were awarded their Master's degrees after completing two years of instruction, under a highly expert international faculty and in accordance with well-developed international curricula in various aspects of shipping and related activities.

The aim of the World Maritime University is to give the highest level of training to maritime teachers, maritime safety administrators, surveyors and other senior technical personnel of developing countries. The training would enable the personnel involved to assume on their return home the most senior technical positions in maritime administration, such as examiners, teachers, inspectors and managers. The courses at the University are geared to provide a thorough knowledge of the most modern professional techniques, an understanding of the organization of a maritime infrastructure, and the application of the international standards developed by IMO in the relevant fields. In the words of its Charter, the University is to "help in developing a uniform international system for the training of experts in the maritime field as a means of facilitating and promoting international cooperation in shipping and related maritime activities."

The World Maritime University is, therefore, a vital part of IMO's global efforts to promote international cooperation in maritime affairs and to assist states and entities engaged in shipping and related maritime operations to derive the maximum benefits from these operations while respecting the legitimate interests of other states and users, as well as safeguarding the overriding concern of the international community for the preservation of the marine environment.

Conclusion

The principal objective of the Convention on the Law of the Sea, as stated in its Preamble, is "to establish a legal order of the seas and oceans which will facilitate international communication and will promote the peaceful uses of the sea and oceans, the equitable and efficient utilization of their resources, the conservation of their living resources and the study, protection and preservation of the marine environment." Several aspects of this noble objective also feature in the aims and purposes of IMO and, indeed, reflect the essential rationale of IMO and its work. For this reason the Convention on the Law of the Sea constitutes a highly important and an extremely useful framework within which IMO will plan, organize and undertake its programs and activities in the years to come. In particular IMO will perform its traditional function of establishing international regulations and rules in full awareness of the need to ensure that these regulations and rules are compatible with the principles of the 1982 Convention. Furthermore, IMO will continue to provide the forum and the machinery through which states may cooperate in reviewing existing international regulations on maritime safety and the prevention of pollution and, where necessary, adopting new or revised regulations and standards. IMO will also give the most serious and urgent consideration to such changes in its mechanisms and its procedures as may be necessary to enable it effectively to undertake the functions and responsibilities which are expressly assigned to it by the Convention or which can contribute to the effective implementation of the Convention's provisions.

Finally, IMO will, through its technical cooperation program, endeavor to contribute, in all appropriate ways and to the maximum extent within its competence and resources, to the global efforts to promote international cooperation in the seas and oceans. In particular, IMO will maintain and increase its efforts to advise and assist all countries, and especially developing countries, in acquiring the human, organizational and material resources which will enable them to participate in maritime affairs with the requisite expertise and efficiency. For, as the Convention clearly indicates, peace and cooperation in the seas and oceans will only be achieved if all states are able to participate in the utilization of marine resources on an equitable and efficient basis. Participation on an equitable and efficient basis presupposes the availability of the requisite expertise and resources. In helping to establish by international agreement the requirements for safety and efficiency, and in promoting a well-considered and pragmatic program for equipping all states with the ability and capacity to operate in accordance with those requirements, IMO seeks, in its limited but important field, to hasten the attainment of the objectives of the Convention on the Law of the Sea. In doing so, IMO will always welcome and take due note of any views, suggestions and recommendations which may come from expert bodies and meetings such as the Law of the Sea Institute Conferences. It is my hope that the deliberations of this Conference, and the ongoing work of the Law of the Sea Institute, will help IMO and its member states in identifying issues of priority emphasis or ways in which improvements may be made in our program or in any of our procedures.

SPECIAL SYMPOSIUM:

MANAGEMENT OF SEAS AND COASTAL ZONES

INTRODUCTION

A.D. Couper
Department of Maritime Studies
University of Wales Institute of Science and Technology

Many of the papers we have listened to so far touch upon certain aspects of the management of sea space and sea resources, especially those dealing with activities such as fishing. This afternoon, we will address the need for a comprehensive management policy for sea areas. This would include the establishment of priorities between alternative uses and users; methods of evaluation in offshore areas of rent, taxes, protection of environment and species; the encouragement of enterprise and innovation; and the uses of the marine environment for education and science as well as for transport, defense, disposal of waste and all the requirements of state and industry. The 1982 Convention has much to say on pollution and navigation, but very little on comprehensive management of sea areas. It contains nothing on the methodology of setting targets or goals in these respects -- and one would not expect that type of detail to be in a Convention. The Convention provides broad guidance and emphasizes that the problems of ocean space are interrelated and must be considered as a whole. This is our point of departure here. We will consider the problems of integrated use with respect to three maritime geographical regions.

First is the case of a regional sea, with a paper from Gerard Peet focusing on activities in the North Sea. Next is the coastal zone, where sea and land processes and activities interact to the greatest extent; the management of this unique zone is covered by Joyce Halliday and John Gibson. Our third paper, by Etty Agoes, is on archipelagic seas. The three commentators, H.D. Smith and C.S. Lalwani of U.W.I.S.T. and Kaldone G. Nweihed of the Venezuelan Embassy in London, will then comment on the presentations, and finally we shall have a discussion.

SEA USE MANAGEMENT FOR THE NORTH SEA

Gerard Peet
Consultant with the S.E.A. Foundation
Delft, The Netherlands

Introduction

The future of the management of seas and oceans will be largely determined by principles set in the framework of the 1982 United Nations Convention on the Law of the Sea. A comprehensive framework has been developed for international cooperation in the management, exploitation, exploration and preservation of the world's seas and oceans. As stated in the Preamble to the Convention, a consciousness has now been developed that "the problems of ocean space are closely interrelated and need to be considered as a whole".[1] Some, like the Chairman of the Third Committee of the United Nations Conference on the Law of the Sea, Mr. Yankov, consider the comprehensive character of the new Convention to be one of its most important features.[2] If such principles are to be put into practice, methods and procedures for integrated ocean management will have to be developed and used.

To what extent have these principles of comprehensiveness already been put into practice? The Regional Seas Programmes of the United Nations Environmental Programme can be considered as a first example. In an Action Plan that was developed for the Mediterranean, "integrated planning of the development of and management of the Mediterranean Basin" was one of four main aspects.[3] In the Action Plans that have been developed for other regions, however, this "integrated planning" is no longer an explicit feature of the Action Plan.[4] These Action Plans are more explicitly aimed at the protection of the marine and coastal environment by, amongst other things, assessing the state of the marine environment and developing guidelines for the management of those activities which have an impact on environmental quality or on the protection and use of renewable marine resources on a sustainable basis. Another example, also limited to environmental protection, is the Convention on the Protection of the Marine Environment of the Baltic Sea Area (Helsinki Convention 1974), which limits its comprehensiveness to all sources of pollution.

These examples represent three levels of integrated management of sea areas on an international level:

1. Comprehensive management of all activities, as formulated in the Mediterranean Action Plan;
2. Coordinated management of those activities which may have an impact on environmental quality, as developed for the other UNEP Regional Seas Programs;
3. Coordinated management of marine pollution from all sources, as, for instance, in the Helsinki Convention.

What about the North Sea? Is there any form of "integrated planning or management" for the North Sea? Is there any need for this "integrated planning or management" for the North Sea? This second question can be answered positively by giving some of the present features of the North Sea, namely:

430

- one of the, if not *the*, most intensively used sea areas in the world;
- one of the world's most productive fishing areas;
- one of the world's major shipping routes;
- one of the world's rapidly developing offshore oil and gas regions;
- and, in a number of parts in the North Sea, one of the world's most polluted sea areas.

These activities and features of the North Sea as such need proper management, but there is also a growing need for proper management of the interrelations between these activities and problems arising from them. This brings us back to the question whether there is any form of "integrated planning or management" for the North Sea.

In a paper Professor Brown wrote for another Conference of the Law of the Sea Institute back in 1978, he observed an overall picture for the North Sea that was "one of considerable complexity."[5] The activities in the North Sea were and are regulated, or managed, by different systems of national law, by European Community law and by public international law. The division of responsibilities between the institutions on these three levels of integration is not always clear on all three levels. Even though this was written in 1978, it still applies fully to the present situation in the North Sea area. The situation has even become slightly more complex on the regional North Sea level.

In 1984 the European Parliament also discussed the considerable complexity of the management of the North Sea.[6] It observed that the present framework of international regulations for the North Sea showed several elements of duplication as well as gaps. It also noted a substantial lack of political will with regard to proper management of the North Sea and especially the protection of its environment. This paper will not discuss all arrangements that constitute this complexity, as these have already been extensively discussed in other publications. The various observations of complexity, duplication, gaps and lack of political will to improve things could very well be interpreted to the effect that at present there is no "integrated management" for the North Sea.

The North Sea Conference (1984)
In November 1984 an International Conference for the Protection of the North Sea was organized in the Federal Republic of Germany. This Conference can be considered as a first effort to establish some form of international cooperation between North Sea states in the management of the North Sea environment. The initiative to organize this Conference was a reaction of the government of the Federal Republic of Germany to a report on the environmental problems of the North Sea by the German Council of Experts for Environmental Affairs.[7] In this report the German government was given a comprehensive assessment of the environmental problems of the North Sea (including the Wadden Sea) such as pollution, offshore activities, land reclamation, industrial developments in coastal regions and fisheries. The initiative to organize the North Sea Conference was announced in June 1982. According to this first announcement the Conference should *not* try to develop new legal regimes for the North Sea, because the existing international treaties, such as the Paris, Oslo, London and various IMO Conventions, already provided the necessary legal frameworks.[8]

One might add that the new legal regimes would only add to the already existing complexity of legal arrangements. The Conference itself may well have added to the complexity of present institutional

431

arrangements by introducing yet another international forum for North Sea policies.

The International Conference for the Protection of the North Sea was originally given the aim of analyzing deficiencies in the execution and enforcement of the articles of those Conventions that apply to the North Sea and to develop a strategy for a "comprehensive, ecologically oriented policy of protection of the North Sea."[9] Decisions were to be taken particularly on:

- an ecological inventory of the North Sea to be prepared by all North Sea states;
- the development of plans gradually leading to a complete ban on the dumping of dangerous substances;
- the development of a management plan setting out acceptable loads for the North Sea;

Due to political changes in the Federal Republic of Germany, especially the change of government and political color, the goals for the Conference were later slightly changed. According to a Memorandum written for the Council of Ministers of the European Communities in February 1983,[10] the aim of the Conference was limited to "reaching decisions on a noticeable reduction of pollution in the North Sea through harmonized action." The ideal of comprehensiveness gave way to a more pragmatic approach towards better anti-pollution management for the North Sea.

The Conference on October 31 and November 1, 1984, was attended by all countries bordering the North Sea and by the Commission of the European Communities; some other states, IMO, UNEP and several inter-governmental organizations joined the meeting as observers. According to the Declaration at the end of the Conference,[11] the North Sea states reached agreement on necessary measures for the protection of the North Sea. They agreed to take timely preventive measures to maintain the quality of the North Sea and to cooperate closely therein. To this end they identified three focal areas of joint action:

1. Reduction of pollution from land-based sources, including rivers and atmospheric inputs.
2. Reduction of pollution at sea, including operational discharges by ships.
3. Further development of the Joint Monitoring Programme.

These three focal areas were elaborated in a long list of conclusions of the Conference, including statements declaring "the firm determination":

- to make every effort at national and international levels as well as at EEC level to protect the marine environment of the North Sea effectively and permanently, and for this purpose to prevent, reduce and control adverse effects on the marine environment which result or are likely to result from human activities;
- to urgently further reduce existing contamination and to prevent additional contamination;
- to implement the existing international agreements for the protection of nature with a view to the conservation of the ecosystem of the North Sea;

- to make highly effective use of the possibilities offered by international agreements on the prevention of marine pollution;
- to take initiatives in international bodies;
- to take the conclusion of this Conference as a basis for concerted action in the competent international bodies.

A number of specific actions were identified for the future. Most of these actions, however, involved a continuation of existing activities, firmly restating the intention to continue. Another firm intention that was stated regularly was that specific objectives and standards would have to be developed. In other words, the Conference did not result in a large number of specific measures; it did result in a large number of firm intentions.

Environmental organizations have been very negative about the results of this Conference, considering these to be vague and insufficient. If the Conference has to be judged by its specific conclusions one might indeed be tempted to a similar judgment. The Conference could, however, also be judged by other criteria such as the question of to what extent the Conference has contributed to a better coordination of North Sea policies on the regional North Sea level, or to the development of a generally accepted basis for North Sea policies in the various North Sea states. To be able to make such a judgment, some preliminary remarks have to be made about the major issues determining present and future North Sea policies, namely: the assessment of the present state of the North Sea environment, and the question of applying quality objectives or uniform emission standards. There are strongly differing positions on these issues, with the government of the United Kingdom on one side, and the Federal Republic of Germany, along with, among others, the Netherlands, on the other side.

The United Kingdom is of the opinion that the present state of the North Sea environment is one of "health" with some local environmental problems in coastal and estuarine regions. The United Kingdom also takes water quality objectives as the basis for its environmental policy. Consequently the United Kingdom is very hesitant in developing stricter rules with regard to discharges of wastes into the North Sea.

On the other side, the most affected North Sea states, the Federal Republic of Germany, the Netherlands and Denmark, take the position that the present status of the environmental quality of the North Sea is such that immediate action towards reducing pollution loads is necessary. For a variety of reasons, including economic ones, they want to impose uniform emission standards when reducing the various discharges into the North Sea.

This conflict of opinion between these states has not just come up in the framework of the North Sea Conference; it has been a basic issue of disagreement within the environmental policy of the European communities for a long time, resulting in a parallel system of applying both quality objectives and emission standards in European environmental regulations. This difference of opinion also proved to be a stumbling block in reaching spectacular results at the North Sea Conference. This is best illustrated by the decision taken with regard to the question of whether an initiative should be taken to have the North Sea designated as a Special Area under the MARPOL 73/78 Convention. At the North Sea Conference it was decided that they will evaluate the effects of MARPOL 73/78 on the quality of the North Sea in order to decide upon this question at a future International North Sea Conference. This was a rather elegant way to avoid admitting to a disagreement of principle on this issue.

This disagreement did show up, however, at a meeting of the Marine Environment Protection Committee of the International Maritime Organization in April 1985. Discussing the necessity of amending the MARPOL 73/78 Convention with a view to designating the North Sea as an optional Special Area, the delegation of the United Kingdom stated that this would be premature in view of the agreement to discuss the question at a second International North Sea Conference, and that the U.K. was convinced that on this occasion no decision was to be expected to that effect because the North Sea did not meet the criteria for a Special Area. The delegation of the Federal Republic of Germany immediately reacted at the same meeting, stating that it considered the North Sea to be an area that already met all criteria to be designated as a Special Area under MARPOL 73/78 in its Annexes I, II and V.[12]

Given this still existing fundamental difference of opinion on the present environmental quality of the North Sea environment, the very fact of all North Sea states discussing North Sea policies, agreeing on a large number of principles for policy and agreeing to have a second International Conference on the Protection of the North Sea should be considered at least a small success as a first step towards a better international management of the North Sea.

Where does this bring the North Sea in terms of international integrated management within the general principles set by the new Law of the Sea Convention?

Earlier in this paper I gave three levels of international integrated management:

- comprehensive management of all activities,
- coordinated management of those activities which may have an impact on environmental quality, and
- coordinated management of marine pollution from all sources.

The North Sea would be at the third level of integrated management, or maybe one should say that the North Sea might be on its way towards this third level of integrated management. The second International Conference on the Protection of the North Sea will determine whether this level of integrated management will be feasible for the North Sea.

The European Parliament's Suggestions for an Umbrella Convention for the North Sea

The European Parliament has adopted a resolution aiming for a higher level of integrated management for the North Sea. In January 1984, before the International Conference on the Protection of the North Sea in Bremen in October 1984, the European Parliament asked the European Commission to present a memorandum in which it should consider possible Community action to combine and harmonize existing international, Community and national legislation to combat North Sea pollution, to create a single and effective central convention on the protection of the North Sea with a view to providing an alternative to the current approach of adopting specific conventions and laws for individual problems and regions. Specific measures regarding fisheries, shipping, oil and gas exploitation, mining of sea floor deposits, land reclamation, recreation and military activities were also asked for.[13] If such an umbrella Convention for the North Sea were developed, quite another level of integrated North Sea management would be the result, comparable to the level of the Helsinki Convention.

Although this resolution was adopted with a very large majority (even though only a limited number of members of the European Parliament were present), no follow-up has been given to this idea so far. The European Commission still has not presented the Memorandum it was asked to write. Reactions to the idea presented by the European Parliament were not all positive. Environmental organizations stated that they saw no need to develop a completely new Convention; they doubted whether those states that did not ratify present conventions would be willing to ratify a new one. The Dutch government[14] considered that there were both advantages and disadvantages to a general umbrella convention for the North Sea and concluded that it would be better to implement first and further develop the existing arrangements. The Dutch government did not, however, dismiss the concept of an overall North Sea Convention; it merely identified other priorities for the time being and set some conditions should such a Convention ever be considered. Norway, not a member of the European Community, has shown some signs of interest in ideas aimed at developing a more coordinated or integrated framework of international North Sea management.

The present management of the North Sea on the international level does not meet, in my opinion, the general principles that will be applicable to the management of the seas once the new Law of the Sea Convention enters into force. The closely interrelated problems of the North Sea are at present clearly not considered as a whole. A successful second International Conference on the Protection of the North Sea could be a first step towards this, but more steps which would introduce policy areas, other than just pollution, into the international North Sea policies are needed. Taking this into account, there could be some merit in the idea of an overall North Sea Convention, not to replace the existing international agreements, but with a view to bringing the existing conventions under one general umbrella, to removing existing duplications in international regulations and to providing a basis for international regulation of those areas for which international regulations are now lacking. The second International Conference on the Protection of the North Sea might seem a logical option, but given the present differences of opinion between the various North Sea states this is also very improbable.

This brings me to the question of whether the European Commission would be an appropriate body to develop such an international convention, or whether the European communities would be the most appropriate framework for it, given the fact that the European Parliament more or less suggested this. At the Oslo Conference of the Law of the Sea Institute in 1983, Clive Archer observed that the European Community had become increasingly involved in the making of policies covering its sea areas.[15] He concluded that the hope that the European Community could provide a source of ocean management seemed to be in vain. The European Community could, however, contribute to ocean management through specific activities. In the framework of the Mediterranean the European Community did develop several specific initiatives within the framework of a general ocean management policy as it is being developed in the UNEP and Barcelona Convention framework.

The European Community could play a similar role for the North Sea in my view. Given the fact that ideas will have to be developed towards a better general management of the North Sea, taking into account all closely interrelated problem areas, the European Community could stimulate the development of such ideas. The Memorandum the European Parliament asked from the European Commission could be used to develop some ideas with regard to a general North Sea Convention for the purpose of further discussing the idea, in the European Parliament and possibly also the second International Conference for the Protection of the North Sea.

National Action

Whilst on the international level the integrated management of the North Sea seems to be in a very early stage of development, there are signs that at national levels more progress is being made. The publication of the report of the German Council on Experts on Environmental Affairs on the North Sea that was mentioned earlier has created a basis for more coordinated North Sea management in the Federal Republic of Germany and the various Lander bordering the North Sea.

In the Netherlands, the government has developed a long-term harmonized North Sea policy.[16] The preparations for this North Sea policy started in 1979 with a systematic inventory of North Sea developments, of administrative involvement in North Sea affairs and of available regulatory instruments. In 1982 the government published a report in which it outlined its future North Sea policy. There were several reasons that the Dutch government embarked on this course of a better coordinated North Sea policy. The present state of the North Sea environment was one obvious reason. Another was the increasingly intensive and varied use of the Dutch part of the North Sea. Even though this part of the North Sea only constitutes 10 percent of the North Sea, 60 percent of all navigation in the North Sea passes through these waters en route to Dutch or other ports. Other factors add to this intensive use such as:

- a rapidly developing offshore oil and gas industry in the vicinity of established shipping routes;
- the presence of sites for dumping or incineration of wastes;
- the presence of several practice areas for the Dutch navy.

For the future a further intensification of the use of this part of the North Sea is to be expected. The number of oil and gas installations is expected to increase from about thirty-six fixed platforms now to over 100 in the last years of this century. There is no need to point out that this will have serious repercussions on the "room to move" for all other activities in this part of the North Sea. New developments may also take place; for instance new land could be reclaimed in coastal waters for urbanization purposes.

In its policy of harmonization for the North Sea, the Dutch government indicated that it wished to promote an increasingly coordinated and balanced development of activities in relation to the North Sea. Such coordination should not be sought in the development of a comprehensive policy view, as this would presuppose the possibility of elaborating in broad outline an all-embracing model of desirable future developments in the North Sea area, involving forecasts both of long-term trends and of the conflicts likely to arise, on the basis of which decisions could be reached in advance. The Dutch government considered such an interpretation of comprehensiveness for its policy as unrealistic, given the close interrelations between many activities in the North Sea. One could again easily refer to Professor Brown who, in 1978, quoted Mr. William Ogden: "...complex systems cannot be planned, they cannot be comprehended well enough; but complex systems can be managed."[17] The Dutch government did choose to manage the complex North Sea system by developing a pragmatic "ongoing process of harmonization of its policies as they relate to the North Sea." This approach should offer the necessary opportunities to give due consideration to all interests involved and to react flexibly to new developments.

The Dutch North Sea policy of harmonization contains three elements:

1. A policy framework, which brings together the various starting points for the government's policy and a continuously updated inventory of developments and problems which have occurred or are about to occur;
2. An action program setting out specific measures to deal with the principal problems as these are identified in the policy framework;
3. An institutional framework comprising existing and necessary procedures and types of consultation to prepare and implement the policy proposals resulting from the action program.

In the policy framework, the following four general objectives of the Dutch North Sea policy were identified:

- the government's efforts are directed towards the safe and efficient use of the various opportunities offered by the North Sea in order that these make an optimal contribution to the national economy;
- the government seeks a harmonious balance between the various activities taking place at the North Sea, limiting and whenever possible preventing any mutual hindrance, partly with the aim of enhancing safety at sea;
- the government aims at the enduring conservation of the North Sea's valuable ecology;
- the government will further develop a balanced and effective set of instruments, both national and international, for management and control.

These general objectives were elaborated into specific policy actions in the action program. Out of a total of some 100 identified problem areas about forty areas of urgent action were selected. Important proposals in the action program included, amongst others:

- drawing up a North Sea navigation policy plan aimed at promoting safety of navigation in the Dutch part of the North Sea;
- compiling a wide-ranging water-quality plan for the Dutch part of the North Sea covering all major sources and types of pollution.

The proposals with regard to this policy of harmonization were discussed by interested organizations, advisory councils and Parliament. Whilst in the discussions with interested groups and advisory bodies, criticism could be heard about the vagueness with regard to priorities in the different policy objectives as well as in the proposed action program, the Parliament accepted and welcomed the newly developed policy for the North Sea in December 1984.

The harmonization of the Dutch North Sea policy is to be a continuous process; the government stresses this point several times. The process started as early as 1975, with a major next step in May 1982, when the government first published its proposals. Several questions still have to be answered, though, as many policy areas require international cooperation, and as many points of action still require further elaboration. In the course of the process, new problem areas will develop and will need to be resolved; new items will have to be added to the action program.

The German and Dutch examples are the only two cases where developments have been initiated towards a North Sea policy taking into account all related interests, towards a North Sea policy that would be in line with the principles as set out in the 1982 Convention on the Law of the Sea. In the other North Sea countries there appear to be no similar processes in the development of their North Sea policy. At the 1983 Conference on the Law of the Sea Institute in Oslo, Mr. Steinar Andresen pointed out that in Norway "little attention has been paid to the need for a comprehensive ocean management policy -- encompassing all ocean related activities."[18] The same can be said of the other North Sea countries.

Conclusions

What then are the prospects for future North Sea management? The present situation is that, on the international level, some very small steps towards an "integrated management" of the North Sea -- a kind of management that, by its structure and instruments, takes into account the closely interrelated character of the North Sea's problems and developments and that considers these problems and developments as a whole -- may have been taken at the level of pollution management. On the national level, the Netherlands seems to have made real progress towards integrated management of the North Sea, within the limits set by their national jurisdiction. But if the process in the Netherlands is to continue towards more harmonization, it is inevitable that the harmonization of the North Sea policies has to be developed on the international (regional) North Sea level as well.

Several very important aspects of North Sea policies can only be organized or regulated at the international level. Pollution control and navigation are two obvious examples. If there is to be some kind of international integrated management for the North Sea, several courses of action can be considered in theory. The first would be that the governments of the North Sea states follow the example of the Netherlands in developing a harmonized North Sea policy for their countries as well. After this, the international aspects of all these national policies could be harmonized on the international level. A major difficulty to this might be the diverging nature of the uncoordinated national activities resulting in various national North Sea policies that because of differences in character, level and structure could not be amalgamated and elaborated into an international North Sea policy. A second possibility would be that the North Sea states discuss, on the basis of, e.g., the Dutch example, ways of developing convergent national North Seas policies aimed at the integrated management of the North Sea on the basis of which in a later stage an international North Sea management policy could be developed. A third possibility would be, as indicated earlier, that a third party inject ideas with regard to an integrated North Sea policy into, e.g., the second International Conference on the Protection of the North Sea in 1987 with a view to stimulating the North Sea countries.

One basic question should, however, be answered before considering any course of action towards an international integrated North Sea management. Is there any political will to develop an integrated management for the North Sea? There is, unfortunately, some doubt as to whether this is the case. The fundamental discussion about the necessity of stricter international regulations with regard to the pollution of the North Sea and the differences of opinion in this respect make it doubtful whether North Sea states could agree on a level of management for the North Sea that goes beyond coordinated pollution management. The fact that in any form of international integrated management for the North Sea, policy areas will have to be included that traditionally have been dealt with only on a national level, such as oil and gas developments or land reclamation plans, will not help the North Sea states in reaching agreement that a more integrated international North Sea management should be developed. And last but not least, it has to be kept in mind that several North Sea states have not signed or ratified the 1982 Convention on the Law of the Sea, and consequently have not embraced officially the principle that all ocean problems are interrelated and need to be considered as a whole, the United Kingdom being a very prominent representative of this position.

Much will have to be done to reach some form of international integrated management for the North Sea, both on the level of convincing all North Sea states of the necessity to do so, and on the level of developing instruments and institutions.

NOTES

1. United Nations Convention on the Law of the Sea, Montego Bay, 1982, Preamble.
2. A. Yankov, "The Significance of the 1982 Convention on the Law of the Sea for the Protection of the Marine Environment and the Promotion of Marine Science and Technology" in *The 1982 Convention on the Law of the Sea*, ed. A.K. Koers and B. Oxman, Law of the Sea Institute, Honolulu, 1983.
3. UNEP, Mediterranean Action Plan and the Final Act of the Conference of Plenipotentiaries of the Coastal States of the Mediterranean Region for the Protection of the Mediterranean Sea, United Nations, New York, 1978.
4. UNEP also developed Action Plans for the East Asian Region, 1983; the Gulfs Area, 1983; the Caribbean Region, 1983; the South Pacific Region; and the South-East Pacific, in 1983.
5. E.D. Brown, "Sea Use Planning in the North Sea, the Legal Framework," in *Law of the Sea: Neglected Issues*, ed. J.K. Gamble, Jr., Law of the Sea Institute, Honolulu, 1979.
6. J. Maij-Weggen, Report on the Combating of Pollution in the North Sea, European Parliament Document 1-1173/83, 1983.
7. Rat von Sachverstandigen Fur Umweltfragen, *Umweltprobleme der Nordsee*, Kohlhammer Verlag, Stuttgart-Mainz, 1980.
8. According to a press release of the German Ministry of the Interior in June 1982.
9. Id.
10. This was included in Ref. 6 as Annex IV.
11. International Conference on the Protection of the North Sea, Declaration, Bremen, October 31 and November 1, 1984.
12. Information based on participation in this meeting by the author.
13. Resolution adopted by European Parliament at its January session in Strasbourg, 1984.

14. Minister van Verkeer en Waterstaat, Harmonisatie Noordzeebeleid deel c: Regeringsbeslissing, Lower House Parliament session 1983-1984, 17408 No. 7-8, The Hague, March 1984.
15. Clive Archer, "Supranational Ocean Management: the Case of the EC," in *The 1982 Convention on the Law of the Sea*, ed. A.K. Koers and B. Oxman, Law of the Sea Institute, Honolulu, 1983.
16. Minister van Verkeer en Waterstaat, Harmonisatie Noordzebeleid, Lower House of Parliament session 1981-1982, 17408 No. 1-2, The Hague, May 1982.
17. Ref. 5.
18. S. Andresen, "National and International Premises in Ocean Management; the Case of Norway," in *The 1982 Law of the Sea Convention*, ed. A.K. Koers and B. Oxman, Law of the Sea Institute, Honolulu, 1983.

IN PURSUIT OF AN ENIGMA:
THE COASTAL ZONE IN MANAGEMENT AND LAW

John Gibson and J.E. Halliday
University of Wales Institute for Science and Technology

Introduction

The coastal zone in both management and law is an enigma. It is the location of some of the most pressing resource management problems facing mankind, a focus for concern. Yet the integrity of the area is typically denied by administration, jurisdiction and perception.

The task of this paper is twofold. Firstly, to reveal some of the most pertinent characteristics of this important, yet disputed, entity. Secondly, to suggest key means by which management and law can be more effectively reconciled with the principles of reality.

The *coastal zone* can be defined at the outset as an area encompassing both the land and the sea adjacent to the coastline. The first element in the enigma therefore is its ambiguous extent. There can be no one satisfactory definition, in terms of a statement of the precise extent; rather the area will vary between regions and within any one region, dependent on the nature of the coastal resource, the use to which it is put, the existing framework of law and management, and the task in hand.

Coastal zone management is literally the way we control, direct and care for (*i.e.*, manage) the coast and its environs. It is the present reality, however inadequate. The same three words have, however, also become imbued with a sense of the ideal: the system required to effectively manage the contemporary coastal resource.

Coastal zone management law is similarly a victim of two superficially inconsistent qualities: it is a modern invention, yet it suffers from the burden of its own history. Most radical developments in administrative law either introduce new legislative controls where none previously existed or replace one legal regime with another. In contrast, the coastal zone is covered by an inherited framework of existing law that cannot simply be swept away, but must be modified and extended to achieve new purposes.

Law, by its capacity for growth and complexity, inevitably invites specialization, and such specializations generally correspond to the sectional concerns of those who utilize the services of lawyers. An initial problem, therefore, in understanding the law relating to the coastal zone is that the subject matter to be assimilated must be abstracted from a wide variety of legal categories which do not merely exist for the convenience of classification, but may also have influenced the content of the rules they contain.

The principal encyclopedia of English law,[1] for example, is oblivious to the concept of the coastal zone, and the reader must search instead for relevant information under such headings as administrative law, admiralty, constitutional law, customs, fisheries, local government, minerals, open spaces, petroleum, ports, public health, shipping, planning and water.

The administration and management of the area on any geographical scale from the international to the local can similarly generally be revealed only by careful study; the identification again of "interested" sectors together with their responsible agencies and the review of, for instance, national attitudes to planning, development and conservation.

The essential truism, therefore, is that the coastal zone is rarely recognized as a distinct area and is thus rarely the possessor of either a discrete body of management or law. The second element of the enigma follows: management undoubtedly occurs around the coastline, the area falls within statutory control, yet coastal zone management *per se* rarely exists; coastal zone law is a concept generally unknown to jurisprudence.

It is possible nevertheless to provide a general framework upon which details of the particular can be hung: a framework which will provide a useful classification mechanism enabling the organization of the growing body of information and the identification of common themes.

A Framework for the Coastal Zone

The Coastal Resource

The first element in any such framework must be the basic physical and ecological attributes of the coastal zones. Variety is again immediately obvious, ranging from the Arctic coastline of Alaska through to the coral reefs of Australia. Within Europe, even within the British Isles alone, a considerable diversity of ecosystems are encountered. Certain salient features can however be established.

Firstly, the coastal zone is a dynamic system. It may be subdivided into the three basic elements, land, sea and shore, elementary subdivisions which are also useful when considering use, administration and law. The elements, however, interact. Intervention in one area cannot therefore be discrete; rather, it will have repercussions for the other components, both spatially (that is, along and across the zone) and temporally removed.

Secondly, the coastal zone is finite. There are still very few ways in which man can physically increase the size of the coastal resource, and for many activities there are a limited number of substitutes for a coastal location. Coasts on a world scale are thus subject to increasing pressures, and the raising of carrying capacities (and hence management) is the only viable way in which the resource can be increased in many areas.

Thirdly, the coastal zone, particularly its biotic element, is frequently fragile. This is a function of a number of factors, including the predominance of serial ecosystems; of areas which have traditionally been remote from disturbance and which are thus increasingly rare and valued examples of relatively pristine habitats; of an increasing number and variety of impacts; and the connectivity of the coastal ecosystem, particularly the fluid, marine environment.

Coastal Use

The second element in the framework is the pattern of use which has evolved, drawing on these biotic and abiotic resources. Again, use varies worldwide but can be classified broadly according to a number of factors.

A basic distinction revolves around the role of the coastal zone in each class of use. In some instances it is a source for raw materials or energy; in others it is the sink for by-products of resource processes; in yet others it provides the link in the communications system. In a further group the coastal zone has a strategic role; in

442

another its role is largely intangible; consider, for instance, recreation and conservation, where the coastal zone contributes to the overall quality of life. Finally the coastal zone may have an enabling role, providing, for instance, the residential and industrial space which enables many of the other coastal resources to be utilized.

Other important attributes of use to be considered, with a pertinence for management and law, include the area utilized. Is use confined, as with many source activities, to a particular locality? What are the characteristics of that locality? Alternatively does it, as with communications or waste disposal, utilize common characteristics of the zone as a whole? One may also profitably consider the strength of its requirements for a coastal location, the period over which the use will extend and whether it is fixed or mobile.

Coastal Zone Law

The third framework element comprises the extant law pertaining to the coastal zone -- a composite that involves aspects of both private and public law. On the one hand, there are major elements of the law of real property concerning the ownership of coastal land and the exercise of rights in tidal waters. Those principles have attracted disproportionate attention from legal writers, because they fall most easily within traditional jurisprudential categories; they tend to be rooted in historic case law, and reflect an obsolescent coastal culture dominated by proprietary disputes between private landowners, the public and the state. A legacy of such litigation in common law countries has been the partition of the coastal zone into three components, each with its separate legal regime: dry land, seabed and the foreshore situated ambivalently in between. Although the distinctions between these sectors are superficially based on natural tidal criteria, in reality they are the arbitrary consequence of judicial compromise and create invisible boundaries that defy precise identification. The physical division of the coastal resource is thus reflected to a degree, but not its unity.

On to this private law foundation must be grafted the predominantly statutory corpus of public law. Here, complex categorization is proportionate to the multiplicity of central government departments, local authorities and quasi-governmental bodies operating in the coastal zone. A fundamental distinction is often evident between organizations whose functions are essentially land-based and those with jurisdiction in the sea, and such differentiation may be emphasized by the use of separate legislative terminology; this is particularly apparent in the variety and incompatibility of maritime boundaries that define the limits of responsibility. A link thus also exists back to the second framework element and forward to the fourth framework element, the diversity of coastal use and the sectoral nature of administration.

Another characteristic of coastal public law that militates against efficient and coordinated management is its tendency to be unnecessarily obscure. This may be exacerbated by a subdivision into general and local legislation. Governments usually accord the greatest publicity to those laws that are of national public interest; unfortunately, these are often of the least significance for the coastal zone, where the precise administrative structure in any place may instead depend on local enactments relating to individual subordinate authorities. Such local and secondary legislation is, however, often difficult for the layman to discover, and may sometimes be known only to the authorities that it directly empowers. Periodic reorganization and transfer of responsibilities further complicates the situation, since pre-existing law is often preserved by reference, but less frequently consolidated. Likewise, it is common for governments to enact primary legislation delegating to the executive a discretion to make further orders for the establishment of coastal authorities. The enabling acts are themselves comparatively uninformative, since they merely indicate the bounds of possibility; it is the secondary and less accessible law that must be scrutinized to determine whether a power has actually been used.

The law becomes, therefore, at best a highly introspective system veiled from public scrutiny; at worse, authorities themselves may be uncertain about their own functions. It is not surprising, then, that within such a framework anomalies abound, and the coastal zone is replete with jurisdictional conflicts, overlaps and legislative omissions.

Management

The final framework element is the way in which the coastal zone is managed at present. Several persistent themes appropriate on the world scale can be identified.

The first concerns the identification of the objectives behind coastal zone management in different areas. This is probably the element where the greatest disparity is evident on the world scale, not just between traditional groupings such as the developed/developing world but also within smaller areas such as the European Continent:[2] a disparity which reflects the intrinsic variety found in the other framework elements, together with key cultural, economic and political differences.

It also offers perhaps the greatest scope for developing a classification of emergent initiatives in the coastal zone. Basic choices revolve, for instance, around the relative priorities given to development and conservation,[3] methods for, and the distributive consequences of, the allocation of the resource within space and time, the freedom of individuals/interests and the weight given to options for the future.

The second theme is that administration tends to be organized around the separate uses of the coast rather than around the area *per se*; that is, it is sectoral in nature rather than zonal.

Thirdly, sectoral interests, as pointed out above, are frequently aligned on either side of the coastline. Differences therefore abound between the administrative practice (the degree of control exercised for instance) and attitudes governing an activity on land and its counterpart at sea. Obvious problems are also posed for the evolution of integrated strategy when decision making and executive action in related fields are the subject of discrete initiatives.

Neither division sectorally nor about the land/sea interface need necessarily pose problems. The connectivity of the coastal state system ensures, however, that decisions taken within any one administrative domain will have repercussions for many other interests. Given the multiplicity of uses at the coast and the pressure on the environment, there is thus an essential requirement for communication. This, however, is frequently lacking, professional training tending rather to emphasize spheres of exclusive competence. Problems are thus internalized and the solutions impinge on others. The overall direction of management tends thus to be reactive rather than purposeful. The other essential requirement if such a system of control, operating through numerous independent agencies, is to work, would appear to be an ability to adjudicate between the numerous competing claims on the coastal resource. National strategy for the coast is, however, again frequently lacking, although important exceptions exist.[4]

In the absence of any such guidance as to how a plethora of separately defined, sectoral objectives can be reconciled, contention is evident in many areas of coastal management. Policies articulated by international, national and local organizations are thus frequently at variance either with the same class of interests operating at a different hierarchical level or with contrasting sectoral concerns.

The fourth characteristic is that the coast rarely occupies a central position on the agendas of the controlling organizations; rather, their interests tend to be wide-ranging. By virtue of its physical location and its generally low political priority, the coast thus tends to be a marginal issue area competing for resources with areas with a higher profile. Consequences are manifold, including lack of available finance, lack of commitment to coastal problems and lack of incentive to intervene.

The third element of the enigma is therefore that the coast has been recognized as being of considerable significance to mankind, yet the concept has failed to emerge strongly from either administration or legislation. The third and fourth framework elements, law and management, remain substantially sub-optimal solutions to the contemporary characteristics of the first two elements, the resource and its use. The next section therefore develops those areas where the present system is perceived as inadequate and outlines some key areas where emergent trends appear to presage a more apposite solution.

Law and Management: Current Inadequacies and Emergent Hopes

A first area of concern centers on the problems that the nature of law itself poses for more effective and appropriate management.

The traditional view of administrative law -- that it provides a medium through which government policy may be translated into executive action and a mechanism for judicial protection against the abuse of power -- is one that bears surprisingly little resemblance to the reality of the coastal zone. It has already been suggested that the structure of coastal law renders it an imperfect channel of communication even to the officials on whom powers are conferred. The corollary is that those officials are also likely to be less than fully informed of the law relating to their neighbors, and thus to function within a specialized and insular legal framework.

It may, however, also be questioned whether coastal legislation genuinely discharges its basic role as a conduit from the source to the exercise of power, since the connection between the word of law and the acts of officialdom sometimes appears more theoretical than real.

The initiative for coastal legislation rarely arises from within the legislature itself, but usually originates in an application for power by the government department or statutory authority ultimately entrusted with its implementation. The legislative process operates to translate their proposals, with or without amendment, into legal terminology that is often so technical that it can only properly be understood by lawyers.[5] The result is that officials are often guided not directly by the law itself, but by extra-statutory explanatory memoranda prepared by their own departments and not always available to the public.

In one sense, then, the role of the law is largely to provide a symbolic gesture of approval for the actions of administrators, who effectively become the interpreters of their own powers. For practical purposes, the courts exercise minimal supervision, since civil litigation is now comparatively uncommon in the coastal zone; maritime authorities only rarely come into conflict with private interests, and are unlikely to sue each other unless financial considerations are at stake.

One further implication of this situation is that the solutions to the legislative burden of the coastal zone must originate from within the wider administration. The need, the political will to change the system, must be perceived by those with executive powers. Too frequently, for instance, there has been a failure even to make full use of the opportunities provided by existing law[6] or an unwillingness to ascertain its limits by litigation if necessary.

There remains, for instance, uncertainty in England and Wales over the fundamental issues of the seaward extent of town and country planning law. Although conventional wisdom assumes that it has no application beyond the low-water mark, a government minister recently advised Parliament that planning control extends to sub-littoral regions in tidal estuaries.[7] The truth could be determined by resort to the courts, but the question remains hypothetical because no local planning authority has the temerity to test it by claiming to exercise such a power.

Provisions exist under several statutes for joint bodies to be formed in respect of uses which impinge on a wide area, coast protection for example. Yet the need is obviously not perceived or is outweighed by a stronger desire for autonomy.

An illustration of the indirect significance of the law may also be seen in both the existence and the effect of the numerous anomalies discoverable in coastal legislation. This is an area of law in which latent theoretical conflicts of jurisdiction abound; yet the paralysis of the system is often avoided by a fortuitous official ignorance of its limitations. Conversely, the executive may sometimes place an idiosyncratic interpretation on a legislative provision that it was not originally intended to bear, but which becomes accepted through long usage, and is never subjected to challenge. An instance is the British practice of requiring licenses under pollution legislation -- the Dumping at Sea Act of 1974 -- in relation to permanent structures on the seabed, even though these are already subject to other more appropriate forms of control.[8]

Paradoxically, despite the infrequency with which the doctrine of *ultra vires* is invoked to curb excesses by the executive in the coastal zone, it is regularly cited by officials themselves to justify their inability to act in the wider public interest. In principle, of course, a coastal authority is less free than a private individual: while the individual may theoretically do whatever he likes as long as there is no law to prevent him, the authority may do nothing at all unless there is a law positively to permit it. Public authorities are creatures of legislation, and only legislation can define the purposes for which they are entitled to act. It is an unfortunate consequence both of the linguistic rigidity implicit in the law and of a legislative process which reinforces specialization that coastal legislation frequently fails to provide the flexibility required for administrative cooperation.

A salutary example of this impasse may be found in the current British attempt to establish marine nature reserves. The Wildlife and Countryside Act 1981[9] seeks to enlist the support of all authorities exercising jurisdiction in coastal waters, by providing that each may use its existing powers to make bylaws for the protection of reserves. Yet, in the course of four years, it has proved impossible to persuade authorities to take advantage of the provision, since each argues that it is statutorily limited to serving objectives different from conservation. Thus, the aid of the law is being used not in a sectarian struggle for power, but rather as an excuse for impotence. The primary fault, however, does not lie with the officials; it is uniquely within the capacity of law to dictate priorities, and this it signally omits to do.

A further way in which law acts to impede coastal zone management is by its inability to respond rapidly to developing situations in an inherently fluid environment. Once legal machinery has been set in motion, it acquires an inexorable momentum that cannot easily be reversed. It may seem scarcely credible, for instance, that in 1984 nearly 10 percent of all British secondary legislation was devoted to the contradictory purpose of designating fixed safety zones around mobile drilling rigs that barely remained in place long enough to enjoy them.[10] A change in the pattern of coastal use found no corresponding flexibility in the law.

The same situation also illustrates the unreal quality of legislation that may never be seen by those whom it most immediately concerns. In such a case, the masters of vessels prohibited from entering safety zones would have learned of their existence not from legislation, but from information in Admiralty Notices to Mariners. Coastal law itself may thus become little more than an unwieldy method of internal communication between administrators. It is far removed from the theoretical model of a powerful, self-regulatory system accessible to officials and the public, providing all necessary powers, coordinating their distribution among authorities and facilitating the translation of policy into practice.

The second major area of concern centers on the requirements for a more effective system of administration and management.

Because of the intimate relationship between law and administration, many of these are implicit in the discussion above or are similar in kind. The need to adjudicate and determine priorities, for instance, has already been mentioned, as have anomalous provisions. In the rapidly changing environment and values of the coast, there is also the same requirement for a flexible system of management as there is for law. Management too must be understood by, and gain the support of, the "managed" and the wider public if it is to be effective.

It is difficult to ascribe relative priorities to the areas where change is needed, but one essential must be the development of an increased coastal awareness. Education is thus vital, for only by achieving increased comprehension and a more accurate perceptual model of the coastal zone can we begin to manage the system sympathetically.

Conferences and directives taking the coastal zone as their focus represent hopeful signs in the emergence of a better informed executive, more aware of the requirements of others and the nature of the coastal resource. At the international level, for instance, the International Union for Conservation of Nature and Natural Resources and the United Nations have both studied the coastal resource and its management. The Regional Sea Programme of the United Nations Environment

447

Programme (UNEP) now covers ten regional seas and involves 120 countries worldwide, and the Organization for Economic Cooperation and Development (OECD) has formulated principles relating to the administration of the coastal zone.[11] The Council for Europe, long active in this field, is presently, through its Steering Committee for Regional Planning, organizing a series of seminars on the development and planning of European coastal regions during the period 1985 to 1987. The European Charter of the Conference of the Peripheral Maritime Regions of the EEC, and, on a smaller scale, the Welsh Coastal Zone Management Conference, are again evidence that the coast is beginning to emerge as an issue area worthy of debate.

Closely allied to recognition and discussion is the idea of increased availability and dissemination of information, for again more informed decision-making should be better decision-making. The coastal surveys carried out in England and Wales, for instance, in the 1940s and the 1960s were early ventures in this field, an initiative which unfortunately was not maintained.[12] The French "Inventaire Permanent du Littoral," however, represents significant progress, not only because the aim in this instance is to maintain a continuous coastal inventory but also because a more comprehensive viewpoint has been taken of the coastal zone. The interaction of land and sea has thus been acknowledged by extending the inventory to include coastal waters.

Considerable information therefore already exists for many aspects of coastal use, but too frequently it is collected for a specific purpose and not disseminated to other potential beneficiaries. Increased cooperation is thus critical if the best use of resources is to be made. The threat to the internationally important wetland, the Wadden Sea, for instance, has lead to combined studies by the countries bordering this sea: Denmark, Germany and the Netherlands. One result has been the resolution that the three countries need a common policy and close cooperation in management, including the zoning of all human activities, if the integrity of this coastal resource is to be maintained. Another has been the assertion that information on all aspects of the Wadden Sea is indeed available, yet authorities charged with decision making are either insufficiently informed or not "assisted" enough in the decision-making process.[13]

A major barrier to cooperation thus exists in the form of narrowly conceived professional and agency domains. Coastal zone problems are essentially inter-agency problems, yet few are prepared to compromise their own organization by establishing and maintaining the necessary formal and informal contacts with other decision-makers.

Reinforcing this idea of continual interplay between law and administration, this same desire to maintain or reinforce traditional roles acts similarly to undermine the process of legislative reform.

Legislation for one authority in the coastal zone again necessarily concerns another, yet there is often a tendency towards territorial protectionism among officials who perceive themselves as custodians of a particular aspect of the public good. Fears may also be exacerbated because administrative law employs general legislation conferring discretionary powers, whose theoretical scope raises visions of possibility far beyond the reality of their ultimate exercise. The price conceded for the withdrawal of opposition may well be a guarantee that the functions of other authorities shall be unaffected by changes in the law. Yet, the result of such savings may be largely to emasculate the new legislation. Once again, the British experience of marine nature reserves provides a depressing illustration, where the express reservation of conflicting rights has rendered the concept of a statutory reserve almost nugatory.

Such progress as has been made towards a more cohesive approach to coastal zone management has tended, therefore, to relate closely to existing administrative configurations. The Scottish planning guidelines, for instance, an approach to a national strategy for the coast, leaves the initiative for realization with the existing authorities. In the final analysis, however, it is only law that can compel the subordination of one interest to another and enforce difficult decisions. It is precisely this role that law is so often unnecessarily prevented from fulfilling in the coastal zone.

Nevertheless, there is increasing evidence of a more fluid and responsive situation emerging, particularly outside what are often seen to be the confines of statute. In England and Wales, for instance, some of the most effective managerial initiatives have come from maritime local authorities, acting singly or in concert, on a non-statutory basis, to reconcile coastal pressures.[14]

The mere spectre of law appears often to exercise a paralyzing influence on executive discretion, and it is thus sometimes easier to achieve an administrative objective independently of legal means. Voluntary marine nature reserves, for instance, already exist in Britain in places where it has so far proved impossible to introduce their statutory equivalent,[15] and Heritage Coasts have been declared without any legislative backing.

Officials thus often seem able to cooperate unofficially, and the achievements made by informal contacts and voluntary initiatives, and the important role of personality, should certainly not be overlooked in our search for coastal progress.

Such a situation, however, has its own inherent dangers. Not the least is that areas of non-statutory initiative are notoriously vulnerable in times of economic stringency and cut-back, whilst the generally low political priority accorded to coastal matters renders vulnerable even statutory initiatives.

Extra-statutory practices also lack one of the essential safeguards of law inasmuch as they cannot be repealed. In Britain, for instance, an emergency extra-statutory recommendation to local councils in 1968 that they should prepare to combat oil pollution within a mile off the coast solidified into an immutable jurisdictional zone creating an impractical dichotomy of administrative functions.[16]

Conclusion

The four framework elements -- the coastal resource, coastal use, law and management -- are thus inextricably linked. Some of the problems encountered by the latter are implicit in any such complex system. It is easy to advocate integration by the centralization of power. Yet, diversity of responsibility is not inherently undesirable, and is dictated in some form by the nature of the task to be performed. It may be observed that although the functions of central government in the three constituent countries of Great Britain are distributed in different degrees among sole and multiple departments of State, there is little discernible difference in the efficiency with which they are performed. It is no solution for all officials to be answerable to a single minister, if his department is necessarily divided within itself.

Informational deficiencies are perhaps the most easily remedied, and while the proliferation of anomalies is a product of human error, they can at least be identified and removed. It is much more difficult, however, to eradicate the impediments that exist simply within the mind. The main consequence of such a perceptual failing is that our legislative and administrative systems are frequently built on inaccurate and dated representations of reality. If we can increase our comprehension of this complex and challenging enigma, then the process of incremental adjustment already in progress may crystallize around a modified system, more appropriate to the control and direction of the coastal resource today.

If we fail, however, to address the area specifically, the imbalance between reality and response, between resource and organization, is likely to precipitate a further crisis. The coastal zone will thus by default still be the target for increased intervention and attention, yet response will remain inadequate because of a continued failure to embrace the coastal zone as a conceptual entity and a fundamental reality.

NOTES

1. Halsbury's Laws of England, 4th Edition.
2. J.A. Steers, "Protection of Coastal Areas," Council of Europe (1974), pp. 1-94. European Information Centre for Nature Conservation.
3. See, *e.g.*, D. Eisma, H. Van Hoorn, A.J. De Jong, "Concepts for Sea-Use Planning in the North Sea," (1979) 5 *Ocean Management* 295-307.
4. See, *e.g.*, Scottish Development Department, *North Sea Oil and Gas. Coastal Planning Guidelines* (1974), pp. 1-15, and the United States Coastal Zone Management Act of 1972.
5. The tendency of legislative draftsmen to force new ideas into the safe confines of traditional formula is a problem encountered in many areas of law, but it is particularly damaging in the coastal zone, where barriers of a geographical, jurisdictional or conceptual kind so frequently need to be overcome.
6. The United Kingdom's ten-year delay in implementing the Control of Pollution Act of 1974, Part II, is an obvious example.
7. 54 H.C. Debs., col. 277 (Feb. 16, 1984).
8. *E.g.*, licenses from the Department of Transport under the Coast Protection Act of 1949, s. 34, and from the Crown Estate Commissioners and harbor authorities. The Dumping at Sea Act of 1974, which on January 1, 1986, was replaced by the Food and Environment Protection Act of 1985, Part II, implements the Oslo Convention for the Prevention of Marine Pollution by Dumping from Ships and Aircraft 1972 and the London Convention on the Prevention of Marine Pollution by Dumping of Wastes and Other Matter 1972.
9. ss. 36-37.
10. 176 statutory instruments were made under the Oil and Gas (Enterprise) Act 1982, s. 21. Parliamentary legislation is now being considered to change the system. The power to create safety zones of up to 500 meters in radius is conferred by the Geneva Convention on the Continental Shelf of 1958, Art. 5.
11. See *e.g.*, United Nations Ocean Economics & Technology Branch, *Coastal Management and Development* (1982). Pergamon Press. The International Union for Conservation of Nature & Natural Resources,

The World Conservation Strategy (1980), and Ekistiks (1982) vol. 49 no. 293 for a special issue on coastal planning and management.

12. See J.A. Steers, "Coastal Preservation & Planning," (1944) 104 *Geographical Journal* 7-27; *ibid.*, "Coastal Preservation & Planning" (1946) 107 *Geog. J.* 57-60; and The Countryside Commission, *The Planning of the Coastline*, 1970, HMSO.

13. W.J. Wolff (Ed.), Proceedings of the Conference of Wadden Sea experts held at the Island of Schiermonnikoog, The Netherlands, 26-28 November 1975 (1977), pp. 1-96.

14. See, *e.g.*, Solent Sailing Conference, *Report of the Working Party* (1983). Hampshire County Council.

15. *E.g.*, Skomer Island (Wales) and Lundy (Devon).

16. *Oil Pollution of Beaches*, Circular 34/68 (Ministry of Housing and Local Government): 29/68 (Welsh Office): 55/68 (Scottish Development Department).

MANAGEMENT OF THE SEAS AND COASTAL ZONES: A BRIEF OUTLOOK ON RECENT DEVELOPMENTS IN INDONESIA

Etty R. Agoes
Department of International Law
Padjadjaran University
Indonesia

Introduction

In the history of international law, the function of the law of the sea has been recognized as that of protecting and balancing the common interests of nations in the use and enjoyment of the ocean while rejecting assertion of special interests in contravention of general community interests.[1] The actual content of the law of the sea at any given time will be a reflection of the underlying pattern of those interests; however, changes in the nature and extent of these interests will inevitably require changes in the substantive rule of law.

Throughout history, the law of the sea has been continuously developed, beginning with centuries-old shipping codes created by one or two dozen seafaring nations. Compatible interests between sovereign states in the sea and international maritime relations during that time basically revolved around sea-borne trade and fisheries. During the eighteenth and nineteenth centuries, it was felt that, in the interest of national integrity, there was a need for the exercise of territorial sovereignty over a limited maritime zone adjacent to the coastal state, known as the territorial sea. Beyond this, all vessels, irrespective of nationality, could proceed essentially without restriction. At that time, it was considered sufficient to leave the regulation and control of all activities beyond the territorial sea to the flag states. This was because, perhaps, at the time the oceans were considered too large to create any problems for the limited number of type and size of ships. At the same time, ocean resources, particularly fish, were thought to be inexhaustible. By the end of the nineteenth century, the law of the sea was still unsettled.

The need for a new law of the sea arose from the necessity of states to reconcile their different interests in the seas, be they strategic, political, or socio-economic. In creating the new law of the sea, the world community had to face all the issues that relate to the oceans, i.e., communications, the arms race, food and energy, management and conservation of resources, and the development of science and technology underlying it.

Divergences over the limit of the territorial sea emerged at the Hague Codification Conference in 1930, which continued during negotiations at the 1958 and 1960 Conferences on the Law of the Sea. Attempts to settle this controversial issue had been made through these conferences, but even after the second conference in 1960, participants from some forty-five countries had been unsuccessful in resolving this problem.

This deficiency of not having been able to reach an agreed limit on the territorial sea, and the reality shown by history that freedom of the seas could only be enjoyed by those who could enforce it, linked with the development of the scientific industrial revolution in the maritime dimension and the discovery of an abundant wealth on the sea-floor, led nations to call for a Third United Nations Conference on the

Law of the Sea. At the UN General Assembly in 1967, Dr. Arvid Pardo drew the world's attention to a proposal that the seabed and ocean floor beyond the limits of national jurisdiction and its resources be considered as the "common heritage of mankind." He proposed that a treaty regarding the peaceful uses of the seabed and ocean floor underlying the seas beyond the limits of national jurisdiction be included in the Assembly's agenda.

In 1967, the United Nations Sea-Bed Committee was appointed, and in 1970 the General Assembly called for the convening of the Third United Nations Conference on the Law of the Sea.

The Conference was burdened with a very difficult assignment -- to set up a comprehensive regime governing all activities in the oceans, which included, *inter alia*:

1. It was obliged to resolve the unfinished tasks of the first and second Geneva Conferences; *viz.*, the limits of the territorial sea and the fishing zone, and to establish a precise criterion for the outer limit of the continental shelf to replace the exploitability criterion.
2. It had to try to find ways to resolve the chaos created by the unilateral extensions of maritime jurisdiction and the conflicting claims resulting therefrom; *i.e.*, the regime for passage of ships and aircraft through straits used for international navigation.
3. The international community was compelled to agree on rules that would govern the seabed and ocean-floor beyond the limits of national jurisdiction;
4. There was a growing alertness within the world community regarding the threat to the marine environment that led states to aspire to adopt new rules to protect and preserve it; and
5. There was a desire among newly independent countries to participate in the creation of the new rules for the oceans as evidence of a progressive development of international law.

The 1982 Convention on the Law of the Sea

After fifteen years of hard work by the largest and longest international conference ever, in December 1982, representatives of 117 nations gathered at Montego Bay in Jamaica to sign the new Convention on the Law of the Sea.[2]

This product of lengthy sessions of the 150 nations' conference, held from 1973 to 1982, and of preparatory work extending over six years by the United Nations Sea-bed Committee, contains the essential provisions governing man's activities in the oceans. The Convention is significant because it is the first comprehensive treaty governing all aspects of the various uses of the oceans and its resources.

In that context, the Preamble to the 1982 United Nations Convention on the Law of the Sea (hereinafter referred to as "the Convention") recognizes the desirability of establishing a legal order for the seas and oceans which will facilitate international communication, and will promote the peaceful use of the seas and oceans, the equitable and efficient utilization of their resources, the conservation of their living resources, and the study, protection and preservation of the marine environment. It then states that the achievement of these goals will contribute to the realization of a just and equitable international economic order.

Another significant aspect of the Convention is that it represents an ambitious effort undertaken by the international community for the codification and progressive development of international law. In general, the Convention provides a comprehensive global framework of ocean management laying down principles governing the rights and duties of states with respect to all matters relating to the different uses of the sea.

First, it updates and codifies some pre-existing law, *i.e.*,

- twelve miles of territorial sea;
- innocent passage in the territorial sea;
- the continental shelf;
- the contiguous zone; and
- the high seas.

Second, it contains many new and innovative concepts, such as:

- transit passage through straits used for international navigation;
- archipelagic baselines and archipelagic sealanes passage;
- the 200-mile exclusive economic zone;
- freedom of scientific research;
- development and transfer of marine science and technology;
- a comprehensive global framework for the protection and preservation of the marine environment;
- mandatory provisions for the settlement of disputes;
- an international regime for the seabed area.

The Convention, with its 320 articles and nine annexes, stands as one of the major accomplishments of the international community in solving complex ocean management problems. However, the significance of these accomplishments has not been fully recognized when the international community has to face the United States' opposition to the Convention.[3] The Convention was open for signature for two years starting from December 1982 and now is subject to ratification. It will enter into force twelve months after the date of the deposit of the sixtieth ratification.

Indonesia and the Law of the Sea[4]

When Indonesia gained its independence in 1945, Indonesian terrirorial waters were still under the 1939 Ordinance.[5] Under this law, the Indonesian territorial sea was established at a width of three nautical miles around each island of the archipelago. By this Ordinance, which generally followed the customary international law of European countries, Indonesian waters were virtually divided, some of which were governed by the regime of the high seas.

In 1957, however, Indonesia declared its new policy on its territorial sea through the Djuanda Declaration, proclaimed on December 13, 1957. With this new policy, a number of provisions of the old 1939 Ordinance were revoked and the width of the territorial sea was extended to twelve nautical miles, measured from the baselines which comprise the lines joining the outer points of the outermost islands surrounding the archipelago.

As an archipelagic state, Indonesia, which lies between the Indian and Pacific Oceans and between the Asian and Australian continents, is of strategic importance and holds an important position in ocean affairs. Geographically, the Indonesian archipelago comprises 13,661 islands, five of which are the principal islands of Sumatra, Jawa (Java), Kalimantan (Borneo), Sulawesi (Celebes), and Irian Jaya (New Guinea or West Irian). In addition, several groups of islands in the eastern part of the country, for instance Maluku (the Moluccas) and Nusa Tenggara (Lesser Sunda) islands, also form an integral part of the archipelago.

The 1957 declaration signified Indonesia's major legal step to establish its position as an archipelagic state.

The Indonesian struggle to gain international recognition for its territorial sovereignty through international fora, particularly the Third United Nations Conference on the Law of the Sea, has been successfully carried out with the acceptance and inclusion of the archipelagic state principles in the Convention.[6] It is a culmination of twenty-five years of the country's effort to get the archipelagic state principle formally accepted as part of the international law of the sea. With this recognition by the international community, Indonesia is aware of the heavy responsibility it faces to provide regulations to implement the Convention.

It might be said that at this moment, legally speaking, there is not yet a Convention. In a formal legal sense, Article 308 requires at least sixty ratifications for the Convention to enter into force. At present, the Convention is still highly controversial.[7] Failing to reach a consensus procedure as agreed upon at the beginning of the Conference in 1973, it was adopted by a recorded vote. Then, the United States blew up the long-time dream of Dr. Arvid Pardo by voicing its opposition and saying that it would neither sign nor ratify the Convention. Further, it has also attempted to ensure that the uncommitted western states, particularly the United Kingdom and Germany, also do not sign. This raises a new status for the Convention: intended as an effort to resolve conflicts, it has now itself become the subject of conflicts.[8]

The next question of importance facing the world today is the degree to which any of the Convention's provisions has any legal force, even though the Convention as such is not yet in force. As a result of developments within the Conference itself, and of the unilateral actions taken so far by states, there is now a new law of the sea. Some of it is already part of the existing law; some is in the process of getting shape and substance. With this understanding, Indonesia faces a much more heavy responsibility not only of implementation but also of deciding on how to use the available law for the maximum benefit of the country.

Like other countries which participated in the Conference, Indonesia's objectives were largely determined by geography and economics. Major concepts arising out of the Convention would have great impact on national jurisdiction over the sea and its resources, likewise, for an archipelagic state.

One of the most important parts of the Convention that cannot be overlooked by Indonesia is Part IV (Articles 46 to 54) on archipelagic states. According to the Convention, an archipelagic state may draw straight archipelagic baselines joining the outermost points of the outermost islands but with a limit to the length of such baselines. Also included in this provision is the ratio of the land territory to the area of water.[9] This provision clearly includes the regulations of the Indonesian archipelago.[10]

However, several other provisions are also of importance for Indonesia. The provisions on the exclusive economic zone[11] and the continental shelf[12] involve Indonesia's interests in the vast resources of the seas and their subsoil under its jurisdiction.

Article 76 shows a radical change in the legal concept of the continental shelf. It no longer uses the 200-meter depth and exploitability criterion of the 1958 Geneva Convention, but gives three basic elements, namely that:

1. The shelf runs from the outer limit of the territorial sea, which is fixed at twelve nautical miles, throughout the natural prolongation of the land territory to the outer edge of the continental margin;
2. If the outer edge of the continental margin does not extend beyond 200 nautical miles, then the right of the coastal state shall end at 200 nautical miles from the baselines;
3. If the outer edge of the continental margin extends beyond 200 nautical miles, then the shelf extends throughout the natural prolongation of the land territory to the outer edge of the continental margin which must be established in accordance with the specific provisions laid down in this Article.[13]

Before the Convention came into existence, Indonesia had already concluded agreements with neighboring states with regard to the delimitation of their respective continental shelves, both in the northern and southern parts of the territory. Because of these borders, the new provisions of the Convention will be of practical significance only to the sea-floor to the west of Sumatra and to the south of Java and Lesser Sunda Islands.

Part V of the Convention concerning the exclusive economic zone constitutes a political confirmation[14] of the acts of those states that have unilaterally declared a 200-nautical miles exclusive economic zone in which the coastal state exercises its rights and jurisdiction only to the extent required to protect and safeguard its legitimate interests.[15] With the Declaration on its exclusive economic zone in 1980,[16] Indonesia has increased its jurisdiction over its natural resources.

Also of importance to Indonesia are the provisions contained in Part III, particularly Articles 41 to 44, which determine the rights and duties of states bordering straits that are used for international navigation. These provisions have succeeded in balancing the responsibility of guaranteeing the smooth passage of ships and aircraft through such straits with the right to protect and secure straits states' interests. Indonesia, along with Malaysia and Singapore, as a state bordering the Straits of Malacca and Singapore, has successfully achieved the reaching of a technical agreement regarding the Traffic Separation Scheme as an interpretative statement on Article 41.

Part XII on the protection and preservation of the marine environment and Part XIII on marine scientific research[17] are also of significant importance to Indonesia. The latter provides coastal states with the authority to regulate and benefit from the collection of data not only within its territorial sea but also in the continental shelf and the exclusive economic zone. These provisions increase Indonesia's valid zones of control.

Perhaps no other part of the Convention is as controversial as the provisions of Part XI on seabed mining. Many years of debate and negotiation of a complex mechanism for this area of the "common heritage of mankind" have been spent. Unfortunately, rather than coming to an agreed principle, on July 9, 1982, the United States announced to the world that it would not sign the Law of the Sea Convention because it viewed the deep-sea mining part of the Treaty as fundamentally unacceptable because "it does not meet the United States' objectives."[18]

456

Indonesia, on the other hand, views the seabed mining provisions as the most important section of the Convention "since it is a realization of the aspiration to use the mineral wealth for the common heritage of mankind."[19] It was clear to Indonesia and other land-based producers[20] that Article 151 concerning production policies was the most important provision of this Part. In order to give land-based producers some protection against the possible adverse economic consequences from the seabed exploitation of the same minerals, this Article contains a formula for restrictions of minerals produced. As a land-based producer state, Indonesia has great interests in this production limitation, particularly in the case of mining nickel ore.

After the Third United Nations Conference concluded its work in December 1982, states have shifted their attention from negotiation and creation of new law to the issues of ratification and implementation. The Convention is of immense significance to Indonesia. Indonesia has gained a solid international recognition as an archipelagic state, thus enabling it to avoid the possibility of obstruction from the outside. However, this acceptance of the archipelagic principle and the inclusion of the exclusive economic zone principle has led to an extension of Indonesian sovereignty and jurisdiction. Therefore, implementation issues are becoming more important.

The Convention will be in force for ratifying states twelve months after the sixtieth deposit of their instruments of ratification. It may be several years before the Convention receives enough ratifications to come into force. However, legal obligations will commence for a state after signature,[21] although the Convention will not be binding until it comes into force.

It is reasonably to be expected that Indonesia will be one of the first nations to ratify the new Convention, with the result that it will have to review its legislation to bring it into harmony with the Convention's obligations. There is, then, the urgent necessity to translate the terms of the new international regime into a new national legal framework.

Formulation of a new national law of the sea requires the support of a national legislative program. Therefore, there is an urgent, high-priority need to place ocean space and resources within a national framework of developmental objectives.

Indonesian Laws and Regulations and Some Recent Developments in the Management of the Seas and Coastal Zones

Efforts towards harmonizing national laws and regulations with the Convention's provisions are already under way in Indonesia. As Minister Mochtar stated after the signing of the Convention, Indonesia must begin to go through the Convention to reap its benefits and prepare for its implementation in national laws and regulations. Three major steps are considered necessary at the moment:

1. Official translation of the Convention into the national language;
2. An in-depth study of the Convention's provisions by government officials through their respective institutions, as well as by members of the parliament and university scholars;
3. The ratification of the new Convention.

Translation of the Convention's provisions was entrusted to the Department of Foreign Affairs, but no official translation has been produced yet. On the other hand, almost every department within the

457

Indonesian government participated in a long study on the possible implementation of the new international law of the sea long before the signing of the Convention. Workshops on the possible implementation have resulted in various papers and reports, some of which are already published as books that are widely used in universities. Research and symposia on the law of the sea have also mushroomed in recent years.

Aside from establishing new laws, efforts have also been made for the revision of some existing laws and regulations to bring them into conformity with the new international law. It should also be noted that Indonesia had successfully concluded boundary agreements [22] with its neighboring countries, and as part of its implementation efforts, Indonesia has recently ratified a special agreement with Malaysia.[23]

It is, therefore, important to go through some present existing laws and regulations governing the Indonesian archipelago.

Law No. 4 of 1960 Concerning the Indonesian Territorial Waters
    This law is constructed of four basic paragraphs:

1. Straight baselines shall be drawn connecting the outermost points of the outermost islands;
2. Waters situated within those baselines, including the seabed and its subsoil as well as the airspace above them and their resources, shall be placed under the country's full sovereignty;
3. The breadth of the territorial sea shall be twelve nautical miles;
4. Innocent passage through the archipelagic waters shall be guaranteed, provided that it is not prejudicial to the country's interests and as long as it does not disturb its security and good order.

Under this law, the breadth of the Indonesian territorial sea was extended from three to twelve nautical miles, measured from some 196 straight baselines, connecting the outermost points on the low-water mark of the outermost islands, with a total length of 8,069.8 miles. The drawing of these archipelagic baselines, however, resulted in substantial changes in the structure and size of the Indonesian territorial sovereignty. Roughly, it more than doubled the previous area mostly due to the additional area of internal waters. It has caused the state's previous land area of 2,207,087 square kilometers to become a land and sea area of about 5,193,250 square kilometers, and increased the territorial waters' area by about 3,166,163 square kilometers.[24]

Government Regulation No. 8 of 1962
    Law No. 4 of 1960 guarantees innocent passage for foreign vessels traversing Indonesian internal waters enclosed by straight baselines. The Indonesian government considered it necessary to further regulate this right, and on July 28, 1962, Government Regulation No. 8 was enacted.

Article 1 of the Regulation stipulates that innocent passage by foreign vessels through Indonesian internal waters, which, before the enactment of law No. 4 of 1960, were part of the Indonesian territorial sea or high seas, was guaranteed. Article 3 provides that passage shall be considered innocent as long as it is not harmful to the security, good order and interests of the country. Vessels are further encouraged to pass through international shipping lanes recognized by the shipping world.

Law No. 1 of 1973 Concerning the Indonesian Continental Shelf
    Indonesia established its continental shelf through a Declaration
of February 17, 1969, to safeguard the exploration for and exploitation
of natural resources (particularly oil and natural gas) beyond the
limits of its territorial waters, especially in the South China Sea. This
Declaration was then followed by Law No. 1 of 1973 on the Continental
Shelf of Indonesia.
    Law No. 1 of 1973 illustrates Indonesia's concern over its natural
resources on the seabed and subsoil beyond its territorial sea. Its
major points are:

1. The Indonesian continental shelf comprises the seabed and subsoil of
the submarine areas beyond the limit of its territorial sea as determined by Law No. 4 of 1960, to a depth of 200 meters or beyond where
the superjacent waters admit the exploration for and exploitation of
natural resources;
2. Full authority and exclusive rights over the natural resources of
the Indonesian continental shelf shall be vested in the state;
3. In the event that the Indonesian shelf, including any depression
found therein, lies adjacent to the territory of another state, a
boundary line shall be established by agreement with that state;
4. Any exploration for and exploitation of the natural resources
therein shall be governed by laws and regulations in force;
5. Anyone conducting exploration and exploitation activities is
required to take the necessary steps to prevent pollution of the superjacent waters and the airspace above the continental shelf.

*Law No. 1 of 1983 Concerning the Ratification of the Treaty Between
Malaysia and the Republic of Indonesia Relating to the Legal Regime of
Archipelagic State and the Rights of Malaysia in the Territorial Sea,
Archipelagic Waters and the Territory of the Republic of Indonesia
lying Between East and West Malaysia*
    According to the Convention, as an archipelagic state, Indonesia
has certain rights and obligations to perform. Of greatest significance
is the obligation to respect the rights and legitimate interests of its
immediately adjacent neighboring states, including those that have
traditionally been exercised in its archipelagic waters.[25] To accommodate such rights, Indonesia has concluded a bilateral treaty with
Malaysia as a result of negotiations between the two countries since
1974. The treaty sets out Malaysia's recognition and support of the
Indonesian archipelagic state regime, and in return Indonesia under-
takes to respect Malaysia's preexisting rights and interests in the
waters of the Indonesian archipelago.
    This agreement and previous boundary agreements concluded by Indo-
nesia with its neighboring countries have a very significant meaning
for the recognition of its archipelagic state regime. Through the
establishment of these boundary agreements, these states have indirectly acknowledged Indonesia's archipelagic state regime since the
limits determined by these agreements are measured from the straight
archipelagic baselines connecting the outermost points of the outermost
islands surrounding the archipelago. The 1982 bilateral treaty between
Indonesia and Malaysia, on the other hand, is an example of explicit
recognition of the archipelagic state concept.

Law No. 5 of 1983 Concerning the Indonesian Exclusive Economic Zone

In 1980, Indonesia made its claim to a 200-mile exclusive economic zone measured from the straight baselines used in determining the outer limit of its territorial sea as regulated by Law No. 4 of 1960. This decision was then followed by the enactment of Law No. 5 of 1983, concerning the Indonesian exclusive economic zone, which grants Indonesia sovereign rights for the purpose of exploring and exploiting, and conserving and managing, the natural resources of its exclusive economic zone which may extend to 200 miles from the baseline from which its territorial sea is measured.

Further, it states that any exploration and exploitation activities shall be carried out with the consent of, or by international agreement concluded with, the Indonesian government. This law also provides for a guaranteed access to the surplus of the allowable catch for foreign legal entities or governments. Also included are provisions concerning an obligation to take the necessary measures to prevent, reduce, and control polluton of the marine environment.

The law also provides for liability for any act which contravenes Indonesian laws and regulations and, in the case of marine scientific research, rules of international law. Strict liability shall be imposed on any act resulting in the pollution of the marine environment or damage to natural resources.

Section VI deals with safeguards relating to the exercise of power of enforcement which shall be carried out in conformity with the Indonesian Code of Criminal Procedure. Liability for any violation of the provisions relating to consent for exploration and exploitation activities and agreement to carry out research[26] is set at a maximum of 225 million rupiahs.[27] Aside from that, vessels and their equipment, along with anything produced from their activities, are also subject to confiscation.

Government Regulation No. 14 of 1984 Concerning the Management of Living Resources in the Indonesian Exclusive Economic Zone

Indonesia realizes its fishing potential in its exclusive economic zone and its need to develop its fishing industry. Until 1963, fishing in Indonesia was mostly confined to shallow and inshore waters along the coasts, employing large traditional fishing gear and small sailing boats. By 1974, through its Second Five Year Development Plan, the government had established various programs to support the development of marine fisheries.

With the enactment of Law No. 5 of 1983, Indonesia has extended its opportunities for the exploitation of the living resources in its exclusive economic zone. To ensure proper management of the living resources in the exclusive economic zone, and to provide a tool for the implementation of Law No. 5 of 1983, Government Regulation No. 14 was enacted on June 29, 1984.

Basically, this government regulation consists of provisions regarding the utilization and conservation of the living resources in the Indonesian exclusive economic zone, and procedures for obtaining licenses and legal sanctions for any violation of these provisions. The major points are:

1. Utilization of the living resources in the exclusive economic zone should be geared toward the development of the Indonesian fishing industry;

2. To improve its fishing capacity the government will provide facilities for joint ventures or any other kind of cooperation between Indonesian and foreign nationals or legal entities;
3. A guarantee of access to the surplus for foreign nationals or legal entities;
4. The Minister of Agriculture shall establish the total allowable catch;
5. To preserve the living resources, the use of explosives and other harmful or dangerous substances or methods is prohibited;
6. Consent through the granting of fishing licenses shall be carried out according to Indonesian fishing laws and regulations;
7. Application for licenses should be accompanied by information concerning vessels used, personnel, types of fishing gear, and fishing sites;
8. Licenses to fish shall be granted for one year, which can be renewed thirty days prior to its expiration date;
9. Fees shall be collected for the registration, amendment or renewal of licenses, and for the catch;
10. The maximum fine for any violation of the prohibition regarding the use of dangerous or harmful methods or substances is seventy-five million rupiahs;
11. For violation of the licensing provisions, the maximum fine is twenty-five million rupiahs.

Law No. 4 of 1982 Concerning Basic Rules Regarding the Management of the Human Environment
Basically, this law imposes an obligation on the Indonesian government to manage and regulate all activities within Indonesian territory to prevent them from disturbing the human environment. Some important characteristics of this law are, *inter alia*:

1. It is simple, yet it gives prospects for future development according to changes in situation, time and place;
2. It gives basic rules for further regulation in its implementation;
3. It covers every aspect of the human environment as the basis for further regulation.

Some Final Thoughts

Having said all this, I think that at present Indonesia has adequate laws and regulations to govern all activities in the seas of this archipelago. However, there are important issues to be considered, especially if Indonesia decides to ratify the Convention.

As mentioned earlier, major concepts arising out of the Convention will have great impact on national jurisdiction over the sea and its resources. Likewise, as an archipelagic state, Indonesia is now faced with the heavy responsibility of reviewing its laws and regulations to bring them into conformity with the Convention, and to provide new regulations for implementation and enforcement of other parts of the Convention that have not yet a place in national legislation.

Most important is the implementation of Part IV of the Convention on archipelagic states. Indonesia will have to establish the outer points of its outermost islands to be able to draw its archipelagic baselines. A review of the present baselines established under Law No. 4 of 1960 would give a picture of what must be done accordingly. Sealanes through the archipelagic waters will have to be established, taking into account the relevant paragraphs on archipelagic sealanes passage.

461

With regard to the exclusive economic zone, the present Law No. 5 of 1983 and Government Regulation No. 14 of 1984 could be considered adequate bases for the management of the Indonesian exclusive economic zone and its resources.

The new definition of the continental shelf is more specific than the 1958 definition. The lack of precision in the latter Convention has now been replaced with a new legal concept of a more precise nature. For Indonesia, this new definition will not have much effect in most parts of the archipelago because Indonesia has concluded continental shelf boundary agreements with its immediate neighboring countries. Some attention, then, should be given to the shelf of the western coast of Sumatra and south of Java for a precise outer limit of the Indonesian continental shelf.

Indonesia, along with Malaysia and Singapore, has done a considerable job in solving the problems of passage through the Straits of Malacca and Singapore. In 1977 the three states successfully concluded a Tripartite Agreement establishing a Traffic Separation Scheme and Under Keel Clearance for vessels traversing the Strait of Malacca.

In the past Indonesia has already taken some legal measures for the protection and preservation of its marine environment. The establishment of Law No. 4 of 1982 is the culmination of these efforts, but as has been stated before, this law serves only as a basis for further regulation in different aspects of environmental management. Indonesia has yet to establish new laws and regulations for the protection and preservation of its marine environment. Also, as the Convention requires states to participate in establishing global and regional rules on the various sources of marine pollution, participation in international law-making is another activity to be engaged in to implement the Convention.

In conclusion, allow me to quote Minister Mochtar Kusumaatmadja at a 1981 Symposium[28] in Bangkok. He said that the Convention "is a result of a decade-long process of balancing and reconciling interests and its conclusion was only made possible by the realization that nobody stands to gain by the failure of this gigantic undertaking and that mankind as a whole is to gain by the successful conclusion of this common effort to create a new order of the oceans."

NOTES

1. Myres McDougal and William T. Burke, *The Public Order of the Oceans: A Contemporary International Law of the Sea* (1982), p. 1.
2. So far there is no uniform nickname for this Convention. Some writers refer to it as the "New Convention"; some attempt to call it the "Montego Bay Convention"; but many prefer to call it the "1982 Convention".
3. In July 1982, President Reagan announced that the United States would not sign the Treaty, and commented that "while most provisions of the Draft Convention are acceptable and consistent with the United States' interests, some major elements of the deep seabed mining regime are not acceptable." The White House, Office of the Press Secretary, *Statement by the President*, July 8, 1982.
4. This part is mostly based on the writer's article "Indonesia and the New Convention on the Law of the Sea," which appeared in the

1985 English edition of *Padjadjaran*, the University of Padjadjaran Law Journal.
5. Territoriale Zee en Marietieme Kringen Ordonnantie, 1939.
6. Part IV, Arts. 46-54.
7. A.W. Koers, "The United Nations Convention on the Law of the Sea: An Overview," in *The International Law of the Sea: Issues of Implementation in Indonesia*, E. Hey and A.W. Koers, eds., Netherlands Institute of Transport, 1984, pp. 24-25.
8. Ted McDorman, "Canada and the Law of the Sea," (1984) 8 *Marine Policy* 2.
9. Art. 47 Paragraph 2 sets the limit to the length of the baselines as 100 nautical miles, with an exception of a maximum of 125 nautical miles for up to 3 percent of the total number of baselines. And as for the ratio between the water to the land area, Paragraph 1 provides for between 1:1 and 9:1.
10. Mochtar Kusumaatmadja, "The Concept of the Indonesian Archipelago," (1982) X *Indonesian Quarterly* 19.
11. Arts. 55 to 75.
12. Arts. 76 to 85.
13. Art. 76, Paragraph 4.
14. Mochtar Kusumaatmadja, *op. cit.*, p. 22.
15. Art. 56 provides for the coastal state's "sovereign rights" to the living resources and "jurisdiction" over certain ocean activities.
16. Declaration on the Exclusive Economic Zone, March 21, 1980.
17. Part XIII, Arts. 192 to 237, and Part XIII, Arts. 238 to 278.
18. See, *supra*, n. 3.
19. Mochtar Kusumaatmadja, *op. cit.*, p. 23.
20. Among the land-based producers are Australia, Argentina, Burundi, Canada, Chile, Colombia, Cuba, Gabon, Guatemala, Indonesia, the Ivory Coast, Nigeria, the Philippines, Peru, Zaire, Zambia, and Zimbabwe.
21. Art. 18 of the Vienna Convention on the Law of Treaties, 1969, states that after signature a nation is obliged to refrain from acts which would defeat the object and purpose of a treaty.
22. Between 1968 and 1979 Indonesia concluded nine boundary agreements with its neighboring countries.
23. Law No. 1 of 1983 concerning ratification of the Treaty between Malaysia and the Republic of Indonesia relating to the Legal Regime of Archipelagic State and the Rights of Malaysia in the Territorial Sea, Archipelagic Waters and the Territory of the Republic of Indonesia lying between East and West Malaysia (done and signed in Jakarta on February 23, 1982).
24. Mochtar Kusumaatmadja, *op. cit.*, p. 17.
25. Art. 47(6) and Art. 51.
26. Arts. 5, 6, and 7.
27. At the current rate of exchange it will amount to about U.S. $20,000.
28. International Symposium on "The New Law of the Sea in Southeast Asia: Developmental Effects and Regional Approaches," Bangkok, December 9, 1981.

COMMENTARY

H. D. Smith
Centre for Marine Law and Policy
University of Wales Institute for Science and Technology

As we move into the aftermath of the 1982 Law of the Sea Convention, heralding the next stage in the development of the law of the sea, the focus shifts to the implementation of the ideas contained in the Convention, whether or not full ratification takes place. In the context of the management of the seas and coastal zones, this commentary briefly considers four points: the relationship between law and management, the historical context, the geographical approach, and the implications of the first three considerations for the further development of management, which increasingly will revolve around the theme of integration highlighted in Mr. Peet's paper.

The cardinal point to make in a management context is the need for a change in perspective from simply the law as viewed in terms of evolution leading up to and including the 1982 Convention, to the law as associated with management, which is concerned with the objectives of sea users and those who govern sea uses. The problems of integration of legislative and management approaches emerges particularly clearly in the discussion by Gibson and Halliday of the relationships between legislation and administration in the coastal zone. The essential point is that the 1982 Convention and existing coastal legislation provide only a framework for management, much of which evolves along lines in part independent of the law as such. It is worth noting, for example, that the North Sea, although lacking the integrated management structures outlined by Peet, is arguably the most managed of all seas, being more intensively managed in a number of respects than the Mediterranean or even the Baltic, in the sense of the number of organizations and diversity of objectives involved. Several frameworks are involved -- northwest European, northeast Atlantic and global. Again, in the Indonesian example discussed by Agoes there appears to be an adequate legal framework, but management as such is arguably only beginning. Management is, in important ways, the outcome of political decisions. In many situations, despite the historic significance of the 1982 Convention, awareness of the seas and coastal zones has far to go to match the thinking behind the Convention.

It is to the perspective of history that we now turn. The post-World War II evolution of the law of the sea took place during the "long boom" of global economic expansion which ended in the early 1970s; it was accompanied by both increased intensity of use and growth of management organizations from the UN agencies to regional arrangements on an unprecedented scale. By contrast, the UNCLOS III negotiations have occupied the first part of a long turndown, accompanied by a restructuring of the global economy which is likely to gather pace between now and the end of the century. The Convention relates essentially to this long time scale in its innovative significance -- politically, in that UNCLOS III was held at all, and, legally, primarily in the Common Heritage provisions. As Castaneda observed at the Law of the Sea Institute Conference in 1983, it is primarily an economic treaty, and as such has a strong focus on the nature of the next long upswing, after 2000, in which environmental considerations are likely to be near paramount in many maritime resource management fields. On such time scales, the evolution of sea uses, together with associated legal and management steps, may be analyzed meaningfully. More work is required to deepen our understanding of the evolution of law and management in an historic context to inform the decisions which lie ahead, especially between now and the end of the century.

The historical pattern has its geographical counterpart in the regional geography of management frameworks. Two points may be made here. The first concerns geographical scale -- global, regional, national and sub-national. Of these, the national scale is crucial and will surely remain so for the foreseeable future, *i.e.*, into the middle of the next century, despite the innovative nature of the Convention with respect to the International Seabed Area, and the increasing complexity of international cooperation of various kinds. This is exemplified by the *North Sea* case. It is significant that the major management initiatives have come from the Netherlands and the Federal Republic of Germany which, together with Belgium, have their primary geographical interest in the North Sea. The Dutch approach to harmonization, encompassing policy, program and institutional components, is of considerable significance. Also, the moves by Indonesia are among the foremost in current developments. Secondly, the challenge of the next long stage will be to strengthen regional arrangements (both international and supra-national) working both downwards from the global approach as in the Regional Seas Programme of UNEP and the work of IMO, and upwards from national cooperation as in some North Sea cases, and in the Baltic. The Law of the Sea Institute examined regional approaches as recently as its 1977 Conference and may have to bear these particular arrangements in mind in the near future. The state will retain the initiative on the seabed and the all-important coastal zone -- the seabed pre-occupation has arguably come nearest to scuppering the Convention. But there is great scope for an integrated approach to the other, water-column based, maritime affairs. In these developments, special cognizance will also have to be taken of the global patterns of economic development and corresponding marine management resource distribution.

The final theme concerns integration. Here, there are three points to be made. The first is the integration of coastal zone and offshore legal and management frameworks (Gibson and Hallliday), primarily a job for each state according to its particular geographical and historical circumstances, including the nature of its maritime communities. The second is the integration of use management -- mainly a question of organization at all four scales outlined above, and in which the organizational approach discussed by Johnston at the Law of the Sea Institute Conference in 1982 is arguably to be favored. As Peet points out, the levels of integration may be variable and relate primarily to uses and environment. Most maritime and coastal zone management is, of course, historically based upon individual uses with very variable degrees of cooperation. Third and most fundamental is the integration of objectives. If every user and management organization at whatever scale has clearly defined objectives, which in most cases will be shared in part (or whole) by others, a sound basis for coordination may be built. That surely needs top priority in the task before us -- the successful implementation of the provisions of the 1982 Convention for the effective management of the seas for the foreseeable future, which is into the middle of the twenty-first century.

465

COMMENTARY

C.S. Lalwani
Department of Maritime Studies
University of Wales Institute for Science and Technology

From the previous papers, it is clear that any approach to the management of the seas is greatly influenced by political developments and the associated legal and administrative changes. Whether these influences are tangible or intangible, a fundamental starting point for sea-use planning will be the integration of existing information systems on legal, environmental and maritime activities. The key systems here are those of the national government departments responsible for navigation, mineral extraction, fisheries, waste disposal, defense and local authorities; non-governmental organizations including classification societies, recreation, research and conservation organizations, ICES; and the developing institutions of the EEC, including the EUROSTAT and ECDIN data bases. The global organizations with regional inputs, including IMO, WMO, FAO and data bases such as IRTPC and oceanographic WDCS, should also be included. There may not be a need for fundamental re-organization but rather for the adoption of common standards required for specific integrated information system objectives.

In this context, a sea-use management system may be looked at in terms of users, key information categories and the organization of specific tasks. The users can be grouped into categories primarily concerned with navigational safety, maritime commerce, marine resources and environmental monitoring.

The navigation systems such as those of the large ports and the Channel Navigation Information System (CNIS) are particularly "planning oriented" as, presumably, are the related strategic systems. Commercial systems, notably those of the ports and classification societies, containing information on ships, cargoes and casualties, are also planning concerns. Marine resources and environmental data are mainly planning and management interests. Therefore, it is likely that substantial data exists for most multiple-use management problems.

A first priority, therefore, is to construct a detailed investigation of specific multiple-use data requirements in relation to existing data bases. Information system development is largely at the user-specific stage in commercial applications related, for example, to the INMARSAT system. For integrated management information system development, the priorities are environmental monitoring, resource assessment and navigation systems.

Formats should be determined by the nature of the planning tasks and are of two kinds. The first is the technical advice notes or manuals, both of standard form such as decision-trees and lists of polluting substances, and of monitoring form such as the state of legislative developments, resource assessments, and environmental monitoring reports. The second is the computer-based information system in the form of an integrated database management system (DBMS). The DBMS is most useful for monitoring formats when continuous updating and periodic format revision are required and which is adaptable enough to carry out mathematical modelling studies.

An ideal approach to an integrated DBMS would be to construct a network of existing data bases using a central processor enabling access by all authorized users to any database available globally. This is now technically possible with fast development in information technology and telecommunication networks such as JANET.

COMMENTARY

Kaldone G. Nweihed
Institute of Technology and Marine Sciences
Simon Bolivar University
Caracas, Venezuela

Faced with three lengthy papers, I have chosen the unorthodox solution for a commentator of putting the three papers in the same basket while trying to find out how they complement or part from one another, and whether, as a whole, they could lead to common conclusions.

Having decided that, it is Mr. Gibson and Ms. Halliday's paper, "In Pursuit of an Enigma: The Coastal Zone in Management and Law," which would set the scene for a normative outlook potentially applicable to the situation of coastal zones *erga omnes*, even if it does not omit specific references within the framework of what may be broadly termed as case studies, drawn from British legislation or from English, Welsh and/or Scottish planning guides and managerial initiatives.

Dr. Gerard Peet's paper on "Sea Use Management for the North Sea," aware of the twin and parallel "amphibious" themes of this symposium, addressed itself to the management of the seas by focussing on the sea-use management of one of the foremost maritime areas in the world, as far as legal and administrative traditions are concerned, perhaps a classic example taking into account the varied experience of the riparian states concerned. It is not by coincidence that the headquarters of the International Maritime Organization (IMO), the Intergovernmental Oceanographic Commission (IOC), the International Court of Justice (ICJ) and the prestigious non-governmental Comite Maritime Internationale (CMI), besides certain fishery and conservation commissions and councils, have found themselves in countries ringing the shores of the North Sea.

The third paper, submitted by Dr. Etty Agoes as a view from a developing country, entitled "A Brief Outlook on Recent Development in Indonesia," not only provides us with the specific background of the country concerned, but also adds the main highlights of the 1982 Convention in a nutshell, neatly separated by a line drawn between the updating and codification of existing law on one side and the establishment of new norms and concepts on the other. Coming from a developing country, the paper on Indonesia offers a by-product which adds a positive element to the subject, for it may be considered as another case study from an archipelagic state, bearing in mind that coastal zone management for this category of states indeed touches upon issues related to their survival and may demand solutions subject to mandatory revision and controlled application.

This dual quality of the Indonesian case is worthy of a specific remark. It should be remembered that almost all states which qualify for the archipelagic definition under the Convention come from the developing world: their clear majority hails from the Indian and Pacific Oceans with Indonesia in the middle, posing as a huge archipelagic bridge, reinforced by the Philippines. I do not wish to trace back the colonial link between third world contemporary archipelagic entities and the development of the law of the sea further than I briefly attempted in my study *La Vigencia del Mar I* (Caracas, 1973), but I do wish to introduce an ecological note which may prove worthy of some reflection.

By weaving threads from the "enigma" paper and the paper on Indonesia, the reader is tempted to question the validity of applying one indiscriminate treatment to coastal management in the developing world. Two dividers, an ecological and a cultural one, may assist us to achieve a functional classification.

The ecological divider should separate countries lying within the intertropical belt -- both north and south of the Equator -- from the temperate zone, mostly in the northern hemisphere. The intertropical belt harbors three sub-categories of coastal states: archipelagic (the Bahamas, Seychelles, Fiji), insular (Cuba, Madagascar, Sri Lanka) and continental (Venezuela, the Ivory Coast and Thailand) -- to mention one example from each continent or ocean. Notwithstanding probable differences of a regional or local nature, the ecological similarity of the coastal zones within the intertropical belt determines and defines the nature of a great deal of the biotic coastal resources, that is to say, the first element in the Gibson and Halliday paper. The law of nature, for reasons better known to natural scientists, has set a distinct pattern for intertropical ecosystems: they are more fragile than in the temperate zone and resources follow a much higher species diversity to a much lower density per given unit of territory.

The other three elements according to the "enigma" paper, namely coastal use, coastal zone law and management vary widely or narrowly according to man-made circumstances, and though the element of coastal use is partly determined by the nature of the resource (*e.g.*, fisheries), it is indeed the cultural or man-made factor that is mainly stressed by separating the element of *resource* from the element of *coastal use* within the proposed framework for the coastal zone.

The cultural divider -- again applied to the third world -- should categorize states which have had a relatively conspicuous and effective tradition in coastal use, law and management from those which have not. In the former category one expects to come across uses, laws and some sort of traditional management even before the rise of the industrial state in the West. It is not correct to assume that there is a necessary correspondence between the categorization arising from the ecological divider and the other resulting from the cultural one, for an intertropical young state in the international law connotation of the word, such as Indonesia, may be a nation of deep-rooted legal traditions reaching through to the property regime applied to coastal lands and uses. Suriname, on the other hand -- part of whose population had actually come from the former Dutch East Indies -- lacks the same tradition as a whole.

Nevertheless, the ecological and cultural dividers are not completely separate. It is a fact that the developing nations from the temperate zone, whether continental or insular, have disposed of the precious gift of two to three millenia of time in order to develop their most convenient versions of the element of coastal use, which, in a way, may have led to the gradual elaboration and later observance of traditional private and public law tenets: the former concerning the rights to the coastal lands themselves and the latter probably dealing with strate-gic, logistical and communications issues which, over the centuries, bore the brunt of what the "enigma" paper describes, while speaking on behalf of coastal zone management law, as the "burden of its own history," thus tending to emphasize the quality of inconsistency when it comes to the modern invention called coastal zone management.

469

In fact, a great or a small deal of this "burden of history" may still be found underlying the coastal zone management enigma in temperate countries as those bordering in Mackinder's Region of the Five Seas (Mediterranean, Black Sea, Caspian, Red Sea and Gulf), as well as in whatever legacy the pre-industrialized societies have still to show in China, Korea and perhaps on the rural face of Japan.

Taking up the North Sea paper again, the same double dichotomy perceived within the Third World concerning coastal zone uses, law and management may be observed regarding the management of corresponding marine areas. Seas have their individual background too, though it is undoubtedly the product of the culture irradiated by the surrounding land masses. Hence their non-scientific division into noble and slave seas.

Both the ecological and the cultural factors would have to be carefully considered. Although the Caribbean has often been called the "American Mediterranean" -- and I should like to evoke the memory of the late Robert D. Hodgson who lectured us on the terminology in Caracas back in 1972 -- it is the burden of history sitting on the Mediterranean of which the Caribbean will feel relatively free when the need arises to carry the local to the international through the regional, or to feed it all back through the same conduit.

The three papers do complement one another quite harmoniously. In the first place, the fact should be stressed that while the enigma pursued in the paper on the coastal zone in management and law is analyzed as a product of rationalized induction, the papers on the North Sea and Indonesia, by espousing the cases of a particular sea and an archipelagic, developing country respectively, seem to point out the same crossing through a process of deduction, highly motivated by a constant and ready supply of a variety of descriptive, pertinent facts. Of course, there is room for further and more varied study cases: the Baltic, the Caribbean, the South China Sea -- to name but a few in maritime space -- as well as other developing countries who may shed new lights on the subject. In fact, if one single conclusion should come out of this symposium, it is the need to build up more literature and expertise on such a fascinating theme. Without being oblivious to the fact that a great deal of research has been and is being done on the management of seas and coastal zones, it is the necessary link with the Law of the Sea Convention that this Conference was meant to stress. It is evident that there is a long way to go before coastal zone and marine management will be associated with, and functionally recognized as, part and parcel of the new order of the oceans. While the gap is being gradually narrowed, the first step to understand the enigma would not only have to be the determination of the extent of the coastal zone within the territorial dimensions of riparian states but also the agreement on a broad standard of reference which would allow room for what the authors of the "enigma" paper have identified as the variation among regions and within any one region.

If enclosed or semi-enclosed seas have already been accorded a generic definition in the 1982 Convention, no such condition has been registered regarding regional seas. Nowhere in the official index to the Convention is there any explicit mention of them, but they have already begun to attract enough attention at academic events and in relevant literature, besides having been espoused by the United Nations Environment Programme (UNEP) in connection with specific programs, action plans and the elaboration of regional conventions. As far back as 1971, one of the so-called twenty-three principles of Ottawa laid down by the Intergovernmental Working Group on Marine Pollution stipulated that states should assume joint responsibility for the preservation of the marine environment outside their national jurisdiction. Section 2 of Part XII of the Convention addresses itself -- as stressed at the outset of the North Sea paper -- to global and regional cooperation in terms which spell out the basis for contingency plans against pollution, research programs and exchange of information.

The process to define and determine the extension of regional seas -- performed conventionally by and through the international system -- needs to be complemented by the definition and determination of the coastal zones in riparian states by and through the national legal systems of individual sovereign states.

The fact that the integrity of the coastal zone is denied by administration, jurisdiction and perception -- as stated at the outset of the "enigma" paper -- is one powerful reason why states should immediately start to rethink their civil divisions (international subdivisions) in terms of an integral, ecological policy, perhaps by attempting what Professor Martin I. Glassner from Southern Connecticut University has suggested may become a sort of "zoning" on a national scale.

An important prerequisite may have to be a due process of creating concern and awareness in public opinion, the media, and, most significantly, in schools, civic centers, community groups and at all apposite events. This should lead to the question of "satisfying the urgent need for a high priority to place ocean space and therefore coastal resource management within a national framework of development objectives" (I am freely quoting from the paper on Indonesia) and subsequently to an answer which draws on "appealing to the law of the highest authority entitled to subordinate one interest to another and enforce difficult decisions" (I am now drawing on the "enigma" paper), in order to avoid the "complexity, duplications, gaps and lack of political will to improve things when nationals of different riparian states and even outsiders converge with a variety of purposes to make intensive use of marine areas" (I am now paraphrasing from the North Sea paper).

I may avail myself of this opportunity to state that the Venezuelan legislature has sanctioned a law on territorial re-organization which empowers the executive to define coastal and other ecological zones with a view of providing them with adequate management. Yet -- as correctly mentioned in the "enigma" paper -- law and management remain substantially sub-optimal solutions to the contemporary characteristics of the first two elements, the resource and its use. The legal framework has not yet generated enough power as to overcome the resistance of well-entrenched economic and local groups, which means that the political will has yet to be marshalled.

With regard to sea management and marine scientific research, President Lusinchi signed a decree last June by virtue of which the National Commission for Oceanology was established. Its main task as a consultative organ would be to coordinate research and narrow the gap between the scientific and productive sectors in the development of marine and coastal resources. The Greater Caribbean Anti-pollution Convention (Cartegena 1983) has just been ratified.

If any final conclusion from the three main papers and the Venezuelan experience be required, I should like to single out the point that coastal zone management and sea management, precisely because of the enigma that shrouds their nature and interrelationship, demand a very careful double approach: sea management -- insofar as applied to regional seas and not necessarily to the inconclusive marine portion of an already-defined coastal zone -- follows the law of the sea from the international community to the coastal state along the afferent conduit of international law; coastal zone management starts at the national legal order and projects itself to the adjacent maritime space through efferent conduits of comparative law and international communication. The former is a lesson to be learnt from the "enigma" paper, the latter is a message of the North Sea paper. It is here that the Indonesian paper, doubling as a voice from the Third World, introduces the dilemma of archipelagoes in its full literal sense: a principal sea whose marine identity is submitted to the plurality of the surrounding insular land. This is exactly where the enigma appears and disappears, for as a frontier between land and sea, it is both and none at the same time. A frontier is intrinsically hybrid and destined to be a constant enigma.

DISCUSSION AND QUESTIONS

Alastair Couper: We've explored several intellectual concepts in this evolving field of sea use management which has been stimulated by the 1982 Convention. Questions or comments?

Kazuo Sumi: I think there is no need to discuss the concept of coastal zone management. The nucleus of the concept is comprehensiveness and integration. The next problems are how to define the special target area, how to formulate a management strategy or a management plan, and how to establish a management authority. So far, the most successful case is the San Francisco Bay Plan, which was created by the San Francisco Conservation Development Commission.

Mr. Peet, what kind of management authority are you thinking of in the North Sea? Are you considering the creation of a new single comprehensive Commission at the international level? What kind of regulatory powers would such a commission have?

We are now making efforts in Japan. We have some precedent in Kagoshima Bay, Omura Bay, and Lake Hamana. But in the case of Tokyo Bay, it is very difficult because there are three main prefectures: Tokyo Metropolis, Kanagawa Prefecture, and Chiba Prefecture. It is very difficult to accommodate and achieve cooperation among local government bodies. There is great fragmentation also among central government agencies such as the Transportation Ministry, Environmental Agency or commercial agencies, so it is very difficult to obtain integration in Japan. This is why the North Sea case is particularly interesting to me.

Gerard Peet: I do not precisely know what kind of management authority there should be for the North Sea. I do not think that there should be a completely new management authority; they should try to combine existing bodies such as the secretariats from various conventions. There should also be the cooperation with the International Maritime Organization, which is doing a lot of very important work for the North Sea. It is a question that needs to be answered: in the future, what kind of management authority is necessary? Maybe the Commission of the European Community could answer it if they finally decide to follow up on an adopted resolution of their own Parliament. The management authority described in my paper is the institutional part; there should possibly also be a political management authority for the North Sea, but I think here as well it might come into existence if the international Conferences on the Protection of the North Sea get more follow-ups.

PART VI:

VESSEL TRAFFIC MANAGEMENT SYSTEMS:
THE FUTURE OF REGULATED NAVIGATION

INTRODUCTION

Edgar Gold
Professor of Law and Director
Dalhousie Ocean Studies Programme[*]
Dalhousie University

This session is concerned with navigation. At the Twelfth Law of the Sea Institute Conference, in the Hague in 1978, shipping and navigation were considered to be one of the neglected areas of the Third Conference on the Law of the Sea. Shipping transit has almost imperceptibly moved into a much more regulated era, and the new law of the sea is providing the legislative "umbrella" under which these changes are occurring. Those directly affecting ships' passage are related to systems which manage, control, route or generally service vessel traffic. These expressions are used interchangeably. This is the issue we intend to address. Douglas Johnston and I presented a paper entitled "Ship-Generated Marine Pollution: the Creator of Regulated Navigation" at LSI XIII in Mexico in 1979 where we discussed how, under the IMO's principle of "clean seas and safe ships", the movement of vessels, particularly in coastal areas, was being subjected to new controls -- some almost akin to air traffic control. It therefore seems timely, in 1985 in Cardiff, at an LSI meeting hosted and co-sponsored by one of the world's principal marine policy and shipping teaching and research centers, to examine this important issue a little further. We have truly an interdisciplinary panel consisting of three lawyers, three master mariners, a shipping transportation economist, a senior UN civil servant, and a representative of the nautical profession!

Dr. Thomas Mensah, the Assistant Secretary-General and Director of Legal Affairs of the IMO, will speak about the IMO's role as the competent international organization in the field of shipping as designated by the Law of the Sea Convention and, more specifically, on the IMO's interest in vessel traffic services and vessel routing.

Professor Richard Goss of the Department of Maritime Studies at UWIST will inject a note of economic realism into the debate by examining the costs versus the benefits of some of these new safety systems. Maritime safety has a significant cost factor which, in an industry facing its worst-ever depression, cannot be ignored. Even if some believe that clean seas and safe ships cannot be discussed in economic terms, it must at least be considered where the costs involved will finally fall. His very extensive paper is co-authored by Ms. Joyce Halliday, of the same department.

Mr. Julian Parker, the Secretary of the Nautical Institute, will remind us that we must not ignore the human factor when considering the viability of greater ship regulation under the new law of the sea. Both on board ships, ashore and, in traffic stations, a new generation of mariners and vessel traffic controllers will require training and expertise not yet universally available. This is of particular concern for developing countries which must keep pace with the requirements of the new systems.

Professor Cadwallader, a professor of maritime law at UWIST, will comment on the legal problems which some of the new vessel traffic regulatory systems will generate. Considering the very high potential of environmental property and personal loss and damage in shipping, particularly relating to liability for negligence, these problems cannot be ignored.

I will now outline the subject a little more specifically and relate it, where appropriate, to the new Law of the Sea Convention.

* now at the International Institute for Transportation & Ocean Policy Studies.

MARINE HAZARDS AND CASUALTIES: THE NEED FOR VESSEL TRAFFIC MANAGEMENT

Edgar Gold
Professor of Law and Director
Dalhousie Ocean Studies Programme*
Dalhousie University

Looking at the future of regulated navigation in which vessel traffic management would play a crucial role, the question arises: "Why is there this need to manage?" It is, unfortunately, in direct response to maritime casualty statistics, which continue to cause concern, not only to all within the shipping world, but also, in particular, to coastal states which, whilst recognizing the benefits of shipping, also regard it as a maritime hazard and a polluting industry.

There is some type of maritime accident involving property damage or injury and loss of life, or environmental damage, or a combination of all, about once an hour somewhere in the world. Serious maritime accidents occur at least four times per day and, in areas of heavy traffic concentration or congestion, such as major straits or approaches to busy ports, accidents are daily occurrences. All this, despite advances in ship technology which have resulted in better ship construction and equipment standards, new navigation electronics, and collision avoidance systems; despite generally strengthened and toughened flag and port state controls; and despite the IMO's efforts, which have developed a whole new generation of maritime safety conventions. At the same time, although there is a general world-wide shipping slump, ships are larger, often faster, and traffic is more concentrated on specific routes for the sake of fuel conservation. Polluting, dangerous, hazardous, and noxious cargoes are carried in greater concentration and variety, as pointed out by Mr. Srivastava in his address, and major spectacular accidents over the years such as the *Torrey Canyon*, the *AMOCO Cadiz*, the *Atlantic Empress*, the *Venpet/Venoil*, and other collisions and groundings, have occurred with dismal regularity.

The damage and loss statistics in the maritime sector would be totally unacceptable in other transport modes and stricter control of navigation was thus an inevitable result. Regulated navigation is a response to the fact that at least 90 percent of all maritime accidents are human-error related. The response to these problems has taken the form of various types of vessel traffic services which have removed some of the traditional autonomy from those in charge of the ship.

In the history of navigation, the subject of vessel traffic services is a comparative newcomer. Nevertheless, it is generating interest, controversy, and discussion analogous almost to the change from sail to steam or the advent of radar at sea. Most of this debate has taken place within the industry itself, *i.e.*, amongst the nautical profession, shipping companies, and governmental marine regulatory agencies. This has resulted in the deservedly technical emphasis on the subject which, after all, is primarily concerned with marine safety. Legal questions have so far been sidelined or reduced to background interest. Legal problems relating to accident liability have been rarely discussed, and when they were, have often been distorted. A discernible realignment of international maritime responsibility has not only taken place in recent years, but this realignment will also provide the background against which vessel traffic services and most other navigational aspects will now have to be established.

479

Within the modern context of navigation, the right of transit for vessels must now be balanced against a complex number of international, economic and ecological considerations. No longer will navigation be the prime ocean use before which all other interests must yield. Rather, navigation will be one of a number of competing ocean uses in the complex marine world. There is no doubt that preservation of the marine environment has become a prime and common interest leading directly and intimately to this new era of regulated navigation.

There is now a newly established international legal right for coastal states to take certain actions under the Law of the Sea Convention. There will be an increasing variety of coastal state initiatives which are designed to prevent or reduce ship-generated marine pollution. The regulation and control of international navigation in coastal waters, as well as in certain parts of the high seas, will thus provide a very significant change in the traditional rules of the international law of the sea. However, it is conceded that, against a history of basically unregulated navigation, the changes forecast here are at a very early stage. If we compare the changes with those in the history of aviation, it will probably be analogous to those existing during the days of early and unregulated flight in the 1920's. Nevertheless, there is a very clear trend towards ocean regulation and it can be predicted that fuller control of vessel traffic in many parts of the sea will, within the next two or three decades, be as commonplace as control of aircraft in the skies. Yet the navigational systems will have to be very different. The various systems comprising vessel traffic services will certainly continue to form the practical route to the regulation of navigation. Therefore, if concern for protecting the environment provided the catalyst, then vessel traffic services will form the means to move navigation into this new era.

As already indicated, the Law of the Sea Convention provides the international legal umbrella beneath which a variety of new regulatory measures relating to the control of navigation can now be established. These new terms of reference are both direct as well as implied. Article 192 of the Convention places a heavy responsibility on all states to protect the marine environment. Article 194 is somewhat more specific about the measures taken to protect the marine environment. It provides, for example, that such measures shall be designed to minimize: "pollution from vessels, in particular measures for preventing accidents and dealing with emergencies, ensuring the safety of operations at sea, preventing intentional and unintentional discharges, and regulating the design, construction, equipment operation, and manning of vessels." Mr. Srivastava has already told us that this article is, in his opinion, one of the most important ones in the Convention on shipping. It would appear that the Article 194 definition of measures could include a number of vessel traffic systems requirements involving training and necessary equipment. However, in the Convention's very difficult Article 211, dealing with pollution from vessels, the power of states to implement these measures is somewhat narrowed.

In the Convention section on innocent passage in the territorial sea, such passage is considered to be "innocent" so long as it is not "prejudicial to the peace, good order, and security of the coastal State." Any activity not having a direct bearing on passage is considered to be prejudicial to the peace, good order, or security of this coastal state!

Under Article 21 the coastal state may make laws and regulations relating to innocent passage concerning the "safety of navigation and the regulation of maritime traffic," as well as relating to the protection of the marine environment. In Article 22, new rules relating to sea lanes and traffic separation schemes are laid out, which give coastal states the right to require vessels to comply with such rules after due consultation with the "competent international organization." It follows that non-compliance with regulations set out under Articles 21 and 22 could well be interpreted to be non-innocent passage and result in proceedings under Article 27. This article gives coastal states criminal jurisdiction over foreign vessels for crimes which "disturb ... the good order of the territorial sea."

Although Article 26 of the Convention specifically prohibits the levying of passage charges on foreign vessels in the territorial sea, charges are nevertheless permitted for specific services rendered to vessels, and it would seem that vessel traffic services could well be so chargeable on a "user pays" principle.

The Convention also mentions sea lanes and traffic separation schemes in the section dealing with navigation in international straits. Under Article 41, states bordering such straits are given the power to establish such schemes after consulting the "competent international organization" as well as other states bordering the strait. The article also requires ships to respect established schemes. Article 43 empowers strait states to make laws and regulations relating to the safety of navigation and regulation of maritime traffic similarly to coastal states in the territorial sea. Strait states are required by the Convention to cooperate by agreement "in the establishment and maintenance in a strait of necessary navigational and safety aids or other improvements in aid of international navigation." Many of these have already been established in a number of important international straits.

In the Exclusive Economic Zone (EEZ) the coastal state's competence relating to navigation regulation is more limited. This is due to the fact that in the EEZ, navigation matters are considered to be more closely related to the high seas than to the territorial sea or straits. Nevertheless, under Article 56, the coastal state has jurisdiction over the establishment and use of artificial islands, installations and structures and, as always, over the protection and preservation of the marine environment. The coastal state may establish "reasonable safety zones around such artificial islands, installations and structures in which it may take appropriate measures to ensure the safety both of navigation and of the artificial islands, installations, and structures." This is already taking place in a number of offshore development areas but, unfortunately, there have also been a number of serious maritime accidents involving collisions between vessels and such structures.

It is, therefore, apparent that the Convention provides a very ample "umbrella" for the establishment for vessel traffic and other safety systems in the territorial sea, archipelagic waters, and international straits, as well as, to a more limited extent, in the international seabed area of the high seas, the EEZ and in its ice-covered areas. Furthermore, the Convention's strict legal requirements to protect the marine environment could be seen to imply that in areas where vessel traffic services would aid the safety of navigation, the lack of such systems may well be a breach of the Convention.

It may now be timely to consider changes and new developments in international navigation brought about by these systems which may well catalyze further needed revisions. Shipping is facing increasing regulation on safety, transit and access, environmental protection, manning and training, commercial and technical matters, and many other aspects at the national, regional, and international level with jurisdiction coming from flag, port and coastal states. Yet at a time when maritime transport faces this difficult challenge it is probably less prepared than it ever was. During the many sessions of the Law of the Sea Conference, shipping played a relatively minor role -- basically reduced to being classified as a polluting industry, defensively fighting for an outdated *status quo*. Even the major maritime states, in carefully weighing their various marine interests, often placed their quickly fading shipping industries in importance below ocean resource and strategic interests.

Developments such as vessel traffic control, which squarely straddle jurisdictional, commercial, technical, legal, and political aspects of international maritime law, will expose these weaknesses. It is, therefore, necessary to consider the need for an all-embracing convention on international maritime transit and transportation which will provide, for the first time, unified legislative terms of reference for all aspects of maritime transportation ranging from access and transit to navigational safety and environmental protection. Such a convention should have as its integral part a section giving the necessary comprehensive powers needed by the IMO to carry out its future tasks.

Although we in the marine fields, particularly in shipping, tend to be very careful -- although the accident statistics do not seem to so indicate -- in using our younger transportation brother, aviation, as an example, in this case it is entirely appropriate. For forty years, aviation has already enjoyed the security of just such a convention as is advocated here. The 1944 Chicago Convention on International Civil Aviation, is a relatively simple, broadly-phrased instrument, providing aviation with an internationally accepted regulatory framework relating to general principles of aviation, overflight and transit, nationality, facilitation of navigation, safety questions, international standards, as well as other terms of reference for the International Civil Aviation Organization (ICAO). Various other aviation agreements and conventions are subordinated to the Chicago Convention. It is not suggested that a general maritime transport convention in the late 1980s will be as easy or as simple to achieve as an aviation convention in 1944. However, aviation has been able to rally broad international agreement on most matters because of its overriding concern for safety. That has not been the prime concern of the shipping industry in the past which, rightly or wrongly, placed commercial questions first. In the *post*-Law of the Sea Conference period, and considering the IMO's principle of "safe ships and clean seas," that has changed radically. There is a growing belief today that maritime safety and environmental protection are so closely related to the prime commercial purpose of shipping that they are interlinked. That also should provide sufficient incentive for an early general diplomatic conference to discuss not only a maritime transportation convention to broaden the powers of the IMO, but also, as suggested in Article 211 of the Law of the Sea Convention, the ultimate protection of the marine environment.

* now at the International Institute for Transportation & Ocean Policy Studies.

THE INTERNATIONAL REGULATION OF MARITIME TRAFFIC: IMO APPROACHES

Thomas A. Mensah*
Assistant Secretary-General
International Maritime Organization

*The views in this paper are solely those of the author and are not in any way attributable to IMO or its Secretariat.

The principal objective of IMO, as stated in its Constitution, is "to provide machinery for co-operation among Governments in the field of governmental regulation and practices relating to shipping engaged in international trade." For this purpose the Organization is enjoined "to encourage the adoption of the highest practicable standards" in a number of specific fields, i.e., maritime safety, efficiency of navigation, the prevention and control of marine pollution from ships and related administrative and legal matters.

IMO's Convention also specifies the functions which the Organization is to undertake in order to achieve its purposes. These are:

(a) to provide for the drafting of conventions, agreements or other suitable instruments and to recommend these to Governments;
(b) to convene conferences when necessary;
(c) to make regulations on matters remitted to it by Governments or other appropriate international organizations;
(d) to facilitate consultation and exchange of information among Governments;
(e) to facilitate technical cooperation.

The last function was only recently added to the list of functions, through an amendment to the IMO Convention adopted in 1977. The amendment entered into force in November 1984. However, this is in fact not a new function, but rather a formal spelling out of what was already inherent in the original functions; since effective technical cooperation is indispensable for the full realization of the goals of the Organization set out in its Convention.

The objectives of IMO and the functions set out in the Convention for the attainment thereof reflect and take account of certain basic assumptions and inescapable realities of international relations. These assumptions and realities place certain limitations on what can reasonably be expected, or feasibly be attempted, in an international organization. The limitations result in part from the nature and history of maritime activity, and the law and practice relating thereto which have developed over the centuries. But, in a more fundamental sense, they are also manifestations of a general principle of international relations -- the principle of state sovereignty to which states, large and small, have always been attached throughout history.

The functions and programs of IMO, like those of any other similar intergovernmental agency, must take due account of this cardinal fact of international life. In the field of shipping, this means that all Governments consider the regulation of shipping as an important responsibility and legitimate prerogative which they are not willing to surrender to other Governments or even to intergovernmental agencies.

However, it is also a fact that Governments appreciate and acknowledge that the effectiveness or otherwise of their measures to regulate the operation of their ships can have significant implications for other states and other users of the marine environment. For that reason, they accept that it may be necessary and appropriate for other states to exercise some regulatory powers over foreign ships in certain well-defined cases. It is also agreed by Governments that regulation of shipping, whether by flag states or by other states, is likely to be better if it is done through cooperation between the Governments concerned, and on the basis of uniform standards accepted by all concerned as appropriate and necessary.

The need for cooperation and uniform standards is now even more accepted because most Governments recognize that activities in the marine environment, undertaken by or under the authority of one state, can have significant effects on the vital interests of other states, including their ability to carry out their own legitimate activities in the environment as well as their enjoyment of certain amenities and facilities related to the seas and oceans. Furthermore, there is now a generally accepted view that the international community as a whole -- and indeed future generations -- have a legitimate interest in the preservation of the marine environment and, consequently, in the regulation of activities conducted in that environment.

The founding fathers of IMO, and the drafters of its Constitution, had these considerations in mind when they established the parameters of IMO's powers and responsibilities in the Convention of the Organization. It is in deference to these assumptions that IMO has, in the more than a quarter century of its existence, operated principally as a machinery for promoting effective cooperation between Governments in regulating shipping and related maritime activity; and has not attempted or pretended to act as an executive supra-national body with the power and authority over states or even over individual operators. In spite of the criticism which has sometimes been levelled, in academic treatises and in journalistic writings, at IMO's "lack of teeth" and regardless of several proposals put forward for making IMO "more effective," the fact remains that no Government Member of IMO has indicated any willingness to concede to IMO the kind of "independent authority" whose absence has been decried, or to endow the Organization with the competence or means to take enforcement action against Member Governments or shipping concerns. It is worth mentioning, in this context, that hardly any Governments have been willing to endow any global agency or body with such enforcement powers in any field of international relations. Thus, IMO's much criticized "lack of teeth" is a feature which is common to all the agencies of the United Nations system and to other intergovernmental bodies outside the United Nations. It is therefore reasonable to assume that IMO will, for the immediate foreseeable future, remain what it is today: a body whose basic function is to provide for the development of standards and regulations which must, ultimately, depend on governmental action for their effective implementation and enforcement.

IMO's work is predicated on the principle that it is the prerogative of states to regulate international shipping. Accordingly, the measures required for the protection of state or private interests and for safeguarding "common" amenities and facilities must ultimately depend on the willingness, readiness and ability of the states concerned to take the measures needed. This is particularly the case in the field of maritime traffic regulation.

Maritime traffic regulation has many purposes, and different states may be interested in some but not necessarily all of these purposes. Among the basic objectives of maritime traffic regulation are the following:

1. the promotion of safety of lives, that is to say the lives of the crew and, where applicable, passengers on board the ships, and also on other ships or vessels, or in port or in the neighborhood of ports;
2. the preservation of the ship itself which may represent for the owner a valuable economic asset;
3. the protection of the cargo and the interests therein of the sellers or buyers, the shipowners and other parties, including states;
4. the improvement of the efficiency of the transportation process on which the commercial health of the parties and the development plans of states may depend;
5. the avoidance of undue constraints on and impediments to other legitimate uses of the seas;
6. the prevention of pollution from ship-borne or ship-generated substances, whether through accidents or careless operations.

Different states give greater attention to some of these objectives, to the exclusion or diminution of others, depending on their interests. For the same reasons the objectives which may be emphasized by one state and the measures taken by it as a result may pose problems for those other states. Because of this, there is general agreement that, to be both effective and fair to all interested parties, regulation of maritime traffic must be undertaken by reference to well-considered and generally-acceptable standards and procedures which can be applied uniformly by all states without fear either of compromising their legitimate objectives or placing others at unjustifiable disadvantage. It is also agreed that such uniform standards must meet certain general criteria. In the first place, international standards and regulations should be such that they enable and obligate all ships to observe certain basic requirements of safety, regardless of where, or under whose authority, such ships may operate. This is essential, because in shipping, safety is not easily divisible and pollution of the sea does not recognize or respect geographical or political boundaries. In the second place, international standards must be capable of uniform application in order to avoid unfair operational and commercial advantage or disadvantage which would result if states are able or permitted to apply different rules and impose varying requirements on ships by reference to arbitrary or discriminatory criteria.

IMO's major contribution to the regulation of international maritime traffic, therefore, consists in the establishment of the rules, regulations, standards, procedures and practices which are essential for safe and efficient shipping and pollution prevention, which meet the requirements of general acceptability because they permit Governments to undertake the measures needed by them in their respective circumstances without placing unnecessary constraints on shipping or inequitable advantages on some states or operators. The establishment of these standards is an essential prerequisite to any meaningful regulation on an international scale. But the implementation of the standards is a matter for states. States are expected -- in some cases required and in others recommended -- to take the necessary measures, in accordance with their laws and circumstances, to implement the standards and to require their ships to observe the standards. In doing so, states exercise their sovereign power and utilize the legal, administrative and economic powers available to them in their constitutional and political systems. These powers and procedures vary from state to state and the machinery for their application may, consequently, differ.

IMO also recognizes that an important ingredient to the success of any regulatory regime -- whether it be national or international -- is acceptance of the necessity and appropriateness of the regulations and standards being enforced or implemented. For it must not be forgotten that shipping is primarily and essentially a commercial activity whose success is of immense economic significance both to the owners or operators of the ships and to Governments. It is no doubt essential that any regulations or requirements adopted by international bodies or enforced by Governments should not be less than what is necessary to achieve the fundamental objective of promoting safety and the prevention of pollution. But it is equally important that such rules should not be or appear to be incompatible with the efficient and economic conduct of the business they seek to regulate. The standards must therefore be such that they satisfy both the need for technical effectiveness as well as the requirement for commercial and technical feasibility. Rules and regulations which go beyond the genuine requirements of safety could make the operation of ships unrewarding for responsible operators. Where responsible operators leave, there is always the possibility that not so responsible operators will be tempted to move in, and attempt to operate outside the rules, in hope of making as much profit as possible before the law catches up with them. This could result in less safety and less protection of the environment. A similar result would occur if the international rules are so unbalanced as not to be accepted universally. If the standards are accepted and applied by some states but not by others, there is the reasonable possibility that operators will be lured to operate in states which apply lower standards or apply the international standards with a lesser degree of diligence. This would tend to lower rather than raise standards. It is, therefore, vital for maximum safety that the international rules be sufficiently high to meet all the reasonable and justifiable requirements for safety while meeting the unavoidable demands for technical and economic viability. In sum, the international rules and standards for traffic regulation must be technically feasible, politically acceptable and economically viable.

Guided by these considerations, the International Maritime Organization has approached the task of promoting international cooperation for the regulation of maritime traffic in a pragmatic and systematic way, through a coordinated set of measures and programs which deal with the various aspects both individually and in relation to each other. The main features of the measures and programs adopted by IMO in this respect are:

(a) the development of international standards through the adoption of international treaty instruments, or non-treaty recommendations, which Governments and operators are expected to implement and enforce in respect of activities undertaken under their authority or within their jurisdiction;

(b) uniform procedures and standards to ensure that the required measures will be undertaken by operators or Governments, on a uniform and non-discriminatory basis;

(c) a credible arrangement to ensure to operators and Governments that ships meeting these standards will be able to operate throughout the world without undue interference; and

(d) an effective system for assisting Governments, where necessary, to take the measures needed to contribute to the implementation and enforcement of the international regulations, both in relation to their own ships and also in relation to other ships within their jurisdiction.

The major standards and regulations adopted in IMO in this context include the Convention on Safety of Life at Sea (SOLAS 74/78), the International Regulations for the Prevention of Collisions at Sea, 1972, the Convention for the Prevention of Marine Pollution from Ships (MARPOL 73/78) and the Convention on Training, Certification and Watchkeeping of Seafarers, 1978. These formal treaty instruments are supplemented by a large number of recommended standards, Codes and guidelines. Among these are traffic separation schemes and routing systems; technical standards for ship-borne navigational equipment, such as radar equipment, automatic pilots and other navigational aids; radio telephony and telegraphy installations; maritime distress and safety systems; and many others.

The means for ensuring that the relevant operators and Governments will implement and enforce the applicable regulations and standards include the treaty provisions requiring or empowering states to enforce these standards in appropriate cases. These are supplemented in many cases by specific recommendations and guidelines developed in IMO to facilitate action by the states concerned. Among these, the procedures for the control of ships in ports deserve special mention, since they provide an important additional incentive to operators to avoid contravention of the standards and regulations, even when their ships are outside the areas of jurisdiction of their flag states.

Another important mechanism for promoting effective implementation and enforcement of the international standards developed in IMO is the Organization's technical cooperation program. Under this program advice and assistance are provided to Governments, particularly of developing countries, to enable them to develop and improve the technical, legal and administrative infrastructure necessary for establishing and operating an effective regulatory regime for maritime transport.

The advisory services provided by IMO's consultants and experts, and by the Secretariat staff where necessary, have already enabled many Governments to establish and enhance their maritime administrations, including the inspection of ships and the examination and certification of ship-borne personnel in order to improve safety on their ships and the requisite action in respect of foreign ships visiting their ports. Governments are also advised and helped in the enactment of appropriate maritime legislation and the promulgation of supplementary technical and administrative regulations, as well as the development of suitable schemes for the training of the requisite personnel for both ship-board functions, other high-level on-shore functions and in their administrations.

The role of IMO in the regulation of maritime traffic, and the various approaches it has so far used to discharge its constitutional mandate, have been recognized and, in some cases, expressly underpinned by many provisions of the 1982 Convention on the Law of the Sea. Specifically, the regulatory and standard-setting activities of IMO in the promotion of maritime safety, efficiency of navigation and the prevention, reduction and control of marine pollution from vessels have been recognized, and IMO is expected or required to maintain and supplement these activities within the framework of the new Convention. In particular, various provisions of the Convention:

(1) require states, through IMO, to adopt necessary rules and regulations and to revise and up-date existing ones;

(2) require or expect IMO to establish uniform standards and procedures to guide states in the exercise of their powers to regulate activities in the marine environment;

(3) urge IMO to establish equity and uniformity in state practice in areas where such uniformity is necessary to safeguard the rights of states under the Convention;

(4) call upon IMO to join in providing advice, assistance and other forms of cooperation to states in order to enhance their capabilities to implement the relevant provisions of the Convention.

In sum, therefore, IMO's role in the regulation of maritime traffic is to enable Governments to cooperate in establishing the highest practicable standards for the regulation of traffic in all contexts; to promote uniformity in the content and application of state measures; and to assist states which need assistance in developing and implementing the requisite measures. But, at the end of the day, the measures which are taken to implement these standards are, and must remain, those of the individual states. IMO is not the regulator of international maritime traffic but an indispensable mechanism for any effective regulation. This is not a limitation on IMO's role: it is a recognition of what the Organization was established to do.

There is considerable evidence that the arrangements and procedures developed in IMO have contributed immensely to improve safety and efficiency in shipping operations worldwide. The work methods and orientation of the Organization require -- and operate on the basis that -- these procedures will be continually reviewed and up-dated to take account of developing needs and changed circumstances. The Convention on the Law of the Sea presents a major change in the situation and IMO has already indicated that it is ready, willing and able to adapt its standards and its procedures to accommodate the new requirements, should this be necessary.

By providing the international community with technically sound and well-considered standards, by establishing acceptable and credible procedures and arrangements to ensure fairness and effectiveness in state regulation on a global basis, and by making pragmatic efforts to assist all states to understand what is expected of them and to be in a position to take the necessary and appropriate measures, IMO plays an indispensable role in promoting the most effective regulation of maritime traffic. It is true that the current regulations and standards of IMO do not specifically require states to institute elaborate Vessel Traffic Management Systems, certainly not on the scale or scope employed in the regulation of aeronautical traffic. It is also the case that very few Governments have indicated the wish or demonstrated the ability to establish such systems. This may be due to essential and fundamental differences between maritime traffic and air transportation; and it may well be that what has worked so well in air-traffic control could not be applied to maritime traffic -- or could only be applied with important modifications. However that may be, there is no doubt that some form of traffic management will be needed and helpful in the near future to make the regulation and control of maritime traffic more effective.

If and when the need and feasibility of such management systems become accepted, IMO will surely be ready and capable of contributing to making them more relevant and more useful. There is nothing in the Organization's Constitution or work method which would make it impossible or inappropriate for IMO to incorporate such systems into its regulatory apparatus. The history of IMO demonstrates clearly that it has the ability and the will to respond to such new developments and needs with expertise and imagination.

THE COSTS AND BENEFITS OF
NAVIGATIONAL SAFETY

R.O. Goss and J.E. Halliday
Department of Maritime Studies
University of Wales Institute of Science and Technology

Introduction

It is a characteristic of maritime casualties -- as of many other forms of accident -- that they often affect a number of parties besides the owners of property (usually a ship) which may be held responsible. Thus, seamen may be killed or injured; holiday-makers' beaches may be fouled by oil, or people's enjoyment of the environment may be spoilt in other ways; and the owners of other property (*e.g.*, ships, or port facilities) may suffer. All of these effects are outside the financial accounts of the person responsible for the casualty and economists therefore term them *externalities*.[1]

These externalities may often be significant; and insurance and other forms of compensation may not always be forthcoming, or fail to provide adequate compensation (*e.g.*, to a drowned sailor or to his dependents). It follows that to rely solely upon the self-interest of ship operators and their shareholders is unlikely, on the whole, to lead to a level of marine safety which adequately reflects the interests of all parties.[2] In practice, most marine casualties attract little public attention, so the usual result of one that is particularly noteworthy is a public scandal and much -- albeit temporary -- political activity. Examples include the *Titanic* (when it was found that there were no rules providing that there should be lifeboat places for all on board and that, accordingly, there were not enough) and more recent instances like the *Torrey Canyon*, the *Amoco Cadiz*, the *Argo Merchant* and the *Christos Bitos*, in some of which creative navigation was added to other faults in ship operation, maintenance or specification. In none of these instances could it be said that reliance upon "the self-interest and emulation of the traders" had proved sufficient, even in combination with the then current rules. The result of such scandals is widespread agreement that *something should be done*. But what?

In principle, there are three solutions to this problem. The first is to arrange for *internalizing the externalities*, *e.g.*, by insisting that the ship operator take out sufficient life and other third party insurance to enable him to compensate crew, passengers and the other interested parties. A perfect insurance market, so the argument runs, will so discriminate between ship operators with different levels of risk as to encourage an appropriate degree of safety. But practical difficulties abound, *e.g.*, in enforcement, in the competitive positions of different flags in the actual, as distinct from the perfect, behavior of the market in marine insurance. Such difficulties are, however, easy to exaggerate and, given the current political climate in Britain and some other countries, it may be thought surprising that there has been so little public discussion of extending this approach, possibly at the expense of the second.

The second approach is, of course, *regulation*; and this is the method which -- *pace* Messrs. Gray and Farrar (see footnote 2) -- has been generally adopted, *e.g.*, through the various conventions of the IMO. It has many advantages but does not take into account the differing positions, costs and practices of ship operators; nor does it rest upon any explicit calculations of the advantages and disadvantages of the measures which are adopted. The decisions, as is frequently said, are "all a matter of judgement"; unfortunately, however, the ability to make such judgements correctly is rare.

Such explicit calculations are the subject matter of the third approach, termed *cost-benefit analysis*. Briefly, CBA aims at *reducing the area in which judgement has to operate in decision-making* by:

(a) *identifying and specifying* the relevant factors (gains and losses) for all the parties affected;
(b) *quantifying* them in physical terms; and
(c) *evaluating* them in economic terms, *i.e.*, by applying the only available common measure of value;

so that the net overall effect may be calculated.

Where, as with investment projects like the dredging of port approach channels, there are significant differences in the timing of costs and benefits, they may be reduced to a common base year by discounting to a net present value (NPV); the process is exactly the same as for the more familiar discounted cash flow calculations. Such an NPV then reflects all identified components of the calculation, including their timing, and may be compared directly with the NPVs of other proposals or of the "do nothing" position. Since all represent sums of money, one selects the biggest; provided that it has a positive sign attached.

Uncertainties, including those of quantification and evaluation, may be explored by sensitivity analysis to determine their significance; often it will be found that the uncertainties in some components may then be ignored; we give some examples of this later in the paper. Those factors which have not been adequately quantified or evaluated may be listed, together with some -- necessarily -- qualitative comments. Given the difficulties and uncertainties inherent in the work, it may be stressed that the object is to *assist* the decision-maker (*e.g.*, the President, the Minister, the Governor, the Mayor or whoever is responsible); *not to take over his job.* It follows that CBA cannot reasonably be expected always to provide unequivocal indications of what should be done.

Outside the U.S., where the Army Corps of Engineers has a long history of evaluating various navigation, flood control and hydro-electric schemes (often in combination with one another),[3] there has been little systematic use of CBA in the maritime field, even though it has become standard practice in several other modes of transport.[4] It is not surprising, therefore, that its absence has sometimes been deplored.[5]

The Department of Maritime Studies at UWIST was therefore glad to have the opportunity to become involved with the EEC and the Marine Directorate of the Department of Transport in London, through the City of London Polytechnic, in an international study concerned with the effects of a variety of Vessel Traffic Management Schemes (VTS) in and around European waters. The study is known by its EEC reference as "COST 301." We began an 18-month program of work in October 1984.

There are many parts to this study and they are being carried on in several different countries. It has, therefore, proved necessary to establish a management center in Brussels to coordinate matters and a number of Working Groups comprising those concerned with the different parts, so that they may work effectively together. As usual when working with bureaucracies, there is a great deal of paper and it is sometimes difficult to convince them that an essential component of research is that one does not know the answer in advance. Worse, one may not be sure that any useful result will be obtained.

This paper therefore represents both a discussion of the general subject of applying CBA to navigational safety and an unofficial progress report on work in this particular field. An earlier and more general outline was presented, in December 1984, to a seminar organized jointly by the Royal Institute of Navigation and the Nautical Institute.[6]

Cost 301: An Outline
The study as a whole aims to:

recommend shore-based aids to navigation which will reduce the potential danger of navigation to human life, the environment, ships and cargoes.[7]

More specifically, it has been suggested that the program be directed at three distinct targets: safety of navigation, traffic efficiency and pollution risk.[8] The first of these is essentially an expression of how marine casualties may be expected to change with the form and location of the shore-based aids (e.g., VTS) in question. The second concerns the change in efficiency, or net speed, with which marine traffic flows through a given area in response to the same changes in the navigational environment. The third refers to the change in the level of risk to which the marine and coastal environment is exposed. Obviously, as far as any given VTS is concerned, some of these may be negative and some positive, besides items which may be negative (such as the cost of establishing and running the VTS itself) and positive (such as reducing the losses of life and property). Again, different VTS proposals will have different effects, possibly in direction as well as in size, upon these components; and this is but one reason why the work of COST 301 is not straightforward. De Bievre[9] has, indeed, identified just this combination of factors as calling for extreme caution by decision-makers in this field.

Cost-Benefit Analysis in Cost 301
Professor John Kemp at the City of London Polytechnic and Dr. Elizabeth Goodwin at the Polytechnic of North London are responsible for calculating the casualty risks associated with particular areas in European waters by means of a "problem area identifier" which reflects a number of environmental and marine traffic parameters. Following on from this, our function at UWIST is to try to ensure that a suitable framework for CBA is developed, capable of application to these areas. Given the development of studies in other transport modes, there has been much work upon which to draw; but, given the paucity of published works in the maritime field, the work has called for careful methodological development, besides extensive borrowing. Whilst, as academic researchers, we are not bound to follow the practices of the Department of Transport, we need to be aware of the differences and to argue them carefully, for there is general agreement on economic principles.[10]

Thus, the costs to be considered are not accounting costs but social opportunity costs. For example, if a VTS authority occupies land which it bought some years ago, in principle we should use the value of that land, in its best alternative use, today; we should not use the price paid some years ago.

Again, the damage to a fishery caused by an oil spill cannot be the loss of the gross value of the catch over the period until the fishery recovers; for, if the boats do not fish, neither do they use fuel nor wear out their nets. It is thus their *net* rather than their gross output (*i.e.*, the value of the catch minus the escapable expenses) that is needed to calculate the loss; and even that assumes that both fishermen and boats spend the whole time standing idle instead of moving to some other fishing ground or activity.

Similar difficulties may ensue when considering the effects of fouled beaches on tourism. The holiday-makers may go elsewhere, though presumably to a less-preferred location or form of holiday. To this loss of *consumers' surplus*[11] should be added the losses of *producers' surplus*[12] for the hoteliers and others serving the holiday trade in the locality. In this context it is helpful to distinguish between the hotels and similar fixed facilities and the staff, some of whom may be highly mobile. Again, the social cost of a fouled beach must be less than the gross cost of trade; for if guests do not come, neither do they have to be fed.

Yet again, the effects on ship patterns of instituting a VTS -- whether to speed their flow or cause delays -- may be represented by the loss or gain of output, not of the costs of achieving it. Since, for ships in commission, many costs are commonly reckoned to be time-related (crew, insurance, repairs as well as capital charges: but certainly not fuel or the costs of handling cargo) these may be counted, but at their long-run opportunity costs, which may or may not resemble their current money costs.

Thus, for example, it is well-known that current shipping freight rates are low because there are too many ships for the business. More-over, following changes in fuel prices and in the pattern of trade, some of the ships are no longer appropriate in design, speed or engine type; turbine ULCCs are an example where both factors are combined. It is not, therefore, the current level of profitability in shipping that is relevant -- nor would this be so if shipping were prosperous. For, it may be argued, if ships are delayed or accelerated, and this is associated with some long-term factor like a VTS, the world will -- to some extent -- need a different size of fleet. It follows that a different amount of capital will be available for investment in other ends, so it is the social opportunity cost of capital that matters. The past, present and prospective rates of return on capital in shipping are all irrelevant, even if we had sufficient information on them, which we do not.

This is merely one example of many possibilities where observable market prices differ from social opportunity costs; the value actually employed is often termed a *shadow price*. Another difficulty arises where we have no market price at all, *e.g.*, because there is no market.

An extreme example of this is the valuation of human life. Many people are revolted by attributing *any* value to this; such a view is equivalent to implying that the proper value is infinity. We may, how-ever, observe that neither public authorities nor people in their individual capacities act in this way. Officials from the former often sound as if every life saved were an unequivocal victory over the forces of darkness: but this is not reflected in the funds they prise out of politicians. Well-informed individuals often take finite risks of death or injury when engaging in certain occupations, in sport or even crossing the road. But it is clearly no use asking people how much money they would accept in order to accept death because they would have no way of spending it.

It is no business of the analyst to tell people what their values ought to be: rather, he should attempt to deduce the values held by society. In this context, various approaches[13] have been tried: courts' compensation awards are generally too inconsistent and tend to compensate the plaintiff rather than society as a whole; the present (*i.e.*, discounted) value of their future contributions to output (which may equal their gross earnings) is likely to be a minimal figure because most of us may be regarded as making other contributions to the welfare of our fellow-beings; and the recently-developed "willingness to accept risk for pay" approach is not yet fully accepted. The standard approach in Britain is the second of these three.

On this and other topics there is a danger in "trying to push our economic appraisal further than our real understanding would currently justify"[14] and it is probably just as well that the number of lives lost in the marine casualties likely to be prevented by a VTS are so few that they are likely to form a minor component of the calculations. Injuries, which are more common, are dealt with essentially by the sum of medical costs and lost pay. Unfortunately, however, the statistics are not nearly as good.

Progress in Applying CBA to Cost 301

Navigational Safety

It is curious that although there are important international agreements concerning the safety of life at sea, most of the harm that is caused by the marine casualties they are designed to prevent seems to concern property -- largely ships and their cargoes, lost and damaged, and the environment. Earlier work by Giziakis[15] covers much of this and will be updated for our purposes. The standard approach is to employ current insurance rather than book values, since these are more likely to reflect the market value of the property -- though without the extreme fluctuations sometimes observed in the market for second-hand ships. Obviously, types of ships and cargoes have to be differentiated largely along Giziakis' lines, and the values of ships and cargoes updated for inflation.

In case anyone should be inclined to rely solely upon the values of ships lost (statistics of gross, net or deadweight tonnages are not much use here), it is worth mentioning that it is very common for the cargo to be worth as much as the ship carrying it. With total losses, cargo values may be taken for bulk, general ("dry, non-bulk") and oil cargoes respectively; the appropriate one will usually be indicated by the ship type, but allowance will have to be made for ships in ballast.

It is more difficult to estimate the extent of cargo damage for ships which are partial losses, *i.e.*, merely damaged and able to continue in service after repair. The cargo may have been undamaged and could stay on board whilst the ship is repaired; though if dry-docking were necessary it might have to be removed.

If establishing a VTS leads to significantly fewer casualties, then it is likely that there will be savings of time and effort in the various forms of search and rescue (SAR) activities. Although our study is essentially Europe-wide, our limited resources make it necessary for us to concentrate on U.K. practices and institutions like the RAF helicopter rescue activities, the Royal National Lifeboat Institution (RNLI) and H.M. Coastguard as the coastwatching and coordinating body. We know that institutions and the division of responsibilities are different in other countries: but the essential activities are rather similar and so, therefore, should be the costs. To study, analyze and report upon the parallel institutions of all EEC Member States would have involved much time, effort and travel. We are not convinced that it would have provided benefits commensurate with the opportunity cost of our time.

For example, the RNLI is a registered charity whose lifeboat crews are volunteers; but we have decided to treat them as if they were being paid. This is because, they are frequently allowed time off work for their activities, so that effectively their employers are incurring the cost. This is an example of the shadow pricing referred to above. It has the advantage of providing a large measure of consistency with other countries where the full costs of life-saving services are borne by the taxpayers.

Moreover, we are impressed by our preliminary findings that the vast majority of all such SAR activities are not concerned with those commercial vessels whose safety is likely to be enhanced by a VTS: they are concerned with such other craft as fishing vessels, yachts, windsurfers, or with holiday-makers cut off by the tide; or they are concerned with casualties to commercial vessels in areas unlikely to be covered by a VTS. Thus, for example, in 1983 a maximum of 11 percent of RAF rescue helicopter activities were concerned with merchant shipping and in 1984 the equivalent figure was only 8 percent; much of these were concerned with areas unlikely to be covered by a VTS. Nor were RAF helicopter rescue services established primarily to deal with civilian needs.

Given, moreover, that many of the costs of such organizations vary little with modest changes in the levels of their activities, it follows that probable cost savings are unlikely to be significant. For example, most RNLI costs are associated with having a lifeboat on its station, not with sending it out. Given the situation described above, it seems unlikely that any VTS would lead to the withdrawal of any lifeboat.

It may be worth mentioning that this apparently simple finding is derived from quite a lot of study of RAF, RNLI and other records, (RNLI, in particular, has a most thorough computer database) besides putting to practical use the economic concepts described above. This is but one of many fields where it is necessary to think in terms of increments and decrements; averages can be quite misleading.

Traffic efficiency

As noted earlier, the second category of effects likely to stem from a VTS is that ships' movements are speeded or slowed, either in the obvious sense or through following a longer route. There is a parallel with traffic engineering on roads. A VTS, especially if accompanied by a routing system, may have positive or negative effects on distance travelled, speed over the ground and therefore on voyage time. This is important for ships and also for cargo, *e.g.*, through effects on working capital.

For the cargo the argument runs thus. Every cargo is being financed by someone. If it takes longer to arrive then he has to employ his capital for a longer time, so he cannot use it for anything else. Again, therefore, the opportunity cost of capital is the required

495

concept, for we are not interested in the financier's identity, nor in legal liabilities, if any, for delay. Nor are we interested in the interest rate he may be paying.

For the ship, some earlier work may be useful[16] since this has outlined a basic methodology consistent with the arguments presented above and again employing shadow prices related to long run costs and the opportunity cost of capital. Whilst there may be problems in obtaining the necessary cost data, these may be modest beside those of estimating the physical extent of speeding or slowing ships' movements. Fortunately these last are not the business of economists.

Pollution effects

This third category concerns the effects of marine casualties on the marine and coastal environments. Obviously oil tanker cargoes are the main concern, but other cargoes, such as flammable, toxic or radio-active substances are also relevant, as are the oil bunkers carried by most ships, usually in their double bottom tanks -- which are most vulnerable to damage in groundings. Matters may be worsened if such pollutants are combined, as in one recent casualty in the Channel. This has been termed "The Hybrid Emergency".[17] Fortunately it seems to be extremely rare.

Specification and quantification are particularly difficult here. The location, season and the types of treatment available are all important determinants of the damage likely to be done. So, too, is the nature of the ecosystem affected, and it is necessary to remember that in real life this is itself likely to be changing from both man-induced and natural causes. Fishing is an example of the first and temperature and salinity changes are examples of the second. In other words, it may be as difficult to establish a base to which changes can be related as to establish the changes themselves.

This is, nevertheless, a class of effects which has assumed increased importance in public discussion. Recent valuations have chal-lenged traditionally accepted levels of social risk. It has, for exam-ple, been suggested[18] that pollution may now be regarded by the public as more significant than the risk to life. There is thus a self-evident need to incorporate this into CBA: yet the problems of specification and quantification remain: and these are not areas of economists' expertise.

Generally, the polluting effects of a marine casualty may be divided into four main classes:

(a) Treatment needs, *e.g.*, by skimming or spraying with dispersant. (It should, however, be noted that the wave action associated with bad weather is one of the most effective treatments, both for the open sea and coastlines.)
(b) Damage to the marine and coastal environment, both biotic (*e.g.*, fish and birds) and abiotic (*e.g.*, beaches).
(c) Damage to marine and coastal uses.
(d) Damage to human health, welfare and amenity.

CBA is, however, concerned with the welfare of people and for our purposes it is more convenient to divide these effects into those affecting consumers' surplus and those with effects on producers' surplus. The first includes the loss of satisfaction from holiday-making, whether in the preferred location with fouled beaches or in a less-preferred one without them. The second (on the arguments presented earlier in this paper) includes the loss of net output from, *e.g.*, fishing and tourism.

Much existing methodology is unsatisfactory, certainly for a predictive model. To equate the value of the environmental damage of an oil spill with the cost of clearing it up is deceptively easy and has many precedents.[19] But are clean-up decisions always right? Who is to say so? And, even if they were, there is a loss of consumers' (and sometimes of producers') surplus that is excluded; yet it is these that justified the clean-up decision. Forgone (net) output will undoubtedly help, though it is not yet clear how loss of consumers' surplus is to be tackled; and there remain formidable problems of specification and quantification.

As with the valuation of life and limb this class of effect -- the damage to marine and coastal biota other than commercial species (dealt with above), damage to abiotic environment and loss of human welfare resulting from reduced aesthetic qualities -- is sometimes held to be outside the scope of formal CBA. Evaluation is generally based on observed or implied willingness-to-pay but there are many philosophical difficulties. Value judgements are often volatile[20] and information inadequate, sensationalized in presentation, or distorted by special interest groups. Moreover, many aspects of the environment are in the nature of "public goods,"[21] in that individuals may often enjoy them whether they make any contribution or not. "Willingness-to-pay" may therefore be seriously inadequate as a criterion. Data collection may also be difficult. There are, however, precedents. The value of a recreational resource for the marginal user has been taken to equal the generalized cost (*i.e.*, including the value of time) of travelling to it. Again, concern for the environment may be considered as a luxury good, increasing with wealth. This would explain the increased interest in and regulation of misuse of recent years and this may be expected to increase. However, it should also be recalled that our knowledge of how to deal with pollution incidents has increased greatly, and coastal communities involving both fishing and tourism have returned to normal after quite catastrophic accidents. Indeed, there is much evidence that the effects of oil pollution, though most unpleasant, are temporary, with many ecosystems returning largely to normal within a year.[22]

Other Effects

Apart from the economic results of the effects already considered, these seem likely to be those on other sea users, *e.g.*, fishermen and yachtsmen, who may well be affected by a VTS, *e.g.*, by being prohibited from using the area for their normal purposes. This can be significant, *e.g.*, in the German Bight, where the traffic regulation scheme covers some 900 sq. n.m., an area which, formerly, constituted some 75 percent of that fishing ground. The result was considerable restriction of fishing effort for sole off the East Frisian coast and of trawling for cod in the inner Bight.

The use of other marine resources, like the extraction of gravel, oil or gas, the use of limited marine space for waste disposal, pipelines, cables, pleasure or naval activities may also be affected; though it is unlikely that these can be considered upon any but an *ad hoc* basis. It may, however, be borne in mind that such effects will increase with the growth of VTS as well as with the growth of such activities. A parallel may be drawn with pleasure flying in many countries, where airspace is so restricted that there is nowhere that it can be done without coming under formal air traffic control.[23]

Conclusions

As noted earlier, this paper is very much an interim report on work in progress in this interesting field. We think, however, that it will be of increasing importance as problems grow and come to be dealt with upon more rational and scientific bases. We are, for example, aware of interesting work in progress in a number of other countries, *e.g.*, by the Canadian Coast Guard. Within the strict context of COST 301 much of our work will depend upon the progress made by our colleagues elsewhere in the organization and, in particular, upon their success in quantifying the physical effects specified above (*e.g.*, through the problem area identifier).

The various tasks within COST 301 are thus closely linked; but it is our hope that our contribution to this general subject will be of wider use, *e.g.*, outside the context of VTS schemes and, indeed, outside Europe.

NOTES

1. Externalities and their economic implications were first described and explored in A.C. Pigou, *The Economics of Welfare*, Macmillan, 1920. They take many forms and may appear on either the demand or cost sides. Thus, on the former, the pleasure a person derives from wearing something is not necessarily independent of what others are wearing nearby; fashion may be a factor. On the cost side, industrial pollution of many kinds would be a social cost if it were not, in many countries, prohibited.
2. This has not prevented authoritative attempts at such reliance. See, *e.g.*, T. Gray, in the prestigious *Journal of the Royal Society of Arts*, vol. 14 (1865-6), p. 239: "...there can be no doubt that government interference is not only unnecessary, but that it may really become vicious if it attempts to attain an end by official inspection and supervision that can be better attained by the development of free and healthy competition and *by the self-interest and emulation of the trader* since it fetters the development of trade, it stands in the way of science and it interferes to the prejudice of the liberty of the subject" (emphasis added). Mr. Gray was, at the time, the Board of Trade official responsible for such safety legislation as then existed and was presenting a paper which attacked it, in detail and in principle. He was no maverick, for he was supported in the subsequent discussion by his then superior, Mr. T. (later Sir Thomas) Farrar. Farrar was subsequently promoted to become Permanent Secretary (*i.e.*, the official head) of the Board of Trade. For a more recent analysis see R.O. Goss (ed.): *Advances in Maritime Economics*, UWIST, 1982.
3. Their studies grew largely from the U.S. Flood Control Act of 1936. Their quality has been much improved since they were criticized in J. Hirshleifer, J.C. De Haven and J.W. Milliman, *Water Supply: Economics, Technology and Policy*, Chicago, 1960.
4. See, *e.g.*, its application to road projects in *COBA 9*, 1981 by the Department of Transport. Many other examples include *The Cambrian Coast Line*, Ministry of Transport, 1960, for railways and *Report of the Commission on the Third London Airport* (Roskill Commission), HMSO, 1971, for aviation.

5. Cf. R. Maybourn, OBE: "Oil tanker operations; today's safety and pollution problems in perspective," the Ferguson-Jones Memorial Lecture, Cardiff, 1984, published in *Journal of the Honourable Company of Master Mariners*, vol. XVI, no. 181, 1985.
6. R.O. Goss and J.E. Halliday, *Cost-benefit analysis of shore support for safety in European waters*, Nautical Institute, 1985.
7. COST 301/PMS/034 *Preliminary project plan*, issue B/09/82, 1982.
8. COST 301 *Objectives and interim plan of work*, Sept. 1984.
9. A. de Bievre, "Navigational safety in European waters" *Journal of Navigation*, vol. 36 (2), 1983.
10. There are numbers of well-known remarks about the disputational propensities of economists, *e.g.*, "wherever 2 or 3 of them are gathered together there will be 3 or 4 opinions and that 2 of these will be Keynes'." The authors would be glad to learn why there appear to be no such standard remarks about lawyers, who seem to make their living by disputation.
11. Consumers' surplus is the gain in satisfaction which is obtained by consuming a given amount of something per unit time over the cost of obtaining it. It should not be confused with *usefulness*.
12. Producers' surplus is the gain obtained by producing a given output of something per unit time over the cost of producing it. "Cost," for this purpose, includes the opportunity cost of everything involved, including, for example, any capital goods. For this and other reasons the concept is quite different from the accountants' or lawyers' definitions of profit.
13. For a review see M.W. Jones-Lee, "Natural disasters: a comparison of alternative methods of evaluating preventive measures," *Geneva papers on risk and insurance*, vol. 9, no. 31, p. 188-205, 1984. This author has done much to advocate the "willingness to pay" approach in respect of death and injury. See, *e.g.*, M.W. Jones-Lee, M. Hammerton and P.R. Philips, "The value of safety: results of a national sample survey" *Economic Journal*, vol. 95, no. 377, March 1985.
14. R.O. Goss, "The costs and benefits of navigational aids in port approaches" in Goss (ed.), *Advances in maritime economics*, UWIST, 1982.
15. K. Giziakis, "Economic effects of marine navigational casualties" *Journal of Navigation* vol. 35 (3), 1982.
16. R.O. Goss and M.C. Mann, "The cost of ships' time," in R.O. Goss (ed.), *op. cit.*, UWIST 1982.
17. The incident involving the *Mont Louis* inspired a conference on "The hybrid emergency" organized by the Greenwich Forum in June 1985.
18. R. Maybourne, *op. cit.*, p. 114.
19. R.O. Goss, *op. cit.*, 1982.
20. See, *e.g.*, D. Fischer, "Willingness to pay as a behavioural criterion for environmental decision-making" *Journal of Environmental Management* vol. 3, pp 29-41, 1975.
21. "Public goods" are an important concept in economics; there are several kinds. The essential feature is they are unlikely to be produced sufficiently or at all by private interests on their own, because it is difficult to collect any fee for providing them, or because they are indivisible and people cannot be excluded from using them, or because people cannot refuse to use them. Classic examples, combining two or more of these, are defense, street lighting, law and -- appropriately for the present context -- lighthouses.

22. Physical and biological agencies were able "to effect the complete removal of moderate oil pollution in some places in 3-4 months" after the *Torrey Canyon* disaster. See, *e.g.*, J.E. Smith (ed.), *"Torrey Canyon", pollution and marine life*; Report by the Plymouth Laboratory of the Marine Biological Association of the U.K., CUP, 1968. The Royal Society, in *The effects of oil pollution; some research needs* (1980) at p. 62, indicate the difficulty in deciding when restoration is complete by suggesting that recovery of conspicuous shore organisms appears to be good if not complete within 1-10 years.
23. A.N. Cockroft, "Routing in the English Channel," *Journal of Navigation* vol. 34, p. 392-413, 1981.

COMMENTARY

C.J. Parker
Secretary, Nautical Institute
London

When I was asked to speak on the training of VTS operators, I believe the organizers had in mind what legal training should operators receive. This in turn may have implied that legal training would improve their performance as VTS operators, make them more positive in their actions and remove any undesirable areas of ambiguity between responsibility and liability.

To look at VTS from the legal point of view is to approach the subject from the wrong direction. After all, there is a limit to the ways that the police can control road traffic accidents. The police can take steps to enforce safer driving practices, but these do not take into account blind spots, vehicle failure, blow-outs, fatigue and so on.

There are quite a number of maritime lawyers who believe that the whole regime of international shipping practice should be changed so that VTS operators can direct ships at will. Aviation has demonstrated the effectiveness of control techniques. The partnership between pilot and traffic controllers is well established and the accident record is exemplary. For some unknown reason nobody seems to question the costs of these air traffic systems but they are astronomic. I must point out that aircraft are separated laterally fore and aft and vertically; ships operate on one plane and in narrow channels. Can you imagine an aircraft with a large cylinder flying from the tail fin as an aircraft hampered in its ability to maneuver? The legal obsession with responsibility and liability stems from the major oil-related disasters of the *Torrey Canyon*, the *Argo Merchant* and the *Amoco Cadiz*. The argument runs like this. The accidents demonstrate that ships cannot be trusted to run safely; therefore coastal states must intervene actively to prevent the same thing happening again. If the coastal state is going to control ships, then the liability for this action should go to the VTS.

This is a most important point because it polarizes attitudes towards VTS: between VTS run by port and harbor authorities who certainly do not want to take on this burdensome and costly liability, and the state-run scheme as in the U.S. and Canada where VTS operators are government employees.

It is important to consider the differences in response by those countries which suffered the above tanker casualties. The *Torrey Canyon* was a British disaster. Pollution control measures were introduced, pressure applied to form a proper compensation fund and nothing further was done about navigation and tanker safety.

When the *Argo Merchant* ran aground, the U.S. through the Coast Guard had to find an answer. Inspections were introduced, the MARPOL convention concerning construction and cleaning methods was initiated, anti-collision radars were developed and their use enforced, and VTS put on red alert.

When the *Amoco Cadiz* went aground on the French coast, the traffic separation scheme was dramatically changed off Ushant, rules were introduced to stop ships using inshore zones, and continuing emphasis is being placed on an integrated VTS system from Ushant to Cap Griz

501

Nez, paid for by the French Government -- although no doubt in the long term, a system of dues will be introduced!

The port of Bremen, on the other hand, uses a VTS to monitor traffic in a long meandering river, where it is very difficult for ships to see round the bends. The port of Rotterdam, with the interface between barge and deep sea traffic, uses VTS to harmonize traffic flow in a busy port, which has so many movements that VTS is primarily concerned with movement control rather than navigation *per se*.

In the Straits of Dover, the surveillance centers at St. Margaret's Bay and Cap Griz Nez exercise surveillance over traffic movements in international waters as vessels use the traffic separation schemes and cross. The main purpose is to impose proper traffic discipline by reporting rogues and vessels which do not cross sharply. The center effectively prevented the loaded tanker *Al Faiha* from going aground with a compass breakdown but failed to stop an unknown ship from nearly ploughing into a cable-laying barge.

Each of these VTS applications demands operators with different attributes, but the most important aspect of training VTS operators is a detailed analysis of the system -- the usual breakdown into knowledge, skills and competence followed by the development of a well thought out training program. Communications skills are vital and simulation is probably the most effective way of providing the training.

Shore Control or Ship Control?

Some observers of the VTS scene believe that shore-based operators can, through direct intervention, prevent marine accidents from happening. This is not always so, as some representative incidents will illustrate. The port of Portsmouth has a narrow entrance which is subject to strong tidal currents. The shore VTS controls the movement of ships and gives precedence to vessels entering or leaving with the current because they are less maneuverable than vessels stemming the tide. The advice was passed to a German frigate to "stop proceeding" into the narrows to let a ferry out. The German vessel stopped. In a few minutes she had drifted down onto a buoy and had severe propeller damage. She was subsequently towed into port.

At the port of Harwich, which is serviced by a VTS, the *European Gateway*, outward bound for the continent, left the channel to go north whilst the incoming *Speedlink Vanguard*, unaware that the *European Gateway* was going north, altered course to starboard and there was a catastrophic collision. The *Gateway* had told the Harwich VTS of its intention and the *Vanguard* had heard the message but did not act on it. Current shipping notices advise ships that they should avoid using VHF between them to avoid collision. The court of inquiry held that it was not the responsibility of VTS to relay the communications of one ship to another. Whether or not you agree with this ruling, the practical solution has been to physically separate incoming and outward bound vessels.

Near Vancouver the *Sundancer* sailed north bound for Juneau, Alaska. Passing through the Seymour Narrows, an error of navigation was made and she struck outlying rocks off Maud Island. The vessel had on board two pilots and well-qualified officers, and the interesting point here is whether or not VTS could have avoided the accident. I do not think so, for the principal reason that the shore-based radar would not necessarily have picked up the drift and would have found it very difficult to give advice to the ship on the appropriate course to steer to counteract the current or take account of instrument errors, etc. In

502

other words, the VTS has only a crude tool for assessing risk of collision and a ship can arrive at a point of no return in a narrow channel before the VTS operator can provide meaningful assistance.

Out at sea the situation is worse, since small echoes which might represent leisure craft or small fishing vessels may not be picked up by the shore-based radar. Should such a VTS operator order a course to be followed which leads to a collision, I would say that the authorities who designed such a system are irresponsible.

It is interesting that Professor Goss in his paper is starting to question the cost of safety. A result of his work may be that shipping is unnecessarily safe and that, within limits, less control should be exercised. Certainly in a busy port like Rotterdam, VTS provides that essential communication and coordination link which allows a greater number of ship movements than would otherwise be possible. What then is the position of the VTS operator whose operations contribute significantly to the commercial success of the port?

In my opinion, the Dutch Government is going as far as is sensible. Safety of navigation and responsibility rest with the ship, but where the port is concerned, the VTS operators are to have the authority and appropriate liability to take avoiding action "*in extremis*."

Conclusion

Errors of navigation, steering gear failures and the like will continue to happen, whether or not there is a VTS in operation. No theoretical model has been able to demonstrate that the control of ships in narrow channels subject to wind and tide can be better achieved from ashore. In coastal waters, the data acquisition of radar targets is such that the ship will have a better appreciation of the local scene than a radar twenty miles away.

The effective control of traffic can be achieved without taking away the responsibility for safety from the ship and the issue of liability is irrelevant.

The training of VTS operators must include detailed examination of the physical limitations implicit in the instruments being used and a style of communication has to be developed which puts VTS in a supporting role rather than a dominant one.

COMMENTARY

F.J.J. Cadwallader
Center for Marine Law and Policy
University of Wales Institute for Science and Technology

I am not an international law of the sea lawyer but a domestic shipping lawyer and a little worried whether some of you get too carried away and commercial fleets get doomed. We used to call it the Merchant Navy, presumably because it was run by merchants. That has wilted a little in the last few years. States now own the so-called merchant navies. We could call them state ship systems (transport).

If we look at the idea of total safety, I owe one comment to Professor Goss, in that the best thing would be to keep your ships in port. It is like total safety for human beings -- if you do not get out of bed, you probably will not suffer too much. I am interested largely in the safety of navigation, but ships must still run at a profit. We are not interested, either, in polluting the sea too much.

I will begin with Dr. Mensah's paper. He talks about the highest practical standards. I underline "practical" as meaning that it would be what we could afford. Professor Goss was kind enough to underline "highest" and put "uneconomic." We have to think about this. I was intrigued to find in Dr. Mensah's paper that one of the functions of the IMO was to ensure that the competitive position of shipping of one state is not jeopardized by the action of other states which either permit their national shipping to operate with lower standards or impose unduly burdensome requirements on foreign shipping. Does the latter include lower freight rates by some state lines? I was interested in Dr. Mensah's point on unprofitability. He said that unprofitable operators may be squeezed out and only the rogues remain. If that is the standard we have reached, then our standards are too high. We do not really want an entire nation of rogues roaming the seas again, although the British did quite well the last time that happened.

I want to take up two points from Professor Goss's paper. First he mentioned insuring life and third party risks. Most ship owners do that through their clubs, but it is a problem in a state system. Insurance is not granted by God to the human race as such. In the United Kingdom those of you familiar with Lloyd's will know that apart from the man at the end of the box (who happens to be an expert), the rest is run by woolly amateurs who think this is the way of making an investment and a living. They have learned otherwise in the last few years. It is necessary to think in terms of insurance as a business, and if standards are set so high that ship owners cannot be insured you will not get anything. On the damages side, Professor Goss recognized that damages at times can be quite ridiculous and that we need to look at reality in the deduction of things. Some of our judges actually could get around to doing that in the future again.

Regarding the legal aspects of traffic guidance systems, I would like to point out that in 1962 a French trawler going about its business was obstructing a major shipping lane. She was cut down by a vessel proceeding at six knots in quite heavy fog (which might be a little fast), but in the resulting case the judge said there was no question of negligence on the part of the trawler merely by reason of her position. He further said there was no rule of the high seas confining a ship to any particular course and that ships were free to cross major shipping lanes if they chose. There is another English case where the judge took the point that one vessel was totally where it should not have been, but nevertheless felt that this could not exonerate one of the other ships involved, and found that the latter vessel was largely to blame and apportioned damages very much in favor of the vessel that was out of its lanes altogether. I am not sure that this is not a case that needs review. Breach of the collision regulations in Rule 10 now deals with the matter, but that is no reason for presuming total fault.

What implications arise out of traffic routing if we get a proper organization? Who will run these matters apart from the state concerned? Do we have United Nations enforcement proper? Or do we rely on states when we report to them and say, "look, one of your ships..." -- anyone who has been through the Channel knows the feeling -- "...is going in the wrong direction" and you report it and what happens? The answer is written on a small piece of paper and handed to the clerk of the court and is not repeatable, or the answer is nothing most of the time.

Is IMO the body to whom these reports are to be given? If so, would they enforce fines on the state in question if the state did nothing about it? You have to start at the top. And also, insofar as the IMO's routing systems are concerned, what happens if there is a mistake there which leads to a very large collision? Do we sue the IMO, and if so can they limit their liability? Let us face one factor in relation to all the points being made in this session about liability. Ship owners can limit liabilities. So can harbors. The right to limit liability returns us to insurance.

Think seriously about these factors in relation to insurance, how far are we will go for safety and whether we can afford it. Are we going to have systems like air traffic control? Of course it is easier with airplanes to say left, right, up a bit, down a bit, but with ships it is only left, right, and not, I hope, down a bit. That system presumably is going to be over the top of the pilots. IMO routing uses professional pilots (which I very much favor, having to represent them time to time). Will we train an international set of pilots for these various areas or for certain areas which are very dangerous indeed, *i.e.*, the Channel? If so, will we have a controlling authority above them, plus pilots and then the ship's master? Is everybody going to have the right to limit liability? If so, we are back to insurance. Pilots in the United Kingdom can limit their liability to 100 pounds per incident. If you are going to have an incident, have a big one, enjoy it, and that is 100 pounds worth. Do not have two or three because it costs more.

The emphasis must lie on enforcement as mentioned by Dr. Mensah. How will we enforce the systems properly? I do not mean putting them in a book. Take for example the International Convention on Training and Certification of Seafarers. We say you must pass an exam which says you have been examined on collisions. It depends on the country. In some countries examinations will be less rigorous than in others. The same is true when it comes to other conventions and the enforcement of the regulations. They have got to be enforced properly and there has to be somebody that can see they are enforced. I do not think we can leave it just with states.

We have talked about CBA (cost benefit analysis) and I will leave you with CWA (can we afford).

DISCUSSION AND QUESTIONS

Edgar Gold: We have time for questions and comments.

Victor Tsarev: The new UN Convention is influencing national legislation and the actions of international organizations. It is a very important document which provides that all states cooperate in the peaceful uses of the ocean and its resources. The main task now is the interpretation of the new Convention.

Among the new concepts adopted by the new Convention, the economic zone is very important, especially for navigation. Navigation is the main problem and the main use by all states of the ocean. But the main problem of the economic zone is whether this area is high seas or if it has a special regime. The answer to this question is settled. The juridical nature of the economic zone is high seas because the economic zone is defined by the principles of common use and non-appropriation, and these two principles are contained in different articles of the new Convention. The first principle is in the part of the Convention concerning the high seas. This principle, common use, is also in Article 58 of the new Convention. All states can use the economic zone for the purposes of navigation and overflight of aircraft. Article 89 of the new Convention provides that states cannot appropriate any areas of the economic zone. This is a principle of non-appropriation. Two principles define the juridical nature of the economic zone.

What is the special regime of the economic zone? Does the special regime damage the principles of common use and non-appropriation? If we analyze the articles of the new Convention, we can see the different jurisdictions of the coastal state, especially on the prevention of pollution and scientific research. These rights of the coastal state do not damage the principle of non-appropriation and common use. The Convention provides a balance between the rights of the coastal state and the interests of the maritime states. This balance shows us that the economic zone continues to be an area of the high seas.

Stuart Johnson: I'm from the Royal Naval College at Greenwich. Speaking as an ex-Merchant Navy officer, an ex-Royal Navy officer, and an ex-Fishery Protection officer, I would like to inform Richard Goss that if he ever fell into the water on the west coast of the United Kingdom, he would be guaranteed to be picked up by a Royal Naval, and not a Royal Air Force, helicopter. My question is: if the French apply a particular set of laws and regime in their traffic separation zone on their side of the English Channel, and the British apply different standards, what is the likely effect on shipping using the Channel and any problems of control of that shipping?

R.O. Goss: This is the third naval officer in the last 35 minutes who has made some such point to me. It was not my intention to annoy the Royal Navy at all, but merely to comment on the fact -- and it is a fact -- that far more rescue work is actually done by Royal Air Force helicopters around the waters of the United Kingdom, largely because they have chosen to be permanently integrated into the search and rescue facilities, rather than by the Royal Navy, who took the attitude that if they were handy, or passing, or if it were near one of the relatively fewer bases that they have, they would be glad to join in -- which is not the same thing at all.

The question of international coordination is a serious one, and there is an excellent precedent in the Dover Straits. Following a ghastly series of collisions, strandings, and hittings of wrecks by successive vessels, none of which seemed to have been looking where they were going, a vessel traffic system was established employing with great success the utmost cooperation between the British and French governments. If possible, the French were even keener on getting to work and doing it than the British were; certainly the whole thing has worked admirably, and I don't wish to run the risk of offending anybody else, but may I say that throughout the French have even been prepared to use the English language, and this is a relatively unusual characteristic for those who are rightly concerned to propagate the glories of French culture. In general, I do not see that there is reason for major disagreement between adjacent countries, providing that they think basically along much the same lines. If they are chronic enemies, then of course there will be difficulties, but those difficulties are likely to extend far beyond the VTS. For example, if you look at what the Foreign Office and the War Office and the Admiralty had to say towards the end of last century about the building of a Channel tunnel: they were apparently under the impression that the French cavalry could charge for twenty-two miles without their horses getting blown -- then you will see an attitude which leads to the opposite result from that which we have achieved in recent years. In other words, if you are good friends, you can do friendly things together, and if you are enemies, you had better not even try.

C.F. Wooldridge: Why has the panel taken such a shore-based perspective of VTS? In ten to fifteen years, we can look forward to satellite and subsea systems that will give us an international, world-wide position-fixing system. Why does so much effort go into shore-based control when the man on the spot, the most trained, and actively doing the work, is still the professional ship's master? The equipment exists to look around corners; you can rebroadcast radar. If you lose your life in an approach channel, it is just as bad as losing your life in the middle of the ocean, and you cannot have shore-based control there, and yet data buoys, real-time information of the parameters that the master wants, can all be made available. Tidal streams, waves, currents can all be broadcast direct to the mariner, which is an interesting legal point in terms of liability. In Dover Harbor, the busiest harbor in the world in terms of ferry movements, their intention is to broadcast VTS information direct to the mariner. They do not want VTS personnel intercept in the harbor board. Liability and decision-making will rest with the master; that is the sort of research that is going on there now. I have just spent nine consecutive high waters parked in the middle of the eastern entrance to Dover; my log shows an average of a shipping movement every thirteen minutes -- a tremendous mix of hovercraft, jetfoil and ferry, often with six ships moving at a time, and the sort of VTS that has been running there for years invites the master, "Would you care to take a more southerly approach?" Either an invitation like that or you may not enter; you stand off at point Alpha -- ten minutes after, they will let you know when to proceed. So what I am asking is: do the panellists not think that, whether it is rules and regulations from IMO or cost-benefit analysis, this sort of approach just creates another "us and them" situation between shore and the mariner at sea, and that more effort should be put into bringing together the technology that we can

507

foresee, much of which is in existence now, and put the VTS decision-making with the professional mariner who is still on the spot?

Edgar Gold: That is a very important comment. You will probably have general agreement from all on the panel. What you have said emphasizes what Mr. Parker and Professor Goss have already said.

C. Julian Parker: I would like to comment on what Dr. Wooldridge said. I am not anti-VTS at all, but you have to examine the situation and you have to examine the type of ships which are using it. In the case of Dover, all the ferries using that port -- maybe all the ships using that port -- use it regularly. They know the people by Christian name terms if they have to call them up on the radio. They are all extremely well qualified and there is really no great ambiguity; they know that the next hovercraft is going to be sailing in two minutes, they know that a ferry was held up because they heard somebody talking about it, they know that a ship is coming in and has got an engine problem and is likely to be late, etc. So I think a ferry port is a bad example when considering international shipping generally, as lots of ships do not have these well-qualified people on board. We must face up to that, and they either need the assistance of pilots or then they need -- coastal states might justifiably say we need -- just that little bit of extra protection.

Going on to other ports and port movements, if you take a busy port like Rotterdam, the main function of VTS is to improve the efficiency of the port by scheduling the traffic movements, improving the speed at which they can operate, maintaining margins of safety, planning barge traffic against deep sea traffic coming in, turning in to basins, getting tugs ready, getting lightermen ready -- generally improving the economic efficiency of the port. That is an extremely valuable tool; it also increases the safety of the port, although you could argue that if it were not there things would move more slowly and the port would be safer without it. Provided one does not have the idea that VTS will solve all problems of a similar type and one looks at each case individually, shore organizations can be useful.

T.A. Mensah: May I just mention one aspect of this which relates to the IMO. We certainly have appreciated over a long period of time the potential and usefulness of satellites in dealing not only with search and rescue but also in the regulation of maritime traffic, and you all are aware of the work that went into producing the International Maritime Satellite System, which is now being run by a separate organization. The point is also relevant to an ongoing program, the development of the Future Global Maritime Distress System. Although the name is "Distress System," its organization and structure will decide that the system will also be used in assisting governments or shore-based systems for the regulation of traffic. I do not believe, however, that this system, or anything that will come from it in the foreseeable future, will do anything more than supplement national or regional shore-based systems, because if it is to be an effective control, then somebody in charge of it -- either the organization or the operators -- should have the right to give instructions or at least make recommendations to the master. That kind of power and that kind of activity will for the foreseeable future still remain with the shore-based organizations because they will have the authority of government behind them, either single governments or governments in cooperation. But certainly

508

the potential of utilizing new technology for locating and communicating with shore-based organizations and with other ships at sea, will play a very important part in the regulation of maritime traffic.

Glen Plant: My question is for Dr. Mensah and Mr. Parker. The previous questioner has pointed out the problem with VTSs of the division of responsibility between the masters on board and the shore-based authorities. It seems to me that traffic separation schemes and VTSs have been talked about in the same breath, whereas I see that as one major difference between them. Other differences are that VTS has tended to do better in shore-based waters, whereas traffic separation schemes are now more of a high seas and EEZ matter. Although VTSs seem to cover a multitude of different forms, the degree of compulsion implied in a VTS seems to be much greater than that in a traffic separation scheme. Traffic separation schemes are not compulsory except in the sense that non-compliance can be used as evidence of negligence in a civil case. My question is: In the case of high seas and EEZ waters, will we have a trend towards increasing compulsion in traffic separation schemes, or will we see an extension of VTS with this modern technology from coastal waters outwards?

T.A. Mensah: The dichotomy that you outlined is a real one. Traffic separation schemes do not necessarily have the same functions as VTSs. But they are very closely related because, since we are now talking in terms of the Convention on the Law of the Sea, they can supplement the role of traffic separation schemes under the Convention. Even in the case of territorial seas, the Convention gives the coastal state the right to prescribe traffic separation schemes; but, in doing so, the state must conform to the recommendations of IMO. In the case of the EEZ and in straits used for international navigation, the responsibilities of IMO go even further. The state has a right to establish traffic separation schemes using the available methods; but VTS could be used to enforce not only the traffic separation schemes but other schemes. This is because the state has got the right to regulate traffic, and traffic separation schemes may be one of the modes of regulation. But they certainly cannot be the only one -- certainly not from the shore-based point of view.

Rowena M. Lawson: My question to Professor Goss relates to a not uncommon situation in developing countries. Suppose your project consists of buying a vessel brought from abroad, and suppose you are shadow pricing the money you are using for buying that vessel and suppose there are three rates of exchange: a government rate of exchange, a commercial rate of exchange, and a black market rate of exchange. Which do you use in your shadow pricing? That is the first question. I have used a vessel as an example, but there are running costs like insurance, hiring the crew and so on. The second question is: Suppose you have a gut feeling that the rate of exchange is going to move before your project is implemented. How do you handle that?

R.O. Goss: This is a general problem in investment appraisal for developing countries, and Dr. Lawson knows this as well as I do. You consult a book written by Little and Merleys many years ago and sponsored by OECD and which states that wherever there are distortions, for example, in exchange rates or internal prices, induced by government actions -- for example, tariffs, exchange controls, etc. -- the best thing to do is to use external prices, and to convert these either into the national currency or sometimes not to go into the national currency at all; to stay in dollars or pounds sterling or whatever it may be. The phrase for economists is that you use "border prices"; you try to abstract a profit from these measures taken by governments which affect market prices in one way or another.

Rowena M. Lawson: I was simply making a point that you have three border prices; you have the fixed rate of exchange for the government rate, you have a commercial rate of exchange, you have a black market rate of exchange. Which of those do you use for your border pricing?

R.O. Goss: I would be very inclined myself to try the black market. The black market is the nearest thing in these circumstances to a free market, and it is sometimes a very good one indeed. Years ago there was a delightful gentleman, Mr. Franz Picke of New York, who produced a volume called *The Black Market Yearbook*, and it actually contained rates of exchange. It did not sell very well under that name because people were not very proud of having it on their bookshelves, so he changed the title to *Picke's World Currency Report*. I am several years out of date; I am not sure whether it is still being produced. If not, there are profitable opportunities for those people who travel around the world and learn about these things.

Andre G. Corbet: I was a little bit disappointed with Mr. Julian Parker's comments; I felt they tended to be a little bit negative. But I think he did put it right in his answer to Dr. Wooldridge just now, and he did accept that VTS have a part to play. But the examples he gave, such as the *European Gateway* case, were examples of bad VTS rather than that VTS is no good. VTS has been with us for many years; as soon as we had port signals: a white light meant you can come in and a red light that you could not -- that was VTS.

I could give another example of bad VTS, where a tanker sailing from Swansea a number of years ago was in the locks, and the lockkeeper had the signal, a red light I assume it was, saying the lock was occupied. When the tanker sailed out, it kept to the port side of the channel as was customary because of the cross-current, and the lock-keeper immediately hoisted a white or green signal -- to say that the lock was clear. An unpiloted coaster outside, seeing that signal, immediately entered the channel, and because it did not know the customs which pilots had adopted in that port, it kept to the starboard side in conformity with international regulations, and there was a collision. But that is a example of bad VTS; the coaster outside did not realize that the signal only referred to the lock and not to the approach channel.

So we are talking about good VTS and bad VTS, and the problem with VTS now is that it is generally not coordinated world-wide. In other words, we can have all different types of terms; some people use different terms for "VTS" even. I must say I am worried about this, and about the negative aspect also from IMO today in this respect: because they did not want to shoulder any responsibilities, apparently, in this field. They just say, "We are there to help, we cannot do anything much about it otherwise." But we should have some authority in this respect. The fact that we have two systems of buoyage in the world despite worldwide conferences does not bode very well for having a uniform system of VTS either. However, having criticized the IMO a little bit,

I should say they have been good in getting the Conventions adopted in relatively short time. So I am not altogether despondent about it; I am sure after I am gone there will be a better VTS system around.

I was also a little bit disappointed with the negative aspects coming again from Julian Parker concerning the control of ships. He said it is necessary to have a man on board who can look at the containers and from that judge how the ship is going to turn and so on. In fact, very often instrumentation and computers are far better in ascertaining the way ships behave, and the technical devices are available or can be developed to cope with that situation. I disagree with Dr. Wooldridge who said everything needs to be put on the ship's master and one should do away with shore control in effect. Perhaps I am overstating his case there, but I am sure that shore control is absolutely essential when we come to time-tabling ships in and out of a waterway or port. Imagine the Suez Canal if we just left it with ship masters to decide when they were going to go through. It would be absolutely impossible. I think the panel is being a little bit negative and hope that they will change their position to that respect. I also had one question to Professor Cadwallader concerning pilots. I had a lot to do with training pilots to get familiar with VTS systems. They often took the attitude of Dr. Wooldridge, that it should all be left to the ship. But there are occasions when the equipment does break down on the ship and a shore radar is available to help. If the pilot does not use the radar, and it could have saved him from going aground, he could be found negligent, I would have thought. We often found that pilots were prepared to accept shore control provided they were the controllers. We conducted a number of tests, and they said they could control the ships better themselves if the shore gave direct instructions to the ship rather than just giving, say, positions and so on. However, pilots are very concerned about loss of job satisfaction and indeed loss of jobs. I was wondering with regard to the recent Government Green Paper on pilots in this country, which suggests that the pilots should be employed by the harbor authorities rather than be self-employed, whether this factor might help with regard to VTS and acceptability of pilots for VTS systems.

T.A. Mensah: I do understand the disappointment about what appears to be the negative attitude. But the point I was making was merely this: it is not that IMO does not think that it would be useful for it to be given more powers or that it does not want them. At the moment we do not have those powers, and if at any time governments come to the view that an organization such as ours should have more powers, then quite clearly there will be the mechanism for exercising that power. I have no doubt at all about it.

C. Julian Parker: I did not want people to think that VTSs were not useful. I just wanted to point out that ship-handling is a very complex affair and that some people have a concept of VTS as controlling the ship. But a person in the radar center ashore only sees that ship as a little blip, two-eighths of an inch in size. It has got no sense of direction, it is just a blip plotting down a radar screen. Some people think that you can control ships in the same way as aircraft and I hope I demonstrated that you cannot. Of course VTS for traffic planning and discipline, keeping people in the lane, stopping the rogues from causing dangerous situations, etc. -- is extremely valuable, so I did not want to be negative.

511

I am glad Captain Corbet brought up this question of good VTS and bad VTS. You get good VTS and bad VTS as you get good ships and bad ships. If you proliferate VTS, you have got to man them. It costs about 100,000 pounds a year to run a fully integrated VTS with just one radar and one man turning over space, time, resources, radars. A proper system with communications and port control will cost about 200,000 pounds a year which a port must pay for. Sooner or later you are probably going to have bad VTS. A port is going to put in unqualified people, because they are cheaper, and try to save on other things. The accident record is going to come down, and then suddenly there will be another big accident. So bear in mind there are practical problems of operating VTS too.

Now the question whether pilots should be in or out of VTS depends on the complexity of the current situation which you are trying to solve. If the situation demands pilot skills and VTS, then you ought to use them. If it does not, you probably should not, because it puts the port out of business because VTS is probably more expensive than the people who give less detailed information. One must be realistic and manage the port according to the demand.

Donald C. Watt: I have a faint doubt about the effectiveness and sophistication of the cost-benefit analysis provided by Professor Goss. The problem with cost-benefit analysis as he applies it is that, while you can show the costs and benefits of doing or not doing a particular thing like introducing a vessel traffic management scheme on a one-year basis, this has to be financed out of public funds with a central control of finance which has to apply similar techniques to a whole range of public expenditure. Where after a year or two the cost of implementing a particular service is going to be a continuing burden on the project and something which people would be worried about as opposed to other public expenditure, the benefits are going to be benefits of non-occurrences. I therefore wonder, if one confined one-self to the risk analysis, particularly of the more sophisticated kind now applied which measures not only the actuarial frequency of certain risks -- a difficult thing to do, anyway, with the absence of statistics -- but also what is actually at stake in terms of particular accidents if they were to occur, whether this would not be a more profitable line of investigation. When my class and I went down to Dover to visit the traffic separation scheme this year, I was impressed by the difference between their projected model of accidents based on past statistics -- which had been developed by the National Maritime Institute -- and the actual rate of the accidents since the introduction of the traffic separation scheme in the Strait. Now there is something, without going into the more sophisticated forms of analysis which Professor Goss tried, which anyone -- even a Treasury official -- might regard as convincing. But ultimately our system does attach very considerable political risk to what on the face of it are very minor accidents, the risks which are attached to the public's view of responsibility and negligence on the part of those whom they have elected or appointed to keep power. One has only to read today's papers to see the enormous amount of political capital which is developing out of a minor case of negligence by a social worker resulting in the death of an, in economic terms, unvaluable black child from a deprived household who was already emotionally retarded. I cannot see how that could have figured in our cost-benefit analysis system in any way proportionate to the actual political consequences of this event. Nor do I think it ought to -- I should make that very clear. Perhaps it is not necessary to pursue the cost-benefit analysis analogy quite as closely in its relation to the political scheme as is being done, and it would be perhaps better to concentrate on developing the skills of risk and hazard analysis which exist already, and on the bringing together of the very considerable sum of knowledge and experience on this which is now scattered over a wide variety of disciplines and schemes. Where they lead to what is basically a measure of prevention, like a traffic separation scheme, there I think one probably has an adequate solution.

Edgar Gold: I think we've had a fairly full morning. I would like to thank the panel and participants.

PART VII:

THE EEC AND THE LAW OF THE SEA

INTRODUCTION

Albert Koers
Professor of International Law
Institute of Public International Law
University of Utrecht

It is perhaps appropriate that the topic of the EEC and the law of the sea comes up last. First, because the EEC is, more often than not, a rather slow-moving organization and the EEC coming in last, at least in my perception, evokes a sense of *deja vu*. Second, in the United Nations Conference on the Law of the Sea, the so-called *EEC issue* -- that is, the participation of the Community in the Convention -- also came up only in the final stages of that Conference.

We may be at the tail-end of this Conference, but let me assure you that we are dealing with a tail, by which I mean the EEC, that in many ways is wagging the dogs -- and by *dogs* I mean, no disrespect intended -- the Member States. This panel will look at the special role of the EEC in relation to the law of the sea -- a role that came about as the result of the Member States transferring powers and competences in certain areas of the law of the sea to the EEC. The fact that the EEC can participate in the 1982 Convention of the Law of the Sea is but one of the results of that transfer of powers.

Against this background Tullio Treves, professor of international law of the University of Milan, will first address the overall issue of the EEC, the United Nations, and the law of the sea. Professor Treves was a member of the Italian delegation to the United Nations Conference on the Law of the Sea, and he was one of the more active members of the Drafting Committee. He is presently on secondment to the Italian Mission to the United Nations.

Then, two papers will address more specific issues. First, Pat Birnie will discuss the EEC's environmental policy and its relation to the law of the sea. Dr. Birnie is a lecturer in law at the London School of Economics and Political Science, and before that, she held a similar position at the University of Edinburgh. Next, Robin Churchill, a lecturer in law at the Centre for Marine Law and Policy of UWIST, will address a specific aspect of the Common Fisheries Policy: the EEC's contribution to state practice in the field of fisheries.

After that, we will hear two commentators, Budislav Vukas, professor of international law at the University of Zagreb, and Markus Ederer, a researcher at the University of Miami and presently an intern at the UN Office of the Law of the Sea in New York.

THE EEC, THE UN AND THE LAW OF THE SEA

Tullio Treves
Professor of Law, State University of Milan, Italy
Legal Adviser, The Permanent Mission of Italy to the UN

Introduction

The EEC, the UN and the Law of the Sea is a challenging subject and also a difficult one. It is challenging because both the EEC and the UN have played and still are playing an important role as regards the law of the sea. It is difficult because there is no obvious link between the roles played by the two organizations.

I will reject the temptation to develop my observations separately for the EEC and the UN. I will instead look at both organizations in their relationship with the law of the sea through a framework that tries to highlight the main functions that both the major universal organization and the most developed regional organization can perform in a context such as that of the law of the sea. These functions seem to be that of:

- a political forum
- a protagonist of international relations
- a provider of ideas and information

In examining, within this framework, the role of the EEC and of the UN, I shall limit my remarks as regards the past to a minimum and focus on the questions of today. These questions may, by and large, all be subsumed under the general title of this Conference. They are either questions of implementation of the UN Law of the Sea Convention or questions of its impact. They include, however, not only the aspect mentioned in this Conference's program, but also deep seabed mining and the specific organ that the Law of the Sea Conference has entrusted with the task of preparing the implementation of the Convention in that particular field: the Preparatory Commission of the International Law of the Sea Tribunal and the International Seabed Authority (the *PrepCom*).

The UN and the EEC as Political Fora

With the conclusion of the Third United Nations Conference on the Law of the Sea, the United Nations General Assembly is the only forum left for general political discussion on the law of the sea to be virtually universal. The other main UN forum, the PrepCom, is not so universal because of the absence from its deliberations of the United States.

Since the opening for signature of the 1982 UN Law of the Sea Convention, the General Assembly has maintained, as an agenda item, the law of the sea. The item has been examined directly by the Plenary, and each year a resolution has been passed.

Even though the debates are relatively short, the preparation of the resolution involves a very intensive exchange of ideas. Up to now it has been possible to reach consensus among the states signatory to the Convention. In fact, in 1984, only the United States and Turkey voted against it, while other non-signatories either were absent or did not participate in the vote.[1] In these discussions, echoed by the official interventions in Plenary, the positions on the Convention, the PrepCom and the activities of the Secreteriat emerge quite clearly.[2] By and large, the resolutions resulting from these discussions have been an

518

exercise in moderation and restraint. This emerges rather clearly if one considers that the non-aligned states have resisted pressure from the Soviet Union and refrained from condemning in the resolution the position of the United States and the other signatories of the 1984 Provisional Understanding Regarding Seabed Mining.

Another interesting UN forum is the General Assembly's Fifth Committee, where the budgetary implications are discussed. Here the concerns of the western states for the most efficient and parsimonious use of the UN's resources have been voiced. The position of the United States, according to which the financing of the PrepCom through the UN's ordinary budget is legally invalid in view of the independence of the PrepCom from the United Nations, has been developed in full detail here.

As regards the Preparatory Commission, it seems that, throughout its first three years of operation, it has been faithful to its functions as provided for in Resolution I of the Third UN Law of the Sea Conference and has not become a general political forum on questions relating to the law of the sea. While it is obvious that some of the questions it considers -- such as those relating to registration of pioneer seabed investors -- have a very relevant political impact, the Commission has, by and large, kept to its assigned task of preparing rules and regulations for the entry into force of the Convention.

The PrepCom has also avoided becoming a forum for discussing reform of the UN Law of the Sea Convention. No discussions are held, even in the corridors, on that matter, even though the question of the implications for Part XI of the Convention of a different general attitude towards the UN and the Convention of a future American Administration is in the minds of many delegates. Moreover, the discussion of the deep seabed mining code, *i.e.*, of the mechanisms for the application of Part XI, although still at a very early stage, seems to confirm the skepticism of those who do not believe that serious changes in the most controversial provisions of the Convention can be obtained through the PrepCom. At the present stage, a little added precision as regards some provisions seems to be all that can be hoped for.

Some general concerns seem, however, to emerge from the work of the PrepCom. The absence of the United States is widely, though not publicly, recognized as the major flaw of the Commission. This has led the PrepCom, though not without meeting strong resistance, to strive for as much universality as possible by ensuring in its rules of procedure, and according to Resolution I, a reinforced observer status to the states signatory to the Final Act of the Law of the Sea Convention but not to the Convention. Such status, whose beneficiaries are now mainly the Federal Republic of Germany and the United Kingdom, permits full participation in the deliberations though not in the taking of decisions of the PrepCom.[3] It is interesting to note that, when it comes to establishing the International Seabed Authority, the Socialist countries have proposed that a similar status be granted in the Assembly of the Authority to signatories of the Convention not having ratified it or not having acceded to it. Western countries have concurred, though proposing that this status should be extended to all potential parties to the Convention. The moderate, though obviously not fully favorable, reaction of the non-aligned delegations seems to confirm that a general concern for universality prevails in the PrepCom.[4]

If we look now at the European Community as a forum of political discussion on the law of the sea, the first observation that comes to mind is that, after the end of the UN Conference of the Law of the Sea, the EC sees much less debate on this matter. The fact that there is no more need to consult on a continuous basis, and to agree or try to agree on common positions, a need that the existence of the Conference imposed in the past, has narrowed the function of the EC as a political forum almost exclusively to matters linked with the activities of the PrepCom.

The structures for consultation and elaborating common positions created during the Law of the Sea Convention (periodic meetings in Brussels and elsewhere of heads of delegations and of experts)[5] are still in place and working in relation to the PrepCom. Their effectiveness is, however, reduced and undergoing a process of transformation into a framework for discussion and reciprocal information.

This is due to the variety of positions and interests represented in the relatively small group of states belonging to the European Community. These countries include ten signatories of the Convention and two non-signatories, the F.R.G. and the U.K. They include deep-seabed miners signatory to the 1984 Provisional Understanding (Belgium, the Federal Republic of Germany, France, Italy, the Netherlands, the United Kingdom)[6] and non-seabed mining countries. Among the former, one has its own seabed mining consortium (France), while the seabed mining companies of the others are parties to consortia with American partners. Among the latter, some (Ireland, Denmark) belong to the group of western "friends of the Convention," while others do not. Moreover, the seabed mining states of the EC, with the exception, since August 1984, of France, cooperate actively in the "Group of Seven" (now Six) seabed mining states of the PrepCom, which includes also Japan but not Canada. Belgium, Italy, the Netherlands and the United Kingdom have, however, some interests in common with Canada, as states whose companies belong to American consortia.[7]

This explains why the EEC coordination effort cannot reach very substantive results in the PrepCom and why, on the other hand, within the EEC group, important information can be exchanged and serious exchanges of views can be held with the confidence and open-mindedness that is proper to states accustomed to working together.

The UN and the EC as Protagonists of International Relations

Under this heading there is much more to say about the EC than about the United Nations. The UN, because of its universal composition, cannot and does not, as such, play a major role as a protagonist of international relations in the law of the sea. The existence of ships employed in the official service of the UN does not change this situation. More interesting may be the role that the UN performs of coordinator of the activities of various specialized agencies in the field of the law of the sea.

As regards the European Community, it is well known that it is competent on various matters falling within the purview of the Law of the Sea Convention. This led the Law of the Sea Conference to include in the Convention various provisions that permit organizations having characteristics similar to the EC -- *i.e.*, organizations to which Member States have transferred competence over matters governed by the Convention -- to become parties to Convention.[8] The most important of these provisions are those containing the following principles:

First, in order for the Organization to be admitted to sign the Convention (and later to become bound by it), it is required that a majority of its Member States sign or become bound.[9]

Second, the Organization has to notify the matters covered by the Convention in which it has competence and will be bound by the Convention to the extent of its competence.[10]

Third, participation of the Organization in the Convention shall not, in any case, confer rights under the Convention on Member States of the Organization that are not parties to the Convention.[11]

When the Convention was opened for signature on December 10, 1982, only five Member States of the EC out of ten signed. Thus the Community could not sign. It was not until a few days before December 9, 1984, when the final deadline for signature was to elapse, that other Member States of the Community signed: Belgium and Luxembourg on December 5 and Italy on December 7.

The problem of whether the EC would sign if this situation were to arise had already been discussed in Brussels. There were no disagreements in analyzing the legal situation as follows. Although, from the viewpoint of the Law of the Sea Convention, the Community could sign as soon as the sixth signature by a Member State was affixed, from the viewpoint of Community law, the signature of the EC was a matter on which a decision had to be taken by unanimity -- in other words, with the concurrence of the non-signatory states, if any. Thus, the decision on the EC signature lay in the hands of those Member States that had decided not to sign: the United Kingdom and the Federal Republic of Germany. On December 6, these two countries abstained in the EC Council of Ministers when it was decided that the Community would sign. Thus the Community could sign on December 7.

Though not signing the Convention, the U.K. and the F.R.G. concurred in deciding that the Community would sign. This, on the one hand, had the effect of making the decision not to sign a little less dramatic for these two countries. As the Special Representative of the UN Secretary-General for the Law of the Sea said in a press briefing on December 10, the U.K. and the F.R.G., being members of the European Community, "were, to a certain extent, indirectly involved" in the Convention. On the other hand, the EC signature had the effect that these two states were placed in a situation permitting them to have some influence in the Preparatory Commission through their participation in the elaboration of the positions of the Community.[12]

When it signed, not only did the Community notify the Secretariat that its Member States had transferred to it competences in the fields of fisheries, protection of the marine environment according to the provisions adopted and the treaties concluded by it, rights of land-locked states from the viewpoint of customs, and seabed mining as regards commercial policy (including the control of unfair economic practices),[13] but it also made a declaration stating that "significant provisions of Part IX of the Convention are not conducive to the development of the activities to which that Part refers in view of the fact that several Member States of the Community have already expressed their position that this Part contains considerable deficiencies and flaws which require rectification." The Community added that it recognized "the importance of the work which remains to be done and hope[d] that conditions for the implementation of a seabed regime that are generally acceptable and which are therefore likely to promote activities in the International Seabed Area, can be agreed."

Thus the Community is instructed to play an active and critical role in the Preparatory Commission. It can play this role in full because, as a signatory of the Convention, it is, since December 7, 1984, a member of the PrepCom entitled to participate not only in deliberations but also in decision making. Its participation as a member, according to Article 55 of the Rules of Procedure of the PrepCom which were adopted before the Community's signature, shall be "in accordance with Annex IX" of the Convention, in other words, within the limits of the Community's competences and in such a way as not to give rights to those Member States that have not signed the Convention.[14]

As far as future developments are concerned, the most interesting questions seem to be the following two. First, will it be possible to see again, as regards ratification of the Convention, the same situation prevailing as regards signature i.e., of the Community ratifying together with only a majority of its Member States? Second, will it be possible for a Member State to ratify the Convention before the Community does so?

The first question refers to a situation that does not seem to be close in time. The ratification process in general, and in particular in the European states, is slow. Moreover, the positions the majority of Member States have taken on deep seabed mining under the Convention make it unlikely that "formal confirmation" of participation by the EC will be discussed in the near future. If, however, a situation similar to that of signature were to rise regarding participation in the Convention, the most difficult legal problems would probably be that of ensuring that Member States which are not party to the Convention would obtain no rights. This might require examining the necessity of modifying some rules of Community law.

The second question might present itself at relatively short notice. Iceland ratified the Convention on June 21, 1985, and it is known that the other Nordic countries, including Denmark, a member of the EC, intend to do the same within a reasonable time.

It seems that the Convention contains no obstacle to ratification on its own by a member of one of the Organizations that are entitled to become parties before the Organization becomes a party.[15] One may, however, ask: how can a state that has transferred to an Organization competence on some matters covered by the Convention fulfill all its obligations under it unless the Organization also becomes a party? And how, from the viewpoint of Community law, can such a state undertake these obligations? It would seem that only the unanimous authorization by the other Member States and the consequent, necessary modifications of Community law would permit these difficulties to be overcome. Such difficulties would, however, become real not when the state in question ratifies, but when the Convention enters into force (assuming that it will not, by then, already be in force).

However interesting the above-mentioned developments concerning the UN Law of the Sea Convention may be, it would seem at least as interesting to mention, under the heading of the EC as a protagonist of international relations in the law of the sea, the achievements reached in the conclusion of agreements in various sectoral fields. Most developments on these aspects are contained in the papers of Patricia Birnie and Robin Churchill. I shall only underscore that the Community has signed a sizeable number of multilateral agreements on fisheries and the prevention of marine pollution. In some of these (one may quote four agreements on fisheries), the EC has become a party without the presence of Member States as parties. In other cases (other agreements on fisheries and all the agreements on the prevention of marine pollution) the EC is a party together with Member States. The status of the Community has sometimes been the object of a declaration by the USSR and by other states of Eastern Europe, but it is a fact that these states, in general the toughest adversaries of the EC and international organizations behaving and being considered as protagonists of international relations, consented to become parties to such treaties together with the

EC. This seems to be a very relevant development, obtained through patient negotiations, whose impact may be at least as important as that of the EC participation in the UN Law of the Sea Convention.[16]

The UN and the EEC as Providers of Ideas and Information

The role of the UN as a provider of ideas and information is at present more far-reaching than that of the European Communities.

The European Community's role, from this angle, is limited to the technical input given by the Commission to Member States and to the PrepCom as regards production limitation by illustrating various mechanisms elaborated within the Community and especially in the Lome Conventions (such as STABEX).

The diversity of interests we have referred to earlier as regards seabed mining has had the effect that in this field the EC is not now a forum in which new ideas are proposed and elaborated. The Member States more directly involved in seabed mining have preferred to cooperate for this purpose with Japan in elaborating various proposals within the "Group of Seven" (now six) mentioned above.

As regards the United Nations, its Secretariat, and in particular its Office of the Special Representative for the Law of the Sea, performs a major role as a provider of ideas, information and services in many areas covered by the Convention.[17] This is true not only for deep seabed mining and the PrepCom, but for other aspects of the law of the sea as well. The Secretariat has to be commended for keeping things in the right perspective and not acting as if seabed mining and the Prep-Com were the only important aspects of the law of the sea. Member States have, by and large, supported the Secretariat, as emerges from the GA's Resolutions and from the major program in marine affairs undertaken by the UN within its medium-term plan for the years 1984-1989.[18]

Within the PrepCom the Secretariat's role goes far beyond that of servicing the meetings. On most questions discussed by the PrepCom, the document on which deliberations are conducted has been prepared by the Secretariat. States or their groupings very often limit themselves to putting forward proposals for modification of some points of the basic proposal by the Secretariat. This seems to be due especially to the lower priority that all states give to the PrepCom as compared to UNCLOS III, a lower priority that translates in employing less manpower and resources for preparations in the capitals. It is due also to the absence of the United States, which was perhaps the main provider of proposals during the Law of the Sea Conference. The "Group of Seven" (now six) seabed mining countries tries to fill this vacuum, but not to such an extent as to replace the Secretariat in the role of the provider of the main input. Moreover, for obvious reasons, the proposals by the Secretariat have the advantage of being more readily accepted as bases for negotiations. Thus, given the importance of the Secretariat's documents, a practice has developed of the Secretariat consulting informally various groups and delegations during the preparations of its proposals.

Outside the field of seabed mining, the Secretariat, which under the relevant provisions of the Convention is the depository of charts and co-ordinates establishing baselines and limits of maritime zones, has already started receiving such charts and lists of co-ordinates even though the Convention is not in force. Even more interestingly, the states sending in such charts and lists of co-ordinates are not in all cases states which ratified the Convention. Some states that have signed only are in this group. The Secretariat is studying the most efficient methods for performing its functions in this matter.

Moreover, the Secretariat has had to respond to inquiries made by states on the implications of signing and of ratifying the Convention, as well as on the implications of declarations made or to be made on signature or ratification. These implications may concern modifications to existing legislation, the adoption of new legislation, and the elaboration of new marine policies.

The UN Secretariat is also co-ordinating the efforts undertaken by various Organizations in the UN system -- ranging from FAO to UNEP, from IMO to ICAO, from IOC to UNDP -- to study the Convention in order to assess its implications for the activities of the various Organizations concerned.

The tasks just mentioned of receiving charts and co-ordinates, in assisting states in assessing the Convention's implications and in co-ordinating the efforts of other organizations, might be seen as involving at least some aspects of application of the Convention before its entry into force. The Secretariat may also be seen as working towards this end, although in a much more indirect way, by its information activities.

These activities consist, firstly, in collecting national legislation and regulations as well as treaties and judicial decisions. This material is in the process of being indexed through a computerized system based on the index the Secretariat has elaborated for the Convention. Important abstracts of this information are given in a Bulletin (the *Law of the Sea Bulletin*), of which four issues have been published to date. It is to be hoped that this very interesting publication will be given wider circulation and easier accessibility beyond the circle of governments and their Missions in New York that presently get to see it.

Another aspect of the information activities of the Secretariat is the undertaking of various analytical studies of the *travaux preparatoires* of the Convention. Considering that many interesting aspects of the *travaux* are contained in documents not included in the seventeen volumes of the "Official Records" of the Conference and in meetings not recorded in them, these studies can be expected to be a very useful addition to the growing library of studies and materials on the legislative history of the Convention.

One must be aware that, when undertaking these studies, the Secretariat treads through a minefield. How will directly interested governments react to analytical studies like those mentioned which, in the words of the Secretariat, aim at constituting "an aid to the interpretation of the treaty provisions"?[19] A possible reaction might be the insistence that the Secretariat be as prudent and restrained as possible in order not to upset some of the many "constructive ambiguities" contained in the Convention.

In one case, however, the Secretariat has been confronted by a request that it behave more boldly than it has up to now. When the Philippines confirmed on ratification a declaration made on signature concerning passage through straits linking its archipelagic waters with the high seas or the economic zone, the Soviet Union, with a note circulated in 1985,[20] not only objected to it but requested that the Secretariat conduct "a study of general nature of the problem of ensuring universal application of the provisions of the Convention, including the question of the harmonization of the national legislation of States with the Convention." Such a study might imply that the Secretariat would be asked to assess whether domestic legislation of various states is in conformity with the Convention, obviously a task on which the Secretariat is at least hesitant to embark.

Concluding Remarks

Both the UN and the EC, each according to its purposes and membership, perform an important task as fora for discussion on the law of the sea. As regards the function of elaborating ideas and providing information, the role of the UN is far more relevant than that of the EC. The Community, however, more than any other international organization, has the status of a protagonist of international relations in the field of the law of the sea. This is true not only as regards its signature, and potential ratification, of the UN Law of the Sea Convention and its participation as a full member of the PrepCom, but also as far as its activities, and especially its treaty-making activites, on those matters upon which competence has been transferred to it are concerned.

The importance of the wide practice of treaties concluded by the Communities, with or without its Member States, in the fields of fisheries and the protection of the environment cannot be underestimated. It is probably the most relevant development in the law of the sea as regards the position of international organizations as protagonists of international relations. It has provided, moreover, one of the most solid arguments for getting the EC accepted as a potential party to the UN Law of the Sea Convention.

As regards the UN Law of the Sea Convention and the PrepCom, there would, however, seem to be a certain lack of proportion between the status the EC enjoys and the input it actually makes. There are many political and legal explanations for this. One cannot, however, fail to remark that this situation can cause disappointment not only to the most fervent Europeans and to the Commission in Brussels, but also, and more relevantly, to third states that look to the Community as a prototype of future developments in international organization and integration and that have contributed, by accepting the Community's participation in the Convention, to give it the particular status it now enjoys. A fund of good-will and expectation might be dispersed unless the EC provides imaginative leadership in the law of the sea.

NOTES

1. U.N.G.A. Res. A/RES/39/73, *Law of the Sea Bulletin*, No. 4, p. 88 (February, 1985).
2. See in particular the debates of 1984: UN Doc. A/39/PV.99 (Plenary meeting of December 13, 1984).
3. Rules 2 and 10, para. 3, of the Rules of Procedure of the Preparatory Commission, Doc. LOS/PCN/28 of November 23, 1983. On these problems, see my paper "Observers Signatory of the Final Act" in "The International Seabed Authority's Preparatory Commission," (1984) 27 German Yearbook of International Law 303-314.
4. For a summary of the various positions, see the Statement of the Chairman of the PrepCom, J. Warioba, in the Doc. LOS/PCN/L.19 of April 3, 1985.
5. Cf. Treves, "The EEC and the Law of the Sea: How Close To One Voice?" (1983) 12 Ocean Development and Int'l Law 173-189.
6. (1984) 24 International Legal Materials 1324.

7. This common interest appears in the letters sent by these five countries to the Chairman of the PrepCom and contained in Docs. LOS/PCN/54,60,61,62,63.
8. UN Law of the Sea Convention, Arts. 1, para. 2(2), 305, para. 1, 306, 307 and Annex IX. For recent critical studies of these provisions, see Gaja, "The European Community's Participation in the Law of the Sea Convention: Some Incoherencies in a Compromise Solution," (1983) 5 Ital. Y.B. Int'l. L. 110-114; Treves, "The United Nations Law of the Sea Convention of 1982: Prospects for Europe" in M.B.F. Ranken (ed.), *Greenwich Forum IX, Britain and the Sea*, 166-182, espec. 176-180 (1984).
9. UN Law of the Sea Convention, Arts. 2 and 3 of Annex IX.
10. UN Law of the Sea Convention, Arts. 2, 3, 4 (paras. 1 and 2), 5 (para. 1) of Annex IX.
11. UN Law of the Sea Convention, Annex IX, Art. 5, para. 5.
12. For a German point of view, see Jenisch, "German non-signature of the new Law of the Sea Convention" [1985] Aussenpolitik 157-173.
13. This notification and the declaration mentioned in the text can be found in the *Law of the Sea Bulletin* of the Office of the Special Representative of the Secretary-General for the Law of the Sea, No. 4, p. 14 ff., February 1985.
14. LOS/PCN/28 Art. 55.
15. Treves, *op. cit.* in n. 8, p. 180.
16. The relevant information is present in a compact form in the following two publications of the European Communities: *The European Community, International Organizations, and Multilateral Agreements*, 3d ed., Brussels, 1984, and *Communautes Europeennes, Conventions et Accords Multilateraux* (I/497/84).
17. A very useful summary of the Secretariat's activities and perspective is in the Report on the Law of the Sea presented by the Secretary-General to the General Assembly. For 1984 see A/39/647 of November 16, 1984.
18. UN General Assembly, Official Records, 37th Session, Suppl. 6A (A/37/6/Add.1) Chap. 25 sect. I.
19. Doc. A/329/647 para. 98.
20. Cfr. C.N. 54 1985 Treaties-4 (Depository Notification) in which the Secretary-General of the UN circulated the Note of the USSR of March 19, 1985 mentioned in the text.

THE EUROPEAN COMMUNITY'S ENVIRONMENTAL POLICY

P.W. Birnie
Lecturer in Law
London School of Economics

Introduction

The EEC has, under Article 305 of the Law of the Sea Convention (LOSC), subject to the requirements of Annex IX, which will be considered in detail later in this paper, become a signatory of LOSC. Although the Treaty of Rome, upon which it is founded, does not require the EC to adopt a Common Environment Policy but does require it to develop a Common Agricultural Policy (CAP) and a Common Fisheries Policy (CFP), the Community has nonetheless adopted a series of Action Programmes on the Environment. Unlike the CAP and CFP, however, the EC's competence in this field is limited by the lack of explicit conferment of competence. A further distinction is that whilst all the EC's coastal Member States that border its northern waters have declared 200-mile fisheries jurisdiction, only France has declared an exclusive economic zone (EEZ); it has not, even so, given effect to pollution control jurisdiction within it. Thus though the CFP applies within the 200-mile jurisdiction, the Action Programmes on the Environment are restricted in geographical scope to the territory and territorial seas, the air above them, and to flagships of Member States; nonetheless, there are many articles and parts of the LOSC which can be implemented on an EEC basis, using its instruments and mechanisms.

Along with Part V, which requires conservation of the Living Resources of the Sea and makes special provision (in Article 65) for marine mammals generally and cetaceans in particular, Part XII on Preservation of the Marine Environment requiring that laws, regulations etc., be developed and enforced for all sources of pollution, is of particular relevance to the role of the Community, since it can provide an international forum for such developments with unusual powers. Since only ten of the twelve Member States have signed LOSC, however, the extent to which the Community can introduce LOSC's more innovative provisions, such as those establishing port state jurisdiction, special areas and protection of fragile habitats, mostly remain uncertain. There is, however, no doubt that the EC's structures have the potential to develop laws and policies on all these issues, as well as on the many other pollution prevention and conservation provisions included in the parts of LOSC referring to the territorial sea, archipelagoes, international straits, semi-enclosed seas, the high seas and the deep seabed. The EC, like other signatories, is, however, faced with the fact that the UN General Assembly, has by a resolution, which attracted a large majority, called upon UN members to do nothing to undermine the package deal nature of LOSC; and that some of its Member States (*e.g.*, the Federal Republic of Germany, Belgium, the U.K.) abstained on this vote.

Preliminary Questions

Before one can consider the policy adopted by the EC to protect the environment of EEC Member States, there are a number of preliminary questions to be asked, to which this paper will attempt to provide the answers.

First, does an organization such as the European Community (hereafter referred to as *the EC* or *the Community*), empowered by its treaties to develop its members' economies in order to raise their standards of living, have the power to include among its policies environmental protection? Second, even if it does, should it in fact do so, in light of the likely political problems, given the economically and environmentally diverse melange of states concerned? Third, if it does embark on an environmental policy, what should be its scope and content and to what extent are any objectives set achievable in practice? Fourth, do the special attributes of the Community -- the existence of permanent organs; the binding nature of some of its instruments; the existence of dispute settlement procedures -- establish it as a more effective and, therefore, more desirable mechanism for protecting the environment than other means available internationally, such as the series of *ad hoc* measures, treaties and commissions already existing in Europe, *e.g.*, the Paris and Oslo Commissions for land-based pollution and ocean dumping respectively; or those developed through the Council of Europe; or the Organization of Economic Cooperation and Development (OECD), outside the EC; or through UN bodies such as the IMO (the International Maritime Organization) or UNEP (the United Nations Environment Program)? Fifth, how can or does the EC harmonize its environmental policies with those of such outside bodies or with third states outside the Community so as to complement rather than undermine their activities?

Underlying all the questions, of course, is the preliminary one of how the Community defines its environment, since this affects its powers, their scope and external applicability.

In endeavoring to answer these questions the paper will concentrate, in deference to considerations of length and of the purposes of this Conference, on examples derived from EC measures to protect the marine environment.

The Aims of the European Community[1]
The Treaty of Rome establishing the European Communities[2] was drawn up in 1957 before the surge of environmental consciousness that led to the convening of the UN Conference on the Human Environment held in Stockholm in 1972. Thus neither it nor later Accession Treaties contain any specific provisions relating to protection of the environment or clearly requiring development of an environmental policy. The main purpose of the original Communities was to establish a Common Market between their Member States based on the free movement of persons and goods, a customs union, a common agricultural policy, non-discrimination in economic affairs and harmonization of Member States' laws to achieve these ends. The thrust of the EC's policies has been to establish this market by progressively approximating throughout the Community a harmonious development of economic standards and stability,[3] thus creating a new international legal order for its Member States. To achieve the mutual benefits that this process is thought to ensure, Member States have been prepared to surrender (some prefer to say "pool") a limited amount of national sovereignty,[4] *inter alia*, involving submission of disputes concerning interpretation of the treaties to the jurisdiction of the European Court of Justice, (ECJ) whose decisions Member States are obliged to accept and implement. In the fields to which the Rome Treaty applies, Community law takes precedence over national law. In some circumstances it takes direct effect; in others it requires further action by Member States to give it effect.

It is important to note that once made effective, the EC legal regime applies not only to Member States but also to their nationals.[5] The result is a body of law consisting of rights, duties, powers and remedies which in the limited spheres to which the Treaty permits its application, represents an effective independent system. This resultant regime, of course, also has external effects on non-member states.

The Community has been equipped with both organs and legal instruments to facilitate these purposes and policies. Whether or not Community law has direct effect depends on the instrument used. The Treaty lays down four types of instruments;[6] the significance of the distinctions between them is of great importance in the context of EC environmental policy. They are:

(i) *Regulations*: measures of immediate general application which bind Member States and, if they so extend them, individuals in those states as part of national law; *i.e.*, they become directly effective without further national legislation and take precedence over national law in the event of a conflict between the two. Several have been adopted on environmental issues.

(ii) *Directives*: measures which can be individual or addressed to all. Though binding as far as their objectives are concerned, directives leave the choice of means of compliance to each Member State, which is also often given an extended time limit within which to bring about compliance. They thus only become effective when implemented and generally, but not invariably, set a time limit for their implementation which is not always strictly observed by Member States, as we shall see in the case of some Directives, *e.g.*, on the quality of bathing beaches. They are required to send the Commission "compliance notices" (which are not published by the Commission) explaining the steps taken by them formally to comply with the Directive; these enable the Commission to determine whether the state concerned has fully complied and the steps to take if it has not. Directives are much used for environmental protection.

(iii) *Decisions*: individual measures addressed to all Member States which are binding both in relation to their objective and the means prescribed for implementation. These are rarely resorted to in practice, though one or two have been taken on the environment.

(iv) *Recommendations or Opinions*: acts of Community authorities which are purely advisory and do not bind Member States.

All these measures require a unanimous vote of the Council of the Community for adoption; since measures (i)-(iii) ultimately become binding following their various procedures,[7] the approval required for their adoption can take a long time to secure. There is no doubt, however, that once adopted the end result is an effective instrument, backed by enforcement provisions of much greater power than is normally the case in international law. As the ECJ has stated succinctly, "the EEC Treaty has established its own system of law, integrated into the legal systems of the Member States, and which must be applied by their courts."[8]

To execute its objectives, to develop and implement the necessary instruments, the Community is equipped with four organs, all of which are now involved in the processes of creating and applying the Community's environmental policy, *viz.*, the Council of Ministers, the Commission, the ECJ and the European Parliament.

(i) *The Council*: This is the supreme and most powerful body; the decision-making body in which voting is weighted according to a formula laid down in the Treaty of Rome.[9] Decisions taken under some Articles -- such as Article 235 on which several environmental measures have been based -- require unanimity, however. The Council tends in any case to aim at unanimity, to avoid invocation of the so-called "Luxembourg Agreement," which endorses the practice of not imposing a decision by qualified majority on a Member State if it regards that issue as a matter of vital national interest. So far that has not arisen on environmental issues. Council meetings are attended by the national Minister whose powers are most appropriate to the subject matter at issue -- in the case of the environment, generally the Environment Minister, though for marine living resources it will be the Fisheries Minister and for non-living resources the Trade Minister. Meeting as the Council of Ministers, they adopt the relevant Regulations, Directives or Decisions proposed by the Commission. Their powers include that under Article 100 of the Treaty of Rome of approximating Member States' own laws, regulations and administrative measures directly affecting the Common Market. It may be even more difficult than before for the Council to act on environmental issues following the enlargement of the Community by the entry of Greece, Spain and Portugal.

(ii) *The Commission*: This is the permanent executive organ consisting of Commissioners, independent of their national governments. It has an important role to play in the process since, as the body charged with ensuring that both the Treaty provisions and the measures taken by the Community in pursuance of them are carried out, it can make legislative proposals to the Council of Ministers for adoption or rejection.[10] The Commission, unlike the Council itself, can exercise its own initiative in putting forward policy proposals without being subject to direction from individual Member States, although working closely with them. The Environment Policy sprang from such initiatives. The Commission tries hard to further integration and inculcate community spirit, encouraging Members to be "communautaire." It can resort to use of formal procedures, to ensure compliance with measures adopted, such as the issue of "Reasoned Opinions" concerning whether Member States have complied with Community law, which can lead to an issue being referred by it to the European Court of Justice, though this procedure has very seldom been used for environmental issues. It can fine and therefore penalize defaulting enterprises but generally strives for compromises. Unfortunately this sometimes means, in the case of marine pollution, that the lowest standard acceptable to one member becomes the common standard. Nonetheless, despite Commission powers under these procedures to take the initiative in developing an environmental policy, ideas can also flow from the member states themselves. As pointed out by Haigh in a recent work, "discussion on policy has a way of leaping between the States and Community institutions so that a matter which starts as a national issue may become 'Europeanised' and so in turn becomes an issue in other Member States,"[11] as happened with the issue of the lead content of petrol. Member States must inform the Commission of their proposals for national environmental legislation; the Commission then has two months to decide whether the proposed measure is appropriate for action at the Community level; if it so decides, the Member State must suspend its proposal for five months to enable the drafting of the Community legislation. Only the numbers of notifications of legislation have been revealed, not their content or significance.

If the Council wants Commission proposals amended, it has to return them to the Commission for re-submission. Though the Commission works closely with Member States, since proposals usually require approval by their national ministers, it does have scope for innovation within the framework of the Rome Treaty and has been making increasing use of this in the environmental field. Moreover, it is the Commission which represents the Community in international bodies based on treaties to which the Community has become party such as the Paris Convention on Land-Based Pollution, or under which it has observer status such as the Oslo Convention on Ocean Dumping or the London Dumping Convention.

(iii) *The European Court of Justice*: This was established by the Treaty of Rome[12] to supervise Member States' observance of that instrument and in order to ensure that in its interpretation and application Treaty law is respected. The ECJ consists of one judge from every Member State and interprets the Community treaties in the context of suits brought before it by the EEC institutions, Member States, companies and individuals, or referred to it by Member State courts concerning matters arising under the Treaty. It can also, if Member States specially agree, decide disputes between individual Member States concerning the Treaty's objects and purposes.[13] Its decisions are binding and must be enforced nationally by Member States by appropriate means.[14] They can and do relate to environmental issues.

(iv) *European Parliament*: This is now a democratically elected body, which exercises, however, not legislative but advisory and supervisory powers conferred on it by the Rome Treaty.[15] As its powers are limited and general, it is not subject to the intense political pressures and need for compromise found in the Council and can be more forward looking. It too, therefore, can play a role in developing an environmental policy; debating the issues and commissioning studies and reports which, if approved by Parliament, can be forwarded, along with any accompanying recommendations, to the Commission which is required to reply (orally or in writing) to any questions put to it by Parliament. Parliament generally acts in these respects by an absolute majority of votes cast. The Rome Treaty requires that Parliament be consulted in certain cases before the Council adopts Commission proposals. In practice the Commission sends all texts (including environmental ones) to Parliament in advance and may amend them in the light of Parliament's views, though it is not required to do so. Parliament has thus exerted considerable influence on such issues as conservation of living resources and prevention of oil pollution. Its greatest power, as yet never used, is that it can censure the Commission, or even dismiss it. Its role could be expanded, though Member States are not at present inclined to do this.

The Role of the Community as Such

In the light of all these roles and powers, the EC, as such, has greater opportunities than almost any other body in the environmental field for organizing international cooperation among its members and developing binding, as well as recommendatory, measures to protect the environment. Though not a state, the Community has its own legal personality in both national and international law under well-established tenets of international law.[16] This means that in its external relations the Community enjoys the capacity to establish contractual links with third countries over the whole field of the objectives of the Treaty.[17] This power is an exclusive one, *i.e.*, in purely economic policies, the Community (represented by the Commission), not the Member States, has been found by the ECJ to have the power to conclude agreements with third states and to take its own place in relevant international bodies. However, while it has been made clear from the case law of the ECJ (despite the fact that the Treaty of Rome does not expressly confer such a power[18]) that the Communities have implied powers deriving from the EC Treaties to enter into treaties with third states in commercial fields and that this power to conclude trade agreements precludes the exercise of concurrent powers by Member States, the Community's role in environmental questions has been much less clear. This is partly because the EC treaties themselves make no reference to the Comunity's role in protecting the environment and partly because, once the Commission begins to consider such a role, the fact that environmental measures are only partially economic in effect clouds the issue. This has led to resistance by some Member States to Community efforts to extend its powers in this field, with the result that, in environmental treaties which are not purely economic in their objectives, such as those dealing with pollution, both the EC and its individual Member States become parties; whereas in fishery conventions and the commissions they establish, though their aims are indirectly environmental insofar as they aim to conserve resources in order to exploit them, since the predominant aim is exploitation, the Community as such has replaced its members, *e.g.*, in NEAFC (North East Atlantic Fishery Commission) and NAFO (Northwest Atlantic Fishery Organization). The extent of the EC's participation in treaties concerning the pollution of the marine environment, such as the Barcelona Convention on the Mediterranean Sea, the Oslo and London Dumping Coventions, the Paris Convention on Land-Based Pollution and the UN Law of the Sea Convention (LOSC), will be dealt with in more detail later. Suffice it to say here that the EC has become a party to the Paris Convention but has not been able to sign the London and Oslo Conventions because of opposition from some of its Member States.

The Community's long-lasting attempt to ensure that the LOSC provided for its signature met with success only at the Final Session. LOSC provides in Article 305 (1)(j) for signature by international organizations constituted by states to which their member States have transferred competence over matters governed by that Convention, including the competence to enter into treaties in respect of these matters, *i.e.*, bodies such as the EC. It permits such organizations to sign if a majority of their member states are also signatories. There are two additional requirements of great significance to the Community: on signing, the EC was required by Annex IX, Article 2, to declare first the matters governed by LOSC in respect of which competence had been transferred to it by such of its members as were also signatories; and, secondly, the nature and extent of that competence. By December 7, 1984, eight of the then ten members had signed LOSC; thus, though the U.K. and F.R.G. did not do so because of their objections to some of the seabed mining provisions, the necessary majority was obtained and the EC signed on December 7, 1984. It declared that "its Member States have transferred competence to it with regard to the conservation and management of sea fishing resources. Hence, in the field of sea fishing it is for the Community to adopt the relevant regulations (which are enforced by Member States) and to enter into external undertakings with Third States or competent international organizations."[19] However, its declaration concerning its competence in other marine environmental matters was markedly less forthright.

It states, "furthermore, with regard to rules and regulations for the protection and preservation of the marine environment, the Member States have transferred to the Community *competences as formulated in provisions adopted by the Community and as reflected by its participation in certain international agreements.*"[20] The latter were listed in an Annex. The list is highly selective as this paper will reveal. It refers to only eight Directives and three Conventions -- the Transboundary Atmospheric Convention, the Paris Convention on Land-Based Pollution and the Mediterranean Convention on Pollution, and the two Protocols to the latter.

The meaning and limitations of this pragmatic and enigmatic declaration will be made apparent by the examination of the series of relevant directives and the instruments adopted by the EC to protect its marine environment, and also by references to Commission proposals that have failed to gain approval.

The Background to the EC's Environment Policy

Although the Community Environment Policy is now well established, initially the Community experienced some difficulty in finding a legal basis for it in the Treaties since no specific article either authorized or required it. Indeed, as some Member States were quick to point out, the Community was established for economic objectives, many of which were arguably incompatible with environmental protection; it was neither obviously appropriate nor advisable, in their view, that the Community should extend its scope to environmental protection; certainly it was not required. The Commission took the view, however, that several Articles, especially Articles 2 and 100, require it to develop such a policy. The legal arguments are discussed in more detail in the section following.

The Preamble to the Treaty of Rome sets out only very general objectives -- closer union of European peoples; promotion of economic and social progress; concerted action to ensure steady expansion; balanced trade and fair competition; and reduction of regional differences. Article 2 lays down basic aims: harmonious development of economic activities throughout the Community; continuous and balanced expansion; increased stability; accelerated living standards; closer relations between Member States. These were to be achieved by the establishment of a common market and the progressive approximation of the economic policies of Member States. The first method requires the free movement of goods, persons, services and capital, the right of establishment and rules governing competition. The Community has used its law-making powers to effect these. The second method is expressed, however, in much more general terms, requiring policy rather than law-making, and affords more scope for applying the treaty to wider fields such as the environment, though the detailed objectives concerning establishment of a common agricultural policy (including fisheries)[21] have environmental implications for protection of living resources.

The Rome Treaty's more general provisions are open to interpretation, allowing the Commission an opportunity to develop policies and regulations in fields not specifically covered and in ways not specifically required. Following the Torrey Canyon disaster in 1969 (in which an oil tanker was wrecked off Cornwall) and the Council of Europe's designation of 1970 as "European Conservation Year" (which focused attention throughout Europe on environmental problems and issues), in 1971 the Commission sent the Council a Memorandum on the environment pointing to the need to take account of natural resources and the quality of life in defining and organizing economic development in the Community and outlining Community action in this field.[22] This was shortly followed by the UN's Conference on the Human Environment (UNCHE) held in Stockholm in 1972; its Declaration of Principles[23] focused attention on a whole range of environmental issues. It recognized, for the first time, the need to take action to protect the environment and related this to the need of states, particularly developing states, to develop economically by adopting their own environmental policies. It also identified the actions most urgently needed, adopted an Action Plan and numerous recommendations (including principles on marine pollution) and established the United Nations Environment Programme (UNEP) as a focal point for environmental action. This acted as a catalyst for EC action.

Thus in 1972 a meeting of the EC Heads of Government (the Paris Summit) recognized that economic expansion was not an end in itself and set eleven principles for a new environmental policy for the Community, which took account of the UNCHE principles.[24] These principles are important since they put the Community on a new course, of which they remain, as supplemented later, the foundation. They included recognition that:

- it was better to counter pollution at its source than to tackle its effects;
- any policy must be compatible with economic and social development;
- exploitation of the environment (including the marine environment) which causes significant damage to the ecological balance must be avoided;
- more encouragement of scientific research was required;
- the polluter must bear the costs of his pollution;
- activities in one state should be not so executed as to degrade the environment (including the marine environment) or another;
- the interests of developing states and effects on their economic development must be taken into account;
- the EEC must make an original and audible contribution in international organizations dealing with the environment;
- for each pollution category a fitting level of action should be established;
- major environmental policy issues in each country must be planned, not implemented in isolation.

Finally, it was determined that the Community environmental policy must be aimed, as far as possible, at the coordinated and harmonized progress of national policies but without hampering projected or actual progress at the national level and without jeopardizing the satisfactory operation of the Common Market. In the event, however, the Community's environmental actions have fallen far short of the aims and recommendations of the UNCHE on which its new policy was based.

In 1973, the EC Council adopted a Community policy and Action Program on the Environment, which has been updated in 1977 and 1981 and soon will be revised once more. All have observed the cardinal principles set out in 1972, especially the "polluter pays" principle; the principle that priority be given to prevention not cure, and the principle that the most appropriate geographical level (local, regional, national, community, international) must be sought for each type of action. Thus the Community only intervenes if national action needs to be set in wider perspective in order to make if fully effective or if it involves common interest (such as protecting the marine or atmospheric environment) or when the adoption of divergent national measures would cause major economic or social problems.[25]

Given the growing economic disparities between Member States, especially relating to specific regions and the political difficulties already experienced, this set of objectives contains the possibility of considerable division and conflict over the need for environmental action on particular issues in the first place, and the level at which such action should be taken and its content and scope in the second place. Moreover, before the Community could embark on such a policy, it had to overcome the objection of some of its members that there was no legal basis for such a policy.

Legal Basis of the EC Environment Policy

Although the EC treaties made no direct reference to protection of the environment, the Commission felt that a number of articles as well as the Preamble[26] provided, in its view, a legal basis for the policy -- if liberally interpreted in accordance with the Rome Treaty's objectives.[27] Their appropriateness has been challenged by critics in Member States and discussed extensively by commentators although, following twelve years of Community action on the environment, these criticisms and arguments are now of academic interest only,[28] particularly as the ECJ has recently found that Article 100 provides an appropriate basis for the adoption of an Environmental Directive.[29] Chief among the objectives relied on is that set out in the Preamble, namely that Treaty Parties shall seek to promote "the constant improvement of living and working conditions of their people." This has been interpreted by the Community as requiring provision of an environment of quality (as laid down in the UNCHE Declaration) based on the cleanest possible air, the purest possible water and the least possible contaminated surroundings.

Another cardinal principle of the Rome Treaty is the creation of a common market in goods and services, which seeks to avoid any distortion created by competition and technical barriers to trade. Differences in national environmental protection legislation could undermine this objective. For example, some Member States might require installation of expensive equipment to abate the discharge of land- or ship-based pollutants into the marine environment; others might not. Thus consumers in the former state would be adversely affected because the serious economic costs of pollution would be passed on to them. It is this linkage that resulted in the Division (now the Directorate) eventually established within the Commission to manage these affairs, somewhat cumbersomely and incongruously designated as "The Consumer Affairs and Environment Protection Division." Harmonizing national environmental laws, a specific aim of the Community, would avoid variance in economic costs passed on to consumers.

Finally, the Community appreciated that it should become involved in development of an environmental policy because of the transboundary and transnational nature of the problems involved. Pollution and living resources, especially the marine and airborne varieties, know no borders. Hydrological and evaporation cycles ensure that one state's waste discharges become another state's pollution -- a perspective that applies within the Community itself, *i.e.*, amongst its Member States, and between the Community and its neighboring states on land and across its surrounding seas, such as the North Sea, North Atlantic, Irish and

Celtic Seas, Western Approaches and the Mediterranean. It should be noted that 80 percent of Community lakes and rivers, major receivers of pollutants, are shared by two or more Member States; the problems of abating salt discharges and chemical dumping in the Rhine, which contribute largely to marine pollution, are familiar and have proved difficult to resolve, as have the problems of transboundary atmospheric pollution -- the so-called "acid rain."[30]

The transfrontier nature of pollution and the migratory nature of species have encouraged and enabled the Community to interpret the provisions of its founding treaty not only to encompass harmonization of its Member States' national laws but also to participate with (not replace) its members in other international bodies concerned with environmental protection, either (when provided for by the relevant treaties) as a full party or as an observer. Some members (notably the U.K.) nonetheless remain critical not only of the legal bases of the EC policy but of its ambitious scope in practice in relation to EC resources, commitments and priorities, and its open-ended definitions. The U.K.'s House of Lords' Select Committee on the European Communities has observed the variety of levels of meaning which the Community has attributed to "common," *i.e.*, Community, policy: in some instances it refers to overall Community jurisdiction and right to legislate in a field (the first level, *i.e.*, the legal competence discussed above); in others it refers to the objectives but it can also refer to the measures (Regulations, etc.) used to achieve them. The Action Programmes are set on the second level but Member States, taking advantage of the legal ambiguities, frequently endeavor to put a brake on the speed with which the Community approaches its environmental objectives by impeding the adoption of the necessary action (the third level). Some articles of the Rome Treaty (*e.g.*, Article 100 and Article 235) require unanimity in the Council, which further seriously inhibits the EC from playing such a progressive a role in environmental regulation as is proposed by the European Commission or Parliament from time to time. Thus environmental action remains only a small part of the Community's activities; nonetheless, the articles and policies on which it is based allow scope for it to develop dynamically, albeit pragmatically, and this it has proceeded to do.

The Community's Definition of the Environment

As pointed out elsewhere, the environment in its simplest definition is what surrounds one and is, therefore, best left to be looked after locally in the first instance;[31] but some issues require action at a broader level. Fortunately, while admitting that everyone probably has their own broad understanding of what is meant by *environment*, for Community purposes, the European Commission has adopted its own all-embracing definition, *viz.*:

> The combination of elements whose complex inter-relationships make up the settings, the surroundings and the conditions of life of the individual and of society, as they are or as they are felt.[32]

It admits this definition is cumbersome and others have criticized it as unduly anthropocentric,[33] but it does have the virtue of covering the natural environment (the countryside, its flora and fauna, rivers, lakes, sea, the atmosphere, wildlife generally, its habitats, etc.) as well as the man-made environment (towns and cities, architectural heritage, etc). The EC does not, of course, hope to regulate all these elements, but it is gradually beginning to identify and control, *ad hoc*, the priorities for such purposes.

There is no doubt that man-made activities, especially those emanating from economic development, increasingly pose a threat, if not controlled, abated or removed, to various of the above aspects of the environment. The chief threat is generally thought to be pollution, and countering this -- especially pollution directly generated by or occurring as a by-product of industrialization -- has been a chief thrust of the EC environmental policy. It is this connection that has encouraged the Community to extend its role to control of certain pollution-generating industries and activities, which diminish the quality of "Community waters,"[34] on land or at sea.

In taking this step, not without criticism from its Member States, the EC has had to define not only the *environment* but also *pollution*. It has adopted a revised version of the GESAMP (Group of Experts on the Scientific Aspects of Marine Pollution, drawn from various international agencies) definition, a definition used, with some variations or additions, by most European bodies for marine pollution control, as well as in the UN Law of the Sea Convention, *viz.*:

> The introduction by man, directly or indirectly, of substances or energy into the marine environment, including estuaries, which results in or is likely to result in such deleterious effects as harm to living resources and marine life, hazards to human health, hindrance to marine activities, including fishing and other legitimate uses of the sea, impairment of quality for use of sea water and reduction of amenities.[35]

This definition also is criticized by some environmentalists because it does not take account of changes in the water or effects on food chains or on ecology generally which do not immediately include apparent harm. Thus it does not preserve the *status quo* and takes a short-term, not a long-term, view of potential harm.

Let us look now at the series of Community Action Programmes and the measures taken to implement them in relation to the marine environment to ascertain the extent to which the Community meets its objectives despite these criticisms.

The EC Environment Action Programme[36]

The three Programmes of Action approved by the Council of Ministers provide the broad framework for the Community's policies and action in this field. The first two state the general objectives and principles of Community action in four areas: reducing pollution and nuisance; use and management of land; environmental natural resources and action to protect and improve the environment; international action.

In its Initial Reflections on the Second Action Programme,[37] the Commission noted that in the period of favorable economic activity prevailing during the First Programme's adoption, the objectives of "helping to bring expansion into the service of man by procuring for him an environment providing the best conditions of life" and reconciling "this expansion with the increasingly imperative need to preserve the natural environment" have been accepted; whereas now, after encountering economic difficulties, "these preoccupations have scarcely lessened," and a Community environment policy "to improve living conditions and protect our natural heritage without creating barriers to trade or distortions to competition is needed as much, if not more, today than it was in the past." It identified three key areas for action: first, continuation of action under the First Programme and its acceleration, if necessary, since the Council still had not taken decisions on some planned projects either because of their complexity or the slowness of procedure; second, clearer definition of guiding principles such as the need to take speedy preventive action, fix common objectives, coordinate national programs, and harmonize policies on a longer-term basis; third, concentration on changes in the economy due to reaction against the types of excess, such as wastage, which the policies encountered. Closer association with development policies of the third world was also advocated to avoid passing on pollution problems to them though the mechanism, *inter alia*, of the Lomé conventions. An environment policy, declared the Commission, should not be swayed by fashion or by short-term economic trends.

Nonetheless, by 1975, the Commission had succeeded only in putting forward a Directive on bathing water quality, though directives on freshwater fish- and shellfish-breeding water quality were being drawn up. It accepted that much work needed to be done to fulfill the aims and planned activities of the First Programme, *e.g.*, objectively evaluating pollution risks to establish criteria based on the concentration and effects of pollution in order to categorize pollutants for action; defining quality objectives and developing common methods to determine measures necessary to achieve these. Some Member States' introduction of "environment impact assessment" procedures should be brought into line with common evaluation criteria, which should, therefore, be developed. Reduction of nuisances at source should be maintained, *inter alia*, by adopting regulations on the discharge into the environment of particularly dangerous pollutants. In pursuing the aim of preventing pollution and waste, the Commission envisaged persistent action by the EC and its members at the international organization level and cooperation with non-members to find common solutions. Prominent among such actions was to be implementation of international conventions to which the Community was signatory. Action to implement such international agreements as the Paris and Barcelona Pollution Conventions and the Convention on Trading In Endangered Species (CITES) is a prime objective of subsequent programs. The Third Action Programme added a fifth area, namely development of an overall strategy, and the Resolution adopting it identifies eleven priority areas of Community action,[38] including several relating directly or indirectly to marine pollution (see below). It aims at promoting the implementation of Directives adopted under the previous Programmes, especially those covering the quality of fresh water and prevention of marine pollution and development of a more coordinated policy for the North Sea.

As Haigh has observed, the programs, though comprehensive, are obfuscated by ambiguities of whether all the items included are appropriate for Community action. The headings of the Council Resolutions approving the programs refer to the resolutions, not merely as Council-generated, but also as instruments of the "Representatives of the Governments of the Member States" and the Resolutions note that the action required "should in some cases be carried out at Community level, and in others by the Member States." Thus there is a continuing argument about what is appropriate to the Community level, though the priority areas indicated for the Third Programme are a guide to the Community's views in this respect. Nonetheless, the necessarily *ad hoc* nature of the adoption of measures in pursuance of these areas means that they are few in practice. Although the Commission, like govern ments, takes various initiatives (commissioning studies and research; giving financial assistance from its limited environmental fund; covering meetings of the conferences; stimulating publication), it cannot take the final decisions on environmental measures -- that must be left to the Member States, although legal questions can be referred to the ECJ. Here the Community has displayed a preference for the use of directives, which allow time for compliance, rather than the instantly binding regulations, for implementing the Programmes. Individual Member States are often reluctant either speedily or fully to implement measures because, in addition to the reasons already given (*e.g.* economic cost, doubtful legal basis), they doubt whether other Member States are effectively enforcing or applying them in the absence of Community inspection.

For purposes of evaluating the Community's progress in protecting the marine environment as a whole, ideally we would need to examine the measures, required and taken under the Action Programmes, which reduce the pollution affecting water and the atmosphere -- particularly the discharge of chemicals -- as well as protection and management of natural resources of marine flora and fauna. To illustrate typical problems which arise, we shall concentrate on the measures directly taken to prevent marine pollution, which in fact have been the main area of Community activity.

Priority Areas
The Community aims to introduce measures to reduce freshwater and marine pollution. Six priority areas have been established:

-    the definition of quality objectives for freshwater and seawater;
-    the protection of the aquatic environment against pollution by dangerous substances;
-    the protection of the sea against oil pollution;
-    the surveillance and monitoring of water quality;
-    measures specific to certain branches of industry;
-    activities under international agreements and organizations.

It has been able to adopt measures on some but not all of these, aiming as far as possible to reduce or eliminate pollution at source and take account of both the type of pollution and the environment into which it is discharged.

Directives Relating to Marine Pollution
The Community has adopted five directives on water quality which indirectly reduce marine pollution:

-    on the standard required for surface water intended for the abstraction of drinking water in the Member States;[39]
-    for bathing water;[40]
-    for fresh waters needing protection and improvement in order to support fish life;[41]
-    for shellfish waters;[42]
-    and for water intended for human consumption.[43]

Some of these have raised problems, but none as acute as the directive on pollution from certain dangerous substances discharged into the Community's aquatic environment,[44] which introduced in the Community forum the problems encountered also in certain regional pollution control commissions concerning the North Sea and North Atlantic areas (the Oslo and Paris Commissions), namely, whether standards set for pollution prevention or control should be strict and uniform emission standards (UES) (*i.e.*, limiting the amount of pollutants discharged at the emission point) or whether environmental quality objectives (EQOs) should be set (*i.e.*, stringent standards for the level of pollutants actually found in the aquatic environment, checked by continuous monitoring). The first approach is easier to apply and ensures parity of economic sacrifice but the second, favored in particular by the U.K., in its view permits the best and maximum use of the capacity of the marine environment to disperse and degrade many pollutants. In the U.K. view it is economically wasteful to prohibit or control the disposal or discharge of such pollutants (or amounts thereof) into the sea to the extent that the sea could safely absorb or reduce them. The Commission and other Member States prefer the first approach.[45]

The problem first arose in the Oslo and then in the Paris Commission since the Conventions on which both are based[46] require that harmful or potentially harmful pollutants be allocated on the basis of criteria laid down in the Conventions to Annexes with the aim of eliminating pollution from so-called "black-list" (List I) substances such as mercury and cadmium which are considered too dangerous ever to be discharged into the marine environment, and reducing pollution caused by so-called "grey list" (List II) substances which can be safely discharged if regulated and controlled according to specific criteria. As the two approaches (UES and EQOs) were irreconcilable, in the end it has been agreed both in these Commissions and later in the EEC that, for an interim period, states parties can adopt the approach of their choice. The EC has become a member of the Paris Commission, having concluded the necessary decisions,[47] and by Resolution has invited Member States also to adhere to the Convention.[48]

The compromise of allowing alternative approaches enabled the adoption of the so-called "parent" Directive on Discharge of Dangerous Substances but left the differences unresolved. They resurfaced when the Commission proposed so-called "daughter" (subsidiary) Directives to establish emission limits and quality objectives for mercury discharges from the chlor-alkali industry and for cadmium. They were eventually adopted on the basis of the compromises, including, as well as UES and EQOs, provisions encouraging the use of the "best available technology" in new plants,[49] allowing yet more flexibility in application. Another on mercury discharges other than from chlor-alkali industry discharges has subsequently been concluded on a similar basis.[50]

Apart from the Paris Convention, the only other marine pollution convention to which the EC has been able to become a full party does not involve the U.K. and has not, therefore, raised such problems, *viz.*, the Barcelona Convention for Protection of the Marine Environment of the Mediterranean Sea, inaugurated by UNEP,[51] and its Protocols.[52] It raises a different set of problems since it involves states that are not members of the EEC, some being developing states. The UNEP Cartagena Convention for the Protection and Development of the Marine Environment of the Wider Caribbean Region, which the EC has also signed, also involves developing countries. The EC is also a party to the Rhine Pollution Convention,[53] which indirectly controls marine pollution and has encountered its own special problems. It too involves a non-EC Member, Switzerland. The EC has not yet been able to become a party to the 1972 Oslo or London Conventions on Ocean Dumping although the EC Commission would like it to do so; neither Convention, since they were concluded before the first Action Programme, makes any provision for EC ratification. The EC does, however, have observer status at Oslo Commission meetings and at the Consultative meetings of the 1972 London Dumping Convention, which is administered by the IMO (International Maritime Organization). The Commission's proposal for a directive concerning dumping of wastes at sea remains pending in the Council.[54] Meanwhile, the European Parliament has urged that a fresh initiative be taken on full membership in both the Dumping Conventions.[55] In the interim, the Commission has established an action program on the control and reduction of hydrocarbons discharged at sea[56] to encourage adoption, as appropriate, of further legislation; an advisory committee to advance this process;[57] and a Community information system.[58]

Directives implementing the Directive on Discharge of Dangerous Substances deal with pollutants *ad hoc*, but the Directives laying down water quality objectives have a different purpose, *viz.*, transforming quality objectives into lists of acceptable parameters and appropriate numerical values which must either be observed or used as guidelines in the waters identified as covered. These Directives, as well as a related one to protect groundwater from pollution, are stated by the Commission as already to have been implemented or about to be so,[59] but all have, in fact, been subject to criticism and delay.[60] In some Member States there is no doubt, however, that a great deal of information is generated by the reporting requirements under these Directives; information which is now incorporated in the UNEP's GEMS (Global Environment Monitoring Service).

There is also a third category of Directive of relevance to marine pollution -- that dealing with specific industrial processes known to introduce pollutants into the environment with a view to reducing such emissions. However, only one, that requiring authorizations by Member States for operation of titanium dioxide plants (responsible for the so-called "red sludge" in the Mediterranean) to avoid deleterious effects on the aquatic environment or on legitimate uses of affected waters, has been adopted,[60A] though monitoring and development of programs for pollution reduction are also required.

Let us look, in the context of notification and compliance dates, at a few illustrations of the effectiveness of some of the Directives referred to above. Only those particularly relevant to the prevention of marine pollution will be discussed. The Directive on the aquatic environment will be discussed in more detail, as that is most important for our purposes.

Directive on discharges into the aquatic environment[61]
This Directive, which provides the framework for eliminating or reducing pollution (defined in terms of harmful effects, as already stated) of all Community waters (inland and coastal) from dangerous substances, was adopted on May 4, 1976, but without any compliance date, although the Commission has suggested September 15, 1978, for the introduction of a system of authorization; September 15, 1981, for introduction of programs to reduce pollution from List II substances; and September 15, 1986, for the full implementation of programs.

Following the system of the 1974 Paris Convention which, *inter alia*, it aims to implement for the Community as a whole (as it does the 1976 Rhine Convention and will later the draft Strasbourg Convention on Pollution of International Watercourses when it comes into effect), this Directive has an Annex comprising List I and List II substances. List I is based on their toxicity, persistence and bioaccumulation and includes mercury, cadmium, organohalogen and organophosphorus compounds and carcinogenic substances: these must be "eliminated." List II consists of less harmful substances such as zinc, copper and lead compounds, cyanide and ammonia. The List I substances are to be regarded as List II substances until specifically regulated by a subsidiary Directive setting their limit values, which means that in the interim they need *not* be eliminated; once limit values are identified, they need only to be appropriately "reduced." Even "elimination" (which will ultimately be required for List I substances) following Paris Commission practice in interpreting this term (the meaning of which was ambiguous and disputed), does not require total removal of all traces of the substance concerned since pollution is defined not in terms of the mere presence of the substance in the relevant waters, but by its effects upon them. Discharge of either category requires prior authorization, *i.e.*, operation of a permit system for List II substances. Permits must eventually lay down emission standards based on quality objectives related to such existing Directives as have been promulgated by the Community. Meanwhile for the List I substances a choice of regime is offered -- either setting limit values which emission standards must not infringe, these values to be set by the Community through a series of subsidiary directives (the system advocated by the Commission and adopted by all Member States except the U.K.), or the decentralized national setting of emission standards for Community quality objectives -- the approach preferred by the U.K. which borders the North Sea but not the Mediterranean, on the grounds, as we have seen, that it takes full account of the varying powers of the receiving waters to degrade and disperse pollutants. It was also argued in the U.K. that emission standards were preferred by the majority of the EC only because the alternative of quality objectives would benefit U.K. industry economically and thus involve unequal competition arguments. The concept of variable emission standards set by reference to quality objectives had been accepted as the basis of the Rhine Convention and in the event was adopted for List II substances under this Directive; the U.K. diverged from fellow members therefore only in relation to List I substances. As we shall see below, for the moment, this is not as important as it may eventually become when more "daughter" directives concerning List I substances are promulgated.

Limit values will be established on the basis of toxicity, persistence and bioaccumulation: these are also terms which have created definitional problems in the Oslo and Paris Commissions, "toxic" not being a scientific term and "persistence" being ambiguous -- definable in terms of surface visibility or residual trace elements in the water mass. Also to be taken into account are the best technical means available for the manufacture of the substance and for the treatment of effluent, understood by the Community to imply that the economic availability of these means is a factor to consider.[62] In the light of these considerations it had proved possible by June 7, 1983, only to categorize on the List I cadmium and mercury discharged by the chlor-alkali industry; all other substances can thus be discharged subject only to the List II controls.

As Haigh has pointed out,[63] this Directive is different from the others on water protection in several ways: it sets no compliance date; the original proposal was for a Decision; the First Action Programme does not provide for the setting of limit values for the substances listed. Its origins ostensibly lay in the need, identified by Belgium, to coordinate the implementation of the three conventions referred to which all impinged on river pollution, but these conventions are neither exclusive to EC members nor inclusive of all EC rivers or waters.[64]

Finally, Member States must draw up inventories of all discharges that contain List I substances, to be supplied to the Commission at its request. They are not required (as had been proposed originally) to make inventories of any List II substances, though almost all substances will be treated in the interim as such until more "daughter" directives on List I substances are promulgated. The inventories will not, therefore, be of much use for the purposes of assessing pollution levels and sources in the waters covered. Moreover, this gap persists despite the fact that the Commission submitted to the Council in 1982[65] a communication stating that studies had pinpointed 1,500 substances included in List I "families" or groups and used for technical purposes. Of these, twenty-five were produced or used in quantities of over 100,000 tons per year (tpy); forty-four over 10,000 tpy; 186 over 1,000 tpy; 1,000 less than 100 tpy. 500 of these were subjected to risk evaluation; 108 of them (in addition to twenty-one already studied) were categorized for priority study and fifteen given the first priority for study. The Commission, stressing that the list was not final, has identified these fifteen. Five have already been the subject of proposals or of decisions not to make any proposal, viz., mercury and its compounds (the subject of one Directive[66] and a proposed Directive[67]); cadmium and its compounds (the subject of a daughter Directive[68]); aldrin, dieldrin and endrin (subject of a proposed Directive[69]); chlordane and heptachlor (no Directive is to be proposed; their use is the subject of another Directive[70]); hexachlorocyclohexane, in particular lindane (the subject of a proposed Directive[71]); arsenic (no Directive is to be prepared[72]).

The Council agreed in 1983 that the list of 129 substances (i.e., the 108 plus the twenty-one already studied) should serve as the basis of the further work program and that within three years Member States should furnish the Commission with such data as was readily available, including data on production, use and discharges by industries; diffuse sources; concentration in water, sediments and organisms; and on remedial measures taken or envisaged and their effect. The focus initially is to be on eleven substances only. This effectively overcomes the limitation of the List I inventory requirement by providing the Commission with information on all these substances.

Further action on List II substances has been confined to the convening of a meeting of EC experts in 1981, setting priorities for comparison of national programs on these substances, selecting six for prior attention, viz., chromium, lead, zinc, copper, nickel, arsenic,[73] and seeking information about Member States' national programs for chromium. The Commission has discussed the possibility of listing arsenic on List I but meanwhile has agreed that it should appear on List II.[74]

Despite the disputes and lack of enthusiasm for centralization of standards, etc., generated by the development of this Directive and its daughters, it is interesting to note that there is evidence that it has had salutary repercussions in the EC, overstepping the limited boundaries imposed by the necessity for political compromise; it has, in EC Member States, concentrated scientific and governmental thought and programs on ways of controlling toxic substances and providing information on them.[75]

Directive on Titanium Dioxide[76]

This Directive was proposed in 1975, promulgated on July 14, 1978, amended in 1983, and was supplemented in 1982 by the Directive on procedures for surveillance and monitoring of environments affected by waste from the titanium dioxide industry. The Directive was notified on February 22, 1978, with a date for formal compliance of February 22, 1979. Pollution reduction programs were to be submitted to the Commission by July 1, 1980, and to be introduced by 1982, in order to meet the program target by July 1, 1987. Triennial reports on progress are to be submitted, the first by February 22, 1981. The Directive, however, has been implemented only slowly by Member States and the timetable for its coming into force has had to be altered.

Discharge or dumping of this waste should be subjected to prior authorization by Member States' competent authorities, each authorization being subject to a time limit and based on information supplied by the applicant in relation to Annex I of the directive. Permits should be granted only if no alternative means of disposal are available and scientific evaluation established. There must be no harmful effects on the marine environment (immediate or delayed) or other legitimate uses of the waters in question. No emission limits are set, but if monitoring shows a higher toxicity peril than specified in Annex II, if there is any degradation of the environment or deleterious effects on other uses, or failure to meet required conditions, the authorities must insist that the situation be remedied, and, if necessary, should prohibit the discharge or dumping concerned.

Member states were required to draw up a program to eliminate titanium oxide pollution by 1979 but were unable to do this until 1982. Though all the industrial premises concerned should be covered, some can be exempted if no further measures are necessary. Delay in implementation prevented adoption of a further Directive, required by the main one, to reduce pollution by 1981. Currently a draft directive for this purpose is under consideration[77] to harmonize Member States' programs and set limit values. New establishments, *i.e.*, those set up after February 1978, now need prior authorization based on the results of an environmental impact survey, and it is required that the firms use processes, etc., which minimize environmental damage.

Waste Oils[78]

The Directive on Disposal of Waste Oils was proposed in 1974 and adopted on June 16, 1975; its compliance date was June 18, 1977; the final date for permits June 18, 1979. Triennial reports on progress are required -- the first by June 18, 1980. States must take the measures necessary to ensure a ban on discharge of waste oils into, amongst other media, internal surface waters and coastal waters. Provisions can be made under it for the licensing of the disposal of waste oils and for the keping of receipts by establishments disposing of more than 500 liters *per annum*. Research had shown that 20 to 60 percent of waste oil was disposed of without restraint in some Member States. The Directive aims at curing the environmental hazard and eliminating waste while avoiding impediments to the functioning of the common market.

States had difficulty complying. The U.K., for example, was the object of the Commission's Reasoned Opinion which assumed U.K. noncompliance because, though it had received some information, it had not been informed that all provisions had been complied with. The U.K.'s final regulations to ensure compliance with most of the Directive took time to enact and were not reported to the Commission until April 1981.

544

Even then, some parts of the Directive had not been met by the U.K. because aspects relating to an absolute ban on certain discharges and recycling requirements were impractical or ambiguous since the U.K.'s system of keeping records and provisions for separate storage presented problems in relation to some of its demands. This, however, remains the only Directive with which the U.K. admits some degree of failure to comply without expressing any intention to do so in the future. Meanwhile, the Commission has taken no further action and does not appear now to regard the U.K. in specific default,[79] presumably preferring to turn a blind eye rather than to force a confrontation over comparatively minor deficiencies.

Polychlorinated biphenyls (PCBs)[80]
This Directive requires Member States to take the measures necessary to ban uncontrolled discharge, dumping and tipping of PCBs, and objects and substances containing them and to ensure that they are disposed of without danger to human health or harm to the environment. It requires that they should as far as possible be regenerated.

It was adopted on April 6, 1976, and required compliance by April 9, 1978, backed by triennial reports, starting on July 18, 1980. The competent authority in Member States must designate enterprises authorized to dispose of PCBs. Again some Member States have had difficulty in complying; the U.K. was late in submitting the necessary information to the Commission which eventually issued a Reasoned Opinion concluding that there had been failure to comply because the information supplied by the U.K. was inadequate. The necessary regulations were eventually enacted in the U.K. and became effective in 1981, though arguably these may not meet all the requirements of the Directive which is, in any case, ambiguous in some respects, *e.g.*, concerning interpretation of "controlled tipping" and "disposal."

Other Actions of the EC to Protect the Marine Environment
The EC has turned its attention to other sources of marine pollution -- such as ocean dumping, vessel-source pollution and seabed (continental shelf) activities, but the Commission has found it more difficult to get the Council's approval to extend its scope to activities which take place in international areas, many of which are already subject to conventions and recommendations concluded in international fora, such as the IMO.

Ocean Dumping.
As we have seen, the EC's attempt to sign the London and Oslo Ocean Dumping Conventions was unsuccessful, since some Member States (who are also members of these conventions) questioned its capacity to do so. It was equally unsuccessful in attempting to promote a Directive to enable the Community to promulgate dumping controls on a similar basis to these conventions, to examine and consider the records of permits issued by Member States and ensure harmonization.[81]

Shipping safety and prevention of vessel-source pollution.
The EC has signed the 1983 Bonn Agreement for Co-Operation in Dealing with Pollution of the North Sea by Oil and other Harmful Substances and has observer status at the IMO, the organization through which EC Member States have so far preferred to work in this field. It is often suggested that the EC could do more to coordinate implementatation of IMO Conventions. So far it has proceeded slowly, pending

conclusion of LOSC, of which it is now a signatory. This event may have considerable impact on its further activity in this field and might enable the two member states that have not signed LOSC (F.R.G. and U.K.) to take advantage of its provisions on marine pollution, especially vessel-source pollution. Meanwhile the Community has adopted a Directive on minimum requirements for certain tankers entering or leaving Community ports,[82] As amended,[83] it requires oil, gas and chemical carriers of 1600 GRT and over to give specified information about themselves before entering a port, to complete a tanker check list detailed in an Annex and to give this to the pilot and, on request, to the port state's competent authorities. Rules are also laid down concerning safe navigation through the territorial sea adjacent to the relevant port.

The EC has also adopted a Directive on pilotage of vessels in the North Sea and English Channel[84] and one has been proposed on enforcement of international standards for shipping safety and pollution (mostly those laid down in IMO Conventions and Recommendations) on vessels visiting Community ports.[85] In its absence, the Community has played a role in implementing, by supervision in Community ports, the Paris Memorandum of Understanding on Port State Control[86] under which participating administrations undertake to inspect a set target number of vessels entering their ports to check their compliance with certain international standards of safety, etc., laid down in specified IMO and ILO Conventions and recommended codes of practice. Fourteen states, including non-EC members, have signed this instrument. It has been suggested, however, that the Community could and should do more to promote shipping safety in order to prevent casualties, rather than to deal merely with their consequences, since Community waters are densely used by vessels, many of which carry dangerous cargoes of chemicals and wastes.[87]

Oil pollution generally

The Community has also established an action program on the control and reduction of pollution caused by hydrocarbons discharged at Sea,[88] under which it is hoped to introduce further measures as appropriate, and to set up an advisory commitee[89] and a Community Information System[90] on the subject. Its attempts to develop controls for prevention of pollution from offshore installations have, however, met with opposition from Member States with offshore activities, notably the U.K.

In 1974, in the early days of continental shelf activity in the North Sea and the UN LOS Conference, the Commission sent the Council a memorandum on action which should be taken by the European Communities in connection with the prevention of sea pollution resulting from the exploration and exploitation of the seabed and ocean floor[91] proposing, *inter alia*, the drawing up by the EC of an outline convention (the broad lines of which it indicated) followed by regional conventions applicable to "homogeneous sectors of the sea-bed." The Commission proposed submission of these to UNCLOS and to non-member EC states, and that states (EC members and non-members) which had participated in the 1973 London Conference on Safety and Pollution Control should be invited to establish one of these regional conventions. It also proposed that other organizations should be encouraged to convene regional conferences taking similar initiatives for other "homogeneous areas," such as the Channel, the northeast Atlantic and the Mediterranean. The Commission saw the conclusion of divergent multilateral agreements on this subject outside the EC framework as creating economic and legal barriers, impairing both the environment and Europe's independence in energy. Nothing came of this proposal, and there have been no further initiatives in this respect; no common policy on energy has been established since Member States in whose continental shelves oil had been found were anxious that it should remain subject to their exclusive jurisdiction as coastal states, unlike the fisheries in the waters above, though they accepted that certain Rome Treaty provisions such as those on freedom of establishment and free movement of goods would apply to their offshore operations. It is notable that though most coastal Member States have established 200-mile fishing zones and some have nominally adopted EEZs, none has yet implemented the non-living resource or pollution control jurisdictions allowed in such zones by LOSC.

Atmostpheric pollution and conservation of marine fauna and flora

As pointed out in our introductions, space does not permit an examination of all the marine aspects of the broad Community Action Programmes. To illustrate how the Community operates in this field and to evaluate its success and its limitations, we have had to concentrate on one area, prevention of marine pollution *per se*, omitting Community actions to preserve air quality and wildlife though these are also relevant. We can only note briefly action on these aspects.

Atmospheric pollution

The EC has become a party to the 1979 Geneva Convention on the Prevention of Long-Range Transboundary Air Pollution in Europe, initiated by the UN's Economic Commission for Europe, and it has adopted Directives on the Sulphur Content of Gas and Oil;[92] Smoke and Sulphur Dioxide in the Air;[93] Lead in Petro and screening for lead and Lead in Air[94] and on Pollution from Motor Vehicles.[95]

Wildlife, including marine species

The EC has adopted a Directive on the conservation of wild birds;[96] two Regulations to protect whales by laying down common rules for the importation of whale and other cetacean products[97] and provisions for their implementation;[98] decisions on the conclusion of the Convention on Conservation of Antarctic Marine Living Resources;[99] the Council of Europe's Berne Convention on the Conservation of European Wildlife and Natural Habitats;[100] and on the Bonn Convention on the Conservation of Migratory Species of Wild Animals;[101] and a Regulation on the implementation in the Community of the Washington Convention on International Trade in Endangered Species.[102]

Conclusion

The Community's adoption of an Environmental Programme and of the Decisions, Regulations and Directives so far enacted to implement parts of it clearly has unusual advantages. Not only does the Community have unique organs and processes for this purpose, but to the extent that measures can or have been taken, they are binding on Member States, and although compliance is not always achieved by the date specified in the instrument concerned and is sometimes deficient in some respects, in general it is fulfilled. The Commission's powers to issue Reasoned Opinions and ultimately bring Member States before the ECJ are powerful sanctions deterring casual failure to comply. The result is that governments in the Member States are now required to take environmental aspects of their maritime and other activities into account to a much greater extent than hitherto, especially since the Council's adoption of the Third Action Programme, promulgated as a structural policy, *i.e.*, one of the central policies of the Community, which must be pursued irrespective of cyclical economic changes, so that the resources of the environment represent both the basis and the limits of economic development.[103]

In some cases the Community Action Programme and legislation has brought about corresponding legislative changes in Member States but, as pointed out by Haigh,[104] there are many other self-evident, long-term effects, on, for example, the flow of information, maintenance of existing legislation, attitudes of industrialists and regulatory bodies, discretionary powers of regulatory bodies, interchange of ideas and experience and techniques between Member States, and Member States' ability to influence each other's law and policies by providing standards to measure up to, evolved through processes different from the purely national. We must await studies like that of Haigh's on the U.K. for each of the Member States, however, before we can document these effects in detail. Meanwhile we can at least conclude that they will be significant, increasing the means available for environmental protection based on common standards and the arrangements for administering and implementing them, and also, of course, as the Community enlarges and increasingly presents a united front on a widening range of issues, influencing more strongly non-member states, especially through the participation as such of the Community in relevant international commissions.

Nonetheless, the Community's role is not without its own limitations and critics, since generally action results only after prolonged political battles from which the Commission's proposals often emerge in an emasculated compromise form, as in the case of the aquatic environment and other directives outlined in this paper. States may drag their heels in implementing even the instruments adopted. Some conflict of goals -- economic and environmental -- is unavoidable given the economic expansion aims of the Treaty of Rome; policies adopted to meet them may not always be "ecologically fitting," as required by environmental bodies[105] who consider that pollution, for example, should be defined in terms of its unpleasant effects rather than just its capacity to harm, and that growth of quality rather than quantity of growth should be the Community's aim. Environmentalists point to the EC's encouragement of growth of transport and energy use, especially of electricity, as a main source of pollution and waste of resources; to the fact that as yet the Community has failed to develop a detailed energy policy; and that when it did set exhaust limits, it set them too low. They call for the air and maritime areas to be protected not only because of their food and resource production capacities but because they are part of the environment -- the latter being also the habitat of wildlife and provider of recreational facilities. It is in this context that the "harmful" definition of pollution is regarded as deficient. The lack of an EC directive on groundwater pollution, one of the major sources ultimately of marine pollution, is regarded by environmentalists as a major gap, protecting industry at the expense of the community.

Finally, the EC's Environment Programmes must be tested by measuring their effects in ameliorating the pollution of the EC's surrounding waters, especially the North Sea and the Mediterranean which have been the subject of particular concern and attention internationally and the subject of conventions involving both EC members and other states as illustrated. It was recently reported that one group had concluded that the North Sea "will be dead in twenty-five years" biologically speaking and that "a devastating environmental catastrophe is imminent."[106] It called, therefore, for a review of industrial plant and port extension plans, the ending of oil and gas prospecting in the coastal areas and on mud flats, and the ending of the discharge of polluting alien substances into the North Sea. This view contradicts the conclusion of the 1984 Bremen Conference on the Protection of the North Sea[107] that there was no evidence of serious pollution effects in central areas although some estuarine and coastal areas were showing effects.[108] The Bremen Conference did not pursue a European Parliament proposal that there should be a single convention for protection of the North Sea.[109] Though it accepted in its final declaration that there was a need "to take timely preventive measures to maintain the quality of the North Sea," it asserted that these should be taken through existing commissions and the EC. The role of the EC as outlined in this paper is thus unlikely to be usurped in the near future by the institution of any other overall body in its area of competence though it will have to continue to coordinate its Action Programme with the other existing concerned bodies and to implement the provisions of conventions to which it is a party and any other relevant environmental conventions to which it may be permitted to become a party.

The Bremen Conference did not move away from the concept of pollution as harmful but recognized the need for more regulation of black and grey list substances through the EC, the Paris and Oslo Commissions and river Commissions, the phasing out of PCBs, new initiatives on "acid rain," and further actions on vessel inputs through the IMO and its Conventions, a policy advocated by the EC itself. The shape of future development of the EC's Environmental Programmes is thus likely to continue to follow the broad form and principles laid down in the three programs concluded to date and their implementation by EC instruments to remain pragmatic, dependent on the achievement of political consent through compromises between scientific advice and economic and environmental requirements. However, the fact that the Third Action Programme was adopted as a Structural Policy, to be pursued despite cyclical economic changes, indicates that in time the Law of the Sea Bulletin will record an increasing number of community texts applicable to protection and preservation of the marine environment and relating directly to subjects covered by LOSC. At present, however, the EC's potential for effective implementation of LOSC has not been fully utilized.

NOTES

1. For an introduction to the legal aspects of the European Community see D. Wyatt and A. Dashwood, *Substantive Law of the EEC* (1980); P. Mathijsen, *A Guide to European Community Law* (4th ed) (1985); D. Lasok and J. W. Bridge, *Law and Institutions of the European Communities* (2nd ed) (1976); L. Collins, *European Community Law in the United Kingdom* (3rd ed.) (1984).
2. Treaty of Rome, UNTS, Vol. 298, p.11; Treaties Establishing the European Communities (1973); European Communities, Luxembourg.
3. *Ibid*, Art. 1.

4. Illustrated by an important Belgian decision, *Minister for Economic Affairs* v *SA Fromagerie Franco-Suisse Le Ski*, [1972] CMLR 330, at p. 373.
5. Case 26/62, *Van Gend en Loos* v *Nederlandse Administratie Der Belastingen*, [1963] ECR 12; [1963] CMLR 105 at 129.
6. Treaty of Rome, Art. 189.
7. Case 6/64, *Costa* v *ENEL*, [1964] ECR 585, at p. 593; [1964] CMLR 425, at p. 455; Case 14/68, *Wilhelm* v *Bundeskartellamt*, [1969] ECR 1, at p. 14; [1969] CMLR 100, at p. 119.
8. *Wilhelm* v *Bundeskartellamt, supra.*
9. Treaty of Rome, Art. 148 (2).
10. *Ibid.*, Art. 155. Its powers have been neatly summarized as: initiator and coordinator of Community policy; execution agency of the Community; and guardian of the Community treaties, Lasok and Bridge, *op, cit.*, p. 112.
11. N. Haigh, *EEC Environmental Policy and Britain* (1984), p. 24.
12. Treaty of Rome, Arts. 164-168.
13. *Ibid.*, Art 173. In 1979, following the rejection by the Commission of the U.K. Government's request for certain exemptions from the requirements of the Directive on Titanium Dioxide, two U.K. companies brought an action in the ECJ against the Commission seeking annulment of the Commission's opinion that the programs were necessary. This was stated in the Bulletin of the European Communities (no. 5, 1979, p. 118) to be the first to come before the Court directly concerning environmental protection; Haigh, *op.cit.*, p. 119; OJ C153, 20.6.79.
14. *Ibid.*, Art. 171 which requires states parties "to take all necessary measures to comply with the judgement of the Court of Justice."
15. *Ibid.*, Arts. 137-144.
16. See I. Brownlie, *Principles of Public International Law* (3rd ed.) (1979), pp. 676-686.
17. Case 22/70, Re ERTA, *Commission* v *Council* [1971] ECR 263, at p. 274; [1971] CMLR 335, at p. 354.
18. Under Art. 210 of the Treaty of Rome the Community is accorded sufficient legal personality to conclude contracts with other states and organizations only; but the ECJ has found that "authority to enter into international commitments may not only arise from an express attribution by the Treaty, but equally may flow from its provisions."
19. *Italy and the Law of the Sea Newsletter*, No. 13, January 1985, p. 7; *Law of the Sea Bulletin*, No. 4, February 1985, pp. 16-19.
20. *Ibid.* Emphasis added. The Directives listed are those on reduction of pollution from hydrocarbons; discharges into the aquatic environment; disposal of waste oils; waste from the titanium dioxide industry; quality of shellfish water; mercury discharges of the chlor-alkali industry; cadmium discharges; mercury discharges other than the chlor-alkali electrolysis industry.
21. Treaty of Rome, Art. 3(d).
22. SEC (71) 2612.
23. Report of the United Nations Conference on the Human Environment, June 5-16, 1972, Stockholm, Sweden, UN DOC. A/CONF. 48/14/Rev.1, Declaration of Principles on the Human Environment, p. 3.
24. EC Commission, *Ten Years of Community Environment Policy*, March 1984, paras. 21-24.

25. Progress Made in Connection with the Environment Action Programme and Assessment of the Work Done to Implement it, Communication from the Commission to the Council, Commission of the European Communities, COM(80)222 final, Brussels, May 7, 1980, p. 2.
26. Articles 2, 84(2), 100 and 235. In a letter to the Times of January 20, 1975, at p.13, Lord Avebury, then President of the Conservation Society suggested an amendment of Article 2 to take full account of the need to conserve natural resources in the interests of successive generations.

   Article 2 states: "The Community shall have as its task, by establishing a common market and progressively approximating the economic policies of Member States, to promote throughout the Community a harmonious development of economic activities, a continuous and balanced expansion, an increase in stability, an accelerated raising of the standard of living and closer relations between the States belonging to it."
   Article 84(2) states: "The Council may, acting unanimously, decide whether, to what extent and by what procedure appropriate provision may be laid down for sea and air transport."
   Article 100 states: "The Council shall, acting unanimously on a proposal from the Commission, issue directives for the approximation of such provisions laid down by law, regulation or administrative action in Member States as directly affect the establishment or functioning of the common market.
   The Assembly and the Economic and Social Committee shall be consulted in the case of directives whose implementaion would, in one or more Member States, involve the amendment of legislation."
   Article 235 states: "If action by the Community should prove necessary to attain, in the course of the operation of the common market, one of the objectives of the Community and this Treaty has not provided the necessary powers, the Council shall, acting unanimously on a proposal from the Commission and after consulting the Assembly, take the approriate measures."

27. Set out in the Preamble and Art. 2.
28. See, for example, Conrad von Moltke, *European Communities: the Legal Basis for Environmental Policy* (1977); Marise Cremona, "The Role of the EEC in the Control of Oil Pollution," (1980) 17 CMLR ev. 171-189; C. Mastellone, "The External Relations of the EEC in the Field of Environmental Protection," (1981) 30 ICLQ 104-117. The U.K. House of Lords Select Committee on the European Communities in its Twenty Second Report (1978) and again in its Fifth Report on the EEC Environment Policy (1979-80) concluded that the EC was certainly not *required* to adopt an Environment Policy. It considered that the purposes of the Treaty of Rome were confined to the economic sphere; that none of its articles provided a legal basis for an environment policy and that limitations of staff and resources indicated that the EC should confine itself to a more general environment "strategy."
29. Re. Detergents Directive: *EC Commission* v *Italy*; Re. Fuel Directive *EC Commission* v *Italy*; [1981] 1 CMLR 331. The ECJ stated: "The Directive has been adopted not only within the Programme of Action of the Communities on the Environment; it also comes under the General Programme for the elimination of technical barriers to trade which result from disparities between the provisions laid

down by law, regulation or administrative action in the Member States ... In this sense it is validly founded upon Article 100. Furthermore it is by no means ruled out that provisions on the environment may be based on Article 100 of the Treaty. Provisions which are made necessary by considerations relating to the environment and health may be a burden upon the undertakings to which they apply and if there is no harmonization of national provisions on the matter, competition may be appreciably distorted."

30. J.G. Lammers, *Pollution of International Water Courses* (1984).
31. N. Haigh, *EEC Environmental Policy and Britain* (1984), pp. 3-4.
32. *The European Community's Environmental Policy* (second edition), European Documentation, Periodical 1/1984, p.7. The EC first attempted a definition in similar but simpler terms in a footnote to its Second Action Programme, *viz.*, "The term environment is used to cover all those elements, which in their complex interrelationships form the framework, setting and living conditions of mankind, by their very existence or by virtue of their impact."
33. Comments of the European Environmental Bureau (EEB) on the Environment Programme 1977-1981 as presented by the Commission of the European Communities, in EEB, Brussels, 1981.
34. Although the EC, not being a sovereign State, has no national waters of its own, it is common practice within it to refer to waters under the sovereignty or appropriate jurisdiction of its Member States (*e.g.*, economic zones, to the extent adopted by them) as "Community waters." For convenience this term will be used hereafter in this paper.
35. There are of course many other ways -- some more subtle and comprehensive -- of defining pollution. See A. Springer, "Towards a Meaningful Concept of Pollution in International Law," (1977) 26 ICLQ; Lammers, *op.cit.* pp.7-17; the latter, for example, in relation to watercourses, suggests that "water pollution means any detrimental change in the composition, content or quality of the water of a water system caused by man through the direct or indirect introduction into the water of substances or energy, provided that the change does not only reduce the capacity of the water to neutralize or carry away those substances or energy or has only been brought about by a change in the volume, velocity or turbulence of the water" (p. 16), which relates the definition to the pollutant-carrying capacity or powers of degradability of the receiving waters. Neither definition, however, covers the introduction by man of alien species of flora or fauna which also can have harmful effects on marine life or water quality or both.
36. *Viz.*, The First Programme of Action on the Environment, OJ C112, 20.12.73; Second Programme of Action on the Environment, OJ C139, 13.6.77; Third Programme of Action on the Environment (1982-1986), OJ C46, 17.2.83.
37. Initial Reflections on the Second Action Programme of the European Communities on the Environment, ENC/137/75-E.
38. Progress Made in Connection with the Environment Action Programme and Assessment of the Work Done to Implement it, COM(80)222 final, Brussels, 7 May 1980, pp. 1-9.
39. Directive concerning the quality requirement of surface waters intended for the abstraction of drinking water in Member States; 75/440/EEC; OJ L194, 25.7.75.
40. Directive concerning the quality of bathing water; 76/160/EEC, OJ L31, 5.2.76.

41. Directive concerning the quality of fresh waters needing protection or improvement in order to support fish life; 78/659/EEC; OJ L222, 14.8.78.
42. Directive on the quality required for shellfish waters; 79/923/EEC; OJ L281, 10.11.79.
43. Directive relating to the quality of water intended for human consumption; 80/778/EEC; OJ L229, 30.8.80.
44. Directive on pollution caused by certain dangerous substances discharged into the aquatic environment of the Community; 76/464/EEC; OJ L129, 18.5.76; for a critique of this Directive see Haigh, *op. cit.* in n. 11, pp. 96-112. The Directive was aimed at coordinating the EC implementation of the Paris Land-Based Pollution Convention; the Rhine Pollution Convention and the draft Strasbourg Convention on Pollution of International Watercourses. It appears that Britain, which strongly favored EQOs, in fact had not set up these processes internally but has begun to do so following the adoption of this Directive.
45. For a brief description of other approaches to standard setting and control and for an analysis of the theory and practice underlying the debate concerning UES and EQO see Haigh, *op. cit.*, Ch. 4: Tools for Pollution Control, pp. 27-36. They include setting biological exposure, process or operating, product or total emissions (the "bubble") standards, as well as EQOs and UES, and use of preventive controls. The Community has used them all in various contexts, often in combination.
46. Oslo Convention for the Prevention of Marine Pollution by Dumping from Ships and Aircraft, (1972) 11 ILM 262; Paris Convention on Prevention of Marine Pollution from Land-Based Sources, (1974) 13 ILM 352.
47. Decision concluding the Convention for the Prevention of Marine Pollution from Land-Based Sources, 75/437/EEC; L194, 25.7.75; Decision Concerning Community participating in the Interim Commission for the Prevention of Marine Pollution from Land-Based Sources, 75/438/EEC; OJ L194, 20.7.75.
48. Resolution on the Convention for the Prevention of Marine Pollution from Land-Based Sources; OJ C168, 25.7.75.
49. Directive on limit values and quality objectives for mercury discharges by the chlor-alkali electrolysis industry, 82/176/EEC; OJ L81, 27.3.82; Directive on limit values and quality objectives for cadmium discharges, 83/513/EEC; OJ L201,24.10.83.
50. *Ten Years of Community Environment Policy*, *op.cit.* in n. 24, p. 21.
51. Decision concluding the Convention for the Protection of the Mediterranean Sea against Pollution and the Protocol for the Prevention of the Pollution of the Mediterranean Sea by Dumping from Ships and Aircraft, 77/585/EEC; OJ L240, 19.9.77; Decision on the conclusion of the Protocol concerning co-operation in combating Pollution of the Mediterranean Sea by Oil and Other Harmful Substances, 81/420/EEC; OJ L162, 19.6.81; Decision concluding the Protocol for the Protection of the Mediterranean Sea against Pollution from Land-Based Sources; 83/101/EEC; OJ L67, 12.3.83. (A proposal for a decision concluding the European Convention for the Protection of International Watercourses remains pending, Text No. 74/2029, OJ C99, 2.5.75.)
52. The Protocols to which the EC is party concern Dumping from Aircraft and Ships; Co-operation in Cases of Serious Pollution by Oil and Other Harmful Substances; Pollution from Land-based Sources

(Athens Protocol) establishing a fund to aid states party to comply; and that on specially Protected Areas in the Mediterranean.
53. Decisions concluding the Convention for the Protection of the Rhine against Chemical Pollution and an Additional Agreement concerning the International Commission for the Protection of the Rhine against Pollution; 77/586/EEC; OJ L240, 19.9.77:
54. Text No. 75/688, OJ C40, 20.2.76; its objectives are to prohibit the discharge into the sea of certain dangerous waste and to set up a uniform EC system of certification.
55. European Parliament Working Document 1-1413/83.
56. OJ 1978, C162/78.
57. OJ 1980, L188/11.
58. OJ 1981, L355/52.
59. *Ten Years of Community Environment Policy, op. cit.* in n. 24, p. 22.
60. For details of this see Haigh, *op. cit.* min. 11: for that on shellfish waters, at pp. 81-84. (He suggests that it is questionable whether Britain is in full compliance with this Directive); on Bathing Water, at pp. 85-95. (Only twenty-seven bathing beaches have been notified by the U.K. as being subject to this directive though bathing takes place from 600 beaches in England and Wales; no beaches at all in Scotland or Northern Ireland have been notified); for surface water for drinking. at pp. 64-68; for water standards for freshwater fish, at pp. 75-80.
60A. See n. 76.
61. For a detailed description and analysis see Haigh, *op. cit.* in n. 11, pp. 96-109; see also J.H. Bates *United Kingdom Marine Pollution Law* (1985), pp. 122-125. Haigh's account of the political problems experienced by the U.K., internally and within the Community, in developing this Directive is particularly illuminating; see also his chapters 2 and 5.
62. Minute of Council Meeting of May 4, 1976, cited in Haigh, *op. cit.,* p. 97.
63. Haigh, *op. cit.,* p. 98.
64. The Convention for the Protection of the Rhine against Chemical Pollution includes all its riparian states (but not, therefore, the U.K.) plus the EC itself; the Paris Convention for the Prevention of Marine Pollution from Land-Based Sources is limited to discharges into the North Sea and North Atlantic; the Strasbourg Convention for the Protection of International Watercourses against Pollution (not yet adopted) is limited to rivers crossing frontiers and therefore excludes the Thames and the Seine.
65. OJ C176, 14.7.82.
66. Directive on limit values and quality objectives for mercury discharges by the chlor-alkali electrolysis industry; 82/176 EEC; OJ L81, 27.3.82.
67. Proposed Directive COM(82) 838; OJ C20, 25.1.83.
68. Directive 83/513; OJ L201, 24.6.79.
69. Proposed Directive COM(79) 243; OJ C146, 12.6.79.
70. Its use is already restricted by Directive prohibiting the Placing on the Market and Use of Plant Protection Products Containing Certain Active Substances; 79/117/EEC; OJ L33, 8.2.79.
71. COM(83) 422; OJ C215, 11.8.83.
72. COM(83)305 final.
73. Interestingly these are already the subject of study at the U.K.'s Water Research Center; see J. Gardiner and J. Mance, *Environmental Standards for List II Substances,* Water Research Center (1982).

74. Haigh, *op. cit.*, in n. 11, p. 104; COM(83) 306.
75. Haigh, *op. cit.*, p. 101-3.
76. Directives 78/76/EEC; OJ 1978 L54/19; 83/29/EEC; OJ 1983 L32/28; and 82/883/EEC; OJ 1982 L378/1. Haigh, *op. cit.*, pp. 113-122; Bates, *op. cit.*, in n. 61, pp. 125-6.
77. COM(83) 189.
78. OJ L194/23, 25.7.75; Haigh, *op. cit.*, pp. 150-156; Bates, *op. cit.*, p. 126.
79. Haigh notes that, in reply to a question in the European Parliament, the Commissioner stated that only Belgium had failed to comply; OJ C177, 4.7.83.
80. OJ 1976 L108/41; Haigh, *op. cit.*, pp. 144-149; Bates, *op. cit.*, p. 126.
81. OJ 1976, C40.
82. OJ 1979, L33/33.
83. OJ 1979 L315/16.
84. OJ 1979 L33/31.
85. OJ 1980 C192/8.
86. (1983) 22 ILM 227.
87. A. de Bievre, *Memorandum on Shipping and the Environment*, European Environment Bureau, Brussels (1984); "Shipping and the European Environment" (1982) 35 Journal of Navigation 451-59.
88. OJ 1978 C162/78.
89. OJ 1980 L188; 22.7.80, Decision (Commission Act) setting up an Advisory Committee on the Control and Reduction of Pollution Caused by Hydrocarbons Discharged at Sea.
90. OJ 1981 L355/52; 10.12.81, Decision establishing a community information system for the control and reduction of pollution caused by hydrocarbons discharged at sea.
91. SEC(74)2213 final, Brussels, 17 June 1974.
92. Directive 75/76/EEC; OJ L307, 22.11.75.
93. Directive 80/779/EEC; OJ L229, 30.8.80.
94. Directives 78/611/EEC; OJ L197, 22.7.78 and 77/312/EEC; OJ L105, 28.4.77; 82/884/EEC; OJ L378, 31.12.82 respectively.
95. There were five relevant directives from 1970-77.
96. Directive 79/409/EEC; OJ L103, 25.4.79.
97. Council Reg. 348/81, OJ L39, 12.2.81.
98. Commission Reg. 3786/81, OJ L377, 13.12.81.
99. Decision 81/691/EEC, OJ L252, 5.9.81.
100. Decision 82/72/EEC; OJ L38, 10.2.82.
101. Decision 82/461/EEC; OJ L210, 19.7.82.
102. Reg. 3626/82; OJ L384, 13.12.82.
103. "Agriculture and the Environment," U.K. House of Lords Select Committee on the European Communities, HL, Session 1983-84, 20th Report, evidence given by Mr. A. Fairclough, DG XI, at p. 149.
104. Haigh, *op. cit.*, in n. 11, Chs. 14 and 15; especially Ch. 15, pp. 299-301.
105. Comments by the European Environmental Bureau (EEB) on the Environmental Programme 1977-81 as presented by the Commission of the European Communities, EEB, Brussels, 1982.
106. The German Tribune, 7 July 1985, No. 1186, p. 12; based on an unpublished study by Professor K. Buchwald of Hanover. The group is mainly German but includes Belgians, Dutch, Danes, Norwegians and British.

107. W.C. Grogan and J. C. Side, *The Bremen Conference, 31 October and 1 November 1984: Retrospect and Prospect*, paper given at Greenwich Forum Conference, 1985.
108. For inventories of emissions and effects of pollutants in this area, see ICES Reports of 1974 and 1978 and European Parliament Document 1-298/81.
109. European Parliament Document 1-1173/83. The EP also proposed more coordination at Community level and involvement of non-EC member states. Leith Nautical College, Edinburgh, U.K. 2-5 April 1985. The Bremen Conference was attended by the Ministers of North Sea riparian states and the EEC, the secretaries of regional bodies (Paris and Oslo Commissions) and international organizations such as IMO, UNEP and WHO.

THE EEC'S CONTRIBUTION TO "STATE" PRACTICE
IN THE FIELD OF FISHERIES

R.R. Churchill
Center for Marine Law and Policy
University of Wales Institute of Science and Technology

The title of this paper may raise a few eyebrows, particularly those from outside Western Europe or unfamiliar with the EEC's Common Fisheries Policy, for clearly the EEC is not a state nor likely to become one in the foreseeable future. Nevertheless it is contended that for fisheries purposes the EEC may be regarded as a single coastal state. After seeking to establish this proposition, the paper will look at EEC practice in the field of fisheries, both as regards the management of fish stocks in EEC waters and as regards relations with third states. In each case a brief comparison will be made between EEC practice and the relevant provisions of the United Nations Convention on the Law of the Sea.

The EEC as a Single Coastal State

Whether the EEC may legitimately be regarded as a single coastal state for fisheries purposes has both internal and external aspects; *i.e.*, it depends on how the position is viewed both by and among EEC Member States themselves, and how it is viewed by third states.

As regards the internal aspect, before 1970 the regulation of fisheries was a purely domestic matter for each Member State. Since 1970 there has been a gradual transfer of the competence to regulate fisheries in the waters of Member States from Member States to the Community. This process culminated in the judgment of the European Court of Justice in *Commission v United Kingdom*,[1] given in 1981, where the Court held that the effect of Article 102 of the Act of Accession[2] is that since 1979 the competence to regulate fisheries in EEC Member States' waters has belonged "fully and definitively to the Community." However, at times and in places where there are no Community fisheries management measures in force, then, according to the European Court, Member States enjoy the competence to maintain pre-1979 measures and amend them in the light of biological and technological developments. At present the only Community waters where there are no Community measures in force are Member States' zones in the Mediterranean. In these waters Member States retain the competence described until the Community lays down management measures (which of course it is competent to do at any time). Elsewhere the Community has in principle exclusive competence: however, the Community has authorized Member States to take management measures in cases where urgent action is required or only local fishermen are affected. But even in these situations Member States' measures are subject to Community control, Community institutions (the Commission and/or Council) having the power to amend or revoke such measures.[3] It should be noted that even where Member States do have some limited competence, this competence must be exercised in accordance with Community law, *e.g.*, measures must be genuine conservation measures, non-discriminatory, notified to other Member States and the Commission, etc.[4]

It is clear that the Community as such is the body primarily responsible for fisheries management in the waters of EEC Member

States, with only a very limited competence being retained by or delegated to Member States. So much for internal aspects.

As regards the Community's relations with third states in fisheries matters, under Community law the Community not only has the competence to enter into treaties with third states on fisheries matters, but since 1977 has had the exclusive competence to do so: in other words, Member States have lost their capacity individually to enter into fishery agreements. This again follows from the case law of the European Court -- see in particular the *ERTA*, *Kramer* and *Rhine* cases.[5]

The Community's competence in this field has been recognized by third states by their entering into bilateral fishery agreements with the Community or by their accepting the Community's participation in a number of multilateral agreements. All these agreements, whether bilateral or multilateral, involve treating the Community as a single coastal state for fisheries purposes. Initially one group of third states -- those of Eastern Europe -- refused to accept the Community as a negotiating partner, but have subsequently not objected to becoming parties with the EEC to a number of multilateral agreements (*e.g.*, the Convention on Future Multilateral Co-Operation in the Northwest Atlantic Fisheries, the Convention on the Conservation of Antarctic Marine Living Resources), although no bilateral fishery agreement between the EEC and an Eastern European state has ever been signed. The number of third states which have some kind of treaty relationship with the EEC in fisheries matters now exceeds eighty.

It therefore appears to be legitimate, for fisheries purposes, to describe the EEC as a single coastal state.

Community Management of Fish Stocks in Community Waters

Coastal state management of the fish stocks in their national waters has become particularly important since the near-universal establishment of 200-mile economic or fishery zones. EEC Member States extended their fishing limits to 200 miles (except in the Mediterranean) at the beginning of 1977. Although the actual extension of limits was a matter for each individual Member State (since the EEC has no competence to establish fishery or any other kind of maritime zone for its Member States), extension was deliberately done in concert and coordinated by means of a Resolution of the EEC Council.[6] There are two reasons why EEC Member States extended their limits at this particular time. First, to counter the threat of third states' fleets being diverted from the waters of those North Atlantic states which were in the process of extending their fishing limits to 200 miles (Canada, Iceland, Norway and the U.S.) to the waters off EEC Member States, with the consequent danger of overfishing. Second, to give the Community a better bargaining position to negotiate access arrangements for Community vessels to waters of those states that had already extended their limits to 200 miles. The extension of EEC Member States' fishing limits to 200 miles meant that the EEC, together with its Member States, became responsible for the management of a significant fishery resource: EEC waters produce an annual yield of about six million tons -- nearly 10 percent of the total world marine fish catch.

Although the Community has had in principle exclusive competence in fisheries management matters since 1979, it was not until the beginning of 1983 that agreement was reached on a Community system of fisheries management.[7] This system has a number of elements. First, the Council, acting on a proposal from the Commission (which in turn is advised by a Scientific and Technical Committee for Fisheries, consisting of twenty-two fishery scientists sitting in an individual capacity) establishes each year a Total Allowable Catch (TAC) for most stocks in Community waters. For some stocks which are not (yet) fully exploited no TAC is set; for other such stocks a precautionary TAC will be set in order to prevent misreporting of catches in areas where catch restrictions would not otherwise operate; or to provide a limit on over-expansion in the case of rapidly expanding fisheries; or to keep a check on by-catch levels in industrial fisheries. The first year of the new Community system (1983) proved something of a fiasco as far as the setting of TACs was concerned, since it was not until nearly the end of 1983 that the Council was able to agree on TACs for that year. However, this was not such a disaster as it sounds, because the TACs laid down for 1982 were simply carried over to 1983. Since 1983 the system has worked much more smoothly, with the TACs for 1984 and 1985 being agreed on at the beginning of the year to which they relate or at the end of the previous year. At the time of writing, the catch statistics were not available in order to see how far the TACs set had actually been observed.

Once TACs have been set, they are divided up into national quotas and allocated to Member States. The criteria for allocation are past fishing performance, the needs of regions (such as Ireland and Scotland) particularly dependent on fishing, and losses suffered as a result of the extension of fishing limits by third states. This is a rather imprecise formula, and it seems that the actual quotas for a particular stock in any given year are the subject of a certain amount of bargaining in the Council. Quotas, like TACs, are set in terms of the Statistical Areas of the International Council for the Exploration of the Sea (ICES). Within the ICES Statistical Area to which a quota relates, vessels from an EEC Member State may fish for the quota anywhere, regardless of which Member State's (or States') fishing zone(s) the Area covers. This follows from the principle of equal access which was laid down in Community law in 1970.[8] The only exception to this is that off each Member State there is a twelve mile zone, access to which is reserved to local vessels -- although in some areas of the zone other Member States may enjoy limited access on the basis of historic rights. As with TACs, the catch statistics are not yet available to see whether quotas are being observed. In areas where no quotas are set (*e.g.*, the Mediterranean) or for species in respect of which no quotas are set (*e.g.*, horse mackerel), any EEC vessel may fish as a result of the equal access principle, apart from the twelve-mile zone already referred to.[8A]

The conservatory effect of TACs is strengthened by a number of other, more traditional, conservation measures which have been adopted by the Council. These include minimum mesh sizes, closed seasons, closed areas and limitations on certain types of gear. Like TACs, these conservation measures are based on scientific advice, principally from ICES, channelled through the Scientific and Technical Committee for Fisheries.

The chief responsibility for enforcing the above measures lies with the national authorities of the individual Member States. Only they, and not the Community, have the competence to arrest vessels and try those alleged, for example, to have broken Community conservation measures or exceeded quotas. Nevertheless, the Community is not entirely uninvolved in enforcement. First, catches must be reported to the Commission, which will order vessels of a particular Member State to stop fishing when that Member State has caught the quota allocated to it for a particular stock. Second, vessels over twenty-six meters fishing in a box around the Shetlands, Orkneys and North of Scotland, an area regarded as particularly sensitive because of pressure on stocks and the needs of local fishermen, require a license, which is issued by the Commission. (This is the only form of Community licensing, though some individual Member States require all or part of their fishing fleets to be licensed.) Lastly, and most importantly, the Commission has set up a small team of Community inspectors to verify that national officials are taking the necessary action to enforce Community measures.

The final element of the Community management system is the action taken to try to reduce the overcapacity in Community fishing fleets, which represents a threat of over-exploitation of fish stocks. A number of measures have been adopted, including grants for scrapping and laying-up vessels, for converting vessels, for encouraging fisheries in new areas and for previously under-utilized species.[8B]

It is obvious that the Community, through its Member States, has exercised the right given to coastal states by Article 56 of the UN Convention on the Law of the Sea, and also undoubtedly now by customary international law, to establish a 200-mile zone in which the coastal state has sovereign rights for the purpose of "exploring and exploiting, conserving and managing" the living resources of the zone. What is not yet clear, and what must now be considered, is whether Community practice conforms to the duties relating to fisheries management imposed by the Convention on coastal states. Of course, such duties may not be binding on the Community. Certainly they are not binding *qua* Convention provisions since the Convention is not in force (though it must not be forgotten that as a signatory to the Convention, the Community is under an obligation to refrain from acts which would defeat the object and purpose of the Convention[9]). Whether the coastal state's fisheries management duties have become part of customary international law is a difficult question, which it is not proposed to answer here. All that will be said here is that it is doubtful whether all these duties have become part of customary international law because some of these duties allow such a latitude of discretion to the coastal state that they would seem not to be of a "fundamentally norm-creating character," which according to the International Court of Justice is a necessary quality for a treaty provision if it is to pass into customary international law.[10] Whether the fisheries management duties of the UN Convention are part of customary international law and thus binding on the Community or not, they are a useful yardstick against which to assess Community practice. (For the purposes of this assessment, only Community practice since the establishment of a Community system of fisheries management at the beginning of 1983 will be considered.)

The UN Convention imposes essentially four duties on the coastal state as regards the management of stocks found in its 200-mile zone. First, coastal states must ensure that the maintenance of stocks is not endangered by over-exploitation (Article 61(2)). This is a duty which the Community would appear in broad terms to fulfill, since its general practice is to set a zero TAC for stocks whose continued existence is threatened. Second, the coastal state is under an obligation to maintain or restore stocks at levels which produce the maximum sustainable yield (MSY), as qualified by environmental and economic factors (Article 61(3)). Again this would seem to be a duty -- vague though it is -- with which the Community in general complies. The broad objective

of the Community system is MSY, subject to the inter-dependence of
stocks and taking into account the socio-economic needs of certain
regions and the desirability of greater economic efficiency.[11] When it
comes to setting TACs, for stocks which are over-exploited the TAC is
set at a level which will decrease past fishing effort and will ultimately lead to stable yields (presumably at or around the level of
MSY). The approach here is a gradualist one, in order to protect
the fishing industry from too sudden changes. In the case of fully
exploited stocks the TAC is set at a level which will maintain stocks
at a stable yield level (again presumably MSY).[12]

The third duty imposed by the Convention on coastal states is
to determine the TACs of the stocks in its 200-mile zone and its own
harvesting capacity (Articles 61(2) and 62(2)). This the Community does
for most stocks. There are one or two under-utilized stocks for which
no TAC is set. There is therefore not a complete compliance with this
duty, but the area of non-compliance would seem to be of little practical significance. Finally, there is a duty on coastal states to promote
the objective of optimum utilization of fish stocks in its 200-mile
zone (Article 62(1)). Assuming that optimum utilization refers to
biological rather than economic criteria, the Community would again
broadly seem to fulfill this duty. Most stocks in Community waters
are fully utilized. For those stocks which are not fully utilized, the
Community permits access by fishing vessels of third states (discussed
in more detail below). The Community also offers financial inducements
-- in the form of grants -- to its own fishermen to encourage them to
fish for under-utilized species.[13]

The general conclusion is that Community practice in relation to
the management of fish stocks in its waters is closely modeled on the
provisions of the UN Convention.

Having looked at EEC practice in relation to the management of
fish stocks in Community waters, the paper will now examine EEC practice as regards relations with third states. This will be considered
under two headings -- first, the access of third states to Community
waters and the acccess of Community vessels to the waters of third
states; and second, the management of joint stocks.

The Access of Third States to Community Waters and the Access of the Community to Third States' Waters

The UN Convention on the Law of the Sea provides that the coastal
state is to admit foreign fishermen to that part of the total allowable
catch for any stock which is surplus to its own harvesting capacity.
For Community waters, this means that the Community should (if this
provision of the Convention is part of customary international law)
admit foreign fishermen to any surplus in its waters. In practice in
most Community waters there is no surplus (at least of normally commercially exploited stocks). Only off the waters of French Guyana is there
any general surplus. Here the vessels of a number of third states --
South Korea, the U.S., Japan, Suriname, Venezuela, Barbados, Guyana,
the Republic of Trinidad and Tobago and, for a time, Brazil -- have
been given access to the surplus (which consists mainly of shrimp and
tuna). These vessels require a license (issued by the Commission), and
limits are set on the number of licenses, the size of catch and number
of fishing days; vessels must also carry a log book, observe all applicable fisheries legislation and transmit certain information to the
Commission. In most cases all or part of the catch must be landed
in French Guyana. These arrangements are enforced by the French

authorities, who must report all infringements detected to the Commission.[14]

The fact that there is no surplus generally in Community waters does not mean that there is no foreign fishing in these waters. On the contrary, there has been quite a high level of foreign fishing. The Community has given access to its waters to the vessels of third states whose waters have traditionally been important for Community fishermen in exchange for the access by Community fishermen to the waters of those states. Preservation of this latter access has been important for two reasons: first, to reduce the dislocation suffered by the Community's distant-water vessels as a result of the world-wide trend to 200-mile limits, and second, to maintain access to species which may not be found, or which may not be so plentiful, in Community waters. The third states whose vessels have been given access to Community waters on this basis are Sweden, the Faroes, Canada, Norway, Finland and, until it became a member of the EEC, Spain. With each of these countries the EEC has concluded a bilateral agreement on access.[15] The agreements themselves are all framework ones, providing the structure and procedures for fisheries arrangements, but leaving the details as to quotas, conservation measures, licenses, etc., to be established in subsequent negotiations between the parties. All the agreements provide that each party is to grant access to its 200-mile zone to vessels of the other party to fish for allotments determined by the first party. In the case of the EEC-Canada agreement this allotment is taken from that part of the total allowable catch which is surplus to each party's harvesting capacity, thus following the provisions of the UN Convention on the Law of the Sea.[16] In the case of the other agreements, however, the concept of surplus plays no role: the allotments are to be determined so as to achieve a balance between the fishing effort of each party in the waters of the other. In the case of the EEC-Norway Agreement, it is an understanding that the balance relates not to the quantity of catches but to their value. All the agreements provide that each party may require the vessels of the other party fishing in its waters to carry a license, and such vessels are subject to the fisheries jurisdiction (both prescriptive and enforcement) of the other party while fishing in its waters. Disputes relating to the interpretation or application of the agreements are to be settled by consultations and, in the case of the agreement with Sweden, where such consultations fail, by arbitration.

The details of the access given by the agreements are laid down from time to time in Community regulations. All these regulations[17] are broadly similar, though naturally there are variations both over time and as regards the different states concerned. The basic pattern of the regulations is as follows. They set out the quota which may be caught by the vessels of each state. In determining the areas where such quotas may be caught, the regulations take into account any historic rights which third states may enjoy in the waters of EEC Member States. Foreign vessels are normally required to carry a license, issued by the Commission on behalf of the Community. In the case of some types of fishing, the number of licenses is limited. Foreign vessels must also "comply with the conservation and control measures and all other provisions governing fishing" in Member States' 200-mile limits.[18] Foreign vessels must keep a log book in which information as to the size of catch and the time, place and method of fishing must be entered, and certain information relating to the vessel's movements and fishing operations must be transmitted by radio to the Commission. As far as the enforcement of these provisions is concerned:

> The competent authorities of the Member States shall take appropriate steps, including the regular inspection of vessels, to ensure the enforcement of [these provisions]. Where an infringement is duly established, the Member States shall, without delay, inform the Commission of the name of the vessel involved and of any action they have taken.[19]

Prior to the adoption of a Community fishery management system for Community waters in January 1983, the agreements providing for the access of third states to Community waters did not function very smoothly. Disagreement on the internal regime sometimes spilled over into the Community's external fishery relations, as one or more Member States from time to time blocked some external development in an attempt to gain a concession in the negotiations over the internal regime. Thus arrangements for the access of third states' vessels to Community waters were often adopted by the Council after considerable delay and for short periods. The result was uncertainty for foreign fishermen, and at times an interruption of their fishing, sometimes for several months at a time. In the case of Norway, Community fishermen on several occasions exceeded the quotas allocated to them in Norwegian waters. Furthermore, the Community at times failed to supply Norway with catch statistics, in spite of an agreement to do so. Since the adoption of the Community's own management system, the position concerning arrangements for third states' vessels fishing in Community waters has markedly improved. On the other hand, not all the blame for the problems encountered with the operation of the agreements lies with the Community. For example, the Faroese authorities have imposed such restrictions on the areas in Faroese waters where Community fishermen may fish that the latter have been unable to catch the full quotas as allocated to them, while Spanish vessels fishing in Community waters have committed an inordinately large number of offenses against conservation legislation.

As far as the access of foreign vessels to Community waters is concerned, it can be seen that Community practice in granting access diverges considerably from the scheme envisaged in the UN Convention. (It is not contrary to the Convention, for there is nothing to prevent a coastal state giving more generous access to foreign fishermen than is required by the Convention.) In particular, the concept of surplus has played little part in Community practice: reciprocity of access has been a much more important principle.

Apart from the reciprocal states mentioned above, the EEC also enjoys access to the waters of a number of other third states on a non-reciprocal basis and we must now examine this practice. These third states fall into three broad categories -- the U.S., a number of African states and Greenland -- with each of whom the EEC has concluded a fisheries agreement.

The Agreement with the U.S.[20] is the standard type of agreement that the U.S. has concluded with third states wishing to fish in its waters. The Agreement permits Community vessels to fish under license in the U.S. 200-mile zone for a portion of any surpluses that may be available, this portion to be determined by the U.S. each year. Under the successor to the original agreement, continued Community access to the U.S. zone is conditional on the Community facilitating access by

U.S. fishery products on Community markets. This is in accordance with recent U.S. practice relating to foreign fishing in its waters, following the introduction of the so-called "fish and chips" policy.

The EEC has concluded fisheries agreements with seven African states -- Senegal,[21] Guinea-Bissau,[22] Guinea,[23] Equatorial Guinea,[24] Sao Tome e Principe,[25] Seychelles,[26] and Madagascar.[27] These agreements are broadly similar. They permit a limited number of Community vessels to fish under license in the 200-mile zones of the above-mentioned states. The agreements do not say whether the amount of fish which the Community can catch (which is generally not precisely specified) comes from the surplus in these states' zones, but it is likely that this is the case. The conditions under which Community vessels have access include an obligation of these vessels to land part or all of the catches in the ports of, and to employ as crew fishermen from, the third states concerned. In return for the access described, the Community pays financial compensation to each of these states. This compensation is used for financing projects connected with fishing and fisheries research, and is in addition both to license fees and to any financial and technical aid under the Lomé Convention. Although the obligations on the Community and Community vessels may appear rather onerous, it is not uncommon to find such obligations contained in fisheries agreements between developed and developing countries, and indeed they are envisaged both by the UN Convention on the Law of the Sea and by the second and third Lomé Conventions concluded between the EEC and some sixty-plus developing states of Africa, the Caribbean and the Pacific.

Finally, there is the rather special category of Greenland. Greenland became part of the EEC when Denmark joined the EEC in 1973, but, following a referendum in Greenland, left the Community on February 1, 1985. Among the arrangements governing Greenland's withdrawal from the EEC is a fisheries agreement.[28] This agreement permits Community fishermen to fish under license in Greenland waters for specified tonnages of fish in return for the payment of financial compensation by the Community. The tonnages for which the Community may fish are fixed, according to Article 2 of the Agreement, as a "quantity which, taking into account the position regarding stocks, ensures that Community fishing activities in the Greenland fishing zone are carried out in a satisfactory manner." It is fairly safe to assume that the Community's quota will, for most stocks in most years, come from that part of the TAC which is surplus to the harvesting capacity of the indigenous population of Greenland. In addition to the tonnages guaranteed in the agreement, the Community is also to have priority access to that part of the TAC which exceeds Greenland's harvesting capacity and the amounts already allocated to the Community in the agreement.

Compared with the position as regards the access of third states to Community waters, the practice of the Community concerning the access of its vessels to the waters of non-reciprocal third states follows much more closely the provisions of the UN Convention, which is based on the idea of foreign states having access to the coastal state's surplus. While the conditions on which Community vessels are given access to third states' waters are generally fairly onerous, these conditions seem to be fully compatible with the UN Convention.

The Management of Joint Stocks

Many fish stocks do not confine themselves to the 200-mile zone of a single state, but migrate to the zone(s) of one or more other states and/or the waters beyond 200-mile limits. In relation to stocks migrating between the 200-mile zones of two or more states, the UN Convention on the Law of the Sea provides that the states concerned "shall seek... to agree upon the measures necessary to co-ordinate and ensure the conservation and development of such stocks" (Article 63(1)).

The EEC shares a number of stocks with third states, notably Norway, Sweden, Canada, Spain and the Faroes. Undoubtedly, too, there are shared stocks in the Mediterranean and in the waters off the French overseas departments, but these appear so far to have been the object of little discussion or investigation. Each of the reciprocal fisheries agreements that the Community has signed (mentioned above), provides that the Community and the third state concerned are to cooperate to ensure proper management of joint stocks. Such cooperation over management would seem to raise three main problems: (1) identifying joint stocks; (2) agreeing on conservation measures; and (3) allocating catches (a matter on which the UN Convention is conspicuously silent).

Cooperation under the reciprocal fisheries agreements is so far most developed with Norway and Sweden. With each of these states the Community has since 1979 concluded a series of annual arrangements. On the identification of joint stocks, agreement has largely been reached, although there is still disagreement between Norway and the EEC over whether North Sea sprat and Western mackerel are joint stocks -- Norway taking the view that they are joint stocks; the Community that they are exclusive to the Community. In the absence of agreement on this matter, each party manages them autonomously.[29] In relation to stocks which are agreed to be joint, however, there is joint management. This takes the form of setting a TAC (based on the recommendations of the ICES), and allocating it between the parties. The main criterion for such allocation is the proportion of the stock which is of catchable size found in each party's zone.[30] The annual arrangements also introduce other limited conservation measures and, in the case of the arrangements between the EEC and Norway, provide that the parties are to consult on fishery regulations with a view to achieving a harmonization of their regulatory measures. In addition to the bilateral arrangements just described, the EEC, Norway and Sweden have since 1979 reached trilateral agreement on arrangements for the Skagerrak and Kattegat.[31] These arrangements are similar to the bilateral arrangements, but they contain more supplementary conservation measures. The above arrangements have not always worked particularly well, especially before 1983, mainly because the Community has been tardy in implementing, or has failed to implement, its side of the arrangements, and because it has failed to ensure that its fishermen observe the arrangements. Furthermore, the appropriate size and allocation of the TAC for North Sea herring has been a largely continuing bone of contention between Norway and the EEC.

The EEC concluded with Canada, in 1979 and 1980, arrangements somewhat similar to those with Norway and Sweden,[32] but no arrangements have been agreed to subsequently, perhaps because of the rather strained fisheries relations between Canada and the EEC in the past few years. With the Faroes no arrangements appear yet to have been discussed to give effect to the obligation to cooperate on the management of joint stocks contained in the reciprocal fisheries agreements between the EEC and the Faroes.

As regards fish stocks which migrate between 200-mile zones and the high seas beyond, Article 63(2) of the UN Convention on the Law of the Sea provides that the coastal state(s) and the states fishing on the high seas "shall seek...to agree upon the measures necessary for the conservation of these stocks." As far as the EEC is concerned, the main area where fish migrate from its 200-mile zone to the waters beyond is the North Atlantic. Here the cooperation between the coastal state and other states called for by the UN Convention is realized through the two fishery Commissions for the North Atlantic, the North-west Atlantic Fisheries Organization (NAFO) and North-East Atlantic Fisheries Commission (NEAFC). The Conventions establishing these two bodies each provide that they and the coastal states of the region (including the EEC) are to coordinate their management measures in regard to stocks migrating between 200-mile zones and the areas beyond.[33]

Viewing the position globally, there appears to have been a relative scarcity of practice in the management of joint stocks. The EEC has therefore made quite a significant contribution to state practice in this area, and has put some regional flesh on the bare bones of the UN Convention's provisions.

Conclusions

Since the latter part of the 1970s a growing body of coastal states has claimed a 200-mile fishing or economic zone, so that today the 200-mile zone has become the basic framework for fisheries management. This development was inspired by the broad consensus on fishing questions which emerged at an early stage of the Third United Nations Conference on the Law of the Sea and which was subsequently incorporated in the UN Convention on the Law of the Sea. Thus even though the Convention is not in force, its provisions on fisheries are, to a greater or lesser extent, reflected in the practice of states.

To this practice a considerable contribution has been made by the EEC, which for fisheries purposes regards itself, and is regarded by third states, as a single coastal state. Through its Member States, the EEC has claimed a 200-mile zone, for the management of whose fishery resources it (rather than its Member States) is primarily responsible. The way in which the Community exercises its management responsibilities is broadly in line with the general fisheries management duties which the Convention lays down for coastal states. In relation to the access of foreign fishermen to a coastal state's 200 mile-zone, Community practice follows less closely the model of the UN Convention. The concept of surplus has not always been the predominant consideration: especially in relation to the access by third states to Community waters; the notion of reciprocity (which is not incompatible with the UN Convention) has been much more important. Finally, the practice of the Community shows how the general duty of cooperation over the management of joint stocks, which is provided for by the UN Convention, may be successfully implemented in practice.

NOTES

1. [1981] ECR 1045; [1982] 1 CMLR 543.
2. Article 102 reads: "From the sixth year after Accession at the latest [i.e., 1979], the Council, acting on a proposal from the Commission, shall determine conditions for fishing with a view to ensuring protection of the fishing grounds and conservation of the biological resources of the sea."

3. Regulation 171/83, *Official Journal of the European Communities* (herafter abbreviated to O.J.), 1983 L24/14, Arts. 18-20.
4. For a full discussion of the relevant provisions of Community law, see R.R. Churchill, *The Common Fisheries Policy of the EEC: A Legal Analysis* (Ph.D. thesis, University of Wales, 1984), pp.279-99.
5. *Commission v. Council (ERTA)* [1971] ECR 263; [1971] CMLR 335; *Officier van Justitie v. Kramer* [1976] ECR 1279; [1976] 2 CMLR 440; and *Opinion 1/76 (Rhine)* [1977] ECR 741; [1977] 2 CMLR 279. For a full discussion of the Court's case law as it applies to fisheries, see Churchill, *op.cit.* in n.4, pp.409-18.
6. Council Resolution of November 3, 1976, on Certain External Aspects of the Creation of a 200-Mile Fishing Zone in the Community with effect from January 1, 1977, O.J. 1981 C105/1.
7. Regulations 170-172/83, O.J. 1983 L24/1. For enforcement aspects of this system, see Regulation 2057/82, O.J. 1982 L220/1. As to why it took the EEC so long to agree on a Community system of fisheries management, see M. Leigh, *European Integration and the Common Fisheries Policy* (1983), Chap. 5 and M. Wise, *The Common Fisheries Policy of the European Community* (1984), Chaps. 6-10.
8. See Art. 2 of Regulation 101/76, O.J. 1976 L20/19.
8A. The allocation and access arrangements described here are considerably modified in the case of Portugal and Spain, which became members of the EEC on January 1, 1986: see Arts. 154-166 and 347-353 of the Act of Accession. Lack of space precludes any attempt to summarize these provisions, which are particularly detailed and complex.
8B. Regulations 2908/83 and 2909/83, and Directive 83/515, O.J. 1983 L290/1, 9 and 15.
9. See Article 18 of the Vienna Convention on the Law of Treaties.
10. See the *North Sea Continental Shelf* cases [1969] ICJ Rep. 3 at 42.
11. See the Commission's Communication to the Council COMS (76) 500, (77) 164, (79) 612 and (79) 687.
12. See the Commission's Communication to the Council COM (79) 687.
13. Regulation 2909/83, O.J. 1983 L290/9.
14. The access of these third states is not provided by means of bilateral agreements, as one might expect, but autonomously by the Community by a succession of regulations, the latest of which is Regulation 8/85, O.J. 1985 L1/73.
15. EEC-Sweden Agreement on Fisheries, 1977. O.J. 1980 L226/2; EEC-Faroes Agreement on Fisheries, 1977. O.J. 1980 L226/12; EEC-Canada Agreement on Fisheries, 1981. O.J. 1981 L379/54; EEC-Norway Agreement on Fisheries, 1980. O.J. 1980 L226/48; EEC-Spain Agreement on Fisheries, 1980. O.J. 1980 L322/3; EEC-Finland Agreement on Fisheries, 1983. O.J. 1983 L192/9.
16. But note that the EEC-Canada Agreement concerning their Fisheries Relations, signed on the same day as the Agreement on Fisheries, O.J. 1981 L379/59, fixes the quotas to be awarded to the Community by Canada for each year up to and including 1987. During this period, therefore, this concept of surplus will play no part as far as allocation by Canada is concerned. These quotas, moreover, are contingent upon the Community continuing to maintain the tariff quotas for Canadian fishery exports to the Community specified in the Agreement.
17. There have been literally dozens of such regulations. For the latest at the time of writing, see Regulation 4/85, O.J. 1985 L1/42 (Norway); Regulation 5/85, O.J. 1985 L1/52 (Faroes); Regulation

7/85, O.J. 1985 L1/64 (Spain); Regulation 3435/84, O.J. 1984 L318/9 (Sweden). For Canada there have, curiously, been no regulations on access since 1980. In the case of Finland, access to Community waters was the subject of Community regulation in 1977. Since then Finnish vessels have not been permitted access, and will not be until the North Sea herring stock has recovered sufficiently to allow a TAC in excess of 100,000 tons to be set.

18. Regulation 4/85, *op. cit.* in n. 17. The "measures and provisions governing fishing" are found in: (1) the licences issued to foreign vessels; (2) in the access regulations themselves; (3) in general EEC conservation measures applying in Community waters; and (4) in the limited legislation enacted by Member States.

19. Regulation 4/85, Articles 7 and 8. Note, however, that one of the penalties for infringement of the regulations, revocation of the license, lies solely with the Commission, and not with the authorities of Member States.

20. EEC-U.S. Agreement concerning Fisheries off the Coasts of the U.S., 1977. O.J. 1977 L141/2. This Agreement has been replaced by a similar agreement with the same title signed in 1984. O.J. 1984 L272/3.

21. EEC-Senegal Agreement on Fisheries off the Coast of Senegal, 1979. O.J. 1980 L226/18.

22. EEC-Guinea-Bissau Agreement on Fishing off the Coast of Guinea-Bissau, 1980. O.J. 1980 L226/34.

23. EEC-Guinea Agreement on Fishing off the Guinean Coast, 1983. O.J. 1983 L111/2.

24. EEC-Equatorial Guinea Agreement on Fishing off the Coast of Equatorial Guinea, 1983. O.J. 1983 L237/15.

25. EEC-Sao Tome e Principe Agreement on Fishing off Sao Tome e Principe, 1983. O.J. 1983 L282/52.

26. EEC-Seychelles Agreement on Fishing off Seychelles, 1984. O.J. 1984 L79/34.

27. Agreement initialled December 1984. Text in O.J. 1985 C86/7.

28. O.J. 1985 L29/9.

29. COM (82) 25.

30. Norwegian Government, *Markedsutvalgets Rapport Nr. XIV om De Europeiske Fellesskap*, Oslo, 1980, p.104.

31. For an example of such an agreement, see Agreement on the Regulation of Fisheries in the Skagerrak and Kattegat in 1983 between the EEC, Norway and Sweden, O.J. 1983 L73/4.

32. See Agreed Record of Consultations with Canada in COMs (79) 74 and (80) 126.

33. NAFO Convention, Art. XI(3); NEAFC Convention, Art. 5(2).

COMMENTARY

Budislav Vukas
Professor of International Law
University of Zagreb, Yugoslavia

My comments address the Declaration of the European Community made upon the signing of the 1982 Law of the Sea Convention, and mentioned in the papers presented by Dr. Birnie and Professor Treves.

One of the merits of the papers of this Panel is that they have shown the complexity of the relationship between national legislation and the Community legal order on matters concerning the law of the sea. For Member States three legal orders exist: a/ domestic, state law; b/ Community law, and c/ international law. For third states, when dealing with individual EEC Member States, Community law is relevant only to the extent to which it replaces state law. Thus, for non-member states, Community law generally has no value *per se*; it is relevant only when it acquires the status of national law. For this reason, the main problem for third states is to find the applicable rule, a task which, in view of the constant growth of the Community's competences and the differing opinions of Community organs, is not a simple one.

The problem of Community or state competence in matters regarding the law of the sea is closely linked to the Community's wish to become a party to the international treaties in the field. The record of the EEC's efforts to be accepted as a party to the LOS Convention is well known. The results of these efforts, generalized in favor of all international organizations to which their member states have transferred competence over matters governed by the LOS Convention, are contained in Articles 305 and 306 of the Convention and in Annex IX. On the basis of these provisions the EEC signed the Convention on December 7, 1984.

In the negotiations on the question of participation by international organizations in the LOS Convention, one of the crucial issues was how to solve the problem of the uncertainty, and even ignorance, of non-member states concerning matters in respect of which such organizations possess competence instead of their Member States. The problem was resolved, as mentioned by Tullio Treves, by the adoption of Articles 2 and 5 of Annex IX, requiring that signatures, final confirmations and accessions of international organizations contain declarations specifying the matters governed by the Convention "in respect of which competence has been transferred to the organization by its member states." In regard to declarations made at the time of signing, it was stated that they shall specify "the nature and extent" of the organization's competence.

Upon signing the Convention, the European Economic Community made a declaration pursuant to Article 2 of Annex IX.[1] In that short text the competence of the EEC with regard to matters governed by the whole Convention of the Law of the Sea was dealt with in five brief sentences to which two lists of relevant legal instruments have been added.

With regard to the conservation and management of sea fishing resources, the Declaration formally confirmed the development in the EEC, according to which Member States have transferred to the Community the competence to adopt relevant rules and regulations and to undertake international obligations. Although this explanation at first seems satisfactory, it does not explain specific situations non-member states are faced with when dealing with states who are members of the EEC.

569

How, for example, could it be understood in view of the above explanation that Italy, a Member State of the Community, is at present individually negotiating a fisheries agreement with Yugoslavia, a non-member state, although the Community itself has the exclusive competence "to enter into external undertakings with third states or competent international organizations"?[2] It is equally confusing that the sovereign rights of a coastal member state -- France -- to the living resources beyond the limits of its territorial sea are established simultaneously by a Community decision and a national law.[3]

It seems that, for the time being third states, parties to the LOS Convention, must disregard the quoted Declaration and instead turn for an explanation directly to the complex Community legislation and to doctrinal writings. According to Annex IX, only after the formal confirmation by the EEC and the entry into force of the Convention may any state party request the Community and its Member States, which are states parties, to provide information concerning their respective competences in regard to any specific question which has arisen.

With respect to the protection and preservation of the marine environment -- a rather complex and somewhat controversial issue concerning the distribution of competences between Member States and the EEC, as demonstrated here by Dr. Patricia Birnie -- the authors of the Declaration have not contributed much to the better understanding of the actual situation. They have stated that "the Member States have transferred to the Community competences as formulated in provisions adopted by the Community and as reflected by its participation in certain international agreements." To this ingenious sentence two lists have been added: the first entitled "Community texts applicable in the sector of the protection and preservation of the marine environment and relating directly to the subjects covered by the Convention," and the second indicating six international conventions in the field, to which the Community is a party. Instead of such information on the relevant material, one would have expected a thorough and competent analysis of the distribution of competences within the EEC and the evaluation of all these developments on the basis of the provisions of Part XII of the LOS Convention. Dr. Birnie calls that part of the EEC Declaration dealing with the marine environment "pragmatic and enigmatic" and devotes many pages of her paper to the scrutiny of the instruments listed in the EEC Declaration.

The picture is even more vague when we look at Part X of the Convention dealing with the right of access of land-locked states to and from the sea and freedom of transit. Here the Community had nothing to say except that it "enjoys certain powers as its purpose is to bring about an economic union based on a customs union." The least that can be said in regards to this "information" is that its authors have forgotten that the Declaration had to specify not only the "nature," but also the "extent" of the Organization's competence.

The comment regarding Part XI where it is said that "the Community enjoys competence in matters of commercial policy, including the control of unfair economic practices" is similar in its scope. Its brevity is apparently caused by the fact, stated in the preamble to the Declaration, that the Community dislikes the "significant provisions" of this Part of the Convention. However, as Professor Treves correctly reminds us, being a signatory of the Convention, the Community is a member of the Preparatory Commission which deals with matters inseparably linked with Part XI. Its participation in the Preparatory Commission, according to Article 55 of its Rules of Procedure, shall be "in accordance with Annex IX of the Convention, in other words within the limits of the Community's competences and in such a way as not to give rights to those member states that have not signed the Convention."[4] On the basis of this, which is taken from the Declaration concerning Part XI, it is impossible to ascertain what the limits of the Community's competences are.

All these deficiencies and flaws in the Community's Declaration could and should be rectified by the declarations required according to Annex IX at the time of the Community's final confirmation and by analogous declarations of Member States. However, the present Declaration warns of the possibility that there will be no formal confirmation, and thus no further declarations. Indeed, in the preamble to the Declaration the Community expressed its position that Part XI "contains considerable deficiencies and flaws which require rectification." In its "revisionist" approach the Community has gone even further than its own Member States. Belgium, France, Italy and Luxembourg expressed their hope that the alleged "shortcomings and defects will in fact be rectified by the rules, regulations and procedures which the Preparatory Commission should draw up."[5] In comparison with the statements by some of the Member States, the Community's Declaration differs in two respects. First, it does not mention that the suggested rectifications in the system of exploration and exploitation of the Area should be brought about through the instruments adopted by the Preparatory Commission. Second, only the Community made its decision on ratification/formal confirmation dependent upon "the results of the efforts made to obtain a universally acceptable Convention." Thus, one of the signatories of the Convention -- the European Community -- conditions its formal confirmation on the revision of the Convention![6] Such a condition for taking a decision on ratification is not in accordance with the meaning which the international law of treaties attributes to the act of signature.

The fact that the Community makes its formal confirmation dependent upon the revision of the Convention will probably affect the decision of other signatories concerning an early ratification of the LOS Convention. Such a hesitation by the EEC is not only disappointing because of the number and importance of its Member States, but especially for the role the Community should have in the question of deep seabed mining. The delay the Community's Declaration could cause in the process of ratification by other signatories could be counterproductive also in regard to the interests of the members of the EEC themselves. More specifically, the delay in the ratification process by developed states could provoke a similar hesitation by developing states, and the joint result of such behavior would not only be the late entry into force of the Convention, but also the impossibility of considering as customary law in the near future the new provisions agreed upon at UNCLOS III, such as those relating to transit passage through straits, the new formula for the outer limit of the continental shelf, some of the provisions concerning the protection and preservation of the marine environment, etc. It goes without saying that all the provisions on institutional and procedural questions depend upon the coming into force of the Convention. Without its entry into force there will not only be no Authority, but also no Commission on the Limits of the Continental Shelf, no International Tribunal for the Law of the Sea and no system of obligatory dispute settlement in matters concerning the law of the sea.

I would like to conclude by expressing my sincere hope that the LOS Convention will eventually become acceptable to the European Economic Community through the work of the Preparatory Commission and that the EEC Member States do not envisage the convening of the Fourth United Nations Conference on the Law of the Sea.

NOTES

1. *Law of the Sea Bulletin*, Office of the Special Representative of the Secretary-General for the Law of the Sea, No.4, February 1985, p. 16.
2. See F. Leita, "La C.E.E. e la pesca nel Mediterraneo," in *La zona economica esclusiva*, Ed. by B. Conforti, Milan, 1983, pp. 81-96.
3. See G. de Lacharriere, "La zone economique francaise de 200 milles," [1976] Annuaire Francais de Droit International 641-652; T. Treves, "La Communaute Europeenne et la zone economique exclusive," *Ibid.*, pp. 653-677.
4. T. Treves, above.
5. Law of the Sea Bulletin..., No. 1, September 1983, p. 26; No. 4, pp. 10, 12 and 13.
6. See U. Jenisch, "German Non-Signature of the New Law of the Sea Convention," German Foreign Affairs Review, 1985, No. 2, p. 171.

COMMENTARY

Markus Ederer
Intern
Office of the Law of the Sea
United Nations

I have been asked to be short and not too technical. These requirements are not easy to meet when we are talking Community law, as the papers have shown. I hope to be forgiven, therefore, for not doing justice to all three papers alike and I will devote myself mainly to Tullio Treves' paper.

I should entitle my remarks "The EEC and the Law of the Sea Convention: What Lies Ahead?" By doing so, I hope to add a third element to this panel. Robin Churchill and Pat Birnie have dealt with the European Community's past endeavors in fields covered by the Convention, and Tullio Treves focused -- as he put it -- on questions of today. I also believe that the question of what can happen to the Convention within the EEC is of considerable interest, particularly for those of us who are not dealing with the legal system of the Rome Treaty on a day-to-day basis.

However, please do not expect me to engage in speculation as to the political decisions which will have to be taken, if the European Economic Community and its Member States are to become parties to the Convention. What I would like to do is to elaborate on some of the salient legal features in that conjunction, which have already been touched upon in Tullio Treves' paper and which will certainly play their role when the relevant political decisions are made.

In most questions concerning the Convention, the EEC and its Member States are balancing on a tightrope, not only politically but also legally. If they fall off on one side, they are likely to be in violation of EEC law; if they fall off on the other side, they are potentially in breach of their obligations under the Convention. This is due to the fact that the provisions in the Convention allowing for participation of international organizations were a necessary but nonetheless not fully satisfactory compromise for the EEC and some of them are indeed in potential conflict with its own legal regime.

Because of the constraints of space I will focus only on the two scenarios Tullio Treves has presented:

1) Member states starting to ratify the Convention individually, *i.e.*, without the Community; and

2) The European Economic Community depositing its instrument of formal confirmation.

I will refer briefly only to the legal issues that are likely to arise under the Convention, if the Community and its member states were actually parties thereto.

Let me begin with individual ratification or accession by some Member States. Chronologically, this is the first step, since Article 3, Paragraph 1 of Annex IX of the Convention requires a majority of its Member States to become parties to the Convention before an international organization may deposit its instrument of formal confirmation.

It will come as a surprise to those unfamiliar with EEC law that ratification or accession of Member States without the EEC would be a violation of the EEC Treaty. This fact, however, was at the very origin of the struggle of the EEC Member States at the Third United Nations Conference on the Law of the Sea to obtain the "EEC clause." The decisions of the European Court of Justice, to which Robin Churchill refers, tell us that the Member States have lost their right to enter into international agreements, individually or even collectively, in fields where they have transferred their competences to the Community. The Law of the Sea Convention would be considered as a so-called "mixed agreement" under Community law, where competences lie partly with the EEC and partly with the Member States. Interestingly, a procedure of individual ratifications by some but not all of the Member States and without the EEC has been suggested for tactical reasons by the Committee on External Economic Relations of the European Parliament, which expressly opposed, in that respect, the Parliament's Legal Affairs Committee. At the other end of the spectrum, the United Kingdom held the view in the Council of Ministers in 1982 that a veto in the Council would not only bar the EEC from becoming party to the Convention but individual Member States as well.

I am not surprised that Tullio Treves nevertheless expects individual ratifications to occur. I also tend to believe that there will be mounting pressure on some Member States, particularly with an increasing number of states ratifying the Convention. Also, there has been an indication that the Member States did not want to close the door to individual ratification. The Commission of the European Communities had urged them to make a declaration when signing the Convention that ratification can only take place together with the EEC. If one looks at the declarations made by the Member States which signed, however, one cannot find anything of that nature. Were it not prohibited by Article 309 of the Law of the Sea Convention, the EEC Member States would still have the option to make a reservation upon their eventual ratifications with regard to their lack of competences in certain fields. However, this is excluded by Article 309 of the Convention.

In anticipation of these problems, the European Parliament, after drawing the attention of the Member States to the risks to the unity of the EEC should they not adopt a common position towards the Convention but act individually instead, solemnly called on the Commission of the European Communities, as guardian of the Treaties, "to ensure that the Member States respect the Community patrimony, in particular the procedures and powers of the Community by invoking, when appropriate, the procedures laid down in the Treaties: including if necessary an application to the Court of Justice under Article 169 or Article 175 of the Treaty." Article 169, for instance, provides that the Commission of the European Communities may bring a matter before the European Court of Justice after giving the Member State concerned the opportunity to submit its observations.

I disagree with Tullio Treves that unanimous consent by the Member States can make individual ratifications legal, even where there is no reasonable chance that the Community can become a party. It is not within the discretion of Member States' governments to violate the Treaty of Rome, nor to acquiesce in such violations. The EEC Treaty is not at the disposition of the Member States except by amendment as provided for by the Treaty itself. As far as such amendments are concerned, as Tullio Treves seems to suggest in his paper, they are unlikely to happen. I will come back to that in a moment.

I do not, however, want to exclude individual ratifications altogether. I do belive that under certain circumstances they would be compatible with the EEC Treaty. However, since the member states have to accede to "mixed agreements" together with the Community, strictly speaking, the criteria for such exceptions must be sought with a close view to Community law and practice.

As to the latter there is a sort of precedent in the field of marine pollution. The EEC, although it had the necessary competences under Community law, was barred from accession to the Helsinki Convention on the Protection of the Marine Environment of the Baltic Sea Area by the refusal of the Eastern bloc states to recognize the EEC as a subject of international law. The two Member States bordering the Baltic Sea, Denmark and the Federal Republic of Germany, thereafter ratified individually the Helsinki Convention.

In its decision in *Commission v. United Kingdom* handed down in 1981 and confirmed in later decisions, the European Court of Justice established the conditions under which Member States could legislate individually in the field of the internal fisheries policy although all the relevant competences had passed to the EEC. There conditions obtain the principal legislative organ of the EEC, the Council of Ministers, was paralyzed by the unanimity rule of the so-called "Accords of Luxembourg."

For reasons of space I cannot go into depth on the issues which arose from these sets of facts, but I believe that the following criteria for individual ratification of the Law of the Sea Convention by Member States can be derived from these cases:

-     Compelling reasons, such as a veto or the threat of a veto in the Council of Ministers, must prevent the EEC from becoming a party to the Convention;
-     The objectives of the Convention must be found to be in accordance with the basic EEC instruments;
-     The Member States concerned must act in close collaboration with the Commission of the European Communities and as trustees of the common interest.

I turn now to the second scenario in which the EEC deposits its instrument of formal confirmation and Tullio Treves' question whether a situation is likely to arise similar to that which prevailed as regards signature when only eight out of ten Member States had signed the Convention. I suppose that one can safely answer this question with a categorical "no."

On the political level, much more will be at stake. Member states unwilling to accede to or ratify the Convention cannot be expected to abstain again in the Council of Ministers as was the case when the EEC signed the Convention. They would, by virtue of at least Article 4, Paragraph 5, Annex IX of the Convention, put themselves at a considerable disadvantage towards the other Member States. This provision provides that participation of an international organization shall in no case confer any rights under the Convention on Member States of the organization which are not parties to it.

Even more importantly, the European Court of Justice would have to declare the Convention incompatible with the EEC Treaty because of this provision as long as not all Member States become parties. Article 4, Paragraph 5, of Annex IX conflicts squarely with Article 7, Paragraph 1, of the EEC Treaty, which prohibits any discrimination on grounds of nationality. That was why the inclusion of Article 4, Paragraph 5, into Annex IX was so vigorously rejected by the EEC member states when it was brought up at the Conference. Even at the Eleventh Session in 1982, the representative of Belgium (which held, at the time, the presidency in the Council of Ministers) expressed the member states' concern in a letter to the President of the Conference that "[a] provision of this kind would in fact be contrary to the letter as well as the spirit of the Treaty of Rome, since it would force the organization to operate discrimination between its Member States." Also, the Vié-Report drawn up on behalf of the Legal Affairs Committee of the European Parliament, stated that Article 4, Paragraph 5, of Annex IX is "prejudicial to Community law and seems to raise serious legal problems."

As long as only some Member States are parties to the Convention, the Community would be simply put into the situation to which I alluded before, where it would have to violate either the pertinent provisions of the Treaty of Rome or of the Law of the Sea Convention. Hence, in 1983 the European Parliament stipulated that in case of "any doubt as to the compatibility of the proposed agreement with the provisions of the EEC Treaty, it would be advisable to obtain beforehand the opinion of the Court of Justice pursuant to Article 228 of the Treaty." Article 228, Paragraph 1, provides that the Council, the Commission or a member state may obtain beforehand the opinion of the Court as to whether an envisaged agreement is compatible with the EEC Treaty. In the case where the opinion or the Court is adverse, the agreement may enter into force only in accordance with the amendment provision of the EEC Treaty.

I understand from Tullio Treves' paper that participation by the EEC and only some of its Member States may make it necessary to modify some rules of Community law. If he wants to declare thereby Article 7 of the Treaty of Rome as endangered species, I would certainly disagree. It is one of the pillars on which the legal system of the EEC rests. The basic freedoms of the Treaty e.g., free movement of workers, goods, establishment and provision of services and even the internal fisheries policy featuring equal access by all Member States' fishermen to all Community waters, can be reduced to the non-discrimination principle of Article 7, paragraph 1, of the EEC Treaty.

In essence, I do not believe that the EEC can deposit its instrument of formal confirmation if not all Member States accede to the Convention or ratify it. Also, it has always been maintained by the Member States' delegations at the Conference that the Community will proceed along these lines.

That brings me to my conclusion.

Under EEC law there are only two situations which do not create any legal problems as regards participation in the Law of the Sea Convention of the EEC and its Member States:

1) The EEC adheres to the Convention together with all its Member States; or
2) Both the EEC and all its Member States remain outside the Convention.

The two scenarios I have concentrated on, however, present serious legal questions including, but not limited to, those on which I have elaborated.

The same can be said for a situation in which the EEC and its Member States actually will have become parties to the Convention. Problems are lurking in the national treatment provisions of the Community's legal instruments which might be incompatible with the non-discrimination rules of the Convention, in which case the Convention prevails according to Article 4, Paragraph 6, of its Annex IX. In this conjunction, the question comes up whether or not the EEC will be considered as a coastal state. In that respect I am somewhat less optimistic than Robin Churchill, mainly because the Community does not have nationals, and third states would have to refer to the member states in these cases. A more refined analysis would also be necessary on the question, already discussed at the Conference, as to whether there can be participation of the Community in the International Seabed Authority, and if so, in which organs and in which form.

This short commentary is intended to show that law of the sea lawyers concerned with both EEC law and international law will have a great deal of trouble in the future in the endeavor to keep the Community on its tightrope. I believe that the foregoing also shows that the admittedly great achievement of the "EEC clause" in the Convention, which is, after long years of negotiations, unique in a comprehensive international agreement, represents not the end but actually marks the beginning of a new opportunity for the EEC to partake in a rather exciting way in the progressive development of international law.

Albert Koers: We will now entertain questions from the floor.

Uwe Jenisch: Panel VII on the EEC has provided us with useful information on the EEC signature as well as on some special aspects of EEC maritime interests and policies. Let me add another neglected issue to this discussion: the internal legal regime in EEC waters.

The 200-nautical mile zones of ten EEC Member States cover a surface of about 3 million square kilometers. Spain and Portugal as new members will add another 3 million square kilometers. Geographically the EEC will increasingly become a maritime community, apart from the fact that its signature has already initiated a political upgrading of the EEC as an entity of international law.

This leads to the legal, if not constitutional, question of whether the whole bulk of EEC treaty law and secondary law applies in the maritime zones of Member States. In particular the four freedoms of the EEC Treaty should be mentioned: the free movement of goods (Articles 9 and 30), the freedom to move (Article 48), the freedom to settle and to set up business (Article 52), and the freedom to provide services (Article 59, *e.g.*, offshore supply shipping), and above all the principle of non-discrimination in Article 7. In the internal "onshore" market these principles have helped to establish free competition in important markets. The same beneficial effects could prevail in marine uses.

To avoid misunderstanding: it is not a question of common sharing of resources but of equal chances for citizens and enterprises from Member States, or to put it differently, of equal rights of access to marine markets free of discrimination and free from protectionist non-tariff barriers.

As regards the geographical extent of the EEC law, the European Court of Justice has confirmed in its judgement of February 16, 1978 (*Irish Fishery Measures*, Cases 61/77 and 88/77), as well as in the *Kramer* case (Cases 3, 4, 6/76) that EEC law applies to all maritime waters within the jurisdiction of Member States and therefore applies to the entire 200-mile zone. The Council of Ministers, meeting on July 20 and 27, 1976, confirmed these ideas. In the meantime equal access of Community fishermen to Member States' fishing zones has been well established. The lesson to learn is that the EEC Treaty is not dependent upon the concept of land territory, provided that extra-territorial competences fall within the broad economic competences of the EEC.

In the field of the continental shelf, the EEC Commission claimed these rights in a memorandum on the applicability of the EEC Treaty to the continental shelf (EC Bulletin 11/1970, p. 51), and there is little doubt that the European Court of Justice would not decide differently if a continental shelf case arose.

Nevertheless, the EEC has still to prove that the Community shelf will be commonly administered. As an example, it may be appropriate to cite the British regulations for the treatment of applications for oil licenses which under the criteria for the Eighth Round of Licensing make the applications dependent upon:

f) The extent of the contribution which the applicant has made or is planning to make to the economy of the U.K., including any contribution to the strengthening of the U.K. balance of payments, the growth of industry and employment;

g) The extent to which the applicant has involved or plans to involve U.K.-owned or controlled organizations in his exploration, development and production activities on the U.K. continental shelf through the generation of new technology, the placement of research and development contracts and the provision of opportunities for the design, demonstration and testing of products and techniques;

h) ...

i) Whether the applicant subscribes to the Memorandum of Understanding to ensure that full and fair opportunity is provided to U.K. industry to compete for orders of goods and services. Where the applicant is, or has been, a licensee, his past performance in providing full and fair opportunity to U.K. industry will be taken fully into account.

The EEC Commission may hold that these regulations are not in conformity with Articles 30, 52 and 59 of the EEC Treaty.

This example illustrates the necessity to elaborate an integral EEC regime for the 200-mile zones as a logical and legal consequence of existing EEC law and emerging sea law. This regime would likewise apply to fisheries, offshore uses, marine scientific research, environmental protection and, I hope, also to navigational and shipping interests.

Patricia Birnie: In my paper I did refer to this question, not quite in the form that you have put it, which is much more complicated, but in the context of the EEC's attempts to propose that the Community should have some scheme for preventing pollution from offshore activities. They did propose that in 1974 and suggested that the seabed should be divided into homogeneous zones and that each state should be responsible for one of these homogeneous zones. This proposal came to nothing because this was in the early days of oil exploration and exploitation, and Member States were very jealous of their national jurisdiction over the shelf. It has been expressed several times that the policies you mentioned, concerning free movement of goods and freedom of establishment, would apply. But you are assuming that everybody will have a 200-mile zone if they ratify the Law of the Sea Convention, and it is already apparent that this is not necessarily the case. It was made quite clear, for example, in the talk by Mr. Darwin that the United Kingdom has not seen the need to have an EEZ and, even if it ever becomes a party to the Convention, certainly does not regard an EEZ as required or automatically resulting from it. This raises the difficulty of the disparate state of play on this issue. Certainly it would be very premature for the Community to start on this now.

Tullio Treves: I fully agree with Dr. Birnie that states are entitled, with or without the Convention, to proclaim a 200-mile economic zone, but even when the Convention is ratified they would not be obliged to do so. This point can be seen in the Convention's articles on the EEZ and on the continental shelf. The latter says explicitly that the shelf pertains to the coastal state with or without express proclamation.

Peter Brueckner: I would make one comment on Professor Treves' paper. He noted that the Community and Member States were not very active in the PrepCom, perhaps due to the various factors that he has explained, and I agree with those. There is some hesitation, however, among Member States of the Community, and the Community itself, that proposals from Member States -- in particular the bigger seabed mining states -- may not be received in the spirit in which they are drafted, despite their virtues at the technical level. There is also the question of time. We are entering into quite a new field of futuristic law. Nobody has ever tried seabed mining, and we are now getting down into the future seabed mining code in all its detail. The PrepCom has progressed faster than we initially thought it would, and delegations have not yet had time to digest the splendid material furnished by the Secretariat.

To Dr. Birnie I would say that I do not think that the absence of an EEZ in some Member States has any effect on the extent of the competence of the Community in environmental matters. It is, as in fishery matters, a functional competence irrespective of where the actual problems lie, and in fact the Community could also exercise competences in the absence of an expressly proclaimed EEZ. I felt, from my experience as a legal adviser in the Community in the 1970s, that she might have exaggerated the role of the Community in the field of environmental protection. The competence, as will be seen from the table annexed to the Community's declaration when signing the UN Convention, is mixed, the Community together with the Member States. Not that we want it to be mixed, but matters as they are presented in these international fora are not determined according to the division of competences between Member States and the Community. So we have to sit there together. When the Commission speaks, it speaks on the mandate of the Council. It is not the Commission in its own name, it is the Commission in the name of the Community on a mandate from the Council. Very often what is said in these fora by others than the Commission may be the result of coordination within the Communities, because the spokesman is not always the Commission, but very often a representative of the Member State exercising the presidency of the Council. That was the case, for instance, during the whole UNCLOS Conference, where the Commission was not able to speak but where the spokesmanship was exercised by the presidency.

To the two commentators, whose exposés draw a dramatic picture, I have two general comments. First, the EEC is a dynamic legal system, and it is therefore not possible to draw the dividing line between the competence of the Community and that of the Member States in matters of the law of the sea. Most important is that we have a system in Annex IX which ensures that third states' interests vis-a-vis the Community and its Member States are protected. The third state can get information in a concrete case, and if there is doubt in litigation, there is a system of solidarity in representation, you might say, so that the third state will always have a competent opponent.

I would comment on Dr. Ederer's last remark concerning the draconian choice that we seem to have. I do not disagree in formal law, but lawyers are here to solve problems, and if the Community and all Member States cannot agree to ratify at the same time, Community lawyers must find a system whereby as many as possible of the member states could accede to, ratify, or confirm the Convention. That would be in the interests of the Convention and the international community. To that end I note Dr. Ederer's three conclusions as to what could be done. In fact there are precedents. As Professor Vukas said when he saw Italy negotiating with Yugoslavia, there are precedents in Community law as stated by the European Court, that under certain circumstances the

Community institutions may delegate the power back to Member States under certain conditions. A solution can be found whereby the overall interests not only of Member States and the Community, but also the international community and the Convention, could be served.

Tullio Treves: Peter Brueckner has made my response to the commentators much shorter.

To Mr. Vukas I would like to say that European law is very much an evolutionary system of law, and the borderline of the competence of the Community is a moving borderline, so that when the Community accepted the clauses on participation, it was with great reluctance, especially of the institutions in Brussels and of those who had to negotiate within those institutions. I participated in part of the negotiations and it was very difficult. On the other hand, third parties have what I would call a solid guarantee, and this is -- as has already been mentioned by Peter Brueckner -- Article 6, Paragraph 2, of Annex IX, according to which any state party may request an international organization or its Member States, which are states parties, for information on who has responsibility for any specific matter. The general declaration may be made precise for a specific case, and I think this guarantees the third state as far as its specific interests are concerned.

As for the Italian-Yugoslav problem, Italy acts on a mandate from the Council.

With regard to Mr. Ederer's remarks, our positions are not as far apart as they might seem at first sight; perhaps he is much more a strict constructionist than I am. He does not think that unanimous consent by the Member States permits ratification by an individual or some individual Member States, because this would require an amendment to the Treaty. I say in my paper that this would require an amendment to EEC law, a slightly more flexible expression that would cover possibly the amendments to regulations and not to the Treaty. One must look at the concrete.

The same applies to his scenario according to which the EEC would give its formal confirmation accompanied only by a majority of its Member States. Would this imply a change in the EEC Treaty and in particular to Article 7, which can be seen as a pillar of the Treaty?

Before we arrive at such a drastic conclusion, we should indeed have a concrete look at which obligations in practice would have to be met by the Community and which would apply only to some of its member states. If you look at the fisheries sector, with its lack of surplus -- at least in European waters; we have learned that in French Guyana there may be some problems -- the questions in practice may become much more simple.

I agree with Peter Brueckner that lawyers are there to solve problems, not to create them. If the political situation arose according to which it was the best judgement of everybody that the Community should become a party to the Convention together with six or seven or eight Member States, I am sure that a practical solution in legal terms -- which might imply some changes, perhaps not to the Treaty but to Treaty-derived law -- could be found. I am sure that in its wisdom the Court would not create a destructive intervention in such a process.

Budislav Vukas: I would like to comment on the interventions of Mr. Brueckner and Mr. Treves. The intent of the clauses concerning declarations and information provided by the Community was to inform third states; there are ten Member States of the Community and 160 states who do not know practically anything about this -- I could say, mess, of the new EEC legal order. We have witnessed today that Dr. Birnie and Mr. Brueckner disagree in certain aspects. Furthermore, concerning the admissibility of Italian negotiations with Yugoslavia, we have heard two speakers say that Italy has been authorized by the Community to negotiate, whereas yesterday a learned colleague, when I mentioned this problem to him, said that these negotiations were unconstitutional under European law. Third states, non-Member States such as Yugoslavia, insisted from the very beginning that the Community being a party to the Convention informs us because we wanted the help of the EEC lawyers to understand this very dynamic distribution of competences. But the first Community declaration, made upon signature -- and as I mentioned in my paper it is very doubtful when we will have another one -- can help no state. It is a political declaration, and I think that every student in the EEC states could have provided more information to serve third states. We have seen from the very informative papers in this panel how complex things are. So how can a state in Asia or a lawyer in Yugoslavia understand better the distribution of competences after this declaration? The duty of the Community under Article 2 of Protocol IX to the LOS Convention was to inform states and explain how the transfer of competences to the Community affects the rights of the Member States.

Markus Ederer: I endorse what Professor Vukas said, and maybe that is why I seem to have this constructionist approach. In law of the sea matters we are mostly dealing with third states and they need some security in dealing with the EEC. In my commentary I do not categorically exclude individual ratification; I set up some conditions and I referred to the Court of Justice and I think that is the least that one can do. As far as specific cases are concerned, with regard to the nondiscrimination principle and the requirement in the Convention that no privileges can be transferred to states not parties, if there is a fisheries agreement with a third state, like an African state, which concerns its surplus, the Community could not give any quota to its Member States which are not parties to the Convention, and that would obviously be in violation of Article 7 of the EEC Treaty.

Pat Birnie: I do not think that Mr. Brueckner and I disagree. There is just one point, however, and that is the reference I made to the geographical scope of the environmental policy. What I had in mind there was not that the EEC would not be able to act on a particular environmental question because it did not have competence for geographical reasons, but simply that having acted, the geographical scope of the action may be affected, unlike the fisheries policy, where most Member States do have 200-mile fishery zones. Thus, for example, if the EEC succeeds in adopting the directive that is proposed on dumping, or if it succeeds eventually in becoming a party to the Dumping Conventions, the application of these instruments would be limited in some cases by the scope of the geographical competence of individual member states.

Donald C. Watt: It has been said that a lawyer's job is to solve problems, not to create them. If this is the case, then they did a singularly unhappy job of the Convention which was signed in 1982. We have a whole series of new problems as a result of abandoning the principle of agreement by unanimity for agreement by majority rule. And it is in this context that I would like to make the comment which originally drew me to my feet. That is to regret the use of the word "revisionism" in the context of our discussions here and in general on the Law of the Sea Convention. "Revisionism" is, or can be, a very neutral word, but as a historian of international relations I know only too well that it is usually used as a very strong pejorative or persuasive element. We are faced with the partial failure of what looked like a major step towards the harmonization of the troubles of our world. All the evidence from 1945 when the United Nations was established has shown that trying to substitute majority rule as a form of pressure on a minority to force that minority to conform, has not worked. It did not work when it was being applied in the United Nations by the majority against the Eastern European bloc in the 1950s, and I do not think that it is working now. If the reality of the European Community does not fit a legal category in the Law of the Sea Convention, perhaps one should alter the legal concept rather than force the reality into the concept. I would make a plea for the return to the principle of unanimity and to ask the lawyers to remember that this is the only way that progress is likely to be made, for majority rule results in the gap which now exists between the signatories and the non-signatories and the ludicrous situation where the resources are not likely to be commercially exploitable by either of the two rival systems. If there is need for rethinking on this point, the adage that lawyers must solve problems, not create them, is one which must be held by all of us here.

Albert Koers: I would like to conclude this session by thanking the speakers for their contributions and the audience for its participation. This meeting is adjourned.

CONTRIBUTED PAPERS

IMPLEMENTATION OF THE 1982 UN CONVENTION ON THE LAW OF THE SEA: SOME ASPECTS

V.I. Andrianov
Senior Research Fellow
Soviet Maritime Law Association
USSR

The 1982 Convention is a complex international law act. It consists of 320 articles and nine annexes. An overwhelming majority of its norms is devoted to the regulation of relations between states *inter se* and between states and other subjects of international law in the field of shipping and other uses of the World Ocean.

The Convention comprises provisions with the main aim to put into action material norms of the law of the sea. Such provisions establish practical and legal means of implementing provisions of the new Convention on the Law of the Sea.

In the Soviet doctrine implementation of international law rules is defined as "purposeful, practical and legal activity of States conducted individually, collectively, or within the scope of international organizations with the aim of timely, comprehensive and complete realization of the obligations undertaken by them in accordance with international law."[1]

As applicable to the UNCLOS we are of the view that it would be useful to add to this definition a reference to the other subjects of law which are able, according to Article 305, to become parties to the Convention.

Provisions of the Convention establishing ways and means of fulfilling obligations have the same legal status as its other rules. Subject to them, Parties to the Convention must strictly adhere to the provision of Article 300 according to which "States parties shall fulfill in good faith the obligations assumed under this Convention and shall exercise the rights, jurisdiction and freedoms recognized in this Convention in a manner which would not constitute an abuse of right."

The Convention's mechanism for implementation of legal provisions is complicated and diverse. It includes legal means, individual and collective actions, and heterogeneous practical forms used in connection with their purpose on national or international levels. Given the complexity and variety of legal ways of realization of the LOS Convention rules, this mechanism reflects expediency and interconnection.

The specific character of the implementation mechanism is stipulated, in our opinion, by the combined character of the object of the "marine convention," the universality of its aims, the family of its subjects able to become the Parties to it, and the content of its rights and obligations. In this respect, the mechanism of realizing the rules of the Law of the Sea Convention 1982 is more complicated than the respective provisions of the 1958 Geneva Conventions on the Law of the Sea.

The leading role in implementation of the new maritime order is allotted to states, *i.e.*, the creators of the Convention. But unlike the Geneva Convention, the Parties to the 1982 Convention may include other subjects of International Law, mentioned in Article 305. It seems that these subjects of the law can play a certain role in the realization of the Convention's provisions to the extent that their appropriate competence is recognized.

As for the role of international organizations in this process, one should take into account a diversity of roles played by the organizations which are not Parties to the Convention, but whose competence is directly connected with problems of the use of marine areas, as well as the role of international bodies whose establishment is provided for by the Convention itself.

A complicated and interesting situation appears in respect of the legal status of the main subjects of rights and obligations, *i.e.*, states. According to Article 1 of the 1969 Vienna Convention on the Law of Treaties, a state which has consented to be bound by a treaty and for which the treaty is in force receives the legal status of a "Party" to it. This legal quality is shared by all states that have accomplished these actions and, in this sense, there is no difference between them.

But in other respects, the Convention, taking into account certain economic, political, geographical and other factors differentiates between participants in the Convention. It seems such distinctions can have a certain juridical significance and be developed in the process of implementation of various provisions of the Convention. In this respect the 1982 Convention goes much further than the Geneva Conventions. The new Convention, taking into consideration peculiarities of the contemporary state of international relations and the reality of the political picture of the world made an attempt in legal form to strengthen the special position of a state in respect of the public order of the oceans.

Thus, the Convention distinguishes between "coastal States," "land-locked States," "developed land-locked States," "archipelagic States," "States bordering a strait," "States bordering enclosed or semi-enclosed seas," "States with special geographical characteristics," "States of origin of anadromous stocks." The list of these categories of states might be prolonged by taking into account those parts of the Convention relating to exploration and exploitation of living and mineral ocean resources.

In the majority of cases the Convention does not give complete definitions of appropriate categories of states. Nevertheless, certain specific juridical features can be seen through the recognition of their special rights and obligations, thus reflecting their interests and characteristics.

The Convention does not prohibit a state from classifying itself simultaneously in several categories of participants. The legal recognition of special interests and rights in the structure of the world ocean order may be seen also in the process of implementation of appropriate provisions of the Convention. For example, land-locked states are not able to adopt national legislation concerning the innocent passage of foreign ships through the territorial sea.

It is also obvious that states parties that are not states of origin of anadromous stocks cannot adopt measures to protect them and regulate the catch.

Specific roles of various types of states in the implementation of appropriate provisions of the Convention can be viewed as an attempt to set a balance between special interests and the common interests of the international community as a whole.

Rules concerning implementation vest states with the power to adopt national laws and regulations. National legislation plays a very important role in implementing the rights and duties of states under international law. Some provisions of the LOS Convention define the object of national laws and regulations. Thus, according to Article 21(2), laws and regulations of the coastal state must not apply to the design, construction, manning or equipment of foreign vessels unless they are giving effect to generally accepted international rules or standards.

A law-creating competence of states in realization of the Convention is specified also in other articles. For example, Article 42(2) provides that the laws and regulations of a state bordering a strait shall not contain discriminatory requirements concerning foreign vessels in respect of the rights of transit passage.

Analogous requirements are laid down not only for the content of laws and regulations but also for their application. So the Convention in authorizing states to adopt national laws for the purpose of the realization of their rights and obligations, at the same time restricts their discretion in respect of the above-mentioned questions. Only those national laws that conform to the provisions of the Convention can be considered lawful.

Another important requirement applied to laws and regulations is the duty to comply with provisions that states adopt national laws and regulations in compliance with the Convention and other norms of international law.

These formulations specify in detail a general provision according to which the sovereignty of the coastal state is to be exercised in conformity with provisions of the Convention.

In respect of internal legislation as a juridical means of implementing its rules, the Convention contains one more important demand. Thus, in exercising its rights and fulfilling its obligations the coastal state shall respect the rights and obligations of other states. Compliance with this provision becomes important in maritime areas where the sovereignty of a coastal state is broad and where collisions of interest between various states and with the international community are possible.

For the purpose of preserving and maintaining a just balance of interests between states, of both coastal and land-locked, the Convention obliges the latter to take into account the interests, rights and obligations of the former as well as the laws and regulations adopted by it in accordance with the Convention. But Article 58, paragraph 3 contains an important addition -- a state must observe such laws and regulations of coastal states only in so far as these are not incompatible with the provisions of Part V of the Convention.

There are two consequences arising from this provision of the Convention with direct relevance to the implementation of its rules. First, states shall harmonize their national (marine) legislation with the provisions of the Convention. Second, non-compliance with this provision gives other states the ground not to recognize national acts of a coastal state where there are reasons to consider them as being inconsistent with the Convention.

As another set of tools, "measures," "other measures," "such measures," and "reasonable measures" can be considered. The Convention does not specify the content of these terms. But it contemplates, probably, the undertaking of concrete actions on appropriate occasions. To support this interpretation certain articles may be quoted. For example, Article 25 paragraph 1 gives coastal states the right to take measures necessary to prevent passage which is not innocent; Article 27, paragraph 2 invites the coastal states to take any steps authorized by its laws and regulations for the purposes of an arrest or investigation on board a foreign ship.

Their purpose is of a dual character. In a majority of cases they are aimed at the protection of the interests and rights of coastal states; the same measures can be applied for the purpose of enforcement of rights and obligations under the Convention, but in this case they originate with the internal legislation of states. "Measures" may include, in our opinion, also the control exercised by coastal states in accordance with Article 33 in the contiguous zone and necessary for preventing and punishing violations of law.

As the general participants in the process of implementation of the Convention, states, besides individual measures, also undertake collective ones, the forms of which are quite variable.

The cooperation of states is important for the process of the Convention's implementation. Some articles declare that States "should by agreement cooperate" (Article 43). The Convention prompts states to establish cooperation in detail and elaborate international rules, standards, recommendations, practices and procedures; (*e.g.*, Article 197).

Creation of additional institutional structures for implementation of some contractual provisions is among other aims of cooperation, including the establishment of regional and subregional international organizations (see, *e.g.*, Article 118).

Cooperation in the field of rule implementation may be of a worldwide character as well as on a regional or subregional basis. It is carried out between the states directly or through the competent international organizations.

Hence, the cooperation of states being a political principle of the Convention, relations between participants are quite important in the implementation of its rules of behavior because the cooperation will mostly be in the form of legislation which interprets and specifies general rules.

These are some of the problems of states' participation in the implementation of the UNCLOS provisions.

NOTE

1. Goverdovski, A.C., Implementation of Rules of International Law, Kiev, 1980, p. 62 (in Russian).

THE JURIDICAL NATURE OF THE EXCLUSIVE ECONOMIC ZONE AND THE LEGAL REGIME OF NAVIGATION OF FOREIGN VESSELS THEREIN

V.F. Tsarev
Senior Research Fellow
Soviet Maritime Law Association
USSR

The institution of the economic zone (EEZ) laid down in the 1982 Convention is justifiably described by Soviet and foreign scholars as an essential modification in contemporary international marine law.[1] No other new concept in marine law emerging from the Third United Nations Conference on the Law of the Sea caused so much discussion and so many conflicting opinions at both the Conference and in juridical literature. Without pretending to give exhaustive coverage to all juridical concepts of the EEZ we shall attempt to examine the most essential problems which, in our opinion, face a researcher into the regime of navigation in the 200-nautical mile EEZ. One such problem is, first and foremost, the juridical nature of the EEZ.

In his study of the juridical nature of the EEZ Professor Scerni from Italy rightly points out that the major matter of principle here is to establish whether the EEZ is the high seas, or whether it has a status different from that of the high seas.[2]

While the concept of the EEZ is still being worked on to achieve a more accurate definition, particularizing its juridical nature is of urgent theoretical and practical significance.

The process of extending the jurisdiction of the coastal state over sea areas has been underway for a long time. It became particularly intensive after World War II. What is important, however, is that the international community has been seeking not to let it get out of hand, to steer and channel it towards reasonable coordinated solutions in the interests of all states, avoiding unilateral advantages in favor of any one group of states to the prejudice of other groups. At the Third UN Conference on the Law of the Sea the "conflict of interests" in respect of the EEZ was so sharp and the division of opinions so wide that the provisions finally adopted boiled down to an obvious compromise subject to varying interpretations which is also true of the juridical nature of the EEZ.

The point is, however, that the juridical nature of the EEZ constitutes the legal basis which predetermines the relationship of rights and interests of the coastal and all other states in the use of the zone. Negation of or disregard for this basis would open up legal channels for a "creeping jurisdiction" of the coastal state, and for priority rights and jurisdiction of the coastal state as compared to the rest of the international community over its EEZ, *i.e.*, over sea areas beyond its territorial waters.

It is not accidental, therefore, that a departure from the traditional division of sea areas into the territorial waters and the high seas was proposed along with a new classification of sea areas that would include the known categories of division (internal waters, the territorial sea, the contiguous zone, etc.) as well as new concepts such as intercontinental waters, pollution zones and international subwater areas.[3]

Under the new classification, the high seas begin only beyond the limits of the EEZ.[4]

The proposals of many developing countries at the Third U.N. Conference on the Law of the Sea to declare the 200-nautical mile EEZ a *sui generis* zone should also be considered in this context.

What is the basic meaning of this concept?

In his introductory note to the unofficial text on the EEZ to be negotiated for inclusion in the Convention, the Chairman of the Second Committee, A. Aguilar, says: "There is no doubt that the EEZ is neither the high seas, nor the territorial sea. It is a *sui generis* zone."[5]

At first glance a good compromise seems to have been found. The definition recognizes neither the views of supporters of the territorial sea concept, nor those of the high seas option, thus making everybody happy. But the point is that instead of clarifying the new institution of marine law this definition of the EEZ makes it even more uncertain and confused.

Several countries sought to read a hidden meaning into the "*sui generis* zone" concept to imply recognition of the coastal state's priority rights[6] which distorted the reasonable relationship between the rights and interests of the coastal and other states with respect to the EEZ. Professor Scerni's caustic comment on the "*sui generis*" concept was as follows: "...when a lawyer resorts to this concept and says here is a *sui generis* solution it means that he does not know what should be done about it in reality."[7] This remark reflects very well how absurd the participants in the Conference felt about being confronted with this approach to the status of the economic zone. It is not accidental that the concept of the "*sui generis*" zone was rejected by most delegations.

What is actually the juridical nature of the EEZ? What are the specifics of the zone's legal regime and how does it affect the regime of navigation in the zone? What is the relationship between the rights of the coastal state in respect of the EEZ, on the one hand, and those of other states, on the other? What juridical principle, in the final analysis, underlies this relationship?

An opinion is sometimes voiced that the juridical nature of the EEZ is based on international treaty. Though this premise is basically correct, it does not reveal the contents of the concept of the zone's juridical nature. Just to say that this is so, is only half-way to a clear-cut identification of such category of law as the EEZ.

Among the first Soviet authors to draw attention to the topicality of the problem was R.V. Dekazonov.[8] Indeed, to lay bare the essence of the zone's juridical nature it is necessary to answer the following question: is the area of the zone a part of the high seas or is it a new category of law different in nature from the high seas?

Practice and experience indicate that the character of the sea area beyond the limits of the territorial sea remains unchanged despite any exceptions to or restrictions of the flag state's jurisdiction over the high seas that may be imposed by international treaties, or any new categories of marine law that may come to exist (the contiguous zone, the continental shelf, etc.). It has always been and continues to be a high seas area. It is subject, as R.V. Dekazonov correctly points out, to the fundamental principles of non-appropriation and common use which constitute the contents of the concept of the high seas' juridical nature.[9]

If this is so, can we claim that under the provisions of the 1982 Convention the EEZ has all the required properties to be classed with the high seas areas? The answer is yes.

And, indeed, as follows from Article 55 of the 1982 Convention the EEZ" is an area beyond and adjacent to the territorial sea, subject to the specific[10] legal regime established in this Part, under which the rights and jurisdiction of the coastal state and the rights and freedoms of other states are governed by the relevant provisions of this Convention." It follows from this provision that, first, the EEZ is geographically beyond the limits of the territorial sea. As soon as it is outside the territory of the coastal state it is not subject to the principle of territorial supremacy of this state. The EEZ, as will be shown below, cannot be an object of territorial rights of the coastal state and its area is thus subject to the common use by all states. Second, it follows from Article 55 that the EEZ is subject to a specific legal regime.

What is the scope of operation of the non-appropriation and common use principles and which other articles of the Convention reflect these principles?

Very important in this context is Article 58 of the Convention which lays down that in the EEZ, all states, whether coastal or landlocked, enjoy, subject to the relevant provisions of the Convention, the freedoms referred to in Article 87 of navigation and overflight and of the laying of submarine cables and pipelines and other international lawful uses of the sea related to these freedoms, such as those associated with the operation of ships, aircraft and submarine cables and pipelines, and compatible with the other provisions of this Convention. Thus, we can see that in the EEZ all states enjoy the major freedoms of the high seas which constitute the main contents of the general principle of the freedom of high seas.

At the same time Article 58 does not mention the freedoms of fishing and marine scientific research. A question may arise in this connection whether this "exception" of some freedoms of the high seas has not affected the operation of the principle of common use as a whole. Of course it has, but the principle as such is not in the final analysis determined by these exceptions. Another important circumstance should not be forgotten, to wit, that in granting the coastal state the rights to utilize the living marine resources and to regulate marine scientific research the Convention makes many reservations and limitations in respect of these rights (Articles 61, 62, 69, 70, 246 to 251). In other words, giving the coastal state basically functional rights to exploit the biological resources of the zone and to regulate marine scientific research the Convention does not completely rule out the rights of other states to use the biological resources of the zone and to conduct, specifically, fundamental marine research in the interests of the whole of mankind.

Moreover, in the above fields of activity the Convention imposes on the coastal state relevant obligations with respect to the international community. For instance, paragraph 2 of Article 56 lays down that in exercising its rights and performing its duties under this Convention in the EEZ, the coastal state shall have due regard to the rights and duties of other states and shall act in a manner compatible with the provisions of this Convention.

This also constitutes a specific feature of the regime of the EEZ.

The aforesaid approach in the Convention to the zone and its natural resources undoubtedly reflects recognition of the EEZ as an area in the common use of all states.

Analysis of Article 58 inevitably poses a question whether the exercise of the relevant freedoms in the EEZ is not made contingent on the discretion of the coastal state. The answer can be only in the negative. The coastal state has no right to restrict under any pretext the exercise of the freedoms of the high seas mentioned in the Convention. As to the freedom of navigation the coastal state is obliged under the Convention to ensure innocent passage of foreign ships even through its territorial sea which, as is correctly noted by Soviet authors, ensures the possibility of these ships exercising their right of freedom of navigation.[11]

In this light any attempt by the coastal state to interfere with the exercise of the freedoms of the high seas legalized in the Convention is absolutely impermissible.

It must be said that the reference in Article 58 (paragraph I) to the duty of all states, including coastal states, to comply with the relevant provisions of the Convention is not a departure from generally accepted practice. Article 2 of the 1958 Convention, for example, says that "freedom of the high seas is exercised under the conditions determined by these articles and other rules of international law." This wording, as is known, leaves no doubt as to the right of all states to a free and unimpeded (with due regard for international obligations) use of the high seas. Soviet scholar Yu. G. Barsegov is quite justified in saying that "absolute freedoms have never existed." The relationship of rights and respective duties is always historically motivated.[12]

In this context the other paragraphs of Article 58 are quite logical. According to paragraph 2 of this Article, "Articles 88 to 115 and other pertinent rules of international law apply to the EEZ in so far as they are not incompatible with this Part."

This is an important provision of principle which decisively confirms that the EEZ (its water mass) is part and parcel of the high seas. Articles 88 to 115 are all in Part VII of the Convention entitled "High Seas." Under Article 88 the high seas shall be reserved for peaceful purposes which is a very significant stipulation, especially if broadly interpreted in the context of the entire Convention.

In this case any departure from the Convention and noncompliance with its provisions would be a violation of the commitment to use the high seas for peaceful purposes. Under Article 89 no state may validly purport to subject any part of the high seas to its sovereignty. Every state, whether coastal or land-locked, has the right to sail ships flying its flag on the high seas (Article 90). It follows from the Convention (Article 89) that no part of the EEZ can be validly subject to the sovereignty of the coastal state. All ships sail in the EEZ under the conditions that constitute the regime of navigation in the high seas. Consequently, the principles of non-appropriation and common use which characterize the juridical nature of the high seas fully apply, as follows from the Convention of 1982, to the EEZ.

Thus, an actual, realistic and non-formal assessment of the provisions of the Convention leads to the indisputable conclusion that it defines the EEZ as part and parcel of the high seas.

It remains to clarify the specifics of the legal regime of the EEZ and how it affects the navigation of foreign vessels therein.

The distinguishing feature of the EEZ is that it encompasses two areas with different legal regimes. This point was raised a long time ago by several authors. Francois Wodle writes that the EEZ includes the seabed, the subsoil and the superjacent waters.[13]

Michael Morris points out that the EEZ includes two areas partially merging though different in their legal regimes -- the EEZ (the author, of course, means the water mass of the zone) and the continental shelf.[14] It follows quite definitely from Article 56, paragraph 3 of the Convention that the sea-bed in the EEZ is subject to the provisions contained in Part VI, *i.e.* those which determine the regime of the continental shelf.

In Soviet literature this peculiarity of the EEZ has been pinpointed by R.V. Dekanozov who points out that the EEZ is a complex formation "because it includes the mass of water and the seabed whose legal natures are different."[15] Unlike other authors, R.V. Dekanozov points, from the start, to the difference in juridical nature between the water mass in the EEZ and the sea-bed within its limits, *i.e.*, the continental shelf.[16]

This peculiarity of the EEZ alone gives grounds for singling out this zone from the other new categories of marine law in the 1982 Convention and to speak of the specific legal regime of the zone as such though, obviously, the specificity of the regime is largely determined, but not exhausted, by this peculiarity.

Under Article 56 in the EEZ the coastal state has sovereign rights for the purpose of exploring and exploiting, conserving and managing the natural resources of the waters superjacent to the sea-bed and of the sea-bed and its sub-soil. These are the basic rights which the developing countries were clamouring for, but their claims with respect to the EEZ did not end there. The Conference emphasized that the principal aspect of the EEZ was recognition of the coastal state's economic rights and interests in a 200-nautical mile area. "The need to protect the economic rights of coastal States," said the delegate from Argentina, "is the underlying concept of the EEZ and of its extension up to 200 nautical miles."[17] These rights, he went on, are basically sovereign and concern exploitation and utilization of the natural resources. The delegate from France stressed that the concept of the EEZ "means that States shall enjoy or exercise specific economic rights in a definite zone."[18] The West German delegation also indicated that in the EEZ "the coastal States shall be given clear-cut rights and jurisdiction with regard to the resources. All other States will continue, as before, to enjoy the freedoms of the high seas with respect to navigation, overflight and other internationally lawful uses of the sea."[19]

Under Article 56 in the EEZ the coastal state has, apart from the aforesaid rights to the resources, jurisdiction with regard to: a) the establishment and use of artificial islands, installations and structures; b) marine scientific research; and c) the protection and preservation of the marine environment.

How can the rights and jurisdiction granted to the coastal state with regard to the EEZ affect the exercise of the freedom of navigation in the zone?

Recognition of the sovereign rights of the coastal state to utilize the natural resources of the EEZ naturally calls for and justifies recognition of its exclusive right to construct and also to authorize and regulate the construction, operation and use of artificial islands, installations and structures designed for the purposes set out in Article 56, *i.e.*, for economic purposes. Such installations and structures may cause certain interference to the exercise of the rights and freedoms of non-coastal states in the EEZ. In this connection the Convention has special safeguards to protect the interests of both the coastal and non-coastal states.

The status of artificial islands, installations and structures, specifically, in the EEZ requires a special study. At this stage we shall confine ourselves to the impact of such artificial facilities on navigation. This problem is dealt with in the 1982 Convention on the basis of the experience of the previous Geneva Convention of 1958 on the continental shelf. Under Article 60, paragraph 3, of the 1982 Convention pertaining to the establishment of artificial islands, installations and structures "due notice must be given of the construction of such artificial islands, installations or structures, and permanent means for giving warning of their presence must be maintained. Any installations or structures which are abandoned or disused shall be removed to ensure safety of navigation, taking into account any generally accepted international standards established in this regard by the competent international organization. Such removal shall also have due regard to fishing, the protection of the marine environment and the rights and duties of other states. Appropriate publicity shall be given to the depth, position and dimensions of any installation or structure not entirely removed." As can be seen from the contents of this paragraph a general solution has been found for some of the problems and the states, obviously, will have to work out in greater detail other problems.

The formula "due notice" also ought to be specified. The competent international organizations will have to develop international standards for the guidance of the coastal states in removing abandoned or disused installations and structures, etc. Solution of these problems is important for ensuring safety of international navigation in the economic zones of coastal states.

In accordance with Article 60 in the EEZ the coastal state shall have the exclusive rights to construct and to authorize and regulate the construction, operation and use of artificial islands, installations and structures for the purposes set out in Article 56 and for other economic purposes, as well as installations and structures which may interfere with the exercise of the rights of the coastal state in the zone. It can be inferred that with respect to artificial islands, irrespective of their nature and purpose, the coastal state enjoys all the aforementioned exclusive rights. As to installations and strutures, the above rights of the coastal state shall be exercised only with regard to those which are designed for the purposes set out in Article 56 and other economic purposes.

Consequently, it may be inferred that in the EEZ other states can put up installations and structures of a non-economic nature without authorization from the coastal state. The jurisdiction of the coastal state cannot extend to such facilities. These may include, according to Soviet scholar P.D. Barabolya, buoys and "barrels" put up by other states for navigational purposes.[20] This right seems to stem from the need to realize the principle of freedom of navigation in the EEZ.

The coastal state may, where necessary, establish reasonable safety zones around the artificial islands, installations and structures under its jurisdiction "in which it may take appropriate measures to ensure safety both of navigation and of the artificial islands, installations and structures." The breadth of the safety zone shall be determined by the coastal state, taking into account applicable international standards.

Under Article 60, paragraph 5 safety zones shall be designed to ensure that they are reasonably related to the nature and function of the artificial islands, installations or structures, and shall not exceed a distance of 500 meters around them, measured from each point of their outer edge, except as authorized by generally accepted international standards or as recommended by the competent international organization. Due notice shall be given of the extent of safety zones. The constantly increasing number of marine installations and structures of various kinds raises very urgent problems in respect of safety of navigation in areas of their heavy concentration, and of ensuring appropriate publicity for their position, and for the breadth of the safety zones, as a means for giving warning of their presence, etc.

As follows from Article 60, paragraph 6, states will have to continue work on international standards regarding navigation in the vicinity of artificial islands, installations, structures and safety zones. All ships must respect these safety zones and shall comply with the mentioned standards.

The Convention forbids the establishment of artificial islands, installations and structures and the safety zones around them "where interference may be caused to the use of recognized sea lanes essential to international navigation." It must be borne in mind that what is meant is obviously that installations may not be established either directly in recognized international sea lanes, or as set out in paragraph 7 of Article 60, where interference may be caused to the use of such sea lanes for navigation, *i.e.*, in their vicinity.

The aforesaid provisions show an obvious preference for the interests of the international community in the exercise of the freedom of navigation in the EEZ over those of the coastal state related to the development of natural resources. Interpreted in this spirit should also be the provisions of Article 78 (paragraph 2) to the effect that the exercise of the rights of the coastal state over the continental shelf must not infringe upon or result in any unjustifiable interference with navigation and other rights and freedoms of other states. This provision has a direct bearing on the EEZ because, as we have established, the zone includes not only the mass of water, but also the sea-bed and the subsoil which form the continental shelf. Fully applicable to the EEZ is also another provision of Article 78 which says that the rights of the coastal state over the continental shelf do not affect the legal status of the superjacent waters or of the air space above those waters. This approach should not be taken as infringement of interests of the coastal state because it stems from the objective need to maintain favorable conditions for international navigation without which normal economic intercourse in the modern era is unthinkable.

Article 60 (paragraph 8) of the Convention lays down that artificial islands, installations and structures have no territorial sea of their own, and their presence "does not affect the delimitation of the territorial sea, the EEZ or the continental shelf."

Another essential aspect for the navigation of foreign vessels in the EEZ is the jurisdiction of the coastal state over the protection and preservation of the marine environment.

The exercise of this jurisdiction is regulated mostly by the provisions of Part XII of the Convention which deals with the protection and preservation of the marine environment.

In accordance with the rules of existing international law coastal states used to enjoy certain competence in matters pertinent to the preservation of the marine environment from pollution from foreign vessels in areas beyond the limits of the territorial sea before the adoption of the 1982 Convention.[21] Their rights in this sphere, however, were essentially less than those enjoyed under the new Convention. Moreover, the earlier rules applied only to those states which were parties to the relevant specific conventions such as the 1954

Convention on prevention of oil pollution as amended in 1962, 1969, and 1971 and the 1972 Convention on prevention of pollution through discharges of wastes and other materials. Under these Conventions the coastal state was expected only to take note of violations by foreign vessels beyond the limits of the territorial sea and notify the flag state of them, and only the latter could penalize the vessel which committed the violation. In other words, under the Convetions only the flag state took direct action against pollution by vessels in the high seas through enforcement of certain measures.

Only the International Convention of 1969 gave the coastal state the right to interfere in maritime casualties in the high seas resulting in a serious and imminent threat of oil pollution to its coastline and to take whatever action might seem justified in respect to the vessel concerned up to, as many authors believe, destroying it.[22]

The 1982 Convention has extended still further the coastal state's rights to prevent oil pollution by foreign vessels. At the same time the Convention has retained the general trend of seeking to do away with pollution through, above all, internationally accepted rules of law which reflects the realism of the participants in the Conference and their awareness of the international nature of the problem[23] that cannot be solved solely or largely through national measures as some of the attending coastal states claimed. Had the attempts of these states to have put through their plans proved a success, the freedom of navigation in the EEZ would have become a fiction because its exercise would have been made largely contingent on purely national measures adopted unilaterally by the coastal state. At the same time it would have been an essential departure from the functional (natural resources, development-oriented) nature of the coastal state's rights in its EEZ and an unjustified actual control over the zone prejudicial to the international community. No wonder that most states attending the Conference turned this solution down.

Under the Convention states must deal with oil pollution from vessels, including within their EEZ, on the basis of international rules and standards adopted through competent international organizations or diplomatic conferences. Such rules and standards shall be re-examined from time to time as necessary. At the same time coastal states may in respect of their EEZ adopt laws and regulations for the prevention, reduction and control of pollution. These laws and regulations, however, must conform to the generally accepted international rules and standards. A departure from this principle may be justified only when the existing international rules and standards are inadequate to meet special circumstances and coastal states have reasonable grounds for believing that a particular, clearly defined area of their respective EEZ is an area where the adoption of special mandatory measures for the prevention of pollution from vessels is required for recognized technical reasons in relation to its oceanographic and ecological conditions, as well as its utilization or the protection of its resources and the particular character of its traffic. In such cases the coastal states may take special mandatory measures (paragraph 6a, Article 211) to prevent pollution from vessels, but these measures cannot be taken unilaterally. The coastal states, after appropriate consultations, through the competent international organization, with any other states concerned may, for that area, direct a communication to that organization, submitting scientific and technical evidence in support and information on necessary reception facilities. It is up to the competent international organization (in this case the IMO) to determine whether the conditions in that area correspond to the requirements set out above and whether the adoption of special measures which are mandatory for foreign vessels as well is justified. But in this case too the laws and regulations adopted by the coastal states must conform to the international rules and standards or navigational practices made applicable, through the organization, for special areas. These laws and regulations shall not become applicable to foreign vessels until fifteen months after the submission of the communication to the organization.

If the circumstances require, coastal states may adopt additional, stricter laws and regulations to prevent, reduce and control pollution from vessels than is provided for by international rules and standards. Such rules and standards may relate to discharges or navigational practices. The relevant states, however, must, firstly, notify the international organization (IMO) of their intention to adopt such laws and regulations; secondly, these laws and regulations shall not require foreign vessels to observe design standards other than generally accepted international rules and standards; and, thirdly, they shall become applicable provided that the organization agrees.

As compared to existing international law the Convention has essentially extended the rights of the coastal states in respect of enforcing the international rules and standards pertinent to prevention of pollution from vessels. Nonetheless, the Convention, as is justly pointed out by Soviet authors, "imposes the main responsibility for the enforcement of generally accepted rules and standards contained in special conventions adopted under the aegis of the IMO and otherwise, on the flag States."[24]

The Convention gives the coastal state (Article 220) considerable rights, including detention of a foreign vessel, its physical inspection, the institution of proceedings and imposition of penalties. But these measures are applicable only in special, clearly-defined cases. For instance, where there are clear grounds for believing that a vessel navigating in the EEZ or the territorial sea of a state has, in the EEZ, committed a violation of applicable international rules and standards, or laws and regulations of that state conforming and giving effect to such rules and standards, resulting in a substantial discharge causing or threatening significant pollution of the marine environment, that state may undertake physical inspection of the vessel for matters relating to the violation if the vessel has refused to give information or if the information supplied by the vessel is manifestly at variance with the evident factual situation.

Where there is clear objective evidence that a vessel in the EEZ committed a violation resulting in a discharge causing major damage or threat of major damage to the coastline or related interests of the coastal state, or to any resources of its territorial sea or EEZ, that state may, provided that the evidence so warrants, institute proceedings, including detention of the vessel, in accordance with its laws.

Besides, a special section of the Convention (7) deals with safeguards designed to protect the interests of international navigation primarily in the economic zone.[25]

As to punishments the Convention lays down that monetary penalties only may be imposed with respect to violations of national laws and regulations or applicable international rules and standards for the prevention, reduction and control of pollution of the marine environment, committed by foreign vessels beyond the territorial sea, except in the case of a willful and serious act of pollution in the territorial sea.

Under the provisions on safeguards states shall not discriminate against vessels of any other state; proceedings to impose penalties on foreign vessels shall not be instituted after the expiry of three years from the date on which the violation was committed; states shall promptly notify the flag state, its diplomatic or consular officials of any measures taken against foreign vessels, etc.

Our analysis of the provisions of the Convention pertinent to the EEZ brings us to the conclusion that the rights and interests of the coastal states and those of other states are proportioned in a relationship that makes it possible to regard the EEZ (its water mass) as an integral part of the high seas. The regime of the EEZ is determined, above all, by its juridical nature which basically boils down to the principles of non-appropriation and common use. Analysis of the provisions on freedom of navigation in the zone clearly indicates that the Convention gives preference to the rights and interests of the international community.

NOTES

1. Bozrikov O., Kiselev V., *Merchant navigation in the economic zone*, Morflot, 1981, No. 2, p. 37; Kolodkin N.L., Kiselev V.A., Savaskov P.V., "Some basic principles of the international legal regime of the World Ocean in the light of the new UN Convention on the Law of the Sea." in Soviet Yearbook of Marine Law, M., 1983, p. 40; Lazarev M.I., *Theoretical problems of contemporary international marine law*, M., 1983, p. 255; Golovatyi S.P., *A 200-mile zone in the world ocean*. Kiev, 1984, p. 64; M. Scerni, "La zone economique exclusive: son importance, sa nature juridique et les problemes principaux et relatifs." in *The Law of the Sea*, Vol. VII, Thessaloniki, 1977, p. 160; Kalinkin G.F., *The Regime of sea areas*. M., 1981, p. 90; Barabolya P.D., "Legal problems related to the establishment of the economic zone." *Contemporary marine law*. M., 1984, p. 123.
2. Scerni M., *op.cit.*, pp. 180-183.
3. Williams S.A., and de Mestral A.L.C., *An Introduction to International Law*, Toronto, 1979, p. 219.
4. Under Art. 86 of the 1982 Convention the EEZ is not formally included in the concept of the high seas. In reality, however, as will be shown below, the EEZ (its water mass) is part of the high seas with its own specific regime.
5. Third UN Conference on the Law of the Sea. Official records, vol. V, p. 226.
6. For more detail see: Molodtsov S.V., *The legal regime of sea waters*. M., 1982, pp. 94-97.
7. Scerni, M., *op.cit.*, p. 181.
8. See: Dekanozov R.V., "The legal nature of the economic zone." Second All-Union Congress of oceanologists. Yalta, December 16-17, 1982. Theses of reports. Issue 8, part 2. Sevastopol, 1982, pp. 47-48.
9. Dekanozov R.V., "On the juridical nature of the high seas and the sea-bed beyond the limits of the continental shelf," in *International law problems of the World Ocean today*. M., 1976, pp. 93-96.

10. In the Russian text of the Convention the word "osobyi" is used which is not a very happy choice as has been pointed out in Soviet literature.
11. Gureev S.A., Freedom of the high seas. "Sovetskoye gosudarstvo i pravo (The Soviet State and Law)", 1982, p. 106. See also: Kisselev V.A., and Sabaskov P.V., "The international law problems of navigation and protection of the marine environment" in *The legal and economic problems of international navigation regulation*. M., 1984, p. 66.
12. Barsegov Yu. G., *The World Ocean: rights, politics, diplomacy*. M., 1983, p. 161.
13. F. Wodle, "Les interets economiques et le droit de la mer" [1976] Revue general de droit international public. 763.
14. Morris Michael A., "Military Aspects of the Economic Zone" in Ocean Yearbook. Chicago, London, 1982, vol. 3, p. 321.
15. Dekanovov R.V., "The legal nature of the economic zone". 2nd All-Union Congress of oceanologists. Theses of reports. Issue 8, part 2. Sevastopol, 1982, p. 47.
16. For more detail see: Dekanozov R.V., and Tsarev V.F., "Some aspects of the juridical content of the continental shelf and the economic zone" in *Present-day problems of marine law*. M., 1983, pp. 53-61.
17. Third United Nations Conference on the Law of the Sea. Official records, vol. II, p. 300.
18. Ibid., p. 282.
19. A/Conf., 62/WS/I6.
20. For more detail see: P.D. Barabolya, *Legal problems related to the establishment of the economic zone*, pp. 152-154.
21. For more detail see: Bozrikov O., Kisselev V., *op.cit.* in n.1, p. 38.
22. Gorshkov G.S., Melkov G.M., *Prevention of pollution of the marine environment*. M., Voyendizat publishers, 1979, p. 45. Bozrikov O., Kisselev V., *op.cit.* in n.1, p. 38.
23. See in: Molodtsov S.V., *op.cit.* in n.6, p. 120.
24. See: Kolodkin A.L., Kisselev V.A., Savaskov P.V., *op.cit.* in n.1, p. 46.
25. For more detail see: Ivanov G.G., "Merchant navigation in the UN Convention on the Law of the Sea" in Soviet Yearbook of Marine Law, 1982. M., V/O "Mortekhinformreklama" publ., 1983, pp. 56-57.

BANQUET SPEECH

THE IMPLEMENTATION PROBLEM IN THE LAW OF THE SEA

Edward L. Miles
Institute for Marine Studies
University of Washington

I should like to focus on the implementation problem in the law of the sea by taking the Convention of 1982 and asking several questions. First, what jobs need to be done by scholars and practitioners even before it comes into force and why? Second, what are states currently doing? And third, how best can we act to preserve the balance negotiated within the Convention so as to avoid undermining its importance as an agreed frame of reference for conduct on the oceans? These questions require some emendation before we turn to the substance of what I think are the jobs to be done.

Why is it relevant to ask what jobs need to be done before the Convention comes into force? The answer to this question is bound up in what public policy analysts know as "the implementation problem" and the attention that must always be given to it. "Implementation" is the installation of new policies and practices in and by public and private organizations. But both policy formulation and implementation are inherently Pandora's boxes in the sense that what is eventually decided is not necessarily what was intended by those who initiated the process; and what is actually implemented may vary considerably from what was decided.

If the decision process is itself fragmented, time-consuming and costly, and if decisions arrived at on most items represent the best compromises that are likely from such a large and complex process, then actions which tend to undermine those compromises unravel agreement without the prospect of being able to do any better. From the perspective of the Convention, therefore, the real issue is: if the Convention is undermined, and if unilateral action is to be the norm, what alternative bases are there which are likely to prove to be more effective for building world order in the global commons of the oceans?

In this connection, one needs also to consider the question of urgency. In the post-negotiation period, and before the Convention comes into force, coastal states are engaged in the making of policy pertaining to most dimensions of ocean use. These policies, as evidenced by domestic legislation, bilateral agreements, national regulations, claims and decisions can either flow from the Convention or differ so greatly from the compromises arrived at therein as to undermine it altogether. It seems to me, therefore, that the urgency relates to protecting the compromises arrived at in Parts II, III, IV, V, VI, VIII, IX, XII, XIII, and XV in particular. I leave out Part XI because the economic realities show that this is primarily a symbolic issue without substance since there is unlikely to be any seabed mining until the twenty-first century. Part XIV is only hortatory. For the rest, however, the beginnings of the future are immediate and of great significance.

What are states actually doing in relation to those parts of the Convention of immediate concern? This turns out to be a very difficult question indeed because only bits and pieces of information are available. The Office of the Special Representative of the Secretary-General for the Law of the Sea is performing a valuable service for the global marine affairs community in making available compendia of national legislation on extended coastal state jurisdiction. FAO is making a similar contribution by its compendia of national legislation relating to fisheries and by monitoring trends in bilateral agreements on fisheries. However, none of the other dimensions of marine policy are covered in a similar fashion by any other agency so we cannot tell comprehensively what the global trends are for straits, pollution, marine scientific research and the like.

Furthermore, in each case, while it is important to know what national legislation is, this never tells the whole story of the pattern of state practice. We need to know what the regulations are which are meant to guide implementation of the legislation in order to compare that with the provisions of the Convention. We also need to know what actual practice is because what states do is not always consistent with what they say they do or will do.

It would be useful, I think, if the Law of the Sea Institute would be willing to marshal its forces and act as a catalyst in seeing whether a global research effort, involving international agencies and other law of the sea research institutes, could be mounted to tackle this problem. The truth is that we cannot now monitor the full range of state practice in any comprehensive sense and the consequences of being unable to do so may be very significant indeed.

The Jobs to be Done

What jobs, therefore, need to be done even before the Convention comes into force? Let me remind you that my concern here is with preserving the balance of interests negotiated within the Convention for the reasons elaborated previously. I shall give most emphasis to the issues of the territorial sea/straits/archipelagoes, the EEZ, the continental shelf, fisheries, and control of marine pollution from ships.

Territorial Sea/Straits/Archipelagoes

Three primary questions are raised by these issues. These can be summarized in terms of limits, status and regulation of navigation via the establishment of sea lanes, traffic separation schemes and vessel traffic reporting and management systems.

With respect to limits, the *Law of the Sea Bulletin*, No. 2 (December 1983), published by the United Nations, provides data on the limits of the territorial sea for 133 coastal states. Of those 109 (82%) have territorial seas of twelve miles or less, with by far the largest majority (83 or 62%) at twelve miles. Twenty-four states (18%) have territorial seas greater than twelve miles with thirteen of those claiming 200 miles. What sorts of relationships will evolve between those states, a definite minority of all coastal states, claiming more than twelve miles and the rest of the international community? Will there be tests of jurisdiction? If so, what forms will they take and how strongly will they be resisted? If the issue does become a cause of conflict, will it be dealt with only bilaterally or in some form of multilateral context, be it regional or otherwise?

Furthermore, what are the implications of extending territorial seas to twelve miles and beyond for straits used for international navigation before the Convention comes into force? Will the constraints on strait state jurisdiction which are written into the Convention be observed in practice even though strait states may deny that they are obligations before the Convention is in force? Clearly, bilateral or multilateral discussions will be necessary between the major maritime powers and strait states in an attempt to reach a mutually acceptable understanding and it is not inconceivable that other bargaining chips may well be brought to bear upon these discussions.

What is important, however, if the balance written into the Convention is to be maintained, is that there be restraint on both sides in the process of claim and counter-claim that will undoubtedly ensue. This can easily get out of hand and quickly escalate into a series of expansive national claims opposed by denials of the permissibility of such action. In a confrontation, or a series of confrontations, the heat of the battle may lead each side to reject the substance of the Convention for tactical reasons. Even in the period before the Convention comes into force, as the great majority of coastal states establish territorial seas of twelve miles, strait states need to think of straits used for international navigation as retaining an international character even when they are encompassed within a twelve-mile claim.

The issue of the archipelagic regime, prior to the entry into force of the Convention, may be a delicate one, especially in certain areas of the world like the South Pacific, the South China Sea, the Indian Ocean and the Caribbean. However, I think that it would be wise for those coastal states claiming archipelagic status to remain within the criteria established in the Convention. If this is done, it would also be wise for the major maritime powers to refrain from raising objections to the legitimacy of doing so even if, in some cases, negotiations concerning route substitution may be involved. Obviously, the point made previously about strait states also applies, *mutatis mutandis*, to archipelagic states.

It should also be noted that so far countries have been somewhat cavalier in the manner in which they have approached announcements of new limits, enactment of new zones and the like. There is clearly a need for much greater specificity here, in terms of maps, charts and coordinates, so that the international community can have a clear idea of what is being claimed, with what geographic effects. While such documentation is supposed to be deposited with the United Nations, this requirement currently seems to be honored more in the breach than the observance.

The last problem which deserves discussion here concerns the regulation of navigation through establishment of traffic separation schemes and vessel traffic reporting and management systems. These may apply not only to the territorial sea, straits and archipelagoes, but also to EEZs for pollution control purposes.

At the Thirteenth Law of the Sea Institute Conference in Mexico City in 1979, Professors Edgar Gold and Douglas Johnston dealt with this issue at some length.[1]

They point out that while IMCO, as it then was, had played a major coordinating role in elaborating international ground rules for the establishment of traffic separation schemes, this had not been true for proliferating vessel traffic reporting and management systems which seemed to be driven primarily by coastal state desires for protection against ship-generated oil pollution. This remains the case (see the papers in Part VI, above).

I think the highly decentralized way in which such regulation of navigation is being developed is a cause for some concern when juxtaposed against the careful system of checks and balances elaborated in the Convention. There are two particular potential issues that seem to be important. The first concerns the setting up of traffic separation schemes in international straits now encompassed within twelve-mile territorial seas or archipelagoes, and the second concerns the regulation of navigation in EEZs in attempts to impose more effective controls against the likelihood of oil pollution damage.

We will return to the EEZ problem a little later. The policy problem which requires resolution is how should strait and archipelagic states deal with the regulation of navigation in international straits prior to the entry into force of the Convention. I suggest that the procedure elaborated in the Convention be employed in order to avoid increasing conflict which would threaten the stability of the compromises arrived at. These policy instruments should be used for the purposes of reducing navigational hazards and controlling pollution and not as surrogates for attaining other objectives which may be contentious. Effective implementation of these safeguards will be facilitated if there is prior international agreement. This argues for utilization of the IMO mechanism as foreseen within the Convention sooner rather than later.

The Exclusive Economic Zone

The problem here is that Part V represents a consensus negotiated globally which requires each coastal state, in effect, to reach its own *internal*, coordinated balance in the implementation of the various provisions. However, state practice seems to suffer from two sources of inherent conflict:

1. Existing domestic legislation, some of it done prior to the Convention in order to influence its outcome, is, in some cases, more expansive of coastal state authority than is the Convention. For example, in the excerpts from the domestic legislation of 54 states provided in the *Law of the Sea Bulletin*, No. 2 (December 1983), 24 states establish exclusive jurisdiction over pollution control and marine scientific research in addition to resources, economic activities and artificial islands and installations. This does not make much difference for marine scientific research but it could imply some conflict with the carefully worked out balance in Articles 213-233 dealing with enforcement of ship-generated pollution controls. State practice here ought at least to be monitored carefully in order to ascertain whether what states actually do is the same as they claim. If not, some discussions will be required within IMO to resolve these differences.
2. Even where there is no conflict between domestic legislation and the Convention, the Conference has been removed as the stimulus for formulating coordinated national ocean policy. Coastal states have, as a consequence, fallen back on the old sectoral approaches to management but not all sectors are equally aware of the compromises and nuances contained within the Convention. Narrow perceptions of management requirements, for instance in pollution control and fisheries, may lead to elaboration of regulations that imply exercise of jurisdiction beyond what the Convention permits. This seems to be a continuing problem which is exacerbated by the absence of an ocean policy integrating mechanism nationally in most states.

It is also apparent that many developing coastal states in Africa, Asia, Latin America and the South Pacific require assistance in aligning their national legislation with the provisions of the Convention in order to facilitate ratification. This is a job that the UN and other international agencies can perform effectively but resources are not being made available for these efforts to be made in any systematic way.

Given the highly decentralized fashion in which customary international law is made, there are no easily available safeguards to ensure that what coastal states claim and do are compatible with the balance of interests worked out in the Convention. One can only caution those who make and implement policy on the need for awareness and moderation. At the same time, it is worth re-emphasizing that continued fragmentation in ocean policy machinery at the national level has also lulled coastal states into relying on the traditional sectoral approaches to ocean management. By thinking in the old way, coastal states miss opportunities to produce innnovative policies which may be facilitated if they attempt to define and maximize national net benefit from the resources and other characteristics of the zone. So far, there does not seem to be even the glimmer of official perceptions of the opportunity and the need to do things differently.

The Continental Shelf[2]

We have here a difficult situation wherein Article 76, containing the Irish Formula, emerged as the focal point of the negotiations on the outer limits of the continental margin and indeed proved to be the only basis for a solution acceptable to the large margin states. The technical requirements for implementing Article 76, on the other hand, are extremely difficult to achieve and, in fact, may be impossible in several important cases.

It will be recalled that the heart of the Irish Formula is contained in Article 76(4). This requires, *inter alia*, determination of the point at which "...the thickness of sedimentary rocks is at least 1% of the shortest distance from such point to the foot of the continental slope." Furthermore, the foot of the slope is defined "...as the point of maximum change in the gradient at its base." These mask two very difficult and costly technical problems. It is extraordinarily difficult to determine precisely where the 1% limit is and the point of maximum change in the gradient of the slope. Data for most states, detailing bathymetric lines normal to the slope and seismic reflection lines out to the 10/0 thickness limit, simply do not exist. The cost of determining the 10/0 limit will be very high as will the cost of determining the point of maximum change in the gradient of the slope.

Given these uncertainties, difficulties and costs, I infer the following:

1. Most coastal states with margins extending beyond 200 miles will have an incentive *not* to declare a firm outer limit.
2. Where attempts are made to determine firm outer limits, the slipperiness of the Irish Formula is likely to produce the permissible maxima, *i.e.*, either 350 nautical miles or 100 nautical miles from the 2,500 meter isobath.
3. The 2,500 m. isobath criterion is likely to be important only in a few areas, *e.g.*, Australia, N.E. Asia, and the Bering Shelf.
4. The existence of the first condition, combined with delays in the operational implementation of Part XI, could facilitate continued creeping coastal state jurisdiction into the international seabed area.

Living Resources

It appears that the new law of the sea is most developed in this dimension and that most coastal state claims and bilateral agreements seem to be quite compatible with, and indeed based on, the relevant provisions of Part V. In this connection, the work by FAO of monitoring national legislation and bilateral agreements has been a major contribution,[3] but we still lack any systematic, comparative analysis of national regulations implementing the legislation.

The early trends in bilateral agreements, *i.e.*, 1976-1978, as analyzed by Carroz and Savini show primary coastal state concern with controlling foreign fishermen. These agreements provided a transitional adjustment to the new regime and were principally of three types:

1. Those phasing out foreign fishing operations and securing their gradual replacement by local fleets;
2. Those providing for reciprocal fishing rights between vessels of both parties in their respective zones of jurisdiction; and
3. Those prescribing terms and conditions of access for foreign vessels.

In this transition, coastal states seemed to be deriving the following kinds of benefits:

1. Income in the form of fees.
2. Increased landings of fish in local ports.
3. Training of local fishermen on board foreign fishing vessels.
4. Financial and economic cooperation.
5. Cooperation in training and research.
6. Trade facilities.
7. Joint ventures.

The later trends in bilateral agreements, *i.e.*, 1979-1983, showed that:

1. Long-term agreements were still not growing significantly in number;
2. There was some movement in the North and Southwest Pacific for framework agreements but these still required negotiation of annual catch quotas and/or fee levels;
3. There seemed to be emerging concern among coastal States about new kinds of regional arrangements in West Africa and West Central and Southwest Pacific; and
4. The EEC achieved the implementation of both the internal and external Common Fisheries Policy.

Interestingly, while we are still in a transitional phase, the later trends seem to show a resurgence of interest by coastal states in certain forms of regional cooperation in fisheries. This will inevitably grow where stocks are shared significantly. Overall, however, the impact of extended coastal state jurisdiction has not solved all problems for fisheries management and development. Extended jurisdiction has certainly solved the international problem of fragmented authority in most cases and has thereby destroyed the traditional common property characteristics of fisheries. In doing so, it has created a significant opportunity for coastal states to do better at management than they have in the past, but the opportunity will be transferred into reality only if coastal states close the loop and show the same concern for regulating their own fleets as they have demonstrated in regulating foreign ones.

So far, a large number of developing and developed countries are getting both direct and indirect benefits from access by foreign vessels where this was not possible before the coming of extended jurisdiction, but there is no clear indication that, in most cases, these benefits amount to more than a small proportion of their hypothetical potential. The result is a modest transfer of income from distant-water fishing nations to coastal states, but this transfer may be limited to the transitional phase since most large-scale distant-water fleets (except perhaps those of the USSR) will decline in the long run. Whether or not coastal states will actually realize the full potential of the opportunity created by extended jurisdiction will depend on the quality of national fisheries policy and the effectiveness of the organizational arrangements they establish. On those dimensions, coastal state performance is not yet cause for admiration.

There are, however, a few problems in the evolution of international fisheries law which may lead to important divergences between state practice and the compromises worked out in the Convention. The first problem is reflected in what seems to be a growing preference for the application of criminal penalties even where there is no agreement allowing for that between the coastal state and the country in which a particular vessel happens to be registered. It would be useful to see a global comparative study of fisheries enforcement in EEZs to determine the extent to which this is a problem. A similar enforcement problem, and potentially more serious for the balance of interests contained within the Convention, concerns the issue of fishing vessels in transit within the EEZ and at least the murmurings of applying something akin to the law of innocent passage to fishing vessels in the zone. This issue carries the seeds of a major conflict with advanced maritime nations if it indeed develops.[4]

Control of Oil Pollution from Ships
The last problem which I would like to mention concerns the tension which exists between the careful balance of interests negotiated within the Convention on enforcement by port, strait and coastal states against ship-generated oil pollution and the fears of these states that the primarily flag state system of enforcement lacks credibility. This issue also touches upon the perceived effectiveness, or lack thereof, of the two IMO Conventions which are meant to control ship-generated oil pollution when seen in the context of an increasing trend of tanker accidents since the mid-1960s. The two IMO Conventions are the International Convention for the Prevention of Pollution from Ships of 1973 and the Protocol to the 1973 Convention enacted in 1978 at the International Conference on Tanker Safety and Pollution Prevention.

The difficulty is that spectacular accidents off major maritime countries stimulate extreme demands for protection by national constituencies. Some governments are thereby pushed, as a result, into adopting regulations which threaten the integrity of the global system which they had a hand in creating. France, for instance, after the *Amoco Cadiz* incident has now imposed criminal penalties, as well as heavy fines, on the master of a ship carrying oil convicted of causing pollution in French territorial waters. Similar strong demands were stimulated in the United States after the *Argo Merchant* incident.

611

It may be that the 1978 Protocol is the last chance for the tanker industry to preserve the balance they achieved in the 1982 UN Convention on the Law of the Sea with respect to enforcement. Unless the flag state system of control is seen to be credible, if the frequency of significant accidents continues to increase, governments will find themselves captured by the angry demands of their populations and unilateral action by significant port, strait and coastal states will be triggered.

Conclusions

I have argued that most parts of the UN Convention on the Law of the Sea of 1982 contain compromises which offer the best balance of interests that is possible in the world which exists today and that these compromises rest on a complex and difficult process which did indeed produce consensus. We cannot expect that a similar balance can be produced out of the decentralized process by which customary international law is made. We should therefore do our best to safeguard those compromises, even before the Convention comes into force, by paying attention to what states claim and do, by being especially sensitive to the potential points of major contention, and by being cautious, restrained, coordinated and mutually responsive in the implementation of policy.

Reliance, instead, on unilateral action can only lead to increased conflict and further extensions of national sovereignty and jurisdiction upon the global commons of the oceans and the international seabed area. Unilateral action cannot now provide an effective basis of building a stable public order of the oceans. We have a valuable opportunity within our grasp. Let us collectively be careful lest we let it slip.

NOTES

1. Edgar Gold and Douglas M. Johnston. "Ship-Generated Pollution: The Creator of Regulated Navigation," in Thomas A. Clingan, Jr. (ed.) *Law of the Sea: State Practice in Zones of Special Jurisdiction,* (Honolulu: University of Hawai Press, 1982), pp. 156-197.
2. I am indebted to G. Ross Heath for his assistance in elaborating the argument in this section.
3. Gerald Moore. *Legislation on Coastal State Requirements for Foreign Fishing,* (Room: FAO, 1981), Legislative Study No. 21, esp. pp. 3-17; J.E. Carroz and M.J. Savini. *Bilateral Fishery Agreements,* FAO Fisheries Circular No. 709, FID/C709, April 1978; and J.E. Carroz and M.J. Savini. "The Practice of Coastal States Regarding Foreign Access to Fishery Resources: An Analysis of Bilateral Agreements," in "Report of the Expert Consultation on the Conditions of Access to the Fish Resources of the Exclusive Economic Zone," FAO Fisheries Report No. 293, FIPP/R293, Rome, 11-15 April 1983, Annex 2, pp. 43-72.
4. This whole issue is treated comprehensively by William T. Burke. "Exclusive Fisheries Zones and Freedom of Navigation," (1983) 20 *San Diego Law Review,* 595-623.

LIST OF PARTICIPANTS

A. Acker
School of Law
University of San Francisco
San Francisco, California

C. M. G. Adams
Research Vessel Services
Natural Environ. Research Council
South Glamorgan, Wales

Etty R. Agoes
Padjadjaran Law School
Padjadjaran University
Bandung, Indonesia

F. Ahnis
Churchill College
Cambridge
England

James H. Aki
Senator
State of Hawaii
Honolulu, Hawaii

Julian M. Ala
Vanuatu Government
Port Vila
Vanuatu

Lewis M. Alexander
Department of Geography
& Marine Affairs
University of Rhode Island

Gunnar V. Alexandersson
Dept. of Geography
Stockholm School of Economics
Stockholm, Sweden

Scott Allen
Law of the Sea Institute
Richardson School of Law
University of Hawaii

Philip J. Allott
Trinity College
Cambridge
England

Lee G. Anderson
College of Marine Studies
University of Delaware
Newark, Delaware

Marvin Anderson
East-West Center
University of Hawaii
Honolulu, Hawaii

R. Anderson
School of Law
University of San Francisco
San Francisco, California

Valery Andrianov
Soviet Maritime Law Association
Moscow
USSR

Thomas C. Archer
Center for Defense Studies
Aberdeen University
Old Aberdeen, Scotland

John E. Bardach
East-West Center
University of Hawaii
Honolulu, Hawaii

Jonathan Bar-Gur
University of Wales
Cardiff
Wales

Peter B. Beazley
Somerset
England

A. K. C. Beresford
Deparment of Maritime Studies
UWIST
Cardiff, Wales

R. J. H. Beverton
Department of Applied Biology
UWIST
Cardiff, Wales

Patricia Birnie
London School of Economics
London

G. H. Blake
Department of Geography
University of Durham

Joaquim G. Boavida
Department of Fisheries
Lisbon
Portugal

G. D. Braithwaite
Royal Naval College
Greenwich
London, England

Roger A. Brooks
The Heritage Foundation
Washington, D. C.

Peter Brueckner
Ministry of Foreign Affairs
Copenhagen
Denmark

F. J. J. Cadwallader
Centre for Marine Law & Policy
UWIST
Cardiff, Wales

A. R. Carnegie
Faculty of Law
University of West Indies
Cave Hill, Barbados

Liang Chen
UWIST
Cardiff
Wales

A. E. Chircop
Law School
Dalhousie University
Halifax, Nova Scotia

Abdul M. K. Choudhury
Supreme Court of Bangladesh
Bangladesh

I.A.E. Clinck
Buisseret, Clinck, Schroeyers
Antwerp
Belgium

M. Coelho
Woodbrooke College
Birmingham
England

E. Bollard
House of Lords
London
England

S. Braunius
Royal Netherlands Navy
Netherlands

E. D. Brown
Centre for Marine Law & Policy
UWIST
Cardiff, Wales

Dennis Bryant
U.S. Coast Guard
Washington, D. C.

Edward W. Cannon
Government Affairs Staff
U.S. Coast Guard

Daniel S. Cheever
Boston University
Center for Int'l Relations
Boston, Massachusetts

Rong-Jye Chen
Faculty of Law
Soochow University
Taipei, Taiwan

T. A. Cho
London School of Economics
London
England

R. R. Churchill
Centre for Marine Law & Policy
UWIST
Cardiff, Wales

Thomas A. Clingan, Jr.
Ocean & Coastal Law Program
University of Miami
Coral Gables, Florida

David A. Colson
Oceans, Int'l, Env. & Sci. Affairs
U.S. Department of State
Washington, D. C.

616

Andre G. Corbet
Dept. of Maritime Studies
UWIST
Cardiff, Wales

Eduardo Ferrero Costa
Peruvian Center for
International Studies
Lima, Peru

W. Cotter
School of Law
University of San Francisco
San Francisco, California

T. Cottier
Faculty of Law
University of Cambridge
Cambridge, England

Alistair Couper
Department of Maritime Studies
UWIST
Cardiff, Wales

C. Couper
Department of Maritime Studies
UWIST
Cardiff, Wales

John P. Craven
Law of the Sea Institute
Richardson School of Law
University of Hawaii

David J. Craven
c/o Law of the Sea Institute
Richardson School of Law
University of Hawaii

K. N. Dahl
Norwegian Federation
of Trade Unions
Oslo

M. Dahmani
Institute of Law
Algiers
Algeria

C. Da Pozzo
University of Pisa
Istituto di Scienze Geografiche
Pisa, Italy

Henry G. Darwin
Foreign & Commonwealth Office
London
England

J. M. B. Da Silva
Departamento da Marinha
Lisboa
Portugal

Arthur Davies
World Meteorological Org.
Brighton
England

P. De Cesari
Istituto di Diritto Internazionale
University of Milan
Milan, Italy

A. Del Vecchio Capotosti
Faculty of Law
Universita Luiss Di Roma
Roma, Italy

F. De Paux
Faculty of Law
Vrije Universiteit Brussel
Brussels, Belgium

Dermot Devine
Institute of Marine Law
University of Cape Town
Rondebosch, South Africa

K. Dharmasena
University of Kelaniya
Sri Lanka

L. Doswald-Beck
University College
London

R. M. D'Sa
Faculty of Law
University of Bristol
Bristol, England

Markus Ederer
Passau
Federal Republic of
Germany

W. R. Edeson
Faculty of Law
Australian Nat'l University
Canberra, Australia

Marlene J. Evans
Faculty of Law
SUNY - Empire State College
Saratoga Springs, New York

P. Fabbri
Department of Geography
University of Bologna
Bologna, Italy

Brit Floistad
Fridtjof Nansen Institute
Lysaker
Norway

P. H. Fricke
Nat'l Marine Fisheries Service
NOAA

Hans-Peter Gasser
International Committee
of the Red Cross
Geneva, Switzerland

H. J. Glaesner
Legal Adviser
Council of European Communities
Brussels, Belgium

Edgar Gold
Dalhousie Ocean Studies Program
Dalhousie University
Halifax, Canada

R. O. Goss
Department of Maritime Studies
UWIST
Cardiff, Wales

Lothar Gundling
Max-Planck Institute
for Comp. Public Law & Int'l Law
Heidelberg, Fed. Rep. of Germany

J. E. Halliday
Dept. of Maritime Studies
UWIST
Cardiff, Wales

C. R. Ellner
Federal Ministry for
Economic Affairs
Federal Republic of Germany

H. Ewang
World Maritime University
Malmo
Sweden

N. C. Flemming
Inst. of Oceanographic Sciences
Wormley, Godalming
Surrey, England

G. P. Francalanci
Survey & Photogrammetry Dept.
AGIP S.p.A.
Milano, Italy

P. Galindo
School of Law
University of San Francisco
San Francisco, California

J. N. K. Gibson
Center for Marine Law & Policy
UWIST
Cardiff, Wales

B. C. Goh
University of Essex
Colchester
England

L. F. E. Goldie
International Studies Program
Syracuse University
Syracuse, New York

G. R. Greiveldinger
Ofc. of the Asst. Sec. of State
for Int'l Security Affairs
Washington, D.C.

S. W. Haines
Center for Defense Studies
University of Aberdeen
Old Aberdeen, Scotland

Robert Halliday
Hydrographic Department
Ministry of Defense
London, England

618

Rognvaldur Hannesson
Norwegian School of
Economics & Business
Bergen-Sandviken, Norway

Jeremy Harrison
Richardson School of Law
University of Hawaii
Honolulu, Hawaii

Ellen Hey
Inst. of Public Int'l Law
University of Utrecht
Utrecht, Netherlands

P. E. Hohnen
Australian Embassy
Brussels
Belgium

Brian Hoyle
Office of Oceans Law & Policy
U.S. Dept. of State

Tsu-Chang Hung
Institute of Chemistry
Academia Sinica
Taipei, Taiwan

M. C. Ircha
Dept. of Civil Engineering
University of New Brunswick
Fredricton, New Brunswick

Guenther Jaenicke
Faculty of Law
University of Frankfurt/Main
Federal Republic of Germany

Uwe K. Jenisch
Kiel
Federal Republic of Germany

L. S. Johnson
London School of Economics
London
England

Sorajak Kasemsuvan
London School of Economics
London
England

Bruce A. Harlow
RADM, U. S. Navy (Retired)
Poulsbo, Washington

Marius Hauge
Ministry of Fisheries
Oslo
Norway

A. H. Hoel
Fridtjof Nansen Institute
Lysaker
Norway

G. Hornsey
Faculty of Law
Queen's University
Belfast, N. Ireland

J. Hoyrup
Ministry of Foreign Affairs
Copenhagen
Denmark

T. A. H. Ijlstra
University of Utrecht
Utrecht
Netherlands

Leon E. Irish
Faculty of Law
University of Michigan
Ann Arbor, Michigan

T. V. C. Jamir
Department of Marine Fisheries
U. of the Philippines - Visayas
Quezon City, Philippines

M. G. Jennings
Ministry of Agriculture,
Fisheries & Food
London, England

S. Kangal
Trinidad & Tobago High Comm.
London
England

W. V. Kattan
Vanuatu Government
Port Vila
Vanuatu

619

J. Keane
PREST
The University
Manchester, England

K. Kemokai
World Maritime University
Malmo
Sweden

J. King
Dept. of Maritime Studies
UWIST
Cardiff, Wales

P. Kirsch
Legal Operations Division
Dept. of External Affairs
Ottawa, Ontario, Canada

U.-D. Klemm
Federal Foreign Office
Bonn
Federal Republic of Germany

Albert W. Koers
Inst. of Public Int'l Law
University of Utrecht
Utrecht, Netherlands

Robert B. Krueger
Finley, Kumble, Wagner, Heine,
Underberg, Manley & Casey
Beverly Hills, California

Barbara Kwiatkowska
Netherlands Institute
for the Law of the Sea
Utrecht, Netherlands

A. Lahouasnia
Bristol University
Bristol
England

Maivan Lam
Law of the Sea Institute
Richardson School of Law
University of Hawaii

Anthony S. Laughton
Institute of Oceanographic
Sciences
Surrey, England

Timothy R. E. Keeney
National Oceanic &
Atmospheric Administration
Washington, D. C.

M. Kennedy
School of Law
University of San Francisco
San Francisco, California

G. D. Kinley
King's College
London
England

L. Kitchen
World Maritime University
Malmo

John A. Knauss
Grad. School of Oceanography
University of Rhode Island
Narragansett, Rhode Island

Elias A. Krispis
Faculty of Law
University of Athens
Athens, Greece

Tadao Kuribayashi
Faculty of Law
Keio University
Tokyo, Japan

Rainer Lagoni
Law of the Sea & Maritime
Law Institute
Hamburg, Fed. Rep. of Germany

C. Lalwani
Department of Maritime Studies
UWIST
Cardiff, Wales

David Larson
Department of Political Science
University of New Hampshire

C. Lavelle
Department of Maritime Studies
UWIST
Cardiff, Wales

Rowena Lawson
Consultant Fisheries Economist
University of Hull
Hull, England

Chun-cheng Lian
Department of Law
Jilin University
People's Republic of China

A. V. Lowe
Faculty of Law
University of Manchester
Manchester, England

Ingo Luge
London School of Economics
London
England

K. MacDougald
School of Law
University of San Francisco

S. Malcher De Macedo Vieira
Paris
France

Gerard J. Mangone
Center for the Study
of Marine Policy
University of Delaware

Francell Marquardt
Law of the Sea Institute
Richardson School of Law
Honolulu, Hawaii

P. V. McDade
Center for Petroleum &
Mineral Law Studies
University of Dundee

M. McNamara Schoen
London School of Economics
London
England

Samuel P. Menefee
Center for Oceans Law & Policy
University of Virginia
Charlottesville, Virginia

Y. L. Lee
Deparment of Geography
Nat'l University of Singapore
Republic of Singapore

Kari Lindbekk
Norges Fiskeriforskningsrad
Trondheim
Norway

Sjarit A. Lubis
Ministry of Mines & Energy
Jakarta
Indonesia

Terry Macalister
Lloyd's List
London
England

Philip J. Major
New Zealand Fishing
Industry Board
Wellington, New Zealand

Mario C. Manansala
Law of the Sea Secretariat
Ministry of Foreign Affairs
Manila, Philippines

Jan M. Markussen
Fridtjof Nansen Institute
Lysaker
Norway

J. McCann
School of Law
University of San Francisco
San Francisco, California

D. J. McMillan
London
England

Donald M. McRae
Faculty of Law
University of British Columbia

Paolo Mengozzi
Faculty of Law
University of Bologna
Bologna, Italy

621

Thomas A. Mensah
International Maritime
Organization
London, England

Edward L. Miles
Institute for Marine Studies
University of Washington
Seattle, Washington

Joseph R. Morgan
Department of Geography
University of Hawaii
Honolulu, Hawaii

Max K. Morris
Arthur Vining Davis Foundation
Jacksonville, Florida

Robert W. Munday
Maritime Command H. Q.
Halifax
Nova Scotia

Gordon R. Munro
Department of Economics
University of British Columbia
British Columbia, Canada

Julius Ndalama
World Maritime University
Malmo
Sweden

L. D. M. Nelson
Law of the Sea Office
United Nations
New York, New York

Jennifer A. Nicholson
Marine Policy
Guildford
England

Tor Nikolaisen
Norwegian Ministry of Defense
Oslo
Norway

Dennis W. Nixon
Department of Marine Affairs
University of Rhode Island
Kingston, Rhode Island

Myron H. Nordquist
Kelley Drye & Warren
Washington, D. C.

M. L. Noronha
London School of Economics
London
England

Kaldone G. Nweihed
Department of Maritime Affairs
Universidad Simon Bolivar
Caracas, Venezuela

W. O'Connor
School of Law
University of San Francisco
San Francisco, California

Shigeru Oda
International Court of Justice
The Hague
Netherlands

Peter T. Orebech
Institute of Fisheries Studies
University of Tromso
Tromso, Norway

J. G. O'Reilly
Department of Geography
University of Durham
Durham, England

Willy Ostreng
Fridtjof Nansen Institute
Lysaker
Norway

Ole J. Ostvedt
Institute of Marine Research
Nordnes-Bergen
Norway

G. O'Sullivan
National Board for Science
& Technology
Dublin, Ireland

Bernard Oxman
School of Law
University of Miami
Coral Gables, Florida

M. Painter
School of Law
University of San Francisco
San Francisco, California

F. Parrish
Crown Estate Commissioners
London
England

Gerard Peet
S. E. A. Foundation
Delft
Netherlands

Glen Plant
Law of the Sea Office
United Nations
New York, New York

Giulio Pontecorvo
Graduate School of Business
Columbia University
New York, New York

J. R. V. Prescott
Department of Geography
University of Melbourne
Parkville, Victoria, Australia

Eldon H. Reiley
School of Law
University of San Francisco
San Francisco, California

S. Ricard
School of Law
University of San Francisco
San Francisco, California

N. Ronzitti
Istituto di Diritto Internazionale
University of Pisa
Pisa, Italy

D. Rush
School of Law
University of San Francisco
San Francisco, California

K. Sato
Ocean Div., Econ. Affairs
Ministry of Foreign Affairs
Tokyo, Japan

C. J. Parker
The Nautical Institute
London
England

J. W. H. Patist
University of Utrecht
Utrecht
Netherlands

L. Pineschi
Torino
Italy

Renate Platzoeder
Stiftung Wissenschaft
und Politik
Ebenhausen, Fed. Rep. of Germany

Alexandria M. Post
Schiller University
East Sussex
England

M. Ramirez
Colombian Embassy
London
England

A. D. Reynders
Netherlands Institute for
the Law of the Sea
Utrecht, Netherlands

R. Robinson
School of Law
University of San Francisco
San Francisco, California

Holger B. Rotkirch
Ministry for Foreign Affairs
Helsinki
Finland

A. C. Salusbury
Hydrographic Department
Ministry of Defense
London, England

O. N. Sav
University College
London
England

M. G. Schmidt
St. Anthony's College
Oxford, England

Jan Schneidern
Netherlands

K. T. Schulz
 San Diego Law Review
University of San Diego
San Diego, California

Niels-J. Seeberg-Elverfeldt
Chamber of Commerce
Hamburg
Federal Republic of Germany

Surya P. Sharma
Faculty of Law
Kurukshetra University
Kurukshetra, India

Hance D. Smith
Department of Maritime Studies
UWIST
Cardiff, Wales

Alfred H. A. Soons
Div. of Maritime Wtrwys & Ports
Ministry of Transport
Netherlands

D. A. Spagni
PREST
The University
Manchester, England

C. P. Srivastava
International Maritime
Organization
London, England

Gerald B. Stanford
Crease & Company
Victoria
British Columbia, Canada

R. C. Stein
Department of Fisheries & Oceans
Government of Canada
Ottawa, Ontario, Canada

Jan Schneider
Washington, D. C.

Wesley S. Scholz
Bureau of Econ. & Bus. Affairs
U.S. Dept. of State
Washington, D. C.

Tullio Scovazzi
Faculty of Law
University of Parma
Milan, Italy

E. Shack
London School of Economics
London
England

S. J. Sigman
London School of Economics
London
England

Robert W. Smith
Office of the Geographer
U.S. Dept. of State
Washington, D. C.

C. R. Sowle
School of Law
University of Miami
Coral Gables, Florida

Michael G. Spang
Verdens Gang
Oslo
Norway

Jorgen Staffeldt
Ministry of Energy
Copenhagen
Denmark

M. J. Starr
School of Law
University of San Francisco
San Francisco, California

Magnus Stene
Forsvarets Overkommando/SST
Oslo
Norway

Carol Stimson
Law of the Sea Institute
Richardson School of Law
University of Hawaii

A. Strati
UWIST
Cardiff
Wales

J. Sullivan
School of Law
University of San Francisco
San Francisco, California

W. M. Sutherland
Hull University
Hull
England

Alberto Szekely
Mexican Foreign Ministry
Mexico City
Mexico

H. Terazaki
Maritime Legislation Section
UNCTAD
Geneva, Switzerland

A. G. Y. Thorpe
Royal Naval College
Greenwich
London, England

D. C. Trefts
House Merchant Marine
& Fisheries Comm., U.S. Congress
Washington, D.C.

Tullio Treves
Permanent Mission of Italy
to the United Nations
New York, New York

Victor Tsarev
Soviet Maritime Law Association
Moscow
USSR

E. Ursua-Cocke
University of Guanajuato
Guanajuato, Mexico

Reid T. Stone
Office of Strat. & Int'l Minerals
Department of the Interior
Long Beach, California

W. C. Strommen
Royal Norwegian Ministry
of Foreign Affairs
Oslo, Norway

Kazuo Sumi
Yokohama City University
Kawasaki
Japan

C. R. Symmons
University of Bristol
Bristol
England

Phiphat Tangsubkul
Faculty of Political Studies
Chulalongkorn University
Bangkok, Thailand

J. S. Thomson
Dept. of History & Int'l Affrs
Royal Naval College
Greenwich, London, England

Magnus Torell
Dept. of Soc. & Econ. Geography
University of Gothenburg
Goteborg, Sweden

Per Tresselt
Norwegian Ministry of
Foreign Affairs
Oslo, Norway

Martin Tsamenyi
Faculty of Law
The University
Papua New Guinea

C. M. Tyson
Case Western Reserve University
Cleveland
Ohio

Mario Valenzuela
Int'l Maritime Organization
London, England

A. Vallega
Department of Geography
University of Genoa
Genoa, Italy

Jon M. Van Dyke
Faculty of Law
Richardson School of Law
University of Hawaii

Budislav Vukas
Faculty of Law
University of Zagreb
Zagreb, Yugoslavia

M. Walker
Office of Ocean Law & Policy
U.S. Dept. of State
Washington, D. C.

Donald C. Watt
Sea-Use Program
London School of Economics

Conrad G. Welling
Ocean Minerals Company
Mountain View
California

Lady White
Chairman of Council
UWIST
Cardiff, Wales

Frederick S. Wyle
San Francisco
California

P. Van Der Vaart
Institute for Public Int'l Law
University of Utrecht
Utrecht, Netherlands

P. M. Varadarajan
Trinity College
Oxford
England

J. M. Walker
Dept. of Maritime Studies
UWIST
Cardiff, Wales

S. M. Wasum
Stiftung Wissenschaft
und Politik
Ebenhausen, Fed. Rep. of Germany

B. Weber
Committee on the Environment,
Public Health & Consumer Protection
European Parliament

J. Wetterstad
Fridtjof Nansen Institute
Lysaker
Norway

C. F. Wooldridge
Department of Maritime Studies
UWIST
Cardiff, Wales

E. Young
London
England

INDEX

In Memoriam

FRANCELL MARBETH MOKIHANA MARQUARDT LASLEY

1959 - 1986

Ua Vilivili Fa'amanu O Matagi.

Persevere Like a Bird Against the Wind.

A young law student of Samoan-Hawaiian ancestry, Fran Marquardt recognized the sustaining role of the ocean and its resources for the peoples of Polynesia and the Pacific islands. She also recognized that, in the interest of self-determination and the wise use of these ocean resources, Pacific islanders would have to develop their own expertise in the law of the sea. It was her original intent to acquire that expertise. When she learned that illness would shortly terminate her life, she resolved to employ her few remaining days as an apostle for education in the law of the sea. Participants at the Cardiff conference will remember her well, injecting and infusing her spirit and intellectual vitality into our deliberations. As we memorialize her in these pages we fulfill her life's mission to serve as a herald of the new generation's role in the development of a peaceable order of the ocean seas.